CONTENTS

•••

CHAPTER 2 **Contending Perspectives on International Politics 44**

PART II **CONTROVERSIES**

CHAPTER 3 **War and "Human Nature" 71**

SPECIAL EDITION FOR UNIVERSITY OF KANSAS

INTERNATIONAL
RELATIONS

PERSPECTIVES AND CONTROVERSIES

KEITH L. SHIMKO
PURDUE UNIVERSITY

Major Assumptions
Arguments?
Examples?

Realism
Liberalism
Constructivism

HOUGHTON MIFFLIN COMPANY   BOSTON   NEW YORK

In memory of my mother, Riitta Shimko (1939-2002)

INTERNATIONAL RELATIONS: PERSPECTIVES AND CONTROVERSIES
by Keith L. Shimko.
Copyright © 2005 by Houghton Mifflin Company. All rights reserved.

Publisher: Charles Hartford
Sponsoring Editor: Katherine Meisenheimer
Editorial Associate: Kendra Johnson
Project Editor: Shelley Dickerson
Executive Marketing Manager: Nicola Poser
Marketing Assistant: Kathleen Mellon
Manufacturing Coordinator: Renée Ostrowski

GLOBAL POLITICS IN A CHANGING WORLD: A READER, THIRD EDITION
by Richard W. Mansbach and Edward Rhodes.
Copyright © 2006 by Houghton Mifflin Company. All rights reserved.

Publisher: Charles Hartford
Sponsoring Editor: Katherine Meisenheimer
Assistant Editor: Christina Lembo
Editorial Assistant: Kristen Craib
Associate Project Editor: Teresa Huang
Editorial Assistant: Jake Perry
Senior Composition Buyer: Sarah Ambrose
Manufacturing Coordinator: Carrie Wagner
Executive Marketing Manager: Nicola Poser
Marketing Associate: Kathleen Mellon

Custom Publishing Editor: Sheila Ellis
Custom Publishing Production Manager: Tina Kozik
Project Coordinator: Janell Sims
Cover Design: Althea Chen
Cover Art: PhotoDisc

Printed in the United States of America.

ISBN-13 : 978-0-618-74452-7
ISBN-10: 0-618-74452-5
N-06166

2 3 4 5 6 7 8 9 – CM – 07 06

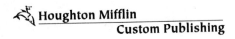

Houghton Mifflin
Custom Publishing

222 Berkeley Street • Boston, MA 02116
Address all correspondence and order information to the above address.

Contents

PREFACE

This text was two years in the writing but more than ten years in the making. As is probably the case with most textbooks, it grows out of many years of teaching the course for which it is intended—introductory international relations. Like others who teach in this area, I have struggled to find the right balance of fact and theory, current events and historical background, as well as breadth and depth of coverage. I am always looking for ways to make complicated ideas accessible without resorting to caricature or talking down to students. I constantly need to remind myself that even though the latest theoretical fad or methodological debate may interest me, it is usually of little interest or value to my students. And though many issues might be old and settled for those of us who have been immersed in the discipline for decades, they can still be new and exciting for students. One of the hardest things about teaching introductory international relations is placing oneself in the position of a student being exposed to the subject for the first time. Undergraduate students are not mini-graduate students, and most do not intend to make the study of international relations their life's ambition. Thus, I begin my class and this text with the assumption that most students are interested in international relations in order to become reasonably informed and thoughtful citizens who are able to think about issues that affect their lives in a manner that goes beyond the superficial coverage of daily headlines. My objective is to help them achieve this goal.

Perhaps the biggest obstacle to introducing students to international relations in one semester is the sheer volume of material. There is so much history that seems essential, so many issues that one can cover, and so many theories that try to make sense of these issues. Choices have to be made. It is simply not feasible to provide all the history and cover every possible issue from every conceivable perspective. It is always easy to find material to add but nearly impossible to identify anything that can be eliminated (a fact that anyone who has ever tried to write a textbook knows well!). The problem is that quantity can sometimes be the enemy of quality. Students presented with an endless catalog of facts, names, theories, and perspectives can drown in a sea of detail. Being exhaustive and comprehensive is certainly desirable in the abstract, but in practice it can become overwhelming. In trying to teach everything, we find that our students end up learning nothing.

GOALS

I have always found it useful to remember that the fundamental goal of this course is getting students to think about international relations. The point is not to provide students with an encyclopedia of facts and theoretical snippets, but rather to instill an appreciation for ideas and the nature and structure of argument. If students can convey, explain, and critique the fundamental arguments for and against free trade, it is not essential that they know the details of every WTO meeting or the results of every GATT round. The debate over the WTO might be a useful entry point into the more enduring questions over free trade, but it is the ideas and arguments that are critical. I am always asking myself whether certain facts are necessary or useful for students to understand the underlying ideas. If they are not, there is no reason to include them.

The danger of overwhelming ideas with facts and detail is not the only challenge. Ideas need to be presented in ways that will allow students to truly engage in the critical issues, not merely be aware of them. It is not enough, for example, that students are able to provide a paragraph summary of balance of power theory. They need to understand its basic assumptions and be able to follow the arguments through its various stages, twists, and turns. They should be able to identify the theory's strong and weak points and do the same for alternative theories. For students to achieve this level of mastery, ideas, and theories must be developed at some length so that they can see how the elements of the arguments come together.

APPROACH

The approach of *International Relations: Perspectives and Controversies* embodies these assumptions. Chapters 1 and 2 are fairly traditional, providing the basic historical and theoretical foundations for thinking about international relations. The remaining chapters are framed differently than most other texts. Each chapter is organized around a basic question that embodies an important issue of controversy in international relations.

- Is war rooted in human nature? (chapter 3)
- Are democracies more peaceful than other societies? (chapter 4)
- Are there alternatives to power politics? (chapter 5)
- Is free trade desirable? (chapter 6)
- What are the obstacles to economic development? (chapter 7)
- Is globalization eroding national sovereignty? (chapter 8)
- Does international law matter? (chapter 9)
- Should the international community undertake humanitarian interventions? (chapter 10)
- Is nuclear proliferation a bad thing? (chapter 11)
- How should we respond to terrorism? (chapter 12)
- Is the global commons in danger? (chapter 13)

Once the question is posed and some essential historical and factual background provided, the chapter presents and develops alternative answers to the question. The questions and the general "debate" format provide a focus that helps sustain student interest. To help students move beyond what they often see as abstract debates and theories and illustrate the real-life relevancy of these ideas, each chapter concludes with a Points of View section containing two primary source documents that bring to life the major issues or positions discussed in the main body of the chapter. For example, the debate about the relationship between democracy and war can be very academic and technical, focusing on conflicting definitions and questions of measurement and methodology. In the chapter dealing with this issue, the Points of View documents debate whether more democracy in the Middle East will bring peace. Given that much of the justification for the 2003 invasion of Iraq rested on the benefits of democratizing the region, this should help students appreciate the real-world implications of theoretical arguments.

My hope is that students will then be able to think about the implications of ideas, critically analyze their own views and those of others, and make better sense of the world around them long after current events have faded into history. Many of the facts and details may be forgotten, but the ability to think about international relations should remain.

FEATURES

Students will learn about the history of international relations in chapter 1, followed by an explanation of the various IR perspectives in chapter 2. Beginning in chapter 3, students will notice a standard set of pedagogical features that will guide their studies of the controversies present in international relations.

- An **opening abstract** introduces students to the chapter's topic and lays the groundwork for the issues and views surrounding the subject at hand.
- An **introduction** gives historical background and perspective to the chapter's issues.
- **Key terms** are boldfaced where they are first introduced in the chapter. The terms are defined in the margins and are listed at the end of the chapter.
- The **Points of View** section includes two readings related to the chapter's issues, often presenting both sides of the debate. An introduction to the readings provides questions for students to ponder as they read the articles.
- A **chapter summary** provides a brief review of the chapter.
- **Critical questions** ask students to apply the concepts they learned in the chapter.
- **Further readings** provide citations of additional sources related to the chapter material.
- Related **websites** give students the opportunity to explore the Internet for more information.

SUPPLEMENTS

International Relations: Perspectives and Controversies provides the following ancillary materials for students and instructors.

The **Instructor's Resource Manual with Test Items**, prepared by the author, includes discussion questions, sample lecture outlines, and a combination of multiple-choice, identification, true/false, and essay test questions.

The **website**, accessible at <college.hmco.com> includes self-test questions for students, web links, and sample answers to the end-of-chapter questions in the book.

ACKNOWLEDGMENTS

The process of writing an introductory international relations text has been a rewarding, yet at times frustrating, experience. I suspect this is the case in any field. Though my name is on the cover, the end product involved the input of many people. First and foremost are all those people who have read and commented on various drafts along the way. Many friends and colleagues at Purdue University have made valuable suggestions for improving several chapters, specifically Berenice Carroll, Harry Targ, Louis Rene Beres, and Aaron Hoffman. Cynthia Weber of Leeds University provided useful input on my discussion of IR theory, especially feminism. Though my debts to Stanley Michalak of Franklin and Marshall College go all the way back to my undergraduate days, for this text he read numerous chapters that are now much better as a result of his insightful, considerate advice and friendly criticism. Stanley was also one of my main sources of encouragement at times when I wondered whether the world really needed another introductory international relations text. In addition to these friends, there is a long list of reviewers arranged through my editors at Houghton Mifflin:

Jason Ackleson, New Mexico State University; Liam Anderson, Wright State University; Robert G. Blanton, The University of Memphis; Rhonda Callaway, Rochester Institute of Technology; Michael Corgan, Boston University; Jane Kellett Cramer, University of Oregon; Douglas C. Foyle, Wesleyan University; Marc Genest, University of Rhode Island; Ivelaw Lloyd Griffith, Florida International University; Terrence Guay, American University; Nancy Haanstad, Weber State University; Joe D. Hagan, West Virginia University; Louis Hayes, University of Montana; Uk Heo, University of Wisconsin–Milwaukee; Jeanne A. K. Hey, Miami University; Stephen Hill, University of Georgia; Matthew J. Hoffmann, University of Delaware; Joyce P. Kaufman, Whittier College; Ed Lynch, Hollins University; B. David Meyers, University of North Carolina–Greensboro; Mark Mullenbach, University of Central Arkansas; John C. Pevehouse, University of Wisconsin; Guy Poitras, Trinity University; Salvatore Prisco, Stevens Institute of Technology; and Andrei P. Tsygankov, San Francisco State University.

Though it was obviously not possible to incorporate all of the ideas and suggestions provided by these reviewers, I can honestly say that this is a much better book as a result of their input.

At Houghton Mifflin, my debts begin with Mary Dougherty, my first sponsoring editor, who saw promise in my original ideas for the book and signed the manuscript; and Katherine Meisenheimer, who took Mary's place early in the process and saw the manuscript through development. Special thanks are due to my developmental editor, Leslie Kauffman, who frequently went a little beyond the call of duty in calming the nerves of an anxious, and not always happy, first-time textbook author.

Finally, this book is dedicated to my mother, Riitta Shimko, who passed away about halfway through the project. Though she is not here to see the final product, I know she would be happy that after many years of talking about it, I finally got off my duff and wrote it. I only regret that she is not here to see it.

Keith L. Shimko

ABOUT THE AUTHOR

KEITH L. SHIMKO is Associate Professor of Political Science at Purdue University. He received his B.A. in 1984 from Franklin and Marshall College (Lancaster, PA) and his Ph.D. from Indiana University. His earlier book, *Images and Arms Control: Perceptions of the Soviet Union in the Reagan Administration* (Michigan, 1991), was selected as a CHOICE outstanding academic book and was the recipient of the Lynne-Reinner/Quincy Wright Award. Dr. Shimko teaches introductory international relations regularly and has been his department's nominee for university teaching awards five times.

INTRODUCTION: THE STUDY OF INTERNATIONAL RELATIONS

YOU AND THE WORLD

Stories of conflict in the Middle East, famine and poverty in Africa, ethnic cleansing in the Balkans, international economic summits, and treaties to slow global warming decades in the future often seem far removed from our daily lives. Given this apparent remoteness, students sometimes wonder why the average person should concern herself or himself with international affairs. Sometimes it is relatively easy to answer this question. Periods of war and conflict in particular bring home the significance of international affairs in dramatic fashion. Anecdotally, it appears that enrollments in international relations courses tend to rise during international crises, probably reflecting an increased awareness of the need to understand what is going on in the wider world. The events of the last few years conform to this pattern. The terrorist attacks of September 11, 2001, the 2003 war in Iraq to oust Saddam Hussein, and ominous stories about North Korean nuclear weapons filled the evening news with an almost unending parade of international crises. In such a charged environment there is an almost intuitive sense that all of this matters, even if most people have some difficulty putting their fingers on exactly how these events affect their daily lives.

But even in more tranquil times, when international affairs recede into the background, our lives are touched by events beyond our shores. Whether the United States is at peace or at war, almost one in five of your tax dollars goes to defend the nation's security, even when no one is quite sure what the threat is. A peacetime army in excess of 1 million troops is the norm. If you are a farmer or work for a company that exports its products, your livelihood may very well depend on continued access to international markets; as a consumer, you pay prices for food and clothes from abroad that are influenced by how much access other nations have to our markets. A crisis on the other side of the globe may require you to shell out more money for the gas you pump into your car. And if you or a loved one is a member of the armed forces, international affairs can literally become a matter of life and death at any moment. Indeed, in the wake of September 11, 2001, Americans now know something people in less secure parts of the world have always known—one need not be wearing a uniform to become a casualty. More civilians died on September 11 than all the American soldiers killed in battle since the end of the Vietnam War. There was a time before bombers, ballistic missiles, and the global economy when the geographical isolation provided by two oceans and the peace of mind that comes from having two weak and friendly neighbors allowed Americans to ignore much of what happened around the world. Very few people and nations have enjoyed this luxury. But that world is long gone. Today we are reminded at almost every turn that our lives are affected, sometimes dramatically, by what goes on thousands of miles from home.

INTERNATIONAL RELATIONS

What is *international relations*? At first glance this appears to be a relatively straightforward and easy question, at least until we try to answer it. We could adopt a fairly narrow view of international relations as the study of state behavior and interaction. In this formulation *international* relations is synonymous with *interstate* relations. Those inclined to this somewhat restrictive definition often prefer the label international *politics* instead of international *relations*. Today the more commonly used *international relations* connotes a much broader focus. Although no one denies that state behavior is *a*, and maybe even *the*, central focus of international relations, few believe this one focus defines adequately the boundaries of the discipline. An emphasis on state behavior is fine, but not to the exclusion of all else. There are simply too many important actors (e.g., multinational corporations and religious movements as well as inter- and nongovernmental organizations) and issues (e.g., terrorism and global warming) that do not fall neatly into a statecentric vision of the world.

[margin note: state behavior is the central focus of international relations]

If a very restrictive definition will not suffice, how much should it be expanded? As we begin adding more and more to what we mean by international relations, it is hard to know where to stop. The line between domestic and international politics blurs as we realize that internal politics often influence a state's external conduct. The distinction between economics and politics fades once we recognize that economic power is an integral component of political power. We also find ourselves dabbling in psychology to understand decision makers, sociology to explain revolutions, and even climatology to evaluate theories of global warming. It may be easier to specify what, if anything, does *not* fall within the realm of international relations. Once we include all the relevant actors and catalog the multitude of issues that can conceivably fall under the general rubric of international relations, we may be tempted to throw up our hands in frustration and define it as "everything that goes on in the world." Though offered somewhat in jest, this definition is not much off the mark of a typically expansive description of international relations as "the whole complex of cultural, economic, legal, military, political, and social relations of all *states*, as well as their component populations and entities."[1] Such a definition covers an awful lot of territory.

[margin note: line between internal state + external policies is Blurry.]

[margin note: This def. basically translates to: "everything that goes on in the world"]

Fortunately, there is no reason we must settle on any final definition. Though it might be an interesting academic exercise to do so at length, it serves no useful purpose at this point. It is enough that we have a good idea of the subjects that would be included in any reasonable definition. It is hard to imagine a definition of international relations that would not, for example, encompass questions of war and peace, sovereignty and intervention, and economic inequality and development. As an introductory text, this book deals with perspectives and issues that almost all agree fall well within the core of international relations, not near its ambiguous and shifting boundaries.

LEARNING AND THINKING ABOUT INTERNATIONAL RELATIONS

The landscape of international relations is in a state of constant flux. Issues, conflicts, and people prominent in today's headlines quickly become yesterday's news. Casual observers are often overwhelmed by the complexity of the subject. The challenge for any introductory text or course in international relations is to bring some order to the confusion by providing you with the necessary tools to make sense of international affairs beyond the level of current events. If the objective were simply to discuss today's most pressing issues, little of lasting value would be gained. Current events may be interesting, but they do not stay current for very long. The goal is to help you think systematically and critically about international affairs in a way that allows you to understand today's headlines as well as yesterday's and, more important, tomorrow's. Once you are able to see familiar patterns in unfamiliar situations, identify recurring puzzles in novel problems, and recognize old ideas expressed in new debates, international relations ceases to be a disjointed and ever-changing series of "events." The names and faces may change, but many of the fundamental problems, issues, and debates tend to reappear, albeit in slightly different form.

The first step in thinking systematically about international politics is realizing that our present is the product of our past. What happened today was influenced by what happened yesterday, and what happens today will determine what happens tomorrow. Even unanticipated and surprising events do not just occur out of the blue: there are always antecedent developments and forces that produced them. The outbreak of World War I, the collapse of the Soviet Union and the end of the Cold War, or the terrorist attacks of September 11, 2001, cannot be understood apart from their historical roots. There is simply no escaping the weight of history. A historical perspective on current events contributes to a deeper understanding of international relations in several respects. First, it allows us to evaluate the significance of today's events in light of historical experience. Without history we would have no way of judging whether a proclaimed "new world order" is really new or merely a mildly updated version of the old world order. Second, knowledge of history helps us move beyond a mere *description* of international relations to the more difficult task of *explanation*, because we begin to wonder about not only *what* happened but *why*. And if we do not move from description to explanation, we cannot make the next move to prescription. If we want to know how to solve or deal with a problem, we need some idea of what causes it in the first place. It is useful to think in terms of an almost logical intellectual progression from description to explanation to prescription.

The move from description to explanation, however, is rarely easy. Anyone who has ever taken a history class knows that knowledge of the "facts" does not necessarily translate into consensus on explanation. Historians might be in total agreement about exactly what happened before and during World War I—who assassinated whom, which nation declared war first, and who won what battles—yet nonetheless disagree about what "caused" the war. And everyone knows that the United States and the Soviet Union never directly fought each other during the Cold War, but there is intense debate about *why* and *how* they managed to avoid war. These debates occur because historical facts do not speak for or explain themselves. Explanation requires that events be interpreted and linked together in a meaningful whole. Unfortunately, there is almost always more than one plausible interpretation of an event, and it is this proliferation of interpretations that makes the study of international relations both frustrating and fascinating.

Competing interpretations result from people's preexisting beliefs. These beliefs act as lenses or filters enabling people to *look* at the same things yet *see* them differently. This applies in all aspects of life, not just international relations. Psychologists have long known that people tend see what they expect and want to see. Firm believers in UFOs, for example, require little evidence to convince them that every flickering light in the sky is a spacecraft carrying visitors from another world. If the facts are ambiguous and open to several plausible interpretations, people will usually accept

current events quickly become yesterday's news

Present is directly influenced by the past.

Historical Perspective on I.R.

① Evaluate significance of today's events in light of hist. experience

② Historical knowledge helps explain "why" things happen

③ History helps us solve problem

Always more plausible than one interpretation of an event

the interpretation that is consistent with their beliefs instead of one that challenges them. As a result, understanding international relations requires knowledge of not only the "facts" but also the belief systems through which people interpret and understand them. If a sufficient historical background is the first prerequisite for thinking systematically and critically about international relations, an appreciation of the various intellectual frameworks that lead to differing interpretations, explanations, and prescriptions is another. Only then is it possible to understand, for example, why some see the United Nations as an invaluable institution for creating a more civilized world and others dismiss it as a pompous and ineffective debating society. International relations is marked not only by conflicts among nations but also by conflicting worldviews.

An appreciation of these competing worldviews is also an essential aspect of critical thinking, which is much more than merely being critical. Critical thinking entails looking at issues and problems from many perspectives, and doing this requires an understanding of, and ability to convey fairly, points of view with which you might personally disagree. This is why students in debating clubs and societies are often required to adopt and defend positions regardless of their personal opinions. Presenting and defending positions other than your own is an intellectual exercise that aids critical analysis, encourages you to think about the structure of argument and the nature of evidence, and makes you aware of the strengths and weaknesses of your own position. Someone who cannot understand or faithfully present an opponent's point of view can never really understand his or her own.

Thus, in order to cultivate systematic and critical analysis, a textbook needs to accomplish at least three tasks. First, it must provide a foundation of knowledge enabling you to think about current events in a broader *historical context*. Second, it has to make you aware of the differing worldviews that influence people's analyses of international affairs so they can analyze events in a broader *intellectual context*. And third, it should examine issues from multiple perspectives so that you can get into the habit of seeing international relations from many different angles.

PLAN OF THE BOOK

With these objectives in mind, this text begins (chapter 1) with a survey of the development of international relations over the last approximately five hundred years, focusing on the emergence and evolution of what we call the modern state system. Although any attempt to summarize more than five centuries in a single chapter inevitably requires that much detail be sacrificed, it is still possible to get a good sense of the most significant elements of change and continuity in international history. This historical survey is followed by an introduction to the major perspectives or worldviews that offer alternative ways of explaining and understanding international relations (chapter 2). Some of these perspectives (e.g., realism, liberalism, and Marxism) have been around for quite some time, whereas others (e.g., feminism and constructivism) have only recently begun to influence our thinking about international relations.

The bulk of the text is devoted to enduring and contemporary controversies in international relations. Each chapter focuses on a central issue or debate, ranging from the very abstract and theoretical (e.g., war and human nature) to the extremely concrete and policy oriented (e.g., nuclear proliferation) and everything in between. Some of the issues are obviously ripped from today's headlines (e.g., international terrorism and nuclear proliferation), and others lurk a little beneath the headlines and between the lines (e.g., the relationship between democracy and war). Whatever the specific issue, the format of each chapter is similar: a brief historical and factual introduction is followed by a discussion of competing perspectives/arguments. The chapter on free trade, for example, begins by tracing the historical and intellectual origins of free trade before turning to the major arguments for and against free trade. Another chapter covers the history of nuclear proliferation before examining the debate over how much we need to be worried about the spread of nuclear weapons.

It is, of course, impossible to do justice to every conceivable position on each and every issue. In the real world there are never just two sides to an argument or debate. On trade issues, for example, some people favor free trade, others oppose it, and many (if not most) fall somewhere in between. There are always nuances of emphasis and gradations of belief that lead to slightly different positions. But before we can even start dealing with nuances, we need to appreciate the more basic and fundamental questions that divide people on important issues. Rather than covering the full range of positions on every topic, we will focus on two or three major positions that reflect differences on fundamental questions. Not only does this perspective allow us to concentrate on the most significant points of disagreement, but we are also able to develop arguments and discuss evidence in some depth. This is a crucial task because critical thinking and intellectual engagement are facilitated by exposure to coherent and fully developed arguments rather than an endless series of short intellectual snippets. It is important to think through ideas and arguments rather than simply reading about them. Once you have mastered the basic ideas, it is easier to think about modifying or combining them to create more nuanced alternative perspectives.

A final element of critical thinking is applying what has been learned in order to think about issues in new ways. You eventually need to make the transition from the classroom to the "real world." The opportunity to do this is provided by the Points of View section at the end of each issue chapter. The Points of View sections are eclectic mixes of official foreign policy statements, government documents, news stories, debate transcripts, and editorials. Not only are they different in form, but they also fulfill slightly different pedagogical functions.

What are you supposed to get out of these documents? Sometimes they are intended to demonstrate that ideas, which can often appear very theoretical in a textbook, have real-world consequences. It is one thing to be exposed to ideas in a textbook or a professor's lecture, but something else entirely to hear them come out of the U.S. president's mouth as he explains why he is taking the nation into war or rejecting a treaty. It is important for you to know that ideas, debates, and arguments about international relations are not confined to the classroom. Other documents require you to think outside the box a little. In order to get across important ideas and debates, professors sometimes have to present them very simply, stripped of complexity and nuance. The real world, however, is not always so simple and tidy. Critical analysis usually involves adding complications and new problems after fundamentals have been taken care of. As a way of introducing complexity, several documents attempt, consciously or not, to reconcile or combine ideas, arguments, and policies that are

Always more than 2 sides to a certain issue

often presented as incompatible. Here you are supposed to evaluate whether these attempts at synthesis are successful or not. Finally, some documents are straightforward news stories reporting on facts or events relevant to the issue at hand, presenting no necessity to take a position. The objective in these cases is for you to think about the nature of evidence by asking whether the evidence supports or undermines particular arguments.

AFTER THE FINAL

Not many of you will make a career of studying international relations. This may be both the first and the last international relations course you will ever take, though I hope it is not. It is also possible you will never read another book about international politics. But whether you like the subject or not, your life will be influenced by international affairs. Long after the exams and quizzes are an unpleasant memory, many of the issues and problems you studied will appear again on the evening news. Even if you do not emerge with a burning interest in international relations and a passionate desire to learn more, I hope you will come away with an appreciation of the important issues at stake. I hope that as you listen to candidates advocate policies you are able to identify and understand the often unstated assumptions and beliefs informing those policies. I hope that you are able to analyze arguments and evidence rather than accept them at face value. In short, you should aim to become an interested, informed, articulate, and thoughtful citizen of a nation and world in which all of our lives and fates are increasingly intertwined. If this text helps in the slightest, its objective will have been achieved.

NOTES

[1] Cathal J. Nolan, *The Longman Guide to World Affairs*
(White Plains, NY: Longman, 1995), p. 178.

HISTORY AND PERSPECTIVES

CHANGE AND CONTINUITY IN INTERNATIONAL HISTORY

CHANGE AND CONTINUITY

In 1989, the Cold War ended as the Berlin Wall, the most vivid symbol of Europe's division for nearly thirty years, came tumbling down and citizens of East and West Berlin mingled freely under the Brandenburg Gate for the first time in over a generation. The peaceful conclusion of the Cold War was undoubtedly a major turning point, but the nature of the post–Cold War world remained in doubt. The first crisis of the post–Cold War era occurred in 1991, when Iraqi forces under the command of Saddam Hussein invaded Kuwait. In response to the Iraqi invasion, the United States created an international coalition under United Nations auspices that pushed Iraqi forces out of Kuwait, liberating the small oil-rich kingdom.

The end of the Cold War, followed closely by the dramatic success of the Gulf War coalition, led some of the more optimistic participants to predict the emergence of a "new world order." There was a sense that the end of the Cold War and the Gulf War marked the beginning of a new period in international relations. Though optimism was the order of the day, it did not take long for civil war and ethnic cleansing in the former Yugoslavia, genocide in Rwanda, and continued conflict in the Middle East to provide reminders of problems that remained. A new world order was not necessarily a better one. In retrospect, these hopes seem somewhat exaggerated. Then, of course, came the terrorist attacks of September 11, 2001, which "changed everything," in the minds of some observers. Again, while undeniably important, the assertion that the attacks changed everything is certainly hyperbole.

Immediate reactions to the end of the Cold War, the 1991 Gulf War, and the September 11 attacks highlight a recurring problem for students of international relations: How does one evaluate the significance of events and changes that one sees in the world? In the abstract, the question of whether a "new world order" is emerging depends not merely on those aspects of international relations that are changing, but also on those that are constant—that is, the relative significance of changes compared to continuities. Unfortunately, continuities are often overlooked. Looking primarily at current events or the very recent past, it is all too easy to focus on those things that appear to be changing because change is interesting and dramatic. The danger is that we will miss important elements of constancy. For this reason it is important to approach current issues from a larger historical perspective, with an appreciation of the events and forces that have shaped the world in which we live.

THE EMERGENCE OF THE MODERN STATE SYSTEM

We take certain features of our world so much for granted that they fade into an unremarkable background. Some things are almost too obvious to need mentioning. If we are asked what a friend looks like, we are unlikely to observe that this person has two arms and two legs. Similarly, someone asked to describe the contemporary world may not begin by noting that it is composed of roughly two hundred entities called states. That may simply be too basic, but it is no less important for being so. So as not to ignore the obvious, it is sometimes useful to play a mind game and imagine how someone with no previous knowledge of our world might see it. An alien visiting planet Earth in order to report back about the way things are done down here would certainly be struck by many of our odd ways. In terms of the political order of our planet, it would certainly want to report all the planet's inhabitants (some 6.5 billion of them) and all the world's territory (about 58 million square miles) are divided up into a relatively small number of very large political entities called states or countries (about 200 of them). It is not only the sheer size of these political units that might seem remarkable, but also their claims to independence. There is no central political authority or world government that unites these different political entities. In pointing out these facts, the alien would be describing the basic features of the **modern state system:** a relatively small number of relatively large (both in terms of population and land) political units that view themselves as independent, recognizing no binding, higher political authority. But had the alien visited a thousand years ago, he would have seen a very different world, and if he returns a thousand years from now, it will certainly look different still. A good place to begin looking at the history of world politics is with how, why, and when the modern state system came into being.

The modern state system has been around (at least in the Western world) for about four hundred years. Some date the beginning of the modern state system to 1648, which was the year the **Thirty Years War** (1618–1648) ended with the **Peace of Westphalia.** Although this is a convenient dividing point, the modern state system did not just appear overnight in 1648: the world of 1647 did not look much different than the world of 1649. The emergence of the modern state system was in reality a slow, gradual process that occurred over a period of several centuries. The process was driven by a number of important economic, religious, and military developments that eventually undermined the feudal order and replaced it with a new way of organizing European politics. As European influence spread throughout the world in subsequent centuries, this new way of organizing things would come, for better or worse, to characterize international politics on a global scale.

A tourist who takes a cruise down the Rhine River in Germany would see the remnants of the feudal order—picturesque castle ruins every few miles. Along the 120 miles from Cologne to Mainz alone, there are 39 castle ruins. Nothing more than quaint tourist attractions today, each castle in its day was the center of one of the many small kingdoms and fiefdoms that dotted the landscape of feudal Europe. That there are so many castles so close together indicates that these political units tended to be quite small (see map 1.1). Each unit was ruled by some member of the nobility—princes, dukes, or other potentates—who ran them largely as personal property. They did not enjoy formal independence but rather were connected to one another in a complicated, chaotic, and often confusing pattern of obligations. Even though one might look at a map of the period and see a few larger countries (e.g., France or England), their appearance is misleading. Political power was not as centralized as the maps suggest. In reality, the kings and central governments were usually very weak and struggled constantly with lesser rulers over whom they supposedly held authority. In general, "the pattern of politics in medieval Europe was . . . a crazy quilt of multiple and overlapping feudal authorities and reciprocal allegiances. . . . Central governments, when they existed at all, were consequently very weak."[1]

As if this division of power were not messy enough, much of Europe was theoretically united under the **Holy Roman Empire.** The basis for this unity was the common Catholic brotherhood of European society. To make things even more complicated, the Holy Roman Empire had both a religious leader (the Pope) and a secular leader, the Holy Roman Emperor, and it was not always clear where their authority began and ended. Furthermore, the empire itself was always a very weak entity in

modern state system The international state system characterized by a relatively small number of relatively large independent/sovereign political units. Though it is the result of several complex economic, religious, and military changes, a convenient date for the foundation of the modern state system is 1648, when the Thirty Years War ended with the Peace of Westphalia.

Thirty Years War (1618–1648) General name given to a series of bloody and devastating wars fought largely on German lands between 1618 and 1648. Though several complex causes and motivations fueled these wars, the conflict between Protestants and Catholics over the authority of the Catholic Church and the Pope was a central issue.

Peace of Westphalia (1648) The agreement that officially closed the Thirty Years War (or wars). Significant in that it marked the origins of modern principles of sovereignty.

Holy Roman Empire The larger political entity that brought some political unity to medieval Europe under the authority of the Pope and the Holy Roman Emperor.

MAP 1.1

Feudal Europe, 1400 C.E. This map of Europe in 1400 illustrates the political fragmentation of the medieval period.

SOURCE: *Periodical Historical Atlas of Europe,* http://www.euratlas.com/big/big1400.htm.

which local nobles and religious figures enjoyed substantial independence from the Emperor and Rome. Thus, feudal Europe was a fragmented place of numerous small political entities entwined in a confusing and complicated mishmash of political authority.

How did we get from that world to one that more resembles our world? Three major developments began to alter the political map of Europe beginning in the 1200s or 1300s (it is not easy to pick any specific date). These three "revolutions" would ultimately create much larger political units organized on the basis of sovereignty and independence. First, the **commercial revolution** (not to be confused with the industrial revolution) provided a powerful economic impetus for the creation of larger entities. Second, the **gunpowder revolution** dramatically altered military strategy and the requirements for defense in ways that gave substantial advantages to larger entities. Finally, the **Protestant Reformation** and the resulting Thirty Years War (1618–1648) destroyed the unity of Europe and led to the modern notion of sovereignty. Let us deal with each of these revolutions in turn.

The commercial revolution Beginning in the thirteenth and fourteenth centuries, Europe began its slow emergence from the stagnation that prevailed since the fall of Rome 700 years earlier. Part of this resurgence was the revival of commerce and the growth of a new commercial class whose livelihood lay not in the production of goods but rather trading. This commercial class faced a problem because conditions in medieval Europe were not conducive to trade. A Europe fragmented into so many small political units was unable to provide many of the prerequisites for commerce. Law enforcement was weak, making the transport of valuable commodities over large distances very risky indeed. The infrastructure was in a terrible state of disrepair—roads, ports, and marketplaces had all deteriorated since the fall of Rome, and the small size of political units inhibited any rebuilding. Individual fiefdoms did not possess the resources to build the infrastructure, and political fragmentation made coordination very difficult. Finally, systems of measurement and currency were unreliable.

All of these obstacles to commerce could be traced to the small size of political units. The emerging commercial class realized that larger political units with more effective central governments were essential. This new social class was not the only player that wanted change. Ambitious rulers also desired larger kingdoms, and kings and their central governments wanted increased power over the local nobility. The result was a convergence of interests in favor of larger political units with more powerful central governments. A tacit alliance emerged between the commercial class and rulers who wanted to expand and centralize their authority. The commercial class provided the resources in the form of taxes, and the rulers gave them in return roads, ports, markets, law enforcement, and reliable currencies needed for trade. Thus, the economic imperatives of trade and commerce contributed to the emergence of larger political units with more effective central governments.

The gunpowder revolution The weapons of the feudal age are familiar from the movies—knights in shining armor on horseback carrying swords, lances, and spears, and archers on foot wielding crossbows. War between kingdoms often turned into long sieges, with the attacker surrounding a fortified castle within which people sought safety. Once a castle had been surrounded, the goal was to harass and starve

▸**commercial revolution**
The revival of trade and commerce as Europe began to emerge from the stagnation that characterized much of the period since the fall of Rome in 476 c.e. This was one of the forces for the creation of larger and more centralized political units, one of the essential features of the modern state system.

gunpowder revolution
The dramatic military, social, and political changes accompanying the introduction and development of gunpowder weapons in Europe, beginning in the fourteenth century, made previous means of defense less reliable and placed a premium on land and larger political units.

Protestant Reformation
Martin Luther's challenge to the Catholic Church in 1517 marked the emergence of a non-Catholic version of Christianity. The growing conflict between Protestants and Catholics was one of the major contributing forces to the Thirty Years War.

The rulers and new commercial class "united" in agreement to forming larger political states / more powerful cent. governments the inhabitants until they surrendered. The military problem was that there was little the attackers could do about the thick castle walls—spears and arrows did not make much of a dent, though catapults might propel fireballs over the walls to wreak havoc within. This type of warfare began to change with the introduction of gunpowder, which had been invented in China. Gunpowder weapons such as guns and cannons significantly altered the military equation. Most important, a kingdom could no longer resist attack by retreating behind the walls of its castles because "from the 1430s onwards the cannons deployed by the major states of Western Europe could successfully reduce most traditional vertical defenses [i.e., walls] to rubble within a matter of days."[2] An adequate defense now required either much more complicated (and expensive) fortifications and/or enough land to be able to absorb an attack and marshal one's own forces in time to meet the attack and defeat it. A kingdom only 40 or 100 miles across with a castle in the middle was now extremely vulnerable. Only larger states had the land and wealth base necessary to conduct war and defend themselves in the gunpowder age. This fact provided a military imperative behind the evolution of larger and larger political units.

The Protestant Reformation Until 1517, being a Christian in Western Europe meant being Catholic. Since the Catholic Church was such a central feature in the social and political life of feudal Europe, the rise of Protestantism had a profound effect on European societies and politics. Martin Luther's challenge to the authority of the Catholic Church marked the emergence of a Christian alternative to Catholicism that spread throughout central and northern Europe. The problem was that many of the Protestant areas and rulers were located within the Holy Roman Empire, a Catholic entity. Protestants eventually tried to free themselves from the authority of the Pope and Catholic rulers. The result was a series of wars known collectively as the Thirty Years War (1618–48). Though these wars involved most nations of Europe, the fighting occurred largely on German lands. By any measure, it was a war of unusual brutality and savagery. Estimates of the numbers of the German population killed in the war range from 30 to 50 percent. Part of the barbarity and savagery of the war can be explained by its religious underpinnings: "Combatants on all sides thought that their opponents were, in a literal sense, instruments of the devil, who could be exterminated, whether they were soldiers or not. Indeed extermination of civilians was often preferred, precisely because it was easier to do away with civilians."[3] One need look no further than Martin Luther's German translation of the Bible for evidence of the depth of this hostility. The only illustrated section was the book of Revelation, which foretells the coming of the Antichrist. The pictures made the identity of the Antichrist perfectly clear—he was the Pope. After thirty years of devastating and unspeakably brutal warfare, not much survived of the notion that the people and countries of Europe were united by a common Christian brotherhood.

The Thirty Years War ended in 1648 with the Peace of Westphalia. The treaty solved the religious question by granting to each ruler the right to exercise authority over his or her territory. In terms of religion, this accord meant that it was up to each ruler to determine questions of religion on the territory they controlled. Rulers no longer had to answer to any higher, external authority such as the Pope. This new freedom, however, did not imply religious tolerance within countries—rulers often brutally suppressed religious dissidents in their countries. What the treaty did establish was the modern notion of national **sovereignty**—that rulers were not obligated to obey any higher authority and that no one else had the right to dictate the internal affairs of another state. The basic principle of sovereignty had been established.

Thus, between the 1300s and the late 1600s the commercial revolution, the gunpowder revolution, and the Protestant Reformation combined to alter the nature of European societies, states, and international relations. The first two revolutions helped usher in an era of larger political entities, and the Protestant Reformation and the Thirty Years War led to the notion of national sovereignty, creating the modern state system—a relatively small number of relatively large independent political units. These are the main outlines of the world our visiting alien would see in 2004. This basic continuity does not imply the absence of important changes. Even though certain essential features of international politics may have endured, the modern state system has certainly evolved in many important respects. And one needs to understand not merely the emergence of the modern state system, but also how it has evolved over the past four centuries.

THE AGE OF ABSOLUTISM AND LIMITED WAR (1648–1789)

The period between the Peace of Westphalia and the French Revolution (1789) was relatively uneventful compared to what came before 1648 and what was to come after 1789. There were no major continentwide wars or political revolutions. Though frequent, wars tended to be modest affairs—professional armies fighting limited wars for limited objectives, with limited casualties and destruction. This period is sometimes viewed as a golden age of diplomacy in which negotiation, compromise, and the balance of power successfully prevented any repetition of the horrors of the Thirty Years War. The relative calm of this period, however, depended on a certain political and social order and would not long survive the erosion of that order in the decades after the French Revolution.

When people tour Europe today, they inevitably visit one of the grand palaces that make for beautiful postcards, such as the Palace of Versailles on the outskirts of Paris. Situated on estates covering many acres of land with finely manicured gardens and dramatic fountains, these mansions have hundreds of rooms, almost every inch of which are covered in gold and valuable art. They are the physical manifestations of the social and political order of this period, which was **absolutist monarchism.** Between 1648 and 1789, monarchs claiming absolute power and authority ruled virtually every nation in Europe. They claimed this authority under the doctrine of the **divine right of kings,** which held that their legitimacy was derived from God, not the people over whom they ruled.

The prevalence of absolutist monarchism helps explain the relative calm of international politics during this period. Domestically, this was not a form of government that encouraged a close sense of connection and loyalty between rulers and their subjects. Indeed, the very term *subjects* hints at the critical point. People who lived in France during this period were not in any meaningful sense "citizens" of France; they were "subjects" of the monarch. But even though their power was "absolute," in

sovereignty In international relations, the right of individual states to determine for themselves the policies they will follow.

absolutist monarchism The political order prevailing in almost all of Europe before the French Revolution in which kings and queens claimed divine sources for their absolute rule and power unrestricted by laws or constitutions.

divine right of kings The political principle underlying absolutist monarchism in which the legitimacy of rulers was granted by God, not the people over whom leaders ruled.

reality monarchs made limited demands on their people. They did not, for example, expect common people to serve in the military and fight wars. For this task the monarchs of Europe maintained professional armies. Unlike volunteer armies of today, soldiers in this period did not have to be from the countries in whose armies they served; these were mercenary, not volunteer, armies. On the eve of the French Revolution in 1789, for example, nearly a quarter of the French army consisted of foreign soldiers.[4] Such armies were very expensive to maintain. Even the wealthiest rulers supported armies of only around 100,000 in peacetime, though these numbers could swell to 400,000 in wartime. Given armies of this size, it was quite rare for battles to involve more than 80,000 soldiers total.[5]

The professional and mercenary nature of European armies of the period reveals a reality in which the masses of people were excluded from political affairs of their country. Politics was synonymous with royal court scheming and intrigue, not elections, political parties, interest groups, opinion polls, and so on. There was no emotional sense of loyalty and connection between people and their rulers or governments. There was no sense of nationalism as we know it today. It was an era of dynastic nationalism, not popular or mass nationalism. Wars during this period were not genuine conflicts between entire nations; they were conflicts among royal families. France *as a nation* did not go to war with Spain or Austria; instead, the Bourbons, France's ruling dynasty, went to war with Austria's Hapsburgs. During these wars people of both states continued to travel in each other's countries and conduct business. Wars involved rulers and their armies, not the populace at large.

The absence of mass nationalism is a large factor in the limited nature of wars and conflicts during this period. The major issues that led to war were territorial disputes, economic and commercial interests, and questions of dynastic and royal succession.[6] Wars were not motivated by intense ideological disagreements because the monarchs of Europe did not disagree about very much. They all adhered to the same basic principles and agreed on the issue of how societies should be organized and ruled. Consequently, "they were not concerned with religion as their seventeenth-century predecessors had been, nor political ideology as their post-1789 successors were to be."[7] The monarchs fought over *things,* not ideas, and wars over things are often less intense and bloody than wars over beliefs.

A final reason wars did not erupt into incredibly destructive affairs was the ability of European monarchs to maintain a balance of power through a constantly shifting pattern of allegiances and alliances. Throughout this period there were usually five or six major powers in Europe—some combination of England, France, Spain, Prussia, Russia, Austria, the Ottoman Empire (Turkey), Sweden, and the United Provinces (i.e., Holland). The major powers were successful in preventing any one power from becoming powerful enough to dominate all of Europe. Whenever one country became too powerful or ambitious, the other major powers simply aligned against it. Because the power of monarchs was so absolute and they had no real ideological differences, they were able to shift allegiances rapidly when the balance was threatened. Absolutism did have its advantages.

THE AGE OF REVOLUTIONS (1789–1914)

As the 1700s drew to a close, few had any inkling of the dramatic changes that would transform European society, politics, and the conduct of international affairs over the next century. Within a span of 120 years, Europe would cease to be a place where kings and queens waged limited wars with professional armies, becoming one in which popular governments fought wars with millions of men, resulting in casualties and destruction on an almost unimaginable scale. The story of how we got from a comparatively gentle world of the 1700s to the horrors of World War I's trenches involves two interrelated developments. The first was the rise of modern nationalism, which altered the relationship between people and their governments and eroded the foundations of absolutist monarchism. And as absolutist monarchism faded, the pattern of international relations it supported also began to change. The second development was the industrial revolution, which would alter the social and political character of European societies and increase dramatically the destructive potential of warfare. When modern nationalism and the industrial revolution came together, it was on the bloody battlefields of World War I. This is a complicated story that begins with two political revolutions, one in the new world and the other in the heart of monarchical Europe.

The American and French Revolutions The American Revolution of 1776 and the **French Revolution** of 1789 signaled the introduction of a new idea that would in time unravel the political order of European societies. Before these revolutions, the rulers of Europe claimed divine sources as the basis for their legitimacy: Louis XIV ruled over the people of France not because the people wanted him to rule but because it was supposedly God's will. At the core of the American and French revolutions was the dangerous, indeed revolutionary, idea of **popular sovereignty**—the notion that in order to be legitimate, governments needed to derive their authority from the people over whom they ruled. *No longer would people accept "God's will" as a legitimate reason.*

The French Revolution did not start out as a revolution but merely as resistance to Louis XVI's attempts to raise taxes (largely to pay off debts incurred when the French sided with American colonists in their war for independence). The resistance rapidly snowballed into a revolt against the monarchy itself, resulting in the overthrow of Louis XVI in 1792 and the establishment of the French Republic. A "Reign of Terror" eventually ensued in which thousands of nobles and supposed enemies of the revolution met with a gruesome end, usually via the infamous guillotine: even Louis XVI and his queen, Marie Antoinette, were not spared.

To understand the significance of the French Revolution, we need to appreciate the status of the French monarch. The King of France was not just another king; he was *the* king, the most powerful and prestigious monarch in all of Europe. As a result, the Revolution and the overthrow of the French monarchy eventually came to be seen as an attack on, and threat to, the entire system of absolutist monarchism. As one might expect, this was not generally viewed as a desirable development in the other capitals of Europe. It did, however, take a while for the full enormity of what had happened to sink in. The initial reaction was not one of great alarm, perhaps because the Revolution was seen as weakening France and unlikely to succeed in the long run. Thus, at first the response was largely to ignore and isolate revolutionary France.[8]

French Revolution The popular revolt against the French monarchy in 1789 that resulted in the establishment of the French Republic. Along with the American Revolution (1776), marked the emergence of modern nationalism.

popular sovereignty The principle that governments must derive their legitimacy from the people over whom they rule. Embodied in the French and American Revolutions, this doctrine challenged the principle of the divine right of kings.

As it became apparent that the Revolution would succeed and maybe even expand beyond the borders of France, the monarchs came to believe that they had a vested interest in crushing the revolution and restoring the French monarchy. The revolutionary government anticipated hostility and possible threats from the rest of Europe and was determined to defend itself. The first step in doing so was the creation of a massive citizen army. The call went out for volunteers, with the appeal being made not on the basis of financial reward but rather loyalty to the revolution and nation. When the call for volunteers proved insufficient, the government instituted the *levée en masse* in 1793, conscripting all able-bodied men between the ages of 18 and 25 into military service. As a result of the *levée en masse*, "by the summer of 1794 the revolutionary army listed a million men on its rolls, of whom 750,000 were present under arms—a great force which, in terms of social class, occupation, and geographical origin, accurately reflected French society. It was the nation in arms composed of the best young men France could offer."[9] Unlike the prerevolutionary French army, the new army required French citizenship as a prerequisite for service.

The citizen army of the French Republic was able to defend the revolution against its foreign enemies. The Republic, however, continued to have its problems. The constant fighting, some military setbacks, domestic political conflicts, and economic problems created an unstable political situation. Taking advantage of domestic strife, Napoleon Bonaparte, a successful and ambitious general of the revolution known for his military brilliance and personal arrogance, staged a military coup, seizing power in 1799. Though he eventually crowned himself Emperor, there was a critical difference between Napoleon and his monarchical predecessors. Echoing the ideals of the revolution, Napoleon continued to maintain that his right to rule was derived from the will of the French people. In claiming nearly absolute power while also insisting that his rule derived its legitimacy from the people of France, Napoleon became the first (but certainly not the last) populist dictator in modern Europe.

After consolidating his power, Napoleon embarked on a program of conquest cloaked in the rhetoric and ideals of the French Revolution. The **Napoleonic Wars** (1802–1815) plunged Europe into another thirteen years of war. Given the unprecedented size of the French army, which was further motivated by emotional appeals to spread the revolution, it was war on a grand scale that had not been seen in some time. Napoleon's forces swept across Europe until most of the continent was under his control. It was not until his armies reached the outskirts of Moscow in 1812 that the tide finally turned against Napoleon. Napoleon's ambitions had gotten the better of him and his invasion of Russia proved to be a fatal mistake. A series of military defeats for France ended with the final failure at the Battle of Waterloo in 1815.

In many respects, the battles of the Napoleonic Wars looked very much like the battles of the 1700s—the soldiers, their weapons, and their horses all looked the same. The major difference was that there were a lot more of them. The ability of France to mobilize and conscript men by the hundreds of thousands forced the other nations of Europe to respond in kind. A few decades before the French Revolution, a battle involving 80,000 troops would have been both extremely large and a rarity. Such battles were dwarfed by the major clashes of the Napoleonic Wars. The Battle of Leipzig (1813), in which France's defeat effectively ended Napoleon's control of German lands, involved more than 200,000 French and another 300,000 Austrian, Russian, Prussian, and Swedish forces.[10] With more than half a million troops on the field, the Battle of Leipzig involved at least five times as many men as a very large battle of the prerevolutionary era. The scale of war had changed to the point where it was no longer just a different level of warfare but a fundamentally new way of preparing for and waging war.

This expanding scale of war was made possible not because of any improvements in military technology but because people were increasingly willing to fight and make sacrifices for their governments—and governments were more willing and able to ask people to make these sacrifices. The French Revolution was a turning point in European and international politics because it marked the beginnings of modern nationalism. The willingness of people from all levels of society to make sacrifices on behalf of their nation was a profoundly important development because "it was this psychological change—this popular sense of identification with the nation—that enabled the French to wage the new kind of war."[11]

After the Napoleonic Wars, the victorious monarchs of Europe formed the **Concert of Europe,** promising to resolve their disputes without resort to force and maintain a balance of power so that no one power would be tempted to dominate the whole continent. In doing so, they attempted to recreate the order of prerevolutionary Europe. But no matter how much they yearned for the days of absolute monarchism and professional armies that waged limited wars, a permanent return would prove to be impossible. The nationalist ideals of the French Revolution and the knowledge of how to organize and fight wars on a grand scale could not be forgotten. Furthermore, Europe was poised on the brink of another revolution—an industrial one—that would change European societies and international relations in ways that would also make it impossible to turn back the clock.

The meaning of nationalism Born with the French Revolution, **modern nationalism** has three major components. First, nationalism involves an emotional or psychological sense of affinity or connection among people who share a common ethnic, cultural, and linguistic heritage. A French citizen who lives in Paris may never meet a French citizen who lives in Lyon, but they nonetheless feel themselves connected as part of a distinct social grouping. Second, modern nationalism entails the belief in popular sovereignty, according to which the only basis for legitimate government is the will of the people. This was the essence of the French and American revolutions. Finally, modern nationalism places a high value on **ethnic** or **national self-determination.** Each ethnic or national group has the right to determine its own destiny, have its own government or state, and rule over itself. Thus, nationalism has both a domestic and an international component. Domestically, it defines what is considered a legitimate political order. Internationally, it demands that political boundaries must coincide with ethnic or national boundaries.

The idea of national or ethnic self-determination was a political time bomb because the political map of Europe after the French Revolution did not reflect its ethnic composition and distribution. There were a few places, such as France, where political and ethnic boundaries overlapped fairly well. Even in this case, however, the fit was not perfect: there were small populations of Germans as well as Basques and others in parts of France. The ideal of self-determination is hard to meet in reality. More problematic in terms of nationalism were Europe's major **multinational states** or empires, in which many ethnic and national groups lived within the boundaries of a

Concert of Europe The informal system in which the monarchs of Europe tried to restore international order after the defeat of Napoleon in 1815. The victors agreed to settle their differences through diplomacy, not war, and maintain a balance of power.

modern nationalism A political creed with three critical aspects: a sense of connection and loyalty between people and their rulers or governments; the belief that governments must derive their legitimacy from the people over whom they rule; and a commitment to national or ethnic self-determination.

self-determination, ethnic or national The principle that each national or ethnic group has the right to determine its own destiny and rule itself.

multinational state A single state or government ruling over people of many distinct ethnic identities.

MAP 1.2

Distribution of Ethnic Groups, 1871–1908 This map showing the distribution of ethnic groups in the Austro-Hungarian Empire illustrates the failure of political boundaries to coincide with ethnic boundaries.

single state. Austria-Hungary, the Ottoman (or Turkish) Empire, and the Russian Empire were the most prominent examples. Within Austria-Hungary, for example, there were at least ten different ethnic groups (Germans, Hungarians, Rumanians, Slovenes, Croats, Czechs, Poles, and so on) (see map 1.2). In addition to the multi-ethnic empires, there were also several **multistate nations,** in which one national or ethnic grouping was divided into several states. The Germans were the most significant example of a multistate nation through most of the nineteenth century. Before 1871, no such country as Germany existed; the area that we know as Germany was divided in several states (Prussia, Bavaria, Hanover, etc.). Nationalism would have a different impact depending on the particular ethnic or political configuration.

In the case of the Austrian-Hungarian and Ottoman empires, nationalism was a disintegrative force. As different ethnic groups demanded greater autonomy, power,

multistate nation A single ethnic group divided into several different, independent political units or states.

and even independence, central governments found it necessary to expend resources and effort to suppress these nationalist movements. The spread of nationalism would gradually weaken states that were composed of many different ethnic groups because they became harder to govern and were forced to devote greater and greater resources to quell domestic conflicts. But nationalism proved to have the opposite effect in places like Germany, where it led to the creation of new, larger, and more powerful political entities. The unification of Italy in 1861 and the German states in 1871 were logical outgrowths of the doctrine of ethnic self-determination. Thus, nationalism was both a destructive, disintegrating force and a creative, integrating force. The weakening of some states and the creation of others altered the map of Europe as well as upset the balance of power in ways that would create new problems and lead Europe down the path to World War I.

Between 1864 and 1871, the Prussian general Otto Von Bismarck, in a series of quick and decisive wars, unified the various German states into a single political entity. This was a monumental geopolitical development. The unification of Germany in a period of only seven years marked the almost overnight creation of a new great power in the heart of Europe. With its substantial population, industrial output, efficient government administration, and military power based on the renowned Prussian army, Germany was a force to be reckoned with. The problem of German power only got worse in the decades immediately following unification. By the turn of the century, German industrial output had soared past that of Great Britain, making the German economy the most powerful in Europe. Within Germany this new productivity led to demands for a more assertive foreign policy and the creation of sufficient military power to sustain it. Most troublesome, especially to Britain, was the increase in German naval power, which was seen as a threat to British naval supremacy. Michael Mandelbaum explains the problems posed by German unification and economic expansion: "Germany's enormous growth was the disturbing element in European affairs. It was a development that could not be accommodated within the existing order. . . . Although surpassing the other powers in military and economic terms, they lagged behind in what were supposed to be the fruits, as well as the sources of power: territorial possessions."[12]

How did the other nations of Europe respond to this new power? France in particular was not happy about being replaced as the dominant continental power and began to look for allies to balance off the growing power of Germany. Germany, on the other hand, feared "encirclement" by hostile powers (France to the west, Austria-Hungary to the south, and Russia to the east). Germany hoped to keep France isolated by forging alliances with Austria-Hungary and Russia. This proved to be a very difficult feat because Russia and Austria-Hungary were often in conflict over issues in the Balkans (the southern part of Eastern Europe). Eventually Germany formed an alliance with Austria-Hungary and Italy in 1882; after years of searching for a partner, France finally formed an alliance with Russia in 1892. This basic division of Europe remained intact up to the outbreak of World War I.

The industrial revolution The industrial revolution changed so much about the way people lived that it is almost impossible to know where to begin or end a discussion of its impact. But in terms of understanding the evolution of international relations, three aspects of the industrial revolution are critical. First, the industrial revolution ① changed European societies in ways that reinforced and exacerbated many of the

MAP 1.3 **Europe on the eve of World War I**

developments associated with nationalism, particularly the erosion of monarchical rule and the rise of mass involvement in politics. Second, the industrial revolution allowed for the production of commodities cheaply and in vast quantities. Not only clothes, canned goods, and railroad cars poured off the assembly lines, however, but also guns, cannons, ammunition, and military uniforms. Third, the wealth, weapons, and technology of the industrial revolution widened the wealth and power gap between Europe and the non-Western world, leading to the expansion of European influence to all corners of the world as the major powers created vast overseas empires.

Before the industrial revolution, societies were primarily agricultural and agrarian, with a majority of people living in rural areas. Advances in agriculture meant that fewer people were needed to produce the same or even larger quantities of food, so people left farms and poured into the cities to work in factories. In addition to large urban populations, the industrial revolution also created new economic and social classes—a small elite of wealthy barons of industry; a substantial middle class of managers, entrepreneurs, and skilled workers; and an ever-increasing and organized urban working class. These new groups eventually demanded a voice in government and politics, contributing to the erosion of monarchical rule.

The monarchs of Europe were increasingly confronted with a dilemma: how to preserve their power while asking their people to make greater sacrifices. In the long run, they did not succeed in resolving the dilemma. As the nineteenth century progressed, the power of monarchs gradually eroded as the power of more representative political institutions increased. Although very few European countries could be considered genuinely democratic by the end of the century, there were also very few genuinely absolutist monarchs. The force of nationalism, the requirements and strains of industrial society, and demands for wider political inclusion slowly transformed European societies from elitist absolutist monarchies to polities characterized by mass political inclusion and involvement.

One of the most obvious and onerous sacrifices governments demanded of their (male) citizens was military service. Conscription was practiced in virtually every nation, some for periods as long as six or eight years. Only Britain among the major powers refrained from conscription. By the end of the nineteenth century, the other European powers were maintaining peacetime armies that dwarfed even the wartime armies of the century before. But despite the tremendous social and political changes of the nineteenth century and the dramatic expansion of military establishments, the period between 1815 and 1914 was deceptively calm. Other than the Crimean War (1854–56), armed conflict among major powers was avoided. The most devastating war during this period, the American Civil War, occurred on the other side of the world. By the end of the nineteenth century, every major power in Europe lived in a state of nearly permanent war readiness. No one knew when or why war might come or what it would be like when it did, but they knew it would come.

In terms of the wider world, the increase in European wealth and military power combined with improvements in naval technology and communications to produce a scramble for overseas colonies, predominantly in Asia and Africa, in the second half of the nineteenth century. By 1900, very few areas of Asia or Africa were not under European domination. Queen Victoria could accurately claim that the sun never set on the British Empire. This was the second major wave of European imperialism. The first, immediately following the discovery of the New World in the 1500s and 1600s, was concentrated on North and South America. The major motive for this earlier imperialism had been the pursuit of wealth, particularly the acquisition of gold and silver to fill the coffers of European monarchs. The reasons for this second wave of over-seas conquest were more complicated and controversial. For some, the major impetus was provided by industrial capitalism's need for overseas markets and access to cheap raw materials, resources, and labor. Others see imperialism as a primarily cultural phenomenon, arguing that notions of ethnic, racial, and religious superiority led Europeans to conquer the "backward" parts of the world in a missionary attempt to spread the virtues of Christianity and Western culture. Whatever the motivating forces, "Europe's domination of the world through the growth of empire reflected the ability of sophisticated weapons and advanced techniques to overcome the inherent advantages of native populations. . . . The machine-gun was only the most concrete military expression of the tactical superiority enjoyed by European armies in Asia and Africa."[13]

At the dawn of the twentieth century the world had been transformed. The age of absolutist monarchism was either over or on its last legs. The spread of nationalism was reconfiguring the map of Europe, creating new powers while weakening old ones. Nationalism and the industrial revolution allowed governments to create war machines capable of unparalleled destruction. European political and military power had spread to even the most remote reaches of the world. On the surface things remained calm, but the calm would not last much longer.

The road to war The division of Europe into rival alliance systems almost guaranteed that a war involving anyone would eventually involve everyone. The only question was which conflict would finally bring the precarious peace to an end. The chances were good that a general war would emerge from the conflicts in the Balkans (the southern portion of Eastern Europe). It was here that the power of the Austrian-Hungarian, Ottoman, and Russian empires intersected in political waters muddied by the conflicts of nationalism. One of the most volatile conflicts was between Austria-Hungary and Serbia. Recall that there were substantial populations of Serbians living within the borders of Austria-Hungary (see map 1.2). Consistent with the sentiments of nationalism, powerful forces within Serbia called for the creation of a Greater Serbia incorporating all the Serbian people, something that did not sit well with the rulers of Austria-Hungary. When a Serbian nationalist extremist assassinated Archduke Franz Ferdinand of Austria-Hungary (next in line to the throne) in Sarajevo on June 28, 1914, the first step on the road to war was taken. What followed was a dizzying round of threats and ultimatums that failed to resolve the crisis. Austria-Hungary declared war on Serbia on July 28. Russia, which generally supported Serbia, mobilized its army on July 30, setting off a chain reaction in Germany and France. By August 4, all of Europe was at war, with Britain joining France and Russia. The peace that had lasted since the defeat of Napoleon was over.

THE AGE OF TOTAL WAR (1914–1945)

When the Great War (as World War I was called before anyone realized there would be a need to number such conflicts) finally came, most expected the troops to be home by Christmas. Men flooded into the recruiting stations to get in on the big adventure. Enthusiastic crowds saw the trainloads of men off to war. This was still an age in which romantic and glorious images of war clouded the popular imagination. The enthusiasm did not long survive the realities of industrial warfare. Instead of the glorious battles of war novels, the soldiers found a bleak, bloody, and impersonal battlefield. The war that was supposed to be over by the holidays dragged on for four years, turning into a horrific war of attrition that destroyed and scarred an entire generation. Machine guns, artillery, massive quantities of ammunition, poisonous gas, and muddy trenches would spell the death of war as a glorious endeavor.

Whereas the Battle of Leipzig a century earlier represented war on an unprecedented scale because it involved 500,000 *soldiers,* during World War I it was not uncommon for single battles to result in more than 500,000 *casualties.* At the Battle of Verdun (1916), over 400,000 men were killed and wounded. The British lost almost 20,000 men on the very first day of the Battle of the Somme (1916). Given the population of Britain at the time, this would be the equivalent of 80,000 Americans dying on the first day of the 1991 Gulf War. Proportionally, the British lost more men in one day at the Battle of the Somme than the United States did during all fifteen years of the Vietnam War. In the end, British casualties exceeded 400,000 at the Somme. At the Battle of Passchendaele (1917), the allies and the Germans suffered over 600,000 casualties. These three battles alone resulted in more than a million total casualties. As if these figures are not astounding enough on their own, they become even more so when compared with the gains achieved. At the Somme, the British captured a grand total of 120 square miles of territory. After losing over 350,000 men, the British gained only 45 square miles at the Third Battle of Ypres (1917). This is not what the enthusiastic young men who boarded the trains and boats in 1914 thought they were getting into.[14]

If it was the enthusiasm of nationalism that brought men to the battlefields, it was the factories of the industrial revolution that supplied them with guns, bullets, cannons, and artillery shells. People who were not fighting the war on the battlefields worked at home in these factories to supply the soldiers. To wage war on this scale, governments had to mobilize populations and take control of economies. War bonds were sold, prices and wages were controlled, consumer goods were rationed, new taxes were imposed, women came out of the home to work in the factories, and even children collected scrap metal to be turned into weapons and ammunition. World War I became the first **total war,** in which every element of society and every aspect of national life were consumed by the conduct of war.

Total war represented the coming together of the two developments that had been transforming European societies and politics over the previous century—nationalism and industrialism. Nationalism allowed governments to make demands of their citizens that would have been impossible in its absence. Industrialization provided the material to equip, transport, and sustain armies on a totally new scale. Commenting on the role of nationalism, Bruce Porter explains, "The feverish nationalism that engulfed Europe in 1914 attested to the status that the nation-state had attained as the supreme claimant on human loyalty. . . . the nationalism of the war and its consequent unifying effect enabled states to mobilize their human resources on a scale previously unthinkable."[15] And the dramatic productive capacities of industrial societies produced almost surreal levels of destruction. It was on the blood-soaked battlefields of World War I that "all the technological and organizational genius of the industrial age culminat[ed] in the mass production of mass destruction."[16]

The carnage continued for three years, and by 1917 the nations and armies of Europe were close to exhaustion. Three pivotal events finally brought the war to an end. First, the armored tank, a new weapon introduced by the British in 1917, offered a way out of the stalemate of trench warfare. Tanks were remarkably successful at advancing across battlefields and through barbed wired without tens and hundreds of thousands of casualties. Second, largely because of the devastation of the war, the demoralization of the army, and the weakness of the government, the Bolsheviks (the communists) seized power in the Russian Revolution of November 1917 and quickly

total war A war in which participants mobilize all available resources, human and material, for the purpose of waging war.

made good on their promise to get Russia out of the war. Although peace with Russia seemed like good news for Germany, this was offset by the bad news of the American entry into the war on the side of France and Britain. German submarine warfare against ships crossing the Atlantic with supplies for Britain finally enraged the United States sufficiently to bring it into the war in April 1917. The tide of the war turned against Germany by August 1918, and Germany was defeated by November. The tragedy of the Great War was over. The troops, psychologically and physically battered and scarred by the horrors of industrialized warfare, headed home. It was now up to the statesmen to pick up the pieces and create a world in which the Great War might be the last one, the "war to end all wars," as it was optimistically called.

The road to war (again) Two major power wars within the lifetime of a single generation are unusual in international history. That Europe would again be plunged into war merely two decades after World War I indicates a connection between the two conflicts. World War II cannot be understood without an appreciation of the impact on World War I on both the victors and the vanquished. As the 1920s and 1930s unfolded, the memories of World War I dominated the thoughts of the generation that fought it. World War I cast a long, dark shadow on these two decades. The legacy of the war was not uniform, however. For some, the horrors of World War I forged a determination to avoid a repeat at any cost. Modern war had become so terrible that nothing could justify the risk of another war. For others, the perception that the Great War's settlement was unfair and unjust fueled resentment. These two ways of looking at the war were to prove a dangerous mix.

Major wars always pose the problem of creating a postwar order, a task that usually falls into the hands of the victors. The first step in this direction was the **Treaty of Versailles** (1919), which spelled out the final peace terms. The treaty was in many senses a quintessential "victor's peace"—harsh on the losers, easy on the winners. Germany was required to accept a host of conditions that applied to no one else—relinquishment of territory, restrictions on the size of its armed forces, and payment of huge reparations to the allies. Most important, Germany was forced to accept sole and total blame for the war. This provision was particularly galling and humiliating for the Germans, who came to feel that they had been unfairly singled out for harsh treatment simply because they were the losers. As a result, "all German parties and statesmen . . . took it for granted that the Treaty of Versailles required drastic revision."[17] A decade later, Hitler and the Nazis were able to take advantage of and exploit these sentiments as they rose to power.

In Great Britain and France, the legacy of the war was somewhat different. Having gone to war in 1914 with the expectation of a short conflict, these two countries instead found themselves trapped in a war of unprecedented horror. Though they were victorious, this victory came at a staggering cost. From the perspective of those who had just been through this experience, the prevailing mindset understandably became one of avoiding another war. During the 1970s in the United States, people often spoke of a Vietnam syndrome, referring to a supposed hesitancy to use force abroad for fear of becoming bogged down in another Vietnam. But if we compare the human and economic costs of the Vietnam War to the United States to the costs of World War I to the nations of Europe, there really is no comparison. The casualties suffered by Britain in World War I (adjusted for the differences in population) were 80 times greater than those of the United States in Vietnam. And World War I lasted

Treaty of Versailles (1919)
Codified the terms on which World War I was concluded. These terms were particularly harsh on the loser, Germany. In addition to requiring the payment of reparations, restrictions on German armed forces, and territorial concessions, the treaty stated that Germany bore full responsibility for World War I. This stipulation was viewed by Germans across the political spectrum as one sided and unjust.

only four years, whereas American casualties in Vietnam were spread over fifteen years. Imagine what the impact of Vietnam would have been in the United States had it suffered 4,000,000 casualties instead of 50,000. Only by trying to comprehend the magnitude of the human losses can we begin to comprehend the effect of World War I on Britain and France. The legacy of war was an incredible war weariness that made a Vietnam syndrome modest in comparison.

Many yearned for the creation of a postwar international order that might prevent another war, and American President Woodrow Wilson attempted to provide one. The cornerstone of his new world order was the **League of Nations**, an international organization that could form the basis for a collective, international response to future threats to peace. The League eventually proved ineffective in dealing with the threats to peace that emerged later in the 1920s. Several obstacles stood in the way of the League's becoming an effective force. First, despite the organization's connection to Woodrow Wilson, the United States failed to join when the U.S. Senate refused to ratify the treaty. Second, the Soviet Union (as Russia was renamed after the communist Russian Revolution in 1917) retreated into isolation. Third, and most important, the League's members were unwilling and unable to do what was necessary to respond to threats to peace. The League of Nations was a voluntary organization of states, not a world government. It did not have its own military forces. If it were to mount a credible response, it would need to convince member states to do so. In the end, the member nations were unwilling to respond.

As the 1920s drew to a close, a dangerous brew was already simmering—Germany was dissatisfied with terms laid out at Versailles, Western European nations were weary of war and determined to avoid a repeat at almost any cost, and the principal postwar institution designed to preserve the peace was not living up to expectations. The Great Depression made things worse, leading to economic hardship and political turmoil everywhere. In Germany, Hitler and his National Socialist German Workers' Party (Nazis, for short) used German resentment and the hardships of the depression to expand their political appeal and bring themselves to power (many forget that although the Nazis quickly destroyed German democracy, they came to power initially through democratic means). Fascist, military-oriented dictatorships emerged in Italy, Japan, and Spain as well. These regimes provided the final tipping point that plunged the world into war for the second time in a generation.

Traditional accounts date the start of World War II with Germany's invasion of Poland on September 1, 1939, although Japan's takeover of Manchuria (part of China) in 1931 or its invasion of China in 1937 can also mark the starting point. As Japan was expanding its empire in Asia during the 1930s, Hitler came to power in Germany in 1933. Ravaged by the Great Depression and limited by the Treaty of Versailles, Germany remained too weak in the early years of Nazi rule to cause much trouble. By 1935, however, the German economy was recovering and Hitler began to implement his plan to restore and expand German power. Conscription was resumed and the new German air force (the Luftwaffe) was unveiled. Though both actions violated the Treaty of Versailles, Germany's neighbors did nothing. Hitler's first major international move occurred in 1936, when German forces moved back into the Rhineland (German territory on the border of France and Germany). The Treaty of Versailles dictated that the Rhineland remain demilitarized. Again, Germany's neighbors did nothing.

Hitler became increasingly bold. During the years 1936–1938, German military

League of Nations International organization created in the aftermath of World War I. Tried to ensure that there would be a collective, international response to any future threats to peace.

Germany never invaded Great Britain

1941
- *Hitler breaks nonaggression act with Soviet Union*
- *Japan attacks Pearl Harbor. USA declares war on Japan*

spending increased dramatically and went largely unmatched and unchallenged. Instead of resisting these initial German moves, the Western nations engaged in a policy of **appeasement.** Rather than risking war over demands that could be seen as moderate and legitimate, France and Britain largely gave in. Though a few lonely voices, such as Winston Churchill in Britain, expressed concern, the policy of appeasement remained popular, in part because the idea of another war was so unpopular. The most infamous act of appeasement occurred in the fall of 1938. The problem (or pretext) was the presence of substantial numbers of ethnic Germans living in a part of Czechoslovakia known as the Sudetenland. With the encouragement of Hitler and the German government in Berlin, the Sudeten Germans demanded to be unified with Germany. As the situation approached war, a conference was held in Munich in which France and Britain (without the consent of the Czechs) agreed to give Hitler what he wanted. Upon his return home, British Prime Minister Neville Chamberlain waved the agreement aloft, proclaiming proudly the achievement of "peace in our time." A few months later, in March 1939, Germany surprised the world again by invading and capturing the rest of Czechoslovakia. The **Munich Agreement** had not satisfied Hitler. It was clear to all now that his goals went well beyond revising the Treaty of Versailles. Few could escape the conclusion that war would come again. But when would it come? And when it came, would the other nations of Europe be ready to fight Hitler's revived Germany?

The next "Great War" Europe did not have to wait long for answers to these questions. After Hitler signed a nonaggression pact with the Soviet Union, German troops invaded Poland on September 1, 1939. If there had been any doubt concerning the expansive nature of Hitler's plans, none remained. Britain and France declared war on Germany. After making quick work of Poland, Hitler turned his sights westward and quickly marched through Holland, Belgium, Luxembourg, and most of France, leaving Britain virtually alone to prevent total German domination of Western Europe. Though the United States provided some critical supplies to Britain, isolationist sentiment kept the United States out of the war. The Germans bombed London and other parts of Britain, which many feared was a prelude to an invasion across the English Channel. Though the bombing caused substantial damage and hardship, the anticipated invasion never came.

In 1941, two developments altered the course of the war. In June, Hitler broke his nonaggression agreement with Stalin and invaded the Soviet Union. Then, in December, the Japanese struck at Pearl Harbor, leading the United States to declare war on Japan. In response, Japan's ally Germany declared war on the United States, which brought the United States into the European conflict. The United States and the Soviet Union were now allies along with Britain in the struggle against Germany (Stalin promised to join the war against Japan shortly after Germany was defeated).

Though the United States declared war on Germany, the vast majority of the fighting in Europe between 1941 and 1944 took place on the Eastern Front between Germany and the Soviet Union. Stalin pressured Churchill and U.S. President Franklin Delano Roosevelt to relieve the burden of fighting on the Soviet Union by opening a "second front" in Western Europe, but this would not happen until June 1944. In the meantime the Soviet Union suffered massive casualties. Whereas previous estimates of Soviet casualties (military and civilian) were around 20 million, "new research

The German city of Dresden destroyed by massive aerial bombardment in 1945. The destruction of cities and civilians was the final step in the brutal logic of total war. Everyone and everything was now a legitimate target.

SOURCE: © Hulton-Deutsch Collection/CORBIS

growing out of the more open atmosphere in recent years has been pointing to figures closer to, and possibly in excess of, 25 million deaths."[18] Furthermore, as German and Soviet forces ground their way back and forth across Soviet territory, cities were leveled to the ground, factories lay in ruins, and farmland was destroyed. It is impossible to overstate the level of devastation and its impact on the Soviet Union. Even though the United States shouldered the burden of fighting Japan in the Pacific, its casualties were modest in comparison, totaling approximately 330,000 in Europe and the Pacific combined, a mere 1 to 2 percent of total Soviet casualties. Since the attack on Pearl Harbor was the only military engagement on United States territory, civilian casualties and physical destruction were minimal. The experience of the countries emerged from World War II as the two major world powers was strikingly different.

The invasion of France on the beaches of Normandy on June 7, 1944 opened the long-awaited second front, requiring Hitler to fight a war on two sides. As allied troops advanced on Germany from the west and Soviet troops closed in from the east, the eventual outcome of the war in Europe became clear. In June 1945, American, British, and Soviet troops met in Berlin and Germany's defeat was final. The war

June 1945 – Germany is defeated

against Japan continued for a few months after the German surrender, with the United States' use of atomic bombs on the cities of Hiroshima and Nagasaki in early August 1945 finally triggering Japan's surrender (just in time to prevent Soviet entry into the war against Japan, a fact some believe to be more than coincidence).[19] The second total war in a generation had come to its conclusion.

Aug 1945, atomic bomb ends WWII

THE COLD WAR (1945–1989)

After waging two wars in the span of thirty years with combined casualties approaching 100 million, the obvious concern was the avoidance of yet another war. As World War II reached its end, it was still unclear what sort of world would emerge from the wreckage. Would the victors be able to construct a postwar order that could avoid a descent into World War III? Would they be able to construct an international organization that might fulfill the failed promise of the League of Nations? Could the world finally learn to avoid the calamity of total war?

Though no one knew the answers to these questions, most realized that the answers depended on whether the United States and the Soviet Union would be able to build on the cooperative relationship established during the war. Everyone knew that these two countries were going to emerge from the war as the dominant powers, and the general character of any international order is usually defined by the nature of relations among its major powers. Before World War II, the relationship between the United States and the Soviet Union had been strained; the United States had refused even to recognize the Soviet government until 1933. Nonetheless, some hoped that their wartime alliance might form the basis for a better relationship. Others remained doubtful, seeing the wartime alliance as a product of unusual circumstances—namely, the presence of a common threat in Nazi Germany. Once that threat was eliminated, conflicts between the United States and the Soviet Union were expected to resurface.

During the war there were indications that the United States and the Soviet Union would have some trouble after the war. One can look to the U.S. atomic bomb program, the Manhattan Project, for one sign of the problems to come. Even though Great Britain was kept informed about the progress of the project, Britain and the United States decided not to share the information with Joseph Stalin, the leader of the Soviet Union, though he certainly knew about the project from spying. Though the United States was allied with the Soviet Union, President Roosevelt "saw no reason to take the Soviets into American confidence about a weapons system of potentially great significance in the post-war years."[20] Even in the midst of war, suspicion was the order of the day.

America kept its development of the atomic bomb a secret from Joseph Stalin.

Keeping the atomic secret was only one sign that the Soviet Union was not viewed as an ally in the same sense as Britain. Another sign of trouble to come was disagreements about the postwar fate of the nations of Eastern Europe (e.g., Poland, Romania, Hungary, and others). The military reality was that at war's end Soviet forces would be in control of these countries. The United States insisted that Stalin promise to hold free elections in Eastern Europe after the war. In fact, Stalin signed the Declaration on Liberated Europe (1945), which called for free and open elections in Eastern Europe. Stalin, however, wanted governments friendly to the Soviet Union. Given

Disagreement between USA and USSR about post-war fate of E. Europe.

Soviet losses in Word War II, Stalin thought this was a reasonable demand to protect Soviet security in the future. Unfortunately, these two objectives could not be met simultaneously: freely elected governments in Eastern Europe would not have been friendly to the Soviet Union. As John Lewis Gaddis explains, "F.D.R.'s superficial knowledge of Eastern Europe kept him from fully recognizing the contradiction between freely elected and pro-Russian governments in that turbulent part of the world."[21]

The secrecy surrounding the Manhattan Project and the future of Eastern Europe were not the only sources of tension between the two allies (the British and American failure to open a second front in Europe in 1942 or 1943 was another), but they are enough to indicate that the United States–Soviet alliance during World War II was more a product of a common threat than of broader common interests and outlooks. To use a familiar adage of international politics: the enemy of my enemy is my friend. It is more accurate to view the United States and Soviet Union as co-belligerents in the war against Germany, not allies in any deeper sense of the term.

US/Soviet alliance in WWII was more the product of a common threat than of anything else.

The Cold War begins: Conflict and containment The earliest signs of deteriorating U.S.-Soviet relations were in Europe. The impossibility of reconciling the Western allies' desires for free elections in Eastern Europe with Soviet expectations of friendly regimes became obvious as Stalin moved to impose communist governments. It was increasingly clear that Stalin had no intention of abiding by the provisions of the Declaration on Liberated Europe calling for broadly representative governments followed by free and open elections. Political dissent throughout Eastern Europe was ruthlessly crushed. These Soviet actions prompted Winston Churchill's famous warning that "from Stettin in the Baltic to Trieste in the Adriatic, an iron curtain has descended across the continent."[22]

In response to these developments, an American diplomat in Moscow, George Kennan, composed an analysis of Soviet policy. Conveyed to Washington as a diplomatic telegram in early February 1946, it was later published in the influential journal *Foreign Affairs* under the title, "The Sources of Soviet Conduct" (signed only as "X"). Kennan argued that the United States needed to understand the expansionist nature of Soviet policy and the threats it posed to U.S. interests. The sources of Soviet expansion, he argued, were deeply rooted in Russia's historical insecurity, Stalin's paranoid personality, the communist regime's need for external enemies, and the imperatives of Soviet ideology. Though in the long run these expansionist tendencies could be modified or tamed, the only immediate option available to the United States was to adopt a policy of **containment.** The United States needed to use its power—political, economic, and military—to prevent further expansion of Soviet influence. Kennan's analysis struck a chord with policymakers in Washington. Though originally focused on Western Europe, the policy of containment was later expanded to other areas of the world.[23]

Because of political pressure to bring American troops home from Europe as soon as possible, many feared a military threat from the Soviet Union. But even those who were less concerned with a direct military attack worried that postwar economic hardship would provide fertile ground for communist parties loyal to the Soviet Union to come to power. Virtually everyone agreed that the economic reconstruction of Western Europe was vital to its security. The primary instrument for recovery was the

containment The United States' policy of resisting the expansion of Soviet/communist influence during the Cold War.

Marshall Plan The program of economic assistance to rebuild the nations of Western Europe in the aftermath of World War II.

Truman Doctrine Announced by President Harry Truman in 1947, this policy committed the United States to assist foreign governments threatened by communist forces. Represented an expansive vision of the policy of containment.

Cold War The conflict between the United States and the Soviet Union from the late 1940s until the late 1980s (the fall of the Berlin Wall) or early 1990s (the collapse of the Soviet Union).

domino theory The belief (and fear) that the spread of communism to one country almost automatically threatened its expansion to neighboring countries.

North Atlantic Treaty Organization (NATO) The Cold War alliance, including the United States, Canada, and many Western European nations, against the Soviet Union and its allies. Has survived the end of the Cold War, even expanding to include many former Soviet allies in Eastern Europe.

decolonization The achievement of political independence by European colonies, especially in Asia and Africa, in the two decades following World War II.

Marshall Plan, announced in May 1947. The Marshall Plan offered massive economic aid to all the countries of Europe (including the Soviet Union) devastated by the war. The Soviet Union refused to accept this aid because some of the conditions were deemed incompatible with its socialist economy. The Soviet-imposed governments in Eastern Europe did likewise. There is universal agreement that the Marshall Plan was a stunning success. By 1952, Western Europe's productive output was almost double its prewar levels. There was no similar recovery in the nations under Soviet domination.

At roughly the same time, the United States also became concerned about a civil war in Greece because the British informed the United States that they could no longer give assistance to the Greek government in combatting a communist insurgency. In a speech to Congress explaining his decision to aid the Greek government (as well as the Turkish government), Truman laid out his policy goals in broad and grandiose terms: "I believe it must be the policy of the United States to support free people who are resisting who are resisting attempted subjugation by armed minorities or outside pressures."[24] This pronouncement, embodying an expansive vision of containment, came to be known as the **Truman Doctrine.** Thus, by the end of 1947 the hope for a cooperative superpower relationship was dead and the **Cold War** had begun in earnest.

The Cold War expands Despite the rhetoric of the Truman Doctrine, which seemed to suggest that the United States would assist *all* "free peoples," it was unclear whether containment would apply everywhere or merely in select, particularly significant, parts of the world. It was also unclear what types of aid would be provided and whether the United States was prepared to go to war to prevent the expansion of communist influence. The fall of China to the communists in 1949 and the North Korean attack on South Korea in 1950 would have the effect of expanding the scope of containment well beyond Europe. The United States decided to take military action under the aegis of the United Nations to prevent the expansion of communism into South Korea. The Soviet Union was absent the day the United Nations Security Council voted on this resolution and thus failed to veto the action. The Korean War, which eventually involved the communist Chinese as well, lasted for four years at the cost of more than 50,000 American casualties. The net effect of the Korean War was to expand containment into a global doctrine. Even if a given country was not strategically very significant, the fear was that if any country "fell" to the communists, others were sure to follow. This belief became known as the **domino theory.** The Korean War also shifted the emphasis of containment. Now the threat and response were seen increasingly in military terms, with one result being the creation of a military alliance, the **North Atlantic Treaty Organization** (**NATO**), in Europe.

The logic of containment and the domino theory would be most severely tested in the Third World. World War II had seriously weakened the colonial powers of Britain and France, and the immediate postwar years witnessed the rise of independence or "national liberation" movements throughout Asia and Africa. The process of **decolonization,** however, was not free of conflict: sometimes the colonial power tried to hold on, usually in vain. But conflicts continued after independence as different groups, including communists, struggled for power. These postcolonial conflicts provided all sorts of opportunities for external meddling, becoming battlegrounds in the larger Cold War.

The most important such conflict of the Cold War occurred in Vietnam. A former French colony, Vietnam was divided between the communist north, supported by China and the Soviet Union, and the noncommunist, though hardly democratic, south. In the late 1950s and early 1960s, a communist insurgency supported by communist North Vietnam threatened the regime in South Vietnam. United States policymakers were determined to support the South Vietnamese government, at first in the form of aid and military advisers. It was not long before the United States was actively involved in fighting the war, and by 1968 there were over 500,000 American combat forces on the ground. Despite repeated promises that victory was at hand, the war dragged on year after year and casualties, which eventually exceeded 50,000, mounted. Public support for the war eroded as protests against the war became commonplace. Despite more than ten years of fighting, the world's most "powerful" nation was unable to prevail. In 1975, communist forces captured Hanoi, the capital of South Vietnam, and television screens around the world were filled with scenes of desperate people climbing to the roof of the U.S. embassy to reach the helicopters carrying the last people out before the communist victory was total.[25]

Easing the Cold War Even as the Vietnam War was being waged, there were attempts to ease the superpower conflict that was at the heart of the Cold War. After being elected president in 1968, Richard Nixon and his chief foreign policy adviser Henry Kissinger embarked upon a policy of **détente** toward the Soviet Union. They thought it was time to move beyond merely reacting to the Soviet Union through containment. They believed that the United States possessed tools that could be used to moderate Soviet behavior. There were things the Soviet Union wanted from the United States that could be offered in exchange for changes in Soviet behavior. The Soviet Union wanted to be recognized as a power on par with the United States, and it wanted greater opportunities to trade with the United States. And there were things the United States wanted from the Soviet Union, such as greater respect for human rights and restraint in Soviet support for communist governments and insurgencies in the Third World. Détente was based on the assumption that these different interests and objectives of the two powers could be "linked" in order to create a relationship based not only on conflict, but also on cooperation when common interests were involved. In the Soviet Union this policy was known as "peaceful coexistence."

Détente was controversial, even within Nixon's own party. A group of conservative Republicans and Democrats, including the former Governor of California, Ronald Reagan, were convinced that détente was a one-way street. Pointing to a dramatic increase in the Soviet Union's nuclear arsenal during the 1970s they were deeply skeptical of the entire arms control process. To make matters even worse, they argued that the promised benefits of détente failed to materialize as the Soviet Union continued to expand its influence in the Third World, including Latin America, through the support of revolutionary movements. Détente had merely lulled the United States into a false sense of security. Whatever the merits of this argument, the Soviet Union's invasion of Afghanistan in 1979 seemed to lend it credence. The invasion was the death knell for détente. After failing to win the Republican nomination in 1976,

détente A policy and period of relaxed tensions between the United States and Soviet Union during the 1970s.

Reagan was successful in 1980, going on to defeat Democrat Jimmy Carter in 1980 by a landslide.

The resurgence and end of the Cold War Reagan was convinced that détente allowed the Soviet Union to surge ahead of the United States in military power and expand its political influence in the Third World while the United States naively waited for Soviet moderation. The new administration pursued policies that many viewed as a return to the coldest days of the Cold War, including an ambitious increase in military spending in both the conventional and nuclear areas. Arms control with the Soviet Union was placed temporarily on hold. The administration was also committed to assisting anticommunist governments and insurgency movements in Third World countries. Most controversial was its assistance to the "contras" in Nicaragua, who were fighting to overthrow the communist government. Opponents in the United States feared that Reagan's policies risked an expensive and dangerous arms race with the Soviet Union as well as possible military intervention in a Third World conflict, another Vietnam. Administration supporters claimed these policies were a necessary demonstration of American power to deter an ambitious Soviet Union. Some may have even hoped that the Soviet Union, suffering from severe economic problems, could never afford to stay in a renewed arms race.

Soviet leadership was in a state of transition during Reagan's first term. Leonid Brezhnev, who had been in power since the 1960s, died in 1982. He was followed by two geriatric remnants of the old guard before a much younger and vibrant figure, **Mikhail Gorbachev,** appeared on the scene. In 1984, Gorbachev had impressed British Prime Minister Margaret Thatcher as someone she could "do business with." It did not take long for people to realize this was a new type of Soviet leader. Not only were he and his wife relatively young and outgoing figures, but on a more important level he was determined to reform the stagnant Soviet system through his twin policies of **perestroika** and **glasnost.** *Perestroika* (restructuring) was intended to loosen government control of the economy and move it in a market-oriented direction. *Glasnost* (openness) was designed to open the Soviet political system to greater dissent and discussion of the problems that plagued Soviet society.

Much to the dismay of many conservatives in the United States, Reagan, like his friend Margaret Thatcher, became convinced that Gorbachev was for real. Chummy summits complete with smiling photo ops soon followed. Progress was made in nuclear arms control talks for the first time in over a decade. But despite the reduction in tensions, the question of how Gorbachev would respond to a real crisis or challenge remained unanswered. If "openness" got too out of hand, would Gorbachev move to crush dissent, as past Soviet leaders had? Was he really different than his predecessors?

By the end of the 1980s, Gorbachev faced a dilemma at home and in Eastern Europe: *glasnost* proved to be a smashing success, whereas *perestroika* was a dismal failure. The result, as David Reynolds explains, was that "[a]s the economy collapsed, freedom to protest grew. Reconstruction became deconstruction."[26] As economies foundered and domestic criticism mounted, the regimes in Eastern Europe grew increasingly fragile. How would Gorbachev respond when pro-Soviet regimes found themselves on the wrong end of *glasnost*?

The answer came in East Germany, which remained one of the most hardline regimes in Eastern Europe until the very end. East Germany's leader, Erich Honecker,

Gorbachev, Mikhail (1931–) Leader of the Soviet Union from 1985 until its dissolution in 1991.

perestroika Mikhail Gorbachev's reforms during the second half of the 1980s, aimed at reforming the Soviet economic system.

glasnost Mikhail Gorbachev's political reforms in the Soviet Union during the second half of the 1980s allowing for greater freedom of expression and dissent.

The Berlin Wall is torn down in November 1989, marking the beginning of the end of the Cold War and the Soviet Union.

viewed Gorbachev and his reforms with alarm. This reaction was not without justification, since Honecker, his cronies, and the infamous East German secret police (the "Stasi") were despised by the East German people. When Gorbachev visited East Germany in October 1989, the crowds chanted "Gorby" as Honecker, as clueless as he was unpopular, stood at his side. Within weeks, opposition to Honecker's regime led to his ouster and desperate attempts to prevent an outright revolution. It was clear that Gorbachev would not save the East German regime from the wrath of its own people. By the middle of November, the Honecker regime was long gone and the Berlin Wall was being torn down. Although Gorbachev did not tear down the wall himself, he did not stop others from doing so. People around the world watched in amazement as Berliners streamed back and forth under the Brandenburg Gate between what used to be East and West Berlin. They celebrated on the very spots where they would have been shot a few months earlier. The same forces that unraveled communism in Eastern Europe would eventually do the same in the Soviet Union. By 1991, the Soviet Union itself joined the list of former communist nations when Boris Yeltsin, Gorbachev's successor, declared communism dead and the Soviet Union itself broke apart in several independent nations.

The curious peace of the Cold War   Students of international relations spend a lot of time trying to understand things that actually did happen. Sometimes, however, it is just as interesting and equally important to ask about and understand those things that did not happen. The peace of the Cold War provides a good example of just such a nonevent. For more than forty years, two of the greatest military powers the world has ever known, divided by an intense ideological rivalry, struggled against each other across the globe. But despite the intensity of the conflict, they never actually went to war with each other. In many ways this is a very curious outcome: it is unusual in international history for two great powers to compete against one another on such a scale and never fight. If any "nonevent" cries out for an explanation, it is the curious peace that was the Cold War.

Why did the Cold War never turn hot? Explanations of why something fails to occur are by their very nature very speculative. In thinking about what one scholar has called the **long peace,** a variety of possible explanations have been put forward.[27] John Mearsheimer highlights two factors, the presence of only two major powers (**bipolarity**) and nuclear weapons.[28] His argument is simple: the chances for war increase when there are more than two major powers because this increases the number of avenues through which war might break out. If there are five major powers, a war could break out between any two of them. When only two major powers are present, there is only one route to war. It is like buying lottery tickets: the more tickets you buy, the greater your chances of winning. Similarly, the fewer major powers, the fewer chances for war, and the less likely war becomes. Furthermore, the fact that the two countries had enough nuclear weapons to destroy the other made them both extremely cautious in their dealings with each other because the potential costs of war exceeded any possible benefits. Many scholars, however, remain skeptical that nuclear weapons were critical in preventing war from breaking out. John Mueller argues that conventional war had become so destructive that this alone was enough to make the two powers extremely hesitant to risk war.[29]

A balance of power between the two superpowers is also credited as the basis for peace. Since each country was roughly equal in military strength, neither side could be confident of victory in war. Since national leaders usually initiate wars when they think they can win, this balance meant that neither side was tempted to start a war because neither was confident of victory. Turning this argument somewhat on its head, Stephen Walt sees the peace as resting on a dramatic imbalance of power, claiming that the combined power of the United States and its allies (Japan, West Germany, France, Britain, etc.) was substantially greater than that of the Soviet Union and its allies (Poland, Hungary, Romania, etc.).[30] Given this imbalance, it was not necessary for the United States to go to war. Soviet leaders realized their inferiority and never challenged genuinely vital American interests, thus avoiding any direct confrontation. Whatever the reason, the absence of war between the United States and the Soviet Union is certainly a remarkable (and very fortunate) feature of the Cold War and its end.

THE POST–COLD WAR WORLD

We are now a little over a decade into the post–Cold War world. The mere fact that almost everyone still describes the period since 1989 as the "post–Cold War era" is in itself telling. This is an era that remains defined by what it is not rather than what it is. Although all agree that we are no longer in the Cold War, there is no consensus about what sort of world has replaced it. In the first few years of the post–Cold War period, expectations about the future of international relations diverged. Some expected a more stable, less conflictual world marked by the triumph of liberal democracy

long peace The "peace" or absence of war between the United States and the Soviet Union during the Cold War.

bipolarity The existence of two major powers in international politics. Usually refers to the structure of the Cold War.

around the globe, economic prosperity, peace dividends, and the reduction of war and conflict. Others feared that the relative stability and predictability of the Cold War order would be replaced by newly unleashed forces of national and ethnic conflicts that would prove more dangerous than the superpower rivalry we had grown accustomed to. Almost fifteen years into the post–Cold War era, these debates about the future of world politics continue to rage without any definitive resolution (we examine many of these questions and debates later in this text). Nonetheless, it is possible to make some general observations about the shape of international politics in the post–Cold War era to which most, if not all, would subscribe. An evaluation of the post–Cold War world is an exercise in examining and judging the relative significance of changes and continuities. Thus, we can approach the post–Cold War era by asking ourselves two questions: What has changed with the end of the Cold War? And what has remained unchanged?

The demise and eventual dissolution of the Soviet Union was unquestionably a major event that transformed critical aspects of international relations, especially in Europe. Germany is unified again for the first time since 1945. Former allies of the Soviet Union now seek admission into NATO, and there is even some consideration of eventual Russian membership. The "artificial" division of Europe has ended. One cannot underestimate the importance of these transformations. Outside the confines of Europe, the United States and Russia retain only a fraction of the nuclear weapons they possessed at the height of the Cold War, and this number is set to go lower still. But the end of the Cold War did not change everything. The world of 2000 would not look totally unfamiliar to someone who had been asleep for twenty years. As John Ikenberry explains, "Only a part of the post–World War II order—the bipolar order—was destroyed by the dramatic events of 1989–1991."[31]

There are still significant elements of continuity, especially in terms of the American influence in the world and the perpetuation of the institutions created under American tutelage during the Cold War.[32] The ending of the Cold War has not brought with it any fundamental alteration in the scope of American power and commitments throughout the world. U.S. forces remain in Japan, Korea, and Europe, though in somewhat smaller numbers, just as they were at the height of the Cold War. The passing of the Soviet military alliance in Europe, the Warsaw Pact, has not been accompanied by the end of the American alliance, NATO. The Gulf War, considered at the time a possible harbinger of a "new world order," demonstrated the continuing centrality of the United States. Though the war involved an international coalition with the blessing of the United Nations, it was fundamentally an American undertaking. A handful of other nations contributed military forces, money, and military bases, but the outcome was determined by the military power of the United States. The 2003 war which toppled Saddam Hussein was, with the significant exception of Great Britain, almost entirely an American undertaking.

Even with the reductions in U.S. military spending that accompanied the end of the Cold War, no other nation possesses the necessary combination of capability and willingness to challenge the military power of the United States. Whether one wishes to refer to this as American "hegemony," "dominance," or "unipolarity," the basic point remains the same. Ian Clark highlights this point in remarking on the "essential continuity in the role of American power. . . . There are institutions that were created during the Cold War, and which were almost defining attributes of it, [that] still endure into the post–Cold War era."[33]

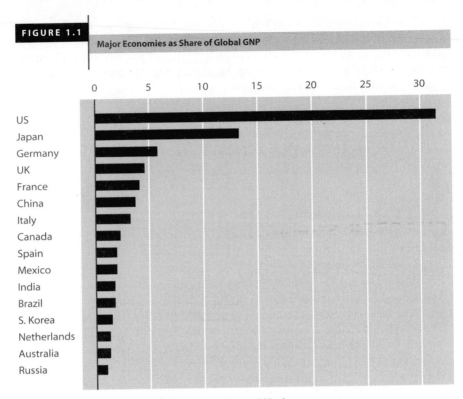

FIGURE 1.1

Major Economies as Share of Global GNP

SOURCE: *Financial Times,* January 20, 2004, p. 7. Figure from World Bank.

There is, of course, more to the character of international relations than the distribution of military power. There are also important continuities in terms of the post–Cold War global economy. Clearly the United States remains the world's largest and most powerful economy (see figure 1.1). Its economy is more than twice as large as that of Japan, the world's next largest economy, and almost five times larger than even that of a unified Germany. Increasing economic cooperation and integration among the nations of Europe, however, is creating an economic unit that rivals the United States. Thus, whereas there is only one real center of military power in the world, the same cannot be said for economic power. Randall Schweller divides the world's power structure into "two separate parts: a unipolar security structure led by the United States and a tripolar economic one revolving around Germany [and Europe], Japan and America."[34] But this economic reality was not the result of the end of the Cold War and represents instead the continuation of a trend that was well under way long before the Berlin Wall came down. Just as important is the continuity of the major economic institutions of the post–World War II or Cold War period. The World Bank, the International Monetary Fund, and the general trading system created under American leadership remain in place (we will say much more about these economic institutions in later sections). Thus, it is hard to disagree with Ikenberry's conclusion that "the post–Cold War order is really a continuation and extension of the Western order forged during and after World War II."[35]

The world, however, is a bigger place, and we must remember that for the vast majority of the world's people life continues much as it did before the end of the Cold War. The gap between the world's rich and its more numerous poor has not been narrowed by the passing of the Soviet Union. Large portions of humanity go to bed hungry every night and have no access to basic necessities of life. The global environmental problems that were emerging as critical global issues before the end of the Cold War remain as pressing as ever: the demise of the superpower rivalry has not restored the hole in the ozone layer, ended global warming, or replenished the world's rainforests. Deadly national and ethnic conflicts continue to rage. If we are living in a new world order, it is one with much continuity from the old world order.

CHAPTER SUMMARY

- The modern state system, characterized by a small number of relatively large sovereign political units, gradually took shape as Europe began to emerge from the medieval period around 1300. The economic pressures of the commercial revolution and the military dynamics of the gunpowder revolution contributed to the creation of larger and larger political units. The Protestant Reformation and the Thirty Years War (1618–1648) brought the origins of the modern conception of sovereignty as embodied in the Peace of Westphalia (1648).

- The period between the Peace of Westphalia and the French Revolution (1789) was a period of relative calm in which wars and conflicts tended to be limited, modest affairs. This calm was rooted in the nature of European societies and politics, particularly absolutist monarchism, the lack of any strong sense of loyalty or connection between people and their rulers, and the absence of ideological conflict.

- The American and French revolutions marked the beginning of modern nationalism and its doctrine of popular sovereignty. Over time, this idea contributed to the erosion of absolutist monarchism and the international order it sustained.

- At the same time, the industrial revolution of the 1800s transformed European societies in ways that had a profound effect on international politics. Increasing wealth and advances in technology solidified European dominance of the globe. Nationalism and the industrial revolution combined to create the "total war" of World Wars I and II.

- In the aftermath of two devastating wars in the span of a single generation, the conflict between the United States and the Soviet Union dashed hopes for a more peaceful world order based on cooperation among the great powers. Although the Cold War never resulted in direct military conflict between the superpowers, it did bring several smaller wars as the United States and Soviet Union engaged in sometimes fierce competition for influence throughout the world, including the recently decolonized nations of Africa and Asia.

- The superpower conflict, political conflict in postcolonial societies, and the policy of containment would eventually lead the United States to war in Vietnam.

- Attempts to moderate the Cold War and control the growth of nuclear arsenals lead to détente and several arms limitation agreements during the 1970s. This thaw in the Cold War proved short lived. The Soviet invasion of Afghanistan in 1979 and the election of Ronald Reagan in 1980 ushered in a period of renewed hostility and conflict between the superpowers.

- By the mid-1980s, the stagnation of communism in the Soviet Union and Eastern Europe prompted a new generation of leaders, particularly Mikhail Gorbachev, to conclude that radical reforms were essential. His policies of perestroika and glasnost, however, ultimately doomed the very communist system they were designed to save. The unraveling of communism was most vividly displayed in Berlin, where the wall between East and West was demolished by the city's citizens in the fall of 1989. This event marked the end of the Cold War.

- Though we have experienced several crises since the end of the Cold War (e.g., the 1991 Gulf War, the terrorist attacks of September 11, 2001, and the 2003 war in Iraq), the fundamental nature of the post–Cold War world remains in doubt.

KEY TERMS

FURTHER READINGS

A classic work on the rise of the modern state system that emphasizes the military aspects is John Herz, "The Rise and Demise of the Territorial State," *World Politics* 9 (July 1957): 473–93. Two more recent treatments are Bruce D. Porter, *War and the Rise of the State* (New York: Free Press, 1994), especially chapters 2 and 3, and Hendrik Spruyt, *The Sovereign State and Its Competitors* (Princeton: Princeton University Press, 1996). For the period between the Peace of West-phalia and the French Revolution, few works surpass the classic account: Edward V. Gulick, *Europe's Classical Balance of Power* (New York: W.W. Norton, 1967).

The rise and impact of nationalism has been the focus of a very large body of literature. Good starting points include Ernest Geller, *Nations and Nationalism* (Oxford: Blackwell, 1983); Eric Hobsbawn, *Nations and Nationalism since 1780* (Cambridge: Cambridge University Press, 1990); and Benedict Anderson, *Imagined Communities: Reflections on the Origin and Spread of Nationalism* (New York and London: Verso, 1991).

The events leading to the outbreak of World War I are given a very straightforward treatment in Laurence LaFore's *The Long Fuse: An Interpretation of the Origins of World War I* (New York: J. P. Lippincott, 1971). A more recent account is Niall Ferguson, *The Pity of War: Explaining World War I* (New York: Basic Books, 1999). An interesting discussion of the legacies of World War I is provided in Porter, *War and the Rise of the State,* chapters 5 and 6.

Not surprisingly, there are many works on the origins and course of World War II. Perhaps the best and most accessible overview is Gerhard Weinberg, *A World at Arms: A Global History of World War II* (Cambridge: Cambridge University Press, 1994). On United States policy during this period, see Robert Dallek, *Franklin D. Roosevelt and American Foreign Policy, 1932–1945* (Oxford: Oxford University Press, 1979). An excellent book on the war against Japan is Saburo Ienaga, *The Pacific War, 1931–1945* (New York: Pantheon, 1978).

A widely respected examination of the early years of the Cold War is John Lewis Gaddis, *The United States and the Origins of the Cold War, 1941–1947* (New York: Columbia University Press, 1971). A more imposing treatment is Melvyn Leffler, *A Preponderance of Power: National Security, the Truman Administration and the Cold War* (Stanford: Stanford University Press, 1992). For a more general overview of the Cold War, see Ronald E. Powaski, *The Cold War, The United States and the Soviet Union, 1917–1991* (Oxford: Oxford University Press, 1998). The Vietnam War is covered in Robert D. Schulzinger, *A Time for War: The United States and Vietnam, 1941–1975* (Oxford: Oxford University Press, 1997). The end of the Cold War is covered in Raymond Garthoff, *The Great Transition: American-Soviet Relations and the End of the Cold War* (Washington, DC: Brookings, 1994). An excellent place to begin making sense of the Cold War's aftermath is Ian Clark's interesting yet theoretically rigorous *The Post–Cold War Order* (Oxford: Oxford University Press, 2001).

NOTES

[1] John Weltman, *World Politics and the Evolution of War* (Baltimore: The John Hopkins University Press, 1995), p. 21.

[2] Geoffrey Parker, "The Gunpowder Revolution, 1300–1500," *Cambridge Illustrated History of Warfare*, ed. Geoffrey Parker (Cambridge: Cambridge University Press, 1995), p. 107.

[3] Weltman, *World Politics and the Evolution of War*, p. 24.

[4] Bruce Porter, *War and the Rise of the State: The Military Foundations of Modern Politics* (New York: The Free Press, 1994), p. 124.

[5] See John A. Lynn, "States in Conflict, 1661–1763," *Cambridge Illustrated History of Modern Warfare*, pp. 164–185.

[6] Kalevi J. Holsti, *Peace and War: Armed Conflicts and International Order, 1648–1989* (Cambridge: Cambridge University Press, 1991), pp. 83–102.

[7] John Owen, "The Canon and the Cannon: A Review Essay," *International Security* 25 (Winter 1998/99): 161.

[8] Paul W. Schroeder, *The Transformation of European Politics, 1763–1848* (Oxford: Oxford University Press, 1994), pp. 68–69.

[9] John A. Lynn, "Nations in Arms, 1763–1814," *Cambridge Illustrated History of Warfare*, p. 193.

[10] Ibid., p. 207.

[11] Weltman, *World Politics and the Evolution of War*, p. 42.

[12] Michael Mandelbaum, *The Fate of Nations: The Search for National Security in the Nineteenth and Twentieth Centuries* (Cambridge: Cambridge University Press, 1988), p. 40.

[13] Hew Strachan, "Military Modernization, 1789–1918," *The Oxford Illustrated History of Modern Europe*, ed. T.C.W. Blanning (New York: Oxford University Press, 1996), p. 75.

[14] Casualty figures drawn from Williamson Murray, "The West at War, 1914–1918," *Cambridge Illustrated History of Warfare*, pp. 284–288; and Weltman, *World Politics and the Evolution of War*, p. 93.

[15] Porter, *War and the Rise of the State*, p. 170.

[16] Ibid., p. 150.

[17] Randall Schweller, *Deadly Imbalances: Tripolarity and Hitler's Strategy of World Conquest* (New York: Columbia University Press, 1998), p. 5.

[18] Gerhard Weinberg, *A World at Arms: A Global History of World War II* (Cambridge: Cambridge University Press, 1994), p. 894. About one-third of the casualties were military and two-thirds civilian.

[19] For the argument that the decision to use the atomic bomb was based on a desire to scare or impress the Soviet Union, see Gar Alperovitz, *The Decision to Use the Atomic Bomb and the Architecture of an American Myth* (New York: Alfred A Knopf, 1995).

[20] Ibid., p. 573.

[21] John Lewis Gaddis, *The United States and the Origins of the Cold War* (New York: Columbia University Press, 1972), p. 173.

[22] Ibid., p. 308.

[23] "X" [George F. Kennan], "The Sources of Soviet Conduct," *Foreign Affairs* 25 (July 1947): 566–82. The best discussion of Kennan's view of containment can be found in John Lewis Gaddis, *Strategies of Containment* (Oxford: Oxford University Press, 1982), chapter 2.

[24] Gaddis, *United States and the Origins of the Cold War*, p. 351.

[25] On the Vietnam War, see Robert D. Schulzinger, *A Time for War: The United States and Vietnam 1941–1975* (Oxford: Oxford University Press, 1997). An insightful explanation of the reasons for the United States' defeat is presented in Andrew Mack, "Why Big Nations Lose Small Wars: The Politics of Asymmetric Conflict," *World Politics* 27 (1975): 175–200.

[26] David Reynolds, "Europe Divided and Reunited, 1945–1995," *The Oxford Illustrated History of Modern Europe*, ed. T. W. C. Blanning (New York: Oxford University Press, 1996), p. 299.

[27] John Lewis Gaddis, *The Long Peace: Inquiries into the History of the Cold War* (Oxford: Oxford University Press, 1987).

[28] John Mearsheimer, "Why We Will Soon Miss the Cold War," *The Atlantic* (August 1990): 35–50.

[29] John Mueller, "The Essential Irrelevance of Nuclear Weapons: Stability in the Postwar World," *International Security* 13 (Fall, 1988): 55–79.

[30] Stephen M. Walt, *The Origins of Alliances* (Ithaca: Cornell University Press, 1987), pp. 274–78.

[31] John Ikenberry, *After Victory: Institutions, Strategic Restraints, and the Rebuilding of Order after Major Wars* (Princeton: Princeton University Press, 2000), p. 215.

[32] This point is emphasized effectively in Ian Clark, *The Post Cold War Order: The Spoils of Peace* (Oxford: Oxford University Press, 2001).

[33] Ibid., p. 23.

[34] Schweller, *Deadly Imbalances*, p. 199.

[35] In Clark, *Post Cold War Order*, p. 23.

CHAPTER TWO

CONTENDING PERSPECTIVES ON INTERNATIONAL POLITICS

MANY QUESTIONS, EVEN MORE ANSWERS

Students in international relations courses are often frustrated by what they see as the absence of any precise answers to questions and problems. On one level, this frustration is justified: we do not have answers in the same sense that problems in math classes have definitive, correct solutions that can be found at the end of the text. On another level, the problem is misidentified. Upon further reflection we realize that frustration emerges not from the absence of answers but their proliferation—too many answers, not too few. The problem is not that we are lacking an answer to the question of why nations go to war, but rather that we have five, six, seven, or more answers. Although each explanation might sound perfectly convincing viewed in isolation, the problem we face is that all of them cannot possibly be correct simultaneously.

This is not a problem unique to international relations but rather a common feature of all social sciences (and more of a feature of the natural sciences than many realize). Anyone who has attempted to get a roomful of economists to agree on how best to combat unemployment quickly recognizes that they also have more answers than they have questions and more solutions than problems. They will offer several explanations about why we have unemployment in the first place and then propose even more potential solutions derived from these differing explanations. Sometimes apparently competing explanations are actually complementary and can be reconciled if one thinks carefully enough about how they might fit together. But there are also times when reconciliation is not possible because the contending positions are manifestations of more fundamental and incompatible assumptions about how the world works.

The existence of alternative and competing paradigms, theories, philosophies, and worldviews characterizes the study of international relations just as it characterizes all other social sciences. As a general rule, different perspectives have two components. Each usually has an analytical component that involves an explanation of why things work the way they do. There is also usually a prescriptive element that suggests what should be done to deal with or solve particular problems. What an economist thinks needs to be done to reduce unemployment (the prescription) depends on why he or she thinks we have unemployment in the first place (the explanation).

Political science and international relations are no different in this respect. Students of international relations disagree intensely about explanations for, and possible solutions to, critical international problems. And frequently these disagreements are outgrowths of fundamental disagreements about the nature of international relations, though the more basic issues at stake often go unarticulated when the debate focuses on a concrete issue. As Stephen Walt explains, "Everyone uses theories—whether he or she knows it or not—and disagreements about policy usually rest on more fundamental disagreement about the basic forces that shape international outcomes."[1]

This chapter presents several of the major alternative perspectives on international relations. These differing views of the nature and dynamics of international relations are themselves rooted in more fundamental and basic social and political philosophies. That is, they represent the extension of more general ideas and assumptions about the nature of humans and society. We will first examine the underlying social or political theory or philosophy upon which each perspective is based and then examine how those ideas have been applied to the realm of international relations.

Over the past two centuries, three dominant social and political philosophies have framed our thinking about social, economic, and political issues—conservatism, liberalism, and Marxism. Each of these philosophies rests on a set of assumptions or ideas that provides a basic intellectual framework for understanding and explaining how the social world works. The basic ideas of each approach have also been applied to understanding the realm of international relations. But these three perspectives do not exhaust the range of potential worldviews. Merely because these have been the dominant perspectives does not imply that they are the only ones. In recent years several alternative approaches, particularly feminism and constructivism, have begun to challenge the dominance of these traditional perspectives.

REALISM

The most influential approach to international relations, especially in the United States since the end of World War II, is **realism.** The realist view of international politics has its intellectual roots in conservative social and political philosophy, and if we want to gain a full and deep understanding of realism as an outlook on the world, we need appreciate its conservative foundations. Though conservatism (like all the philosophies we will examine) is a rich and complex system of thought developed over many centuries, and there are dangers in trying to summarize and entire philosophy in a few pages, we can highlight several of conservatism's central beliefs/assumptions.

The first critical element of a conservative social and political philosophy is a pessimistic view of human nature. The conservative worldview holds that people are flawed, imperfect, and imperfectible creatures. Human nature is a mix of good and bad features, and the latter can never be completely eliminated. Conservatives of a more religious orientation emphasize the notion of original sin that can be traced to the biblical story of Genesis, involving humankind's fall from grace with God in the Garden of Eden. This is why those Christians who attend church every Sunday, for example, pray for forgiveness of their sins. The minister or priest does not ask just those who might have sinned in the past week to pray; the assumption is that no one in attendance could possibly have made it through an entire week free of sin. The Christian theological view of people as tainted by original sin is one of humans as flawed creatures. More secular versions of conservatism emphasize that even though people are capable of rational, thoughtful, and ethical behavior, they are also motivated, perhaps even more so, by the baser impulses of lust, passion, and greed. As Edmund Burke (1729–1797), the founder of modern conservatism, noted, "politics ought to be adjusted, not to human reason, but to human nature, of which reason is but a part, and by no means the greatest part."[2]

The second critical element of a conservative social and political philosophy is a view of people as essentially social creatures. By this is meant that people are driven, and have a deep-seated need, to belong to groups. People are not, and do not want to be, isolated, unattached beings. People are not individualists; they derive a great sense of belonging and comfort from their group and social identities. Family groups, social groups, political groups, and so on define who we are and allow us to feel like we

realism A perspective on international politics emphasizing the inevitability of conflict among nations, the centrality of power, and the ever-present threat of war.

are part of something larger than ourselves. In and of itself, the social or group impulse is not a bad thing. Nonetheless, the desire for group identity has a dark side. The problem with group identity is that it entails both inclusion and exclusion. Groups are defined not merely by whom they include but also by whom they exclude. A group to which everyone belongs is not really a group at all, at least not one that provides any special sense of belonging. This is why social groups almost always exist with opposing groups. How many colleges or universities have only one sorority for all of the women? Why do so many religions spend as much time talking about the nonbelievers outside the group as they do the believers in the group? The tendency for people to form group identities has the inevitable consequence of dividing human societies. But even this might not be necessarily bad. The existence of groups and the recognition of difference are essential for diversity, which can often be a very good thing.

The more problematic aspect of people's social nature is the almost irresistible tendency for people to view themselves and the groups with which they identify as not merely separate and different but also superior in some way. This is what we might call **collective** or **group egoism.** How many people view themselves as belonging to one religious group while thinking another religion is actually the true one? How many people believe that their fraternity or sorority is the worst on campus? It is very difficult for people and different social groups to see themselves consistently as merely different but in no sense better or superior to other people and groups. This perception obviously sets the stage for all sorts of problems and conflicts.

The third critical element of conservative social and political philosophy is a belief in the *inevitability of social conflict.* People and groups will always find themselves in conflict with others. We need to find ways to manage conflicts, not waste our time on utopian schemes to eliminate conflict. But why are such conflicts inevitable? Social conflict has both *rational* and *irrational* causes, according to this view. Part of the problem is group or collective egoism. When people and groups believe that they are not merely different but also better than others, this is a recipe for conflict—people do not like to be told that they are not as good or have the ways and beliefs of others imposed on them. But conservatives do not see social conflict as resulting solely from irrational feelings of group superiority. There is a more fundamental, rational reason why social conflict is inevitable. Conservatives argue that it is impossible to create a social, economic, and political order that benefits everybody and every group equally. In any society there are always people and groups that benefit from the status quo and other people and groups that would benefit from a change of the status quo. And those who would benefit from changing the status quo will always come into conflict with those who benefit from the existing order. This is the essence of social, economic, and political conflict. Politics is about the management of conflicts, finding ways to deal with conflicts so that they do not become violent conflicts. There may be more or less effective ways of dealing with and managing social conflict, but social conflict has always existed and always will. American theologian and social commentator Reinhold Niebuhr (1892–1971) provided the most succinct statement of conservatism, arguing that "the easy subservience of reason to prejudice and passion, and the consequent persistence of irrational egoism, particularly in group behavior, make social conflict an inevitability in human behavior, probably to its very end."[3] Here we see the three critical elements of conservatism: flawed human nature, group identity and egoism, and the inevitability of conflict. That is the conservative worldview in a nutshell.

collective or group egoism
The tendency of social groups to view themselves as not only different from other groups but also better in some respect. An element of conservative or realist thought particularly important for understanding the dynamics of social conflict.

[handwritten margin notes: people in social groups inevitable conflict]

[handwritten margin notes: people for the status quo vs. people for the change of the status quo]

[handwritten margin notes: (1) Flawed Human Nature (2) Group Identity + egoism (3) inevitability of conflict]

The school of thought that applies these conservative insights to the study and understanding of international relations has come to known as _realism._ Though real- ist ideas can be traced as far back as the ancient Greek historian **Thucydides** (c. 460 – c. 400 B.C.E.), a number of twentieth-century thinkers have exerted a more profound and direct impact on the development of realist thought. Some of the thinkers who have contributed to the development of realist thought include British historian Edward Hallet Carr (1892–1982), University of Chicago political scientist **Hans Morgenthau** (1891–1976), and **George Kennan** (1904–), an American diplomat and specialist in Soviet Russian affairs. These thinkers are sometimes considered _clas- sical_ realists. Their ideas are more closely and obviously derived from conservatism than is the case with some more contemporary realists. This distinction can be seen, perhaps most dramatically, in the classical realists' view of human nature, which was certainly quite pessimistic. According to Hans Morgenthau, "it is the ubiquity of the desire for power which . . . constitutes the ubiquity of evil in all human action. Here is the element of corruption and sin which injects itself into the best of intentions at least a drop of evil and thus spoils it." It is this inevitable element of power lust and sin that accounts for "the transformation of churches into political organizations, of revolutions into dictatorships, [and] love of country into imperialism."[4] George Ken- nan wished he "could believe that the human impulses which give rise to the night- mares of totalitarianism were ones which providence had allocated to other people and to which the American people had graciously been left immune." Unfortunately, "the fact of the matter is that there is a little bit of totalitarian buried somewhere, way deep down, in each and every one of us."[5]

Although some classical realists placed greater emphasis on flawed human nature than others, the conservative view of humans as imperfect and imperfectible creatures was clearly a major element of the realist vision of international relations and conflict. In Morgenthau's words, "the world, imperfect as it is from a rational point of view, is the result of forces inherent in human nature."[6]

Similarly, realists see group identity and conflict as central to understanding in- ternational relations. According to Robert Gilpin, "Realism . . . holds that the foun- dation of political life is what Ralf Dahrendorf has called 'conflict groups.' . . . This is another way of saying that in a world of scarce resources and conflict over those re- sources, human beings confront one another ultimately as members of groups, not as isolated individuals."[7] At the international level the primary group identity is the nation-state, though this does not mean that other identities, such as religious loyal- ties, are not also present. For realists, international relations is fundamentally about the interactions and conflicts between and among states. This is not to say that real- ists fail to recognize the existence of nonstate actors (international organizations, multinational corporations, human rights organizations such as Amnesty Interna- tional). Such groups and actors can be important and influential, but they have yet to replace the nation-state as the key actor. The realist argument is that national identi- ties and loyalties are generally more important than others and that the nation-state has been and remains the major actor, or _conflict group,_ at the global level.

Finally, realists argue that just as conflict between and among individuals and groups is an inevitable feature of social life, conflict between and among nations on the global level is also unavoidable. The reasons for this state of affairs are straight- forward extensions of what the conservatives view as the irrational and rational sources of social conflict. First, feelings of national, ethnic, and cultural superiority are sources of "irrational" international conflict. Second, there is no such thing as international order that benefits all nations equally. E. H. Carr warned scholars and statesmen that it was dangerous wishful thinking to ignore "the unpalatable fact of a fundamental divergence of interest between nations desirous of maintaining the status quo and nations desirous of changing it."[8] The central conflicts of international politics are those between *status quo* states—that is, those that derive benefits from the existing international order—and *revisionist* states—that is, those states that would benefit by altering, changing, or "revising" the existing order. Put even more simply, "Like all politics, international politics involves conflicts between those who want to keep things the way things are and those who want to change them."[9] And realists believe that there will always be states benefiting from the status quo as well as states that would benefit from changing that status quo. These nations will always come into conflict. Thus, conflict among nations is an unavoidable feature of international politics.

The fact that conservatives and realists view social or group conflict as inevitable does not mean we must simply throw up our hands in despair because there is nothing we can do. Even though conflicts are inevitable, we can seek ways to deal with and manage social conflicts in order to prevent or minimize the chances that these conflicts will become violent conflicts. At the national level (within countries) we have governments that help people and groups deal with their conflicts through laws, police, and courts in ways that reduce (but of course never completely eliminate) violent group conflict. This observation leads to what virtually all realists see as perhaps the most critical aspect of international relations—international **anarchy**. Though many realists (especially those known as *neorealists*) have totally abandoned the classical realists' emphasis on a flawed human nature, they continue to place international anarchy at the center of their understanding of international politics. By *anarchy* we mean the absence of a central authority or government. Anarchy is not to be confused with chaos and a lack of order—there is a lot of order in international relations. Still, the fact that there is no government on a world scale that does for states what governments do for their citizens on a domestic level is what makes international relations fundamentally different from domestic politics (or *domestic relations*, a term no longer in use). E. H. Carr was succinct on this point: "In domestic affairs it is clearly the business of the state to create harmony if no natural harmony exists. In international politics, there is no organized power charged with the task of creating harmony."[10] This, according to Stanley Michalak, is "the first fact of life about international politics: The international system is a system without government."[11]

anarchy the absence of a central governmental/political authority.

But why is the absence of a central authority on a global level so critical for realists? The reason is simple: there is no entity that does for states what our government does for us. One of the things our government does for us (usually) is provide protection. If we see an armed band of thugs coming down the street toward our home, we can pick up the phone, call the police, and the police will come to our aid. The police do not sit around at the station for hours debating whether it is in their interest to come help the endangered citizen. Nor must we rely on neighbors with whom we negotiated previous alliances for mutual aid. Though the absence of a world government means that states are not obligated to obey any higher authority, it also means that no state can rely on others to come to their aid. As Kenneth Waltz, an influential neorealist, observes: "Citizens need not prepare to defend themselves. Public agencies do that. A national system is not one of self-help. The international system is."[12]

security dilemma The problem nations face when the actions taken to make one nation feel more secure inevitably make other nations feel less secure.

This lack of world government in turn creates a **security dilemma** in which states "must be, and usually are, concerned about their security from being attacked, subjected, dominated or annihilated" by other states. As states acquire the power and means to defend themselves, "this, in turn, renders the others more insecure and compels them to prepare for the worst. Since no one can ever feel entirely secure in a world of competing units, power competition ensues, and the vicious cycle of power accumulation is on."[13] The critical dilemma nations face is how to increase their security without doing things that make other nations feel less secure. On the domestic level, the police provide both you and me with security simultaneously; my feeling of security does not come at the expense of your security. This is not the case for nations. For realists, the anarchic nature of international relations and the dynamics of the security dilemma are the cornerstones for understanding how and why states behave as they do. It is the central reality that states must come to terms with, and it is the critical fact those seeking to understand the behavior of states must grasp.

How, then, do realists propose we deal with the problems of international conflict? Is there anything that can be done to reduce the chances that these conflicts will become violent conflicts? How about the creation of a world government that could provide states with security and overcome the security dilemma? At a theoretical level, realists would concede, this would be a solution. Realists, however, are skeptical that this theoretical solution can be translated into any practical scheme. Historically, realists have focused on more modest (more realistic, they would maintain) solutions. The most prominent has been the balance of power. When nations find themselves in a conflict in which war becomes a possibility, realists have traditionally argued that the chances for it are lessened if the parties in conflict are relatively equal in power. The reason for this argument is quite simple to grasp. We assume that nations start wars because they expect to win them. Rarely would a nation start a war it expects to lose. Nations are more likely to anticipate victory when they perceive themselves as more powerful than their potential opponent. Thus, when two sides are relatively equal, neither side will be confident of victory, so neither is likely to initiate war. There is some debate about this point among realists—some argue instead that peace is actually more likely when one power is much more powerful than others, that is, when there is a great imbalance of power. The logic here is that the very powerful nation need not resort to war to get what it wants and the much weaker states avoid war because they recognize how futile war would be. Despite these differences among realists, there is general agreement that the management and distribution of power is critical for realists when they think about international conflict and the chances for war.

So we can see that realism presents us with one way of looking and understanding the world, one that grows out of conservative assumptions about the nature of people and human societies. It is a vision of world politics in which states must interact and deal with their conflicts without the benefits of a central authority to do for them what governments do for their citizens. It is a world in which some states benefit from the existing world order, and these nations inevitably find themselves in conflict with others who would benefit from changing the existing order. Though conflicts of interest are common, violent conflict among nations (war) remains relatively rare. Nevertheless, the anarchic nature of international politics drives nations to prepare

PART I *History and Perspectives*

for and occasionally fight wars. As Robert Gilpin observes, "the fundamental nature of international relations has not changed over the millennia. International relations continues to be a recurring struggle for wealth and power among independent actors in a state of anarchy."[14]

LIBERALISM, IDEALISM, AND LIBERAL INTERNATIONALISM

The dominant alternatives to conservatism and realism as an approach to understanding social reality and international relations are **liberalism** and **idealism.** In some sense the latter term is unfair because it suggests that people who hold "idealist" views are somehow woolly-headed dreamers devising fanciful plans for world peace while ignoring the hard realities of world politics. Though this may have been the case for some of the more utopian idealists of the interwar period who hoped that international treaties could outlaw war, it is generally an unfair characterization. Idealism is merely a different way of looking at and understanding the world that grows out of different beliefs and assumptions than those that support realism. For this reason, it is better to label this alternative to realism as **liberal internationalism** or, more simply, *liberalism,* which refers to the political and philosophical tradition from which it emerged.

Liberalism is a social and political philosophy that began to flourish as Europe emerged from the medieval world which existed from the fall of the Roman Empire in 476 C.E. until the beginnings of the Renaissance in the 1300s and 1400s. The Renaissance was a period of scientific, artistic, intellectual, and cultural revival that ended the stagnation of medieval times. It was a period of renewal, and liberalism provided a more optimistic social and political philosophy that challenged the major elements of conservative thought. Among the thinkers associated with the development of liberal thought were John Locke (1632–1704), Jean Jacques Rousseau (1712–1778), and Immanuel Kant (1724–1804), although the historical roots of liberal thought can be traced to the ancient Greeks. It is important to know the key elements of liberalism and how they differ from conservatism in order to understand how they lead to a very different vision of international relations.

Like conservatism, liberalism is a rich and varied intellectual tradition that is not easily reduced to a few paragraphs. That having been said, there does appear to be a core set of beliefs that define a liberal worldview and set it apart from a conservative outlook. "In simplest terms," David Sidorsky explains, liberalism is "first, a conception of man as desiring freedom and capable of exercising rational free choice. Second, it is a perspective on social institutions as open to rational reconstruction in the light of individual needs. It is, third, a view of history as progressively perfectible through the continuous application of human reason to social institutions."[15] Liberalism, thus, parts company with conservatism on almost every critical point. In contrast to conservative philosophy, liberalism portrays people as essentially rational, ethical, and moral creatures capable of controlling their baser impulses. No doubt people have often behaved in irrational and immoral ways, but this is not seen as the inevitable result and manifestation of a flawed human nature.

liberalism Social, political, and economic philosophy based on a positive view of human nature, the inevitability of social progress, and the harmony of interests.

idealism An approach to international politics based upon liberal assumptions and principles. Its more optimistic (or utopian) versions envision a world in which law, institutions, and diplomacy replace power competition and the use of force.

liberal internationalism Another term, along with **idealism,** for the application of liberal assumptions and principles to international relations.

Liberals usually see such behavior as being the result of ignorance and misunderstanding, which can be overcome through education and reforming social and political institutions.

In addition to possessing a more optimistic view of human nature, liberals are much less inclined to view social and individual conflicts as inevitable. Liberals believe that it is possible to create a social, political, and economic order that benefits everybody—an order that maximizes individual freedom and material/economic prosperity. This element of liberal thought is sometimes referred to as the **harmony of interests.** The belief in a harmony of interests, for example, is the cornerstone of the liberal belief in the free market. In terms of justifying the free market, liberals claim that when each individual is left alone to pursue and advance his or her individual economic interests without government interference, the long-term result is growth and prosperity, which benefits everyone. Yes, Bill Gates has become a multibillionaire, but his wealth did not come at the expense of my well-being. In fact, his creations and inventions have improved my life as well. There is no conflict between his interests and mine. Much of what we see as social conflict results not from an inevitable and irreconcilable clash of interests, but the failure of people to understand their deeper mutual interests.

Thus, when realists look at the world, they tend to focus on conflicts of interests and the clashes that result; liberals are more drawn to the common interests that, they believe, people and nations share and the prospects for cooperative activities that will satisfy these interests. Liberals see the realist emphasis on international conflict and war as a distortion of reality. The overwhelming majority of interactions among nations are cooperative and nonconflictual. Certainly, wars do occur, but the vast majority of nations spend the vast majority of their time at peace, and the reason they are at peace has little to do with any balances of power (is it a balance of power that preserves peace between Finland and Sweden, the United States and Mexico, or Argentina and Chile?). Emphasizing conflict and war in trying to understand international relations while paying less attention to cooperation and peace would be like trying to understand New York City by focusing on the several hundred people murdered every year while ignoring the fact that the other 8-plus million people got along without killing one another. Not that wars and murders should be ignored; it is a matter of looking at such things in the context of the totality of relations. International relations is not all about conflict and war; in fact, it is not even mostly about conflict and war.

Finally, and perhaps most important, liberals believe in the possibility, perhaps inevitability, of human progress. The human condition is better today than it was two hundred years ago, and it is likely to be better two hundred years from now than it is today. Why? In part this belief in progress goes back to the liberal view of people as essentially rational creatures. As time goes by, people learn more about their world, both the physical or natural world (e.g., the causes and cures for diseases) as well as the social world (e.g., the causes of poverty, prejudice, and violent conflict). As people learn more about how their world works, they use this knowledge to solve problems. Human history is a story of the application of reason and knowledge to the solution of problems. There are, of course, some temporary setbacks (e.g., no one argues that Nazi Germany constituted "progress" over what came before), but the general trend of human history is one of scientific, social, and moral progress. Institutions almost universally accepted in recent human history, such as human slavery and the disenfranchisement of women, are now almost universally rejected. There is such a thing as progress.

Those who follow American politics can be forgiven if they are slightly perplexed by this discussion of liberalism and conservatism. The confusion stems from the fact that the labels *conservative* and *liberal* are used somewhat differently in everyday political debate than in discussions of political philosophy. For example, in American political discourse we usually think of free market capitalism and limited government as conservative principles, with liberals favoring greater regulation and big government. Philosophically, however, free markets and limited government are central tenets of liberalism. What we have in the United States is really gradations and variations of liberalism. Ronald Reagan may have been a conservative president and Edward ("Ted") Kennedy may be a liberal senator, but both embrace the more fundamental and basic assumptions of liberalism.

In the realm of international relations this belief in progress is central to the liberal view of the world. Although realists argue that the main features and dynamics of international politics are relatively enduring, liberals believe that we are witnessing some profound changes that, among other things, are reducing the importance of force and war in relations among states while increasing the significance of such things as human rights as major concerns. We will have an opportunity to address many of these developments later in our discussion of specific issues, but let us briefly highlight some here. One of the forces that liberals see as transforming international relations is the spread of democratic institutions around the world. Not only is this a good thing for the people within newly democratic states, it is also good news for international relations. **Democratic liberalism** argues that democracies are more peaceful than nondemocracies, particularly in their dealings with one another. As a result, liberals anticipate that as the world becomes a more democratic place, it will also become a more peaceful place.

The spread of democracy has also been accompanied by another trend—the growth of economic interdependence. This interdependence takes many forms—from the more obvious and recognizable growth in trade among states (very few things Americans buy were made wholly in the United States) to the somewhat less obvious increase in investments people and corporations make in other countries. According to **commercial liberalism,** trade and interdependence are forces for peace. The logic is quite simple—the greater the level of interdependence, the more one nation's well-being depends on another nation's well-being. This interdependence creates common interests. As Richard Rosecrance observed in one of the most forceful and persuasive liberal statements of recent years: "It is nonetheless true that interpenetration of investment in industrial economies provides a mutual stake in each others success that did not exist in the nineteenth century or before World War I."[16] As a result, "the incentive to wage war is absent in such a system for war disrupts trade and the interdependence on which trade is based."[17]

The growth of international institutions has also helped ameliorate many of the conflicts and insecurities that have traditionally characterized international politics. One of the dilemmas states have historically faced is the difficulty of cooperating even in the face of common interests because of the lack of trust in an anarchical environment. According to **liberal institutionalism,** international organizations can often

democratic liberalism
A strain of international liberal thought that claims democracies are more peaceful than nondemocracies, especially in their relations with each other.

commercial liberalism
A version of liberal international thought that stresses the importance of interdependence in trade and investment as a force for peace.

liberal institutionalism
A version of liberalism that stresses the positive role of international organizations and institutions in promoting cooperation and peace.

help states reduce the uncertainties of anarchy by building trust. Perhaps nowhere is this more evident than in Europe, which is a much different place today than it was fifty or sixty years ago. Whereas suspicion, rivalry, conflict, and war were once normal among Europe's major powers, war among Germany, France, and Britain today would be ludicrously unimaginable. In large part this situation results from the post–World War II institutions such as the European Union that have helped nurture and sustain peace, cooperation, and commerce. The citizens of modern Europe no longer live in the "brooding shadow of violence" as their grandparents and great-grandparents did.

A final positive development that is reducing the importance of war and force is the growth and spread of new ethical and moral norms. In particular, the way people view war has changed dramatically over the previous two centuries. John Mueller argues that this transformation in the common view of war has been so profound that war is rapidly becoming obsolete in large parts of the world. He begins by pointing out that a mere two hundred years ago people tended to view war as in and of itself a good thing. War was noble, invigorating, exciting, and romantic. This view did not long survive the horrors of World Wars I and II. War then came to be viewed as a regrettable necessity in certain circumstances but not something to be valued and welcomed. Increasingly, the prevailing view of war is shifting to something more resembling our current view of dueling or slavery—a barbaric and outdated institution. Mueller explains that "dueling finally died out not so much because it became illegal, but because it became ridiculous—an activity greeted not by admiration or even grudging acceptance, but by derision and contempt." Similarly, "when the notion of war chiefly inspires ridicule rather than fear, it will have become obsolete. Within the developed world at least, that condition seems to be gradually emerging."[18]

We can see in these liberal perspectives on international relations the more basic elements of liberal social and political philosophy—assumptions of basic human rationality and morality, the belief in reforming institutions as solutions to problems (i.e., spreading democracy), and, most important, a belief in human progress. Liberals reject the assumption made by realists that the basic dynamics and fundamental realities of international relations remain unchanged. People are rational enough to know that certain things (e.g., war) are irrational and undesirable, and they are capable of learning how to eliminate practices that are deemed undesirable. Robert Gilpin noted that realism "is founded on a pessimism regarding moral progress and human possibilities."[19] In contrast, as the liberal arguments highlighted here indicate, liberalism is founded on an optimism regarding moral progress and human possibilities. According to Mark Zacher and Richard Matthew, liberal thinking about international relations is characterized by a belief that "the changing interests of inhabitants of states . . . [and] the underlying forces for change are creating opportunities for increased cooperation and a greater realization of peace, welfare and justice."[20] Perhaps this is the best way to distinguish realists from liberals in debates about international politics. Liberals are generally optimistic about the prospects for positive change and "progress," whereas realists are fundamentally pessimistic about the chances for any lasting improvement in the conflictual nature of international relations.

MARXISM

In many respects it is difficult to talk about a Marxist approach to international relations, particularly with American students. The first problem is that most students enter college with virtually no exposure to **Marxism,** whereas many at least have some familiarity with liberalism and conservatism. The second problem, though this has become less so as the Cold War fades into what constitutes the distant past for many students, is that intellectual discussions of Marxism as a philosophy are hard to disentangle from the heated issues of capitalism and democracy versus communism that defined the Cold War. Finally, it is somewhat of a misnomer to refer to a "Marxist" view of international politics because Marx himself had relatively little to say about international relations. Marx was mainly concerned with the internal foundations and dynamics of capitalist societies. The Marxist view of international relations is largely the result of attempts by subsequent thinkers (some Marxists, some merely influenced by Marx) to extend his basic ideas and concepts to the realm of international relations.

In order to understand Marxism, we must appreciate the times in which Marx lived and the prevailing conditions he was reacting to. **Karl Marx** (1818–1883) lived and wrote in the middle decades of the nineteenth century—that is to say, the early years of industrial capitalism (indeed, it was Marx who coined the term *capitalism*). Most of his intellectual life was spent in the cradle of the industrial revolution, England. Here he saw a world of capitalism that bore little resemblance to the capitalist societies we live in today. It was a world of 60- and 70-hour work weeks where children worked alongside adults for low wages. Workers lived in slums and tenements, not comfortable suburbs. There were no child labor laws, no overtime, and no paid vacations. It was a world without an Occupational Safety and Health Administration to ensure that fire exits were open and clean drinking water was provided to workers. It was a world without health insurance, either from government or an employer. There was no unemployment insurance, no worker's compensation, no retirement accounts and 401Ks. It was a world in which the vast majority of people worked long hours for little reward and lived lives of nearly unending misery and drudgery. But amidst the hardship and squalor of the masses, some people lived lives of great affluence and comfort. Mansions with fifty or a hundred rooms for families of five or six people littered with expensive artwork and gold-plated bric-a-brac, summer villas, private schools for children dressed in fancy clothes who got to play with ponies and swim in private lakes. What made this disparity of living conditions even worse was that the very people leading miserable lives worked on the land and in the factories of those leading such opulent lives. The lifestyles and wealth of the elite relied upon the labor and effort of the impoverished.

Given the world in which he lived, it is not surprising that Marx saw class division and conflict as the defining feature of capitalist society. Class divisions and conflict are not unique to capitalism—ancient Western society was characterized by a division between slaveowners and slaves, and feudal society between nobles and serfs. All previously existing societies were class societies, but the nature and basis of these class divisions changes over time. The classes that defined capitalist society were the **bourgeoisie** (i.e., the capitalist class) and the **proletariat** (i.e., the working class). The classes are distinguished by what Marx referred to as their different *relationship to*

Marxism Social theory emphasizing the importance of class conflict for understanding social relations, including international politics.

Marx, Karl (1818–1883) German philosopher whose writings form the basis for the social, political, and economic theory that bears his name, Marxism.

bourgeoisie Karl Marx's label for the economic class that controls the "means of production." More colloquially known today as the *capitalist class*.

proletariat Karl Marx's label for those people who sell their labor to those who own the means of production (i.e., the bourgeoisie or capitalists). More colloquially known today as the *working class*.

Although Karl Marx did not have much to say about international relations, his view that capitalist societies were marked by class division and conflict influenced those who see the contemporary world in similar terms.
SOURCE: © Bettmann/CORBIS

the means of production. This simply means that the bourgeoisie control the means of production (that is, the land, mines, factories, banks, etc.) whereas the members of the proletariat earn their income by selling their labor for wages to the bourgeoisie. The bourgeoisie owns the means of production; the proletariat works in or on the means of production. Marx argued that the relationship between the classes was not merely unequal but also based on exploitation. Marx viewed this relationship as exploitive because the workers who produce all the goods and services receive only a portion of the value of what they produce in the form of wages—the remainder goes to the capitalists in the form of profits. Because the relationship is based on inequality and exploitation, there is a fundamental conflict of interests. Economic inequality and exploitation are the basic causes of social conflict in a Marxist worldview. As long as some people exploit other people, conflict will result.

Marx saw this economic reality as the foundation of capitalist society and argued that all aspects of capitalist society—art, culture, literature, religion, and politics— must be understood within this context. A society's economic structure, or *base,* forms the foundation for everything else, the *superstructure.* Religious doctrines that tell people that wealth and material well-being in this world are unimportant because it is spiritual health and the afterlife that really matter are actually part of the system of class domination. Ideas and doctrines that encourage people to accept the inequalities of capitalist society have the effect of supporting and perpetuating capitalism. This is why Marx characterized religion as the "opiate" of the masses—that is, it is a drug that prevents them from seeing the world around them for what it really is.

Just as religion cannot be adequately understood without reference to the central economic realities of capitalism, politics also needs to be put in the same economic context. In simple terms, economic power and control of economic resources brings political power and control of political institutions. The state or government in capitalist society is controlled by and serves, protects, and advances the interests of the capitalist class. This concept is referred to as the **nonneutrality of the state.** The government is not a neutral actor—it is systematically biased in favor of the dominant, controlling economic class. As Gabriel Kolko explains, "the *essential, primary* fact about the American social system is that it is a capitalist society based on a grossly unequal distribution of wealth and income . . . *political power in America is an aspect of economic power* [emphasis added]."[21] Consequently, the actions and policies of capitalist governments, domestically and internationally, can only be understood in the context of class interests and class conflict. Take, for example, social welfare programs that might seem to benefit the lower, working classes. Marxists tend to view such reforms of capitalism as minor crumbs intended to placate the working class into not revolting against a system that is fundamentally not in their interest. Although social welfare programs might seem to undermine and work against the logic of capitalism, their actual effect is to uphold and sustain an unequal and exploitive system. Eventually, Marx believed that the misery of the working class and the inequality inherent in the system would become so great that the proletariat would revolt against the system and the bourgeoisie.

When these basic insights are applied to international relations, the result is a very different view of the world than that offered by realists or liberals. At the level of individual states, Marxism emphasizes the significance of their internal class structure. One cannot understand the policies of the United States without recognizing that it is a capitalist society. As such, the government pursues policies designed to protect and advance the interests of its economic elite. The international policies of capitalist states must be placed in the same conceptual framework as their domestic policies. Whether one is trying to understand why the United States was at war in Vietnam or the Persian Gulf or why it wanted the North American Free Trade Agreement (NAFTA), we must base our analysis on the economic and class dynamics of capitalism. This is very different than either a realist or liberal perspective. A realist account of the U.S. involvement in Vietnam might not even mention the fact that it is a capitalist system, whereas for Marxists this is the essential starting point for analysis. In applying their basic economic and class analysis to the behavior of states, then, Marxists present a very different picture of why states act as they do.

But the Marxist economic and class analysis goes beyond this. Not only are the policies of individual states to be understood in terms of economic and class interest, the international system as a whole is conceptualized in class terms. For Marxists, the starting point for understanding international relations is the recognition that it is a capitalist international system that (like domestic capitalist systems) is based on

nonneutrality of the state
The Marxist assumption that the state or government inevitably serves, protects, and advances the interests of those with economic power.

beneficial to the capitalistic class

inequality, exploitation, and class conflict. Whereas realists and liberals look at the world and see two hundred-odd sovereign states interacting with one another, Marxists look at the world and see the division between the wealthy, industrial, capitalist states of the north and the poor, weak states of the south as its essential feature. There is a parallel to Marx's perspective in the nineteenth century. Marx looked at capitalist societies that surrounded him and concluded that their defining feature was their class structure. Contemporary Marxists look at the world and see its defining feature as the division of the world into the powerful **core** of states that control economic resources and use their power to exploit the states and people of the weak and powerless **periphery.** Whether one labels the division as core versus periphery or north versus south, haves versus have-nots, or First World versus Third World, the underlying reality of inequality remains the same. Marxists take this analysis one step further. Not only can we see the world as divided into different classes as a whole, but class interests themselves transcend national boundaries. Elites in the powerful, wealthy states of the core have created alliances with elites in the poor countries of the periphery to the detriment of the lower, working classes in both the core and periphery. Whatever aspect of international relations we are looking at, it always comes back to class.

This vision of the world leads Marxists to a different set of concerns than those that normally animate realists and liberals. Despite their profound philosophical and theoretical differences, realists and liberals tend to focus on questions of war and peace. They may disagree about whether or not democracies are more peaceful than nondemocracies, but the problem of war and conflict is at the core of both liberal and realist thought. Marxists, on the other hand, are more focused on understanding the institutions and processes that sustain what they see as an unequal, exploitive, and unjust international order. Whether it is states (through military intervention or imperialism), quasistate actors (such as the World Bank or International Monetary Fund) or nonstate actors (such as multinational corporations), Marxist analysis always returns to the central reality and problems—understanding the role these actors play in maintaining and perpetuating a global capitalist order.

FEMINISM

Feminist approaches to international relations share some things in common with Marxist approaches, even though the vast majority of feminists are not Marxists. One similarity is that both Marxism and **feminism** are dissident approaches within the discipline of international relations in the sense that they are often ignored in debates where realist and liberal perspectives are assumed to exhaust the alternatives. Feminist and Marxist approaches also share a belief that the dominant approaches of realism and liberalism ignore the most significant variable for understanding social reality: for Marxists that variable is economic class, whereas for feminists it is gender. When Marxists look at the world around them, they think it is obvious that class inequality and conflict are critical for understanding how that world works. When feminists look at the world, they think it is obvious that gender inequality and male dominance are, if anything, even more pervasive. Indeed, there are few areas where male dominance is more pronounced than international relations: one can count on

core and periphery Refers to the division of the world into classes somewhat analogous to Marx's bourgeoisie and proletariat. The **core** is the small group of wealthy and powerful states exploiting the larger group of weak and impoverished states (i.e., the **periphery**).

the political view of, bourgeoisie vs. proletariat

feminism A perspective on social phenomena focusing on issues of concern to women while theoretically emphasizing the importance of gender.

A meeting of the leaders of the world's major economies in 1989. Britain's Prime Minister Margaret Thatcher is the lone woman. Half the world's population is usually not even this well represented at such gatherings. Can we really understand international relations without coming to grips with its gendered nature? Feminists think not.
SOURCE: © Peter Turnley/CORBIS

a few fingers the women who have been present in the meetings of "world leaders" in the past fifty years (former British Prime Minister Margaret Thatcher and U.S. Secretary of State Madeline Albright being the only two who come immediately to mind). How one can possibly understand international relations while ignoring this fact is incomprehensible to feminists. A final similarity is that Marxism and most varieties of feminism are self-consciously emancipatory perspectives in that both look forward to the creation of a social order free of the inequalities, domination, and injustices that characterize the contemporary world.

There is no single feminist theory of international relations. A core of concerns and beliefs may unite a variety of feminist perspectives, but there is also a range of significant issues on which feminists disagree. Rather than cataloging all the different variants of feminist thought, it is more useful to focus on the assumptions, issues, and concerns that unify most feminist analyses. Feminists of all stripes appear in agreement in their conviction that traditional approaches and research have systematically excluded women and issues of concern to them. For example, the literature on war in international relations could fill a large library. There are endless studies on whether war is more likely when only two major powers or three or more powers are present. The numbers of studies on how war affects the lives of women could fit on a very small shelf. Discussions of "human rights" in international relations focus on "political" rights such as free speech and extrajudicial executions, but much less attention is paid to the widespread and systemic violations of the human rights of women, whether it be sexual slavery, genital mutilation, the denial of access to education, or the acceptance of violence against women. The imprisonment of political opponents prompts governments to protest and people to write letters, but the failure of governments to prosecute men who kill their wives because of insufficient dowries is written off as a cultural difference. Whatever their other theoretical differences, feminists of all persuasions decry the exclusion of women and the issues that affect women from the agenda of international relations scholars. But feminist perspectives go much further than simply demanding a greater empirical focus on women.

In her article "Well, What Is the Feminist Perspective on Bosnia?" Marysia Zalewski explains that "there is an easy and a difficult answer to such a question. The easy, but no less important, answer is to look at what is happening to women in Bosnia. No one can deny that women suffer in gender specific ways in wartime."[22] Here Zalewski is talking about an empirical focus on women's experiences, such as the systematic use of rape as a weapon of terror in ethnic cleansing. But she goes on to note that "this, at first sight easy, answer feeds immediately into the difficult one . . . Changing the empirical focus . . . make[s] us start questioning how beliefs and myths about gender play an important role in creating, maintaining and ending war, including the one in Bosnia."[23] That is, one should not stop once one has detailed how certain practices and institutions affect women. There is a more fundamental question of how and why such practices and institutions came into being and are perpetuated. Studying the experiences of women should inevitably lead to trying to understand the conditions and social dynamics that shape these experiences. This requires that we look not only at women, but also at gender and the gendered nature of all social relations, including international relations.

If feminist approaches to international relations are marked by their empirical focus on women, feminist theories are distinguished from other approaches by their focus on **gender.** This may seem a little confusing since in everyday language people often use *sex* and *gender* as if they were the same. Feminist analysis draws a distinction between the two. A person's *sex* is a biological matter: the nurse could tell, with a few rare exceptions, whether you were a boy or a girl the moment you were born. *Gender,* on the other hand, has to do with those behavioral traits we associate with "masculinity" and "femininity." When we say that someone's "manhood" is being questioned, we do not mean that there are doubts about whether he is a man in a strictly biological sense. His masculinity, not his sex, is being questioned. Gender refers to those socially constructed images of what a "man" or a "woman" should be and how they should behave. As Steve Niva explains, "gender does not refer to biological differences between men and women but to a set of socially constructed and defined characteristics, meanings, and practices associated with being a man (masculinity) and being a woman (femininity)."[24]

Although some feminists see behavioral differences between men and women as biologically based, most assume that there are virtually no inherent or "essential" differences between men and women beyond a few minor biological and physical variations associated with procreation. The dramatic differences in social roles assigned to men and women and the vast inequalities in power that exist cannot be the result of these relatively minor inherent differences. They result instead from socially formed conceptions of what it means to be a man or woman. Most of the traits or behaviors

gender Socially constructed categories and traits of "masculinity" and "femininity."

we commonly associate with men or women (e.g., men are more aggressive, women are more nurturing) are not biologically determined, but socially constructed.[25] This can be demonstrated anecdotally by the fact that we can all think of men who seem to embody many "feminine" traits and, conversely, women who exhibit "masculine" traits.

Feminists go on to observe that "masculine" and "feminine" traits are typically defined in opposition to one another—that is, if men are "competitive," women are "cooperative"; if men are "aggressive," women are "peaceful"; if men are "rational," women are "irrational"; and if women are "nurturing," men are "emotionally distant." To be a "man" means to not be a woman, and vice versa. Furthermore, societies have systematically placed greater value on those traits associated with masculinity than femininity. A woman who displays "masculine" behavior will be more accepted than a man who is considered "feminine" because masculine traits are preferable to feminine traits. Social reactions to boys who engage in typically feminine behaviors are more judgmental than to girls when the situation is reversed. Most women can wear typically "male" clothes without raising any eyebrows, but the same cannot be said for men in "women's" clothes. When a woman politician, such as Margaret Thatcher, is combative, competitive, and confrontational, this is seen as a good thing (almost as if she had "overcome" her femininity). A male politician who is seen as possessing feminine traits, on the other hand, is considered a "wimp."

These socially constructed definitions infuse all aspects of social, political, and economic life and result in a myriad of gendered practices and institutions that effectively perpetuate male dominance. Take, for example, one of the gendered dualisms that has been part of our culture for centuries, if not millennia: that of the *private* versus the *public*. The idea that home and family life, dubbed the private sphere, is the natural domain of women whereas politics and commercial life, the public sphere, is the natural domain of men has had a profound impact on the status of women. The most glaring example was the exclusion of women from the franchise (i.e., the right to vote) in every democracy until the first quarter of the twentieth century, though even in the first part of the twenty-first century women are still excluded and wildly underrepresented in these areas. When one combines socially constructed notions of masculinity and femininity with the exclusion of women from the institutions of public power, this inevitably means that the institutions and practices of the public sphere will reflect masculine traits. If men are supposed to be competitive, aggressive, and rational, then the institutions dominated by men will reflect these traits. In this way, institutions and practices become gendered.

What does this perspective have to do with our understanding of international relations? To begin with, there is no reason to think that the processes and dynamics of international relations are immune to the impact of gender. The nature and conduct of international relations is profoundly shaped by the effective exclusion of women and prevailing social constructions of masculinity. When masculinity is socially defined as competitiveness, lack of empathy, self-reliance, aggressiveness, and power seeking, it should come as no surprise that a realm of activity dominated by men will reflect these values and characteristics. Socially constructed notions of masculinity are projected onto world politics. But feminists maintain that there is nothing inevitable about this state of affairs, since neither male dominance nor social constructions of masculinity are unchangeable.

But it is not merely the "real world" that reflects this male dominance. Our philosophical and theoretical thinking about international relations has also been shaped almost completely by men. This fact affects both what we think constitutes international relations and how we think international relations works. This way of thinking helps account for why many of the issues of concern to women have typically been ignored on the ground that these issues are "not really international relations." Male dominance also influences prevailing theories and perspectives on international relations. When (male) theorists portray international relations as a "naturally" competitive realm marked by conflict and strategic rationality and calculation, they are treating as inevitable and universal something that is actually the consequence of socially constructed conceptions of gender and the exclusion of women. Feminists have been particularly critical of realism in this area because they see it as a theory of international relations of, by, and for men. Realism sees the world through a masculine lens but pretends to provide an "objective" portrait of how the world works. Realism treats a world shaped by men and permeated to its core by masculine gender assumptions as a genderless and universal reality.

A common misperception of feminist theories is that they are only about women. Given the label "feminist" theories, this is a somewhat understandable mistake. In reality, the focus on the construction of gender norms and the impact of these norms on international relations is just as much about men as women. Though the empirical focus on women naturally leads to an emphasis on how women are adversely affected by these gendered norms, men are also frequently harmed as well. After all, if war is a consequence of the gendered nature of international politics, the millions of men who died on the battlefields of World War I were hardly beneficiaries of gendered practices.

There are some differences among feminists (as there are among realists, liberals, and Marxists). *Liberal feminists* tend to downplay the notion that any inherent differences exist between men and women and believe that women are equally well equipped to occupy positions of power. There is no great sense that things would be all that much different if they did (except, of course, for the women who would now enjoy equal opportunities). *Standpoint feminists* are more inclined to argue that there are some basic differences between men and women, whether rooted in biology, socialization, or varying life experiences. Women do approach issues from a different perspective or standpoint than men. Consequently, the fact that men dominate international relations does have a profound impact, and a greater role for women could help alter the nature and dynamics of international politics. *Postmodern feminists* reject the liberal feminist attempt to ignore the importance of socially constructed gender differences and the standpoint feminist tendency to perpetuate the notion that there are inherent differences between men and women. Postmodernists agree that notions of masculinity and femininity as socially constructed are important, but they see these norms as unstable and alterable. Though it is important to be aware that the feminists do not agree on all points (just like realists, liberals, and Marxists often disagree among themselves), at this point we are more interested in the values and assumptions that most feminists share.[26]

Many find feminist approaches to international relations difficult to grasp. The diversity of feminist thought is part of the problem. But the main problem is that feminism presents a way of looking at international relations that is noticeably different from the perspectives we have become accustomed to. It requires us to look at something—the consequences of male dominance—that is so obvious and pervasive that it often escapes our notice. What is staring us in the face is often the very thing we overlook. Though feminist approaches may appear difficult to grasp at first, the basic elements that shape a feminist approach are quite simple. First, the empirical fact is that men have dominated and still dominate the institutions of public power. Perhaps nowhere is this dominance greater than in those areas that have traditionally been the focus of international relations—foreign policy, diplomacy, and the military. And male dominance has consequences in terms of the conduct of international relations. Second, male dominance is no less absent among scholars who have shaped our theoretical thinking about international relations, whether it be realism (Morgenthau), liberalism (Kant) or Marxism (Lenin). This dominance has consequences for how we have traditionally thought about international relations. Third, there is no doubt that socially constructed gender roles and norms remain a central feature of our social and political life. Thus, to assume that the reality of male dominance and social conceptions of gender can be ignored in our attempts to understand international relations is simply not tenable.

CONSTRUCTIVISM

Feminism, which stresses the socially constructed nature of gender norms, segues well into a discussion of the most recent approach to understanding international relations, **constructivism.** Feminists argue that behavioral differences between men and women are not rooted in essential biological characteristics. Instead, men and women behave as they do largely because of deeply and widely held beliefs and norms about the content and boundaries of acceptable or desirable male and female behavior. That is, men and women learn what it means in our society to behave like a man or woman and act accordingly. Males and females are socialized into becoming "men" and "women." Over time, however, changing norms can alter behavior even though sexual biology remains the same, which in itself demonstrates the socially constructed nature of behavior.

constructivism A perspective that stresses the importance of identities and shared understandings in shaping the behavior of social actors.

Feminist observations about the socially constructed nature of masculinity and femininity are actually a particular example of a broader phenomenon. One can restate this specific insight in a more general form: any actor's behavior is shaped by socially transmitted and reinforced beliefs, norms, and identities that define that actor within the context of its society. Being a "man," for example, is only one social identity. "College professor" is another. A professor's behavior is also shaped by prevailing beliefs, norms, and conceptions about what it means to be a professor and how professors should behave. And how professors relate to students and vice versa is shaped by their mutual identities and conceptions of how they should behave toward each other, of what sorts of behaviors are appropriate and inappropriate. Thus, when we look at why people behave as they do, there is no escaping the overwhelming importance of beliefs, social norms, and identities.

Constructivists attempt to apply this basic insight to understanding why states and other international actors behave as they do. Daniel Thomas explains: "According to . . . constructivist theories of international relations, actors [states] seek to behave in accordance with the norms relevant to their identities . . . [which are] definitions of the self in relation to others that provide guidance for how one should behave in a given context."[27] The focus is on how actors, in this case largely statesmen and elites, view themselves, others, and the norms of appropriate behavior. Richard Rosecrance explains that "one reason why no single theory of international politics has ever been adequate is that nations modify their behavior in face of experience and theory. If statesmen believe that the balance of power must determine their policies, then they will act in such a way as to validate the theory." And "because leaders and statesmen have been acting on different and contrasting theories of international politics," no single theory will be able to capture all of international politics.[28]

Rosecrance states the point so casually that its significance might be lost. Most theories of international relations, and especially realism, begin with the assumption that there is an objective reality that they seek to reveal. The preeminent realist Hans Morgenthau claimed that "political realism believes that politics, like society in general, is governed by objective laws . . . the operation of these laws being impervious to our preferences, men will challenge them only at the risk of failure."[29] Realists assume that states would act as they do regardless of whether there exists a theory telling them that is how they should behave. The realities of world politics exist, they are not "created." Constructivists disagree. They see no inherent and inevitable reason that states must behave in any particular way. States behave as they do because they adhere to certain notions of how they should and do behave. Their behavior is determined by their identities, which are neither given nor constant. "Constructivism," notes Cynthia Weber, "argues that identities and interests in international politics are not stable—they have no pre-given nature."[30] States that behave as realists (or liberals) predict they will only so long as they accept and internalize the norms of state behavior embodied in these theories. This is not to suggest that there is no "real" world out there or that the world is and can become whatever we imagine it to be. There are realities: no world government exists, some nations do have nuclear weapons, and some nations are stronger than others. Constructivism holds, however, that the implications of these facts for the conduct of international relations depend on how people understand their significance.

An example (which we will deal with at greater length later) may help illustrate the point here. Most constructivists accept the fact that there is no world government— that is, international politics is anarchic. Realists tend to argue that anarchy creates insecurities and leads states into conflict with one another (the security dilemma). Constructivists are quick to note that this is not always the case. Sometimes the insecurity of anarchy leads states into conflict, but other times it does not. France and Great Britain, enemies or rivals for much of their history, no longer fear each other. Why? Has a world government been created to eliminate uncertainty and insecurity? No. What has changed is how British and French statesmen view themselves and each other. They have come to see themselves as democracies that do not threaten each other. In the words of a prominent constructivist, "anarchy is what states make of it."[31] That is, anarchy exists, but what this means in terms of how states relate to one another depends on what statesmen think, how they identify themselves and others, and how they believe they should act toward each other.

In this sense, constructivists highlight the distinction between theory in the natural sciences such as biology, chemistry, and physics as opposed to theory in the social sciences. The laws of physics, for example, operated long before we knew what they were. Gravity will force a dropped book to the ground regardless of whether we think this will or should happen. Theories about how cells behave or chemicals interact do not influence their behavior. But this sharp line between theory and behavior does not hold in the social realm. In the social sciences there is an intimate relationship between theory and practice, between what leaders think about how the world works and how they choose to behave in the world.

PERSPECTIVES AND LEVELS OF ANALYSIS

There are a number of ways we can organize and make sense of the complexities of international relations. One is to identify distinct schools of thought or worldviews and see how they apply to particular issues and problems. This is the approach emphasized in this text. Others have found it useful to focus on different **levels of analysis** in which international phenomena such as war or foreign policy are examined from several different "levels." At the *individual level,* for example, we might focus on general aspects of human nature or traits of individual decision makers (e.g., perceptions, beliefs, and personalities). At the *state level,* we can try to understand how societal characteristics influence state behavior (e.g., are democratic states more peaceful or capitalist states more expansionist?). Finally, at the *international level,* we can attempt to understand the impact of international anarchy or given distributions of power (e.g., does a balance or imbalance of power lead to peace?).

> **levels of analysis** An organizational scheme for thinking about international politics. The most general focuses on causes and dynamics of the individual, state, and systemic levels.

Though various analysts tend to emphasize different levels, any reasonably complete understanding of international relations in general or a specific event will probably incorporate all the levels of analysis. Indeed, the various perspectives discussed in this chapter usually cut across these different levels. Liberals, for example, make some assumptions about human nature (individual level) and the peacefulness of democracies (state level). Similarly, realists make assumptions about human nature (individual level) as well as the consequences of international anarchy (system level). Whether we organize our thinking about international relations primarily in terms of competing theories and philosophies or different levels of analysis is largely a matter what seems most useful. Neither approach is necessarily better than the other; they are simply different organizational schemes for thinking about, and making sense of, international relations.

CONCLUSION

Though this diversity of perspectives might seem confusing enough, matters actually get a little worse because even within each perspective there are differences of opinion on theoretical and practical/policy issues. As a result, it is very rare that we can identify *the* realist, liberal, Marxist, feminist, or constructivist position. An answer to the question, "What is the realist position on such and such?" is not always straightforward. On a theoretical level, for example, realists disagree among themselves about whether the chances for war are minimized with one, two, or multiple major powers. On a policy issue, there was no single realist position on U.S. intervention in Vietnam:

some realists favored involvement, whereas others remained staunch opponents. Muddying the waters further, representatives of differing perspectives may find themselves in agreement in an issue.

Thus, it is not always useful to think in terms of *a* realist, liberal, Marxist, feminist, or constructivist *position*. Instead, it is better to approach debates in terms of *arguments* or *rationales*. Let us use the Vietnam example to illustrate. Realists disagreed among themselves about the wisdom of U.S. policy in Vietnam. But if we look at the type of arguments and rationales offered in defense of their differing positions, certain similarities are evident. Realist opponents of the Vietnam War claimed that Vietnam's strategic significance was insufficient to warrant the costs associated with war. Other realists, emphasizing the broader ramifications of a loss in Vietnam to American prestige and interests in the world, supported the war. In this case there was agreement that national and strategic interests need to guide decisions to go to war. Realists were united on this point. They disagreed about whether Vietnam in particular was strategically important enough to justify war. The underlying issues and concerns were the same, but their application to the specific case was different. On the question of Vietnam, one could make an argument for or against the war on realist terms. It is the type of argument made, not necessarily the conclusion reached, that usually allows one to distinguish a realist from a Marxist or liberal. Thus, people who share the same basic assumptions may arrive at different positions.

Conversely, people who start with different assumptions may arrive at the same position. An example we will examine later is free trade. This is an issue on which one finds some strange bedfellows, with opponents of free trade often coming from both the far right and far left. But this apparent agreement frequently masks underlying differences. When we look at the arguments offered for their skepticism about free trade, we begin to notice that their similar positions are based on divergent rationales. Thus, we cannot always assume that realists will always agree with other realists (or liberals with liberals and so on) or that people from different perspectives will always be at odds. In textbooks such as this one, ideas are often neatly divided into sections and subsections. The real world, however, is not always so tidy.

CHAPTER SUMMARY

- Theoretical and policy debates in international relations are usually rooted in competing perspectives or worldviews that provide differing ways to look at and understand the world around us. The chapter focused on five competing visions of international relations: realism, liberalism, Marxism, feminism, and constructivism.

- Realism provides a somewhat pessimistic outlook that stresses the centrality and inevitability of conflict among nations. Many classical realists trace these conflicts to a flawed human nature, whereas neorealists are more inclined to see it as a consequence of an inherently insecure anarchical international system.

- Liberalism is a more optimistic outlook that sees a greater scope for international cooperation and peace. Whether the stress is on expanding commerce, spreading democracy, changing ethical norms, or strengthening international institutions, liberals believe that common interests and shared values offer hope for a fundamentally better and more peaceful world.

- Marxists analyze society, domestic and international, in terms of class interests and conflicts. The behavior and policies of states are seen as reflections of class (not national) interests, and the dynamics of world politics as whole are understood in terms of the unequal and exploitative relations between the wealthy, powerful nations of the North and the impoverished, weak nations of the South. Social conflict generally, and international conflict in particular, is an inevitable consequence of inequality and exploitation.

- Feminists argue that social dynamics and institutions cannot be understood without a recognition of the reality of male dominance and the importance of gender. International relations is no exception, especially because there are few other areas where male dominance is so pronounced. Male dominance and socially constructed notions of masculinity and femininity have helped shape the reality of international politics as well as our theories of international politics.

- Constructivists argue that the behavior of social actors (e.g., individuals, groups, nations) is shaped by ideas, norms, and identities. As a result, they are skeptical of theories that portray certain types of behaviors as inevitable.

KEY TERMS

anarchy 49
bourgeoisie 55
collective or group egoism 47
commercial liberalism 53
constructivism 63
core and periphery 58
democratic liberalism 53
feminism 58
gender 60
harmony of interests 52
idealism 51
Kennan, George F. (1904–) 48
levels of analysis 65
liberal institutionalism 53
liberal internationalism 51
liberalism 51
Marx, Karl (1818–1883) 55
Marxism 55
Morgenthau, Hans (1891–1976) 48
nonneutrality of the state 57
periphery (see core and periphery) 58
proletariat 55
realism 46
security dilemma 50
Thucydides (c. 460–c. 400 B.C.E.) 48

FURTHER READINGS

A good place to begin is with two of the most influential statements of classical realism: Edward Hallett Carr, *The Twenty Years' Crisis, 1919–1939* (New York: Harper Collins, 1964 [1945]), and Hans Morgenthau, *Politics among Nations: The Struggle for Power and Peace* (New York: Alfred A. Knopf, 1967). The essential presentation of neorealism is Kenneth Waltz, *Theory of International Politics* (Reading, MA: Addison-Wesley, 1979). A forceful recent restatement of realism is John Mearsheimer, *The Tragedy of Great Power Politics* (New York: W.W. Norton, 2000). The literature on liberalism is more diverse. Some essential works reflecting various strains of liberal thinking include Bruce Russett, *Grasping the Democratic Peace* (Princeton: Princeton University Press, 1993); Richard Rosecrance, *The Rise of the Trading State: Commerce and Conquest in the Modern World* (New York: Basic Books, 1986); John Mueller, *Retreat from Doomsday: The Obsolescence of Major War* (New York: Basic Books, 1989). Those interested in Marxist approaches should begin with Lenin's classic *Imperialism: The Highest Stage of Capitalism* (New York: International Publishers, 1939) and John Hobson's *Imperialism: A Study* (Ann Arbor: University of Michigan Press, 1965). A more recent survey is Anthony Brewer, *Marxist Theories of Imperialism: A Critical Survey* (London: Routledge, 1990). Some important recent feminist works include J. Ann Tickner, *Gender and International Relations* (New York: Columbia University Press, 1993), and Christine Sylvester, *Feminist Theory and International Relations in a Post-Modern Era* (Cambridge: Cambridge University Press, 1994). One of the classic and most interesting feminist works is Cynthia Enloe, *Bananas, Beaches and Bases: Making Feminist Sense of International Relations* (Berkeley: University of California Press, 2001, updated edition). The essential work in the constructivist tradition is Alexander Wendt, *A Social Theory of International Politics* (Cambridge: Cambridge University Press, 1999).

NOTES

[1] Stephen Walt, "International Relations: One World, Many Theories," *Foreign Policy* 110 (Spring 1998): 29.

[2] Quoted in Hans Morgenthau, *Scientific Man versus Power Politics* (Chicago: University of Chicago Press, 1946), ii.

[3] Reinhold Niebuhr, *Moral Man and Immoral Society: A Study in Ethics and Politics* (New York: Charles Scribner's Sons, 1934), xx.

[4] Morgenthau, *Scientific Man*, pp. 194–95.

[5] George Kennan, *Memoirs 1925–1950* (Boston: Little, Brown, 1967), p. 319.

[6] Hans Morgenthau, *Politics among Nations: The Struggle for Power and Peace* (New York: Alfred A. Knopf, 1967), p. 3.

[7] Robert Gilpin, "The Richness of the Tradition of Political Realism," in *Neorealism and Its Critics*, ed. Robert Keohane (New York: Columbia University Press, 1986), p. 305.

[8] Edward Hallett Carr, *The Twenty Years' Crisis, 1919–1939* (New York: Harper & Row, 1964), p. 53.

[9] Stanley Michalak, *A Primer in Power Politics* (Wilmington, DE: Scholarly Resources, 2001), p. 45.

[10] Carr, *Twenty Years' Crisis*, p. 51.

[11] Michalak, *Primer in Power Politics*, p. 2.

[12] Kenneth Waltz, *Theory of International Politics* (Reading, MA: Addison-Wesley, 1979), p. 104.

[13] John Herz, *The Nation-State and the Crisis of World Politics* (New York: David McKay, 1976), pp. 72–73.

[14] Robert Gilpin, *War and Change in World Politics* (Cambridge: Cambridge University Press, 1981), p. 7.

[15] David Sidorsky, ed., *The Liberal Tradition in European Thought* (New York: Capricorn Books, 1970), p. 2.

[16] Richard Rosecrance, *The Rise of the Trading State: Commerce and Conquest in the Modern World* (New York: Basic Books, 1986), p. 148.

[17] Ibid., p. 24.

[18] John Mueller, *Retreat from Doomsday: The Obsolescence of Major War* (New York: Basic Books, 1989), pp. 217, 244.

[19] Gilpin, *War and Change in World Politics*, p. 305.

[20] Mark Zacher and Richard Matthew, "Liberal International Theory: Common Threads, Divergent Strands," in *Controversies in International Relations Theory*, ed. Charles W. Kegley (New York: St. Martin's, 1995), p. 140.

[21] Gabriel Kolko, *The Roots of American Foreign Policy* (Boston: Beacon Press, 1969), pp. 9, 6.

[22] Marysia Zalewski, "Well, What Is the Feminist Perspective on Bosnia?" *International Affairs* 71, no. 2 (1995): 355. The interesting title of this article reflects the widespread frustration feminists feel when their work is attacked on the grounds that it lacks "real-world" relevance.

[23] Ibid., pp. 355–56.

[24] Steve Niva, "Tough and Tender: New World Order Masculinity and the Cold War," in *The "Man" Question in International Relations*, ed. Marysia Zalewski and Jane Parpart (Boulder, CO: Westview Press, 1998), pp. 111–12.

[25] There are those (mostly nonfeminists) who see many behavioral differences as biologically determined. See, for example, Francis Fukuyama, "Women and the Evolution of World Politics," *Foreign Affairs* 77, no. 5 (September/ October 1998), and Richard Wrangham and Dale Peterson, *Demonic Males* (Boston: Houghton Mifflin, 1996).

[26] A good, accessible summary of differences among feminists can be found in Jacqui True, "Feminism," in *Theories of International Relations*, ed. Scott Burchill and Andrew Linklater (New York: St. Martin's Press, 1995), pp. 210–52.

[27] Daniel C. Thomas, *The Helsinki Effect: International Norms, Human Rights and the Demise of Communism* (Princeton: Princeton University Press, 2001), p. 13.

[28] Rosecrance, *Rise of the Trading State*, p. 41.

[29] Morgenthau, *Politics among Nations*, p. 4.

[30] Cynthia Weber, *International Relations Theory: A Critical Introduction* (New York: Routledge, 2001), p. 60.

[31] Alexander Wendt, "Anarchy Is What States Make of It," *International Organization* 46, no. 2 (Summer 1992): 392–425.

CONTROVERSIES

WAR AND "HUMAN NATURE"

Is there something about human nature that leads to war? Pointing to its obvious irrationality, many believe there must be some uncontrollable force that drives people to engage in warfare. For many centuries, contrasting philosophical and religious views of human nature have framed this debate. More "scientific" versions of this argument focus on psychological and biological impulses or instincts that supposedly lead to aggression and war. Though most realists do not explicitly endorse instinctual theories of war, there are some obvious parallels with their negative view of human nature, especially for classical realists. The opposing view sees war as a culturally learned practice, a form of collective violence rather than a manifestation of any individual-level aggressive instinct. This perspective is more consistent with liberalism's positive assessment of human nature as well as feminist and constructivist perspectives stressing the socially constructed nature of many human behaviors. Though much of this debate has been defined in terms of the familiar nature-*or*-nurture divide, in the final analysis it might be more useful to think in terms of a combination of nature *and* nurture.

Sometimes we have to think about human behaviors and institutions in the starkest possible terms before we realize how truly bizarre they are. In his exploration of the roots of human aggression and war, psychologist Anthony Storr pulls no punches: "That man is an aggressive creature will hardly be denied. With the exception of certain rodents, no other vertebrate habitually destroys members of his own species. No other animal takes positive pleasure in the exercise of cruelty upon another of his own kind."[1] When we say that in war humans behave like animals, this is something of an insult to most animals, since there are virtually no members of the animal kingdom who do to their own kind what we do to ours. We might indeed be better off if we behaved a bit more like the animals. The question of why human beings systematically prepare for and carry out the large-scale slaughter of members of their own species is perhaps the central question, not merely for students of international relations, but for anyone interested in the human condition and our fate on this planet.

Though Anthony Storr's indictment is certainly a harsh one, it seems to be supported by the depressing statistics of war. By one estimate, there have been only 292 years of peace in the world over the last 5,600 years, and during that time more than 3,500,000,000 people have died in, or as a result of, more than 14,000 wars.[2] Such a figure includes not only the obvious military and civilian casualties associated with actual conduct of war, but also those who die from the common consequences of war—disease, famine, and civil violence. Other studies arrive at somewhat different figures, but they do not change the overall picture: war is almost certainly the second leading cause of death in human history, behind only the diseases and conditions associated with old age.

It does not take long, in most discussions of the causes of war, for someone to voice the opinion that war is an outgrowth or part of what we call "human nature." Even though this view has fallen out of favor with scholars and academics, it remains part of the common wisdom. Exactly what it is about human nature that supposedly leads to war varies, and the concept of human nature is itself quite fuzzy and elastic. Some treat human nature in a philosophical or theological sense involving foundational assumptions about human motivation, whereas others approach it from a perspective based on biology, instinctual behavior, and evolution. For some, the element of human nature that leads to war is an innate aggressive drive or instinct. Others see war as resulting not from aggression per se, but rather from human greed, irrationality, or group-forming tendencies. Whatever the specifics, "human nature" explanations of war imply, either explicitly or implicitly, the inevitability of war, a belief that war has always been with us and always will be. Virtually all other explanations for war—those that see it as derived from cultural, political, or economic sources—hold out at least the theoretical possibility that we can eliminate war. The only theories that genuinely regard war as an inevitable fact of human existence are those that see war as rooted in some inherent psychological or biological aspect of human nature. Political, economic, cultural, and social institutions and practices can be altered (perhaps not easily), but human nature, by definition, cannot.

On the other side of the debate are people who see war as learned behavior, the culmination of a process of socialization that encourages us to think about aggression, violence, and other social groups in ways that make systematic killing acceptable, even desirable in some situations. War does not come "naturally," like sex; it is something we must learn to do and sometimes must be forced to do. It is more like slavery and

[handwritten margin note:] For some, the element of human nature that leads to war is
- Aggressive Drive/ Instinct
- Greed, irrationality, group forming tendencies
- ..derived from political, economic, cultural, social sources
- Learned Bhehavior

the practice of wearing black to funerals (learned, created social practices that can be eradicated) than sex (a biologically based drive). In very simplistic terms, disagreements about the relationship between war and human nature are no more than specific examples of the age-old **nature-versus-nurture** debate. The debate involves differing perspectives on which aspects of human behavior and society are inevitable reflections of some unchangeable part of the human makeup and which are social creations and practices that are amenable to alteration. Because any explanation for something as complex as war inevitably combines elements of both nature and nurture, it is probably better to view explanations as lying along a nature–nurture continuum. Nonetheless, there is usually a sufficient difference in emphasis so that it is possible to place different theories on either side of the fundamental debate.

AGGRESSION, INSTINCTS, AND WAR

Philosophical and theological assumptions about human nature are not susceptible to scientific test or argument; they are simply foundational beliefs that one either accepts or rejects. There have, however, been attempts to trace the origins of human aggression and war to certain biological and physiological instincts, creating what can be seen as modern or "scientific" versions of philosophical and theological doctrines. Sigmund Freud, for example, argued that people have both a life instinct (Eros) and a death instinct (Thanatos), with aggression, whether it is directed toward oneself in the form of suicide or others in the form of violence, resulting from the deep-seated death instinct. Though he would later express some doubts about this position, in his *Civilization and Its Discontents* Freud was clear about his view of human nature: "Men are not gentle creatures who want to be loved, and who at most can defend themselves if they are attacked; they are, on the contrary, creatures among whose instinctual endowment is to be reckoned with a powerful share of aggressiveness. . . . [this instinct] manifests itself spontaneously and reveals man as a savage beast."[3]

The most coherent and influential attempts to theorize about the causes of war in terms of human instincts have been advanced by **ethologists** (those engaged in the study of animal behavior). Books such as Desmond Morris's *The Naked Ape,* Lionel Tiger and Robin Fox's *The Imperial Animal,* and Robert Ardrey's *The Territorial Imperative* have argued that human beings possess an aggressive instinct and that war is a manifestation or result of this instinct.[4]

The most prominent and influential exponent of this viewpoint is **Konrad Lorenz,** a German ethologist, whose book *On Aggression* provided the intellectual and theoretical foundation for the more popularized works of Morris, Tiger, Fox, and Ardrey.[5] Lorenz's approach to understanding war and aggression begins with the implicit puzzle contained in Anthony Storr's observation about the near uniqueness of human slaughter: How do we explain the fact that human beings kill each other with such frequency and enthusiasm? "Undeniably, there must be," Lorenz concludes, "superlatively strong factors which are able to overcome the commands of individual reason so completely and which are so obviously impervious to experience and learning."[6] What might these factors be? To approach this question, it is useful to break the big puzzle into two smaller ones. First, why do humans fight with one another? Second, why do they fight to the point where they kill one another? That is, how do we

nature versus nurture The debate over which human behaviors are biologically or instinctually determined as opposed to being socially or culturally conditioned.

ethology The study of animal behavior. Many ethologists have been influential proponents of the view that war has an instinctual basis in human behavior.

Lorenz, Konrad Influential and controversial German ethologist famous for drawing the distinction between lethal and nonlethal animals and placing humans in the latter category. Claimed that the ability of humans to craft lethal weapons upset the balance between our ability to kill and inhibitions against killing.

account for human aggression in general, and how do we explain *lethal* human aggression in particular? The distinction between aggression and *lethal* aggression is critical. If we all just fought each other without killing each other, the problem of war would not be nearly that important.

The "functions" of aggression Lorenz and his fellow ethologists begin with the assumption that humans are animals. They mean this not in a bad, normative sense, but simply in the sense that we are living, breathing creatures. Though we are different from other animals of the world in important respects, we are still animals nonetheless. One similarity with other animals is that we are a product of an evolutionary process that has endowed us with certain instincts. We may have fewer instincts than other animals, but we still have them. This apparently straightforward and uncontroversial set of assumptions immediately raises a number of misleadingly simple questions. First, what exactly is an instinct? And second, how does one know which behaviors are instinctual and which are learned? These questions are not as easy to answer as might be assumed.

There is substantial agreement on an abstract definition of an **instinct** as a psychologically and biologically predetermined behavioral response to external stimuli. Hibernation, for example, is an instinct in some animals because it is a predetermined behavioral response to changes in the weather that announce the coming of winter. Agreement on this definition, however, does not preclude intense debate on what behaviors meet the definition. Lorenz and Morris argue that one way to distinguish instinctual from learned behaviors is to see whether the behavior is accompanied by biological or physical "symptoms." Sexual arousal provides one example: external stimuli, such as the appearance of an attractive mate, elicit specific physical changes and activate desires to engage in sexual behavior. For Lorenz and Morris, it is significant that aggression and fighting are also accompanied by physiological changes, such as rapid breathing, increased blood pressure, heart rate, higher levels of adrenaline, a cessation of food digestion, muscle tension, and various neurological changes.[7] These are all seen as indicators of an instinctual response. In comparison, culturally learned behaviors, such as wearing black to funerals, are not associated with similar physiological indicators.

Ethologists view instincts in the context of evolutionary theory. In their view, instincts emerge and survive because they serve useful functions or purposes. To use a more technical terminology, instincts exist and persist because they are "adaptive"; they help assure the survival of a species. Among the instincts that virtually all animals have are fear, sex, hunger, and aggression. The usefulness of sex and hunger for species survival are too obvious to comment on at length since procreation and nutrition are necessary at the most basic level. Fear helps protect us from unknown dangers. The evolutionary purpose of aggression is not as immediately clear and requires some explanation.

What are the positive or adaptive functions of aggression? Ethologists see aggression as fulfilling several useful functions in animals. The first purpose of aggression is **spacing.** Any given area has sufficient resources to support a certain level of population. As the animal population expands, fights over resources (land, food, mates) increase. These fights tend to repel the animals, driving them away from each other. This distributes or spreads the population out in a manner that prevents overpopula-

instinct A biologically or psychologically predetermined behavioral response to external stimuli.

spacing The tendency of animals to disperse themselves over a given territory so as to prevent overpopulation and depletion of resources. Cited by ethologists as one of the useful functions of aggression in animals.

PART II *Controversies*

tion. The second function of aggression is the establishment of a **hierarchy** in animal groups. Fights among animals within their groups basically determine who rules, who is the top dog and bottom dog. This hierarchy is an integral element of social structure. It is also usually linked to reproduction in that those animals at the top of the social hierarchy have the most access to mates and produce more offspring. As a result, the strongest and fittest members of the species mate the most, which contributes to the health and perpetuation of the species. Finally, aggression is necessary for the defense of the young. There are some other potential functions of aggression, but these are among the most common and important. According to Lorenz and his followers, there is every reason to believe that aggression performed these same basic functions in human history and evolution. Thus, Lorenz argues that humans have developed an aggressive instinct over the course of evolution for very much the same reasons as all other animals.

But this is not the real puzzle. This critical issue is not why human beings fight each other but rather why we kill each other. It is not our aggression that makes us stand out among the animals of the world but rather our lethal aggression. All animals fight with members of their own species; the difference is that they rarely kill members of their own species. This is the genuinely puzzling thing about war: not why we fight one another, but why we kill one another. It is in his explanation of the uniqueness of human lethal aggression that Lorenz made his most original (and controversial) contribution.

The curse of intelligence: Weapons In looking at the animal kingdom as a whole, Lorenz makes a fundamental distinction between two types of animals. On one hand, there are those animals that do not possess the physical endowments necessary to kill with any ease. Doves, gerbils, and rabbits, for example, do not possess the powerful limbs and jaws or sharp claws and teeth required for lethal aggression. On the other hand, animals such as lions, tigers, wolves, and bears do possess the physical tools necessary to kill their own kind. Explaining why doves, gerbils, and rabbits do not run around slaughtering other doves, gerbils, and rabbits is easy. These animals do not kill each other because they cannot, even if they wanted to. They still fight members of their own species, but they are unable to kill each other. No real puzzle there.

The more difficult question is why animals that can kill members of their own species rarely do. As Desmond Morris observes, "Species that have evolved special killing techniques for dealing with their prey seldom employ these when fighting their own kind."[8] But why not? Why aren't the plains of Africa littered with the corpses of great game killed by their own kind? The answer, according to Lorenz, is that animals with the capacity to be lethal to their own kind have developed in the course of evolution a set of signals, repertoires, and behaviors that inhibit the killing of members of their own species. In a fight between potentially lethal members of the same species, there is almost always a point where the fight ends well short of a participant's death. This happens in one of two ways. The most obvious means of avoiding death is flight; the loser simply runs away, effectively conceding whatever it was that caused the fight. The victor seldom chases in order to inflict further harm. But flight is not essential to avoid death. In instances where flight is not feasible, the loser "must somehow signal to the stronger animal that he is no longer a threat and that he does not intend to continue the fight . . . if he can signal his acceptance of defeat . . . he will be

hierarchy The unequal distribution of power and authority in an animal grouping. The social hierarchy is often established by in-group fighting. Cited by ethologists as one of the useful functions of aggression in animals.

able to avoid further serious punishment." According to Lorenz, "this is achieved by the performance of certain characteristic submissive displays. These appease the attacker and rapidly reduce his aggression, speeding up settlement of the dispute."[9]

This submissive posture is also sometimes referred to as an **appeasement gesture.** It might involve lying down passively and/or exposing a vulnerable part of the body, but it is something that signifies and is recognized as a symbol of defeat. Death rarely follows. Thus, potentially lethal animals rarely kill members of their own species because "all heavily armed carnivores possess sufficiently reliable inhibitions which prevent the self-destruction of the species."[10] A species with the ability to kill its own kind that does not possess the necessary inhibitions is unlikely to thrive in the long run.

How do human beings fit into the Lorenzian scheme of things? In terms of the division between lethal and nonlethal animals, humans fall into the latter category. Our natural physical endowments are not terribly menacing. We do not have sharp teeth, powerful jaws, strong limbs, or dangerous claws. Two naked people would find it very difficult to kill each other using only their own body and physical capabilities. In this sense we are more like rabbits than wolves. As essentially nonlethal creatures, we should have no need to develop mechanisms that might prevent us from killing each other because we are not able to kill each other. The problem is that our intellect, creativity, and ingenuity have allowed us to develop tools that allow us to become lethal. In the 150,000 or so years humans and their earliest ancestors have been around, we have gone from using sticks and rocks to cannons and missiles. Although 150,000 years seems like a long time to you and me, from an evolutionary perspective this is an eyeblink. And it has been less than ten thousand years from the development of many close-range weapons to the development of bombers and missiles. So in an evolutionary sense we have gone almost overnight from being relatively harmless animals to being incredibly lethal. Lorenz lays out the basic problem: "All of his [mankind's] trouble arise from his being a basically harmless omnivorous creature, lacking in natural weapons with which to kill prey, and, therefore, devoid of the built-in safety devices which prevent 'professional' carnivores from abusing their killing power." Unfortunately, "in human evolution, no inhibitory mechanisms preventing sudden manslaughter were necessary because quick killing was impossible . . . the invention of artificial weapons upset the equilibrium of killing potential and social inhibitions."[11]

On some level there undoubtedly do exist certain inhibitions. Many people would find it very difficult to kill someone in hand-to-hand combat when they were crouching and crying helplessly in a corner. Many would take this behavior as a sufficient appeasement gesture. The problem, however, is that not only have human beings developed the capacity to be lethal, they have also fashioned weapons that allow them to be lethal from great distances: a few dozen feet with spears and arrows, a few hundred feet with guns, a mile or two with artillery, several miles from above with a bomber, and thousands of miles away with missiles. A few individuals can press some buttons in an underground bunker and vaporize millions of their fellow human beings without ever seeing a drop of blood or a single anguished expression. Again, Lorenz makes the implications of this clear: "The distance at which all shooting weapons take effect screens the killer against the stimulus situation which would otherwise activate his killing inhibitions. . . . The man who presses the releasing button is so completely screened against seeing, hearing or otherwise emotionally realizing the consequences of his action, that he can commit it with impunity."[12]

appeasement gesture
A concept popularized by Konrad Lorenz involving displays or signals made by lethal animals while fighting with members of their own species in order to indicate defeat and avoid death.

PART II *Controversies*

Thus, according to Lorenz and Morris, what we have is a form of **evolutionary lag** or **disequilibrium.** Human intellectual evolution, reflected in our ability to build increasingly destructive weapons that allow us to kill from greater and greater distances, has outstripped our moral evolution. We are the evolutionary equivalent of bunny rabbits running around with machine guns, amazed at their newfound lethality while lacking the internal devices that stop them from killing their own kind. This is not a very pretty picture.

In some respects, these theories of instinctual human aggression seem to mirror conservative and realist views. If people do have an aggressive instinct that leads to war, this would seem to be consistent with the conservative and realist view of humans as an imperfect and imperfectible species. Very few realists, however, have explicitly adopted any particular biologically based theory of human aggression. Realists who emphasize the imperfections of human nature are generally content to rely on generic assertions of human lust, greed, passion, and will to power. Nonetheless, it is difficult to avoid the similarities. And when those who believe in the innateness of human aggression turn their attention to international relations, they tend to adopt a decidedly realist approach. We can recall Reinhold Niebuhr's observation about the inevitability of conflict in human history until its very end and easily imagine the same words coming from the pen of Konrad Lorenz. And the arguments of Robin Fox and Robert Ardrey echo George Kennan's lament that humankind cannot do anything about the beast within. For this reason, theories of instinctual human aggression are often grouped with realist approaches to international relations.

The curse of intelligence: Abstract thought Even if Lorenz is correct about the presence of an aggressive instinct and the consequences of our ability to produce lethal weapons, this in and of itself could not completely account for war. The argument presented thus far could just as easily lead to the expectation that individuals would be running around killing each other *as individuals* on a grand scale, but this is not what happens. War is not merely lethal aggression; it is a particular form of lethal aggression. It is lethal aggression among and in the name of organized political or social entities. The aggressive instinct alone cannot account for the prevalence of war. It may be a necessary part of explaining war, but it is not sufficient. As Robin Fox explains, "There is no question that aggression is related to war, just as sex is related to prostitution. . . . but neither *institutional* form follows directly from the basic instinctive drive."[13] If we want to understand why people engage in this type of lethal aggression, we need to add something to the equation. In a sense, there are three questions we need to answer in order to understand war: Why do people engage in aggression? Why do they engage in lethal aggression? Why do they engage in that type of lethal aggression we call war? Thus far, we have only answered the first two questions. Lorenz and Morris give the final explanatory answer by incorporating our ability for abstract, symbolic thought and our innate sociability. These things combine with our innate aggressiveness to explain war.

Though Lorenz and those who agree with him see people as animals with instincts, they would also agree that we are probably less instinctual than other creatures because of our intelligence and capacity for abstract, conceptual thought. It is this intelligence that distinguishes us from other creatures and has allowed us to thrive in an evolutionary sense. Paradoxically, it is also our intelligence, our greatest asset, that is the root cause of our war problem. It is our intelligence, after all, that provides us with

evolutionary lag (disequilibrium) Konrad Lorenz's idea that humans' intellectual evolution and ability to kill has not been matched by the development of inhibitions against using these abilities to kill members of our own species.

the ability to invent the weapons that place our survival as a species in danger. It is also this intelligence that "aids and abets" our innate aggressiveness to produce war as we know it. Not only does our intelligence allow us to think of new ways to kill each other, it allows us to conceive of the world in ways that are part of the equation of war. As Lionel Tiger and Robin Fox explain, "Only an animal with brain enough to think of empires and try to manage them could conceive of war. Only an animal so wedded to the truths inside his skull could travel many miles and expend endless, precious calories and hours and artifacts to destroy others."[14] Animals fight over things—mates, food, territory—but people fight over ideas: "Since we are an animal that lives primarily by ideas and only secondarily by instincts . . . we react fanatically when our basic ideas—those that decide our identities individual and collective—are threatened."[15] And as Lorenz states with characteristic boldness, "All the great dangers threatening humanity with extinction are direct consequences of conceptual thought."[16]

The notion of a collective identity hints at another fundamental human motivation—our "natural tendency to form in-groups."[17] Though not necessarily an instinct in the strictest sense of the term, this is a basic human motivation that has been deeply rooted in our psyche over the course of human history and evolution. Echoing some of the same ideas we saw in conservative and realist thought, people are seen as inherently social creatures who inevitably identify themselves with social groups. These social groups provide people with a sense of meaning and belonging. Earlier in human history, they were also essential to survival in very harsh environments in which individuals on their own stood little chance. Group identity, however, requires differentiating one's in-group from out-groups. Anthony Storr elaborates: "We define ourselves, psychologically as well as physically, by comparison and differentiation. Colour does not exist except in relation to another colour; personality has no meaning except in relation to other personalities. . . . The maintenance of human identity requires oppositions."[18] People are generally able to maintain peaceful relations within their in-group when an out-group exists upon whom aggression can be discharged. But it is this division of human society into distinct social groupings combined with our attachment to ideas that accounts for the particular form of lethal aggression we call war. Fox combines these elements in observing that "the occasions for each particular will vary. . . . But ultimately 'we' fight 'them' because they are different, and their difference is threatening in its challenge to the validity of these ideas we live by. Thus, all wars are ideological wars."[19]

For Lorenz, Morris, Fox, and Storr, war results from the combination of innate aggressive instinct, the ingenuity that produces artificial weapons, our capacity for conceptual thought, and the divisive consequences of social group formation. Our creativity and intelligence are at the same time humankind's greatest blessing and curse. One might wonder whether the same intelligence that got us into this dilemma might ultimately provide a way out. But there is little reason to expect a nice ending to this story. The result is gloomy assessments about the fate of humankind. Though Lorenz tries to maintain a cautious optimism that human reason and culture may eventually help control our aggressive instincts, he is usually drawn to more pessimistic conclusions: "An unprejudiced observer from another planet, looking upon man as he is today, in his hand the atom bomb, the product of his intelligence, in his heart the aggressive drive inherited from his anthropoid ancestors, which this same intelligence cannot control, would not prophesy long life for the species."[20]

CULTURE, SOCIAL LEARNING, AND WAR

Those who believe that war is the inevitable result of human nature are fond of pointing out how common war is in human history. Using the figures cited at the beginning of this chapter, we can point to less than three hundred years of peace in the last fifty-six centuries. Robin Fox confidently asserts that "war has been a constant of human history."[21] Indeed, it would seem to make sense that something that derives from a basic human instinct would be a constant: if human nature is by definition an unchanging constant, the behaviors that spring from it should also be constant.

But before we deal with theoretical disagreements over war and human nature, we need to ask whether this assertion that war is a constant is empirically accurate. What do we mean when we say that war has been a constant? Do we mean that every person, every society, and every nation is "constantly" engaging in warfare? This would be a ludicrous assertion because it is patently not the case. Even though war is constant in the sense that at any given moment a war is probably going on somewhere in the world, this is not the same as saying that people and nations are constantly at war. Others look at the evidence on the frequency of war and conclude the exact opposite—that war is a relatively rare occurrence. In any given year, the vast majority of people and nations are at peace, not war. The majority of the world's people has never fought in a war, has never killed anyone, and will never kill anyone. Furthermore, few people will go to their graves considering their life to be diminished and incomplete if they have never engaged in warfare. Does this sound like aggression, lethal aggression, and war are an integral part of human nature? Could we say the same thing about other supposedly instinctual behaviors such as sex? Certainly not. Thus, many reject the empirical characterization of war as a constant feature of human existence. And if war is actually a rare event, then its inevitability and connection to what we call human nature can be called into question.

Beyond the fact that war does not seem to be a constant feature of human existence, those who fall on the nurture side of the debate see several other major flaws in human nature explanations for war. First, the presence of peaceful societies contradicts the expectations of human nature theories. Second, when we look at the actual behavior of those who fight wars, there are reasons to believe that people may in fact possess a fundamental aversion to lethal aggression. Third, even if there is an individual instinct of aggression, this may have nothing to do with war. Finally, it is more compelling to view aggression, lethal aggression, and war as the result of social learning, cultural norms, conditioning, peer influence, and other environmental forces that shape our behavior.

Peaceful societies If a behavior is an inherent part of human nature or derives from a fundamental instinct, it seems reasonable to assume that the behavior in question would be universal. That is, the behavior (or, at least, the desire to engage in that behavior) should be in evidence across time and space in human existence. Again, sex provides a somewhat less controversial example. Almost every human being has sexual desires and every human society we know of has engaged in sexual behavior. Those groups that refrain (such as religious leaders or sects that take vows of celibacy) do not claim to be free of sexual impulses but merely pledge to resist the desire. There are no examples of sexless human societies.

One piece of evidence that seems to work against the notion that war is inherent

peaceful societies Historical and contemporary human communities that do not engage in war or even have a concept for it. These rare examples are often used to counter the argument that human nature or instincts make war an inevitability.

in human nature is the presence of so-called **peaceful societies.** Many anthropologists have identified contemporary and historical human societies that appear to have no experience with anything we would recognize as war. Some do not even have a word or concept that embodies the notion of war. Commonly cited examples include the Copper Eskimos in Canada, the Polar Eskimos of Greenland, the King Bushman of the Kalahari Desert in Africa, and the Hutterites and Zuni Indians in North America.[22] These are obviously societies of human beings, but they seem to have no war. In the modern world there are also countries that have gone generations without any involvement in war, such as Sweden and Switzerland. If there is such as thing as human nature and human instincts, we can assume people in these societies possess that nature and those instincts. Nonetheless, war does not seem to be part of their world. For many, this fact in itself refutes the idea that war is the consequence of some essential, inherent human characteristic.

Studies of peaceful societies remain controversial on several counts. A few supposed examples, such as the Tasaday in the Philippines, a primitive society supposedly "discovered" in the 1970s, have been exposed as frauds. Most, though genuine, raise questions of interpretation. For example, does any act of violence by someone from one group against someone from another group constitute a war? When a group attacks another group and takes food or captures mates, are these raids or wars? These interpretive debates aside, there are certainly a few unquestionable examples of human societies that appear to have been free of war. But even in these cases, many remain skeptical of their larger significance, pointing to both the rarity of these societies and their very unusual characteristics. After emphasizing that only a handful of such peaceful societies exist "in all the world and all history," Joshua Goldstein goes on to explain that "these societies all exist at the fringes of ecological viability, in circumstances where small communities are scattered in a harsh environment with little contact with each other. These cases demonstrate the extremes to which one must go to find a society where war is absent."[23] Still, their existence cannot be denied. Examining the evidence on peaceful societies, Lawrence Keeley concludes that "while it is not inevitable, war is universally common and usual."[24] The fact that war does not seem to be inevitable is a theoretically significant finding, even if it does not offer much of a basis for practical hope.

The reluctance to kill An intriguing body of evidence that might help us assess the relative merits of the nature–nurture positions is studies of how people actually behave in battle, a subject often ignored by those interested in the causes of war. When people find themselves in combat situations, do they behave as innate aggression theories would lead us to believe? Apparently not. In fact, some argue that the evidence seems to point exactly in the opposite direction: that people possess an instinctual aversion to lethal aggression that is extremely difficult to overcome.

There are surprisingly few systematic studies of how soldiers actually behave in battle, though anecdotal accounts are common. Before World War II, there were no genuinely systematic studies of combat behavior. Recognizing this dearth of evidence, during that war the U.S. Army decided that it needed to understand what soldiers actually did in combat. The purpose was to figure out better ways to train soldiers, not to test theories of human aggression, but the findings have some bearing on the issue of motivations for aggression and what it actually takes to get people to kill. Under the direction of General S. L. A. Marshall, soldiers were asked what they did in combat situations. Their answers came as something of a shock to the military establishment. Marshall found that only 15 to 20 percent of soldiers actually took part by firing their weapons at the enemy. The majority, in even situations where their lives might be endangered, did not take part. Though they did not run from battle, they would simply not fire their weapons or would do so in ways that posed little danger of actually killing anyone. These findings seemed consistent with some anecdotal evidence from previous wars in which large amounts of ammunition were fired with relatively few casualties. The idea that soldiers might purposely try to miss the enemy did not occur to most people. But unless they were simply very bad shots, this should have been the unavoidable conclusion. There is also evidence that soldiers are particularly unlikely to fire their weapons when they are isolated—that is, when others are unable to witness their refusal to shoot.[25] This has become known as the phenomenon of **nonfirers,** or the reluctance of soldiers to actually fire their weapons to kill the enemy.

How are we to interpret this evidence, and what does it tell us about the nature–nurture debate? For critics of the innate aggression thesis, this avoidance of lethal aggression hardly seems consistent with the notion that the violence of war is the consequence of some uncontrollable instinct. The fact that soldiers are even more reluctant to engage in lethal aggression when they are isolated from their commanding officers and comrades suggests that social pressures are essential to get soldiers to do things they would prefer not to do. What sort of instinct can this possibly be, when social pressure is so important and when so many soldiers refuse to kill even when their own lives are in danger? This sort of avoidance does not appear to be an action that is the result of an innate instinct.

In fact, some have gone one step further, suggesting that studies on nonfirers point in precisely the opposite direction. General Marshall himself concluded that "the average and healthy individual . . . has such an inner and usually unrealized resistance towards killing a fellow man that he will not of his own volition take life if it is possible to turn away from the responsibility."[26] From these studies, the military learned that much of its previous training had been based on the faulty assumption that it needed to overcome the soldier's fear of death before he could become effective. Marshall's study demonstrated that the real problem was overcoming the average soldier's reluctance to kill. And even after all the drills, training, indoctrination, social pressure, and threat of discipline, the military is not always successful in doing so. What kind of instinct is this when so much effort meets with so little success in eliciting the desired behavior? Would such effort be necessary, and would success be so scant, in trying to get people to engage in sex, for example?

War is violence, not "aggression" One of the more powerful criticisms of the Lorenzian thesis begins with the seemingly odd assertion that war has nothing (or very little) to do with aggression in the first place. Ashley Montagu, perhaps the harshest critic of theories of instinctual or innate aggression, makes the startling observation that "the truth is—and this is perhaps the greatest paradox of all—motivationally, war represents one of the least aggressive forms of man's behavior."[27] This is an observation that takes some time to digest. How can one look at the slaughter of millions of men on the battlefields of World War I and seriously contend that this killing represents one of the *least* aggressive forms of human behavior? There are two keys to

nonfirers Soldiers who refuse to fire their weapons in battle (or deliberately try to avoid killing enemy soldiers). The frequency of this phenomenon is often cited by those who reject instinctual theories of aggression and war.

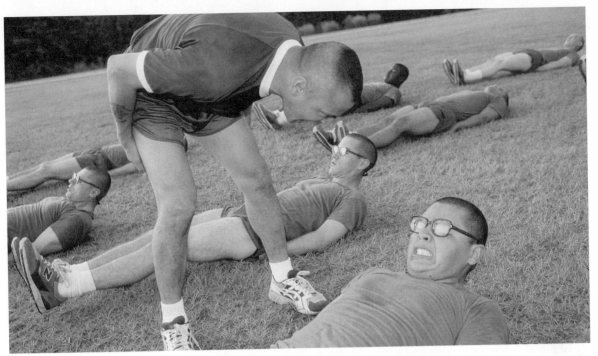

Basic training at Paris Island, North Carolina, designed to turn civilians into soldiers. The transformation is as much psychological as physical.
Source: Andrew Lichtenstein / The Image Works

understanding Montagu's argument—his careful use of the word *motivationally* and the distinction between violence and aggression.

An analogy might help illuminate Montagu's point. If asked why people eat, we might be tempted to say that they do so to satisfy their hunger. In this case, hunger provides the motivation for the behavior of eating. But does this mean that every time we witness someone eating, we can conclude that person was motivated by hunger? No. Certainly hunger leads people to eat, but people often eat for reasons that have nothing to do with hunger, such as habit, social custom, or some psychological compulsion. Sometimes we eat lunch just because it is lunchtime. Other times we might sooth our depression with a pint of ice cream. Everyone eats at social functions such as wedding receptions, though it is unlikely they all happened to be hungry at the same time. Thus, even though hunger drives people to eat, we cannot assume that every act of eating is the result of hunger. There are many motivations for eating.

Similarly, although aggression may lead to acts of violence, we cannot assume that every act of violence is motivated by aggression. To use another analogy, a robber who shoots a bank teller after the teller refused to hand over the cash has used violence in order to get something, not because any internal desire or drive led to the violence. Had the teller handed over the cash, the shooting would not have taken place. He was motivated in this case by greed, not aggression. This is sometimes referred to as **instrumental violence**—violence employed to accomplish a particular objective. It is very different, for example, from someone who kills in an aroused state of anger in

instrumental violence Violence employed in pursuit of some identifiable objective.

PART II *Controversies*

the midst of a heated argument. Though there is certainly some relationship between violence and aggression, they are not one and the same.

Montagu sees the violence of war as more like the bank robber who shoots in order to get the money than someone who kills in a fit of rage and anger. War is the organized, planned use of violence by political and social units that is designed to accomplish particular political, economic, or social objectives. Even if people do have an instinct for or drive toward aggression, it is difficult to see how this need is satisfied in war. The people who make the decision to go to war are rarely participants themselves, and the soldiers who actually engage in the violence are picked out of their normal settings (often by force) and transported to distant battlefields to fight. Montagu quotes French biologist Jean Rotund: "In war . . . man is much more like a sheep than a wolf. War is servility . . . but not aggressiveness."[28] The soldier's behavior "is not instinctively but state-directed toward the enemy."

Montagu's argument is very clever and formidable. Even if one concedes almost all of Lorenz's major points (which Montagu does not, by the way) Montagu's basic position still stands. Even if people do have instincts, and even if aggression is one of them, this does not necessarily bring us any closer to understanding war. Theories of human aggression only help us understand war if one believes that war is aggression. It is the linkage between war and aggression that Montagu rejects, which makes theories of aggression interesting but largely irrelevant. For Montagu, war has as much (or as little) to do with aggressive instincts as gluttonous Roman feasts where people stuffed their faces for hours and days on end had to do with their hunger.

Social learning and conditioning Human nature, by definition, is a constant. War, on the other hand, is variable. Some periods in history reveal more frequent and intense wars than others: the first half of the twentieth century was much bloodier than the last half of the nineteenth century. Certain countries and societies have been extremely warlike in the past but are relatively pacific today: the Swedes used to be fierce warriors but have not been in a war for almost two centuries. Within societies some groups are more warlike than others: the Amish, for example, refused to fight even in World War II. Whenever we see behavior that varies over time, across societies, and even within societies, we are dealing with something that has, at the very least, a significant social or cultural component. The variability of war across and within societies and cultures leads anthropologist Margaret Mead to conclude that warfare "is an invention like any of the inventions in terms of which we order our lives, such as writing, marriage, cooking our food instead of eating it raw, trial by jury, or burial of the dead, and so on."[29] If war is an invention, it can be "uninvented"; if it is learned, it can be unlearned.

When we say that war is a learned behavior, we mean this in a much broader sense than explicit instruction, such as that which occurs in the classroom. Learning in this context refers to the complex process by which people are socialized—that is, how they learn what behaviors are acceptable in what settings. People learn in a variety of ways. One mechanism is observation and imitation. As people grow in any culture, they see how others behave in certain situations and they are likely to behave likewise in similar settings. People also learn through a process of **stimulus and response** based on the consequences of a particular behavior. If people receive rewards for a behavior, they are more likely to continue that behavior. Conversely, if people are

stimulus and response
Used in social learning theory to indicate that human behavior is shaped by social stimuli—that is, people engage in those behaviors for which they receive social rewards and refrain from behaviors that bring social punishment.

punished for a behavior, they will be inclined not to repeat it. "Rewards" and "punishments" need not be financial but can also be praise, prestige, and adulation (as rewards) or criticism, denigration, and social ostracism (as punishments). To use a common example, nobody requires or instructs all the teenagers in high school to dress alike, but they almost always do. Why? Because they fear the social "punishments," and value the social "rewards," that result from various forms of dress. These processes of socialization that shape our behavior are so pervasive and subtle that people are usually not even conscious of what is going on.

There are potentially many forms and manifestations of aggression. All cultures have norms and rules regarding what types of aggression are acceptable and in what settings. Almost nobody believes that it is permissible to beat up a cashier who gives you the wrong change or kill someone who cuts you off on the highway. Killing someone in this context would get you a long jail sentence. These are forms of aggression that our society rejects and punishes. As a result, they are also extremely rare forms of aggression. But if the government sends you a draft notice, cuts your hair, puts you in uniform, and sends you thousands of miles away to kill people you have never met, you are praised for this. If you are very good at it, you may even get medals for it. Richard Barnet put his finger on the irony of this situation: "Individuals get medals, promotions and honors for committing the same acts for the state for which they would be imprisoned in any other circumstance."[30] In relation to nonfirers, this is one of the problems for military training: How do we get people to do something (kill) when they have been taught their whole lives that killing is wrong? Overcoming these previously learned social inhibitions is apparently fairly difficult. Even if there is some instinctual basis for aggression, the forms this aggression will take and the contexts in which it is deemed acceptable are shaped by our culture. These sorts of distinctions are culturally, not biologically, determined.

Margaret Mead also saw a connection between a culture's treatment of aggression and violence in general and in war. In this context it is interesting to look at the subtle and not-so-subtle messages our culture conveys about violence. War films provide an obvious example. At any time of day we can turn on the television and see films that portray the mass slaughter of people in war in positive and heroic terms. Such films are not relegated to late-night viewing accompanied with warnings about the content. The same holds for video stores, where there are usually never any restrictions on who may rent films containing incredible levels of violence in the name of "entertainment." David Grossman emphasizes in graphic terms society's disparate treatment of violence and sex by pointing out that "in video stores the horror section repeatedly displays bare breasts (often with blood running down them), gaping eye sockets, and mutilated bodies. Movies rated X with tamer covers are generally not available in many video stores and, if they are, are in separate adults-only rooms. But horror videos are displayed for every child to see." The implicit lesson is that "breasts are taboo if they are on a live woman, but permissible on a mutilated corpse."[31]

What sort of message does this send about what types of behavior are acceptable and desirable? Why is boxing, in which two men (and, now, women) beat each other up, considered a "sport" that can be seen on television at any time of day but certain types of nudity need to be reserved for after 9 p.m.? Why do people automatically become tempting presidential candidates because they successfully fought a war and not because they avoided one? These examples can be multiplied many times over. What is the cumulative effect of these images, messages, and practices over the course of a lifetime?

Though images and messages conducive to war are prevalent even in times of peace, in times of war they become dominant in the form of explicit propaganda. How war propaganda portrays the enemy is particularly significant. In his study *Faces of the Enemy,* Sam Keen demonstrates that societies at war tend to use very similar visual and rhetorical imagery to convey an image of the enemy as less than human.[32] Whether the picture is a savage brute who commits atrocities without regret or, at the most extreme, the depiction of the enemy as a literal animal or vermin, the prevalence of such imagery, and perhaps the need for it, is instructive. The process of constructing images of the enemy has been characterized as **dehumanization** or **psuedo-specification,** which is the tendency to view members of our own species as if they are not members of our species — that is, to falsely (hence *pseudo*) divide the human race into different species.[33] Keen and others argue that process of dehumanization is an almost necessary component of war because "as a rule, human beings do not kill other human beings. Before we enter into warfare or genocide, we must first 'dehumanize' those we mean to eliminate. . . . The hostile imagination systematically destroys our natural tendency to identify with others of our species. . . . The purpose of propaganda is to paralyze thought . . . and to condition individuals to act as a mass."[34]

This dehumanization is particularly important for soldiers who have to do the actual fighting and killing. As Richard Holmes explains, "The legitimate need to defuse deep-seated cultural and psychological taboos against killing is an inseparable part of military training." Part of this "defusing" of taboos is the "almost obligatory dehumanisation of the enemy."[35] William Broyles, an author and veteran of the Vietnam War, pointed out that the soldier's greatest weapon was not his rifle but rather his idea of the enemy.[36]

The ubiquity of dehumanization in war is both depressing and a grounds for hope. It is depressing in the sense that we are able with such ease to create and accept images of other people as less human than ourselves. On another level, however, the fact that we do this suggests that people may indeed have a resistance to killing other people whom they recognize as like themselves. If we were able to kill other human beings on a grand scale while viewing them as being on a par with ourselves, this would be even more troubling. This process of dehumanization also suggests the importance of culture and socialization for understanding war. It is obvious that inhibitions against killing, the social "taboos" Holmes refers to, can be created. The fact that efforts need to be taken to overcome these taboos suggests there is nothing natural or inevitable about it. The images and ways of thinking that allow or encourage people to do the killing that is part of war are social and cultural artifacts. There is nothing inevitable or biologically instinctual about them. Part of the answer to problems of war, then, is how we make the "taboos" against killing stronger while refraining from actions to "defuse" these taboos. If we can consciously "defuse" these taboos, we can also reinforce them.

Are people peaceful? If people are not by nature aggressive and warlike, does this mean that we are by nature peaceful? Most alternatives to instinctual theories of aggression do not make this leap. It does not automatically follow that a negative view of human nature needs to be replaced with a positive one. Logically, one can also

dehumanization The portrayal and/or perception of other people as less than human.

pseudospecification Viewing other humans as if they were not members of one's own species. Wartime propaganda depicting the enemy as animals or insects facilitates this process. This tendency is often cited by those who see war as a culturally and socially learned phenomenon.

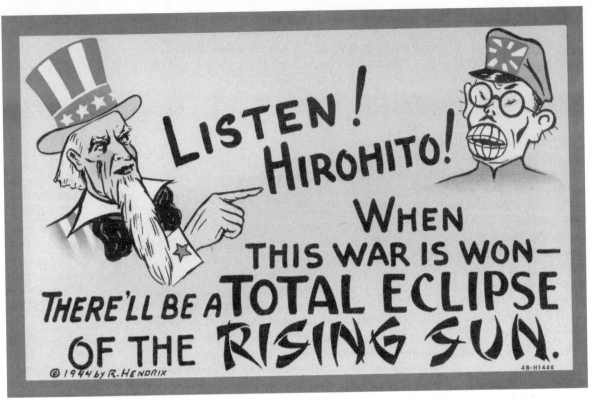

A typical propaganda poster from World War II. Crude stereotypes, such as the horn-rimmed glasses and buckteeth, have the effect of minimizing the humanity of wartime opponents.
<small>SOURCE:</small> © Lake County Museum/CORBIS

claim that people have no "nature" at all—that is, we are not naturally good or bad, moral or immoral, rational or irrational, peaceful or warlike. Exactly where social learning theorists come down on this question is often unclear. When David Grossman refers to the difficulties of overcoming people's fundamental resistance to killing, he does appear to be suggesting the existence of an innate peaceful disposition. Similarly, in pointing to the essential role played by dehumanizing rhetoric and propaganda, Sam Keen also seems to be leaning in this direction because he suggests that people would be much less inclined to kill other people if they recognized them for what they are—other people. If ethological theories of instinctual aggression lent support to conservatism and realism, these approaches would appear more in line with liberalism's optimistic view of human nature.

Most social learning theories, however, reject the very notion that we can identify a "human nature" independent of social circumstances. There are no (or almost no) human behaviors that are not socially derived. It is not a matter of social forces or pressures reinforcing or defusing preexisting drives, but rather of creating them in the first place. Skepticism about the utility of the concept of human nature is a characteristic of Marxist, feminist, and (obviously) constructivist approaches. These approaches may differ in terms of which social forces are viewed as most important in shaping human behavior. For Marxists it is the underlying economic forces that drive behavior, whereas for feminists it is beliefs about gender roles and gendered social and political institutions. From these perspectives, debates about the relationship between war and human nature are pointless and distracting.

Conclusion

Within this debate about whether war is a biological, instinctual phenomenon or a cultural and social invention there is actually more common ground than might be assumed. We can see the point of convergence in Robin Fox's admission that war as an institutional form of aggression does *not* follow directly from what he sees as the basic instinctual drive. In order to make the link between the supposed instinct of aggression and war, Lorenz, Fox, and Morris are compelled to add cultural and social factors. The causal arrow is not a direct one. That is, even though they see aggression, like sex, as an instinct, they admit that our culture conveys norms about the contexts in which aggression is acceptable and the targets against whom it may be directed. That is, war is seen as the result of both nature and nurture—a basic drive and a culture that channels that drive in certain directions. The question then becomes whether those cultural and social factors that complete the link between the aggressive instinct and war can be altered. If so, the instinctual drive, even if it exists, becomes irrelevant. One need not always eliminate the "root" cause in order to deal with a problem. We do not need to get rid of the sun to eliminate skin cancer; sunscreen can do the job. Thus, the real debate is not about whether there is an aggressive instinct that leads to war, but rather whether those social and cultural forces that everyone seems to agree are a significant part of the equation of war can be altered.

To say that war is a learned behavior that can be unlearned is not necessarily a basis for much optimism. Even if this is theoretically true, we may conclude that the practical obstacles to unlearning war are insurmountable. Tiger and Fox are led in this direction when they ask: "If we are not by nature violent creatures, why do we seem to inevitably create situations that lead to violence?" After conceding that a substantial element of learning and social conditioning goes into war, they conclude that "we are creatures who are by nature *easily* aroused to violence, we *easily* learn it, and we are wired to create situations in which the arousal and learning readily take place and in which violence becomes a necessity [emphasis added]."[37] When Tiger and Fox look at the world, they are amazed by how little it takes to get people to fight and kill. The ease with which they think this is done indicates to them that it strikes a cord with a deep and fundamental part of our being.

As in disagreements about whether the glass is half empty or half full, still others are drawn to the exact opposite conclusion. Those who lean more toward the nurture side of the debate are amazed at how much effort it takes to get people to fight and kill: a lifetime of socialization into a culture of violence, social pressure and government compulsion to get soldiers to serve, and a continual dehumanization of the enemy that is to be fought and killed. According to Sam Keen, "*Homo hostilis* must be created by the media and the institutions that subject him to a constant indoctrination by way of hero stories, ideology, rationalizations, tribal myths, rites of passage, and icons of the enemy. . . . The entire institutional and symbolic apparatus of society is necessary" to get people to engage in war. And even after all this, "the effort is successful for only a small minority." Rather than being easy, Keen thinks "it is so *difficult* to mold us into killers [emphasis added]."[38]

So the debate about whether war reflects some fundamental drive or instinct becomes transformed slightly. The question becomes not whether people learn to engage in war, but how easily they learn it. Not whether it can be unlearned, but how difficult this will be. Like many debates, the debate over war and human nature has been defined by the extremes. The true insights are likely to be found in between. Even though looking at the "purer" or more extreme sides of a debate is often a useful approach for focusing on the central issues of contention, one need not be trapped into these positions. The debate over war and human nature, like most debates, has more than two "sides."

POINTS OF VIEW

Are People (or Men) "Hard Wired" for War?

The relationship between war and human nature is one of those abstract and theo-retical topics that people rarely talk about explicitly. Assumptions about human nature are more likely to remain implicit in most discussions of war and peace. Oc-casionally, however, those who reject or endorse the notion of a tie between innate human aggressiveness and war feel compelled to restate their position. One of the more powerful and succinct attempts to refute the instinctual theory of violence and war in recent decades is the Seville Statement on Violence. Drafted in 1986 by a group of natural and social scientists, the statement was subsequently adopted by the United Nations Educational, Scientific and Cultural Organization (UNESCO) as an official expression of its position on war and violence. This statement, included here, clearly reflects the view that war is a culturally learned and conditioned prac-tice. Yet there are those who remain convinced that some connection must exist between aggressive instincts and war, though the exact nature of the connection is sometimes unclear. This viewpoint is evident in the ABC News report that follows, on recent research relating to the question of whether people (or men in particular) are "hard wired" for war.

In many respects, these two documents reflect the basic positions presented in this chapter, though often with different emphases and evidence. To what extent do they reflect the familiar arguments in the nature–nurture debate, and in what ways do they move beyond the traditional positions? In particular, how might the evi-dence about war and violence for societies with a high proportion of young males fit into the larger nature–nurture debate? Though this evidence is presented as if it supports an instinctual theory of violence and war, can one also argue that it is more in line with cultural theories (and even feminist theories)?

Seville Statement on Violence, Spain, 1986 (Subsequently Adopted by UNESCO at the Twenty-fifth Session of the General Conference on 16 November 1989)

Believing that it is our responsibility to address from our particular disciplines the most dangerous and destructive activities of our species, violence and war; recognizing that science is a human cultural product which cannot be definitive or all-encompassing; and gratefully acknowledging the support of the authorities of Seville and representatives of the Spanish UNESCO; we, the undersigned scholars from around the world and from rele-vant sciences, have met and arrived at the following Statement on Violence. In it, we chal-lenge a number of alleged biological findings that have been used, even by some in our disciplines, to justify violence and war. Because the alleged findings have contributed to an atmosphere of pessimism in our time, we submit that the open, considered rejection of these mis-statements can contribute significantly to the International Year of Peace.

Misuse of scientific theories and data to justify violence and war is not new but has been made since the advent of modern science. For example, the theory of evolution has been used to justify not only war, but also genocide, colonialism, and suppression of the weak.

We state our position in the form of five propositions. We are aware that there are many other issues about violence and war that could be fruitfully addressed from the standpoint of our disciplines, but we restrict ourselves here to what we consider a most important first step.

IT IS SCIENTIFICALLY INCORRECT to say that we have inherited a tendency to make war from our animal ancestors. Although fighting occurs widely throughout animal species, only a few cases of destructive intra-species fighting between organized groups have ever been reported among naturally living species, and none of these involve the use of tools designed to be weapons. Normal predatory feeding upon other species cannot be equated with intra-species violence. Warfare is a peculiarly human phenomenon and does not occur in other animals.

The fact that warfare has changed so radically over time indicates that it is a product of culture. Its biological connection is primarily through language which makes possible the co-ordination of groups, the transmission of technology, and the use of tools. War is biologically possible, but it is not inevitable, as evidenced by its variation in occurrence and nature over time and space. There are cultures which have not engaged in war for centuries, and there are cultures which have engaged in war frequently at some times and not at others.

IT IS SCIENTIFICALLY INCORRECT to say that war or any other violent behaviour is genetically programmed into our human nature. While genes are involved at all levels of nervous system function, they provide a developmental potential that can be actualized only in conjunction with the ecological and social environment. While individuals vary in their predispositions to be affected by their experience, it is the interaction between their genetic endowment and conditions of nurturance that determines their personalities. Except for rare pathologies, the genes do not produce individuals necessarily predisposed to violence. Neither do they determine the opposite. While genes are co-involved in establishing our behavioural capacities, they do not by themselves specify the outcome.

IT IS SCIENTIFICALLY INCORRECT to say that in the course of human evolution there has been a selection for aggressive behaviour more than for other kinds of behaviour. In all well-studied species, status within the group is achieved by the ability to co-operate and to fulfil social functions relevant to the structure of that group. 'Dominance' involves social bindings and affiliations; it is not simply a matter of the possession and use of superior physical power, although it does involve aggressive behaviours. Where genetic selection for aggressive behaviour has been artificially instituted in animals, it has rapidly succeeded in producing hyper-aggressive individuals; this indicates that aggression was not maximally selected under natural conditions. When such experimentally-created hyper-aggressive animals are present in a social group, they either disrupt its social structure or are driven out. Violence is neither in our evolutionary legacy nor in our genes.

IT IS SCIENTIFICALLY INCORRECT to say that humans have a "violent brain." While we do have the neural apparatus to act violently, it is not automatically activated by internal or external stimuli. Like higher primates and unlike other animals, our higher neural processes filter such stimuli before they can be acted upon. How we act is shaped by how we have been conditioned and socialized. There is nothing in our neurophysiology that compels us to react violently.

IT IS SCIENTIFICALLY INCORRECT to say that war is caused by "instinct" or any single motivation. The emergence of modern warfare has been a journey from the primacy of emotional and motivational factors, sometimes called 'instincts', to the primacy of cognitive factors. Modern war involves institutional use of personal characteristics such as obedience, suggestibility, and idealism, social skills such as language, and rational considerations such as cost-calculation, planning, and information processing. The technology of modern war has exaggerated traits associated with violence both in the training of actual combatants and in the preparation of support for war in the general population. As a result of this exaggeration, such traits are often mistaken to be the causes rather than the consequences of the process.

We conclude that biology does not condemn humanity to war, and that humanity can be freed from the bondage of biological pessimism and empowered with confidence to undertake the transformative tasks needed in this International Year of Peace and in the years to come. Although these tasks are mainly institutional and collective, they also rest upon the consciousness of individual participants for whom pessimism and optimism are crucial factors. Just as a "wars begin in the minds of men," peace also begins in our minds. The same species who invented war is capable of inventing peace. The responsibility lies with each of us.

Seville, 16 May 1986

David Adams, Psychology, Wesleyan University, Middletown, CT., U.S.A.

S.A. Barnett, Ethology, The Australian National University, Canberra, Australia

N.P. Bechtereva, Neurophysiology, Institute for Experimental Medicine of Academy of Medical Sciences of the U.S.S.R., Leningrad, U.S.S.R.

Bonnie Frank Carter, Psychology, Albert Einstein Medical Center, Philadelphia (PA), U.S.A.

José M. Rodriguez Delgado, Neurophysiology, Centro de Estudios Neurobiologicos, Madrid, Spain

José Luis Diaz, Ethology, Instituto Mexicano de Psiquiatria, Mexico D.F., Mexico

Andrzej Eliasz, Individual Differences Psychology, Polish Academy of Sciences, Warsaw, Poland

Santiago Genovés, Biological Anthropology, Instituto de Estudios Antropologicos, Mexico D.F., Mexico

Benson E. Ginsburg, Behavior Genetics, University of Connecticut, Storrs, CT., U.S.A.

Jo Groebel, Social Psychology, Erziehungswissenschaftliche Hochschule, Landau, Federal Republic of Germany

Samir-Kumar Ghosh, Sociology, Indian Institute of Human Sciences, Calcutta, India

Robert Hinde, Animal Behaviour, Cambridge University, Cambridge, U.K.

Richard E. Leakey, Physical Anthropology, National Museums of Kenya, Nairobi, Kenya

Taha H. Malasi, Psychiatry, Kuwait University, Kuwait

J. Martin Ramirez, Psychobiology, Universidad de Sevilla, Spain

Federico Mayor Zaragoza, Biochemistry, Universidad Autonoma, Madrid, Spain

Diana L. Mendoza, Ethology, Universidad de Sevilla, Spain

Ashis Nandy, Political Psychology, Centre for the Study of Developing Societies, Delhi, India

John Paul Scott, Animal Behavior, Bowling Green State University, Bowling Green, OH., U.S.A.

Riitta Wahlstrom, Psychology, University of Jyväskylä, Finland

SOURCE: United Nations Educational, Scientific and Cultural Organization. Accessed at http://www.unesco.org/shs/human_rights/hrfv.htm.

Hard-Wired for War?

Violence Part of Being Human

June 2, 1999

Humankind has lived through a hideously violent century.

World War I, World War II, wars in Vietnam, Cambodia, China, Bangladesh, Korea, Nigeria and elsewhere have extinguished millions upon millions of lives. The killings continue today in Sierra Leone, East Timor and Sudan, to name a few.

Waging war is nothing new for us humans. Bloody conflicts from the Crusades to Kosovo have been a hallmark of our history. Which raises the questions: Is such behavior simply part of human nature? Are we hard-wired for war?

There's certainly no definitive answer. But enough scientists have looked into our past—and present—to shed a bit of light on why we do what we do.

New Environment, Old Brain

When interpreting human behavior, it's best to remember that the strongest human instincts are to survive and reproduce. What we need to satisfy those instincts hasn't changed much since our primitive ancestors roamed the globe; it's about getting enough food, water and mates.

Like it or not, write Leda Cosmides and John Tooby, co-directors of the Center for Evolutionary Psychology at University of California, Santa Barbara, "our modern skulls house a Stone Age mind."

Though modern-day aggressors may not be aware of it, those primitive instincts drive their behaviors too. A strong group benefits from attacking a weaker group if in the process the aggressors gain fertile lands, reliable water, greater market share—any resources that improve their collective livelihood.

There's no denying that aggression has been a good survival strategy. Which is why we humans are genetically hard-wired to fight.

But what triggers that aggression and what can magnify it to the point of a Rwanda or a Kosovo?

Richard Wrangham of Harvard University sees two conditions necessary for what he calls "coalitional aggression," or violence perpetrated by groups rather than individuals. One condition is hostility between neighbors.

Human aggression got more organized with the introduction of agriculture about 10,000 years ago, says J. William Gibson, author of *Warrior Dreams: Violence and Manhood in Post-Vietnam America*. With farming came the concept of land ownership—and defense—and the development of more complex and organized societies. Suddenly, there was more to covet, more to protect and more people around to help do both.

The other condition for group violence is an imbalance of power great enough that aggressors believe they can attack with virtually no risk to themselves. Majorities have persecuted minority groups, whether religious, ethnic or tribal, again and again, believing they're immune from punishment. The tangled turmoil in the former Yugoslavia is only the most immediate example.

Animals Do It, Too

Humans aren't the only ones who gang up. Chimpanzees, with whom we share 98.4 percent of our DNA, are another. Wrangham, who wrote *Demonic Males: Apes and the Origins of Human Violence,* describes five chimps attacking one. Four will hold the victim while the fifth breaks bones and rips out the victim's throat or testicles.

Examples of taking such advantage of imbalances of power are rare in the animal kingdom because that kind of behavior requires a sophisticated level of coordination and cooperation. However, both chimps and humans are certainly capable of it.

"There's always conflict in societies," says Neil Wiener, an associate professor of psychology at York University, "The issue is, when do these conflicts erupt into violence?"

Young Men More Likely to Wage War

According to Wiener, a critical factor in the escalation from conflict to violence, is the percentage of young, unmarried males in a population. He and co-author Christian Mesquida studied the demographics of 153 nations since the 1960s, comparing those that have remained peaceful and those that have been at war. Turns out, there is a difference.

"Whenever young people represent a relatively small portion of the population ... times are relatively tranquil," they wrote in their study. "But when a large portion of a country's population is young there is likely to be turmoil and political violence."

Examples include the Congo, Rwanda, Sudan, even the former Yugoslavia.

Aggressive wars seem to happen when the percentage of young men—ages 15 to 29—reaches 35 to 55 percent of the adult male population. "I think that young males are hard-wired to form groups ... and under the right circumstances, to act aggressively in groups," Wiener says.

If Wiener is right, some areas ripe for conflict are China and India—the world's two most populous nations—as well as Pakistan, parts of the Middle East and Africa.

So with evolution and demographics against us, what can be done to lessen the chances of war?

Natural selection over millions of years has brought us to this violent point and it won't be swinging the other way any time soon.

Besides, says Wiener, "what drives this stuff ultimately is demographics."

That may be, but there are certain actions that can be taken to derail our baser human tendencies.

Peace has a better chance in a more interconnected world, where all nations keep tabs on one another. International watchdogs big and small—the United Nations, NATO, Amnesty International and others—are already helping to keep imbalances of power in check.

Population control can reduce conflicts by making sure that every nation has adequate resources.

Such efforts may not bear fruit for generations, but they do provide seeds of hope for a more peaceful twenty-first century.

Source: ABCNEWS.Com.

CHAPTER SUMMARY

- The nature–nurture debate is one that appears in some guise in virtually all social sciences. At issue is which behaviors are best understood as reflections of basic and unalterable aspects of human nature or instincts as opposed to cultural conditioning and socialization. Whether or not the persistence of war can be explained by some element of human nature is only one specific manifestation of this more general debate.

- A "nature" or instinctual explanation for war often begins with the assumption that the persistence of such an irrational and destructive behavior must be rooted in some uncontrollable drive.

- The ethologist Konrad Lorenz claimed the human beings possess an aggressive instinct, just like virtually every animal. For animals this instinct is "adaptive" because it helps preserve, protect, and perpetuate species.

- Lorenz divided the animal kingdom into two categories—lethal and nonlethal creatures. In the case of nonlethal animals, there is no danger that aggression will become lethal aggression. Hamsters do not kill each other because they cannot. Though lethal animals can kill members of their species, over the course of evolution they tend to develop inhibiting mechanisms that prevent them from killing.

- The problem is that humans are essentially nonlethal animals who have become lethal because of the technology afforded by our intellectual evolution. Humans can now kill their own kind with great efficiency and often at great distances. This adaptation has happened so quickly, however, that inhibiting mechanisms have not emerged to prevent humans from killing members of their own species.

- When we add the basic human need for social belonging and identity to this aggressive instinct and weapons, the result is war.

- The proposition that war is an inevitable reflection of human nature or instincts can be criticized in several ways. The existence of peaceful societies and others that go very long periods without war suggest that war is not an integral feature of human existence. The lengths to which societies and governments must go to get soldiers to engage in war seems to undermine the instinctual argument. Finally, some question whether it even makes sense to view war as aggression. Perhaps war is better viewed as instrumental, socially organized violence that has little or nothing to do with individual aggression.

- Instead of viewing war as rooted in human nature or instincts, it can also be viewed as a cultural or social practice shaped and reinforced in countless and often subtle ways as people are bombarded with messages, lessons, images, and ideas about violence and war.

- Perhaps a better approach is to understand war as a result of instincts *and* learning. In this view, aspects of human nature certainly can lead to war, but they do not do so on their own. It is a matter of whether those elements of human nature that contribute to war are reinforced or discouraged by learning and socialization.

CRITICAL QUESTIONS

1. How do we distinguish instinctual from learned behavior?

2. Assuming that war is a learned behavior, is it easily learned or difficult to teach?

3. Might there be other aspects of human nature that lead or contribute to war apart from an aggressive instinct?

4. If war is a learned behavior, does this necessarily imply that it can be "unlearned"?

5. Why is the distinction between aggression and violence potentially critical for understanding the causes of war?

KEY TERMS

appeasement gesture 76
dehumanization 85
ethology 73
evolutionary lag (disequilibrium) 77
hierarchy 75
instinct 74
instrumental violence 82
Lorenz, Konrad 73
nature versus nurture 73
nonfirers 81
peaceful societies 80
pseudospecification 85
spacing 74
stimulus and response 83

FURTHER READINGS

The classic statement of the instinctual aggression thesis is Konrad Lorenz, *On Aggression* (New York: Harcourt, Brace and World, 1963). The major critique of this position is Ashley Montagu, *The Nature of Human Aggression* (Oxford: Oxford University Press, 1976). The classic statement of the social/cultural perspective is Margaret Mead, "Warfare Is Only an Invention—Not a Biological Necessity," *Asia* 40 (1940): 402–405. A more recent example of this position is David Grossman, *On Killing* (Boston: Little, Brown, 1995). Another interesting perspective on this debate is found in Joanna Burke, *An Intimate History of Killing* (New York: Basic Books, 1999). And Barbara Ehrenreich's *Blood Rites: Origins and History of the Passions of War* (New York: Henry A. Holt, 1998) tries to integrate and transcend the nature–nurture divide.

WAR AND HUMAN NATURE ON THE WEB

www.culture-of-peace.info
> Organization dedicated to creating a "culture of peace" to replace the "culture of war." The group's perspective in terms of the issues discussed in this chapter are obvious.

www.seedsofpeace.org
> Organization dedicated to promoting peace by teaching children to "develop trust and empathy for another." The underlying assumption guiding the organization's mission obviously place it on the "nurture" side of the debate over war and human nature.

www.killology.com
> Website of Lt. Col. David Grossman (cited in this chapter) focusing on how people are socialized into violent behavior.

http://www.globalissues.org/HumanRights/Media/Military.asp
> Discusses and illustrates media coverage of war issues as well as propaganda.

www.classroomtools.com/faces2.htm
> Contains some good examples of the dehumanizing propaganda that is often part and parcel of modern war.

www.warandgender.com
> Deals with issues and controversies surrounding questions of war, gender, biology, socialization, and war.

NOTES

[1] Anthony Storr, *Human Aggression* (New York: Atheneum, 1968), introduction, n.p.

[2] These are the conclusions of Norman Cousins cited in Francis Beer, *Peace against War* (San Francisco: Freeman, 1981), p. 20.

[3] Sigmund Freud, *Civilization and Its Discontents* (New York: W. W. Norton, 1961), p. 58.

[4] Desmond Morris, *The Naked Ape: A Zoologist's Study of the Human Animal* (New York: McGraw-Hill, 1967); Lionel Tiger and Robin Fox, *The Imperial Animal* (New York: Holt, Rinehart and Winston, 1971); and Robert Ardrey, *The Territorial Imperative* (New York: Atheneum, 1966).

[5] Konrad Lorenz, *On Aggression* (New York: Harcourt, Brace and World, 1963).

[6] Ibid., p. 237.

[7] James A. Schellenberg, *The Science of Conflict* (New York: Oxford University Press, 1982), p. 32; Morris, *Naked Ape,* pp. 149, 159.

[8] Morris, *Naked Ape,* p. 156.

[9] Ibid., p. 156.

[10] Lorenz, *On Aggression,* p. 241.

[11] Ibid., p. 241.

[12] Ibid., p. 242.

[13] Robin Fox, "Fatal Attraction: War and Human Nature," *The National Interest* (Winter 1992/3): 15.

[14] Tiger and Fox, *Imperial Animal,* p. 212.

[15] Fox, "Fatal Attraction," p. 17.

[16] Lorenz, *On Aggression,* p. 238.

[17] Morris, *Naked Ape,* p. 176.

[18] Storr, *Human Aggression,* p. 57.

[19] Fox, "Fatal Attraction," p. 16.

[20] Lorenz, *On Aggression,* p. 49.

[21] Fox, "Human Attraction," p. 13.

[22] David Fabro, "Peaceful Societies," in *The War System: An Interdisciplinary Approach,* ed. Richard Falk and Samuel Kim (Boulder, CO: Westview, 1980), pp. 180–203; Lawrence Keeley, *War before Civilization: The Myth of the Peaceful Savage* (New York: Oxford University Press, 1996), pp. 27–32.

[23] Joshua Goldstein, *War and Gender* (New York: Cambridge University Press, 2001), pp. 32–33.

[24] Keeley, *War before Civilization,* p. 32.

[25] See S. L. A. Marshall, *Men against Fire* (New York: Morrow, 1967). The implications of this study are addressed by David Grossman, *On Killing* (Boston: Little, Brown, 1995), pp. 15–16, 29–30; Sam Keen, *Faces of the Enemy: Reflections of the Hostile Imagination* (San Francisco: HarperCollins, 1986), p. 178; and Richard Holmes, *Acts of War: The*

Behavior of Men in Battle (New York: The Free Press, 1985), pp. 325–27.

[26] Quoted in Grossman, *On Killing,* p. 29.

[27] Ashley Montagu, *The Nature of Human Aggression* (New York: Oxford University Press, 1976), p. 273.

[28] Ibid., p. 272.

[29] Margaret Mead, "Warfare Is Only an Invention-Not a Biological Necessity," in *War,* ed. Leon Bramson and George Goethals (New York: Basic Books, 1964), p. 270.

[30] Richard Barnet, *Roots of War* (New York: Atheneum, 1972), p.13.

[31] Grossman, *On Killing,* p. 310.

[32] Keen, *Faces of the Enemy.*

[33] See David Barash and Judith Eve Lipton, *The Caveman and the Bomb* (New York: McGraw-Hill, 1985), pp. 139–40.

[34] Keen, *Faces of the Enemy,* p. 25.

[35] Holmes, *Acts of War,* p. 366.

[36] From the documentary video by Sam Keen, *Faces of the Enemy,* produced in 1987 and based on the previously cited book.

[37] Tiger and Fox, *Imperial Animal,* p. 208.

[38] Keen, *Faces of the Enemy,* p. 178.

CHAPTER FOUR

WAR AND DEMOCRACY

The idea that democracies are more peaceful than nondemocracies has been part of liberal international thought for more than two hundred years, and it is one of those ideas that has seeped from the realm of theory to real-world policy. Though proponents of what has become known as *democratic peace theory* suggest a variety of reasons that democracies might be less willing and able to wage war, all versions of the theory share one basic prediction: democracies will not fight other democracies. If the theory is correct, a more democratic world will also be a more peaceful world. The most important evidence offered in support of the theory is the absence of any wars between clearly democratic states. Skeptics question this evidence, pointing to what they see as convenient and shifting definitions that omit troublesome cases. Some even claim that there have been wars between democratic states. Realists in particular are generally unconvinced by the theory and its supporting evidence. Even if we have not yet seen a war between democratic states, realists think our luck is likely to run out. In time, democracies will be subject to the same insecurities and conflicts that have driven nondemocratic states to war. The coming decades are likely to put the theory to a real-world test as the number of democracies in the world continues to grow.

MAP 4.1a

Government in 1937

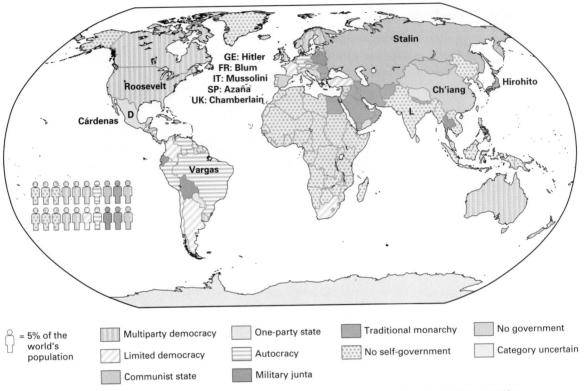

SOURCE: Historical Atlas of the Twentieth Century, http://users.evols.com/mwhite28/govt1937.htm.

The spread of democratic political institutions has been one of the most remarkable trends in world politics over the past few decades (see maps 4.1a, 4.1b, and 4.1c). The period around 1989 marked something of a watershed in global political history when, for the first time, a majority of the world's population lived under some form of democratic government. One might debate a few of the specifics in terms of which countries deserve to be classified as democracies, but the overall trend of global democratization seems clear. This is not to suggest that global democratization is inevitable or irreversible; it is merely to point out that the world is a much more democratic place today than it was a hundred, fifty, or even fifteen years ago. On this point there is little dispute.

Most people, particularly in long-established democracies such as the United States, view the globalization of democracy as a good thing. But why? Why should anyone care whether people in other countries live under democratic forms of government? To the extent that democracy is associated with a greater respect for human rights, political and otherwise, the positive assessment of global democratization is welcomed as the triumph of those values that people in existing democracies hold dear and wish to see shared. That is, the spread of democracy is seen as a good thing

MAP 4.1b

Government in 1967

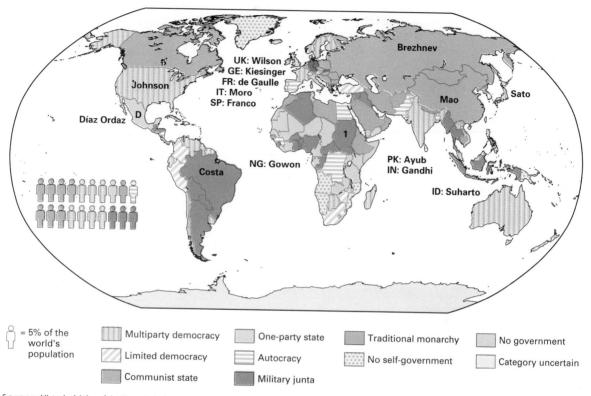

= 5% of the world's population

Multiparty democracy	One-party state
Limited democracy	Autocracy
Communist state	Military junta
Traditional monarchy	No government
No self-government	Category uncertain

SOURCE: Historical Atlas of the Twentieth Century, http://users.evols.com/mwhite28/govt1960.htm.

in and of itself, not necessarily because there is anything to be gained from it. Not everything boils down to self-interest.

Nonetheless, the spread and preservation of democracy around the world is often presented as a matter of national interest. The argument is that democracy elsewhere in the world is a good thing not only for the people who live in other countries, but also for the United States and other established democracies. Why might this be the case? What difference does it make to Americans in South Dakota whether or not people in the Middle East, Latin America, Asia, or Africa live under democratic governments? A number of possible connections might be drawn. To the extent that democracy is related to capitalism, free markets, and trade, one could argue that the spread of democracy contributes to the growth of the global economy, something that serves the interests of Americans. This chapter, however, focuses on another claim, namely, that democracies are more peaceful than nondemocracies. It is the assumed peacefulness of democracies that provides the connection to American national interests: the United States has an interest in peace, democracies are more peaceful, and thus the spread of democracy is a vital interest.

The notion that democracies are more peaceful than nondemocracies is widely

MAP 4.1c

Government in 1997

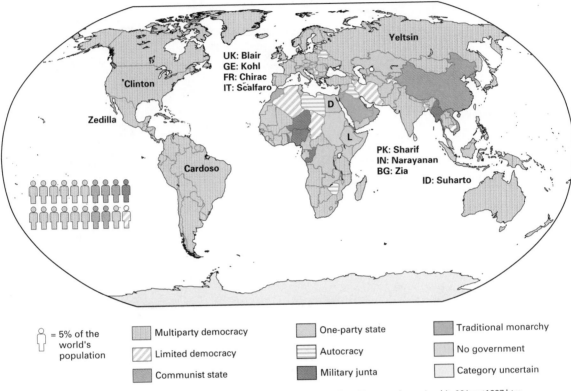

SOURCE: Historical Atlas of the Twentieth Century, http://users.evols.com/mwhite28/govt1997.htm.

accepted at many levels—among the general public, policymakers, and academics. If American post–Cold War foreign policy has had any central objective to replace the containment of communism, it is the spread of democracy (that is, at least, until the war on terrorism, success in which is frequently linked to spreading democracy). Indeed, few ideas about international politics share the same level of widespread acceptance. Exactly what we mean when we say that democracies are more peaceful is more refined and nuanced in policymaking and academic circles, but the general idea that democracies behave differently than nondemocracies in their relations with other nations has permeated both elite and public thinking about international relations and foreign policy.

THE SOURCES OF DEMOCRATIC PEACEFULNESS

The proposition that democracies are more peaceful than nondemocracies is a central tenet of liberal international theory whose origins can be traced to writings of **Immanuel Kant** (1724–1804). Living in an era where the predominant form of nondemocratic government was absolutist monarchism, Kant argued in his classic work, *Perpetual Peace,* that the emergence and spread of "republican" (or liberal democratic) political institutions would be accompanied by the emergence of a zone of peace among democratic nations. Kant referred to this as a republican or **democratic pacific union.** He did not argue that democracies would cease being involved in wars; if he had, his prediction would have proven wrong many times already. Democracies have been involved in dozens of wars during the past two centuries. Kant did not maintain that democracies would be pacifists, that they would never start wars or would turn the other cheek if attacked. Kant simply argued that democracies would not wage war against other democracies. More democracies would mean a larger zone of peace, and universal democracy would entail universal peace.

But why would we expect democracies to behave any differently than nondemocracies? Do democracies not have conflicts of interest with other democracies? Do they not also live in an anarchic international system and have to deal with the same insecurities and security dilemmas as all other states? Other than the natural tendency to assume that one's preferred system of government embodies all that is good, are there any compelling theoretical arguments underlying expectations of a democratic peace? In fact, Kant and others who came after him have put forward several theoretical arguments about why we might expect democracies to be more peaceful, particularly in their dealings with one another.

Kant begins with the basic observation that in a republic or democracy people are citizens of the state as opposed to the mere subjects of a king or queen as they were in a monarchical order. As citizens, the people in general have access to means by which their desires and interests are allowed to influence government policy, including decisions to go to war. Kant assumed that the average citizen has much more to lose than gain from war: the common people are the ones who shoulder the burdens of war. As essentially rational creatures (another fundamental assumption of liberalism), people are generally unwilling to pursue policies that do them harm. In *Perpetual Peace* Kant expressed his belief that people in a democracy "will have a great hesitation in embarking on so dangerous an enterprise [as war]" because "this would mean calling down on themselves all the miseries of war." These miseries include not only the obvious, such as "doing the fighting themselves, supplying the costs of war from their own resources," but also "making good the ensuing devastation, and, as the crowning evil, having to take upon themselves a burden of debts which will embitter peace itself and which can never be paid off on account of the constant threat of new wars."[1]

We might refer to this as the **rational** or **pacific public thesis** because it sees democratic peacefulness as the political consequence of the rational self-interest of democratic publics in peace. Such a view is no longer very popular as an explanation of democratic peace. The past century and a half of real-world democracy provides too many examples of public support, even enthusiasm, for war, despite the negative consequences highlighted by Kant. Even people in democratic states, for example,

Kant, Immanuel (1724–1804) German political philosopher who first proposed that democratic (or "republican" states) would be unlikely to wage war against each other.

democratic pacific union The separate peace that Immanuel Kant predicted would exist among democratic states. Many believe that this democratic peace has in fact emerged.

rational/pacific public thesis The view that democracies are more peaceful because their foreign policies reflect the desires of an inherently rational and peaceful public.

greeted World War I with tremendous enthusiasm. In some cases, such as the Spanish-American War of 1898, public opinion, spurred by a pro-war press, actually appears to have pushed a reluctant political leadership into war.[2] As Robin Fox, a critic of democratic peace theory, observes, "there is rarely very effective opposition to a successful war."[3] For Fox, the absence of effective antiwar movements while wars are being won suggests that there is no general preference for peace among democratic publics, merely a reluctance to fight losing wars. The hesitance for war, which seemed "natural" to Kant, appears not to exist in reality.

Most theories of democratic peace, however, do not rely on such optimistic assumptions about the general populace's pacific nature. Indeed, even Kant was not content to rely on the proposition that popular opposition to war would be sufficient to create the democratic peace. Kant and others also point to more foundational aspects of democratic systems, in particular their institutional structure and political-cultural underpinnings. On an institutional level, the manner in which political power and decision making are constructed and distributed in democratic societies is seen as presenting an obstacle to war making. Furthermore, the successful functioning of democratic institutions depends on the widespread adherence to certain political and cultural values that shape international behavior of democracies. These institutional and cultural constraints are generally seen as particularly significant in terms of relations between and among democratic states.

The **institutional thesis** rests on the fact that democratic political systems are usually distinguished from nondemocratic regimes by their dispersion of political power. Although there are significant differences among various forms of undemocratic governance, one characteristic they tend to share in common is the concentration of political power in the hands of a single person or a small group of people. Whether the ruler is Louis XIV, Joseph Stalin, or Saddam Hussein, these leaders do not generally operate with many domestic constraints on their authority. When Saddam Hussein invaded Kuwait in 1991, he did not have to worry about getting the approval of an elected legislature, hostile newspaper editorials, or the next election. This is not to say that he had no worries, since even undemocratic leaders can be overthrown. The point is simply that, as a general rule, leaders in nondemocratic societies face fewer political constraints than those in democracies.

Democratic societies, on the other hand, are characterized by the dispersion of political power. There are competing political parties, elections that can be lost, and public opinion that cannot be consistently ignored. There are also separate institutions within the government that operate to limit the executive's freedom of action. Legislatures commonly possess budgetary authority, which gives them leverage over anything that requires expenditures, as wars certainly do. In the United States we use the terms **checks and balances** to describe the relationship between the executive (i.e., the president), the legislature (i.e., the House of Representatives and Senate), and the judiciary. Other democracies have slightly different institutional structures, but the general point remains valid. This dispersion of power makes it very difficult for democracies to do anything, from reforming social security or the tax code to going to war. As America's founders made clear in *The Federalist Papers,* making government action difficult was precisely the point of dispersing political power. As a result, a certain degree of consensus and political mobilization is required for a democratic government to adopt or change policies, particularly when those policies represent radical changes or are very controversial. Thus, the essential element of the institu-

institutional thesis A variant of democratic peace theory that sees the dispersion of power in democracies (see **checks and balances**) as the most important reason they are less likely to wage war, especially against each other.

checks and balances The division of power in democracies among different branches of government (e.g., the president and Congress in the United States). The institutional version of democratic peace sees this dispersion of powers as a critical factor in why democracies are less likely to engage in war, especially with each other.

tional thesis is that democracies will find it more difficult to go to war, and certainly more difficult to initiate a war, than nondemocratic governments.

Although the institutional thesis stresses those characteristics that affect a democracy's *ability* to wage war, the **political-cultural thesis** emphasizes the relative *unwillingness* of democracies to go to war. Here the argument is that democratic institutions only work when they are rooted in widely shared norms on how political conflicts are to be dealt with. In particular, political democracy requires a consensus that conflicts among people and groups should be resolved without resort to force. The observation that democracies substitute the counting of heads for the breaking of heads captures the point well. However deep our disagreements are over certain issues, very few resort to violence once they have lost the contest in the political arena. Al Gore loyalists did not circle the White House with guns to prevent George Bush from moving in, despite their reservations about the outcome of the election. In the absence of a general acceptance of the norm of peaceful conflict resolution, democracy is unlikely to prove very durable. In terms of international relations, the political-cultural thesis maintains that democracies are prone to externalize this fundamental norm that shapes their domestic affairs. Thus, the norm of peaceful conflict resolution predisposes democracies to favor nonviolent approaches to international conflicts.[4]

Constructivists present a slightly different explanation for the democratic peace. It is not that something inherent in democracies prevents them from waging war against each other. What keeps democracies at peace is the widely accepted and internalized norm that democracies do not fight each other. The prohibition on fighting other democracies has become part of what it means to be a democracy—that is, an integral component of the democratic self-image, or how democracies view, define, or "identify" themselves. When and if all democracies share this self-image, an "intersubjective understanding" emerges and the peace among democracies holds. In a sense, democratic peace theory is an almost self-fulfilling prophecy—the more people, especially elites in democratic societies, tell themselves that democracies do not fight each other, the more they come to believe it; and the more they believe it, the more their behavior reflects this belief.[5]

Most formulations of the democratic peace thesis, including Kant's, do not predict a generalized predisposition for peace. The democratic preference for peace is assumed to operate primarily (or maybe even only) when democracies deal with one another. Kant's pacific union was a zone of peace among democratic states: he fully anticipated that this zone of peace would not extend to relations between democratic and nondemocratic states. But why would democracies prefer peace in dealing with fellow democracies but not exhibit the same peaceful nature in their relations with nondemocracies? Part of the reason is that the institutional and cultural factors that supposedly inhibit democracies from going to war will be more successful in preventing war when they are present in both nations as opposed to just one. But there is more to it than that.

Peace among democracies is also rooted in mutual expectations. When a democracy finds itself in conflict with another democracy, it is willing to proceed on the expectation that their conflict will be resolved peacefully because it assumes that the opposing democracy is operating on the same set of values and expectations. As Spencer Weart explains, "Peace follows if leaders come to recognize that their preference for negotiation is shared."[6] The expectation of reciprocity is what allows the democratic peace to flourish. When the potential opponent is not a fellow democracy, the

political-cultural thesis
A variant of democratic peace theory that sees political and cultural norms or peaceful conflict resolution as the most important reason that democracies are less likely to wage war, especially against each other.

assumption of a shared preference for peaceful resolution cannot be made. In fact, democracies may assume the exact opposite—that nondemocracies will be unwilling to resolve disputes peacefully. The insight that what matters most is a democracy's expectations about what sort of conduct it can expect from another nation has led one scholar to revise the democratic peace proposition slightly, pointing out that the critical factor is whether two states *perceive* each other as democratic, not whether they are democratic according to some previously set criteria. There are a few cases where this distinction may be critical. For example, it may be possible to argue that Germany, by some standards, was a democracy on the eve of World War I (we will have more to say about this shortly), and since Germany ended up fighting Great Britain and the United States, this example could invalidate the democratic peace proposition. John Owen and Ido Oren, however, try to demonstrate that at the time Germany was not perceived as a democratic state by Britain and the United States. Since they did not think they were dealing with a democracy, the obstacles to war were not operative.[7]

What Is "democracy"? The assertion that democracies are more peaceful than nondemocracies seems straightforward, but a number of issues need to be resolved before it can be refined or systematically examined. One of the trickiest is the meaning of the word *democracy*. Though casual observers are sometimes exasperated by the academic tendency to argue over the definition of terms whose meanings appear obvious, sometimes it really does matter precisely what definition we adopt. Virtually any definition of democracy would include nations such as the United States, Japan, and India today, yet many contemporary and historical cases are less clear cut.

If asked what makes a country democratic, most people would probably list universal adult suffrage (i.e., the right to vote) as an essential component. Though this criterion seems straightforward enough, it is not always easily applied to the real world. For example, a strict application of this standard would exclude the United States before 1920: women were not allowed to vote and in large parts of the country citizens of African descent were effectively denied their right to vote well into the 1960s. Can a country be considered a democracy when more than half the adult population is excluded from the franchise, either by law or practice? If universal adult suffrage is not an absolute requirement, can South Africa under apartheid be classified as a democracy (even though it certainly was for whites)? We could solve this problem by applying different criteria in 1960 than we would in 1860. The extent of suffrage, however, is not the only question. Another concerns the durability of democratic practices. Should a country be considered a democracy after a single round of elections, or do we need to see a pattern sustained over time? Although this is not the place to work through all the fine details and complications, these examples illustrate some of the questions that arise. How these definitional issues are resolved is potentially critical to answering the question of whether democracies have, in fact, ever waged wars against each other.

Despite some minor differences in definition, most attempts to examine democratic peace theory have agreed on those features that make for a democracy: regular elections for major government offices, competitive political parties, near-universal adult suffrage, and certain basic political and individual rights.[8] The inclusion of basic rights that are protected even from democratic majorities leads many to prefer the

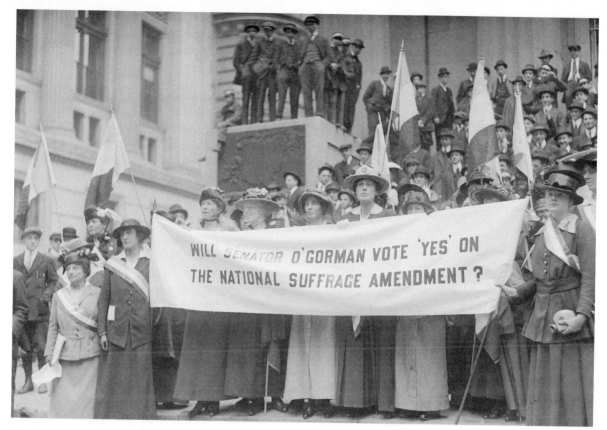

What is a democracy? Here women protest in 1915 for the right to vote. We consider the United States a democracy before World War I even though half the adult population was disenfranchised. Today universal adult suffrage is considered a necessary condition for a nation to be classified as a democracy.
SOURCE: © Bettmann/CORBIS

description *liberal democratic states.* The criteria are usually relaxed somewhat when we move back to the nineteenth century, particularly on the issue of voting rights. A country that denied women and others the right to vote (e.g., on racial grounds or with property restrictions) in 1840 can still be classified as a democracy, but similar practices today would be disqualifiers.

After we have decided what constitutes a democracy, we need to figure out how to judge "peacefulness." Should we look simply at a crude measure, such as whether democracies have been involved in fewer wars than nondemocracies? This is certainly the easiest thing to look at, but is it an adequate measure of peacefulness? Perhaps the important question is not mere involvement in war, but the initiation of the use of force. But what about covert operations, threats of force, and military interventions that fall short of a formal state of war? And what about the provision of military aid and assistance that enables wars to go on, which might be considered an indirect form of war involvement? The range of behaviors that we might look at to get a handle on the issue of peacefulness is quite broad, and our conclusions might be different depending on what we choose to focus on. Although research has tended to focus on war narrowly defined, some attention has been directed toward other behaviors that fall short of war but might be part of an evaluation of peacefulness.

The evidence At first glance, the claim that democracies are more peaceful seems odd. A long list of democracies at war is easy to compile: the United States in the Vietnam War, British imperialism and all the wars that accompanied it, and the French war in Algeria, to name just a few. One of the earliest studies of democracy and war demonstrated that over the last two centuries there has been no difference between democracies and nondemocracies in terms of the frequency or duration of their involvement in war.[9] This was also not the result of democracies always being attacked, since there was also no difference in incidence of war initiation. Rather than disputing these findings, democratic peace theorists have argued that they are not good tests of the theory. Recall that Kant and others did not predict that democracies would refrain from any involvement in war. Democratic peace theorists have usually not predicted a generalized preference for peace. The expectation was that democracies would not fight wars against one another. Thus, the test of democratic peace theory is whether democracies deal with their conflicts among themselves differently than they do with conflicts with nondemocracies. So the question is not how many wars democracies have been involved in, but rather whom these wars have (and have not) been fought against.

The most commonly cited piece of evidence in support of democratic peace theory is the absence of any wars between democratic states. There have been many wars between democracies and nondemocracies as well as among nondemocracies. But, as Bruce Russett asserts, "there are no clear-cut cases of sovereign stable democracies waging war with each other in the modern international system."[10] Several of the important qualifications in this observation need to be highlighted. Russett's observation does not include civil wars, only wars between or among sovereign states. War is defined as an armed conflict between at least two sovereign states resulting in at least 1,000 battle casualties. This definition eliminates civil wars, many colonial wars, and small clashes, such as border skirmishes. Note also the qualifier of "stable" democracies. Russett also shows that conflicts between democracies are less likely to involve threats of force, displays of force, and uses of force below the threshold of war, though there are cases involving these lower levels of force.[11] Russett also makes an attempt to examine democratic peace theory in the premodern era by looking at ancient Greece, finding that democratic city-states were "reluctant to fight each other," though it did happen.

Russett and others recognize some cases that might be classified as wars between democracies: the War of 1812 between the United States and Great Britain, the American Civil War, the Spanish-American War (1896), and the allies against Finland in World War II. In each case, however, these end up not being wars between democracies. Britain was not a democracy in 1812, nor was Spain in 1898. The North and the Confederacy were not sovereign states in the American Civil War. And even though Finland was aligned with Germany in World War II (thanks largely to its conflict with the Soviet Union), Finland never fought against the Western democracies. Other supposed examples of democratic wars are usually rejected on similar grounds. Some boldly assert that democracies never have and never will wage war against each other, whereas others are content to make the more limited claim that democracies are

PART II *Controversies*

much less likely to fight one another. But whichever version one is examining, the empirical fact that no democracy has ever gone to war against another democracy appears to many as strong evidence supporting Kant's prediction that democracies do not wage war against one another, thereby forming a democratic pacific union.

ARE DEMOCRACIES REALLY ANY DIFFERENT?

Despite the apparently compelling fact that democracies have never fought each other, those who approach international relations from perspectives other than liberalism are, at a minimum, skeptical of democratic peace theory. This skepticism is to be expected since someone who sees war as the result of flawed human nature, international anarchy, the dynamics of capitalism, or the gendered nature of international politics would fail to see how these underlying causes are eliminated by altering the domestic political arrangements of states. In terms of the larger debate among the competing visions of international relations, the question of democratic peace is extremely significant. If, in fact, something about the nature of democratic regimes prevents them from going to war with each other, the presence of this quality would strongly support the liberal worldview and undermine other perspectives, particularly realism.

But how does one get around the "fact," as Russett describes it, of democratic peace? In reality, the "fact" of democratic peace is not immune to legitimate criticism. First, it is possible to accept the empirical observation that we have not yet seen a war between two democracies while questioning whether this is a sufficiently significant finding upon which to reach any broader conclusions. Second, some see the failure to find any democratic wars as an artifact of definitions of democracy and war that appear designed to exclude uncomfortable disconfirming cases. Finally, merely because two democracies have not fought each other yet does not automatically prove that their democratic nature explains the absence of war. Other factors may account for their failure to fight one another.

No democratic wars—So what? Much of the impetus behind the democratic peace proposition is provided by the absence of any clear-cut examples of wars between democratic states. It is, after all, rare in a discipline filled with qualifications and exceptions that we are able to say that something has *never* happened. This nonevent seems to cry out for an explanation. It is a puzzling finding that requires some solution. Then again, maybe it does not. Perhaps the nonoccurrence of democratic war is not as anomalous as it first appears.

To understand why some analysts remain unimpressed by the absence of a democratic war, let us draw an analogy. If a given person has never won the big jackpot in the state lottery, would anyone find this at all surprising? Would this nonevent be viewed as something requiring an explanation or investigation? Probably not. The mere fact that something has *never* happened does not automatically create a puzzle. Since the odds of winning the lottery are so small to begin with, the fact that someone has never won is to be expected and is explained simply by the statistical improbability of winning. In fact, winning the lottery is the real anomaly, and winning twice would require some investigation. Thus, the nonoccurrence of an event is surprising only if there was a good reason to expect it to happen in the first place.

David Spiro has made the same basic point about the absence of democratic war, which he describes as a statistically insignificant fact. His argument is quite simple and rests on two basic observations. First, over the last two hundred years there have been very few democratic states. No more than a handful could be considered democratic prior to 1945, and it is only in the past decade or so that democracies have constituted a majority of the world's states. So even the existence of democracy has been a historically rare event. Second, the occurrence of war is also a rare event. Even though a war is usually going on somewhere in the world at any given moment, virtually all countries spend most of their time at peace, not war. Peace is the norm in international relations; war is the exception. Spiro demonstrates that when we take into account the statistical rarity of both democracy and war, the absence of a war pitting one democracy against another is not in the least surprising. In fact, this is precisely what we should have expected. Thus, this absence of war is not an anomaly that cries out for an explanation.[12] The "puzzle" of democratic peace is explained by the statistical improbability of war between two democracies.

Empirical fact or definitional artifact? As we have noted, proponents of democratic peace theory usually recognize the existence of some potential examples of war between democracies, usually labeling them as "close" or "ambiguous" cases. They also go to great lengths to explain why these cases are not what they seem. The typical response is that either one of the states in question was not really democratic or was not a sovereign state (which means that it could not be involved in a "war"). Critics, however, see a pattern of shifting and loose definitions that always manage to save the theory. Sometimes the requirements for being classified as a democracy appear quite lenient (e.g., the United States in 1840), whereas at other times they become curiously exacting (e.g., Germany in 1914).

The definition of war is also a very restrictive one. Proponents of democratic peace theory, for example, usually reject the American Civil War as an instance of democracies fighting because the North and the Confederacy were not sovereign states in the sense of being recognized as such by other states. This is true. But given the underlying logic of democratic peace theory, it is not clear why this criterion should be so important. Why should the theory not hold merely because the states in question were not recognized as independent by other states? This objection seems to be relying on a theoretically irrelevant technicality. Russett appears to admit as much when he notes that the American Civil War is "readily eliminated" as an exception "by the straightforward use of the definitions."[13] But for critics of democratic peace theory, the American Civil War raises serious questions that cannot be dismissed by its definitional elimination. Ted Galen Carpenter points to "the inconvenient matter that Southerners considered their new confederacy democratic (which it was by the standards of the day) and that most Northerners did not dispute that view (they merely regarded it as beside the point) is simply ignored. The willingness of democratic Americans to wage enthusiastic internecine slaughter fairly cries out for more serious discussion." The experience of the Civil War leads him to ask "if democratic people could do that to their own, how confident can we be that two democracies divided by culture or race (e.g., the United States and Japan) would recoil from doing so?"[14]

The example of Germany and World War I is a particularly controversial case, largely because of the magnitude of the conflict. As Christopher Layne explains, "Even if World War I were the only example of democracies fighting each other, it would be so glaring an exception to democratic peace theory as to render it invalid."[15] To some, Germany in 1914 seems reasonably democratic—there were regular and competitive elections, political parties represented a full range of political views from right to left, there was a free and vigorous press, and adult males were allowed to vote. In a largely undemocratic world, this was not too bad. So why is Germany (frequently labeled "Imperial" Germany) not generally considered a democracy? The problem is that unelected government officials who were not responsible to the legislature, the Reichstag, controlled German foreign policy. Though this may be true, Layne believes Germany is being held to a higher standard and subjected to a degree of scrutiny that France, Britain, and the United States manage to escape. Looking more closely at these "democracies," Layne concludes that most foreign policy decisions in London and Paris were also made with little or no legislative involvement, oversight, or control. Maria Meginnes reaches the same conclusion: "Through universal male suffrage, Germans elected a legislature, the Reichstag, in contested elections between multiple parties. German civil rights, protected under the constitution, were consistently observed." Though conceding that "the issue of foreign policy control is slightly problematic," she notes that "minimal popular influence was common practice among other 'liberal' states of the era. In short, Imperial Germany was indeed 'democratic.'"[16] Democratic peace theorists, however, will have none of this. Spencer Weart reacts almost angrily, insisting that anyone who classifies Germany in 1914 as a democracy "display[s] either their ignorance of modern history, or a willful indifference to the explicit meaning of this proposition."[17]

Critics of democratic peace theory would counter Weart's charges of ignorance or willful indifference by noting that all democracies in 1914 were imperfect. One would not have to look very long to find legitimate grounds to deny the democratic credentials of virtually any country in 1914, starting with the denial of the right to vote to half their adult citizens. Many democracies look a lot more democratic on the surface than they do when they are placed under the magnifying glass that always seems to be pulled out in the close cases. Thus, there are suspicions that new criteria emerge because the classification of Germany as a democracy in 1914 would, as Layne observes, be a fairly devastating blow to the theory. But just as the American Civil War was "readily eliminated" by using a certain definition of war, World War I is eliminated by using a certain definition of democracy. A charitable interpretation of the whole debate would highlight the inherent problems of making clear distinctions between democratic and undemocratic states in a messy world. A less charitable characterization would be that democratic peace theorists are more interested in finding ways to "eliminate" troublesome cases than subjecting their theory to rigorous examination.

The charge that democratic peace theorists play fast and loose with definitions in order to protect their theory from problematic cases is frequently made by realists, who are anxious to demonstrate that democracy has no significant impact. But there are also criticisms from the political and theoretical left. From this perspective it is the manner in which terms such as *peaceful* are used that comes under fire. On one level, democratic peace theory makes a very specific claim: that democracies are unlikely to fight other democracies. The difficulty is that this very narrow theoretical prediction and (maybe) empirical fact almost imperceptibly is inflated into self-congratulatory assertions about being more "peaceful" in general. Robert Latham, for example, argues that there is a tendency to see refraining from war as synonymous with being peaceful, which allows people to ignore the myriad ways in which the policies of liberal democratic states contribute to war and conflict all over the world. In his view, "Islands of liberal democratic peace have not only waged war on non-democracies, they have also been responsible for—and are uniquely successful at generating—high levels of global militarisation in, and conflict among, non-democratic states." He focuses in particular on the role of democratic states in the development and spread of arms in the world: "In the post second–World War period liberal democratic states—above all, the U.S.—have been in the lead in arms sales and the development and transfer of technology . . . in this sense . . . liberalism is the most effective interstate social organization for the production of military force in modern history."[18] Latham does not quarrel with the fact that no two democracies have fought each other. He is simply unable to get terribly excited about this fact. For Latham, the absence of a democratic war is a relatively insignificant point that indicates little about the "peacefulness" of democracies in any broader and more meaningful sense of the term.

One could add to this evidence of democracies using covert action to undermine or even overthrow other democratically elected regimes. As Ted Galen Carpenter notes, "during the Cold War the United States government overthrew democratic regimes in other countries." Even though democratic peace theorists would be quick to point out that these efforts did not count as "wars," Carpenter sarcastically responds that "this will come as a tremendous comfort to the people of Iran, Guatemala and other countries that were saddled with thuggish dictatorships." Technically, of course, such policies do not undermine the narrow claim that democracies will refrain from war with each other, but it does seem relevant to democratic peace theory's underlying assumptions of how democracies would view and treat each other. In these cases, "U.S. policy exhibited extreme hostility to democratic regimes that were not deemed 'friendly' to the United States."[19] That is, strategic considerations dictated U.S. policy, and the fact that these regimes were democratic did not save them. This being the case, critics wonder, can we really be so sanguine about the future of the democratic peace?

Cause or coincidence? Let us accept for the moment the proposition that no two democracies have ever fought each other. Would we be able to infer from this claim that they have managed to avoid going to war *because* they were democracies? Not necessarily. *New York Times* columnist Thomas Friedman also points out that "no two countries that both had a McDonald's has fought a war against each other since each got its McDonald's."[20] Would anyone seriously infer from this fact that eating fast-food burgers and fries leads nations to be more peaceful? Probably not. Though the "McDonald's peace thesis" is obviously somewhat frivolous, the underlying point is critical: empirical correlation is not sufficient grounds for inferring a causal relationship. There is always the possibility that the observed relationship is **spurious**—that is, explained by other variables. There is, for example, an empirical correlation between height and income—taller people earn more money than shorter people. When we look closer, we find that the real explanatory variable is age—eight and nine year olds, who happen to be short, earn little income. The causal link is between age (or, more precisely, the education, skills and experience that come with age) and income despite the empirical link between height and income. Perhaps the relationship between democracy and peace is similar to that between height and income—empirically true but not causal.

spurious In statistics, a relationship that might appear to indicate a causal relationship but that actually reflects the impact of a third variable. For example, democracies may not fight each other for reasons other than the fact that they are democracies (e.g., wealth).

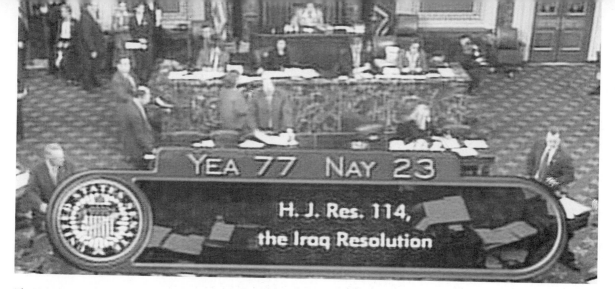

The United States Senate approves almost certain war against Iraq in October 2002. The belief that democracies are inherently more peaceful obviously needs to be qualified.
SOURCE: Pool/Pool/Getty Images

In many respects the peace that has prevailed among democracies has been "overdetermined"—that is, there are many forces that appear conducive to peace. Until the post–World War II era the rarity of democracies and their distance from each other severely restricted even the possibility of going to war. Peace between Finland and New Zealand in 1920 can be explained by the fact that they were on opposite sides of the globe, not by their shared democracy. There is also the existence of common, unifying threats. One of the standard observations about social conflict is the **in-group/out-group hypothesis,** which says that the internal cohesion of any group increases in the face of an external enemy. It is plausible to argue that the peace that has prevailed among democracies in the twentieth century can be explained by the presence of such external threats—for example, fascism in the 1930s and early 1940s and communism throughout most of the post–World War II period. That is, the democratic peace has been the product of strategic circumstances that provided a powerful incentive for cooperation. Still others have argued that peace is a consequence of economic wealth, growth, and prosperity, and since most democracies have been relatively wealthy and prosperous, this seems plausible as well. Most natural science researchers rule out alternative variables through their manipulation in the laboratory. In the social sciences, it is usually more difficult to disentangle the relative significance of variables that might plausibly produce an outcome.

Perhaps one way to look at the influence of alternative factors is to examine closely cases in which democracies came into conflict but managed to avoid going to war. The historical record might reveal what considerations prevented the outbreak of war. Christopher Layne examined several crises involving democracies between 1861 and 1923 in which democracies came very close to going to war. The United States and Great Britain came close to war twice: once in 1861, after a naval blockade of the Confederacy prevented British commerce with the South, and again in 1895–96,

in-group/out-group hypothesis The proposition that the internal unity of a social group increases when it is faced with an alternative social group, particularly if that other group is seen as posing a threat.

when the U.S. injected itself into a border dispute between Great Britain and Venezuela. Great Britain was also a party to the third close call, though this time with France in a crisis involving a contest for advantage in Egypt (and the critical Suez Canal) in 1898. The final crisis pitted France against Germany in 1923, when France militarily occupied German territory known as the Ruhr (war was averted only because Germany concluded it was too weak to resist the French occupation). Though none of these crises escalated to war, Layne thinks they are relevant for two reasons. First, they were instances where democracies seriously contemplated going to war with one another, which in and of itself seems inconsistent with democratic peace theory. Second, the reasons they managed to avoid war had little if anything to with the fact the countries were democracies. In each case, the decision against war was based on assessment of how vital the interests at stake were and the relative power of the states in conflict. Even Russett concedes that "in each of Layne's cases, power and strategic considerations *were* predominant."[21] That is, the democracies remained at peace, but not necessarily for the reasons suggested by democratic peace theory.

CONCLUSION

We began this chapter by noting the recent trend of global democratization. Although the historical evidence concerning the democratic peace remains controversial, the next few decades should go a long way to resolving the debate. For the first time there are a lot of democracies in the world representing many different cultures and levels of economic development. Many of these democracies are located next to each other and have histories of conflicts and war. Referring back to the argument about the statistical insignificance of the democratic peace thus far, every year that passes without a democratic war makes for greater significance. If a hundred or more democracies around the world can go the next four or five decades without a war among them, it would be hard to deny the reality of democratic peace. In this sense, we are about to live through a massive real-world test of democratic peace theory.

As the world becomes a giant laboratory, the debate over the democratic peace is sure to rage in the interim, with implications for both the somewhat abstract world of international relations theory as well as the real world of policymaking. On the level of theory, Russett goes so far as to claim that "the theoretical edifice of realism will collapse" if democratic peace theory is proven correct.[22] Though not everyone would see the stakes in such extreme terms, there is a general recognition that the issues raised strike near the heart of different theories. If internal democracy has a profound effect on the behavior of states, this would clearly undermine realist notions that international anarchy or human nature are the fundamental causes of war. But it is not only realism whose days might be numbered. Marxism is also challenged because liberal democratic states are for the most part capitalist states. Since Marxism sees the underlying dynamics and requirements of capitalism as a basic cause of expansionism, militarism, and war, we can extend Russett's warnings about the collapse of realism to Marxism as well. Perhaps it is the realization that the stakes are so important that explains why the debate over the democratic peace has become so central to contemporary research in international relations. The high stakes involved may also explain why the debate has become so testy, and at times downright nasty.

In terms of policy, critics of democratic peace theory see its acceptance by policymakers as dangerous. Some worry that it will lead to "crusades" to spread democracy throughout the world, and others fear that it will blind the United States to emerging strategic threats because of the optimistic assumption that other democracies cannot possibly be threatening. Ever the realist, Christopher Layne warns that "if American policymakers allow themselves to be mesmerized by democratic peace theory's seductive—but false—vision of the future, the United States will be ill-prepared to formulate a grand strategy that will advance its interests in the emerging world of multipolar great power competition."[23] For Russett, however, the failure to "grasp the democratic peace" would represent a tragedy of historic proportions, a lost opportunity to create and nurture a more civilized and peaceful world.

POINTS OF VIEW
Would Democracy Bring Peace to the Middle East?

Though it is one thing to understand the logic of democratic peace theory in the familiar context of Europe or North America, there is no reason its logic should be so restricted. The interesting question is whether the introduction of democracy into places of intense war and conflict would have the same pacifying effects. When we think of conflict in the contemporary world, perhaps the first place that comes to mind is the Middle East. This raises the inevitable question: Would the spread of democracy bring peace to the Middle East? The conviction that it would was part of the rationale for regime change in Iraq in 2003. This general question is addressed in the following two essays. Charles Krauthammer argues for the proposition that democracy would bring peace, or at least dramatically increase the chances for peace, even in this troubled region. James Pinkerton is not so sure and holds out the possibility that democracy might actually increase conflict. How do these two essays reflect the various arguments presented in this chapter? Do the authors present any arguments that have not already been discussed? Which prediction about democracy and peace in the Middle East do you find more persuasive?

Peace through Democracy

Charles Krauthammer

The president's speech on the Middle East this week unveiled a radically new idea that goes far beyond the "Arafat has to go" headlines. Of course Arafat has to go. He has spent his eight years in control of Palestinian society encouraging and glorifying violence. "Asking Arafat to give up terrorism," explains Bernard Lewis, the dean of Middle East scholars, "would be like asking Tiger Woods to give up golf." As long as Arafat is in control, the blood is guaranteed to flow. Of course he has to go.

But President Bush went far beyond the obvious. He dared to apply the fundamental principle of American foreign policy—the promotion of democracy—to the one area where it has always been considered verboten: the Middle East.

Why is that important? Because the Middle East conflict is often dismissed as one of those incurable they-have-been-killing-each-other-for-centuries ethnic conflicts. So what can we do?

Do what Europe did. Europeans have been killing each other for millennia (see Herodotus, Thucydides, Caesar). But not anymore. Why? They discovered democracy and the peace that comes with tolerant, open societies.

There is never any guarantee of peace, but democracy comes close. There is no reason in principle why an open and democratic Palestine could not resolve what is essentially a border dispute with an open and democratic Israel.

The president's proposal for democratizing Palestine is a fundamental rejection of the Oslo conceit that you could impose upon Palestinian society a PLO thugocracy led by the inventors of modern terrorism and then be surprised that seven years later it exploded in violence.

After a decade of ignoring the Palestinian Authority's corruption, its incitement to hatred, its militarization of Palestinian society, its glorification of violence, indeed, its creation in Palestine, as nowhere else on earth, of a deeply disturbed cult of death, the United States has declared that with this leadership there can be no peace.

The Bush proposal is grounded in the larger American idea that the spread of democracy is fundamental not only to the spread of American values but also to the achievement of peace. Ironically, the man who first insisted that this idea had to be applied to the Middle East is Natan Sharansky, hero of the gulag. Drawing on his experience in the struggle against Soviet tyranny, Sharansky has for years argued that there could be no progress in peacemaking until the Arabs democratized. This earned him the sneers of the Oslo sophisticates as just another right-winger trying to derail the Oslo "peace process" by making "impossible" demands on the Palestinians.

Sharansky was right. Had he been listened to earlier, we might have derailed the "war process" that was Oslo.

Some in the State Department had been pushing—and leaking—a Bush Middle East initiative that would begin with the immediate granting of "provisional statehood" to Palestine. They lost. It was just too absurd that in the midst of its own fight against terrorists, the United States should gratuitously confer the powers of statehood upon a Palestinian Authority, as the president put it, "trafficking with terrorists."

Instead, insisted the president, there will be no American support for a Palestinian state until "the Palestinian people have new leaders, new institutions and new security arrangements with their neighbors." Close call. A policy that was headed for a shipwreck—a "provisional" state run by terrorists—has turned into a new and promising American initiative.

The test, however, is implementation. Already, those who once gave us Oslo and who were pushing for immediate "provisional" Palestinian statehood are now urging a more fixed timetable to statehood—presumably to give the Palestinians "hope." But what if the Palestinian Authority goes unreformed? What if the terrorism continues? What if the president's conditions are flouted? You can be sure that the Arabs, the Europeans and the clever ones at State (and their semiofficial spokesmen at the New York Times) will be pushing to explain away or just ignore Palestinian noncompliance in order to stay on calendar and get us to the ultimate goal of "peace."

They never learn. That is precisely how Oslo ended in catastrophe. Every condition imposed on the Palestinians—Arafat's written pledge to renounce terrorism, to end incitement, to limit the size of his "police," to truly recognize Israel's right to exist—was systematically violated. The Labor governments in Jerusalem and the Clinton administration in Washington ignored the violations, equally systematically, so as not to disturb the "peace process."

We cannot make that mistake again. There is a road to peace. If the Palestinians show a genuine willingness to reform and accept a settlement with Israel, there can be peace. But we cannot let the benchmarks be eroded and the conditions be ignored. If they are, then the promise of the president's bold new policy will have been irrevocably lost.

SOURCE: **"Peace Through Democracy,"** by Charles Krauthammer, *Washington Post,* June 28, 2002, p. A29. © 2002, The Washington Post Writers Group. **Reprinted with permission.**

Bush Mixes Democracy and Hypocrisy

James P. Pinkerton

Yesterday, President George W. Bush and his negotiating partners made a good start toward peace in the Mideast. Now there's only one thing that can screw it up: democracy.

Of the four participants in the Aqaba Summit, three—Bush, Israeli Prime Minister Ariel Sharon and Palestinian Prime Minister Mahmoud Abbas—mentioned "democracy." The exception was Jordan's King Abdullah, the unelected leader of a country rated by Freedom House, the human-rights group, as "partly free."

And what of the other Arab leaders Bush met with the day before, in Sharm el-Sheikh? The same Freedom House rates both Egypt and Saudi Arabia as "not free." Of course, that didn't stop Egyptian President Hosni Mubarak from praising democracy—in other countries.

And maybe that's what the Mideast needs: some Mubarak-like hypocrisy about democracy. Why? Because it appears that democratizing and peacemaking are two different things. But wait a second: Bush has said many times that democracy is the future of the Mideast. In his February 26 speech to the American Enterprise Institute, for example, he extolled the "d" word, declaring, "The world has a clear interest in the spread of democratic values, because stable and free nations do not breed the ideologies of murder."

That may be the case, but nations and peoples, democratic or not, have goals that are sometimes expressed in violence. One might consider the Palestinians: According to a poll conducted last month by the Organization of International Solidarity for Human Rights, 95 percent of Palestinians insist on the "right of return" to the homes and lands they claim within Israel. Indeed, 84 percent of Palestinians say that they oppose the creation of a Palestinian state if it includes the formal renunciation of this "right of return." Israelis, of course, consider such a return to be a deal-breaker, tantamount to national suicide for the Jewish state.

So Abbas knows that if he is to have any success in negotiating with the Israelis and their American allies, he will have to keep the "return" issue in the background. But such backgrounding could explain why Abbas—who was, in effect, appointed by the United States—has an approval rating among Palestinians of between 2 and 4 percent. That's right, 2 and 4 percent.

To be sure, Abbas' popularity could surge if his summiteering delivered tangible benefits to the folks back home. But in the meantime, opinion polls show that anti-Israeli and also anti-American feeling is rising—in the Palestinian territories, in the Arab world, in the Muslim world. A survey released on Tuesday by the Pew Global Attitudes Project found that 98 percent of Palestinians have an unfavorable view of the United States. And that percentage was exceeded in King Abdullah's country of Jordan, where 99 percent saw the United States unfavorably. Indeed, 71 percent of Palestinians and 55 percent of Jordanians said they believed that Osama bin Laden was the world leader most likely to "do the right thing" in foreign affairs. No wonder Jordan's king made no reference to popular sentiment in his speech yesterday.

The numbers were almost as bleak elsewhere. In countries such as Lebanon, Morocco and Pakistan, 70 percent or more of respondents held strongly anti-Israeli and anti-American views.

Does this matter? Not if the countries aren't democracies. But what if they are democracies, where public opinion—and popular passion—rules? For example, in Turkey, eight

PART II *Controversies*

in 10 have a negative view of the U.S., according to Pew. Three months ago, a high-level deal to let the United States use Turkish territory as a jump-off point for Operation Iraqi Freedom was undone because the masses erupted in opposition. Nine in 10 Turks opposed the war.

And speaking of Iraqi freedom, what's up with that? Answer: not much. American liberators have decided to put Iraqi democracy on hold indefinitely, until they can be more sure of the electoral outcome. In other—words, Bush is praising democracy for Arabs—but thwarting it for the Arabs whom America controls.

Oftentimes, dictators can make deals—even good deals, such as peace deals—that democrats can't. Such deals might hold, until the people speak. And that always happens, sooner or later. But until that time, let's be thankful for hypocritical dictators/peacemakers.

SOURCE: *Newsday* (New York), June 5, 2003. Copyright © 2003 LexisNexis, a division of Reed Elsevier Inc. All Rights Reserved.

CHAPTER SUMMARY

- The idea that democracies are more peaceful than non-democracies, which has long been central to liberal thinking about international politics, can be traced to Immanuel Kant's vision of a "democratic pacific union" in which democratic (or "republican") states would refrain from war in their relations with each other.

- With the end of the Cold War and the dramatic spread of democracy in the 1980s and 1990s there has been renewed interest in democratic peace theory among academics and policymakers alike.

- Democratic peace theory has two major variants. The institutional variant claims that the division or dispersion of power in democratic states makes it very difficult for them to initiate and wage war. The cultural version argues that the norms and values that permeate democratic societies, especially the commitment to resolving political disputes without resort to force, also shape the foreign policies of democratic states. These institutional and cultural constraints are particularly powerful when democracies deal with each other.

- The empirical record appears to support democratic peace theory because there is no example of an unambiguously democratic state engaging in war with another unambiguously democratic state.

- Critics and skeptics remain unconvinced by the evidence. The rarity of war and (until recently) the rarity of democracy mean that we should not have expected to see wars among democracies. As a result, the lack of a war between democracies is neither surprising nor compelling.

- Skeptics also see a very convenient pattern of constantly shifting definitions, particularly when it comes to the requirements for classifying a country as a democracy. Whether or not Germany on the eve of World War I deserves the label of democracy is the most controversial example of these definitional problems.

- The spread of democracy over the last two decades will provide for a real-world test of democratic peace theory in coming years because many new democracies are geographically close to each other and have long histories of conflict.

CRITICAL QUESTIONS

1. Why might democracies be more peaceful in their relations with each other than with nondemocracies?

2. What other factors might explain the absence of war among democratic states?

3. Why is democratic peace theory inconsistent with realism?

4. Does the United States' 2003 war in Iraq shed any light on democratic peace theory? Why or why not?

5. What are the necessary characteristics of a "democratic" state?

KEY TERMS

checks and balances 102
democratic pacific union 101
in-group/out-group hypothesis 111
institutional thesis 102
Kant, Immanuel (1724–1804) 101
political-cultural thesis 103
rational/pacific public thesis 101
spurious 110

FURTHER READINGS

Contemporary interest in democratic peace theory was sparked by Michael Doyle's seminal "Liberalism and World Politics," *American Political Science Review* 80 (December 1986): 1151–69. A number of subsequent works have since become standards in support of the democratic peace theory, including Bruce Russett, *Grasping the Democratic Peace* (Princeton: Princeton University Press, 1993), and Spencer Weart, *Never at War: Why Democracies Will Not Fight One Another* (New Haven: Yale University Press, 1998). Stressing the importance of mutual perceptions of democracy is John Owen, *Liberal Peace, Liberal War: American Politics and International Security* (Ithaca, NY: Cornell University Press, 1997). Critiques from several different perspectives can be found in Christopher Layne, "Kant or Cant: The Myth of the Democratic Peace," *International Security* 19 (Fall 1994): 5–49; Joanne Gowa, *Bullets and Ballots: The Elusive Democratic Peace* (Princeton: Princeton University Press, 1999); and Robert Latham, "Democracy and War-Making," *Millenium: A Journal of International Affairs* 22 (1993): 139–64.

WAR AND DEMOCRACY ON THE WEB

www.hawaii.edu/powerkills

Explores the relationship among freedom, democracy, and war.

www.worldaudit.org

Evaluates and ranks the nations of the world on various scales, including democracy, press freedom, civil liberties, and others.

www.cidcm.umd.edu/inscr/polity

Classifies nations of the world according to their type of government.

NOTES

[1] Quoted in Michael Doyle, *The Ways of War and Peace* (New York: W. W. Norton, 1997), p. 280.

[2] This not a universally shared interpretation. See Louis A. Perez, *The War of 1898* (Chapel Hill: University of North Carolina Press, 1998), pp. 70–77. Still, even those who reject the notion that popular opinion pushed President McKinley into war over Cuba cannot plausibly argue that public opinion was a force for peace in the crisis.

[3] Robin Fox, "Fatal Attraction: War and Human Nature," *The National Interest* (Winter 1992/1993): 17.

[4] The best summary of the institutional and cultural theses can be found in Bruce Russett, *Grasping the Democratic Peace* (Princeton: Princeton University Press, 1993), pp. 29–42.

[5] Thomas Risse-Kappen, "Democratic Peace-Warlike Democracies: A Social Constructivist Interpretation of the Liberal Argument," *European Journal of International Relations* 34, no. 1 (1995): 489–515.

[6] Spencer Weart, *Never at War: Why Democracies Will Not Fight One Another* (New Haven, CT: Yale University Press, 1998), p. 90.

[7] John Owen, *Liberal Peace, Liberal War: American Politics and International Security* (Ithaca, NY: Cornell University Press, 1997) and John Owen, "How Liberalism Produces the Democratic Peace," *International Security* 19, no. 2 (Fall 1994): 87–126. Also Ido Oren, "The Subjectivity of the Democratic Peace: Changing U.S. Perceptions of Imperial Germany," *International Security* 20, no. 2 (Fall 1995): 147–84.

[8] More radical or Marxists theorists might take issue with this statement. They would be inclined to argue that the formal processes mask the fundamentally undemocratic nature of most contemporary democracies because the skewed nature of economic power prevents the emergence of anything that could be considered democratic in the deeper sense of the term.

[9] J. D. Singer and Melvin Small, "The War Proneness of Democratic States," *Jerusalem Journal of International Relations* 1 (1976): 49–69.

[10] Bruce Russett, *Grasping the Democratic Peace* (Princeton: Princeton University Press, 1993), p. 11.

[11] Ibid., p. 21.

[12] David Spiro, "The Insignificance of the Liberal Peace," *International Security* 19, no. 2 (Fall 1994): 50–86.

[13] Russett, *Grasping the Democratic Peace*, p. 16.

[14] Ted Galen Carpenter, "Review Essay: Democracy and War," *Independent Review* 2 (Winter 1998): 435–441.

[15] Christopher Layne, "Kant or Cant: The Myth of Democratic Peace," *International Security* 19, no. 2 (Fall 1994): 41.

[16] Maria A. Meginnes, "Defining the Democratic: Imperial Germany and Democratic Peace Theory," *The Undergraduate Journal of Politics and Government* 1, no. 2 (Spring 2001): 32.

[17] Weart, *Never at War*, pp. 311–12. In general, Weart provides a comprehensive overview of the "close" cases and the reasons why he thinks none of them invalidates the democratic peace proposition (pp. 297–318).

[18] Robert Latham, "Democracy and War-Making: Locating the Liberal International Context," *Millenium: A Journal of International Affairs* 22, no. 2 (1993): 139, 153, 154.

[19] Ted Galen Carpenter, "Democracy and War: Reply," *Independent Review* 3 (Summer 1998): 107.

[20] Thomas Friedman, *The Lexus and the Olive Tree* (New York: Farrar Straus Giroux, 1999), p. 195.

[21] Bruce Russett, "And Yet It Moves," *International Security* 19, no. 4 (Spring 1995): 166.

[22] Ibid., p. 164.

[23] Layne, "Kant or Cant," p. 49.

CHAPTER FIVE

POWER POLITICS

International politics is often considered a realm of power politics. Without a world government, nations do not have the luxury of security and must strive for power or live at the mercy of their powerful neighbors. According to realists, international politics is fundamentally a struggle for power in which nations must always be wary of the power of other nations. Nations that naively ignore these realities and try to avoid power politics will suffer the consequences of their folly. Historically, liberals have rejected this pessimistic assessment and sought alternatives to power politics. Though some utopian liberals have embraced world government, most have proposed more modest alternatives. Assuming a widely shared interest in peace, many liberals believe that the international community as a whole can effectively organize to deter aggression and war. Constructivists also reject the realist view that states must pursue power to ensure their security, pointing out that many states have created stable and secure relations that do not rest on calculations of power.

What are the causes of war? What, if anything, can be done to preserve and promote international peace? Although there is little agreement on the answers, at least there is consensus that these are the most important questions for students of international relations. Most would concede that some measure of international conflict, like social conflict in general, is unavoidable. People, groups, and nations are unlikely to agree about everything all the time. Accepting the inevitability of social/international conflict, however, does not necessarily entail the inevitability of *violent* social or international conflict. And even if it is unrealistic to eliminate all violent social or international conflict, there might still be ways to significantly reduce its likelihood. As we saw in the previous chapter, some hold out hope that the spread of democracy in the world can reduce, or perhaps even eliminate, the chances for war. Others argue that the prospects for war and peace have more to do with the nature of the international system—including anarchy, the distribution of power, and/or the existence of international institutions—and suggest we need look here for ways to preserve peace. But which international arrangements or institutions are conducive to peace? Does a balance of power lead to peace? Does peace require the presence of a hegemonic power capable of enforcing it (i.e., a great imbalance of power)? Can the global community as a whole come together to preserve peace? In short, what are alternative mechanisms for preserving peace, and how feasible are they?

PEACE THROUGH STRENGTH?

It is almost impossible to get through a national political campaign in the United States without hearing the phrase "peace through strength." It is usually displayed prominently in the background when candidates speak at military bases and defense factories. It is one of those slogans that is more frequently invoked than explained or justified. What should we make of this geopolitical catchphrase? What exactly does it mean? The political attraction of the slogan is clear: both peace and strength are desirable, especially since the implied alternatives are war and weakness. Being against peace and strength would be tantamount to opposing motherhood and apple pie. For our purposes the interesting word in the phrase is *through*, because it suggests a causal connection between peace and strength. Perhaps this is meant to inoculate candidates who favor increasing military power from charges of warmongering: more military power will lead to peace, not war, so do not worry about electing me. Political motivations aside, is there any reason to believe that peace and strength go hand in hand, that the latter leads to the former? Is there any evidence, for example, that strong nations are involved in fewer wars than weaker nations? Probably not. The United States, arguably the strongest nation for most of the twentieth century, fought many wars while much weaker nations such as Sweden and Switzerland fought none.

But these may be nitpicking criticisms. Those who invoke peace through strength probably do not intend it to be taken as a social scientific hypothesis. More likely, it is rhetorical shorthand for a foreign policy orientation that identifies national power as the essential currency of international affairs. It embodies an underlying message that nations must be concerned about strength and power if they value their independence and security. The expression "peace through strength" reflects a commitment to **power politics,** a perspective in which international politics inevitably entails

"PEACE THROUGH STRENGTH"

power politics A perspective portraying international relations as inevitably a realm of conflict and competition for power among states.

"perceptions of insecurity (the security dilemma); struggles for power; the use of Machiavellian stratagems; the presence of coercion; attempts to balance power; and the use of war to settle disputes."[1] The guiding assumption is that nations have no choice, or at least no good choice, but to engage in power politics. If nations neglect considerations of power and place their fate in the hands of international institutions or the good will of others, they will only imperil their survival. In the international realm, nations face a choice between two options: "the alternatives . . . [are] probable suicide on the one hand and the active playing of the power-politics on the other."[2] The imperatives and logic of international anarchy compel states to pursue power. Without a truly fundamental (and highly unlikely) transformation of the international order, there is no feasible alternative to power politics. As Stanley Michalak argues, "We like to think that solutions exist 'out there,' new ideas that . . . could usher in a new era of peace and amity among nations," but regrettably, "the truth is: none exists. The few alternatives to military force have been well known for centuries . . . and whenever they have [been] tried, they have failed."[3] Thus, the operation or "playing" of power politics is not an alternative to international peace; it is the only feasible, though admittedly imperfect, means for achieving international peace.

Not surprisingly, Michalak's pessimistic conclusion is not universally shared. Though the wisdom of "peace through strength" may not be questioned very often on the campaign trail, there is an enduring debate about the wisdom and inevitability of power politics. Critics find the association of power and peace to be disingenuous at best and morally irresponsible at worst. If the history of international politics reveals anything, it is that the pursuit of power has not produced anything that deserves to be called peace, and the security it supposedly ensures is fleeting and illusory. Strong powers may be *less insecure* than others, but in a world of relentless power competition no nation enjoys security in any meaningful sense of the term: there are simply varying degrees of insecurity. Critics also challenge the assertion that there are no alternatives to power politics as a dangerously self-fulfilling part of the realist catechism, a statement of faith and ideology rather than a reflection of reality.

THERE IS NO ALTERNATIVE TO POWER POLITICS

In vivid terms Kenneth Waltz tells us that "the state among states . . . conducts its affairs in the brooding shadow of violence." Because "some states may at any time use force, all states must be prepared to do so—or live at the mercy of their militarily more vigorous neighbors." In international relations, as in any other sphere of social interaction, "contact without at least occasional conflict is inconceivable; and the hope that in the absence of an agent to manage or manipulate conflicting parties the use of force will always be avoided cannot be realistically entertained."[4] It is hard to imagine a clearer or more concise statement for the inevitability of power politics. Waltz captures all the essential elements of the argument: international politics is anarchic, nations must provide for their own security, nations can never be certain what others are up to, war is always a possibility, and alternatives to national power as the final guarantor of safety and independence are unrealistic. Let us dissect and trace the elements of the argument.

From anarchy to power politics Why do nations in international society worry about their strength and power in ways that people and groups within nations usually do not? Is it because nations come into conflict with each other, whereas as people and groups within nations manage to live in harmony? Certainly not. Domestic societies are rife with all kinds of conflicts, personal, social, and political. Is it that people within domestic societies are never threatened with violence, whereas nations are? Again, this is obviously not the case. Even though nations differ greatly in their level of domestic violence, none is able to eliminate it entirely. The difference is that in domestic society conflicts and violence occur in a context where there is a central political authority to deal with and manage these conflicts. Waltz explains that "the difference between national and international politics lies not in the use of force but in the different modes of organization for doing something about it." In the domestic realm we have governments with "a monopoly on the *legitimate* use of force, and legitimate here means that public agents are organized to prevent and counter the private use of force." Because there is a government, "citizens need not prepare to defend themselves. Public agencies do that. *A national system is not one of self-help. The international system is.*"[5]

International society is **anarchic** in that there is no central political authority. There is no world government that has the right and capacity to use force to protect nations. The United Nations is a voluntary organization of independent states; it is not, nor was it ever intended to be, a world government. Without a central authority to protect nations from threats, they have no alternative but to protect themselves as best they can. In a domestic setting people are not responsible for providing their own security. Even though police do not offer foolproof protection, "states . . . do not enjoy even an imperfect guarantee of their security unless they set out to provide it for themselves."[6] States can protect their security by relying on their own resources, or they can combine power with others in alliances. But either way, nations have to make their own security arrangements. There is no escaping the reality that "**self-help** is *necessarily* the principle of action in an anarchic order."[7] And, according to Frederick Dunn, "so long as the notion of self-help persists, the aim of maintaining the power position of the nation is paramount to all other considerations."[8]

If self-help is the necessary corollary of anarchy, the **security dilemma** is the logical consequence of self-help. The dilemma nations face, even those that do not intend to threaten others, is that many, if not most, of the actions that make them feel more secure will increase the insecurity of other nations. Even measures that appear purely defensive at first glance are potentially menacing to others. Though nations usually claim that their armies and weapons are intended purely for defense, there are not many weapons that lack offensive potential. Take, for example, a strategic defense system (e.g., the "Star Wars" plan proposed by U.S. President Ronald Reagan) designed to intercept incoming missiles. How can a system intended to defend against an attack be viewed as threat by others? The answer is simple: because this system also allows the nation possessing it to attack others and then prevent any effective retaliatory response. A nation armed with an effective defense could then carry out offensive plans with impunity (this is why the United States worried about the Soviet Union's acquiring such a system during the Cold War). It does not require great stretches of logic to see how a defensive system can be an integral part of a larger

anarchy, anarchic The absence of a central governmental or political authority.

self-help The necessity for actors to make provisions for their own security in the absence of any central authority to protect them from potential threats.

security dilemma The problem nations face when the actions taken to make one nation feel more secure inevitably make other nations feel less secure.

offensive plan. Although every increase in one nation's security does not necessarily lead to an equivalent reduction in another nation's security, there is usually some tradeoff. The contrast with domestic society is critical. Police protection provides everyone with security without undermining anyone's security. As a result, individuals usually do not have to worry about their power vis-à-vis their neighbors. When there is a central authority, the security dilemma can be solved. Because international politics is anarchic, there is no lasting solution to the security dilemma of nations.

The security dilemma has two facets. First, states must be aware of how their security measures will be viewed by others; there is no reason to provoke unnecessary anxiety since this might prompt other nations to take actions that will in turn reduce your security. Second, nations have to worry about the capabilities and intentions of other states. The relatively easy part of this assessment is determining capabilities. Trying to decipher what others intend to do with their capabilities is another matter. Though people sometimes assume that intelligence efforts are directed at measuring the capabilities of potential adversaries, differing intelligence analyses usually have little to with disagreements about capabilities. There was not much uncertainty, for example, about the size of the Soviet nuclear arsenal during the Cold War. Spy planes and satellites gave the United States a fairly reliable count of Soviet weapons. Debates revolved around conflicting views of what the Soviet Union planned on doing with its weapons. This is the unavoidable element of uncertainty in international politics, and uncertainty in a world of armed states translates into insecurity, which easily escalates into fear. And because "fear is endemic to states in the international system . . . it drives them to compete for power so that they can increase their prospects for survival in a dangerous world."[9]

So the argument for the inevitability of power politics follows a clear line of development: "Because the international system has no central authority, every nation must fend for itself, and states can do that only by utilizing their power; therefore, they will always be trying to increase their power."[10] According to Waltz, "the requirements of state action are *imposed* by the circumstances in which all states live."[11]

Power politics I: The balance of power We have already seen that it requires a little work to interpret the expression "peace through strength." In the field of international relations, terms and concepts are often ambiguous and contested. *Power* and *balance of power* are two other examples of commonly used concepts whose meanings are not always crystal clear. Even though "power lies at the heart of international politics . . . there is considerable disagreement about what power is and how to measure it." As a starting point, we can think of **power** as the ability to prevail in conflict, the capacity to influence and alter the behavior of other actors. The measurement of power, or the evaluating resources needed to wield influence, is more problematic. Most operating within the tradition of realism and power politics would probably have few quibbles with Mearsheimer's observation that "states have two kinds of power: latent power and military power. These two forms of power are closely related but not synonymous." Whereas military power is fairly self-explanatory, "latent power refers to the socio-economic ingredients that go into building military power; it is largely based on a state's wealth and overall size of its population. Great powers need money, technology and personnel to build military forces and to fight wars, and a state's latent power refers to the raw potential it can draw on when competing with

power Influence over the behavior of others and the ability to prevail in conflict.

A May Day parade in the former Soviet Union, where the most recent military hardware was usually on display. This is a vivid illustration of the arms races that realists believe are the result of the insecurities produced by international anarchy.

SOURCE: © Dean Conger/CORBIS

rival states."[12] Some will undoubtedly find this definition a little narrow, preferring to include such things as ideological and cultural power. Though we could go on for several pages with different definitions of power, Mearsheimer's is a good starting point for a discussion of power politics.

The expression "balance of power" can also be confusing. As Inis Claude notes, "balance of power is assigned a number of different, and not always compatible, meanings in discourse on international relations." This can be illustrated by looking at two common uses of the term. In some cases, it is clear that the balance of power refers to a situation in which two nations or alliances are roughly equal—that is, when the power of one nation or alliance is literally balanced or offset by the equal power of another. Here balance of power indicates an *equilibrium* of power. But there are also instances in which people refer to a "favorable balance of power." This usage seems like a contradiction in terms, since the very idea of "favorable" balance suggests that power is not balanced at all. In this case, the balance of power actually refers to a *distribution* of power that is not in balance. So when we see references to the "balance of power between X and Y" or someone promises to create a "balance of power," it is necessary to look closely to determine if "balance" in fact means a balance or imbalance.

Definitions of these terms are critical because they are central to many theories of international relations, especially **balance of power theory,** sometimes referred to as "the grand old theory of international relations."[13] Balance of power theory begins by accepting the basic premises of power politics: international relations is a struggle for power and security in an anarchic world of insecure states. Kenneth Waltz, probably

balance of power theory
Predicts that the pursuit of security by nations tends to result in the creation of balances of power on a systemic level. This is often accompanied by the prediction that war is less likely when power is balanced because no nation can be confident of winning a war (and, thus, no nation is tempted to initiate one).

the theory's leading proponent, claims that "balance of power politics prevail wherever two, and only two, requirements are met: that the order be anarchic and that it be populated by units [states] wishing to survive."[14] Some states undoubtedly wish to do more, but survival is assumed to be the minimal objective of all states. Since no central authority restrains states or provides protection and because intentions are always uncertain, states inevitably focus on the capabilities of other states. Balance of power theory predicts that states will do exactly what the name of the theory suggests—that is, balance against the power of other states. In order to prevent any one state or alliance from achieving dominance, states try to check their power by forming countercoalitions. Individual states do not always intend for an overall strategic balance to emerge, but "according to the theory, balances of power tend to form whether some or all states consciously aim to establish or maintain a balance."[15] States merely set out to safeguard their security and in the process "the various nations group themselves together in such a way that no single nation or group of nations is strong enough to overwhelm the others."[16]

Balancing, however, is not the only option states have. There is also the possibility of joining forces with the stronger power. To use the common terminology, states could *bandwagon* with, rather than balance against, the most powerful state or alliance. Balance of power theory predicts that **bandwagoning** is unlikely because "to ally with the dominant power means placing one's trust in its continued benevolence. The safer strategy is to join with those who cannot readily dominate their allies, in order to avoid being dominated by those who can." Furthermore, "joining the weaker side increases the new members' influence within the alliance, because the weaker power has greater need for the assistance."[17] To use an illustrative metaphor, the balance of power operates like a seesaw: whenever one side gets powerful enough to tip the contraption in its favor, nations scoot over to the other side to keep it on an even keel.

In addition to preventing any one power from becoming powerful enough to dominate the international system, the tendency for states to balance may have the added benefit of contributing to peace and stability. Preserving peace is not the goal of states, and indeed wars are sometimes needed to check the power of other states. Nonetheless, some argue that when the overall system is in balance, the chances for major war are greatly reduced. The argument is straightforward. It begins by assuming that nations start wars because they expect to win them (i.e., they anticipate that gains will outweigh losses). When potential antagonists are roughly equal in power, neither side can be confident of victory. The cost of war with equals is likely to be high and the prospects for victory uncertain at best. In such a situation, no one is tempted to initiate war. When power is not balanced, the stronger side is more likely to be tempted to aggression.

Balance of power theory is not universally accepted. Even many who accept the inevitability of power politics question whether it presents an accurate picture of how the world works. Part of the problem is that the theory is very difficult to test. Waltz himself admits that "because only a loosely defined and inconstant condition of balance is predicted, it is difficult to say that any given distribution of power falsifies the theory."[18] The theory only predicts a tendency toward balancing, not an actual balance at every point in time. So the fact that power might not be balanced does not au-

bandwagoning When less powerful actors align with (rather than against) the most powerful. Inconsistent with balance of power theory, which predicts that nations will align against (and hence "balance") the most powerful nation.

tomatically undermine the theory. Furthermore, measuring power, and thus determining if it is actually in balance, is also notoriously difficult. Scholars cannot even agree on whether there was a balance or large imbalance of power between the United States and the Soviet coalitions during the Cold War.

In addition to these problems, there are also many historical examples that appear to run counter to the theory's prediction that nations will align against the strongest power. In the early years of the Cold War, for example, the United States was undeniably the world's most formidable military and economic power. If ever there were an undisputed strongest power in the world, the United States was it. According to balance of power theory, other nations should have been flocking to align against the United States. This did not happen. Nations do not seem to balance automatically against power. At a minimum, there are many other considerations that come into play.

Power politics II: Balance of threat theory An alternative to balance of power theory that still accepts the basic precepts of power politics is **balance of threat theory.** Balance of power theory assumes that states are primarily concerned about power because intentions can never be known for certain. When intentions are excluded from the equation, states assume that those with the greatest capabilities pose the greatest potential threat and balance against them. On an abstract level, this is probably true: all else being equal, the most powerful states do pose the greatest danger. In the real world, however, all else is never equal. States do not ignore intentions merely because they cannot be established beyond a reasonable doubt. States make assessments, however imperfect, of both power and intentions. Balance of threat theory agrees that states do in fact engage in balancing; the disagreement is about what they balance against (see figure 5.1 for a summary and contrast of the two theories).

Stephen Walt, who provides the most persuasive statement of balance of threat theory, explains: "Perceptions of intent are likely to play an especially crucial role in alliance choices . . . states that are viewed as aggressive are likely to provoke others to balance against them. . . . even states with rather modest capabilities may prompt others to balance if they are perceived as especially aggressive."[19] Many historical examples that appear to contradict balance of power theory make more sense in the context of balance of threat theory. Again, Walt notes that "balance of threat theory helps explain why the coalitions that defeated Germany and its allies in World War I and World War II grew to be far more powerful than their opponents . . . the answer is simple: Germany and its allies . . . were more threatening (though weaker) and caused others to form a more powerful coalition in response."[20] This approach also helps explain the alignment pattern of the early Cold War. Even in the face of its obvious advantage in virtually every component of power, most nations aligned with the United States rather than the Soviet Union because the latter was seen as posing the greater threat despite its more limited power.

Nations balance against others that are *perceived* as posing a threat. Of course, assessments of threat may be wrong, just as measurements of power can be mistaken. The failure of an adequate deterrent coalition to emerge against Nazi Germany in the mid-1930s is an example of just such a failure. But balance of threat theory does not claim that perceptions of threat are correct, merely that they play a critical role in

balance of threat theory
Predicts that nations align against whichever nation is seen as posing the greatest threat, not necessarily against the powerful nation.

FIGURE 5.1   **Balance of power versus balance of threat theory**

BALANCE OF POWER THEORY

Imbalances of power ————————cause————————▶ Alliances against the strongest state

An imbalance of power occurs when the strongest state or coalition in the system possesses significantly greater power than the second strongest. Power is the product of several different components, including population, economic and military capability, technological skill, and political cohesion.

BALANCE OF THREAT THEORY

Imbalances of threat ————————cause————————▶ Alliances against the most threatening state

An imbalance of threat occurs when the most threatening state or coalition is significantly more dangerous than the second most threatening state or coalition. The degree to which a state threatens others is the product of its aggregate power, its geographic proximity, its offensive capability, and the aggressiveness of its intentions.

SOURCE: Stephen Walt, *The Origins of Alliances* (Ithaca, NY: Cornell University Press, 1989), p. 265.

preponderance theory
Argues that nations tend to align on the basis of interests—those that are satisfied with the status quo as opposed to those that are dissatisfied. Peace and stability are more likely when there is a great imbalance of power in favor of the status quo states—that is, when there is a preponderance of power in support of the existing order.

degree of power In power preponderance theory, refers to a state's position in the international power hierarchy—that is, whether it is a great power, a middle-range power, or a weak state.

degree of satisfaction In power preponderance theory, the extent to which a state is essentially satisfied or dissatisfied with the existing international order.

alliance choices. And it is also important to note that the emphasis on threat as opposed to power alone does not make the theory an *alternative to* power politics, but rather an *alternative vision of* power politics.

Power politics III: Preponderance theory A final version of power politics is **preponderance** or **hegemonic stability theory,** in which states are distinguished by their **degree of power** and **degree of satisfaction.** *Degree of satisfaction* refers to whether a state is essentially satisfied or dissatisfied with the current international order and its place in it. Satisfied states are interested in preserving the international status quo, whereas dissatisfied states are revisionist states that want to change the existing order. On the basis of power and satisfaction, the theory draws a distinction among four types of nations: (1) the powerful and satisfied, (2) the powerful and dissatisfied, (3) the weak and satisfied, and (4) the weak and dissatisfied. There are, of course, more subtle gradations of power. At the top of the power hierarchy is the dominant power or hegemon, which typically emerged from the last major war as the most powerful victor. By definition, the hegemon is a status quo power interested in preserving the existing order (the United States can be viewed as the hegemon from the end of World War II until the present). Below this hegemon are great powers, middle powers, small powers, and dependencies. In each category there are typically both status quo and revisionist powers (see figure 5.2).[21]

FIGURE 5.2

The power transition

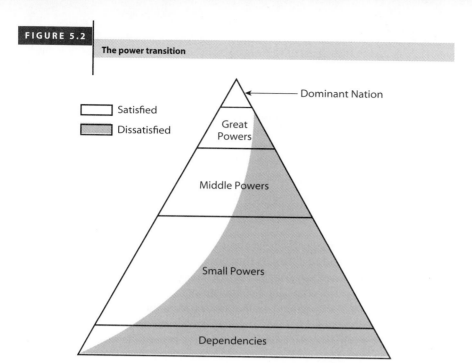

SOURCE: A. F. K. Organski, *World Politics* (New York: Alfred A. Knopf, 1968), p. 369.

This theory holds that states tend to align on the basis of interests—that is, status quo nations against revisionist nations. Though the alliances may not always be formal alliances based on explicit treaties, status quo states will come together if the existing order is threatened by revisionist states. In the mid-1930s, for example, the United States, France, and Great Britain (status quo powers) did not form an alliance against Nazi Germany (a revisionist power), but they did eventually align in the face of German aggression.[22] In this sense, preponderance theory has more in common with balance of threat theory than with balance of power theory.

To illustrate the differences among the theories, consider their predictions for the post–Cold War world. The collapse of the Soviet Union has clearly left the United States as the dominant nation in the world. No other nation possesses the same combination and economic and military power. The United States is the only nation with the ability to project military force on a global scale. Balance of power theory predicts that lesser powers will eventually align against the United States in order to prevent American domination. Balance of threat theory, on the other hand, does not automatically predict the emergence of a counter-American coalition. The important variable is not the power of the United States per se but whether it comes to be viewed as a threat. Hegemonic stability theory predicts that a counter-American coalition will not emerge because the other major powers (Japan, Germany, Britain, France) are all essentially satisfied powers interested in preserving the existing international order. Though there may be some occasional conflicts and disagreements, the fundamental similarities of interests will keep these status quo nations in line with each other.

Preponderance theory also parts company with balance of power theory on the issue of which power distribution is most conducive to peace. According to Organski, it is not a balance of power that leads to peace but rather an imbalance of power: "World peace is guaranteed when the nations satisfied with the existing international order enjoy an unchallenged supremacy of power . . . major wars are most likely when a dissatisfied challenger achieves an approximate balance of power with the dominant nation."[23] Though it is true that a balance of power "means that either side might lose, it also means that either side may win."[24] When there is a great imbalance of power, the challenger knows there is no chance of winning a war and the dominant status quo power has no need to resort to war. The peace that results when the dominance of the status quo powers is unquestioned "is not necessarily a peace with justice," but it is peace if we define this to mean the absence of war.[25]

The common vision of power politics The differences among balance of power, balance of threat, and hegemonic stability theories are clearly significant. Whether states balance against power or threats or align on the basis of interests is a critical question, not only for academic theorists but also for policymakers. But the issues on which these theories disagree should not be allowed to obscure the underlying vision of international politics that they share. It is not unusual for people to share certain beliefs but nonetheless disagree on the implications of those beliefs. The analogous example of religious sects that agree on most issues and accept the same texts but argue vociferously about relatively marginal questions is only one example (and it is often the minor points of disagreement that attract the most attention). This is what we have here. For our purposes, the most important point is that all of the theories we looked at in this section share a commitment to power politics in that they agree on the fundamental features and dynamics of international relations: anarchy is the central fact shaping relations among states, nations have to be concerned about their power vis-à-vis other states, and the pursuit of power and security by independent states is the driving force of international politics. There is no suggestion of any feasible alternative to the reality of international power politics. In the words of Gwynne Dyer, "it is practically impossible for a sovereign state to behave well (by ordinary human standards) within the existing international system."[26]

ALTERNATIVES TO POWER POLITICS

Even those who believe there is no realistic alternative to power politics concede it is not ideal. Though a balance or imbalance of power may be more conducive to peace, there is no guarantee that peace can be preserved indefinitely. Eventually, the balance breaks down or revisionist states gain power and war results. Within a system of power politics, war is always possible and periodically inevitable. Even when peace prevails, states must conduct their "affairs in the brooding shadow of violence."[27] At least this is what realists tell us. But is it so? Is the world really doomed to power politics marked by periods of peace and stability punctuated by spasms of war and violence? Or are there alternatives to the relentless and ruthless logic of power politics?

World government? If power politics is driven by the insecurities that inevitably arise when there is no government on a world scale to do for states what national governments do for their citizens, then world government would appear to be the most obvious alternative to power politics. To the extent that anarchy is the "root cause" of power politics, the creation of a world government would constitute a frontal assault on the problem. But because we have no experience with world government, the argument in its favor is made largely on the basis of logic and analogy. On the level of theory and logic, the case for world government is impeccable and simple. Just as national governments eliminate the security dilemma for individuals by providing protection and mechanisms for dealing with conflicts, a world government is essential if the same result is to be attained on a global scale. A truly effective world government would entail "the establishment of an authority which takes away from nations, summarily and completely, not only the machinery of battle that can wage war, but also the machinery of decision that can start a war."[28]

Though arguments for world government have been advanced for centuries, the problem is getting there. As Inis Claude notes in his discussion of the prospects for world government, "I do not propose to deal extensively with the question of the *feasibility* of world government in the present era, or in the foreseeable future. This abstention is in part a reflection of my conviction that the answer is almost self-evidently negative." He sees "no realistic prospect of the establishment of a system of world government as a means for attempting to cope with the critical dangers of world politics."[29] Realists, such as Kenneth Waltz, generally concede that on a theoretical level world government presents a solution to the problems of anarchy. But world government is "unattainable in practice" because the world lacks the sense of shared values and community that are essential preconditions for effective government. "In a society of states with little coherence," Waltz predicts, "the prospect of a world government would be an invitation to prepare for world civil war."[30] The solution could end up being worse than the problem. Fortunately for those who seek an alternative to power politics, world government is not the only option.

Collective security Though there has never been a serious attempt to establish a world state, efforts have been made to transcend power politics through what is known as **collective security**. Though there is some minor variation in how this term is used, collective security generally refers to "a system of states that join together . . . and make an explicit commitment to do two things: (1) they renounce the use of force to settle disputes with each other, and (2) they promise to use force against any of their number who reject rule 1."[31] "The animating idea of collective security," Earl Ravenal explains, "is that each outbreak of aggression will be suppressed, not by a partial alliance directed specifically against certain parties, but by a universal compact, binding *all* to defend *any*."[32] Under collective security, peace is preserved not by individual states shifting alignments in order to offset the power of specific potential aggressors, but rather by the prospect of the entire community of nations coming to the aid of victims of aggression. Though sometimes portrayed as being global or "universal" in scope, collective security pacts can also be more limited, such as a European or Southeast Asian collective security arrangement.

It is important to note what collective security does and does not do. Though

collective security A system in which states renounce the use of force to settle disputes and also agree to band together against states that resort to the use of force. In such a system, the threat of collective response by all states deters the use of force by individual states. Collective security was the initial goal of the League of Nations.

there would certainly be institutions for making decisions about how and when to respond to aggression, no attempt would be made to create a world government. Individual states are not disarmed and replaced by some global police force. In this sense, international politics remains anarchic. Nor does collective security reject power and deterrence as vital components of preserving peace. Proposals for collective security "recognize that military power is a central fact of life in international politics, and is likely to remain so for the foreseeable future."[33] In fact, collective security seeks to keep the peace by threatening any aggressor with the overwhelming power of the international community as a whole. In this sense, collective security shows some similarities with hegemonic stability theory, in which an imbalance of power is seen as more conducive to peace than a balance.

Rather than transcending international anarchy, collective security tries to ameliorate its consequences. Because the protection of each state's security becomes the responsibility of the wider international community, states would no longer be in a pure self-help situation. In committing themselves to come to the aid of any state threatened with aggression, all nations become part of what we can think of as an international police force, albeit one that is more like a volunteer fire department than a full-time police department. The element of self-help and national interest is removed because states are obligated to help whenever the peace is broken, not merely when it is in their interests to do so. And the fact that this aid would be available to all members of the community allows states to escape the security dilemma. The security afforded to all does not come at anyone else's expense.

The most significant experiment with collective security was the League of Nations during the 1920s and 1930s. In urging the creation of the League, U.S. President Woodrow Wilson laid out the basic logic of collective security: "If the peace presently to be made is to endure, it must be a peace made secure by the organized major force of mankind. . . . Right must be based upon the common strength, not the individual strength, of nations upon whose concert peace will depend."[34]

Though the League of Nations provided for means short of force to punish and deter aggressors, such as economic sanctions, the military option remained the ultimate deterrent. According to Article 16 (1) of the League Charter, "Should any Member of the League resort to war . . . it shall *ipso facto* be deemed to have committed an act of war against all other members of the League," and after other measures had failed to restore the peace, "the Members of the League should severally contribute to the armed forces to be used to protect the covenants of the League."[35]

There is no debate about whether the League was a success or a failure, but there is some debate about why it failed so miserably. Some trace its failure to specific historical circumstances that doomed the League from the outset, particularly the unwillingness of the United States to join. It is also clear that even though members paid lip service to the principles of collective security, they proved time after time that they were unwilling to actually do what had to be done to make it work. There was a huge gulf between the rhetoric and treaties on one hand and the real world of policy on the other. Others go further and attribute the League's failure to the inherent weaknesses of collective security that render it unworkable in almost any context.

A few of the problems likely to be encountered in any collective security system are obvious from the outset. One is the identification of the "aggressor." Sometimes this is relatively clear, such as when Iraq invaded Kuwait in 1990. But there are also

The League of Nations meets in 1923. It was one of the most ambitious attempts to implement the principles of collective security. Unfortunately, the world's great powers failed to live up to expectations. World War II followed sixteen years later.
SOURCE: © Hulton-Deutsch Collection/CORBIS

many instances in which there is disagreement. A vote in the United Nations on whether Israel is an "aggressor" vis-à-vis the Palestinians would certainly not be unanimous. A vote on whether the United States was the aggressor in Vietnam would have also yielded a similarly divided verdict. The point is not that these judgments are right or wrong, but merely that such things are not always unambiguous in international politics. And if nations cannot agree on who the aggressor is, how can they be expected to fall into line in punishing and/or deterring the aggressor?

Critics see even deeper flaws than the difficulty of agreeing on the identity of aggressors. In rejecting as illegitimate any forceful change of the existing order, collective security systems are inevitably biased in favor of those nations that benefit from the status quo. Hochman observes the League's goal of collective security "was, of course, identical with the defense of the post–World War I status quo."[36] Unfortunately, Germany and other nations viewed the World War I settlement as illegitimate, and they eventually possessed the power to challenge and change it. From the perspective of nations disadvantaged by the existing international order, collective security arrangements look very different. Rather than seeing collective security as a noble and high-minded attempt to preserve peace, they view it as a scheme for protecting the interests of those who benefit from the status quo. As E. H. Carr argues, "just as the ruling class in a community prays for domestic peace, which guarantees its own security and predominance . . . so international peace becomes a special vested interest of predominant powers."[37] Interestingly, both realists and Marxists tend to dismiss the lofty pronouncements about preserving peace as mere smokescreens for the underlying interests of dominant states.[38]

Even those who support collective security admit that it only works if the major powers share an interest in upholding the status quo. In considering whether collective security could work in post–Cold War Europe, for example, Charles and Clifford Kupchan hold out the possibility that "Russia will emerge as a benign democratic great power and that all of Europe's major states will share similar values and interests." If this happens, "the underpinnings for the successful functioning of a collective security system" will be in place.[39] Note the critical concession here: in order for collective security to work, all major powers must "share similar values and interests." Skeptics are quick to point out that if all major powers share the same basic values and interests, the chances for war are exceedingly low to begin with. Thus, collective security arrangements are most likely to work under conditions where there is no major threat to peace and most likely to fail when they are needed most.

Finally, in order for collective security systems to work, nations must be willing to respond to, punish, and deter acts of aggression whether or not their interests are threatened. Woodrow Wilson recognized that "the central idea of the League of Nations was that States must support each other *even when their national interests are not involved.*"[40] Wilson could have gone one step further: in some circumstances collective security could require states to act in *opposition to* their national interests. This is what differentiates collective security from power politics: the idea that nations can and will refrain from the use of force to advance their national interests and will use force when their interests are not at stake. Putting aside for the moment the issue of whether nations *should* do this, realists doubt that they *will* because there is no evidence that states ever have. Thus, realists argue that collective security arrangements are bound to fail for two basic reasons: the necessary common interests and values among great powers will rarely be achieved, and states will place their national interest above the security of others.

If realists have been the traditional critics of collective security, its supporters have been found among liberal ranks. Given the two major criticisms leveled by realists, the basis for liberal support should be fairly obvious. One of the basic assumptions of liberalism is the existence of a harmony of interests. Though few liberals have been so naïve as to believe that conflicts among nations do not exist, they have always been more inclined to see common interests as a basis for international cooperation. Collective security assumes that the common interest in preserving a peaceful international order outweighs any particular interests that might be advanced through war. A commitment to upholding international peace need not be predicated on any moral attachment to peace per se (though there is no reason to assume this cannot be part of the motivation) but rather enlightened self-interest. Though not part of a formal collective security arrangement, the international coalition that reversed the Iraqi conquest of Kuwait in 1991 is often cited as an example of the world community's coming together to resist aggression. Advocates of collective security concede that the League of Nations was a failure, but they warn against assuming that every effort at collective security is doomed. After all, the operation of power politics did not prevent World War II, either.

Security amidst anarchy Even if we conclude that world government and collective security are not terribly practical alternatives to power politics, we are still not without hope. Though there are certainly many examples of interstate relations that conform to the basic "anarchy leads to power politics" proposition, many others run counter to these expectations. According to Inis Claude, "in sober fact, most states coexist in reasonable harmony with most other states, most of the time; the exceptions to this passable state of affairs are vitally important, but they are exceptions nonetheless."[41] Consider for a moment relations among the Scandinavian states of Norway, Sweden, and Finland. No one seriously believes there is any chance these nations will go to war with each other, and even though they each have armed forces, there is no evidence they worry about the potential threat these forces pose. Why not? Is it a balance of power in Scandinavia that preserves the peace? Is it because one nation enjoys a preponderance of power? Is there a central Scandinavian government? Have they created a collective security system? No, no, no, and no. Why have these states managed to escape the sort of power politics we are told is the inevitable result of anarchy, self-help, and the security dilemma, and is there any larger lesson we can draw from their experience?

Scandinavia provides an example of what Karl Deutsch referred to as a **security community**—that is, a group of nations that shares a reasonable and prevailing expectation of nonviolence.[42] There is nothing that makes the use of violence impossible—they are still sovereign states possessing armed forces. It is simply that the use of force has become sufficiently improbable that it no longer guides or shapes their relations. Deutsch identified several critical factors for the development of security communities, the most important being shared political and social values among political elites and a history of reliable and predictable behavior. Someone who tried to convince the president of Finland of the need to prepare for war with Sweden by giving a lecture about anarchy, self-help, and uncertainty would be confronted with a question: sure, Sweden could invade tomorrow, but since it has not invaded on any other day over the past two centuries, why worry about it doing so now? Assuming that a Swedish invasion is not in the cards is a gamble in some sense, but it is a pretty safe one. Though the emergence of security communities may be uncommon, they nonetheless make a significant point: international anarchy does not *inevitably* lead to power politics. There have been and still are parts of the world that are anarchic yet "seem not to be subject to the kind of interstate relations that realists talk about."[43]

In recent years, constructivists have offered a more direct challenge to the realist proposition that international anarchy necessarily leads to power politics. Alexander Wendt states the question succinctly: "Does the absence of centralized political authority force states to play competitive power politics?" Realists answer this question in the affirmative. Wendt's answer is equally straightforward: "Self-help and power politics do not follow logically or causally from anarchy."[44] Understanding exactly why not is somewhat complicated.

The basic premise of constructivism is that the behavior of social actors, be they individuals like you and me or nations, is shaped by their identities and prevailing beliefs and norms about how actors with those identities should behave. Men and women, for example, often engage in different behaviors because their actions are

security community A group of nations among whom exists the prevailing and widely accepted expectation of nonviolence.

shaped by prevailing norms that they are socialized into accepting about what is appropriate for "men" and "women." Men, for example, are overwhelmingly more likely to make marriage proposals in our culture than women. Why is this? If you asked men why they believed they were responsible for making the proposal, you would find out they have a certain image in their mind of the way men are supposed to behave and they behave accordingly. There is nothing "natural" or "inevitable" about this practice; it is simply a socially constructed behavioral norm that men (and women) have come to accept.

Constructivists argue that nations (or the people who make decisions in their name) are influenced by prevailing beliefs and norms about how states should behave. On the question of power politics, John Vasquez offers a good summary of the constructivist perspective. He begins with a simple restatement of constructivism's basic premise: "I assume that any theory of world politics that has an impact on practice is not only a tool for understanding, but also helps construct a world." If nations engage in power politics it is "not because that behavior is natural or inherent in the structure of reality, but because realism has been accepted as a guide that tells leaders (and followers) the most appropriate way to behave." Thus, if we tell ourselves that nations should and will act in certain ways, we create "a kind of self-fulfilling prophecy."[45] It is not anarchy but rather "realist folklore [that] has provided a guide and cultural inheritance for Western states that has shaped and patterned the behavior of major states."[46] It is no accident that realism seems most accurate when we look at the behavior of European states over the past few centuries, since this is where realist theory has been most influential. But "once you move to the periphery where nations were not socialized to realist theory, states do not behave this way."[47]

Even within the context of anarchy, according to constructivists, there are alternatives to power politics. If prevailing conceptions of how states should behave change, there is nothing about anarchy that dictates that they continue to engage in power politics. We saw this in the last chapter on the democratic peace. If leaders of democratic states accept the proposition that democracies do not go to war with other democracies, they will not view fellow democracies as threats even if the international system remains anarchic. If Finland and Sweden view each other as peaceful social democratic states that will not pose a threat to each other, there is nothing about anarchy that forces them into a competitive relationship. Anarchy does not have to lead to power politics. "Anarchy," according to Wendt, "is what states make of it."

CONCLUSION

Even those who see no alternative to power politics do not exactly sing its praises; it is treated as a regrettable inevitability, like death and taxes. It is hard to make a case in favor of insecurity, power struggles, and war. A recent statement of the inevitability of power politics begins with the caveat: "Nothing in this primer should be taken as an endorsement or glorification of power politics."[48] If we asked whether there were any *desirable* alternatives to power politics, almost everyone would answer yes. It is easy to imagine systems of international relations preferable to the one that has produced violence, death, and destruction on such a massive scale. The shortcomings of power politics are plain for all to see. The critical question, however, is whether there are any *feasible* alternatives.

It is often in the aftermath of great wars that people begin to reevaluate the nature of international politics and create institutions that might help prevent the recurrence of war: the creation of the Concert of Europe in the wake of the Napoleonic Wars, the League of Nations after World War I, and the United Nations after World War II are cases in point. Though the Cold War never resulted in a literal war, its ending has also prompted a reexamination of international politics. President Bush's vision of a "new world order" after the 1991 Gulf War was typical of the hopes for a better world that frequently emerge after major wars. But have we seen the emergence of a new world order, or just a slightly reshuffled version of the old world order? And if a new world order proves unattainable, is this because efforts to transform the international system are inevitably doomed to failure? Is there a better and feasible way to preserve international peace? These are the fundamental and enduring questions addressed by the debate over power politics.

POINTS OF VIEW
Does Power Politics Shape United States Strategy?

U.S. presidents are now required by law to provide the Congress with National Security Statements laying out their administration's foreign policy goals and objectives. Attached are the introductory summaries of the two most recent such statements in which the Clinton and Bush administrations spelled out their foreign policy visions. On one level both administrations were still trying to come to grips with the post–Cold War world, though the Bush administration's statement was profoundly influenced by the events of September 11, 2001. Like most public pronouncements on foreign policy, these National Security Statements try to strike a balance between realism and optimistic idealism. The statements also reflect many of the ideas and theories we have discussed in this chapter. Examine the statements with an eye toward how they deal with the question of power and power politics in international relations. Do they seem to be particularly influenced by one of the perspectives in this chapter? Do the two statements differ in their emphasis? What are some of the different ideas from both sides of the power politics debate that have shaped each administration's strategy? Have these different ideas been combined to create a coherent strategy or a contradictory mish-mash of conflicting ideas and objectives?

The National Security Strategy of the United States of America

Preface
William Jefferson Clinton
The White House, January 11, 2000

As we approach the beginning of the twenty-first century, the United States remains the world's most powerful force for peace, prosperity and the universal values of democracy and freedom. Our nation's challenge—and our responsibility—is to sustain that role by harnessing the forces of global integration for the benefit of our own people and people around the world.

These forces of integration offer us an unprecedented opportunity to build new bonds among individuals and nations, to tap the world's vast human potential in support of shared aspirations, and to create a brighter future for our children. But they also present new, complex challenges. The same forces that bring us closer increase our interdependence, and make us more vulnerable to forces like extreme nationalism, terrorism, crime, environmental damage and the complex flows of trade and investment that know no borders.

To seize these opportunities, and move against the threats of this new global era, we are pursuing a forward-looking national security strategy attuned to the realities of our new era. This report, submitted in accordance with Section 603 of the Goldwater-Nichols Defense Department Reorganization Act of 1986, sets forth that strategy. Its three core objectives are:

- To enhance our security.

- To bolster America's economic prosperity.

- To promote democracy abroad.

Over the past five years, we have been putting this strategy in place through a network of institutions and arrangements with distinct missions, but a common purpose—to secure and strengthen the gains of democracy and free markets while turning back their enemies. Through this web of institutions and arrangements, the United States and its partners in the international community are laying a foundation for security and prosperity in the twenty-first century.

This strategy encompasses a wide range of initiatives: expanded military alliances like NATO, its Partnership for Peace, and its partnerships with Russia and Ukraine; promoting free trade through the World Trade Organization and the move toward free trade areas by nations in the Americas and elsewhere around the world; strong arms control regimes like the Chemical Weapons Convention and the Comprehensive Nuclear Test Ban Treaty; multinational coalitions combating terrorism, corruption, crime and drug trafficking; and binding international commitments to protect the environment and safeguard human rights.

The United States must have the tools necessary to carry out this strategy. We have worked diligently within the parameters of the Balanced Budget Agreement to preserve and provide for the readiness of our armed forces while meeting priority military challenges identified in the 1997 Quadrennial Defense Review (QDR). The QDR struck a careful balance between near-term readiness, long-term modernization and quality of life improvements for our men and women in uniform. It ensured that the high readiness levels of our forward-deployed and "first-to-fight" forces would be maintained. The priority we attach to maintaining a high-quality force is reflected in our budget actions. This fiscal year, with Congress' support for the Bosnia and Southwest Asia non-offset emergency supplemental funds, we were able to protect our high payoff readiness accounts. Next year's Defense Budget increases funding for readiness and preserves quality of life for military personnel.

Although we have accomplished much on the readiness front, much more needs to be done. Our military leadership and I are constantly reevaluating the readiness of our forces and addressing problems in individual readiness areas as they arise. I have instructed the Office of Management and Budget and the National Security Council to work with the Department of Defense to formulate a multi-year plan with the necessary resources to preserve military readiness, support our troops, and modernize the equipment needed for the next century. I am confident that our military is—and will continue to be—capable of carrying out our national strategy and meeting America's defense commitments around the world.

We must also renew our commitment to America's diplomacy—to ensure that we have the superb diplomatic representation that our people deserve and our interests demand. Every dollar we devote to preventing conflicts, promoting democracy, and stopping the spread of disease and starvation brings a sure return in security and savings. Yet international affairs spending today totals just one percent of the federal budget—a small fraction of what America invested at the start of the Cold War when we chose engagement over isolation. If America is to continue to lead the world by its own example, we must demonstrate our own commitment to these priority tasks. This is also why we must pay our dues to the United Nations.

Protecting our citizens and critical infrastructures at home is an essential element of our strategy. Potential adversaries—whether nations, terrorist groups or criminal organizations—will be tempted to disrupt our critical infrastructures, impede government operations, use weapons of mass destruction against civilians, and prey on our citizens overseas. These challenges demand close cooperation across all levels of government—federal, state and local—and across a wide range of agencies, including the Departments of Defense and State, the Intelligence Community, law enforcement, emergency services, medical care providers and others. Protecting our critical infrastructure requires new partnerships between government and industry. Forging these new structures will be challenging, but must be done if we are to ensure our safety at home and avoid vulnerabilities that those wishing us ill might try to exploit in order to erode our resolve to protect our interests abroad.

The United States has profound interests at stake in the health of the global economy. Our future prosperity depends upon a stable international financial system and robust global growth. Economic stability and growth are essential for the spread of free markets and their integration into the global economy. The forces necessary for a healthy global economy are also those that deepen democratic liberties: the free flow of ideas and information, open borders and easy travel, the rule of law, fair and even-handed enforcement, protection for consumers, a skilled and educated work force. If citizens tire of waiting for democracy and free markets to deliver a better life for them, there is a real risk that they will lose confidence in democracy and free markets. This would pose great risks not only for our economic interests but for our national security.

We are taking a number of steps to help contain the current financial turmoil in Asia and other parts of the world. We are working with other industrialized nations, the International Monetary Fund and the World Bank to spur growth, stop the financial crisis from spreading, and help the victims of financial turmoil. We have also intensified our efforts to reform international trade and financial institutions: building a stronger and more accountable global trading system, pressing forward with market-opening initiatives, advancing the protection of labor and the environment and doing more to ensure that trade helps the lives of ordinary citizens across the globe.

At this moment in history, the United States is called upon to lead—to organize the forces of freedom and progress; to channel the unruly energies of the global economy into positive avenues; and to advance our prosperity, reinforce our democratic ideals and values, and enhance our security.

SOURCE: Accessed at: http://clinton2.nara.gov/WH/EOP/NSC/html/documents/nssrpref.html.

The National Security Strategy of the United States of America

George W. Bush
The White House, September 17, 2002

The great struggles of the twentieth century between liberty and totalitarianism ended with a decisive victory for the forces of freedom—and a single sustainable model for national success: freedom, democracy, and free enterprise. In the twenty-first century, only nations that share a commitment to protecting basic human rights and guaranteeing political and economic freedom will be able to unleash the potential of their people and assure their future prosperity. People everywhere want to be able to speak freely; choose who will govern them; worship as they please; educate their children—male and female; own property; and enjoy the benefits of their labor. These values of freedom are right and true for every person, in every society—and the duty of protecting these values against their enemies is the common calling of freedom-loving people across the globe and across the ages.

Today, the United States enjoys a position of unparalleled military strength and great economic and political influence. In keeping with our heritage and principles, we do not use our strength to press for unilateral advantage. We seek instead to create a balance of power that favors human freedom: conditions in which all nations and all societies can choose for themselves the rewards and challenges of political and economic liberty. In a world that is safe, people will be able to make their own lives better. We will defend the peace by fighting terrorists and tyrants. We will preserve the peace by building good relations among the great powers. We will extend the peace by encouraging free and open societies on every continent.

Defending our Nation against its enemies is the first and fundamental commitment of the Federal Government. Today, that task has changed dramatically. Enemies in the past needed great armies and great industrial capabilities to endanger America. Now, shadowy networks of individuals can bring great chaos and suffering to our shores for less than it costs to purchase a single tank. Terrorists are organized to penetrate open societies and to turn the power of modern technologies against us.

To defeat this threat we must make use of every tool in our arsenal—military power, better homeland defenses, law enforcement, intelligence, and vigorous efforts to cut off terrorist financing. The war against terrorists of global reach is a global enterprise of uncertain duration. America will help nations that need our assistance in combating terror. And America will hold to account nations that are compromised by terror, including those who harbor terrorists—because the allies of terror are the enemies of civilization. The United States and countries cooperating with us must not allow the terrorists to develop new home bases. Together, we will seek to deny them sanctuary at every turn.

The gravest danger our Nation faces lies at the crossroads of radicalism and technology. Our enemies have openly declared that they are seeking weapons of mass destruction, and evidence indicates that they are doing so with determination. The United States will not allow these efforts to succeed. We will build defenses against ballistic missiles and other means of delivery. We will cooperate with other nations to deny, contain, and curtail our enemies' efforts to acquire dangerous technologies. And, as a matter of common sense and self-defense, America will act against such emerging threats before they are fully formed. We cannot defend America and our friends by hoping for the best. So we must be prepared to defeat our enemies' plans, using the best intelligence and proceeding with deliberation. History will judge harshly those who saw this coming danger but failed to act. In the new world we have entered, the only path to peace and security is the path of action.

As we defend the peace, we will also take advantage of an historic opportunity to preserve the peace. Today, the international community has the best chance since the rise of the nation-state in the seventeenth century to build a world where great powers compete in peace instead of continually prepare for war. Today, the world's great powers find ourselves on the same side—united by common dangers of terrorist violence and chaos. The United States will build on these common interests to promote global security. We are also increasingly united by common values. Russia is in the midst of a hopeful transition, reaching for its democratic future and a partner in the war on terror. Chinese leaders are discovering that economic freedom is the only source of national wealth. In time, they will find that social and political freedom is the only source of national greatness. America will encourage the advancement of democracy and economic openness in both nations, because these are the best foundations for domestic stability and international order. We will strongly resist aggression from other great powers—even as we welcome their peaceful pursuit of prosperity, trade, and cultural advancement.

Finally, the United States will use this moment of opportunity to extend the benefits of freedom across the globe. We will actively work to bring the hope of democracy, development, free markets, and free trade to every corner of the world. The events of September 11, 2001, taught us that weak states, like Afghanistan, can pose as great a danger to our national interests as strong states. Poverty does not make poor people into terrorists and murderers. Yet poverty, weak institutions, and corruption can make weak states vulnerable to terrorist networks and drug cartels within their borders.

The United States will stand beside any nation determined to build a better future by seeking the rewards of liberty for its people. Free trade and free markets have proven their ability to lift whole societies out of poverty—so the United States will work with individual nations, entire regions, and the entire global trading community to build a world that trades in freedom and therefore grows in prosperity. The United States will deliver greater development assistance through the New Millennium Challenge Account to nations that govern justly, invest in their people, and encourage economic freedom. We will also continue to lead the world in efforts to reduce the terrible toll of HIV/AIDS and other infectious diseases.

In building a balance of power that favors freedom, the United States is guided by the conviction that all nations have important responsibilities. Nations that enjoy freedom must actively fight terror. Nations that depend on international stability must help prevent the spread of weapons of mass destruction. Nations that seek international aid must govern themselves wisely, so that aid is well spent. For freedom to thrive, accountability must be expected and required.

We are also guided by the conviction that no nation can build a safer, better world alone. Alliances and multilateral institutions can multiply the strength of freedom-loving nations. The United States is committed to lasting institutions like the United Nations, the World Trade Organization, the Organization of American States, and NATO as well as other long-standing alliances. Coalitions of the willing can augment these permanent institutions. In all cases, international obligations are to be taken seriously. They are not to be undertaken symbolically to rally support for an ideal without furthering its attainment.

Freedom is the non-negotiable demand of human dignity; the birthright of every person—in every civilization. Throughout history, freedom has been threatened by war and terror; it has been challenged by the clashing wills of powerful states and the evil designs of tyrants; and it has been tested by widespread poverty and disease. Today, humanity holds in its hands the opportunity to further freedom's triumph over all these foes. The United States welcomes our responsibility to lead in this great mission.

SOURCE: Accessed at www.whitehouse.gov/nsc/nss.html

CHAPTER SUMMARY

- Fear and insecurity, the pursuit of power, the use of force, and the ever-present possibility of war—that is, power politics—are often presented as inevitable, if regrettable, realities of international politics. For realists in particular, there is no avoiding power politics in an anarchic international system that lacks any mechanism but self-help to provide security for states.

- Despite this agreement on the inevitability of power politics, realists differ on the dynamics of power politics. Balance of power theorists assume that states tend to align with the most powerful nations. Balance of threat theorists predict that states will align against whatever powers appear to pose the greatest threat, regardless of whether they are the most powerful. Similarly, preponderance theorists argue that nations align on the basis of interests, with the generic distinction being status quo versus revisionist states.

- Balance of power theory predicts the emergence of balances of power in international politics, whereas balance of threat and preponderance theories anticipate imbalances of power.

- Despite their differences, all three theories assume the inevitability of power politics.

- Liberals have historically rejected the realist claim that there is no alternative to power politics. Though some more idealistic liberals have advocated the creation of world government, most have sought more modest collective security arrangements.

- Collective security, which was the principle behind the League of Nations, posits an organized community of states whose combined power will preserve peace by deterring possible aggressors. Collective security transcends power politics, not by eliminating the need for power, but by replacing self-help with community assistance.

- Critics claim that collective security arrangements have rarely worked and have several fundamental flaws. The requirement that states be willing to use force even when their national interests are not threatened is considered unrealistic. Most important, collective security is unlikely to work when it is needed most—that is, when major powers reject the status quo and are willing to change it by force.

- More recently, constructivists have argued that world government and/or complex collective security arrangements are not essential to overcome power politics.

Power politics can be (and has been) transcended by shared expectations, beliefs, and images that allow states to see each other as nonthreatening.

CRITICAL QUESTIONS

1. How and why does anarchy supposedly lead to power politics?

2. What are the similarities and differences between power politics and collective security?

3. Is world government necessary to overcome the negative consequences of anarchy?

4. How do balance of power and balance of threat theory explain the peace of the Cold War?

5. Does the post–Cold War world appear to conform to balance of power, balance of threat, or preponderance theory?

KEY TERMS

anarchy, anarchic 123
balance of power theory 125
balance of threat theory 127
bandwagoning 126
collective security 131
degree of power 128
degree of satisfaction 128
hegemonic stability theory 128
power 124
power politics 121
preponderance theory 128
security community 135
security dilemma 123
self-help 123

FURTHER READINGS

A classic analysis of power politics and balance of power theory that remains essential reading despite the passage of time is Inis Claude, *Power and International Relations* (New York: Random House, 1962). A recent argument for the inevitability of power politics is presented in Stanley Michalak. *A Primer in Power Politics* (Wilmington, DE: Scholarly Resources, 2001). An influential restatement of balance of power theory is Kenneth Waltz, *Theory of International*

Politics (Reading, MA: Addison-Wesley, 1979). Balance of threat theory is most clearly presented in Stephen Walt, *The Origins of Alliances* (Ithaca, NY: Cornell University Press, 1989). Randall Schweller's *Deadly Imbalances: Tripolarity and Hitler's Strategy for World Conquest* (New York: Columbia University Press, 1998) is a fascinating application of balance of power and threat theories for understanding the origins of World War II. The best statement of preponderance theory is still A. F. K. Organski and Jacek Kugler, *The War Ledger* (Chicago: University of Chicago Press, 1980). In addition to Inis Claude's *Power and International Relations,* a good (though critical) overview of collective security is presented in Earl Ravenal, "An Autopsy of Collective Security," *Political Science Quarterly* 90 (Winter 1975–76): 697–714. A more favorable assessment is provided by Charles Kupchan and Clifford Kupchan, "The Promise of Collective Security," *International Security* 60 (Summer 1995): 52–61. The constructivist critique of power politics can be found in Alexander Wendt, *Social Theory of International Politics* (Cambridge: Cambridge University Press, 1999), especially chapter 6, and John Vasquez, *The War Puzzle* (Cambridge: Cambridge University Press, 1993), especially chapter 3.

POWER POLITICS ON THE WEB

www.wfa.org
Website of the World Federalist Organization, which seeks the "establishment of a democratic federal world government." Its president is John Anderson, former Republican congressman from Illinois and Independent Presidential candidate in 1980.

www.yale.edu/lawweb/avalon/leagcov.htm
The full text of the Covenant of the League of Nations, a classic statement of the ideals of collective security, especially Article 16.

www.cunr.org
Website of the Campaign for United Nations Reform. One of this organization's main goals is strengthening the United Nations so that it can fulfill the mission laid out in its charter, including "preserving peace."

www.whitehouse.gov/nsc/nss.html
The full text of the Bush administration's 2002 National Security Strategy statement.

NOTES

[1] John Vasquez, *The Power of Power Politics: From Classical Realism to Neotraditionalism* (Cambridge: Cambridge University Press, 1998), p. 168.

[2] Kenneth Waltz, *Man, the State and War* (New York: Columbia University Press, 1959), p. 205.

[3] Stanley Michalak, *A Primer in Power Politics* (Wilmington, DE: Scholarly Resources Books, 2001), p. 173.

[4] Kenneth Waltz, *Theory of International Politics* (Reading, MA: Addison-Wesley, 1979), p.102.

[5] Ibid., pp. 103–104, emphasis added.

[6] Waltz, *Man, the State and War,* p. 201.

[7] Waltz, *Theory of International Politics,* p. 111, emphasis added.

[8] Quoted in Waltz, *Man, the State and War,* p. 160.

[9] John Mearsheimer, *The Tragedy of Great Power Politics* (New York: W.W. Norton, 2001), p. 345.

[10] Michael P. Sullivan, *Power in Contemporary International Politics* (Columbia, SC: University of South Carolina Press, 1990), p. 76.

[11] Waltz, *Man, the State and War.,* p. 160.

[12] Mearsheimer, p. 55.

[13] Geoffrey Blainey, *The Causes of War* (New York: The Free Press, 1973), p. 110.

[14] Waltz, *Theory of International Politics,* p. 121.

[15] Ibid., p. 119

[16] A. F. K. Organski, *World Politics* (New York: Alfred A. Knopf, 1968), p. 274.

[17] Stephen Walt, *The Origins of Alliances* (Ithaca, NY: Cornell University Press, 1989), pp. 18–19.

[18] Waltz, *Theory of International Politics,* p. 124.

[19] Walt, *Origins of Alliances,* p. 25.

[20] Ibid., pp. 265–64.

[21] The best overall statement of preponderance theory, which this discussion draws heavily on, is provided by A. F. K. Organski, *World Politics* (New York: Alfred A. Knopf, 1968), pp. 338–76; and A. F. K. Organski and Jacek Kugler, *The War Ledger* (Chicago: University of Chicago Press, 1980).

[22] See Randall Schweller, *Deadly Imbalances: Tripolarity and Hitler's Strategy of World Conquest* (New York: Columbia University Press, 1998).

[23] Organski, *World Politics,* pp. 371–72.

[24] Inis Claude, cited in Sullivan, *Power in Contemporary World Politics,* p. 79.

[25] Ibid., p. 370.

[26] Gwynne Dyer, "World War, Change and the Bankrupt Nation-state System," *Chicago Tribune,* May 23, 1989, p. 13.

27 Waltz, *Theory of International Politics,* p. 102.

28 Norman Cousins, cited in Inis Claude, *Power in International Relations* (New York: Random House, 1962), p. 207.

29 Ibid., p. 208.

30 Cited in Thomas L. Prangle and Peter J. Ahrensdorf, *Justice among Nations: On the Moral Basis of Power and Peace* (Lawrence: University of Kansas Press, 1999), p. 246.

31 David W. Ziegler, *War, Peace and International Politics* (New York: HarperCollins, 1993), p. 302.

32 Earl C. Ravenal, "An Autopsy of Collective Security," *Political Science Quarterly* 90, no. 4 (Winter 1975–76): 702.

33 John Mearsheimer, "The False Promise of International Institutions," in *Theories of War and Peace,* ed. Michael Brown, Owen Cole, Sean Lynn-Jones, and Steven Miller (Cambridge, MA: MIT University Press, 1998), p. 355.

34 Cited in Claude, *Power in International Relations,* pp. 96–97.

35 Charter provisions cited in Michalak, *Primer in Power Politics,* p. 195.

36 Jiri Hochman, *The Soviet Union and the Failure of Collective Security* (Ithaca, NY: Cornell University Press, 1984), p. 174.

37 Edward Hallett Carr, *The Twenty Years' Crisis, 1919–1939* (New York: Harper & Row, 1964), p. 82.

38 For the Marxist view, see C. Dale Fuller, "Lenin's Attitude Toward an International Organization for the Maintenance of Peace, 1914–1917," *Political Science Quarterly* 64, no. 2 (June 1949): 245–61.

39 Charles Kupchan and Clifford Kupchan, "The Promise of Collective Security," *International Security,* 60, no. 1 (Summer 1995): 60.

40 Quoted in Ravenal, "Autopsy of Collective Security," p. 712.

41 Claude, *Power in International Relations,* p. 213.

42 Karl Deutsch et. al., *Political Community and the North Atlantic Area* (Princeton: Princeton University Press, 1957).

43 Vasquez, *The Power of Power Politics,* p. 211.

44 Alexander Wendt, "Anarchy Is What States Make of It: The Social Construction of Power Politics," *International Organization* 46, no. 2 (Spring 1992): 391, 394.

45 John Vasquez, *The War Puzzle* (Cambridge: Cambridge University Press, 1993), p. 87.

46 Ibid., p. 196.

47 Ibid., p. 116.

48 Michalak, *Primer in Power Politics,* xii.

CHAPTER SIX

FREE TRADE

Debates over the North American Free Trade Agreement (NAFTA) and protests at global economic forums indicate that conflicts over trade issues are deepening. This chapter focuses on a critical aspect of these debates—the desirability of free trade. A basic principle of the post–World War II global economic order, free trade has been part of a liberal prescription for international relations for almost two hundred years. Free trade is seen as desirable because it allows consumers to buy what they need and want for the lowest price regardless of where in the world it is produced. Free trade serves the interests of consumers (and everyone is a consumer) while promoting economic efficiency. Just as nations practice free trade within their borders, they should practice free trade across their borders. Critics reply that there are times when, and very good reasons why, nations might not want to pursue free trade. Marxists and feminists (and even many liberals) fear the impact of free trade on economically vulnerable segments of society. Even if free trade does promote economic efficiency, there may occasionally be other social considerations and values that take precedence. Realists, who tend to think about international economics in terms of national security, worry about becoming dependent on other nations for essential commodities. These intellectual conflicts are likely to fuel political conflicts over trade for some time to come.

By now the scene is familiar: the heads of the world's major economies meet amid tight security as protestors and police clash in the streets. In recent years these protests have become more intense and violent, leading many to consider abandoning such high-profile summits altogether or convening them in remote settings where large protests are more difficult. It is no coincidence that these protests are taking place at summits that focus on international economic issues policy. Twenty or thirty years ago, similar meetings did not elicit the same reactions. The frequency and severity of these protests are perhaps the most vivid indicator of the increasing significance and contentiousness of international economic issues.

Though it might be fair to say the protesters share a general unease about the shape and direction of their global economy, one is struck by the diversity of groups as revealed by the signs and banners. The protesters run the gamut from traditional liberal social activists and environmentalists to more radical Marxist and anarchist revolutionaries. The issues and concerns that animate these divergent groups are also extremely varied. Some protest because they think the global economy increasingly benefits wealthy nations and multinational corporations at the expense of already marginalized groups in the world economy, locking poor nations in a cycle of poverty and misery. Others worry that workers in the advanced industrialized nations are seeing their wages and social welfare benefits pushed down because they are forced to compete with much cheaper labor in the developing world. Many fear that the world's environment and resources are being sacrificed to the demands of growth and corporate profits. Still others worry that international economic institutions and multinational corporations are taking power and authority away from democratically elected governments, eroding their sovereignty in the process.[1]

The list of grievances is long and complex. But it is possible to see unity in this diversity if we frame these issues as interrelated elements of a larger debate over *globalization*. Indeed, the general descriptor *antiglobalization* is often used to characterize these protests and protestors. Though it is certainly important to recognize that these diverse issues may be just facets of a single larger issue, it is still useful to examine the critical concerns separately. Doing this allows us to focus on the most important points of contention. For the sake of clarity and focus, it is occasionally necessary to make somewhat artificial separations and look at issues in isolation before we can understand how they fit together. The next three chapters focus on issues that all agree are at the heart of debates about the nature and future of the global political economy—trade, inequality, and sovereignty.

THE LIBERAL INTERNATIONAL ECONOMIC ORDER

In order to examine debates and concerns about the future of the global political economy, we need to begin with an understanding of the nature and origins of the current global economic system, particularly the rules and institutions that govern international trade. In general terms, the main outlines of the current global economy were set in place in the years immediately following World War II largely by the United States, which emerged from the war not only as the dominant military power in the world but also as the most powerful economy. The global economy it created was shaped by the recent historical experience of war and depression, the U.S.

economic interests, and a commitment to liberal economic theory. The system that emerged became known as the **Liberal International Economic Order (LIEO)**. The cornerstone of the postwar liberal economic order was the principle of free and open trade. As Stephen Krasner explains, "The fundamental objective of American foreign economic policy after the Second World War was to establish a regime in which the impediments to the movement of capital and goods were minimized."[2]

In formal terms, several institutions were designed to help create and sustain a liberal international order. The **World Bank** (officially known as the International Bank for Reconstruction and Development) and the **International Monetary Fund (IMF)** were established in 1944 at a conference in Bretton Woods, New Hampshire (which is why the postwar economic order is also sometimes referred to as the **Bretton Woods system**). The World Bank is a global lending agency whose initial purpose was, as its official name suggests, to aid in the reconstruction of Europe after the war. Later it would become a prime source of loans for economic development to the world's developing nations. The International Monetary Fund's major function is to provide short-term assistance to nations with balance of payments difficulties. Both institutions are supposed to operate in a manner that promotes liberal policies domestically and internationally—that is, free trade among nations and limited government intervention in domestic economies. The final element of the postwar liberal order was the **General Agreement on Tariffs and Trade (GATT)**. Created in 1947, GATT is the most important institution for international trade because its fundamental goal is the reduction of international tariffs (taxes on goods imported from other countries) to the lowest possible level. Since 1947, there have been a number of summits or talks (known as *rounds*) intended to move nations closer to a system of free trade. In January 1995, GATT became the **World Trade Organization (WTO)**. Even though the world has never achieved a completely free and open trading system without any barriers to sale of goods and services among nations, this is the ideal, the principle, upon which these institutions are based. And it is these international institutions—the IMF, the World Bank, and the WTO—that arouse the hostility of the protestors who have become fixtures at international economic summits.

The critical question, however, is *why* the United States and others believe that a liberal order based on free and open trade is a desirable objective. What was the motivation behind the creation of the LIEO? Part of the explanation lies in the perceived "lessons" derived from the Great Depression and World War II. After World War II, American decision makers traced the causes of the Great Depression of the 1930s to the **economic nationalism** of the 1920s. That is, throughout the 1920s the world's major economies, the United States included, used ever-increasing tariffs and quotas on foreign imports to protect domestic industries from foreign competition. Eventually, these tariffs and quotas undermined world trade, which contributed to the collapse of the global economy and the Great Depression. The Great Depression, in turn, was seen as critical to the collapse of democracy and the rise of fascism, and thus war. Free trade, it was believed, was necessary to prevent a repetition of this course of events. In this way free trade was seen as providing political as well as economic benefits: free trade brings prosperity, which helps sustain democracy, which helps keep the peace.

There was also a good measure of self-interest driving the creation of the LIEO. Since the United States emerged from World War II as the only intact industrial economy, free trade was clearly in its economic interests—after all, where else would other nations buy things from? But the commitment to free trade was also based on a broader conviction that it would serve every individual's and every nation's interests in the long run. It was not merely self-interest, but enlightened self-interest. By promoting economic growth and prosperity, a system of free and open trade would be, to use a common metaphor, a rising tide that lifts all boats. It is this argument asserting mutual gains from free trade that ultimately provides the intellectual rationale for the postwar liberal order.

THE CASE FOR FREE TRADE

Why is free trade such a good idea? Why shouldn't governments protect their workers and industries from foreign competition? If there are winners and losers in the economic competition of free trade, how is it possible for everyone to benefit? If we want to answer these questions, it is best to return to those economists who first developed a theoretical defense of free trade, particularly **Adam Smith** (1723–1790) and **David Ricardo** (1772–1823). Even though Smith and Ricardo lived two centuries ago, the arguments in favor of free trade have not changed much in the interim. In their time Smith and Ricardo advocated free trade in place of prevailing policies and doctrines of **mercantilism.** Mercantilism was a set of trade policies designed to increase the wealth of each state through trade. This involved rigging trade rules so as to promote exports and reduce imports. The rationale was that if a country sold more goods than it bought from abroad, more gold would flow in than out, increasing the state's wealth. Mercantilist doctrine viewed a nation's trade policy as a means to increase a state's relative wealth and thus its power. It was economics in the service of politics. Smith and Ricardo opposed mercantilism, arguing for the removal of barriers to the importation of foreign goods because such restrictions reduced economic competition, promoted economic inefficiency, and harmed consumers by making them pay more for goods.

The origins of free trade Conflicts over trade issues are not new to our time. In the middle of the 1800s, England faced intense domestic debate over the repeal of what were known as the **Corn Laws.** These laws gave British growers of wheat, corn, and other grains a monopoly on the domestic market through a variety of means—government subsidies as well as restrictions on the export and import of grains. The practical result of these policies was that the price of grain and bread for the average person in Britain was much higher than it needed to be because there was restricted access to cheaper products from abroad. Part of the problem was that many poor people were still excluded from voting and political power and these laws benefited powerful landowners. Influenced by the writings of Smith and Ricardo, **Richard Cobden,** a prominent figure in the British Liberal Party, pushed for the repeal of these laws on the grounds that they benefited a few at the expense of the many (he also advanced the liberal argument that free trade would also lead to peace since it was cheaper to acquire commodities through trade than conquest). Though the Anti-Corn Law League had been founded in 1837, it took almost a decade to abolish the laws. Their repeal in 1846 marked the emergence of free trade as a theory converted

General Agreement on Tariffs and Trade (GATT) World organization of nations created in 1947 for the purpose of reducing tariffs and other obstacles to international trade. Resulted in series of meetings and agreements in subsequent decades (so-called "GATT Rounds") that reduced tariffs. Replaced in 1995 with the World Trade Organization (WTO).

World Trade Organization (WTO) Created in 1995 as a successor to GATT, the World Trade Organization is supposed to enforce international trade rules promoting free and open trade.

economic nationalism Policies designed to protect domestic industries from foreign competition.

Smith, Adam (1723–1790) A liberal economist and philosopher who argued for free trade. Coined the famous expression "the invisible hand" to describe the operation of a free market economy.

Ricardo, David (1772–1823) English economist known for his defense of international free trade and theory of comparative advantage.

mercantilism Trade policies designed to increase the wealth and power of a state vis-à-vis other states.

Corn Laws In the first half of the 1800s, these laws gave English farmers protection from foreign competition. Supporters of free trade claimed they protected inefficient farmers and forced consumers to pay too much for basic food items. Attempts to repeal these laws succeeded in 1846.

Cobden, Richard (1804–1865) Prominent figure in the British Liberal Party and a leading crusader for free trade and the repeal of the Corn Laws.

division of labor Individuals and/or nations specializing in the production of certain commodities.

comparative advantage, theory of The idea that all nations benefit when they produce those commodities each produces most efficiently. David Ricardo argued that free trade allows nations and consumers to benefit from their different comparative advantages.

autarky A policy of self-sufficiency in which a state attempts to cut itself off from the outside world. A policy of economic autarky would attempt to meet all a society's needs from its own resources.

into policy.[3] The historical popularity of free trade has fluctuated since then. For the next few decades of the mid- to late 1800s, trade barriers declined, especially within Europe. The last decades of the nineteenth century saw a waning enthusiasm for free trade. The years between World War I and World War II also witnessed increasing barriers to international trade.

Smith and Ricardo's defense of free trade was based on two relatively simple economic concepts, the division of labor and comparative advantage. The **division of labor** refers to the simple fact that people do not produce everything they need and want. We do not all build our own houses, make our own clothes, educate our children, or even change the oil in our cars. In all but the most primitive economies, there is a division of labor. Different people specialize in the production of certain commodities, and then they trade what they produce with people who produce other things. In modern economies this exchange occurs through the medium of currency, not barter: when we buy things with money, we are really exchanging what we produce (and got paid for) for things others have produced. This is the most efficient way to organize an economy. If we all had to make and provide for ourselves all the things we need and want, it would be wildly inefficient. We would all end up with fewer of the things we want and need. Thus, an efficient economic system at any level (local, national, or international) is based on a division of labor. And if there is a division of labor, trade is necessary to meet people's wants and needs.

But why does this trade have to be "free" trade, without taxes, tariffs, and other barriers? The answer is provided by Ricardo's **theory of comparative advantage.** Simply stated, the theory holds that people and nations should specialize in the production of those things they produce most efficiently and cheaply (that is, those commodities where they have an advantage compared to others) and trade these commodities with others who are specializing in what they do best. Nations possess different resources that lead to different comparative advantages—some nations produce oil or other scarce commodities, some have plentiful and cheap labor, some have agriculturally productive land, and others have favorable geographical locations for trade. Japan will probably never produce its own oil, Saudi Arabia will never grow a lot of rice, landlocked Chad will never be a center of shipping, and Canada is unlikely to produce much coffee. If these nations want to meet the needs and wants of their people, they need to specialize and trade. **Autarky,** or complete self-sufficiency, is not a practical or economical option.

In his *Principles of Political Economy and Taxation,* Ricardo illustrated his theory using the simple example of Portugal and England and the production of wine and cloth, arguing that Portugal produced good, cheap wine (while England did not) and England produced good, cheap cloth. Free trade allows the people of both England and Portugal to have good and cheap wine and cloth.[4] Thus, England should produce cloth, Portugal should make wine, and they should trade.

Let us use a different example to demonstrate the operation of comparative advantage. The people of Vermont and Florida all occasionally like to have maple syrup and orange juice as part of their breakfast. How are the people of these states to meet their desire to consume these commodities? One option is that the people of each state could produce both juice and syrup. Producing maple syrup would be no problem for the people of Vermont because the climate conditions are ideal for growing maple trees. Orange juice would be another matter because it would probably involve constructing huge greenhouses to grow orange trees and heating them in the winter. Vermonters *could* make their own orange juice, but it would end up costing a lot of money. The reverse can be said of the people of Florida and their production of orange juice (easy) and maple syrup (difficult and expensive). What to do? For Ricardo the answer was simple—each state should specialize in producing that commodity for which they have a comparative advantage and trade the commodity with others producing commodities for which they have an advantage. The Vermonters make maple syrup, Floridians make orange juice, and they trade with one another.

The problem is that free trade in orange juice will chase all the juice producers in Vermont out of business. Who, after all, would pay several more dollars a gallon for orange juice from Vermont than juice from Florida? In order for the orange juice producers of Vermont to survive, an import tax would have to be applied to artificially raise the price of juice from Florida. The same would have to be done to protect the maple syrup producers in Florida. But Ricardo would have argued that Vermont's orange juice and Florida's maple syrup producers should not be protected from competition. Protection would simply promote economic inefficiency and increase prices to consumers (thus reducing their ability to buy other things they want and need). Certainly there are interests that are harmed by free trade in the short term, most notably Vermont orange juice producers and Florida maple syrup producers. But from a larger long-term perspective, everyone is better off as a result of the efficiency that comes from free trade. This is the same argument Ricardo made for England and Portugal and the production of cloth and wine.

From the standpoint of economic theory, tariffs and other barriers to imports are bad because they distort the market. In the market, prices convey information to consumers about who is producing a commodity most efficiently. People reward efficient producers by buying their lower-priced goods and punish the inefficient by not purchasing their products. When these purchasing decisions are aggregated, the inefficient producers are driven out of business. When prices are artificially raised (or lowered) by government intervention, this information is not conveyed. As a result, inefficiency is not punished and efficiency is not rewarded. And in the long run the inefficient use of resources serves no one's interests.

Free trade within nations, free trade among nations Interestingly, virtually all nations accept the logic of free trade within their borders. In the United States, for example, one of the functions of the federal government under the Constitution is to prevent the adoption of restrictions on interstate trade. The state government of Tennessee, for example, could not impose taxes on cars imported from Michigan in order to protect the jobs of workers at the Saturn production plant located in that state. Such taxation would be considered a restraint on interstate trade and thus illegal. Everyone would probably agree that it would be a disaster if individual states within the United States could impose tariffs on goods coming from other states. The harm to the American economy if individual states pursued protectionism policies would be immense.

Advocates of free trade argue that the same basic logic that supports free trade *within* nations should be applied to trade *among* nations. If it makes sense to practice free trade between Minneapolis and St. Paul or Vermont and Florida, it makes just as much sense to practice free trade between the United States and Germany or Japan and Botswana. The economic logic of free trade is not altered merely because a political boundary is crossed. As Jagdish Bhagwati explains, "If one applies the logic of efficiency to the allocation of activity among all trading nations, and not merely *within* one's own nation—that alone would ensure that goods and services would be produced where it could be done most cheaply."[5] We can refer to this argument as the logic of extension—extending the logic that justifies free trade within nations, which virtually no one questions, to trade among nations.

The primacy of the consumer The interests of consumers lie at the heart of the case for free trade. But it is important to realize that from Smith and Ricardo's perspective everyone is a consumer. The distinction between producers and consumers is artificial—almost everyone is both a consumer and a producer. And as consumers, people are *always* better off if they can buy the things we want and need for the lowest possible price no matter where in the world it is produced—whether it comes from across town, across the state, from another state, or from the other side of the world. It should not matter where an item is made. We are better off because this arrangement leaves us with more money to buy other things we want and need. Consumers are never better off paying more.

Within this argument is also an implicit assumption about the compatibility of individual and collective interests. That is, if every individual consumer in a community is better off, it follows that the community as a whole is better off. In the case of free trade, this means that if free trade is in the best interests of every American consumer, it must follow that free trade is also in the best interest of the United States as a whole. The individual and collective interest is in harmony. Ricardo makes this implicit assumption explicit: "Under a system of perfectly free commerce, each country naturally devotes its capital and labor to such employments as are most beneficial to each. The pursuit of individual advantage is admirably connected with the universal good of the whole."[6]

It is here that the liberal roots of free trade doctrine become most apparent. One of the key assumptions of liberalism is the existence of a harmony of interests. This is also the underlying assumption of free market capitalism in general and free trade in particular: each individual and each nation pursuing their own economic self-interest unrestricted by government regulation results in a long-term situation where the interests of all are advanced. There is no conflict in terms of the economic interests of individuals and nations. In promoting economic efficiency, a system of free trade works to the benefit of all. To use some technical terminology, international trade is not a **zero-sum game** in which one consumer's or nation's gain is someone else's loss, but rather a **positive-sum game** in which all can benefit simultaneously. Economist Paul Krugman, one of the leading advocates of free trade, emphasizes the harmony of interests in an essay tellingly entitled "The Illusion of Conflict in International Trade." If trade is treated as something involving conflicts of interests among nations, Krugman fears that "trade will be treated as war, and the current system of relatively open world markets will disintegrate. . . . And that will be a shame . . . [because] the conflict among nations that so many policy intellectuals imagine prevails is an illusion; but is it an illusion that can destroy the reality of mutual gains from trade?"[7] It would be impossible to state the liberal argument more clearly: conflict is an illusion.

Given this analysis, advocates of free trade view government interventions and restrictions such as tariffs and quotas as devices that advance and protect sectional in-

zero-sum game A situation in which one actor's gain is another actor's loss (as opposed to a **positive-sum game**, in which actors can all gain simultaneously).

positive-sum game A "game" or situation in which the actors involved can all gain or benefit at the same time.

One of the major political battles involving trade occurred in 1993 over the North American Free Trade Agreement (NAFTA). Here Vice President Al Gore and Ross Perot debate its merits, with the former in favor and the latter opposed.
SOURCE: Markowitz Jeffrey/CORBIS SYGMA

terests and the expense of the broader public interest. A tariff on automobiles imported from abroad, for example, serves the short-term interests of the domestic automobile industry. Although this may seem like the wise course to pursue, in the long run it is not. The consequence of such a policy merely protects a relatively inefficient industry from competition, removes incentives to become more efficient, increases the price people must pay for automobiles, and thus decreases the amount of money they have to spend on other things they want and need. The benefits of protectionism may be immediate and tangible to that sector of the economy, but the benefits are short lived and illusory and come at the expense of consumers (who are often not as organized and politically powerful as particular industries and workers).

Contemporary challenges to free trade Even though the cornerstone of the postwar liberal order has been a commitment to free trade, the ideal of completely free and open trade has never been achieved. All nations, even those supposedly most committed to free trade, including the United States, have an array of tariffs and other restrictions. Nations have proven very ingenious in devising methods of protectionism. Though tariffs and quotas are the most obvious means of restricting imports, they are by no means the only ones available. There are a host of restrictions to trade known as **nontariff barriers.** Nations could impose a series of regulations on imported commodities that serve the same purpose as an outright tariff. An example is regulations requiring that imported agricultural goods meet certain quality and inspection requirements. Although these demands might seem reasonable on their face, if the result is that the imported goods have to sit around for days to be inspected, this can be as much of a problem as an outright ban. Perishable commodities sitting on the dock

nontariff barriers Policies designed to inhibit trade and imports without imposing direct tariffs on imports. Safety regulations that make it nearly impossible for foreign producers to sell their goods are an example.

or in warehouses are at disadvantage compared to domestic produce that can go right to market.

Another means of government intervention that runs contrary to the logic of free trade is government subsidies. If a government gives money to a company or industry that enables it to sell its product for a price that does not accurately reflect the costs of production, this is as much a violation of the principle of comparative advantage as a tariff that raises prices. When politicians accuse other countries of **dumping,** this is what they mean—selling something on the world market for less than it costs to produce, which is often made possible by government subsidies. Recent GATT and WTO negotiations have tried to deal with such practices, but this is much harder than dealing with explicit tariffs and quotas.

But even when nations agree in principle that free trade is a good thing, it has historically been difficult to maintain. Part of the problem is that even though people may agree in the abstract that free trade is in everyone's long-term best interest, there are short-term negative consequences. There are losers in the game of trade. Companies go out of business and workers lose their jobs. Such is the nature of economic competition and efficiency. These companies and workers are seldom comforted by the economic logic that they will be better off in the long run. Their dissatisfaction creates political problems for governments, which often feel strong pressures to protect industries from the negative consequences of international trade. This situation creates an incentive for governments to find ways to enjoy the benefits of free trade (i.e., access to others' markets) while avoiding the costs (i.e., threats to domestic industries). The temptation is to be a **free rider**—that is, let others practice free trade while you do not. The free rider enjoys all the benefits but pays none of the costs.

When we hear about disputes between the United States and its major trading partners in Western Europe and Japan, there are frequent accusations of unfair trade practices. This dispute largely boils down to nations who object to others as free riders: we practice free trade while you do not. The charge of "cheating" embodies this dilemma. But many contemporary conflicts over trade go further and are more deeply rooted than this. It is not merely the difficulty of actually practicing free trade when everyone agrees it would be desirable. The problem is that there is disagreement about whether free trade is always the best policy and the circumstances under which free trade might be a bad idea. There are some compelling arguments against free trade, and these tend to be more widely accepted in Europe and Japan than in the United States. There are alternatives to the theory (some might say ideology) of free trade.

WHAT'S WRONG WITH FREE TRADE

The case against free trade is not really an argument against free trade. There are very few who believe that nations should never practice free trade or that foreign imports should always be subject to tariffs and quotas. No one seriously believes that complete autarky is possible or desirable. The argument against free trade really amounts to skepticism about whether free trade is always the preferable policy. Even critics agree that much of the time, maybe most of the time, unrestricted trade is wise. But, they argue, there are other times when, and very good reasons why, nations might opt not

dumping Selling commodities to other nations for less than it costs to produce them.

free rider When an actor enjoys the benefits of policy without paying its share of the costs associated with that policy.

to practice free trade. The objection is that free trade has become an ideology within certain academic and policy circles, particularly in the United States, and those who question this ideology are viewed as the equivalent of people who deny that the earth is round. Paul Krugman, who was quoted earlier, suggests that anyone who does not see the wisdom of free trade is stupid and uniformed. The notion that there is any intellectually respectable position against free trade is simply not entertained. But the fact is that Adam Smith and David Ricardo have not been alone in thinking about international trade, and everyone who has thought seriously about the issue has not come to the same conclusion.

After spending several years in Asia, columnist and author James Fallows was struck by the difference between the way many there think about international trade compared to the perspective of decision makers in the United States. One symptom of this divergence in thinking about trade is the popularity of the German economist **Friedrich List** (1789–1846). Most Americans can get an economics degree without ever having read List; one certainly hears a lot less about him in the United States than Adam Smith and David Ricardo. Fewer still have actually read List's *The Natural System of Political Economy* (1841), which is probably the most powerful critique of Smith and Ricardo.[8] In Europe and Asia, according to Fallows, List's work remains influential. List did not argue that nations should never practice free trade. He did not reject free trade in principle, and this point needs to be emphasized. Most of the time and for most commodities, free trade is probably a good idea. Instead, List argued that Smith and Ricardo failed to recognize that there were also certain circumstances in which, for very good reasons, states might want to engage in some form of protectionism.

List's criticisms of free trade are not the only ones. List offered a decidedly conservative or realist critique of liberal trade doctrine. This will become evident as we deal with his major arguments. Criticisms of free trade have been offered from other perspectives as well. Marxist critiques analyze free trade within the general context of international capitalism. Feminists often worry about the impact of trade on women, an issue they feel is usually ignored. Interestingly, these seemingly odd ideological bedfellows make many of the same arguments. This paradox is reflected in the somewhat unusual coalition that has emerged in opposition to the economic aspects of contemporary globalization in which many on the political right and left find themselves aligned.

More efficient, but so what? The first major justification for free trade is that it promotes economic efficiency. When production and trade are based on the operation of comparative advantage, the most efficient producers survive and the less efficient go out of business. On purely economic grounds, critics of free trade such as List concede this point: free trade probably does lead to greater economic efficiency. But so what? This does not therefore settle the matter. Merely because something is economically the most efficient thing to do, does this automatically imply that it is what we should do? Not necessarily. This would be the logical conclusion only if economic efficiency were the be-all and end-all of economic policy. In the real world, however, policies need to balance a variety of values and considerations.

The fact is that as a society we do things and follow policies all the time that are inconsistent with strict standards of economic efficiency. For example, most societies

List, Friedrich (1789–1846) German economist critical of David Ricardo and free trade. Rejected the liberal notion that individuals advancing their own interests inevitably serve the interests of the larger community or nation. Argued that nations need to approach trade from the perspective of the national interest and the interests of the community as a whole.

spend the majority of their health care dollars on people in the last few years of their lives, people who have ceased being economically productive. If societies allocated their resources based solely on economic efficiency, there would certainly be other areas where this money could be better spent. If we adopted policies simply on the grounds of economic efficiency, what sort of health care systems would we have? What would we do with people who were no longer economically productive? Why do we spend all this money on the economically unproductive elements of out society? The fact is that we do so because other values and criteria influence our decisions. Economic efficiency is only one thing we take into consideration. Demonstrating that a policy promotes economic efficiency is an important component of policy debates, but it does not end these debates. Thus, even if we concede the economic efficiency argument to the proponents of free trade, this does not mean that they have carried the day.

Applying this point to international trade, we might imagine considerations that lead states not to practice free trade, even if the result is less economic efficiency. Take, for example, the case of Japan and rice. Rice produced in Japan costs a lot more than rice grown in the United States. If the logic of free trade were adopted and the principle of comparative advantage put into play, Japan's rice farmers would almost certainly be chased out of business as Japanese consumers bought the cheaper foreign rice (though there are some questions about whether foreign rice tastes the same to Japanese palates). But for the Japanese rice is more than just another food; it is a deeply meaningful part of their history and culture. A Japan that did not grow its own rice would be like a Germany that did not produce beer, a France that did not make cheese, or a United States that did not make automobiles. To an economist, these are just commodities and it should not matter where they are made. But most people are not economists. If preserving this part of Japanese culture requires them to restrict foreign imports, can we say this is wrong?

Other countries have a similar problem with small family farms, which are almost never competitive with huge agricultural corporations or cheap foreign imports. Pure free trade would almost certainly chase these small farms out of business because they are inefficient in many respects. But what if people like to have a quaint countryside with small villages and cute farms they can return to on the weekends? If a government restricts cheaper imports in order to protect these farms and the rural way of life, is this necessarily a wrongheaded policy? Smith and Ricardo would think so, but others might not be so dismissive. If the people of a country have to pay a bit more for domestic agricultural produce in order to preserve something else they value, perhaps this is an acceptable tradeoff in which strict considerations of economic efficiency lose out to broader cultural and lifestyle concerns.

The particulars of cases will vary, but the general point here is to question the underlying assumption often implicit in arguments for free trade that economic efficiency is *the* basis on which policies should be chosen. John Gray, a critic of global free trade, concedes the economic argument: "There is not much doubt that the free market is the most *economically efficient* type of capitalism." He goes on to note that "for most economists that ends the matter."[9] For Gray and others, obviously, it does not end the debate. Instead, economic efficiency is portrayed as *a* criterion. Evaluating the implications of policies for economic efficiency is only the beginning of the debate, not its beginning and end.

A traditional Japanese rice farm whose product cannot compete with cheaper rice from the United States. The Japanese government protects domestic rice producers from foreign competition. David Ricardo would not have approved.

SOURCE: © Robert Essel NYC/CORBIS

Free trade within nations, free trade among nations? No. Friedrich List's most forceful criticism of theorists such as Smith and Ricardo stemmed from what he saw as their failure to recognize the critical difference between how states related to one another and how people interact within states. When this distinction between international and domestic relations is taken into account, it does not follow that because free trade makes sense within nations it makes just as much sense among them. Within national boundaries people do not have to worry much about becoming dependent on others for things they need because this dependence is unlikely to be used as leverage. For example, someone who is pro-choice does not have to worry that the grocery store will withhold food until they change their position. The people of Florida do not have to worry that the people of Vermont will refuse to sell them maple syrup unless they vote the right way in the presidential election. Within nations, people do not have to be concerned with becoming dependent on one another. Nations, however, do need to worry about dependence and power vis-à-vis other nations. International economics cannot be divorced from considerations of international politics.

Thus, List argued that if a nation can produce commodities that it really needs, it should do so rather than become dependent on others, even if these commodities can be purchased more cheaply from abroad. Take, for example, something like steel or computer chips. These are commodities that a modern industrial and technological economy needs to function. Let us assume that country A can manufacture steel for $20 a ton and chips for $.50 a piece. If country B can produce steel for $18 and chips for $.40, what should country A do? The logic of free trade and comparative advantage would dictate that country A should buy steel and chips from country B and get out of the steel and chips business. Country A should not impose a tariff or quota on steel and chip imports in order to protect its own industries. For List, however, this would be a ludicrous policy. If A becomes totally dependent on B for these vital commodities, B will have potential power or leverage over A in the future. In this case, it may be advisable for A to impose tariffs in order to stay in the steel and chip businesses even though these commodities could be purchased more cheaply from abroad.

Sometimes nations have no option but to be dependent on foreign sources. Japan, for example, needs oil but produces none of its own. There is nothing Japan can do about the fact that it does not have any domestic oil reserves. Furthermore, for most things it really does not matter if a nation becomes dependent on others. Being dependent on another nation for honey or sneakers is not the same as being dependent on that nation for oil or steel. List would simply argue that there are some vital commodities that nations should retain the ability to produce for themselves if they can. If it requires some deviation from the rules of free trade to do so, then so be it.

List also argued that it is sometimes necessary to protect **infant industries** from foreign competition. When a nation first begins producing a commodity, it might be difficult for that industry to compete with established producers elsewhere in the world. If the logic of free trade were applied, these industries would "die in the cradle," so to speak. List pointed out that many industries in the United States and Britain developed behind a wall of protection before the adoption of free trade. Foreshadowing some of List's themes, Alexander Hamilton made a very similar argument in the early years of the American republic: "to maintain, between recent establishments of one country, and the long-matured establishments of another, a competition upon equal terms . . . is in most cases, impracticable."[10] So there are times when some level of protection from more efficient foreign competition is necessary to promote economic and industrial development.[11]

Some take List's argument one step further, arguing that nations can, and sometimes should, use trade policy not merely to protect their industries but also to undermine the industries of other countries. Assume, for example, that country A produces steel for $20 a ton and B for $18. Under free trade, country A would go out of the steel business and buy its steel from B. But country A could stay in the steel business by imposing a tariff of $2 or more to protect its domestic steel industry. And country A could go one step further by subsidizing its domestic steel industry and selling its steel on the world market at a loss (maybe $17.00 a ton) in order to drive country B out of the steel business and make it dependent on A. This turns the logic of free trade and comparative advantage on its head. This sort of **predatory pricing** policy is an example of what is sometimes referred to as **strategic trade policy,** or consciously using trade policy to enhance national power and leverage over others.

These types of policies and concerns derive from List's conviction that trade and economic policy cannot and should not be separated from national security policy. In an anarchic world nations have to worry about their security in ways that people and groups within nations do not. This is why free trade might not make as much sense among nations as it does within. The economic logic may be the same, but the political situation is very different. Nations have to consider the implications of trade policy in terms of their power over, and dependence upon, others. List criticizes "Adam

PART II *Controversies*

---

infant industries Industries at early stages of their development, particularly when the same industries are already well developed (i.e., mature) in other nations.

predatory pricing Setting the price of a commodity with the intention of driving others out of business, even if this requires selling the commodity for less than it costs to produce.

strategic trade policy Policies designed to enhance national power and encourage other nations to become dependent as a means of gaining leverage over them.

Smith's doctrine. . . . [because it] ignores the very nature of nationalities, seeks almost entirely to exclude politics and the State, presupposes the existence of a state of perpetual peace and of universal union, underrates the values of national manufacturing power, and the means of obtaining it, and demands absolute freedom of trade."[12]

In the international realm, trade and economics cannot be divorced from issues of politics, conflict, and the ever-present possibility of war. And in the final analysis a nation's power rests on its ability to produce, not consume. In this sense, List's criticisms of, and reservations about, free trade are consistent with a realist perspective. His emphasis on the different environment in which states operate, his focus on economic power and production as the foundation of national power, and his concern about the consequences of dependence on other nations embodies and is consistent with a realist view of the world. Whereas liberals tend to see international trade as a positive-sum game in which all can become better off at the same time, List and realists are more inclined to approach trade as a zero-sum affair in which the gains of one are losses for others. Recall that List entitled his treatise on international trade *The National System of Political Economy*. He chose his title carefully and purposefully. List thought that Smith and Ricardo provided a theory of *private* political economy that spoke to the interests and motivations of individuals. List thought it necessary to approach issues of trade in terms of the motivations and interests of nations as well.

Consumers and the nation We have already noted that the consumer lies at the heart of the case for free trade. Consumers are better off when they can buy things for the lowest price regardless of where it is produced. This allows them to buy more of what they want and need. And since everyone is a consumer, everyone's interests are advanced by free trade. Furthermore, if each individual in a nation is better off, it follows that the nation as a whole is better off. For critics of free trade, this logic is deceptively attractive but wrong. When individuals do what is in their best interest, this does not "add up" to the best interests of that community of individuals. Understanding why not requires some explanation.

Every day consumers are faced with discrete purchasing decisions. Someone goes to the mall to buy a pair of jeans. There are two pairs to chose from: one made in the United States costing $40 and the other made in Malaysia for $20. The two pairs are pretty much identical. In this situation most consumers would buy the cheaper pair because it would leave them $20 to buy other things. In the world of Smith and Ricardo, this is as it should be. This one decision by the consumer is good for that person and has no wider social or economic consequences. But if we take this one decision and multiply it by thousands and millions of identical decisions, there are larger social and economic consequences. Perhaps the plant making jeans in the United States will go out of business or the workers will have to accept lower wages. If the workers are fired, they will be collecting unemployment insurance that has to be paid for through other people's taxes. If enough factories go out of business, maybe the entire local community's economy will collapse. As factories leave and unemployment goes up, tax revenues go down. Schools have less money. As schools decline, the community's downward spiral accelerates. Crime may increase and the quality of life as a whole is eroded. The problem is that we cannot reasonably expect consumers to think out and take into account these consequences each time they make a purchasing decision. Emphasizing this point, List asks, "Can the individual . . . take into consideration in promoting his private economy, the defense of the country, public security, and the thousand other objects which can only be attained by the aid of the whole community?"[13] The manner in which the question is posed suggests the answer.

Contrary to the liberal assumption that the individual and collective interests are in harmony, List explicitly rejects the conflation of individual interests and the broader national interest: "nor does the individual merely by understanding his own interests best, and by striving to further them, if left to his own devices, always further the interests of the community."[14] It does not necessarily follow that whatever serves the best short-term interests of each consumer is consistent with the long-term interests of the community as a whole. In such situations it is reasonable for the government to step in and protect the interests of the larger national community. This is what governments do. As James Fallows points out, people live in nations and communities and "in the real world happiness depends on more than how much money you take home. If the people around you are also comfortable. . . . you are happier and safer than if they are desperate."[15]

How do we deal with this problem? List did not think it unreasonable to use trade restrictions to promote the broader interests of the national community. To continue with our jeans example, the national government might impose a tariff to make the foreign jeans less attractive. Again, Fallows explains that "the answer to this predicament is to pay explicit attention to the welfare of the nation. If a consumer has to pay 10 percent more for a product made by his neighbors than for one from overseas, it will be worse for him in the short run. But in the long run, and in the broadest definitions of well-being, he might be better off."[16]

One can see these types of concerns manifest themselves when the **European Union** (EU) considers new nations for inclusion. The EU is an organization of European states that essentially practices free trade among themselves. They are wealthy and prosperous nations with high wages and generous welfare states. When poorer nations with lower wages seek admission, the current members experience some hesitancy. If poorer nations with much lower wages are allowed to compete on a free basis, the fear is that this will exert downward pressure on wages throughout the EU. Regulations that determine who may and may not join the EU are in part designed to protect European workers from the effects of competing with cheaper labor.

Although it is primarily realists who express concerns about the impact of free trade on the economic bases of national power and security, worries about the effects on workers and the general standard of living come from a broader range of perspectives. Those with a Marxist perspective, for example, see free trade (which is part and parcel of global capitalism) as potentially harmful to workers in developing as well as developed countries. Because capital (i.e., multinational corporations) is free to set up shop wherever wages are lowest, the net effect of free trade is to push and keep wages down. Part of the problem is that on a theoretical level completely free trade should allow labor to move as freely among nations as capital and commodities. In the real world, however, this is not possible. Thus, business can go in search of the lowest wages anywhere in the world, but workers cannot go in search of the highest wages. This fundamental difference in the mobility of capital and commodities as opposed to labor places workers at a great disadvantage.

Feminists are also often critical of free trade and its consequences. They tend

European Union An organization of European states designed to promote economic and political cooperation, founded in the 1950s as the European Common Market. Creates a "common market" within which barriers to trade are eliminated.

to agree with Marxists that workers in all parts of the world are harmed by free trade. But feminists also point out that women in particular usually bear the brunt, because women often find themselves as second-class economic citizens, occupying the lowest-paying and most "expendable" jobs, their interests are usually the first to be sacrificed. Even many liberals, who are generally predisposed to free trade, worry about the potential consequences, especially unrestricted trade between nations at very different levels of development. There are also issues that go well beyond those mentioned already, such as the impact on the environment when factories are moved to low-wage countries with fewer environmental protections. But an overall concern about the impact of free trade on workers and other vulnerable groups unites critics from a very broad range of viewpoints.

CONCLUSION

Conflicts over issues of international trade are likely to increase both among the world's major trading partners and within them. One source of these conflicts is the political ramifications of free trade. Even those who support free trade concede that even if everyone benefits in the long run, in the short term there are winners and losers. Free trade, when it works as it is supposed to, drives comparatively inefficient producers out of business. Industries go under, investors and stockholders lose money, and workers lose jobs. We cannot expect these groups to be happy about their losses. In democratic societies, where the success of politicians depends on keeping people happy, there will continue to be strong political pressures to protect domestic interests from the inevitable consequences of free trade and competition. Even if the long-term benefits of greater efficiency work to the benefit of all, these benefits are often dispersed. The costs of free trade, however, are very concentrated. People who lose their job feel the costs more than people who save a dollar on a pair of jeans notice the benefits. Economic logic and political imperatives sometimes point in opposite directions. This is a dilemma even when there is agreement on an intellectual level that free trade would be desirable.

The problem goes beyond this because there is not a consensus, either within or among nations, that free trade is in fact always desirable. Among the advanced industrialized nations the belief in free trade is probably greatest in the United States. The Japanese and Europeans do not always share this country's enthusiasm. They see a greater scope for legitimate government intervention and are more inclined to recognize potential conflicts between the short-term interests of the consumer and the long-term well-being of the national community.

For many, it seems as though disagreements over trade issues are becoming more widespread and intense. Some cite declining American hegemony and the end of the Cold War as reasons for increasing conflicts over trade. The argument is that the decades immediately after World War II were characterized by American economic and military dominance over Japan and Western Europe. The United States was able to use its power to keep others in line with its policy preferences, and the common threat of the Soviet Union created a need for unity and desire to avoid conflict. Today the unifying threat of the Soviet Union is gone and the recovery and growth of other economies has eroded American hegemony. As a result, we are witnessing increasing conflict and tension over trade issues between the United States and its allies in Europe and Asia. Whether the liberal international order can be sustained in the face of declining American hegemony is subject of intense debate.[17] If the thesis about the importance of American hegemony is correct, we are likely to see more, not less, conflict over trade issues.

When we look at disagreements at the level of governments, we are largely in the realm of differences of degree. The Europeans and Japanese do not reject free trade in principle, but their commitment and attachment to free trade is weaker and more conditional. The same cannot be said of many of the social movements and groups protesting the move toward economic globalization. Many of these groups are animated by a much deeper and pervasive skepticism about the impact of free trade in the context of the contemporary global economy that approaches an outright rejection of the principle of free trade. Whether these movements and groups prove to be a powerful enough force to erode the liberal trading order remains to be seen.

POINTS OF VIEW

Whose Interests Does the World Trade Organization Serve?

In recent years the intellectual and political battle over free trade has been waged in the context of debates over trade agreements, such as the North American Free Trade Agreement (NAFTA), and international organizations designed to promote trade. The organization at the center of the controversy is the World Trade Organization (WTO). This was particularly evident in the fall of 1999, when the WTO convened in Seattle and was greeted by throngs of protestors. The following two documents (reflecting three positions) come from the debate over the WTO in 1999. Beyond the focus on the WTO, they reflect a more fundamental disagreement over the benefits and consequences of free trade. The text of an interview/discussion with Ralph Nader and Patrick Buchanan is a good example not only of the arguments against the WTO and free trade, but also the odd political alliance that has developed on trade issues between normal political antagonists from the right and left. The other document is a Thomas Friedman essay reacting to the protests in Seattle. Though he does not criticize Nader and Buchanan directly, Friedman does so implicitly by taking on the protestors who echoed the same themes as Nader and Buchanan.

Even though Nader and Buchanan are both critical of the WTO, can you identify differences in the rationales that lead them to the same position? To what extent do their concerns reflect typical criticisms of free trade discussed in the chapter? Why does Thomas Friedman think the protestors, and by implication Nader and Buchanan, are misguided? In what ways does his position appear to reflect traditional arguments for free trade?

The Battle in Seattle

Patrick Buchanan and Ralph Nader
November 28, 1999

Timehost: Our guests tonight, Pat Buchanan and Ralph Nader ... two very different political figures, who are coming down on the same side of a hotly debated issue ... globalization. Patrick Buchanan has just joined us! Welcome, Mr. Buchanan. Thanks for coming by....

Timehost: Mr. Nader has just joined us ...

Ralph Nader: I would not use the language of the adversary. It isn't free trade. If it was free trade, why do they need hundreds of pages of rules and regulations? If it was free trade, they could do it in two sentences. GATT [General Agreement on Tariffs and Trade] and WTO is a massive global regulatory system concocted by corporations, lawyers and their minions without any accountability. It's an autocratic system.

BlueSilkBebe asks: I would like to know how the two of you ended up on the same side of the issues?

Pat Buchanan: What brought me to the issue is the massive loss of good-paying jobs, the decline of America's economic independence, and the emergence of a global government unresponsive to the people.

Ralph Nader: What attracted me to the WTO was the fact that it's government of the big corporations, by the big corporations, for the big corporations, that undermined our democracy, that gave up more of our sovereignty than we have ever given up in our entire history in order to subordinate all human values for workers consumers, small taxpayers and the environment and our democratic processes to the dictates of international commerce.

Pat Buchanan: It's trade *über alles*.

Louisk39 asks: For Buchanan, why lock our workers into old nineteenth-century factory jobs via protectionism? The best examples of protectionism are in North Korea and Cuba. We have 20 million new jobs under freer Clinton/Gore trade.

Pat Buchanan: The gentleman is ignorant of history. The greatest growth in American history was from 1860 to 1913, when we averaged 4 percent a year. We had an economy half the size of Great Britain at the start, and ended up with an economy twice the size of Great Britain's, while the British embraced free trade and we embraced protectionism. And how can you say these are nineteenth-century jobs, building cars, motorcycles, textiles, toys, etcetera, when Americans, on the eve of the twenty-first century, are consuming them in greater volumes than ever before? …

Every nation that has risen to greatness, and preeminence, Britain before 1860, the U.S. prior to World War I, Bismarck's Germany prior to World War II, postwar Japan, all of them, protected their domestic markets and invaded foreign markets. They all used the same Hamiltonian formula. And none of them rose to prominence by throwing open their borders.

andrew93_2000 asks: All the jobs leaving the U.S.A. are no-tech and low-tech, though they are unionized. Why not focus on the new hi-tech labor force we need rather than save the low-tech jobs?

Pat Buchanan: Look, we have working men and women in this country many of whom do not have advanced degrees and computer skills. For years, these Americans had a yellow brick road right to the middle class: tens of millions of manufacturing and industrial jobs in a country that produced at one point 30 percent of all the world's manufactured goods. It's these jobs we're sending overseas. And it's these workers and Americans who we are selling out when we deprive them of a manufacturing job with health insurance and force them into a service job that may pay only two thirds of their previous wages.

Ralph Nader: The jobs that are staying at home are the $6 an hour low-tech, McDonald's food jobs. And the capital-intensive jobs moving over the Rio Grande into Mexico are not low-tech jobs. They are capital-intensive jobs. So the reality is just the opposite of what the questioner poses.

hyde_volpe asks: Pat and Ralph: Do either or both of you see this coming together of the old liberal and conservative politics over the sovereignty and corporate power issues as the beginnings of a truly new populist movement that may have equal significance to the one of the last century?

Pat Buchanan: I think there's a realignment coming in American politics. It will leave Newt Gingrich and Bill Clinton and their minions in the same party. And there will be a new party that's rooted in traditionalism and economic patriotism and that puts America and the American people first. And I think the battle will be between globalism and patriotism.

Ralph Nader: It began a few years ago on corporate welfare issues, where liberal and conservatives got together to defeat the Clinch River breeder reactor boondoggle. And most recently in the testimony by the same groups at the first-ever congressional hearing on the corporate welfare issue conducted by John Kasich. That was in June 1999, stimulated in part by the great *Time* magazine cover story on the issue, by Bartlett and Steele, from whom nothing has been heard of since. We want to hear more from them. Giant corporations are on a collision course with democracy. Whether liberals and conservatives disagree on all sort of issues, they have got to agree on one: they can't operate without democracy.

Pat Buchanan: The transnational corporate interests are repeatedly coming into conflict with U.S. national security interests, as we see in the China WTO deal. Some of my conservative friends on Capitol Hill should wake up to that reality.

SOURCE: Timehost transcript, November 28, 1999.

Senseless in Seattle

Thomas Friedman
December 1, 1999

Is there anything more ridiculous in the news today than the protests against the World Trade Organization in Seattle? I doubt it.

These anti-WTO protesters—who are a Noah's ark of flat-earth advocates, protectionist trade unions and yuppies looking for their 1960s fix—are protesting against the wrong target with the wrong tools. Here's why:

What unites the anti-WTO crowd is their realization that we now live in a world without walls. The cold-war system we just emerged from was built around division and walls; the globalization system that we are now in is built around integration and webs. In this new system, jobs, cultures, environmental problems and labor standards can much more easily flow back and forth.

The ridiculous thing about the protesters is that they find fault with this, and blame the WTO. The WTO is not the cause of this world without walls, it's the effect. The more countries trade with one another, the more they need an institution to set the basic rules of trade, and that is all the WTO does. "Rules are a substitute for walls—when you don't have walls you need more rules," notes the Council on Foreign Relations expert Michael Mandelbaum.

Because some countries try to use their own rules to erect new walls against trade, the WTO adjudicates such cases. For instance, there was the famous "Flipper vs. GATTzilla" dispute. (The WTO used to be known as GATT.) America has rules against catching tuna in nets that might also snare dolphins; other countries don't, and those other countries took the U.S. before a GATT tribunal and charged that our insistence on Flipper-free tuna was a trade barrier. The anti-WTO protesters extrapolate from such narrow cases that the WTO is going to become a Big Brother and tell us how to live generally. Nonsense.

What's crazy is that the protesters want the WTO to become precisely what they accuse it of already being—a global government. They want it to set more rules—their rules, which would impose our labor and environmental standards on everyone else. I'm for such higher standards, and over time the WTO may be a vehicle to enforce them, but it's not the main vehicle to achieve them. And they are certainly not going to be achieved by putting up new trade walls.

Every country and company that has improved its labor, legal and environmental standards has done so because of more global trade, more integration, more Internet—not less. These are the best tools we have for improving global governance.

Who is one of the top environmental advisers to DuPont today? Paul Gilding, the former head of Greenpeace! How could that be? A DuPont official told me that in the old days, if DuPont wanted to put a chemical factory in a city, it knew it just had to persuade the local neighbors. "Now we have six billion neighbors," said the DuPont official—meaning that DuPont knows that in a world without walls if it wants to put up a chemical plant in a country, every environmentalist is watching. And if that factory makes even a tiny spill those environmentalists will put it on the World Wide Web and soil DuPont's name from one end of the earth to the other.

I recently visited a Victoria's Secret garment factory in Sri Lanka that, in terms of conditions, I would let my own daughters work in. Why does it have such a high standard? Because anti-sweatshop activists have started to mobilize enough consumers to impress Victoria's Secret that if it doesn't get its shop standards up, consumers won't buy its goods. Sri Lanka is about to pass new copyright laws, which Sri Lankan software writers have been seeking for years to protect their own innovations. Why the new law now? Because Microsoft told Sri Lanka it wouldn't sell its products in a country with such weak intellectual property laws.

Hey, I want to save Flipper too. It's a question of how. If the protesters in Seattle stopped yapping, they would realize that they have been duped by knaves like Pat Buchanan—duped into thinking that power lies with the WTO. It doesn't. There's never going to be a global government to impose the rules the protesters want. But there can be better global governance—on the environment, intellectual property and labor. You achieve that not by adopting 1960s tactics in a Web-based world—not by blocking trade, choking globalization or getting the WTO to put up more walls. That's a fool's errand.

You make a difference today by using globalization—by mobilizing the power of trade, the power of the Internet and the power of consumers to persuade, or embarrass, global corporations and nations to upgrade their standards. You change the world when you get the big players to do the right things for the wrong reasons. But that takes hard work—coalition-building with companies and consumers, and follow-up. It's not as much fun as a circus in Seattle.

Source: *New York Times*, December 1, 1999.

CHAPTER SUMMARY

- Debates over trade policy, both within the developed world as well as between the developed and developing worlds, have become increasingly intense in recent years. Occasional violent protests at global economic summits are among the more dramatic manifestations of this debate.

- The Liberal International Economic Order (LIEO), which emphasizes the importance of free and open trade, was created in the aftermath of World War II under the auspices of the United States.

- Free and open trade was deemed essential to the health of the U.S. economy, the preservation of democracy and peace, and the prospects for growth and prosperity around the world.

- In terms of reducing barriers to trade, the General Agreement on Trade and Tariffs (GATT), created in 1947, was the most important element on the LIEO. GATT was replaced by the World Trade Organization in 1995.

- The intellectual case for free trade was first made by liberal economists Adam Smith and, more importantly, David Ricardo, whose theory of comparative advantage remains the foundation of the case for free trade.

- According to the theory of comparative advantage, nations should produce those commodities they produce more efficiently and trade these for those commodities that others produce more efficiently. Tariffs, quotas, and any other barriers to trade interfere with this process and promote economic inefficiency.

- Supporters of free trade emphasize that consumers (and everyone is a consumer) are always better off when they can buy the things they want and need for the lowest possible price, no matter where in the world they are produced. And if every consumer in a nation is better off, the nation or community as a whole is better off.

- One of the earliest critiques of Ricardo's case for free trade was provided by German economist Friedrich List.

- Opponents of free trade usually concede that free trade promotes economic efficiency but argue that economic efficiency is not the only consideration that needs to be taken into account. There may be social, political, and strategic priorities that might outweigh purely economic considerations.

- List argued that nations, unlike the individuals within them, need to be worried about becoming dependent on other nations for necessary commodities. He suggested that in such cases nations should maintain their industries, even if the commodities could be purchased more cheaply from other nations.

- List also claimed that nations sometimes need to protect "infant" industries from foreign competition in the early stages of their development.

- The idea that the pursuit of individual interests necessarily results in the common good, an essential element of the case for free trade, is, according to List, profoundly mistaken. Individual consumers cannot possibly know and evaluate the larger social consequences of their aggregated decisions. Thus, it is essential that the government regulate trade to protect the long-term interests of the nation as a whole.

CRITICAL QUESTIONS

1. Why and how might domestic political forces prevent nations from practicing free trade?

2. Are consumers always better off paying less for the goods they want and need regardless of where in the world they are produced?

3. Tariffs and quotas are the most obvious ways governments can interfere with free trade. What are some other examples of barriers to free trade?

4. What is the significance of List's distinction between private economy and political economy in terms of evaluating free trade?

5. How and why does free trade promote economic efficiency?

KEY TERMS

autarky 150
Bretton Woods system 148
Cobden, Richard (1804–1865) 150
comparative advantage, theory of 150
Corn Laws 149
division of labor 150
dumping 154
economic nationalism 149
European Union 160

FURTHER READINGS

A good place to start with the debate over free trade is the original sources, since the main outlines of the debate have not really changed very much. The case for free trade was first fully developed by David Ricardo in *On Protection to Agriculture* (London: J. Murray, 1822) and *On the Principles of Political Economy and Taxation* (London: J. Murray, 1819). Ricardo's most forceful critic was Friedrich List, whose ideas are best conveyed in his *The National System of Political Economy* (New York: August M. Kelley Publishers, 1966 [1885]). The best contemporary defense of free trade are Jagdish Bhagwati, *Protectionism* (Cambridge, MA: MIT University Press, 1988) and Douglas A. Irwin, *Free Trade under Fire* (Princeton: Princeton University Press, 2002) and *Against the Tide: An Intellectual History of Free Trade* (Princeton: Princeton University Press, 1996). A good summary of the major arguments against free trade is presented by James Fallows, "How the World Works," *The Atlantic* (December 1993), pp. 61–87. An interesting, though certainly opinionated, treatment of the debate over the North American Free Trade Agreement (NAFTA) is John R. MacArthur, *The Selling of "Free Trade": NAFTA, Washington and the Subversion of American Democracy* (Berkeley: University of California Press, 2001).

FREE TRADE ON THE WEB

http://www.wto.org
Website of the World Trade Organization, which has been at the center of attempts to promote and halt multilateral open trade.

http://www.freetrade.org
A pro–free trade website, sponsored by the libertarian CATO Institute, that is intended to "increase public awareness of the benefits of free trade and the costs of protectionism."

http://www.usft.org
Site of United Students for Fair Trade. The focus is on how college students can work for "fair trade."

http://www.maketradefair.com
Another fair trade organization, focused on ensuring that the farmers and producers in Third World nations receive fair prices for the goods they produce.

NOTES

[1] See Manny Fernandez, "Diverse Foes: Wide Range of Protestors Unites against IMF, World Bank," *Washington Post*, September 23, 2001, p. B1.

[2] Stephen Krasner, "United States Commercial and Monetary Policy: Unraveling the Paradox of External Strength and Internal Weakness," ed. Peter Katzenstein, *Between Power and Plenty: Foreign Economic Policies of Advanced Industrial States* (Madison: University of Wisconsin Press, 1978), p. 51.

[3] An excellent account of the campaign to repeal the Corn Laws is William D. Grampp, *The Manchester School of Economics* (Stanford: Stanford University Press, 1960). Oddly, even though Ricardo influenced those who favored repealing the Corn Laws, he actually opposed their repeal. Grampp explains the unusual reasoning behind Ricardo's opposition. See also Charles Kindleberger, "The Rise of Free Trade in Europe, 1820–1875," *Journal of Economic History* 35, no. 1 (1975): 20–55.

[4] David Ricardo, *Principles of Political Economy and Taxation* (London: George Bell and Sons, 1908), pp. 115–16.

[5] Jagdish Bhagwati, *Protectionism* (Cambridge, MA: MIT Press, 1988), p. 33.

[6] Ricardo, *Principles of Political Economy and Taxation*, p. 114.

[7] Paul Krugman, *Pop Internationalism* (Cambridge, MA: MIT University Press, 1998), p. 84.

[8] Friedrich List, *The National System of Political Economy* (New York: August M. Kelley Publishers, 1966 [reprint of 1885 edition]).

[9] John Gray, *False Dawn: The Delusions of Global Capitalism* (London: Granta, 1998), pp. 82–83.

[10] Edward Earle Meade, "Adam Smith, Alexander Hamilton and Friedrich List: The Economic Foundations of Military Power," in *Makers of Modern Strategy: Military Thought*

from Machiavelli to Hitler, ed. Edward Earle Meade (Princeton: Princeton University Press, 1971), p. 131.

[11] The argument that industrial development has usually included elements of protectionism is also made in William Lazonick, *Business Organization and the Myth of the Market Economy* (Cambridge: Cambridge University Press, 1991).

[12] List, *National System of Political Economy,* p. 347.

[13] Ibid., p. 165.

[14] Ibid., p. 166.

[15] James Fallows, "How the World Works," *The Atlantic* (December 1993), p. 70. See also James Fallows, *Looking at the Sun: The Rise of the New East Asian Economic and Political System* (New York: Pantheon, 1994).

[16] Fallows, "How the World Works," p. 70.

[17] An influential examination of this issue is Robert Keohane, *After Hegemony* (Princeton: Princeton University Press, 1984).

THE IMF, GLOBAL INEQUALITY, AND DEVELOPMENT

Through the lens of the controversy surrounding the International Monetary Fund (IMF), this chapter explores the debate about the nature of the global economy and the obstacles to development. The immediate issue is the consequences of reforms enacted in many developing countries as a condition for receiving IMF loans. The purpose of these reforms was to promote economic development and reduce poverty. But as is often the case with disagreements on specific policies, there is a much deeper and more fundamental clash of worldviews informing this debate. The IMF's policies embody a liberal worldview in which pro-market policies and integration into the global (capitalist) economy are considered prerequisites for economic growth and development. From this perspective, the misguided policies of developing states have been the main obstacles to development. Critics of the IMF disagree. In their view, the primary obstacle to development is a global economic order that works systematically to the advantage of the wealthy and powerful at the expense of the poor and weak. Heavily influenced by a radical/Marxist analysis of global capitalism, this perspective portrays the IMF as an integral part of a global economic system that perpetuates poverty and inequality.

In the previous chapter we noted that a central element of the case for free trade is that it benefits everyone in the long run—to reuse the cliché, a rising tide lifts all boats. This means that free trade is supposed to be good not only for the wealthy industrialized nations and their citizens but also for developing nations and the world's poor. Even though trade issues often appear in the news in the context of trade disputes between the United States and Japan or Western Europe, they are equally, if not more, important for understanding relations between the developed and developing nations. The issues of trade, inequality, and development are inextricably intertwined and are central to most debates about the dynamics and future of the global economy. And these issues collide most vividly in the politically and intellectually charged controversy over the IMF and its relationship with developing nations.

At anti-globalization demonstrations the **International Monetary Fund** (IMF) is usually singled out for particularly harsh criticism, with a host of social and economic ills in the Third World laid at its doorstep. Indicative of prevailing sentiment, Conn Hallinan relates a riddle making the rounds among critics of the IMF: "What is the difference between Tony Soprano and the International Monetary Fund? Nothing, except that Tony and his Mafia pals, who extort and impoverish a handful of people in New Jersey, are television creations. The IMF, on the other hand, does this to hundreds of millions of people in the real world."[1] A harsh evaluation indeed.

Given the seemingly innocuous mission of the IMF, it might appear odd that the organization has become the object of such stinging criticism. Founded in 1947, the IMF was given its original mandate to help nations experiencing balance-of-payments problems and to stabilize currency exchange rates with short-term loans, not exactly the sort of thing that leads people to take to the streets in protest. Criticism leveled against the IMF today, however, has relatively little to do with the somewhat arcane monetary matters that occupied the IMF during the first two decades of its existence. The origins of the contemporary controversy can be traced to the mid-1970s, when the IMF became increasingly involved in providing loans to developing economies in the Third World. At this point, the IMF and its policies became entwined in the emotionally and intellectually charged debate about the causes of, and remedies for, global economic inequality. The question is whether the IMF is a savior providing a recipe for growth and poverty reduction or an integral part of a global economic system that serves the interests of the wealthy and powerful at the expense of the world's poor.

International Monetary Fund (IMF) One of the critical institutions of the post–World War II Liberal International Economic Order. Initially intended to help nations deal with balance-of-payments deficits, since the 1960s it has played an increasing and controversial role in assisting developing nations.

From Decolonization
to Structural Adjustment

The wave of post–World War II decolonization may have transformed the political map of the world, but it had relatively little impact on its economic landscape. The optimistic expectation that economic development would follow rapidly on the heels of independence was quickly dashed. Independence and formal political equality (sovereignty) proved perfectly compatible with dramatic economic inequality. It soon became evident that decolonization did nothing to alter the **international division of labor** that emerged over the previous century of colonialism. Manufacturing was still concentrated in the industrialized economies of the North, whereas the newly

international division of labor In critiques on the global economy's impact on developing nations, the division between the core nations, which have diversified manufacturing-based economies, and peripheral nations, which have specialized economies that rely on raw material exports.

independent countries of the South remained sources of primary products (e.g., unprocessed raw materials and agricultural goods). Not only were Third World economies still reliant on primary product exports, but most also depended on just one or two products for the bulk of their export earnings. They were highly specialized compared to diversified economies such as the United States. It was (and still is) not unusual for a developing country to receive more than half of its export income from the sale of a single commodity. More than two decades after independence, for example, 96 percent of Uganda's export earnings came from coffee, 89 percent of Zambia's from copper, and 59 percent of Ghana's from cocoa.[2] A diversified economy can survive a slump in any single economic sector, but if the price of coffee falls by 50 percent in a given year, Uganda is in real trouble.

By the late 1950s, this economic division of labor and specialization came to be viewed as an obstacle to development. Argentinean economist Raul Prebisch and others associated with the Economic Commission on Latin America (ECLA) highlighted two major problems. First, prices of many primary products often fluctuated wildly from year to year. The resulting instability in income creates difficulties for planning and development. Imagine, for example, individuals trying to borrow money or make investments if their incomes went up or down unpredictably by 50 percent from year to year. Second, there was also a general tendency for the price of primary products to fall without any similar fall in the price of manufactured goods. The result was what economists refer to as **declining terms of trade**—that is, the prices for those commodities developing nations sell are going down, whereas the prices for the manufactured goods they buy are not. For example, when fiber optic cable began replacing copper wire beginning in the 1980s, the price of copper on the world market fell by nearly 80 percent. Nations like Zambia were devastated. Left unchecked, these declining terms of trade would inexorably lead to even greater poverty and inequality.

The logical solution to this dilemma was for Third World nations to reduce their reliance on primary products and shift their economies to manufacturing. This was easier said than done. The problem was that in the initial stages manufactured goods from Third World countries would not be very competitive with those of established industries in North America, Europe, and Japan. How could developing nations create a manufacturing base in the face of competition from the already industrialized economies? The solution adopted in much of the Third World, particularly in Latin America and Africa, was known as **import substitution.** That is, domestically manufactured goods would be substituted for previously imported manufactured goods. There were two components to a strategy of import substitution. First, governments had to direct or channel investment into selected industries. Second, so-called infant industries had to be protected from the international market until they could compete on their own, which entailed the imposition of tariffs and quotas on manufactured goods from abroad.

Import substitution policies met with some initial success during the 1950s and 1960s, with many Latin American and African countries experiencing high rates of economic growth. During this period the focus was largely on low-tech, labor-intensive industries such as nondurable consumer goods (shoes, clothes, etc.). These industries did not require huge investments and were labor intensive, allowing Third World nations to take advantage of their large pools of low-wage labor. Making the transition to high-tech, capital-intensive manufacturing (e.g., electronics and durable

declining terms of trade
The tendency for the prices of raw material to decline relative to manufactured goods.

import substitution
A policy designed to promote economic development by restricting foreign imports in order to replace them with domestically produced goods.

consumer goods such as appliances) was more problematic. Poor countries lacked large reserves of domestic capital for investment because their populations had low rates of saving (poor people do not put much of their meager incomes in the bank). Third World nations were forced to look abroad for the needed investment capital. There were two potential sources for this investment capital—multinational corporations and northern financial institutions, both public and private. Each of these sources had its drawbacks. Relying on corporations would increase the power and influence of foreign economic interests, something viewed with great suspicion in recently decolonized nations. Borrowed money, on the other hand, would ultimately have to be paid back with interest. But since this investment was supposed to produce more economic growth, paying back the loans a few years down the road was not expected to pose much of a problem.

By the 1970s, however, rates of economic growth throughout much of the Third World began to stagnate. The situation was exacerbated when oil-producing nations, acting through the **Organization of Petroleum Exporting Countries (OPEC),** raised prices substantially, beginning in 1973 and again in 1979. Although higher oil prices inconvenienced the wealthy industrial economies, they proved crippling to many developing nations, which had to pay, but could ill afford, the same higher prices. Thus, by the mid- to late 1970s, many developing countries saw their economic growth rates plummet and the costs of imported energy soar.

The cumulative result of these developments was what became known as the **debt crisis.** Several major developing countries, especially in Latin America, found themselves unable to pay back the money they had borrowed during the 1970s. The most significant of the early crises involved Mexico, largely because of the sheer amount of money it owed. Throughout the 1970s, Mexico's debt burden grew faster than its economy as a whole. By the early 1980s, it became clear that Mexico would be unable pay back its loans on schedule. Fearing the consequences of Mexico's defaulting on its loans, especially for major international banks, the IMF agreed to loan Mexico enough to prevent a default. The money did not come without strings, however. The IMF insisted that Mexico enact certain economic policies and reforms in order to receive assistance. The IMF deemed these reforms necessary for promoting the economic growth needed if there was to be any hope that Mexico's loans would eventually be repaid. This action set the precedent for many subsequent IMF bailouts throughout Latin America, Africa, and Asia over the next two decades. The practice of requiring reforms in order to get IMF assistance came to be known as **conditionality.** Though some details differed, the same basic conditions were imposed on all nations seeking IMF assistance. Taken together, this bundle of reforms came to be known as **structural adjustment policies,** and it is these policies that prompted the rising chorus of criticism directed against the IMF.

Structural adjustment: Cure and diagnosis The IMF's structural adjustment programs were designed to solve a very real problem. Mounting debts to Northern governments and banks combined with low rates of economic growth left many Third World nations on the verge of bankruptcy. On this there is not much disagreement. But Jagdish Bhagwati reminds us that in economic policy as in medicine, "the cure is defined by the diagnosis."[3] To continue the medical metaphor, the debt crisis was the symptom and structural adjustment policies were the cure. But the nature of this cure

Organization of Petroleum Exporting Countries (OPEC) Founded in 1960, OPEC was and remains an attempt to create a cartel of major oil producers for the purpose of raising the global price of oil.

debt crisis The inability of many developing nations to pay back foreign debts beginning in the early 1980s.

conditionality The IMF's policy of requiring certain economic policies and reforms in order to receive loans.

structural adjustment policies The bundle of market-oriented reforms required for developing nations to receive IMF loans.

depended upon the IMF's diagnosis of the problem. From the IMF's perspective, the immediate problem was the lack of economic growth, but this explanation begs the more basic question: What was the cause of this poor growth? The IMF believed it was the misguided economic policies of developing nations, which needed to be replaced with policies to spur economic growth.

In locating the cause of poor growth and underdevelopment in the policies of Third World nations, the IMF stepped into the center of the most enduring debate in development studies: the relative importance of domestic versus international obstacles to development. For the last several decades, debates about the causes of underdevelopment have been defined by two basic positions. One perspective contends that the capitalist global economic system presents obstacles that make genuine development, if not impossible, at least extremely difficult. The dynamics of global capitalism ensure that the rich get richer and the poor get poorer. Some take the argument further, claiming that the wealthy have a vested interest in keeping other nations in poverty. If this is correct, the international economic order as a whole needs to be reformed if development is to be achieved. An alternative analysis locates the obstacles to development in the policies of developing states. Thus, we can view the debate over IMF policies (the cure) as stemming from a more fundamental disagreement about the causes of underdevelopment (the diagnosis).

The IMF and Neoliberalism

The late 1970s and early 1980s were not only a period of emerging crisis in much of the developing world but also of changing intellectual currents in the industrialized world. Since the end of World War II, economic thought in the United States and Europe was dominated by the ideas of British economist **John Maynard Keynes** (1883–1946). While supporting the essential features of capitalism, Keynes advocated a greater role for government in regulating the ups and downs of the capitalist business cycle through fiscal and monetary policy. During recessions, for example, when growth is low and unemployment high, governments should spend at a deficit in order to inject money into the economy to encourage growth and employment. By the mid-1970s, Keynesian ideas and policies came under attack by economists such as **Milton Friedman** (1912–), who favored a diminished role for government and a greater emphasis on the free market. The election of Ronald Reagan in the United States and Margaret Thatcher in Great Britain was an indication of these shifting intellectual currents. Domestically, both Thatcher and Reagan pursued similar agendas: tax cuts, lower government spending, fewer regulations, scaled-back social welfare programs, and privatization (moving government-provided services into the private sector).

The growing influence of free market policies was bolstered by the total failure of state socialism and communism in the Soviet Union and Eastern Europe. Decades of state planning and government control in these nations led to economic stagnation, social malaise, and a host of other problems, including environmental degradation. Even though the Soviet model of development appeared attractive to some during the 1950s and 1960s, by the 1980s it had lost all of its luster. The political and intellectual triumph of liberal democratic capitalism appeared universal. This vision of

Keynes, John Maynard (1883–1946) Influential British economist who advocated a substantial role for government in regulating the ups and downs of the business cycle through fiscal and monetary policy.

Friedman, Milton (1912–) Nobel Prize–winning economist influential in the resurgence of liberal/neoliberal (i.e., pro-market) economic policies and thought in the 1970s and 1980s.

"smaller" government and increased reliance on the market came to be known as **neoliberalism.**

The debt crisis in the developing world coincided with the emergence and eventual dominance of neoliberalism. Comparing the structural adjustment policies imposed by the IMF with those that Reagan and Thatcher tried to enact in their respective countries, it is obvious that they were cut from the same intellectual cloth. There were several key reforms in virtually every structural adjustment plan, including:

1. *Fiscal austerity,* or balancing government budgets. This usually entailed either increases in government revenues (usually new fees for government services) or, more commonly, reductions in government spending.

2. *Reductions in government subsidies to domestic industries.* These subsidies had often been part of import substitution strategies.

3. *Reduction of tariffs, quotas, and other barriers to imports.* This would subject domestic industries to international competition.

4. *Capital market liberalization.* This is a technical term for easing restrictions on foreign investment.

5. *Privatization,* or selling off government-owned industries to the private sector.

Taken together, these policies reflected the IMF's worldview "that market forces, liberalized trade and payments, and general freedom in economic matters are usually more efficient and promoted greater prosperity and a better allocation of resources than a system characterized by controls and restrictions."[4] This bundle of policies and the underlying liberal or neoliberal economic philosophy that informed them became known as the **Washington consensus,** reflecting the United States' significant role in shaping these policies.

Growth is possible: The market and development The IMF and its supporters reject the argument that a liberal international economic order stands in the way of development. If all the development efforts of the past fifty years had met with failure, there might be good reason to believe that the global economic system was the main culprit. If different nations pursuing different policies had ended up with the same results, it would be logical to assume the presence of a common obstacle. But this has not been the case. The past fifty years has produced some abject failures, some modest development, and even some truly remarkable success stories. David Landes notes that "since independence, the heterogeneous nations that we know collectively as the South, or as the Third World. . . . have achieved a wide diversity of results. These have ranged from the spectacular successes of East Asia, to mixed results in Latin America to outright regression in such places as Burma and much of Africa."[5] This diversity of outcomes can be illustrated with some striking comparisons between Africa and East Asia. In the early 1950s, for example, Egypt had roughly the same average income as most nations in East Asia, but today incomes in East Asia are between five and thirty times larger than those of Egypt. Landes is struck by the different trajectories taken by Nigeria and Indonesia: "In 1965, Nigeria (oil exporter) had higher GDP per capita than Indonesia (another oil exporter); twenty-five years later, Indonesia had three times the Nigerian level."[6] An even more dramatic reversal of fortunes is provided by Ghana and South Korea: in 1957 Ghana had a larger gross national product (GNP)

neoliberalism A contemporary version of economic liberalism, emphasizing the importance of limited government, reduced regulation, and the market economy.

fiscal austerity Controlling government spending and taxation with a preference for balanced budgets. Demands for fiscal austerity were central elements of the IMF's structural adjustment programs.

capital market liberalization Removing barriers to foreign investment, a key element of IMF structural adjustment programs.

Washington consensus A label for the liberal ideas of free trade and limited government that guide many of the policies of the IMF toward developing nations, especially in the context of its structural adjustment loans.

A tale of two cities: Poverty-stricken Lagos, Nigeria (this page) and prosperous Hong Kong (facing page). How can we explain the difference?
SOURCE: © Campbell William/CORBIS SYGMA

than South Korea, but by 1996 Ghana's GNP stood at $7 billion whereas South Korea's GNP had soared to $485 billion, almost seventy times larger than Ghana's.[7] So any blanket assertion that development is impossible within the existing liberal-capitalist economic order cannot be sustained.

But beyond the mere fact that development is possible, what does this diversity tell us about the causes of development and underdevelopment? Can we identify any answers to Keith Richburg's pointed question, "Why is Africa eating Asia's dust?" The variance is not easily explained by histories of colonialism because some of the most successful East Asian nations had also been colonies. To many observers, the fact that some nations have achieved genuine development and others have not indicates that "the basic obstacles to economic development [can be found] within the less developed countries themselves." But what might these obstacles be? The list of possibilities is long indeed: war and frequent civil unrest, political instability, rampant government corruption, cultural and religious beliefs that inhibit initiative, and cumbersome bureaucracies, to identify just a few. One of the most commonly cited problems, however, is bad or misguided government policies. From the IMF's perspective, one thing is clear: excessive government control of the economy and attempts to cut off developing economies from foreign trade and investment are definitely *not* routes to development. If excessive government intervention and control explain the failure of development efforts, "market openness, fiscal discipline and noninterventionism constituted the route to economic development."[8]

The poster children for successful economic development are, of course, the so-called East Asian "tigers" or newly industrializing countries (NICs). As Robert Gilpin notes, "The most successful economies among the less developed countries are precisely those that have put their houses in order and that participate most aggressively in the world economy. They are the so-called Gang of Four: Hong Kong, Singapore, South Korea, and Taiwan."[9] Do these cases lend support to the neoliberal view that free market policies and integration into the global economy lead to development? This is a hard question to answer, and all sides of the debate are anxious to claim that the East Asian experience supports their position. On one hand, there is no denying that East Asian governments were often heavily involved in directing investment into targeted industries. This was development with a heavy dose of state guidance of the sort the IMF frowns on today. Nonetheless, many still conclude that their policies were more market oriented and trade dependent than the import substitution policies of Latin America and the socialist policies pursued in many African nations. According to Stephen Haggard, "Intervention may have been extensive in the East Asian NICs . . . but it has been less extensive than in Africa, South Asia and Latin America."[10] In Gilpin's opinion, East Asian development policies "have worked with the market and not against it . . . Japan and the NICs have encouraged a well-functioning market that spurs individual initiative and economic efficiency. They have demonstrated that the liberals are quite correct in their emphasis on the benefits of the price mechanism in the efficient allocation of resources."[11] Most important, the East Asian nations clearly embraced international trade as the engine of the economic growth.

India provides a somewhat more clear-cut example of successful market-oriented policies. In the two decades following independence, India's economic performance was disappointing. According to Jagdish Bhagwati, "The main elements of India's policy framework stifled growth until the 1970s." These elements included "extensive bureaucratic controls over production, investment and trade" as well as "inward looking trade and investment policies" and "a substantial public sector, going well beyond the conventional confines of public utilities and infrastructure."[12] Beginning in the 1980s (and especially in 1991), India undertook reforms designed to reduce government control, free the economy, and open its economy to foreign trade and investment. The result has been higher rates of economic growth and a substantial reduction in poverty. In fact, virtually all the poverty reduction in the Third World during the 1990s occurred in just two nations, India and China (which was also instituting market reforms). Though India's reforms were not part of an IMF adjustment program, its experience is seen as additional confirmation of the IMF's underlying market-oriented philosophy.

A more controversial case is Chile. In the late 1970s, under the influence of economists trained by University of Chicago economists, the Chilean government adopted a truly radical free market agenda of opening Chile's economy to imports and foreign investment while reducing government spending (going so far as to privatize Chile's version of social security). After some initial hardship, Chile enjoyed more than a decade of sustained economic growth unrivaled elsewhere in Latin America. Chile's example remains controversial for two reasons. First, its market reforms were indeed radical, going well beyond anything the IMF demands under structural adjustment. Second, the reforms were enacted by a military dictatorship that did not have to worry about their unpopularity.[13] The connection between military dictatorship and market reforms was not exactly a public relations success for advocates of similar reforms elsewhere in Latin America.

When these experiences from the Third World are combined with the failure of state socialism in the former Soviet Union and Eastern Europe, the general lessons seem clear. First, government interventions that work against the market are a recipe for economic inefficiency, stagnation, and underdevelopment. Second, those areas of the world that have prospered the most are the those that have participated most extensively in the global economy, whereas those that have tried to cut themselves off have stood still or regressed. P. T. Bauer, who advocated neoliberal policies before they became fashionable, saw this correlation: "The materially more advanced societies and regions of the Third World are those with which the West established the most numerous, diversified and extensive contacts." Conversely, "the level of material achievement usually diminishes as one moves away from the foci of western impact. . . . the poorest areas of the Third World have no external trade. Their condition shows that the causes of backwardness are domestic and that commercial contacts are beneficial."[14]

Recent evidence seems to support this position. In December 2001, the World Bank released a study on the performance of developing economies during the 1990s, focusing on the importance of trade as a measure of globalization. The most important indicator was a nation's ratio of international trade to overall national income (e.g., how significant is foreign trade in terms of the whole economy?). For the two dozen developing nations for whom trade was most significant, there was an average increase in per capita GNP of nearly 5 percent a year as well as increases in life expectancy and schooling levels. This was better than the 2 percent increase registered by the developed nations. It was also much better than the rest of the developing world, for whom trade was less significant: their GNP actually declined by 1 percent

FIGURE 7.1

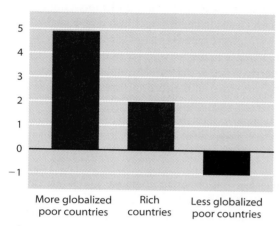

Trade pays GDP (PPP*) per person, 1990s growth rates, %

More globalized poor countries   Rich countries   Less globalized poor countries

SOURCE: *The Economist,* December 8, 2001, p. 67. Figure from World Bank.

a year over the same period (see figure 7.1).[15] The conclusion: trade is good for the developing world and its people.

Despite the protests, the value of trade is understood by most in the Third World. Though it might be chic in intellectual and academic circles in the North to denounce the evils of trade and globalization, "Latin American governments are persevering with integration, as they cut tariffs and sign regional trade agreements." They do so because "no Latin American politician would want to deny their constituents the imported goods they have become accustomed to . . . [so] they line up for a free trade agreement with the United States as they duck the stones thrown by U.S. and European college students who claim to be acting on behalf of the world's poor."[16] Whatever qualms they might have about the specifics of IMF policies, they understand that its basic vision is valid: the market and the integration into the global economy offer the best hope for an end to the cycle of poverty.

A moral hazard? Criticism of the IMF and structural adjustment comes from every part of the theoretical and political spectrum. Surprisingly, however, some of the strongest criticisms come from those who share the IMF's commitment to economic growth, free trade, and limited government intervention. According to this perspective, IMF actions actually violate the very principles the organization supposedly stands for. Remember that the need for IMF assistance arises when nations can no longer meet their loan payments. If this were to happen to you or me, we would have to default on our loans and declare bankruptcy. As a result, the bank would lose its money (or at least most of it). This is why banks are careful to check an applicant's creditworthiness before they make loans. But even with these checks, banks still make some mistakes. When a debtor does go bankrupt, the bank merely chalks it up as a business loss, part of the inevitable costs of a business that comes with some measure of risk. If we allowed the market to work at the international level, nations that could not pay up would essentially go bankrupt and the banks would lose their money. Nations that default on loans would then find it very difficult to borrow money again until they got their act in order, and banks would be more careful about their loans. But this does not happen. Instead, the IMF steps in and saves nations and banks from the consequences of their unwise borrowing and lending. IMF actions, therefore, constitute a form of interference in the operation of markets. This creates what critics refer to as a **moral hazard**—a policy that actually undermines efforts to enact needed reforms by relieving the parties of the consequences of their failures. Thus, banks and nations know that they can continue to make bad decisions because the IMF will be there to rescue them. Even though critics from this perspective have problems with IMF policies, they still share the organization's basic belief in capitalism, the market, and trade as the remedy for underdevelopment.

moral hazard Situation created when policies promote the very problems they were intended to solve. Many argue that IMF loans to debt-ridden developing nations serve to relieve them from the consequences of their mistakes and rescue banks that made bad loans. In doing so, these loans only encourage further irresponsibility.

The (neo)liberal vision It is important to understand how IMF and neoliberal policies are rooted in the fundamental assumptions of liberalism. The emphasis on the market in neoliberal prescriptions for development stems not only from a belief that it promotes economic efficiency, but also from a deeper assumption of a harmony of interests. When everyone pursues his own economic self-interest in the market, we are all better off in the long run. People and businesses prosper when they provide others with goods and services they want for prices they are willing to pay. In advancing their own interests, they are also satisfying the needs and wants of others. Applying this assumption of the harmony of interests to the global economy, liberals reject any zero-sum analysis in which the wealth of the North is seen as coming at the expense of the South. The developing nations are not poor *because* the industrialized nations are rich. Egyptians did not become poorer as South Koreans grew richer. There is no need to chose between Northern prosperity and Southern development. There is no need to choose between multinational profits and Southern development. The rising tide of global economic growth can lift all boats. Development and wealth is possible for all in a global capitalist economic system.

NEOLIBERALISM AS NEOIMPERIALISM

How can one argue with the apparent success of those policies and international trade in promoting development? Critics of the IMF, neoliberalism, and structural adjustment make three basic arguments. First, the neoliberal vision fails to recognize the fundamentally unequal terms on which developed and developing nations participate in the global economy. Second, after twenty years there is little evidence that structural adjustment policies work in promoting economic growth and development or reducing poverty. Third, developed nations are hypocritical in imposing a model of development that virtually none of them followed themselves.

The political economy of dependence and exploitation Since IMF structural adjustment policies reflect a neoliberal view of the global economy, it should come as no surprise that the IMF's critics see the global economy in a very different light. Though criticisms of the IMF come from many perspectives, the dominant critique is strongly influenced by **dependency theory,** which emerged in Latin America during the 1950s and 1960s to explain the region's lack of development. Dependency theory sees international capitalism as the major obstacle to Third World development. Unlike neoliberals, "all dependency theorists maintain that underdevelopment is due primarily to external forces of the world capitalist system and is not due to the policies of LDCs [less developed countries] themselves."[17] Dependency theorists portray a world divided between an industrial **core** and an underdeveloped **periphery** (a category of **semiperiphery** has also been included to account for the very few nations that have managed to move out of the periphery, such as the East Asian economies). Though the troops and governors of formal colonialism went home long ago, a new form of economic imperialism, which could be called **neoimperialism** or **neocolonialism,** has taken its place. The primary agent of this new imperialism is the multinational corporation, which is "the embodiment of international capital."[18] Multinational corporations benefit from an impoverished periphery because it provides cheap commodities and inexpensive labor that allows them to reap windfall profits. This profiteering is done in conjunction with a domestic political-economic elite within Third World nations that has been bought off by, and serves the interests of, international capital. This **comprador class** collaborates with foreign capital in its domination of peripheral nations and forms an "antination" within the nation. Even when developing nations do experience high rates of economic growth, the benefits are not distributed evenly. The new wealth goes disproportionately to economic elites "who are able to enjoy the lifestyle and consumption patterns of developed countries of the North . . . [while] large segments of the population experience no significant improvement in their standard of living."[19] The benefits of growth do not "filter" or "trickle" down to the masses. So-called economic growth in many developing nations has not always resulted in the reduction of poverty or improved living standards. Growth and development are not the same thing. Impressive statistics about economic growth are misleading and all too often obscure the growing inequality within developing nations.

This increase in domestic inequality is accompanied by a growing gap between developed and developing nations in the global economy. The periphery is systematically impoverished or underdeveloped as multinationals earn substantial profits that are sent back to line the pockets of shareholders and corporate executives. Profits are not reinvested in the Third World nations where they were made. This constitutes a massive transfer of wealth from the periphery to the core. The contrast with the economic development of nations such as the United States is critical here. Although Andrew Carnegie and John D. Rockefeller raked in hundreds of millions in profits during the late 1800s and early 1900s, at least they reinvested most of their profits back into the American economy, producing genuine development. This is why even Marx agreed that capitalism was a "progressive" force: it is very good at developing a society's resources. But when corporations earn huge profits in the periphery today, these profits are *not* reinvested but rather siphoned away. This constitutes an exploitive process of unequal exchange that produces underdevelopment and exacerbates global inequality.

The fundamental difference between dependency theory and neoliberalism hinges on whether a harmony or a conflict of interests is perceived between North and South. As we have already noted, neoliberalism argues that Northern wealth does

dependency theory
A theory of global economics influenced by a Marxist understanding of capitalism. The world is seen as divided between a wealthy and powerful core and a poor and impoverished periphery that are locked in an unequal and fundamentally exploitative relationship. From this perspective, it is the global economic system, not just bad policies pursued in developing nations, that perpetuate international inequality.

core and periphery The division of the world into classes somewhat analogous to Marx's bourgeoisie and proletariat. The **core** is the small group of wealthy and powerful states exploiting the larger group of weak and impoverished states (i.e., the **periphery**).

semiperiphery In dependency theory, the small number of developing nations that have developed to the point where they can no longer be considered part of the periphery.

neocolonialism A pattern and policy of economic inequality, exploitation, and domination that has persisted despite the end of formal colonialism.

comprador class From the perspective of dependency theory, the ruling elite in developing nations that collaborates with foreign capital in the exploitation of peripheral nations.

not require Southern underdevelopment. Brazil and Nigeria are not poor *because* the United States and Great Britain are rich. Northern and Southern nations can prosper simultaneously. Dependency theory makes the opposite assumption: there is a basic conflict of interest in which Northern prosperity depends on the exploitation of an underdeveloped South. As Paul Baran explains: "Economic development in underdeveloped countries is profoundly inimical to the dominant interests in advanced capitalist countries. Supplying many important raw materials to the industrialized countries, providing their corporations with vast profits and investment outlets, the backward world has always represented the indispensable hinterland of the highly developed capitalist West."[20]

The influence of the Marxist view of capitalism is evident. Though not all dependency theorists are Marxists, there are clear parallels between this understanding of the global economy and Marx's original analysis of capitalism. The distinction between core and periphery is roughly, though not perfectly, analogous to Marx's distinction between the bourgeoisie and proletariat. Just as the relationship between the bourgeoisie and proletariat was unequal and based on exploitation, so it is with the relationship between core and periphery.

It is into this general worldview that the IMF is situated as a vehicle for advancing the interests of the dominant capitalist states. As an almost physical manifestation of its role in the global economy, the IMF is headquartered just a few blocks from the White House and the World Bank in Washington, D.C. This alone is a telling fact. Voting within the IMF is weighted according to a nation's contributions to the fund. Because it contributes 18 percent of total IMF funds, the United States has an equivalent share of voting power; as a result, it is almost impossible for the IMF to do anything over the objections of the United States. Seven nations (the United States, Britain, France, Britain, Germany Italy, and Japan) enjoy a combined voting share of 40 percent, more than the entire African continent. In what some found to be a moment of rare candor, U.S. Trade Representative Mickey Kantor once characterized the IMF as a "battering ram" for U.S. interests.[21]

There are also less direct sources of bias. Most IMF economists were trained at American universities, where they were inculcated into the dominant economic ideology of neoliberalism. They attend cocktail parties in Georgetown and dine in swanky Manhattan restaurants where they discuss abstract economic theory without ever confronting the reality of global poverty. Many of the fund's top officials have close ties to investment firms and multinational corporations. Even though they may sincerely believe they have the best interests of the developing world at heart, they are deluding themselves. In the words of William Greider, the IMF and World Bank "serve as paternalistic agents of global capital—enforcing debt collection, supervising the financial accounts of poor nations, promoting wage suppression and other policy nostrums, preparing the poorer countries for eventual acceptance into the global trading system."[22]

The failure of structural adjustment The impact of structural adjustment programs is exhibit A in the brief against the IMF. No one has been able to argue that these programs have been a smashing success. The IMF itself has only been able to muster cautious and lukewarm evaluations of its own programs. Withering critiques, on the other hand, are almost too numerous to count. The list of negative effects attributed to structural adjustment programs could fill an entire volume. It is difficult to think of any problem in the developing world that has not supposedly been exacerbated by IMF policies. Putting aside some of the more extreme critiques, the most common criticism is that structural adjustment policies have had a devastating impact on the poor and most vulnerable in developing nations.

Take, for example, the demand for fiscal discipline and balanced budgets. There are only two ways to bring an unbalanced budget into balance—bring in more revenues or reduce expenditures. In most instances the latter course is pursued, and reductions in government spending usually concentrate on social and welfare programs for political reasons (cutting military spending runs the risk of angering powerful military establishments). As a result, "governments find it easier to trim their budgets by charging fees at rural clinics and schools than by firing soldiers or well-connected cronies."[23] Cuts in social and welfare spending usually fall most heavily on those who are already living on the edge. Even minor increases in fees could be crushing for people who live on the equivalent of one or two dollars a day.

Feminists have drawn particular attention to the impact of such cuts on women: "A measure which has an immediate impact on women is the reduction of state expenditures on social services, with women expected to expand their domestic responsibilities to compensate for decreasing state investment in children's education or health."[24] Increases in fees for government services such as health care and education can also have a perverse impact on girls from poor families in societies that have gender bias in favor of male children. Faced with choices about which children get medical care or go to school, girls often lose out. And when government subsidies to industry are reduced, it is often women workers who are the first to be laid off.

Trade liberalization and opening economies to unrestricted foreign investment also have a deleterious impact on the poor. Without government subsidies or protections from foreign competition, domestic industries are forced to reduce costs by lowering wages or laying off workers. Forced to compete with cheap labor elsewhere in the developing world, they exert downward pressure on wages. Multinational corporations, when they are willing to invest at all, are attracted by the lure of cheap labor. It is, after all, a large and inexpensive workforce that provides developing nations with their primary competitive advantage.

Some of the most significant disagreements between the IMF and its critics concern foreign investment and its consequences. One of the goals of structural adjustment is to reduce barriers to foreign investment and create a stable economic environment that will attract investment. Building factories, hiring and training workers, and introducing new technologies all supposedly contribute to economic growth and development. Critics disagree. Foreign corporate investment tends to be limited to those things that contribute to the bottom line, profits. In the long run, genuine development requires a basic infrastructure—transportation systems, hospitals, and schools—that facilitates commerce and creates a healthy, educated workforce. Foreign corporations, however, do not build roads, schools, and hospitals because the economic returns from these investments would be too distant and remote. Only governments can undertake these basic public investments. But saddled with huge debts, and under IMF pressure to balance budgets and reduce spending, most developing nations are simply unable to make these sorts of investments. When such nations are denied the resources to provide the infrastructure that only governments can, escape from poverty and underdevelopment is unlikely. In this context, foreign investment will take advantage of underdevelopment, not reverse it. Foreign investment may contribute to economic growth in the sense that some people get richer, but this does not necessarily result in development or the alleviation of poverty.

Structural adjustment has even failed on its own terms. According to the IMF, the primary goal of structural adjustment was economic growth. The problem is that it does not appear to have created much growth. The IMF's own study concluded that growth rates in countries under structural adjustment increased from −1.5 percent in the 1980s to .3 percent in the early 1990s and 1 percent by the mid-1990s. This is certainly improvement, but nothing to get terribly excited about.[25] Other studies failed to find any improvement whatsoever. A 2001 report by a World Bank economist found "no evidence for a direct effect of structural adjustment on growth."[26] And according to one independent analysis, "participation in IMF [structural adjustment] programs reduces growth while the country remains under [them] and has no salutary effect once a country leaves."[27]

One can also make some fairly direct comparisons between those countries that implemented IMF policies versus those that refused. Faced with some problems in paying back loans in 1997, several Southeast Asian countries, most notably Thailand and South Korea, approached the IMF for short-term loans. Rather than simply granting the request, the IMF insisted on conditional loan packages, requiring recipient countries to enact a whole series of reforms to liberalize their economies. Critics charged that the IMF unnecessarily turned a minor problem into an excuse to impose major restructuring. According to Harvard economist Jeffrey Sachs, IMF officials arrived in Thailand caught in the grips of their own ideology, "filled with ostentatious declarations that all was wrong and that fundamental and immediate surgery was needed."[28] The results proved disastrous (even the IMF admits its response "was not flawless")—gross domestic products actually declined and unemployment increased. Faced with a similar problem and IMF demands for wide-ranging reforms, Malaysia simply refused the IMF's offer yet was able to resolve its loan payment problem without the negative consequences experienced by Thailand and South Korea.[29]

The hypocrisy of neoliberalism: Do as we say, not as we did Developing nations also see a large measure of hypocrisy in the IMF's imposition of a neoliberal model of development. Not only are neoliberal policies unlikely to lead to development in the future; they have never done so in the past. The United States and other developed nations are caught in the grips of a mythology about their own history and development that bears very little resemblance to reality. In his book, *Business Organization and the Myth of the Market Economy,* economic historian William Lazonink examined the policies today's developed states followed during their development. The notion that markets and free trade propelled their development is, as his title suggests, a myth. Every nation (except the first to develop, Great Britain) followed the same pattern— they protected industries from foreign imports until they were able to compete. In the United States, for example, basic industries were protected from European, especially British, competition in the latter part of the 1800s and early 1900s by substantial tariffs that allowed them to mature. Only after World War II, when it emerged as the world's only unscathed industrial economy, did the United States become a convert to free trade. It is almost comical to hear U.S. officials pontificate about the evils of tariffs and quotas, given their nation's history. The Japanese economic revival after World War II also took place thanks to government protection that shielded critical industries. As Michael Mandelbaum explains, "Japan carefully regulated its trade. Although its volume of imports was substantial, the Japanese government tightly controlled what could be brought into the country. Almost all imports were raw materials necessary for industry. . . . Industrial products of the kind the Japanese themselves made we kept out."[30] And contrary to what neoliberals would have us believe, the East Asian NICs were not paragons of limited government and free trade. In reality, "they practiced a purposeful medley of state intervention . . . [including] government policies that steered and subsidized enterprise, that suppressed domestic interest rates and controlled foreign capital, [and] that protected their infant industries from the raw market forces.[31]

Harsher critics of the IMF find it both curious and telling that the developed world imposes policies that have not led to development in the past. This suggests that the IMF is not really interested in promoting genuine development. Perhaps the real purpose of these policies is to advance the economic interests of the developed states, Northern banks, and multinational corporations.

CONCLUSION

In 2002, the World Bank reported that the percentage of people living in poverty throughout the world had declined from 28 percent to 24 percent between 1987 and 1998 (poverty being defined as an income of less than $1 a day). Virtually all of this reduction occurred in just two nations, India and China, the two most populous nations of the developing world. For the rest of the developing world there was little good news. As is usually the case with these kinds of studies, the report set off a ferocious debate among economists that rapidly degenerated into a mind-numbing battle of competing statistics, measures, methodologies, and interpretations. But any way you slice the data, the fact remains that a very large portion of the world's population lives under conditions that most people in the United States and Europe can barely imagine, never mind tolerate. Even if the World Bank's figures are reliable, 24 percent of the world's population translates into well over 1 billion people subsisting for an entire year on what many in the North spend on a single outfit. Even if the cost of living is lower, a dollar a day is still very little money in any setting.

A United Nations study released a few years before the World Bank's put a slightly less optimistic spin on the data, highlighting what it labeled "grotesque" inequalities in the global distribution of wealth (see box 7.1). Though the fortunes of Bill Gates and the Walton family fluctuate with the value of their stock, even in a bad year for Wall Street their relative wealth is still striking. One need not be a radical egalitarian socialist in order to think there is something not quite right about a world in which one or two families possess more wealth than entire nations.

Though the debate over the IMF touches on many of the critical issues facing developing economies, it barely scratches the surface in other respects. For large parts of the Third World in which the prospects for development are bleakest, the bad news just keeps coming. The obstacles to development appear so numerous, intractable, and interrelated that it is hard to know where or how to begin addressing them. One

UN Reports "Grotesque" Income Gaps

Washington Post Service, July 14, 1999
UNITED NATIONS, New York

The world's 200 richest people have doubled their wealth in just four years, and the assets of the three richest families now exceed the combined gross national products of all the least-developed countries, according to a UN report released Tuesday.

"Global inequalities in income and living standards have reached grotesque proportions," according to the Human Development Report, an annual survey that focuses this year on the costs and benefits of globalization, a vaguely defined term that includes developments as diverse as the liberalization of markets and the expansion of the Internet.

As of 1998, the three leading billionaires —Bill Gates, head of the Microsoft Corp., the Sultan of Brunei and the Walton family that owns the Wal-Mart grocery store chain—had amassed at least $135 billion in combined assets, more than the total GNP of all 43 countries categorized by the United Nations as "least developed," said a spokeswoman for the UN Development Program.

If the world's 200 richest people each donated 1 percent of their wealth per year, the report said, they could ensure access to primary education for every child in the world.

SOURCE: **U.N. Cites Disparities in Wealth, by Colum Lynch, Washington Post, July 13, 1999. © 1999, The Washington Post, reprinted with permission.**

feels trapped in an endless series of catch-22s. The interrelated problems of poverty, political instability, and investment provide one example. Extreme poverty often contributes to political instability as various segments of society compete over meager resources. As long as the political situation remains volatile, foreign companies are hesitant to risk investment (and because domestic savings are so low in poor countries, foreign investment is essential). But without this investment, it is hard to overcome the poverty that creates the political instability in the first place. Societies end up caught on the horns of a dilemma: without economic growth there will be no stability, but without stability there can be no economic growth. One can also look at the relationship between economic growth, education, and health care. Economic growth requires a decently educated and healthy workforce, but without economic growth how do developing nations provide the education and health care their people need? The list goes on and on. Poverty and the lack of development seem *overdetermined*—that is, there are so many obstacles that the elimination of just one or two would barely make a dent in the larger scheme of things.

To make matters even worse, many of the most desperate nations in the developing world, particularly in sub-Saharan Africa, are being decimated by the AIDS crisis. As many as one in five Zambians is HIV positive, and between 1993 and 2003 the population of Botswana declined from approximately 1.4 million to under 1 million.[32] Demographically, the disease tends to strike the most vital and economically productive segments of society—young urban professionals. Health care systems, which had a hard enough time dealing with relatively easy-to-treat conditions, find it nearly impossible to cope with this complicated and very expensive illness. As a result, AIDS taxes health and social welfare systems that were already straining to meet people's most basic needs. And this does not even begin to take into account the psychological toll on a society that witnesses its young people dying in large numbers.[33]

The 1980s and 1990s are sometimes referred to as Africa's "lost decades," during which economic stagnation left the continent further behind the rest of the world. If anything, the next decade is likely to be even worse, regardless of what the IMF does. Economic stagnation could easily be replaced by outright regression. Following the "right" economic policies might help bring development in some parts of the world, but in others the problem of poverty and underdevelopment resemble the proverbial Gordian knot in that we have no idea which string to pull to loosen the knot without fear of making it even tighter.

POINTS OF VIEW
Do Trade Barriers Prevent Development?

Though this chapter has focused on the IMF, it has done so as a means of getting at some of the larger issues in debates about development, inequality, and the nature of the global economy. One of the most politically explosive issues in terms of North–South relations, development, and trade concerns subsidies and tariffs in developed nations. From the perspective of developing nations, this is perhaps the most significant example of how the global economy is often rigged against them. To be blunt, the charge is that developed nations preach free trade, and insist through organizations such as the IMF that developing nations eliminate subsidies and open their markets, while they hypocritically provide subsidies and erect barriers that impede imports from developing nations.

The following editorials by Wole Akande and Jagdish Bhagwati deal with the tricky issue of subsidies and tariffs in developed nations. For Akande, the hypocrisy of developed nations is merely another indicator of how the global economy is systematically biased against developing nations. When liberal policies work to the benefit of developed nations, they are perfectly content to follow and impose them, but when these same liberal policies work against the interests of the developed states, they are quickly abandoned. Though Bhagwati is also critical of these subsidies and tariffs, he presents a very different take on the whole question. Despite their agreement that subsidies and tariffs should be eliminated, Bhagwati and Akande see the global economy and the motives of organizations such as the IMF very differently. They may arrive at the same conclusion, but they get there via different routes. How does this debate over tariffs and subsidies fit into the controversy over the IMF? How do the disagreements between Bhagwati and Akande relate to the larger debate about the nature of the global economy and the causes of underdevelopment?

How Agricultural Subsidies in Rich Countries Hurt Poor Nations

Wole Akande
YellowTimes.org October 19, 2002

There is trouble ahead on the farm front, despite assurances made to poor countries by the World Trade Organization's Agreement on Agriculture promising drastic reductions in agricultural subsidies being doled out in the Western countries. Agricultural subsidy is the process whereby governments give large sums of money to agriculture traders and farmers to increase their overall profits; this allows these exporters to drastically reduce the prices of their goods. Earlier this year, President Bush signed into law a new farm bill worth $180 billion that will raise U.S. agricultural subsidies up to 80 percent a year for the next 10 years.

Behind the 2002 Farm Security and Rural Investment Act is a simple principle: U.S. producers will market crops at very low prices, and then have their incomes topped up by government transfers. For 2002–03, wheat and maize growers will get a 30 percent top-up, rising to almost 50 percent for rice and cotton farmers. The result will be that giant grain traders, such as the Cargill Corporation, will be able to buy commodities from farmers at artificially low prices and farmers will get fat government checks to make up for their losses.

With agricultural subsidies already accounting for 25 percent of the value of farm output in the United States, the new farm bill will lead to greater American overproduction, further distort agricultural commodity markets around the world and restrict access to the United States market for poor farmers in the developing world.

While the 2002 farm bill acts as a welfare program for agribusiness, with U.S. taxpayers footing the bill, it also robs the world's poor. Wielding the World Bank, the International Monetary Fund (IMF), and international trade agreements, the U.S. is opening up foreign markets for exports by forcing poor countries to remove government subsidies and lower import tariffs while the U.S. shields itself from foreign competition by increasing its subsidies and maintaining tariffs.

These measures have allowed the U.S. to dump its farm surplus on world markets. For example, the U.S. exports corn at prices 20 percent below the cost of actual production, and wheat at 46 percent below cost. This has resulted in Mexican corn farmers being put out of business. The dramatic increase in U.S. agricultural subsidies will further jeopardize the livelihoods of those in developing countries. Poor regions, like Africa, depend on agriculture for about a quarter of their total output, most of it coming from low-income families.

Exporters in Africa will also suffer. According to the World Bank, West African cotton exporters already lose about $250 million a year as a direct result of U.S. subsidies; this figure will rise sharply. In West African countries like Burkina Faso, Mali and Chad, where cotton accounts for more than one-third of export earnings, the losses already represent around three times the savings provided through debt relief.

This is a classic example of trade policy undermining aid. In the cotton-growing basin of Sikasso, in southeast Mali, where 80 percent live in poverty, the consequences will be devastating. The Texas cotton barons will be cashing in at the bank while desperately poor Africans suffer more.

Staple food producers in developing countries face particularly bleak prospects as IMF imposed import liberalization exposes them to intensified competition with subsidized imports. For instance, since Mexico's import barriers started tumbling under the North American Free Trade Agreement, U.S. maize imports have tripled, Mexican smallholders have been forced out of local markets, undermining rural economies and fuelling migration. The U.S. Department of Agriculture is now targeting countries such as Brazil and the Philippines.

Import liberalization in markets distorted by subsidies can have devastating implications for efforts to combat rural poverty and improve self-reliance. When the IMF bulldozed Haiti into liberalizing its rice markets in the mid-1990s, the country was flooded with cheap U.S. imports. Local production collapsed, along with tens of thousands of rural livelihoods. Self-sufficient a decade ago, Haiti today spends half of its export earnings importing U.S. rice.

The wider danger is that the U.S. farm bill will undermine local agriculture and foster dependence on imports. This will be particularly damaging in sub-Saharan Africa, where staple food production lags behind population growth and imports have risen 40 percent over the past decade.

Even the World Bank president, James Wolfensohn, acknowledges "these subsidies are crippling Africa's chance to export its way out of poverty." The developing world faces trade barriers costing them $200 billion per annum—twice as much as they receive in aid. Industrialized nations currently spend about $350 billion a year assisting their farmers, more than the economic output for all of Africa.

Flipping the script, if developing countries were able to increase their share of world exports by just 5 percent, this would generate $700 billion. The potential for this to translate into poverty reduction for hundreds of millions of people is enormous. Economic modeling by Oxfam indicates that if Africa, East Asia, South Asia and Latin America were each to increase their share of world trade by 1 percent, the resulting gains in income could lift 128 million people out of poverty.

Not surprisingly, the double standards of the U.S. administration that professes allegiance to market economics and fiscal probity have unleashed a wave of indignation among countries whose development prospects largely depend on farm exports. Agriculture and food are fundamental to the well being of all people, both in terms of access to safe and nutritious food and as foundations of healthy communities, cultures, and environment. All of these have been undermined by dependence on the vagaries of the free market promoted by the World Bank, the International Monetary Fund, and the World Trade Organization. Instead of ensuring the right to food for all, these institutions have created a system that prioritizes export-oriented production and has increased global hunger and poverty while alienating millions from productive assets and resources such as land, water, and seeds.

For millions in poor countries, the "world market" of agricultural products simply does not exist. What exists is an international trade of grain, cereals, and meat surpluses dumped primarily by the European Union, the United States, and other members of the Cairns Group. Behind the faces of trade negotiators are powerful transnational corporations such as Cargill and Monsanto, which are the real beneficiaries of domestic subsidies and international trade agreements. Fundamental change to this repressive trade regime is essential.

The Poor's Best Hope—Trading for Development— Removing Trade Barriers Is a Job for the Poor as Well . . .

June 22, 2002

The poor's best hope—Trading for development—Removing trade barriers is a job for the poor as well as the rich.

By invitation

Removing trade barriers is not just a job for the rich. The poor must do the same in order to prosper, says Jagdish Bhagwati. . . .

Proponents of trade have always considered that trade is the policy and development the objective. The experience of the post-war years only proves them right. The objections advanced by a handful of dissenting economists, claiming that free-traders exaggerate the gains from trade or forget that good trade policy is best embedded within a package of reforms, are mostly setting up and knocking down straw men.

But if trade is indeed good for the poor countries, what can be done to enhance its value for them? A great deal. But not until we confront and discard several misconceptions. Among them:

- The world trading system is "unfair": the poor countries face protectionism that is more acute than their own;

- The rich countries have wickedly held on to their trade barriers against poor countries, while using the Bretton Woods institutions to force down the poor countries' own trade barriers; and

- It is hypocritical to ask poor countries to reduce their trade barriers when the rich countries have their own.

In fact, asymmetry of trade barriers goes the other way. Take industrial tariffs. As of today, rich-country tariffs average 3 percent; poor countries' tariffs average 13 percent. Nor do peaks in tariffs—concentrated in textiles and clothing, fisheries and footwear, and clearly directed at the poor countries—change the picture much: the United Nations Council for Trade, Aid and Development (UNCTAD) has estimated that they apply to only a third of poor-country exports. Moreover, the trade barriers of the poor countries against one another are more significant restraints on their own development than those imposed by the rich countries....

The wicked rich?

These facts fly in the face of the populist myth that the rich countries, often acting through the conditionality imposed by the World Bank and the International Monetary Fund (IMF), have demolished the trade barriers of the poor countries while holding on to their own. Indeed, both the omnipotence of the Bretton Woods institutions, and the wickedness of the rich countries, have been grossly exaggerated.

The World Bank's conditionality is so extensive and diffused, and its need to lend so compelling, that it can in fact be bypassed. Many client states typically satisfy some conditions while ignoring others. Besides, countries go to the IMF when there is a stabilisation crisis. Since stabilisation requires that the excess of expenditures over income be brought into line, the IMF has often been reluctant to suggest tariff reductions. These could reduce revenues, exacerbating the crisis.

Then again, since countries are free to return to their bad ways once the crisis is past and the loans repaid, tariff reforms can be reversed. Countries do not "bind" their tariff reductions under the IMF programmes, as they do at the World Trade Organisation (WTO). Equally, tariff reductions may be reversed when a stabilisation crisis recurs and the tariffs are reimposed to increase revenues.... For instance, Uruguay in 1971 increased trade protection during an IMF programme that began the year before, and even managed to get another credit tranche the year after. Kenya's 1977 liberalisation was reversed in 1979, the year in which another arrangement was negotiated with the IMF....

But even if rich-country protectionism were asymmetrically higher, it would be dangerous to argue that it is therefore hypocritical to suggest that poor countries should reduce their own trade barriers....

In fact, the protectionism of the poor and the rich countries must be viewed together symbiotically to ensure effective exports by the poor countries. Thus, even if the doors to the markets of the rich countries were fully open to imports, exports from the poor countries would have to get past their own doors.

We know from numerous case studies dating back to the 1970s (which only corroborated elementary economic logic) that protection is often the cause of dismal export, and hence economic, performance. It creates a "bias against exports" by sheltering domestic markets that then become more lucrative. Just ask yourself why, though India and the far-eastern countries faced virtually the same external trade barriers in the quarter-century after the 1960s, inward-looking India registered a miserable export performance while outward-looking South Korea, Taiwan, Singapore and Hong Kong chalked up spectacular exports. Just as charity begins at home, so exports begin with a good domestic policy. In the near-exclusive focus on rich-country protectionism, this dramatic lesson has been lost from view.

A strategy for change

Rich-country protectionism matters too, of course. And it must be assaulted effectively. But here, too, we witness folly. The current fashion is to shame the rich countries by arguing that their protection hurts the poor countries, whose poverty is the focus of renewed international efforts....

If shame were sufficient, there would be no rich-country protectionism left. Trade economists and international institutions such as UNCTAD and the General Agreement on Tariffs and Trade (the GATT) have denounced the rich countries on this count over three decades....

The argument to rich countries should be made in quite a different way: If you hold on to your own protection, no matter how much smaller, and in fact even raise it as the United States did recently with steel tariffs and the farm bill, you are going to undermine seriously the efforts of those poor-country leaders who have turned to freer trade in recent decades. It is difficult for such countries to reduce protection if others, more prosperous and fiercer supporters of free trade, are breaking ranks.

CHAPTER SUMMARY

- Originally founded to help nations deal with balance of payments problems, since the late 1970s the IMF has played an increasingly controversial role in providing loans and policy advice to developing nations in response to the so-called "debt crisis."

- As a condition for granting these loans, the IMF required economic reforms reflecting a neoliberal view of the global economy and development. Convinced that previous development strategies failed because of excessive government interference in the economy and misguided attempts to limit foreign trade and investment, the IMF's structural adjustment programs called for reducing the role of government and opening developing economies to greater trade and investment.

- By requiring these reforms to spur economic growth and development, the IMF implicitly assumes that the major obstacle to development has been the policies of developing nations themselves.

- Pointing to the success of several East Asian nations, the IMF and its supporters reject the notion that development is impossible within the existing global economy. Only the differing policies of developing nations, not some fundamental feature of the global economy, can explain the diversity of outcomes.

- From the IMF's perspective, the evidence of the past fifty years reveals one basic lesson: market-oriented policies at home and integration into the global economy through trade and investment are the route to growth and development, but socialism, state control, and isolation are a recipe for stagnation.

- Though the IMF draws criticism from across the ideological spectrum, the harshest and most sustained critiques are informed by dependency theory, which sees poverty and inequality as inherent features of the global capitalist economic order.

- From this perspective, IMF policies are designed to advance the interests of the wealthiest states and multinational corporations at the expense of the poorest and most vulnerable in developing countries.

- As a result, critics are not surprised that structural adjustment policies have failed even on their own terms — they have not produced economic growth or reductions in poverty.

- More important, critics reject the underlying assumption that limited government interference and opening the domestic economy to foreign competition and investment are the path to development. This is not the model successful nations have followed in the past, and it will not work in the future. Such a development strategy is actually a recipe for inequality, poverty, dependence, and exploitation.

- Concerns about the IMF and structural adjustment aside, it is important to recognize the magnitude of global inequality and the multitude of obstacles to development that many Third World nations confront. Even the "right" policies, whatever those are, might not be enough in some of the most problematic areas.

CRITICAL QUESTIONS

1. Do people in the developed world benefit from continued poverty in the developing world?

2. What are the major differences between dependency and neoliberal views of the global economy?

3. Why do the East Asian economies such as Taiwan, South Korea, and Singapore play such a controversial role in debates over the causes of underdevelopment?

4. Why are many in developing nations skeptical about the role of multinational corporations in their development?

5. In what areas does the debate over structural adjustment policies reflect deeper disagreements about the causes of underdevelopment?

KEY TERMS

capital market liberalization 175
comprador class 181
conditionality 173
core 181
debt crisis 173
declining terms of trade 172
dependency theory 181
fiscal austerity 175
Friedman, Milton (1912–) 174
import substitution 172
international division of labor 171
International Monetary Fund (IMF) 171
Keynes, John Maynard (1883–1946) 174
moral hazard 180
neocolonialism 181
neoimperialism: see neocolonialism

FURTHER READINGS

For those interested in the IMF and structural adjustment policies, the most recent and comprehensive account is James R. Vreeland's *The IMF and Economic Development* (Cambridge: Cambridge University Press, 2003). In terms of the larger debate about the global economy and development, it might be useful to begin with two influential statements of dependency theory: Fernando Enrique Cardoso and Enzo Faletto, *Dependency and Development in Latin America* (Berkeley: University of California Press, 1979) and Peter Evans, *Dependent Development: The Alliance of Multinational, State, and Local Capital in Brazil* (Princeton: Princeton University Press, 1979). One of the few attempts to subject dependency theory to empirical testing is Vincent Mahler, *Dependency Approaches to International Political Economy* (New York: Columbia University Press, 1980). Perhaps the most forceful (and quite harsh) critique of dependency theory is Robert Packenham, *The Dependency Movement: Scholarship and Politics in Development Studies* (Cambridge, MA: Harvard University Press, 1992). Though not explicitly intended as critiques of dependency theory, two works that reject its underlying assumptions are David Landes, *The Wealth and Poverty of Nations: Why Some Are So Rich and Some Are So Poor* (New York: W.W. Norton, 1998), and Nathan Rosenberg and L. E. Bridzell, Jr., *How the West Grew Rich: The Economic Transformation of the Industrial World* (New York: Basic Books, 1987). An effort to explain the success and failure of development in terms of cultural values is Lawrence E. Harrison and Samuel Huntington, *Culture Matters: How Values Shape Human Progress* (New York: Basic Books, 2001). And an excellent overall survey of international economics is Robert Gilpin, *Global Political Economy: Understanding the International Economic Order* (Princeton: Princeton University Press, 2001).

THE IMF, GLOBAL INEQUALITY, AND DEVELOPMENT ON THE WEB

www.imf.org
The official website of the International Monetary Fund.

www.50years.org
Site highly critical of the IMF and dedicated to a radical change in the organization's policies and priorities.

www.grassrootsfreemarket.org.
Organization dedicated to promoting development through free market policies.

www.unicef.org
Website of a United Nations organization that deals extensively with the developing world. Its yearly "Progress of Nations" reports can be found on this site.

www.cedpa.org
Site of the Center for Development and Population Activities, an organization that emphasizes the role and status of women in developing countries.

www.jubileeusa.org
Organization dedicated to relieving developing nations of crippling foreign debts.

www.oxfam.org.uk
One of the oldest and most influential organizations interested in assistance to developing nations.

NOTES

[1] Conn Hallinan, "The Global Goodfellas at the IMF," *San Francisco Examiner,* January 11, 2002, p. 23.
[2] Peter Korner, Gero Maass, Thomas Siebold, and Rainer Tetzlaff, *The IMF and the Debt Crisis: A Guide to the Third World's Dilemma* (London: Zed Books, 1986), p. 35.
[3] Jagdish Bhagwati, *India in Transition: Freeing the Economy* (Oxford: Clarendon Press, 1993), p. 71.
[4] Bahram Nowzad, *The IMF and Its Critics,* Essays in International Finance, no. 146 (Princeton: Princeton University Department of Economics, 1981), p. 8.
[5] David Landes, *The Wealth and Poverty of Nations: Why Some Nations Are So Rich and Some Are So Poor* (New York: W. W. Norton, 1998), p. 433.
[6] Ibid., p. 499.

[7] This comparison is drawn from Keith R. Richburg, "Why Is Africa Eating Asia's Dust," *The Washington Post National Weekly Edition,* July 20–26, 1992, p. 11.

[8] Robert Gilpin, *Global Political Economy: Understanding the International Economic Order* (Princeton: Princeton University Press, 2001), p. 312.

[9] Robert Gilpin, *The Political Economy of International Relations* (Princeton: Princeton University Press, 1987), p. 268.

[10] Stephan Haggard, *Pathways from the Periphery: The Politics of Growth in Newly Industrializing Countries* (Ithaca, NY: Cornell University Press, 1990), p. 14.

[11] Gilpin, *Political Economy of International Relations,* p. 302.

[12] Bhagwati, *India in Transition,* p. 46.

[13] See Juan Gabriel Valdes, *Pinochet's Economists: The Chicago School in Chile* (Cambridge: Cambridge University Press, 1995), and Daniel Yergin and Joseph Stanislaw, *The Commanding Heights: The Battle between Government and the Marketplace That Is Remaking the Modern World* (New York: Simon and Shuster, 1998), pp. 238–40.

[14] P. T. Bauer, *Equality, the Third World, and Economic Delusion* (Cambridge, MA: Harvard University Press, 1981), pp. 70, 76.

[15] "Going Global: Globalisation and Prosperity," *The Economist* (December 8, 2001), p. 67.

[16] Andres Velasco, "Dependency Theory," *Foreign Policy* (November/December 2002): 45.

[17] Gilpin, *Political Economy of International Relations,* p. 286.

[18] Peter Evans, *Dependent Development: The Alliance of Multinational, State and Local Capital in Brazil* (Princeton: Princeton University Press, 1979), p. 34.

[19] The Report of the South Commission, *The Challenge to the South* (Oxford: Oxford University Press, 1990), p. 38.

[20] Paul A. Baran, *The Political Economy of Growth* (New York: Monthly Review Press, 1962), pp. 11–12.

[21] Cited in Michael Camdessus, "A Talk with Michael Camdessus about God, Globalization and His Years Running the IMF," *Foreign Policy* (September/October 2000): 34.

[22] William Greider, *One World, Ready or Not: The Manic Logic of Global Capitalism* (New York: Touchstone Books, 1997), p. 281.

[23] "Nothing to Lose But Your Chains: Aid for Africa," *The Economist* (May 1, 1993), p. 44.

[24] Robert O'Brien, Anne Marie Goetz, Jan Aart Scholte and Marc Williams, *Contesting Global Governance: Multinational Economic Institutions and Global Social Movements* (Cambridge: Cambridge University Press, 2000), p. 37.

[25] IMF Policy Development and Review Group, "Experience under the IMF's Enhanced Structural Adjustment Facility," *Finance and Development* (September 1997): 32–35. Another study that departs from conventional wisdom and offers a modestly positive assessment of the effect of structural adjustment is David E. Sahn, Paul A. Dorosh, and Stephen D. Younger, *Structural Adjustment Reconsidered* (Cambridge: Cambridge University Press, 1997).

[26] William Easterly, "IMF and World Bank Structural Adjustment Programs and Poverty," paper prepared for the World Bank, February 2001.

[27] Adam Przeworski and James Raymond Vernon, "The Effect of IMF Structural Adjustment Programs on Economic Growth," *Journal of Development Economics* 62 (2000): 401.

[28] Cited in Joseph M. Grieco and G. John Ikenberry, *State Power and World Markets: The International Political Economy* (New York: W. W. Norton, 2003), p. 280.

[29] See Joseph Stiglitz, *Globalization and Its Discontents* (New York: W. W. Norton, 2002), p. 132.

[30] Michael Mandelbaum, *The Fate of Nations: The Search for National Security in the Nineteenth and Twentieth Centuries* (Cambridge: Cambridge University Press, 1988), p. 359.

[31] Greider, *One World, Ready or Not,* p. 276.

[32] Hugh Russell, "It's Worse Than You Imagined," *The Spectator* (March 1, 2003), p. 22.

[33] See also "AIDS in the Third World: A Global Disaster," *The Economist* (January 2, 1999), pp. 42–44.

CHAPTER EIGHT

GLOBALIZATION AND SOVEREIGNTY

This chapter explores a central aspect of the larger debate over what has become known as *globalization*—whether national societies and governments are becoming part of a single global society. The question is whether globalization is robbing national communities and governments of their ability to shape their own policies and destinies. Some believe that economic and technological trends are taking critical decisions out of the hands of national governments, placing them at the mercy of supranational forces, actors, and institutions. Economic actors such as multinational corporations are increasingly able to escape the power of national governments. Observers from a variety of perspectives—liberal, Marxist, and feminist—agree that globalization is occurring, though they disagree on whether this process is essentially beneficial or harmful. Others, particularly realists, believe these arguments are wildly exaggerated: national boundaries, communities, and governments are still paramount and the world remains fundamentally a collection of national communities rather than a truly global society or economy.

A walk down the Kurfürstendam, Berlin's major shopping street, would come as something of a disappointment to a first-time visitor hoping to be overwhelmed by the sights and sounds of a different culture and society. Were it not for the fact that most people were speaking German, one might just as well be walking down Fifth Avenue in New York or Michigan Avenue in Chicago. The clothes would look familiar—Levi jeans and Nike sneakers abound. The food would taste familiar—it takes little effort to find a McDonald's, Pizza Hut, or Starbucks. The music would sound familiar, and larger-than-life Brittany Spears posters grace the windows of Virgin Records. Automatic teller machines make access to one's checking account no more difficult than at home. After a long day buying items you could just as easily have purchased in the United States, you could duck into an Internet café to check the day's e-mail messages. Back at the hotel, the latest episode of *Friends* is likely to be on television and you could catch the news on CNN before falling asleep. This would not have been the experience of someone making the same transatlantic journey thirty years ago when traveling to another country was, well, like traveling to another country.

The sense that Berlin is no longer much different than Chicago is a superficial manifestation of something we call **globalization,** a term more widely used than defined. When people refer to globalization, they generally mean that traditional divisions and boundaries that used to mark global society are no longer what they once were. In clichéd terms, the world is becoming a smaller place. Anthony Giddens sees globalization as "the intensification of worldwide social relations which link distant localities in such a way that local happenings are shaped by events occurring many miles away and vice versa." But Martin Albrow provides the most succinct and general definition of globalization as "all those processes by which the people of the world are incorporated into a single world society."[1]

Globalization is, of course, a multifaceted phenomenon. Though many focus on its economic aspects, and perhaps rightly so, this is not the be-all and end-all of globalization. There are important environmental, cultural, and even medical consequences of globalization. It is no understatement, for example, to note that "the globalization of trade is inextricably linked to the globalization of disease . . . with globalization, widespread diseases are literally a plane ride away."[2] The worldwide spread of AIDS is perhaps the most dramatic example of the globalization of disease. And the same technologies that allow us to move consumer goods and legitimate investments around the world with ease can be utilized to traffic in illegal narcotics and funnel money to terrorist organizations. The Internet might undermine totalitarian governments by making it easier for people to access ideas and information, but it also helps hate groups develop and maintain international networks. The technology and process of globalization are neutral and can be used for good or ill.

globalization The multi-faceted process by which the nations and societies of the world are increasingly being merged into a single global society and economy.

WHAT IS AT STAKE

Beneath some very general observations about our shrinking world lie tremendous debate and unease about the nature and consequences of globalization, ranging from seemingly petty concerns that English is corrupting the French language to worries about the impact on global economic inequality. These debates are both empirical and normative. Empirically, the disagreement is about the extent of globalization—are nations, economies, and cultures really as interconnected as some believe, or is talk of globalization just so much trendy "globaloney"? Normatively, the issue is whether globalization is a progressive force to be welcomed and encouraged or a malignant process to be condemned and resisted. For those who reject globalization as faddish exaggeration, the normative debate is largely beside the point. After all, it makes no sense to waste time debating the consequences of something that is not really happening. The normative issues arise only if the empirical question is answered affirmatively.

Obviously, it is not possible to do justice to all aspects of the globalization debate in a single chapter. Fortunately, many of the issues associated with globalization are dealt with in other chapters. We have already looked at the debates over free trade and development, both central elements of the larger globalization controversy. Later we will examine global environmental issues. This chapter focuses on another issue that lies at the heart of debates about globalization—whether or not there are forces at work undermining what many believe has been the defining feature of international politics for several centuries—national sovereignty. As Ian Clark explains, "According to conventional wisdom it is sovereignty which is most at risk from globalization. . . . [thus] if we wish to trace the impact of globalization, then it is within the realm of sovereignty that the search must properly begin."[3] The fear is that nations are gradually losing the ability to determine their own fate as the forces of globalization shift the locus of meaningful decision making to other entities. According to this **constrained state thesis,** "changes in the international political economy have radically restricted policy choice and forced policy shifts that play to the preferences of global investors and mobile corporations, rather than to the needs of the domestic political economy and its citizenry."[4] The fundamental question is whether national political communities can still shape the policies and tame the forces that affect the lives of their citizens.

> **constrained state thesis**
> The idea that the forces driving globalization are profoundly weakening or limiting the ability of national states to shape their own policies and destinies.

THE VISION OF A BORDERLESS WORLD

Interdependence was the buzzword of the 1970s. Middle East crises, oil embargoes, and long gas lines brought home how interdependent the economies of the world had become. Although it is always difficult to locate the first usage of new terminology, *globalization* appears to have entered the lexicon of international relations in the early 1980s. The need for a new concept arose from the sense that *interdependence* no longer captured the full magnitude of how much our world was changing. Interdependence suggested that increasing levels of international trade and investment were creating mutual dependencies among different national economies. Globalization conveys something more—not merely that national economies are increasingly dependent on each other, but that for all intents and purposes they are becoming a single economic system. To use an analogy, we usually do not describe the economy of Minneapolis as being dependent on the economy of St. Paul. These are not two separate economies dependent on each other but rather part of a single economy. Though the difference between interdependence and globalization might seem to be only a matter of degree, there comes a point where differences in degree become so great as to become differences in kind. This is what globalization implies—not just greater interdependence, but something well beyond that. An interdependent world is one in which borders and nations are still meaningful. In a truly globalized world, they are not.

No one has been more articulate in presenting a vision of globalization as eroding national sovereignty than Kenichi Ohmae. In his books *The Borderless World* and *The End of the Nation State,* Ohmae makes a forceful case for the proposition that economic and technological trends are rendering the nation-state increasingly irrelevant and impotent. This effect can be seen most vividly in the dynamics of the global economy: "On the political map, the boundaries between countries are as clear as ever. But on the competitive map, a map showing the real flows of financial and industrial activity, those boundaries have largely disappeared."[5] If we removed the political borders from a map of the world and looked only at the patterns of economic activity, we would no longer be able to redraw the world's political boundaries.

This means there is an increasing disjuncture between political and economic realities. This disconnect, however, cannot last forever. Ohmae thinks the readjustment is already well under way: "the modern nation-state itself—the artifact of the eighteenth and nineteenth centuries—has begun to crumble."[6] Nicholas Negroponte outdoes even Ohmae in consigning the nation-state to the dustbin of history: "Like a mothball, which goes from solid to gas directly, I expect the nation-state to evaporate."[7] And Anthony Giddens has joined the funeral chorus: "Nations have lost the sovereignty they once had, and politicians have lost their capability to influence events . . . the era of the nation-state is over."[8] But why? Why might globalization be eroding the sovereignty of the nation-state, or even threatening its extinction? The answer is to be found in technological and political changes that have made it easier to move, communicate, and trade without regard to location and national borders.

Ending the tyranny of location Two or three hundred years ago, most people lived in local economies. They either grew their own food or bought it from local producers, and most of their possessions were made by local crafts workers. Today, hardly anything on our supermarket shelves is grown locally—the tomatoes are from New Jersey, the pineapples from the Philippines and the broccoli from Chile—and virtually nothing in our homes was produced within 100 miles of where we live. We no longer live in localized economies. Certainly global trade is nothing new—the Dutch East India Company was global in scope back in the 1500s and 1600s and people in Europe enjoyed spices from Asia. But in the larger scheme of things, the volume of such trade was miniscule and unimportant in the lives of most people.

The evolutionary process of moving from local to national economies and from national economies to an international economy has taken several centuries. To explain this transformation, one needs to focus on developments that have allowed people to overcome previous obstacles to long-distance commerce. Before the industrial revolution, transporting goods across great distances was either extremely expensive or impossible (e.g., one could hardly transport fresh produce from Brazil to France without artificial refrigeration). The advent of the internal combustion engine, the railroad, the steamship, and the telegraph helped overcome many of these obstacles. Advances in transportation drove the first wave of globalization in the 1800s and early 1900s. The current wave of globalization rests more on revolutions in communications (though easy and cheap air travel and transport are a part of contemporary globalization). As Thomas Friedman explains, "Today's era of globalization is built around falling telecommunications costs—thanks to microchips, satellites, fiber optics and the internet . . . technologies now allow companies to locate different parts of their production, research and marketing in different countries, but still tie them together . . . as though they were in one place."[9] The head of Levi-Strauss provides an illustration: "Our company buys denim in North Carolina, ships it to France where it is sewn into jeans, launders these jeans in Belgium, and markets them in Germany using TV commercials developed in England."[10]

Limited technology, however, was not the only obstacle to the emergence of a genuinely international economy. Except for relatively rare periods of free trade, tariffs, quotas, and other barriers made international commerce difficult. In order for a truly global economy to emerge, the technological *and* political obstacles had to be overcome. It had to be so easy and cheap to move goods around that it no longer mattered very much where production took place. And businesses needed to be able to buy and sell supplies and products from and into different markets without politically erected barriers. The creation of a liberal trading order after World War II provided the political foundation for the emergence of global economy.

Thus, until very recently economic production and exchange suffered from the **tyranny of location**—that is, a business's prospects for success depended to a significant degree on where it was located. In the contemporary world, location does not matter nearly as much as it used to. A company that makes cars 10 miles from my home enjoys no significant competitive advantage in terms of inducing me to buy its product instead of a car made on the other side of the globe. The conjuncture of free trade policies and technological advances that liberate commerce from the shackles of geography permitted the emergence of national and, now, international economies. Once we come to grips with this basic economic transformation, we are in a position to understand the threat globalization poses to national sovereignty.

The mobility of capital When location mattered a great deal, businesses often had no alternative but to locate in certain places. Take the hypothetical example of a tire company. If it wants to sell tires to the people of Cleveland and the U.S. government imposes a tax on tires imported from other countries, the company will need to build its tire factories within the United States. If it costs a lot of money to ship tires 1,000 miles, the company should probably locate its factory close to Cleveland so that it does not lose out to more local producers. But if transporting products is not very expensive, the company can locate anywhere within the United States. And if there are no barriers to importing tires from abroad, it can locate anywhere in the world. Diminishing technological and political obstacles to trade increases what we call the **mobility of capital.** Thus, today our tire company can open its factory in Cleveland, Georgia, or Indonesia.

When corporations enjoy this sort of freedom, the relative power between governments and business shifts. This is the critical point. If a business needs to locate in a certain place, the government that controls that territory has leverage that allows it to tax and regulate. The stronger the shackles of location, the stronger are the powers of governments to control and regulate business. But as businesses enjoy greater mobility, they are free to move elsewhere if governments enact policies they do not like.

tyranny of location Conditions in which a producer's geographical proximity to sources of supply or markets is a critical determinant of its ability to compete effectively.

mobility of capital The ease with which businesses and investment can move from one part of the world to another. Potential obstacles might include costs associated with commerce over long distances or government policies that make trade difficult.

So if you want to sell tires to the people of Cleveland, but the city wants to tax or regulate you in ways you do not like, move to Georgia, and if the United States government wants to do the same, move to Indonesia.

We can see this in a small way when companies shop around for places to build plants. The scenario is familiar to most communities. Company X announces that it has narrowed its choice for a new factory down to three cities. City leaders then engage in a feverish competition to see who can offer the best deal, usually involving exemptions ("abatements") from local taxes. In such cases, it is easy to wonder who is really in charge. Are governments regulating businesses, or are businesses regulating governments? Martin and Schumann frame the problem in stark terms: "It is no longer democratically elected governments which decide the level of taxes; rather, the people who direct the flow of capital and goods themselves establish what contribution they wish to make to state expenditure."[11] The fear of "capital flight" allows businesses almost to dictate what policies, regulations, and tax levels governments can impose: give us what we want, or we (and our jobs) move elsewhere. This shifting of power from governments to mobile capital is one of the developments threatening the sovereignty of states.

The race to the bottom The ability of capital to dictate policies is most clearly seen in what critics of globalization refer to as the **race to the bottom.** If corporations and investors are no longer tied to any particular location, what determines where they will set up shop? There are, of course, a host of considerations that businesses take into account. But surely the costs of doing business are a paramount concern. All other things being equal, businesses prefer to locate where the costs of production are lowest, since this maximizes profits. The story of Nike, the familiar American sports apparel company, provides an illustration of this drive to minimize costs:

> All but 1 percent of the 90 million shoes Nike makes each year are manufactured in Asia. If the costs in a particular country or factory move too far out of line, productivity will have to rise to compensate, or Nike will take its business elsewhere. . . . Until recently, almost all of Nike's shoes were made in South Korea and Taiwan, but as labor costs there have soared, the firm's contractors in these two countries have moved much of their production to cheaper sites in China, Indonesia, and Thailand. Now, Vietnam looks like the next country on the list.[12]

But there is no need to look to Asia for examples. Immediately south of the U.S.-Mexican border a host of U.S. companies are manufacturing everything from auto parts to kitchen appliances. Why not locate in Texas instead? A large part of the answer has to be the lower costs of production—lower wages, fewer benefits, and less regulation. Because they can import the final product into the United States without barriers (largely as a result of NAFTA), it would make little economic sense to locate these factories in the United States, where the costs of production are higher.

This ability to move around in search of lower costs is what propels the race to the bottom. In a globalized free market economy, workers everywhere have to compete as companies like Nike go shopping for the best deal. If the workers in Taiwan ask for too much, Vietnam awaits with its workers who will make footwear for less. The problem is exacerbated by the fact that labor does not share the same level of mobility. Be-

race to the bottom The proposition that globalization is exerting downward pressure on wages, regulations, taxes, and social welfare benefits as corporations relocate in search of lower wages, fewer regulations, and lower taxes.

The "race to the bottom"? Many fear that workers in the United States and Europe cannot compete with these Vietnamese workers in an athletic shoe factory.
SOURCE: Lou Dematteis/The Image Works

cause restrictions on immigration remain in force throughout the world, workers are not free to move around in search of the highest wages. This imbalance of mobility puts workers at a tremendous disadvantage.

Declining wages are only part of the story of the race to the bottom. Complying with government regulations, such as environmental or workplace safety rules, is also a cost of doing business. In a globalized economy, those states that impose the fewest regulations will be most attractive to corporations. This fact in turn puts pressure on states to reduce regulations that increase the cost of doing business. In terms of environmental regulations, John Gray explains the result: "The countries that require businesses to be environmentally accountable will be at a systematic disadvantage. . . . Over time, either enterprises operating in environmentally accountable regimes will be driven out of business, or the regulatory frameworks of such regimes will drift down to a common denominator in which their competitive advantage is reduced."[13]

There is still more. Globalization also poses a danger to social welfare programs that protect the poor. Businesses, like individuals, generally prefer lower taxes to higher taxes. Though celebrities and sports stars can escape to tax havens such as Monaco, most people do not have the same luxury. The average person is stuck paying whatever taxes the government imposes. In a globalized economy, corporations enjoy the advantage of movement. Not only can they relocate factories to wherever labor and regulatory costs are low, they can also move in search of lower taxes. This freedom of corporations places national governments with generous welfare programs in a bind. If governments impose high taxes on business to finance social welfare spending, they run the risk that the businesses will pick up and move. This leaves two unpalatable options—raising taxes on people and those businesses that cannot move or reducing social welfare expenditures, neither of which is very popular.

Thus, the mobility of capital creates a race to the bottom on many levels—wages, environmental and safety regulations, and social welfare benefits. Jeremy Brecher and Tim Costello summarize the problem in their appropriately titled *Global Village or Global Pillage*: "Corporations can now outflank the controls governments and organized citizens once placed on them by relocating . . . so each [government] tries to reduce labor, social, and environmental costs below the others. The result is a 'downward leveling'—a disastrous 'race to the bottom' in which conditions for all tend to fall toward those of the poorest and most desperate."[14] And to the extent that individual states must respond to these pressures or risk the flight of capital, they have been robbed of their effective sovereignty. Corporations tell governments what they can and cannot do rather than the other way around. Governments that do not toe the line are "disciplined" by the global market and capital. National governments either conform to the dictates of the global market or suffer the consequences.

It is not only business and the global market that threaten national sovereignty. Nations also have to deal with powerful international organizations, such as the International Monetary Fund and the World Bank. As we discussed in chapter 7, many Third World nations borrowed money from First World governments and banks during the 1970s but found themselves unable to pay back these loans in the 1980s, when the hoped-for economic development failed to materialize. The IMF and the World Bank stepped in to deal with the debt crisis in the 1980s. As a condition for rescheduling debt payments or granting new loans, the IMF required nations to adopt structural adjustment programs, which included reductions in social spending, the elimination of deficit spending, privatization, and opening markets to international competition. The IMF deemed these policies essential for attracting foreign investment and thus for promoting economic growth. Not coincidentally, critics are quick to point out, these policies also "neatly coincide with the agenda of mobile capital."[15] Such is the power of the IMF over many Third World nations that noted Harvard economist Jeffrey Sachs describes it as "an all-too-constant presence, almost a surrogate government in financial matters . . . these governments rarely move without consulting the IMF staff, and when they do they risk their lifelines to capital markets, foreign aid and international respectability."[16] The characterization of the IMF as a surrogate government highlights the issue of lost sovereignty.

Taken as a whole, the thesis of a race to the bottom embodies three of the key worries about the consequences of globalization. First, there is concern about the erosion of national sovereignty and the ability of governments to pursue independently determined policies. Second, there is the prediction that globalization will work to the disadvantage of poor, working class, and marginalized people around the world, who will see their wages depressed further, their environments degraded, and their social welfare benefits slashed. Third, the power of international markets, transnational corporations, and international organizations to shape, influence, or even dictate policies to national governments is viewed as a threat to fundamental values of democratic governance. When the corporations and the unelected leaders of the IMF and World Bank are able to tell elected leaders what to do, both sovereignty and democracy are compromised. As a result of globalization, national policies are increasingly determined by forces, people, and institutions that no one ever voted for. The result is a **democratic deficit.** "The fear is that the global economy is undermining democracy by shifting power from elected national governments to faceless global bureaucracies . . . power is going global but democracy, like politics, still stops at frontiers."[17]

THE MYTH(S) OF GLOBALIZATION

One of the recurring difficulties in analyzing world politics is trying to look simultaneously at changes and continuities. The hard part is evaluating the significance of that which is new relative to what is enduring. This is problematic because there is always a tendency to focus on those things that are changing, if only because the novel is more interesting than the familiar. When it comes to whether globalization is taking place, the question is not whether international trade, investment, and cultural diffusion are increasing. It would be silly to contend otherwise. The issue is whether patterns of international interactions are changing in ways and to a degree so that it makes sense to even begin talking about a borderless world or the end of the nation-state. For globalization skeptics, such talk is wildly premature at best and rests on a persistent pattern of exaggeration and selective use of evidence.

Location still matters No one can deny that advances in transportation and communications have helped overcome the obstacles of distance. Skeptics caution, however, that this should not be confused with an "end" of geography in which location no longer matters at all. Is location less important for commerce today than two hundred years ago? Certainly. Is geography even close to becoming irrelevant? Certainly not. That we are moving in the direction of an outcome (the irrelevance of geography, in this case) does not mean we have achieved or will ever achieve that outcome.

Most accounts of globalization focus on companies and plants that relocate production from one country to another in order to illustrate the irrelevance of location. But do these examples tell the full story? What about those plants that do not move? Skeptics charge that there is a tendency to focus on examples (often derided as "anecdotes") that conform to the thesis of globalization. The technical term for this problem is *selection bias.* That is, focusing on those firms that relocate while ignoring those that stay inevitably biases the analysis in favor of the declining significance of location. But a full and fair evaluation requires that we look also at those firms and plants that chose to remain. Only then will we have an accurate picture of how much location matters.

Somewhat tongue in cheek, Micklethwait and Wooldridge wonder what Bill Gates and Microsoft's legal troubles tell us about globalization and the mobility of business. Even though his company has been the object of extremely expensive antitrust lawsuits by the U.S. Department of Justice, Gates has not moved from the comfortable confines of Seattle in order to escape the long arm of the law. Why not? If companies can move for cheaper labor and/or discipline governments by threatening to relocate, why hasn't Bill Gates moved and why has the U.S. government not been disciplined? The answer is that "Bill Gates could not have threatened to move his operation to the Bahamas, even though Microsoft has relatively few fixed assets. Microsoft depends not just on a supply of educated workers (who would have refused to move) but also on its close relationship with American universities."[18] Focusing on the same case, Thomas Friedman reminds us "even when a U.S. firm becomes a much-envied world-class gem, like Microsoft, it still has to answer to a Justice Department antitrust lawyer making $75,000 a year."[19] The news that national governments are impotent would come as something of a surprise to Microsoft's lawyers.

Microsoft, however, is a high-tech firm. Would the same apply to a company making t-shirts or notepads? There are also plenty of examples of low-tech firms staying put. "Wander around Los Angeles, America's main manufacturing center, and you will find squadrons of low-tech factories turning out toys, furniture, and clothes, all of which could probably be made cheaper elsewhere." Why so do they remain in Los Angeles? Micklethwait and Wooldridge explain that "they stay partly for personal reasons (many are family owned), partly because they can compensate for high labor costs by using more machines, but mostly because Los Angeles is a hub of all three industries—a place where designers, suppliers and distributors are just around the corner."[20] That is, in many respects it does still matter where businesses are located. These examples are also just anecdotes. But for skeptics they at least indicate that proclamations of the end of the tyranny of location and the consequent erosion of government power are at best premature.

The myth of a borderless world Kenichi Ohmae claims that if we look at a map of the world indicating flows of trade, investment, and production, we would not be able to redraw the political map. In a nutshell, he is saying that economic flows no longer conform to political boundaries. Interestingly, Ohmae does not actually provide a map that allows us to test his neat idea. For globalization skeptics there is a very good reason he does not—instead of supporting his position, such a map would actually prove him wrong.

In his book *How Much Do National Borders Matter?* John Helliwell takes up Ohmae's challenge to see whether economic flows no longer follow political borders. He focuses on the United States and Canada—two of the world's closest trading partners who share one of the most porous borders in the world. If Ohmae is correct, the political border separating these two nations should be nearly unnoticeable if we look at economic statistics. Given the specifics of the U.S.-Canada case, this should be a relatively easy test of the borderless-world thesis. If it does not apply here, one could reasonably wonder if it holds anywhere.

Helliwell's findings are not good news for Ohmae. Even though the importance of trade between the United States and Canada has been increasing in recent decades, the significance of trade within both nations still dwarfs trade between them. He provides the example of trade between Ontario and British Columbia, both Canadian provinces, compared to trade between Ontario and Washington State, which is the same distance from Ontario as British Columbia. If Ohmae is correct about the borderless world, there should be little difference in the pattern of trade between the two Canadian provinces and trade between the Canadian province and the American state. The national border should be meaningless. In fact, there is a marked difference: "Ontario's exports to British Columbia were more than twelve times larger than those to Washington."[21] On a map showing trade flows there would be twelve arrows pointing from Ontario to British Columbia for every one connecting Ontario and Washington. On this basis, most people would probably assume that British Columbia and

Ontario were part of the same political unit but Washington and Ontario were not. And, of course, they would be correct. The same pattern is found elsewhere. Despite the creation of a single market under the auspices of the European Union, people in Europe are still six times more likely to trade within their own national boundaries as opposed to across them. Again, there is no denying that the relative importance of trade across national borders is on the rise, but skeptics see this as a far cry from becoming a borderless world.

The continuing significance of national borders is even more evident in areas other than trade. Timothy Taylor points out that investors still behave as if national borders mattered. Within the confines of the United States, investors do not let location shape their decisions. Investors who live in Los Angeles exhibit no greater preference for companies located in their city as opposed to New York or Chicago. In a truly borderless world economy, we would see the same pattern: investors in the United States or Japan would display a similar lack of concern about the nationality of companies they invest in. But evidence on patterns of investment reveals a striking correlation between an investor's nationality and his or her investments: "U.S. investors [hold] 90 percent of their stock portfolios in U.S. stocks. Canadian investors [hold] 88 percent of their equity in Canadian stocks. Ninety-four percent of stock owned by Japanese investors is in Japanese stocks."[22] Thus, if we had a map of the world showing where investors are and where they choose to invest their money, national borders, far from being undetectable, would stand out like sore thumbs. Thus, even though "international flows of goods, services and financial capital have increased dramatically . . . we are still a long way from a single global market."[23] Are we closer to having a single global economy and a borderless world? Probably. But we are not close enough to begin acting as if we are there or even assuming we will get there anytime soon.

The myth of a race to the bottom   The race to the bottom is usually presented as an integral part of the processes of globalization, particularly (but not exclusively) by radical and Marxist analysts who see globalization as resulting in greater inequality, lower wages, and declining environmental protections. The ability of capital to move around the globe, which is what drives the race to the bottom, is also a major force behind the supposed erosion of national sovereignty. Either national governments pursue the policies desired by corporate interests or they run the risk of punishment in the form of capital flight. The argument makes intuitive sense. And the confirmation of the race to the bottom seems obvious to many—one need look no further than all those manufacturing plants right across the U.S.-Mexican border. Newspapers seem to provide almost daily examples of plants closing in the United States and moving to nations with lower wages and laxer regulations. According to Daniel Drezner, however, although "the race-to-the-bottom hypothesis appears logical . . . it is wrong. Indeed, the lack of supporting evidence is startling."[24] No doubt there are examples of companies moving plants in order to reduce their costs of production. But the race-to-the-bottom hypothesis suggests more than that. This movement of capital is portrayed as a significant, if not dominant, feature of the global economy that is occurring on a scale sufficient to depress wages and reduce regulations on a worldwide basis. It is not just a matter of a handful of companies or even a few economic sectors; it is a fundamental feature of the new global economy.

What sort of evidence beyond specific examples of plant relocation would we need to validate the race-to-the-bottom hypothesis? According to Drezner, we should see an inverse relationship between overseas investment on one hand and wage and regulation levels on the other. That is, countries with relatively high wages and costly regulations should attract little (or at least a declining share of) investment from overseas, whereas countries with low wages and few regulations should attract a lot of investment. As a general rule, wages and regulations are highest in North America, Europe, and Japan while they are lowest throughout the developing world. Thus, according to the race-to-the-bottom thesis, investment should be pouring into the developing world as corporations shop the world and relocate to lower their production costs.

When Drezner examines the destination of foreign direct investment during the 1990s (see figure 8.1), one thing becomes clear: when multinational corporations invest abroad, they are much more likely to do so in other high-wage, high-regulation nations. Between two-thirds and three-quarters of foreign direct investment takes place among the wealthy industrialized economies of the North, sometimes referred to as the *triad* (North America, Europe, and Japan). Hirst and Thompson reach the same conclusion: "Capital mobility is not producing a massive shift of investment and employment to the developing countries. Rather, foreign direct investment (FDI) is highly concentrated among the advanced industrial economies."[25] That is to say, there is no shift toward investing in countries with lower wages and less stringent regulations.

There are also many specific examples that illustrate this trend. In the spring of 2002, for example, the company that produces lifesavers candies in Michigan announced it was relocating its factory outside the United States. What is interesting is where the factory was being moved to: not Mexico, but Canada, another high-wage, high-regulation economy. The company was not looking for lower wages or fewer regulations but rather cheaper sugar. Because tariffs on sugar imported into the United States nearly double its price compared to elsewhere in the world, a number of candy manufacturers have made similar moves. The critical point is that it did not relocate to a developing country where sugar *and* wages were cheaper (and making candy is not exactly a high-tech undertaking). Recall also the description provided by the head of Levi-Strauss. Where were the jeans assembled? France. Where were they laundered? Belgium. France and Belgium can hardly be considered low-wage, low-regulation economies. Because assembling and washing jeans requires low-skilled labor, these are precisely the types of jobs that should be moving to low-wage areas. Though plant relocations to other high-wage, high-regulation economies rarely receive the same attention as those that flee to Mexico, Drezner argues that the aggregate data suggest that the former are more representative than the latter.

But why aren't companies flocking to places where they can take advantage of lower wages and regulatory costs? According to Micklethwait and Wooldridge, fears of a race to the bottom rest on a simplistic misconception that reducing wages verges on an obsession for businesses seeking to improve their bottom line. This misconception stems from a failure to distinguish the *cost of labor,* which is not terribly important, from the *value of labor,* which is critical: "What really matters to [businesses] is the value of labor." Although "some companies will undoubtedly move routine tasks to parts of the world where hourly wages are lower . . . what employers want is not cheap workers but productive ones. And the most productive workers are usually

FIGURE 8.1

Destination of worldwide foreign direct investment

■ Developed countries
▨ Developing countries
☐ Transition economies

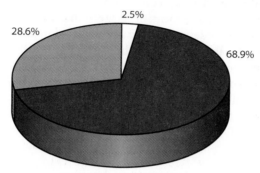

1992

2.5%
28.6%
68.9%

Total: U.S. $173,761 (millions)

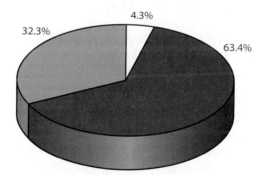

1995

4.3%
32.3%
63.4%

Total: U.S. $316,524 (millions)

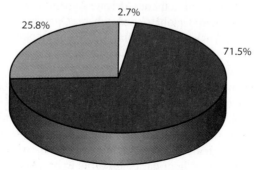

1998

2.7%
25.8%
71.5%

Total: U.S. $643,879 (millions)

SOURCE: Daniel Drezner, "Bottom Feeders," *Foreign Policy* (Nov/Dec 2000) 121:67. From *World Investment Report* (UNCTAD, various years).

those with the best education, access to the best machinery, and a support system that includes things like a good infrastructure."[26] All other things being equal, businesses would prefer to pay their workers less rather than more. But in the real world all other things are rarely equal. In addition to lower wages, businesses also prefer political stability, the absence of government corruption, and the rule of law, all of which are in much greater supply in high-wage, high-regulation countries. This is why most transnational corporations continue to invest two-thirds to three-quarters of their overseas investment in Europe, the United States, and Japan despite having the option of many places where wages and regulations are much lower.

The counterargument, of course, is that it is not necessary for businesses to actually move in order to reap the advantages of mobility. According to Hoogvelt, "The point about the 'discipline' of the market is that such companies do not have to move. It is sufficient for them to threaten to move." Though many, even most, firms remain in higher-wage nations, the option of relocation "has imposed a social discipline on workers all over Europe, indeed all over the world, that unless they conform, companies have the power to move plant [sic] to another country."[27] As a result, governments and workers have preemptively given corporations what they want in order to prevent them from fleeing. This is a plausible argument, but not one that is easy to evaluate.

CONCLUSION

Are we seeing the emergence of a single global society in which traditional divisions are increasingly meaningless? Is this process beneficial or detrimental? These are the two questions that lie at the heart of the debate over globalization. This chapter has tried to focus on the first, but it is extremely difficult to deal with the empirical and normative issues in isolation. In the most general sense, answers to these questions combine to provide three general perspectives on globalization. The skeptics, who tend to be realists, answer "no" to the first question, believing that the case for globalization relies on selective trends and statistics at the expense of more substantial evidence that points to the continuing centrality of nations and national communities. Since the first question is answered in the negative, the second becomes moot. Liberals and Marxists generally answer the first question in the affirmative but part company on the second. Liberals, despite some reservations, are essentially optimistic in their assessment of globalization, whereas Marxists, who see globalization in the context of their analysis of capitalism, offer a more pessimistic analysis.

Realist skepticism Realists are predisposed to focus on the enduring features of world politics; as a result, they are always skeptical of claims that the world is in the midst of some fundamental transformation. Realists see globalization, which Kenneth Waltz refers to as "the fad of the 1990s," as either wildly exaggerated or a complete myth. They like to begin by reminding us that many of the same arguments associated with contemporary globalization were made a hundred years ago, another period in which national boundaries appeared to be giving way to transborder interactions. International trade exploded in the second half of the nineteenth century and by the eve of World War I reached levels comparable to what we see today. In 1999, for example, U.S. exports were 20.5 percent of GDP, which was more than double the

9.5 percent of 1960. Advocates of globalization frequently point to such statistics while failing to add that the 20.5 percent figure is roughly the same as it was in 1900. So even though trade as a percentage of GDP has doubled since 1960, it is unchanged since 1900. On the issue of overseas investment, Robert Wade notes that "today the stock of U.S. capital invested abroad represents less than 7% of the U.S. GNP. That figure is, if anything, a little less than the figure for in 1900."[28] Robert Gilpin summarizes the basic argument: "Trade, investment, and financial flows were actually greater in the late 1800s, at least relative to the size of national economies and the international economy, than they are today."[29] Furthermore, in some respects the world was even more globalized in 1900 than today: people moved with greater ease, with large-scale immigration to the United States being the most prominent example. In addition to the economic aspects of globalization in 1900, the telegraph (the so-called "Victorian Internet") made communication to distant parts of the world cheap and instantaneous.[30] At the time there were also optimists who saw an emerging world of trade, prosperity, and peace, at least until World War I and the Great Depression put a damper on things.

In terms of contemporary globalization, realists do not reject the evidence usually provided to demonstrate globalization. Most of the facts are not in dispute. But facts do not speak for themselves. Facts need to be selected and interpreted. Between 1970 and 1995, for example, U.S. exports rose from 5 percent to 13 percent of GNP. There is no disagreement about this. Those who see a process of globalization underway find it remarkable that the importance of exports more than doubled in just twenty years. But even after this large increase, 87 percent of all goods and services produced in the United States were consumed in the United States. Which figure tells us more about the extent of globalization, 13 percent or 87 percent?

Realists also reject the proposition that globalization is an irreversible process that threatens states. On the contrary, realists see globalization as a process promoted and enabled by the policies of states, not something driven just by technology and economics. Whether it be free trade policies, rules and regulations conducive to foreign investment, or the adoption of common currency in Europe, states have advanced globalization as a political project. Globalization will come to a screeching halt if the major states reverse the policies that sustain it. A century ago, many argued that the economic and technological forces bringing the world together were irreversible. They proved to be woefully wrong. Realists argue that those enamored of contemporary globalization (both pro and con) are equally wrong.

Liberal optimism Whenever he is asked what he thinks about globalization, Thomas Friedman answers that he "feel[s] about globalization a lot like I feel about the dawn. Generally speaking, I think it's a good thing that the sun comes up every morning. It does more good than harm. But even if I didn't much care for the dawn there isn't much I could do about it."[31] This observation embodies two of the typical liberal reactions to globalization—that it is largely an irreversible process driven by technology and economics and that on balance it is a beneficial process. The growth of trade and the elimination of barriers are embraced for the same reasons liberals have always favored free trade. The belief that globalization works to the advantage of all reflects the underlying liberal assumption of the harmony of interests. But there is more to the liberal vision of globalization than economics. Globalization is as much about the spread of ideas as commerce, particularly notions of human rights and political democracy. As we have observed elsewhere, the world has witnessed a dramatic expansion of democracy over the past two or three decades, and this is just as much a part of globalization as the spread of McDonald's and Starbucks. Globalization, trade, and democratization are all part of the same process. When all the various elements are brought together, liberals view globalization "as the latest in a series of Enlightenment grand narratives purporting to outline a universal civilization and a common destiny for mankind: in this sense it simply incorporates and resurrects the belief in progress and becomes its current embodiment."[32]

Even though Thomas Friedman thinks that globalization does more harm than good, this still implies that it does some harm. There are forces in the world that have reacted negatively to the modernizing dynamics of globalization, such as fundamentalist religious movements that feel threatened by what they see as the secular and amoral values that are part of the emerging global culture. For these movements, opposition to globalization is easily converted into hostility toward the United States because for many in the world globalization is tantamount to Americanization.

Perhaps the most troubling aspect of globalization, however, is the widening gap between the haves and have-nots of the world. Whereas some critics see this widening gap as an integral and unavoidable consequence of globalization, liberals are more inclined to see insufficient globalization as the primary culprit. The problem is not that people and nations are being impoverished by globalization, but rather that some are being left behind, excluded from the process of globalization. The poorest of the poor among and within nations lack the basic resources—technology, infrastructure, and education—to take advantage of the opportunities that globalization presents. This holds for large sections of the Third World, particularly Africa, and the former Soviet Union as well as some groups within wealthy nations. For liberals, the solution is to find ways to include these people and nations in the process of globalization: we need more, not less, globalization.

Marxist resistance For Marxists, globalization is inseparable from global capitalism. According to Bertell Ollman, "'Globalization' is but another name for capitalism, but it's capitalism with the gloves off and on a world scale. It is capitalism at a time when all the old restrictions and inhibitions have been or are in the process of being put aside."[33] And since the current global(izing) order is at its core a capitalist system, it suffers from all the shortcomings of capitalism that Marx identified more than a century and a half ago: the concentration of capital, the increasing misery of the working class, the widening of economic inequalities, and the sacrifice of all values to the imperatives of the market. Although Marx might not have foreseen globalization in all its details, he would not be surprised by it, either. William Greider believes that "the ghost of Marx hovers over [today's] global landscape, perhaps with a knowing smile" because "the gross conditions that inspired Karl Marx's original critique of capitalism in the nineteenth century are present and flourish again." In Greider's view, "the world has reached . . . the next great conflict over the nature of capitalism. The fundamental struggle, then as now, is between capital and labor . . . and capital is winning big again . . . and the inequalities of wealth and power that Marx decried are marching wider almost everywhere in the world."[34]

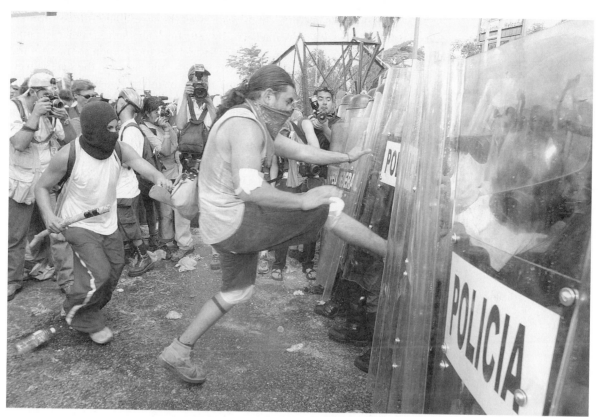

A violent clash between protesters and police at the WTO summit in Cancun, Mexico, in 2003. Such clashes have become a vivid symbol of the debate over the impact of globalization.
SOURCE: © Daniel Aguilar/Reuters Newmedia Inc./CORBIS

Hopes and fears For critics, the notion of globalization conjures up images of tacky fast-food joints, escapist Hollywood entertainment, rampaging multinational corporations, the loss of cultural identities, and faceless, unelected international bureaucrats telling national governments what they can and cannot do. For its supporters, globalization means increased trade, prosperity, the spread of liberal values of democracy and human rights, the sharing of cultures and traditions, and the erosion of the artificial boundaries that have divided human societies. Following the debate over globalization, one is reminded of the famous inkblot (Rorschach) tests psychologists use to gain insight into their patients' mental state. Because the images are so nebulous, they are open to many possible interpretations. The assumption is that the patients' interpretation will reveal more about them than it does about the image. It is tempting to see the Rorschach test as an especially good metaphor for the globalization debate. Because globalization is such a multifaceted phenomenon encompassing social, cultural, economic, and political trends, there are many places we might look for evidence, much of which remains vague, preliminary, and contradictory. It is not surprising that observers from different perspectives can find evidence that allows them to see wildly divergent realities.

Though in this sense no different than other debates we examine, the controversy over globalization appears more intellectually and politically charged. What accounts for this intensity? Perhaps it is because very few debates touch upon so many of the basic issues that divide competing perspectives—e.g., the nature of the state system, the dynamics of international conflict, the nature of international capitalism. But there is more to it. If globalization is occurring, it portends a fundamental transformation of international relations and global society on a scale we might not have witnessed since the rise of the modern state system. Because the ambiguities of globalization combine with the possibility of a historic transformation, it engages not only divergent beliefs about how the world works today, but also our hopes and fears about the future of global society.

POINTS OF VIEW

Are Governments Losing Control?

Discussions about globalization, the loss of national sovereignty, and the power of global capital can often seem very abstract and theoretical. Making the connection between these ideas and more concrete issues that people can get a handle on is challenging. The following news articles try to illustrate these larger issues by using a few very specific examples of diminished sovereignty. The story on offshore tax shelters deals with one facet of the loss of sovereignty—the ability of corporations to escape regulations of states by moving to places were laws are more to their liking. The story about local business regulations in Canada focuses on another aspect of eroding sovereignty—whether international treaties and/or organizations are undermining the authority of local governments to regulate activities that have traditionally been within their purview.

Do these examples convince you that loss of sovereignty is something local and national governments should be worried about? How might those who question the loss of sovereignty thesis respond to the fears raised in these cases? The articles also make it clear that local and national governments are trying to find ways to preserve and reassert their power and authority, particularly in the case of tax shelters. What tools are available to governments faced with an erosion of power? Is there any reason to think these attempts to protect and regain power might or might not prove successful in the long run?

Offshore Tax Shelters Under Fire

William M. Welch
Washington, July 31, 2002

With a new law cracking down on corporate cheaters in place, Congress is turning its focus to companies that have moved offshore to escape paying U.S. taxes.

Democrats and Republicans are looking at ways to halt corporate flight to tax havens such as Bermuda, where Connecticut-based Stanley Works has proposed to follow a number of other companies that have set up corporate addresses but kept most operations in the USA. Some in Congress also propose a sanction that could hit those companies where it hurts— banning them from lucrative contracts for business with the federal government.

Ten of the biggest companies that have already relocated to Bermuda or have proposed it did more than $1 billion in business with the federal government in the 2001 fiscal year. Three-fourths of the value of those contracts, or $763 million, was for defense or homeland-security related work. The contracts ranged from security and technology consulting to underwear for the U.S. military, made by Bermuda-based Fruit of the Loom.

"For these folks to escape in the dark of night and subsequently bid on defense and security work strikes me as unfair," says Rep. Richard Neal, D-Mass., who is leading the fight for one of several bills aimed at stopping the exodus.

After seeing opposition to financial reform collapse in the face of public outrage over accounting deceptions by big companies, some in Congress think similar support will lift legislation to punish or at least block corporate tax flight. The companies that moved their addresses offshore to avoid federal corporate income taxes may find themselves whip-sawed by twin forces—post-Sept. 11 patriotism and a crisis of confidence in corporate management.

Tax avoidance by corporations in offshore tax havens could cost the U.S. Treasury $4 billion in lost taxes over the next 10 years if Congress does not act, according to an estimate by the Congress' Joint Committee on Taxation.

Last week, California state Treasurer Phil Angelides announced that the state's two big pension funds, Calpers and TIAA-CREF, would stop investing in U.S. corporations that relocate offshore to avoid taxes.

The House last week overwhelmingly approved a move by Democrats to prevent a proposed new homeland security department from doing business with companies incorporated in tax havens. Republican leaders opposed the measure, but when it appeared likely to pass, 100 GOP lawmakers switched their votes to approve it.

Democrats who see corporate misdeeds as a political problem for President Bush and the Republicans have begun branding offshore companies "corporate traitors." Neal's bill would eliminate tax benefits for companies that moved offshore since Sept. 11.

The issue has touched off vigorous lobbying by big-spending corporations on both sides of the issue.

Accenture, a consulting company spun off from the accounting firm Arthur Andersen, is one of several corporations that has been quietly but intensely lobbying to preserve its status. But competitors of some offshore companies are fighting for legislation that would crack down on the tax flight. They argue that the zero tax rate on profits claimed in Bermuda and other tax breaks provide an unfair advantage.

Spokesmen for Accenture declined to comment. But the company issued a statement calling itself "a global organization with 75,000 people working in 47 countries" that was justified in incorporating in Bermuda.

House Ways and Means Committee Chairman Bill Thomas, R-Calif., has proposed a three-year moratorium on corporate relocations offshore. His plan is part of a larger corporate tax bill that he hopes Congress will act on this year.

The Bush administration also backs a moratorium. On Tuesday, David Aufhauser, general counsel for the Treasury, told a Bermuda audience that the federal tax code is to blame for chasing companies offshore.

House Majority Leader Dick Armey, R-Texas, in a letter to House members, said penalizing businesses for minimizing their tax burden by legally moving offshore "is akin to punishing a taxpayer for choosing to itemize instead of taking the standard deduction."

In the Senate, Finance Committee Chairman Max Baucus, D-Mont., and Republican Charles Grassley of Iowa are pushing a different bill. It would recapture taxes from corporations that move offshore if most of their shareholders remained the same as under the U.S. company. The outlook there is uncertain, but lawmakers say growing political pressure could prompt action.

The issue has become a focus of one of the hottest congressional elections this year in Connecticut, where Republican Rep. Nancy Johnson and Democratic Rep. James Maloney are each competing to show how much they are doing on the issue. The district is home to workers of Stanley, which voted in May to reincorporate in Bermuda. Stanley's decision touched off a storm of protest, and its board of directors has authorized a second vote.

Globalization—Coming to Your Town?

Sherry Peters
March 3, 2002

The power of Canadian municipalities to pass zoning regulations and control such things as retail store hours may run afoul of an international trade agreement.

World Trade Organization negotiators have listed local bylaws that could favour smaller businesses over larger ones as potential violations of the General Agreement on Trade in Services (GATS). The details of GATS are being worked out during the current round of WTO negotiations in Geneva.

Signed by the federal government, GATS is binding on all levels of government in Canada, including municipalities. If municipal powers become subject to GATS, large retailers that claim local bylaws covering store density and hours of operation give smaller retailers an advantage could challenge those bylaws at the WTO as unfair trade barriers. "This is what globalization is all about," says Toronto Councillor Jack Layton, who is also president of the Federation of Canadian Municipalities. "It starts with the nation-state, then it hits at the provincial and local level."

"This should send a chill down the spine of every local councillor and mayor in Canada."

GATS "potentially strips away municipal power," adds West Vancouver Councillor Victor Durman. "I believe that any local community represented by their municipal representatives should be able to set regulations that reflect local concerns and desires and not have it overruled by an international tribunal."

Representatives of the WTO's 144 member nations, including Canada, are preparing a list of grounds for challenging domestic regulations they believe create barriers to trade.

Trade rules permit one country to challenge another member country's domestic policies if they are seen to be trade-restrictive. Insiders say some countries have been under significant pressure from large retailers to target regulations they believe favour smaller businesses.

According to leaked minutes of a meeting last fall, at least two delegations to the trade talks argued that regulations governing zoning and hours of operation should be subject to GATS. And a second internal document indicates that WTO staff agree that such local regulations be included as possible trade restrictions.

Under these circumstances, municipalities would have to ensure that any regulations they placed on development, such as prohibiting the construction of a 24-hour, big-box store in a residential neighbourhood, met the GATS test of being "no more burdensome than necessary." ...

If things such as zoning are included in the new international agreement, "any regulations local councils pass in order to restrict the building of big-box stores, limit housing developments that are out of character with the neighbourhood or restrict how long stores can stay open could be challenged," she said.

Ellen Gould, an independent trade researcher from Georgetown University, explained the burdensome test could be a difficult one for municipalities to meet: "If there are neighbourhood concerns about excess noise from traffic to Wal-Mart, (municipalities) may not be able to simply zone to prohibit a big-box retail store. They might have to accept Wal-Mart's proposal to buffer the noise through landscaping, changes to access roads, etc."

Some observers suggest that the push to curb regulations that may favour small stores is coming from firms such as Wal-Mart and large European retailers, including IKEA and Boots. Wal-Mart was to have opened 11 so-called Supercenters in the United States last month. The 24-hour stores range in size from about 110,000 to 230,000 square feet.

The fact that zoning and hours of operation are being put forward for discussion in Geneva has added to the concerns of Canadian municipalities about international trade deals.

"This confirms our worst fears— that an unelected panel of officials meeting in secret would be able to decide local matters like zoning and hours of operation," Layton says.

"We know that the Wal-Marts of the world are out there putting significant resources to try to stop the kind of techniques that local government use to try to protect the character and local businesses of their area."

But federal trade representatives say municipalities have nothing to worry about.

Vince Sacchetti, senior policy analyst with Industry Canada, suggests matters like municipal zoning and restrictions on hours of operation are simply "a garbage list of examples" that might be covered under GATS.

"I can't believe it would go to the WTO," he says. "We have not yet had a full discussion. It's ongoing ... We're just compiling a list. So far, only three out of the 144 members have submitted their lists."

Gould, however, says a member of the European Union's trade negotiation team has approved the inclusion of zoning and hours of operation in GATS.

"If the federal government doesn't want it on there, they better speak up now," she says. "There is a critical meeting to define what's up for grabs on domestic regulations in March."

Andre Lemay, a spokesperson for Foreign Affairs in Ottawa, also says municipal concerns are not warranted.

"GATS was basically made to measure for Canada. In 95 per cent or more of the cases, we are already playing by the rule of the WTO. What GATS wants to do is provide market access," Lemay says. "But no municipality will lose its right to create regulations. This is protected right in the preamble."

Gould says the right to regulate is not guaranteed in the preamble, but has to be balanced with the commitment to expand trade....

Lemay says that if municipalities want issues of zoning and hours of operation off the negotiating table, "then we will promote that position at the WTO."

But if, after federal-municipal consultations, "51 or 55 per cent of municipalities say they want it on (the list), then who are we to say no?"

The Federation of Canadian Municipalities has prepared a list of written questions it would like answered by the federal government.

"It will be very clear from those answers the extent to which they are prepared to get into the truth of the matter," says federation lawyer Donald Lidstone.

Municipalities believe "that land use planning and land use control historically, traditionally and constitutionally are a matter of local jurisdiction." Lidstone also says Ottawa should already be well aware that municipalities do not want zoning or hours of operation on the trade list.

According to the June 11, 2000, issue of *World Trade Agenda,* a newsletter published by a former communications director with the WTO, large retailers and wholesale firms expect to see the distribution services sectors a priority in GATS.

"Despite accounting for between 25 and 30 per cent of all enterprises in most economies, distribution services have largely been ignored in past WTO services negotiations," the newsletter said.

But big-name chains like Wal-Mart and Marks & Spencer "have global strategies for which market access conditions and domestic regulatory restraints in new markets are crucial."

CHAPTER SUMMARY

- Over the last twenty years, the concept of globalization has gradually made its way from academic to popular thinking about international relations. In general terms, globalization refers to the multifaceted social, cultural, technological, economic, and political processes that are gradually merging the world's nations and societies into a single larger global society.

- Though references to globalization are common, there is an intense debate about the reality and consequences of this process. One of the major points of disagreement is the effect of globalization on the ability of national governments and communities to shape their own destinies in the face of multi- and supranational actors, forces, and institutions.

- Those convinced that globalization is real claim that technological trends and economic policies are reducing the importance of geographic location, particularly in terms of economic production and commerce. The economic map of the world is increasingly "borderless."

- The declining significance of location is seen as shifting power away from nations and governments to forces and actors that are able to transcend national boundaries, including multinational corporations, mobile capital, and more amorphous global "market forces."

- This shift in power is most vividly demonstrated in the notion of a "race to the bottom" in which wages, regulations, and social welfare programs are reduced as corporations and mobile capital move freely about the world in search of low wages, regulations, and taxes.

- Skeptics question the evidence supporting dramatic claims of a "borderless" global economy and society. The data on economic production, trade, and investment demonstrate the continued relevance, not disappearance, of national boundaries.

- Globalization skeptics also point out that contrary to the predictions of those who see a race to the bottom, the overwhelming majority of corporate investment occurs in those nations with high wages, regulations, and taxes.

- The debate over globalization involves at least two basic questions. First, are we seeing the emergence of a single global society? Second, if so, is this a beneficial or harmful development? Realists tend to answer the first question in the negative, which makes the second irrelevant. Others, including liberals and Marxists, answer the first question in the affirmative but disagree on the second. On balance, liberals are inclined to see globalization as a positive force. But largely because globalization is synonymous with global capitalism, Marxists view it as a harmful process.

CRITICAL QUESTIONS

1. This chapter has focused largely on the economic aspects and political consequences of globalization. What are some of the other manifestations of globalization? Do you consider these good or bad?

2. How does globalization differ from interdependence?

3. Do you think globalization is a force for greater peace and cooperation or discord and conflict in the world?

4. Can globalization be stopped?

5. How might globalization look different for people in other societies than it does for Americans?

KEY TERMS

constrained state thesis 197
democratic deficit 203
globalization 196
mobility of capital 199
race to the bottom 200
tyranny of location 199

FURTHER READINGS

For those interested in globalization, there are few better places to start than Thomas Friedman's popular *The Lexus and the Olive Tree* (New York: Farrar Straus Giroux, 1999), an enjoyable yet informative analysis of globalization in terms that laypersons can easily understand. The borderless-world thesis is advanced most forcefully in Kenichi Ohmae's two works *The End of the Nation-State* (New York: Free Press, 1995) and *The Borderless World* (New York: Harper Business, 1999). One of the more favorable and enthusiastic analyses of globalization is John Micklethwait and Adrian Wooldridge, *A Future Perfect: The Challenge and Promise of Globalization* (New York: Random House, 2002). A very critical and influential critique of globalization is Naomi Klein, *No Logo: No Space, No Choice, No Jobs* (New York: Picador, 2002). Another interesting and more eclectic critique is John Gray, *False Dawn: The Delusions of Global Capitalism* (London: Granta Books, 1998). Paul Hirst and Grahame Thompson's *Globalization in Question* (Cambridge: Polity, 1999) casts doubt on the extent of globalization. A recent work skeptical of claims of the constrained state thesis is Linda Weiss, ed., *States in the Global Economy: Bringing Domestic Institutions Back In* (Cambridge: Cambridge University Press, 2003).

GLOBALIZATION ON THE WEB

http://yaleglobal.yale.edu/globalization/index.jsp
An interesting and constantly updated collection of articles and studies on all aspects of globalization, with a tendency to challenge simplistic and widely held assumptions (e.g., cultural globalization is synonymous with "Americanization").

http://www.globalpolicy.org/nations/soverindex.htm
Examines the threat to national sovereignty from the forces of globalization.

http://globalization.about.com
Covers all issues and sides of the globalization debate.

http://www.fantasyworldorder.com
Contains a questionnaire that allows people to determine where they stand on globalization debates.

NOTES

[1] Both the Giddens and Albrow quotations are found in Jan Aart Scholte, "The Globalization of World Politics," in *The Globalization of World Politics,* ed. John Baylis and Steven Smith (Oxford: Oxford University Press, 2001), p. 15.

[2] Richard Ernst, "Globalization of Disease is Overlooked," *The Gazette* (Montreal, Quebec), March 6, 2001, P. B2.

[3] Ian Clark, *Globalization and International Relations Theory* (Oxford: Oxford University Press, 1999), p. 71.

[4] Linda Weiss, "Introduction: Bringing the State Back In," in *States in the Global Economy,* ed. Linda Weiss (Cambridge: Cambridge University Press), p. 3.

[5] Kenichi Ohmae, *The End of the Nation-State* (New York: Free Press, 1995), p. 7.

[6] Kenichi Ohmae, *The Borderless World* (New York: Harper Business, 1999), p. 18.

[7] Quoted in John Gray, *False Dawn: The Delusions of Global Capitalism* (London: Granta Books, 1998), p. 68.

[8] Anthony Giddens, *Runaway World: How Globalization Is Reshaping Our Lives* (New York: Routledge, 2000), p. 26.

[9] Thomas Friedman, *The Lexus and the Olive Tree* (New York: Farrar Straus Giroux, 1999), xv–xvi.

[10] Quoted in Jan Aart Scholte, "Global Trade and Finance," in Baylis and Smith, *Globalization of World Politics,* p. 526.

[11] Hans-Peter Martin and Harald Schumann, *The Global Trap: Globalization and the Assault on Democracy and Prosperity* (New York: Zed Books, 1996), p. 201.

[12] James C. Abegglen, *Sea Change: Pacific Asia as the New World Industrial Center* (New York: Free Press, 1994), pp. 26–27.

[13] Gray, *False Dawn,* p. 80.

[14] Jeremy Brecher and Tim Costello, *Global Village or Global Pillage: Economic Reconstruction from the Bottom Up* (Boston: South End Press, 1994), pp. 20, 4.

[15] David Ranney quoted in ibid., p. 56.

[16] Quoted in William K. Tabb, *The Amoral Elephant: Globalization and the Struggle for Social Justice in the Twenty-First Century* (New York: Monthly Review Press, 2001), p. 79–80.

[17] R. C. Longworth, "Resisting Globalization's 'Democratic Deficit'," *Chicago Tribune,* October 15, 2000, pp. 1, 6.

[18] John Micklethwait and Adrian Wooldridge, "The Globalization Backlash," *Foreign Policy* (September/October 2001): 22.

[19] Friedman, *Lexus and the Olive Tree,* p. 301.

[20] Micklethwait and Wooldridge, "Globalization Backlash," p. 20.

[21] John Helliwell, *How Much Do National Borders Matter?* (Washington, DC: Brookings Institution Press, 1998), p. 17.

[22] Timothy Taylor, "The Truth about Globalization," *The Public Interest* (Spring 2002): 27.

[23] Ibid.

[24] Daniel Drezner, "Bottom Feeders," *Foreign Policy* (November/December 2000): 64.

[25] Paul Hirst and Grahame Thompson, *Globalization in Question* (Cambridge: Polity, 1999), p. 2.

[26] Micklethwait and Wooldridge, "Globalization Backlash," p. 22.

[27] Ankie Hoogvelt, *Globalization and the Post Colonial World* (Baltimore: Johns Hopkins University Press, 2001), p. 134.

[28] Robert Wade, "Globalization and Its Limits: Reports of the Death of the National Economy Are Greatly Exaggerated," in *National Diversity and Global Capitalism,* ed. Suzanne Berger and Ronald Dore (Ithaca, NY: Cornell University Press, 1996), p. 72.

[29] Robert Gilpin, *Global Political Economy: Understanding the International Economic Order* (Princeton: Princeton University Press, 2001), p. 364.

[30] See Thomas Standage, *The Victorian Internet: The Remarkable Story of the Telegraph and the Nineteenth Century Online Pioneers* (London: Weidenfeld and Nicholson, 1998).

[31] Friedman, *Lexus and the Olive Tree*, xviii.

[32] Clark, *Globalization and International Relations Theory*, pp. 41, 35.

[33] Bertell Ollman, "Bertell Ollman on Globalization." Accessed at: www.pipeline.com/~rgibson/OllmanGlobalism.htm.

[34] William Greider, *One World, Ready or Not* (New York: Touchstone Books, 1997), p. 39.

INTERNATIONAL LAW

Discussions of international law have often been framed by the extremes—those who dismiss international law as a meaningless sham and others who see it as a tool for dramatically improving international order. Those who question the value of international law argue that because it is so diverse, vague, and contradictory, nations can find a legal basis or justification for just about anything they do. And given the absence of an effective international legal system, it is easy for states to ignore international law when it is in their interests to do so. Though realists usually do not dismiss international law completely, they are inclined to see its role as extremely limited, especially when international law conflicts with the interests of powerful states. Liberals have historically offered a more favorable assessment of international law. Although few contemporary liberals suggest that signing treaties can eradicate war or other problems simply by making them illegal, they believe that international law embodies norms widely shared in international society. The existence of these laws does influence the behavior of states in the same ways that domestic laws influence the behavior of individuals. Despite the weaknesses skeptics dwell on, nations usually do abide by international law. Constructivists share this more robust view of international law: international law may not prevent states from pursuing their national interests, but it does influence how states define their national interests and what behaviors are considered acceptable in pursuit of national interests.

Discussions of international politics and foreign policy are often filled with references to international law. States are always anxious to claim that they are acting in accordance with international law and that their opponents have violated these same laws. Teams of international lawyers at foreign ministries the world over provide detailed legal justifications for almost everything their nations do. Supposed violations of international law are even cited as grounds for using force against other states. But at some levels the whole concept of international law might appear puzzling. After all, one of the central features of international society is anarchy, or the absence of a central political authority. Unlike domestic politics, there is no higher authority that states feel obligated to obey. This raises the obvious question: How can there even be international laws if no international government exists to make and enforce them? The absence of government would seem to imply the absence of law. International politics is the realm of power, not law; of might, not right—an arena where the strong take what they can and the weak grant what they must. In the famous passage from his *Leviathan*, Thomas Hobbes expressed this point of view: "Where there is no common power, there is no law."[1]

Despite the "no law without government" argument, most people agree that international law does exist despite the anarchic nature of international society. In fact, the origins of modern international law are often traced to the early seventeenth century when the modern sovereign state emerged from the maelstrom of the Thirty Years War and the Peace of Westphalia (1648). Reacting in part to the horrors of that conflict, **Hugo Grotius** (1583–1645), sometimes referred to as the "father of international law," attempted to devise a system of rules specifying acceptable and unacceptable behavior in the making and conduct of war. Though there was no overarching government, he argued that sovereign states still formed a society or community in which regular interactions took place within the framework of rules and norms of behavior. Some of these rules could be found in formal agreements; others were revealed by the customary behavior of states. More ambitiously, Grotius argued that states were also bound to obey a higher moral code. But where did this code come from? One possible source was God (or religious texts). Perhaps because he lived through the Thirty Years War and witnessed the devastation religious conflicts could bring, Grotius preferred a more secular foundation. He argued that human reason allows us to devise a code of moral conduct that is necessary for the preservation of a civilized community of people or states. Though he accepted the existence and legitimacy of sovereign states, Grotius provided a vision of a more humane international order in which shared moral values and norms could tame the excesses witnessed during the Thirty Years War. For Grotius there was no necessary contradiction between state sovereignty and international law.[2] This position stands today.

The debate over international law, however, does not focus on whether it exists, but rather on its impact on the behavior of states. On one hand, there are those who remain skeptical that international law offers much of a constraint on state behavior. At the margins and on some relatively insignificant issues international law may influence states, but power and interests usually trump law and justice in international politics. On the other hand, international law can be seen as providing not only direct constraints on state behavior, but also norms that influence how states think about the world and their role in it.

Grotius, Hugo (1583–1645)
Dutch philosopher often considered the founder of international law. Even without a world government, he argued that nations still formed a community and were bound to obey a higher moral code.

What Is International Law and Where Does It Come From?

Is there such a thing as international law? The answer depends largely on what we mean by *law*. If we adopt a very strict definition that laws are rules and regulations enacted by political authorities that have the ability to enforce them, then there is no such thing as international law. By definition, if there is no central political authority, there can be no law. But those who argue that international law can exist even without a world government define law more broadly. Though there are some minor definitional differences, *international law* is generally viewed as "the customs, norms, principles, rules and other legal relations among states and other international personality that establish binding obligations."[3] Hedley Bull provides a similar definition: "International law may be regarded as a body of rules which binds states and other agents in world politics with one another."[4] This is, admittedly, a messier way of thinking about law. Domestic (or *municipal*) law has the virtue of centralization—it usually originates from easily identifiable government institutions and is enforced by agents of the state. International law is decentralized both in origins and enforcement mechanisms.

Historically, international law has involved states—that is, the rights and obligations of states vis-à-vis each other—though both of the preceding definitions of international law make some allowance for "other" agents that might have standing. This provision is incorporated largely because international law over the past few decades has gradually moved beyond a sole focus on states. Human rights, for example, are increasingly part of international law. This area of law entails that states have some obligations toward their citizens and citizens have rights that their governments are required to respect. Though we will have more to say about this new role for individual rights in international law in a later chapter, at this point it is enough to note that the general strengths and weaknesses of international law are relevant in this area as well.

If there is no international government to pass and enact laws, where do they come from? Article 38 of the Statute of the International Court of Justice identifies four (or five, depending on how one counts) sources of international law:

1. International conventions, whether general or particular, establishing rules expressly recognized by consenting parties
2. International custom, as evidence of a general practice accepted as law
3. The general principles of law recognized by civilized nations
4. Judicial decisions and the teachings of the most highly qualified publicists of the various nations[5]

The sources are listed in order of declining significance, with treaties and conventions being by far the most important sources of international law. *Treaties* and *conventions* are formal, written documents that specify behaviors that states agree to engage in or refrain from. Some treaties, such as nuclear arms control agreements signed by the United States and Soviet Union during the Cold War, are bilateral (i.e., involving only two nations), whereas others, such as the Nuclear Non-Proliferation

Treaty (1968) involve virtually all nations. But whether a treaty involves two or two hundred nations, it obligates signatories to abide by its terms. The difference is in the scope of the treaty, not its nature. Treaties in international law are equivalent to what we refer to as *contracts* in domestic law. Thus, when we say that a state has violated international law, this assertion is usually accompanied with a reference to the specific treaty or convention whose terms have been contradicted.

The fact that most international legal obligations derive from treaties and conventions automatically indicates one of the major differences between domestic and international law. Domestic laws are usually binding on everyone. If a state legislature decides to impose a 55 mph speed limit, the law applies to all regardless of any individual's approval. Laws are not circulated among citizens for signatures. In the domestic context we do not get to choose which laws apply to us. In international law, nations are only obligated to abide by those treaties and conventions they consent to. Edward Carr explains that "a treaty, whatever its scope and content, lacks the essential quality of law: it is not automatically and unconditionally applicable to all members of the community whether they assent to it or not."[6] If a nation has not signed the Nuclear Non-Proliferation Treaty, it cannot be charged with violating this treaty. Thus, international law relies on voluntary consent to a much greater degree than domestic law.

Not all international law is codified in written documents. Practices and norms that states have come to adopt over time and that are routinely observed form a sort of unwritten body of law. We generally refer to this as **customary law.** Customary law does not require explicit consent, like treaties; consent is inferred from behavior. Sometimes these customary rules eventually find their way into actual agreements, but often they do not. Many of the laws regarding the conduct of diplomacy, such as diplomatic immunity (about which there will be more to say later), began as customs that evolved gradually over time. It was only with the Vienna Conventions on Diplomatic (1961) and Consular Relations (1963) that these norms acquired the status of written law. The prohibition on slavery and the slave trade was part of international customary law before the formal Slavery Convention of 1926. Until recently, the issue of how far offshore a nation's sovereignty extended was also a matter of customary law. The limit used to be 3 miles because this was about as far as a cannon could reach, though it was eventually extended to 12 miles and was codified in the U.N. Convention on the Law of the Sea (1982). The same convention contained another example of the codifying of custom. In the early 1950s, several South American countries claimed exclusive fishing rights out to 200 miles, which was viewed at the time as violating freedom of the seas beyond the 12-mile limit. In subsequent years, other nations, including the United States, decided to follow the lead of the South Americans and asserted the 200 mile limit. The 1982 convention recognized this new norm by specifying a 200-mile exclusive economic zone (EEC).

Interestingly, though customary international law is often more difficult to identify than treaty-based law, it can in exceptional cases be more powerful because it may apply universally, irrespective of state consent. David Bederman provides the example of genocide. Though there is an international convention against genocide, it is possible to argue that genocide is also a violation of customary law. As a result, "two states may not conclude a treaty reciprocally granting themselves the right to commit genocide against a selected group." The rule against genocide may be one of those "rules

customary law One of the major sources of international law. The fact that states routinely and consistently abide a particular norm is often considered sufficient for that norm to attain the status of law, even if it is not codified in any actual agreements or treaties.

of custom that are so significant . . . that the international community will not suffer States to 'contract' out of them by treaty."[7] Similarly, the fact that a nation had not signed the Slavery Convention (1926) would assuredly not excuse that nation from abiding by the international custom against slavery.

Though custom should not be overlooked as a source of international law, it remains very difficult to know when a norm has entered the realm of customary international law. How many states, one might wonder, must abide by the norm and for how long before it can confidently be classified as a binding law? It is even harder to gauge when an international custom has reached a level where it becomes binding on all states even if they claim not to accept it, as would be the case with genocide and slavery. Even experts in international law have no clear answer: "How these particular rules of 'super-custom' are designated and achieve the exceptionally high level of international consensus they require is a bit of mystery."[8]

THE WEAKNESS OF INTERNATIONAL LAW

As we have already noted, the harshest rejections of international law simply dismiss it by definition: law is something made and enforced by governments. Since there is no international government, international law does not exist. Indeed, if a world government existed, there would still be no *international* law, so the very notion of "international law" is a contradiction in terms, an oxymoron. This argument might be a clever debating strategy, but it does not really help us understand how most people, critics and supporters alike, have thought about the role of law in international politics. The view of international law as a body of norms and rules that states usually feel obliged to obey is the more common conceptualization. Most critics agree that international law exists. What remains uncertain is its influence in actually shaping the behavior of states. Those who doubt the value of international law make several basic arguments. First, international law is a contradictory and vague mass of agreements and norms that offers few clear guidelines for action. Second, even if we could specify the contents of international law, the absence of an effective legal system severely limits its impact. Third, to the extent that international law does influence state behavior, it is on issues of relatively minor importance. When it comes to the most pressing issues of international politics involving the great powers, international law gives way to power and national interests.

Vague and conflicting obligations What exactly is the content of international law? Which behaviors are condoned and which are condemned under existing international law? These are the first questions students of international law have to answer. Even when we rely on written agreements, it is not easy to answer them. The first problem is that most nations are parties to literally thousands of treaties, conventions, and other international agreements entered into over decades, if not centuries. Since 1945 more than 40,000 international treaties, agreements, and conventions have been signed throughout the world. It would be unrealistic to expect all of these agreements to be perfectly consistent with one another (indeed, it is not unheard of for the same treaty to contain seemingly contradictory provisions). This lack of consistency sometimes makes it very difficult to even know what a nation's treaty obligations are. Of course, this is also a problem domestically—legislatures might pass laws that contradict other laws already on the books and states might pass laws that are inconsistent with federal law. On the domestic level, there are mechanisms for dealing with conflicts of laws, such as courts that decide which laws take precedence. But the problem is much greater at the international level for two reasons: first, the decentralized nature of laws (not only treaties but also nebulous customary law) increases the likelihood of conflicts; and second, the lack of an authoritative legal system makes the resolution of these conflicts problematic.

Treaties create not only problems of conflicts of laws but also vagueness. This is particularly the case when it comes to treaties and conventions that are signed by many nations. Morgenthau explains what frequently happens in the process of creating documents many nations can sign: "In order to find a common basis on which all those different national interests can meet in harmony, rules of international law embodied in general treaties must often be vague and ambiguous, allowing all the signatories to read the recognition of their own national interests into the legal text agreed upon."[9] And since nations are often interested in preserving their freedom of action, escape clauses are often built in, specifying exemptions in cases of "self-defense" or "aggression." As with conflicts of laws, vagueness and ambiguity are not unknown in domestic laws. Lawmakers often adopt vague wording in order to get the votes needed to pass legislation. This is one of the reasons that courts frequently have to "interpret" the law—if the law were crystal clear in the first place, interpretation would not be necessary. And to repeat a point that should not need repeating, there is no judiciary to do the same at the international level.

Laws that are contradictory and vague create dilemmas for even the disinterested observer. For those with a vested interest in a conflict, there is much room for self-serving uses (or abuses) of international law. With references to the right treaties and a generous interpretation of ambiguous wording, critics charge, almost any action can be supported with a plausible legal justification. Foreign ministries in all countries, including the U.S. State Department, employ staffs of very smart lawyers whose job it is to provide a legal rationale for the policies of their governments. The number of times when they have been unable to do so can be counted on a few fingers. Nations rarely alter their behavior in order to conform to international law. It is more likely that nations will do the exact opposite—twist international law so that it conforms with their policies. Since international law is plagued with ambiguity and contradictions, it is simply too flexible to provide much of a restriction on state behavior.

No effective legal system   In order to be meaningful and effective, laws must come with machinery capable of implementing them. It is not enough that there be laws; there must also be a legal system equipped with the necessary tools and powers to enforce them. And in order for a legal system to work properly, it must enjoy **compulsory jurisdiction.** Carr explains that domestic legal systems are effective because "the jurisdiction of national courts is compulsory. Any person cited before a court must enter an appearance or lose his case by default; and the decision of the court is binding on all concerned."[10] When individuals within domestic society are charged with crimes, found guilty and sentenced, they do not have the option of failing to appear in court or refusing to abide by the court's decision, should it not be to their liking. Just imagine the state of domestic law if people were free not to appear in

compulsory jurisdiction
When legal bodies can force parties to appear before them and be bound by their final decisions. Domestic legal systems usually enjoy compulsory jurisdiction, whereas international legal bodies do not.

court and were able to ignore verdicts they disagreed with. That would be a mess. But this is precisely the state of the international legal system. Among existing international courts, the **International Court of Justice** (ICJ), also known as the World Court, headquartered in the The Hague, Netherlands, is the most important. This court is the judicial branch of the United Nations. Any state is free to bring a case when it feels its rights under international law have been violated (and only nations, not individuals, can brings suits). The ICJ, however, is not a terribly busy court—between 1946 through the end of the 1980s, the court heard fewer than ten cases in each decade. By comparison, the U.S. Supreme Court hears more cases in just two or three years than the ICJ has heard in almost fifty. Nonetheless, it provides something that at least gives the appearance of an international legal system.

The problem is that nothing compels the relevant parties to attend trials or even abide by the courts final decision. The Statute of the International Court of Justice (the treaty creating the ICJ) contains what is known as the **optional clause.** This clause gives nations the ability to choose whether they want to be subject to the compulsory jurisdiction of the ICJ. Less than one-third of United Nations member countries have accepted the compulsory jurisdiction of the ICJ by signing the optional clause. Even nations that sign the optional clause can specify conditions under which they will not automatically recognize the court's jurisdiction. When the United States signed the optional clause in 1946, it stipulated reservations that were broad enough to totally negate the principle of compulsory jurisdiction. And faced with a likely adverse decision by the ICJ, the United States withdrew its endorsement of the optional clause.

This lack of compulsory jurisdiction can be illustrated with a case involving the United States. During the 1980s, the Reagan administration pursued a controversial policy of aiding anticommunist rebels fighting to overthrow the Marxist Sandinista government of Nicaragua. In addition to providing money and arms to the "contra" rebels, the United States mined Nicaraguan harbors (i.e., within Nicaragua's legally recognized territorial waters). In 1984, the government of Nicaragua asked the ICJ to determine whether U.S. support for the contras and harbor mining constituted violations of international law. The United States responded that the ICJ did not have jurisdiction over the matter. The ICJ ruled that it did have jurisdiction and would hear the case over the United States' objections. At this point the court issued a preliminary opinion ordering the United States to cease its mining of Nicaraguan harbors. The United States ignored the order and decided to remove itself from the entire process in January 1985. In 1986, the ICJ ruled in support of Nicaragua, declaring the United States in violation of international law. The United States simply ignored the court's ruling. When Nicaragua brought the matter before the United Nations Security Council in order to have sanctions imposed, the United States used its veto. That was pretty much the end of the matter.[11] To those skeptical of the value of international law, this is perhaps its most critical weakness, because "no legal system can be effective in limiting the activities of its subjects without compulsory jurisdiction over their disputes."[12] To paraphrase Thomas Hobbes, laws without an effective legal system are mere words.

The ability of the United States to ignore international law and the decisions of the ICJ in the Nicaraguan case reveals another weakness. In principle, all states might be equal in the eyes of international law. In practice, however, this application of international law cannot be divorced from considerations of power. Great powers have

International Court of Justice (ICJ) Also known as the World Court, the legal judicial branch of the United Nations. Any state that feels its rights under international law have been violated is free to bring suit in the ICJ against the offending parties.

optional clause A critical component of the treaty that created the International Court of Justice, this clause gives states the option of agreeing or not agreeing in advance to be bound by the decisions of the ICJ.

always had a greater capacity to escape the restrictions imposed by international law than weak states. Of course, even in domestic society the wealthy and powerful can manipulate legal systems to their advantage in ways that the poor cannot (e.g., by being able to afford better legal representation). The ideal of equality before the law is rarely achieved in any context. But at the international level this problem is magnified because of the absence of a central authority to coerce great powers into obedience.

In addition to compulsory jurisdiction, a clear **judicial hierarchy** is another essential element of an effective legal system. Such a hierarchy requires the existence of lower and higher courts with a definite line of command or authority. Higher courts fulfill several functions. First, parties who are unsatisfied with lower court decisions can sometimes appeal to higher courts for another hearing. Second, when lower courts issue contradictory rulings, higher courts decide which ruling prevails. Third, the highest courts, such as the Supreme Court in the United States, establish precedents, or interpretations of laws, that lower courts are bound to obey. The international legal system does not have an effective legal hierarchy. The ICJ does not stand over national courts in the same way that the U.S. Supreme Court reigns supreme over lower district or state courts. Although treaties signed and ratified by the United States become the law of the land and acquire the status of domestic law, the U.S. Supreme Court does not have to abide by the decisions of the ICJ. Indeed, in conflicts between the U.S. Constitution and international law, the Constitution prevails: "It is now a well-established principle that neither a rule of customary international law nor a provision of a treaty can abrogate a right granted by the Constitution."[13] This demonstrates the absence of legal hierarchy in which international law and courts could take precedence over national laws and courts. The U.S. Supreme Court might take the ICJ's decisions and interpretations into account in its own deliberations, but it does not recognize the ICJ as a superior authority.

judicial hierarchy The chain of command in legal systems in which the decisions of higher courts possessing greater authority are binding on lower courts.

Law and power Historically, realists have been the most skeptical about the value of international law. Some of those who reject the very existence of international law are realists. The majority of realists concede that international law is a reality but downgrade its importance. There are several reasons that critiques presenting international law as a weak force in international politics appeal to realists. First, realists typically place a great deal of emphasis on the fundamental divide between domestic and international politics, with the critical difference being the absence of a central political authority on the global level. This is the "first fact" of international politics for realists. To the extent that criticisms of international law stress the absence of institutions to create and enforce laws, they reflect this basic realist tendency to see the international realm as distinct from the domestic realm.

Realists would no doubt concur with James Brierly's conclusion that "the fundamental difficulty of subjecting states to the rule of law is the fact that states possess power."[14] On the rather mundane day-to-day issues that nations deal with, they may indeed abide by thousands of international laws. But this is not the point. The real test of international law is not whether it constrains relatively weak states on issues of lesser importance. The test is whether it has any impact on the actions of great powers on the pivotal issues of international politics, war and peace, and the use of force. When national power and interests come into conflict with international law, which prevails? Is there any chance that law trumps power and interests in such cases? For realists, the answer is no. Realists are also inclined to argue not only that international law will not prevail in such cases, but also that it *should not.* Nations abide by international law as long as it is in their national interests to do so. When states do make reference to international law, it is "as a source for the manufacture of *ad hoc* or *ex post facto* justifications for decisions taken on the basis . . . of power politics and national interests."[15]

At an even deeper level, realists (and, interestingly, Marxists) sometimes argue that international laws and norms are themselves reflections of power. International law does not just appear out of nowhere. It originates in concrete social-political settings in which power and resources are not equally distributed. The norms and rules that prevail at any point in time are likely to be consistent with the interests of those actors with the power to enforce them and the power to exert control over international institutions. Most contemporary international law originated in Europe beginning in the 1600s and developed over the course of the last four hundred years. As Malanczuk points out, "most developing countries were under alien rule during the formative period of international law, and therefore played no part in shaping that law."[16] As a result, it would be naïve to assume that international law has not been influenced by the particular values and interests of European societies: "Law has the inclination to serve primarily the interests of the powerful. 'European' international law, the traditional law of nations, is no exception to this rule."[17] Such principles as freedom of the seas and the protection of private property no doubt serve the interests of those with the power to use the seas and who possess the property. According to Lenin, law (domestic and international) is but the "formulation, the registration of power relations . . . and expression of the will of the ruling class."[18] On this issue at least, realists would agree with Lenin.

THE ENDURING VALUE OF INTERNATIONAL LAW

Defenders of international law would appear to have an uphill battle, and a fairly steep one at that, to make the case for it being a meaningful force in international politics. Most of the critics' basic points need to be conceded at the outset: "International law has no legislature . . . there is no system of courts. . . . and there is no executive governing authority . . . there is no identifiable institution either to establish rules, or clarify them or see that those who break them are punished."[19] How does one make a case for international law in the face of this void? There are essentially three arguments advanced by those who see international law as a powerful constraint on state behavior. First, critics of international law tend to exaggerate its shortcomings by focusing on a small handful of spectacular failures and attacking an unrealistic, almost straw-man, vision of what international law can accomplish. Second, nations almost always abide by international law for many of the same reasons people abide by domestic laws even in the absence of a government to enforce them. Third, critics tend to underestimate how powerful international laws and norms can be in altering and shaping state behavior.

The false lessons of spectacular failures Extreme criticisms that international law is a worthless sham and that it is violated all the time often highlight some of the more spectacular failures, and there are plenty to chose from. A favorite example from the 1920s is the **Kellogg-Briand Pact** (1928), or the "General Treaty for the Renunciation

Kellogg-Briand Pact (1928)
Formally known as the General Treaty for the Renunciation of War, the agreement obliged signatories to renounce war as an instrument of policy and to settle their disputes peacefully.

United States President Calvin Coolidge presides over the signing in 1929 of the Kellogg-Briand Pact, intended to outlaw war. In retrospect, this was a naive attempt to alter the character of international relations by legalistic fiat. World War II followed just ten years later.
SOURCE: © Hulton-Deutsch Collection/CORBIS

of War," which was signed by sixty-five states, including Italy and Japan. The pact obliged signatories to renounce war as an instrument of policy and to settle their disputes peacefully. Though many at the time realized the treaty for what it was—an unenforceable statement of moral aspirations—others actually believed that it could transform international politics. Although the attempt to abolish war by treaty is silly in retrospect, the failure of the Kellogg-Briand Pact provides a good basis to begin understanding what international law realistically can and cannot accomplish. Even those who think that international law is generally effective and worthwhile recognize that it does have limits, as does domestic law (after all, laws prohibiting the production, sale, and consumption of alcohol in the United States during the 1920s and 1930s fared about as well as the attempt to outlaw war).

In thinking about the promise and limits of international law, we need to understand two very different approaches to law, or how we go about deciding what actions should and should not be illegal. Over the past several centuries, the **natural law tradition** and the **positive law tradition** have shaped thinking about the sources and functions of law, domestic and international.[20] A natural law approach is driven by a moral analysis, whereas a positivist approach rests on a behavioral analysis. Natural law begins by identifying an abstract standard of moral absolutes—the delineation of what behaviors are morally right or wrong—and attempts to translate these absolutes into laws and regulations. "Natural lawyers," according to Lea Brilmayer, "suggested that international law followed from the basic universal principles of morality."[21] These moral principles are derived without reference to the actual behavior of people. Morality, after all, is not a popularity contest. If people are already behaving in ac-

natural law tradition
A tradition that holds that universal moral principles should form the basis for laws. Usually contrasted with the **positive law tradition.**

positive law tradition
A tradition that holds that laws need to take into account the ways in which people (and states) actually behave. Attempts to rigidly translate moral principles into law without regard for the realities of human behavior are unlikely to be very successful.

cordance with these absolutes, so much the better. But what if they are not? In this case, the law becomes a tool for changing the way people behave. If something is wrong, it should be illegal, regardless of how people are really behaving.

Positivist legal theory adopts a very different approach: "Applied to international law, positivism . . . regard[s] the actual behavior of states as the basis of international law."[22] Positivists try to identify those norms of behavior that are generally adhered to in the real world (it is assumed that routine adherence to norms constitutes a form of tacit consent). These norms then become the basis for law. In many cases, these behavioral norms are also consistent with moral absolutes. We are fortunate, for example, that laws against murder are consistent with both moral absolutes and actual behavior. But there are also many instances in which behavior and abstract principles diverge. In these cases, the law needs to be reconciled to prevailing behavior. Laws that dictate behaviors that are at great variance with actual behavior are doomed to failure. Brierly explains that "the real contribution of positivist theory to international law has been its insistence that the rules of the system are to be ascertained from observation of the practice of states and not from *a priori* deductions."[23] One of the earliest positivists, Niccolo Machiavelli (1469–1527) warned of the dangers of excessive moralism: "The gulf between how one should live and one does live is so wide that a man who neglects what is actually done for what should be done learns the hard way to self-destruction."[24] From a positivist perspective, the purpose of law is not to radically alter the way most people are behaving, but rather to punish and influence the behavior of the small handful of people who are inclined not to follow these norms. The requirement that laws embody existing norms of behavior is even more important in the international realm than the domestic. Since there is no central authority with the power to enforce laws in international society, it is critical that laws are based on consent and be consistent with prevailing behavior.

The problem with treaties such as the Kellogg-Briand Pact is that they attempted to apply a moral norm to states that was in great variance with the way statesmen actually thought and behaved. Although the signatories of the treaty certainly consented to its terms, there was an almost surreal disconnect between the treaty's lofty sentiments and the depressing realities of world politics. The logic of Kellogg-Briand was simple: if war was wrong, it should be illegal, case closed. Its goal was to transform the basic dynamics of international politics. It tried to alter political reality rather than work within it. The pact was the international equivalent of domestic laws against alcohol consumption. It should come as no surprise that these laws failed. But it is easy to overlearn the lessons of such failures. It would be a wild exaggeration to use these examples such as Kellogg-Briand to support any sweeping denunciation of international law as a worthless collection of rules that states violate at will any more than the failure of Prohibition can support a blanket criticism of domestic law. The point here is simple: we need to have a reasonable expectation of what international law can accomplish. Criticizing international law for failing to achieve the unattainable is a decidedly pointless endeavor.

States usually abide by international law It is easy to produce a long list of violations of international law. But what does this prove? Not much. It would be just as easy to create a similarly long list of violations of domestic laws. Merely because domestic laws are violated, we do not conclude that they are worthless or nonexistent. In fact, if laws were never violated, there would not be much of a need for them in the first place. The value of international law does not depend on universal compliance. The occasional violations of law should not be allowed to obscure the frequency with which it is obeyed. Unfortunately, compliance never draws much attention: there are never headlines announcing the millions of people who are not robbed or murdered every day. It is the violations of law that everyone remembers. But an accurate evaluation of international law requires an assessment of both compliance and violation. And virtually everyone who has looked at the issue agrees with Stanley Michalak's assessment that "most of time states do obey international law; most of the time they do get along with their neighbors; and most of the time, they do cooperate on countless issues and problems."[25] And even Hans Morgenthau, a realist who spends a lot of time discussing the weaknesses of international law, concedes "that during the four hundred years of its existence international law has in most instances been scrupulously observed."[26]

Why do states abide by international law? If there is no central enforcement mechanism to assure that states abide by international law, why do they, even when they might derive some immediate benefits from ignoring it? As with individuals and domestic law, states typically have a variety of reasons for following international law. The first set of reasons fall under the rubric of **identitive compliance.** When we think about why we usually abide by our domestic laws, the most prominent reason is that they embody norms of behavior we agree (or "identify") with. How many of us would engage in rape, murder, or theft even if we were certain that we would never be caught or punished? Not many. For the vast majority of laws, especially those that seek to protect people from direct harm, the threat of punishment is not the primary reason that people comply. Undoubtedly, "some people do in fact obey laws because lawbreaking will bring them into unwelcome contact with the police and courts . . . but no community could survive only through an ever-present fear of punishment."[27] The threat of punishment is there to deter the relatively small handful of people who would not be restrained by their own conscience. Most nations refrain from attacking their weaker neighbors, committing genocide or kidnapping foreign diplomats, not because they fear punishment, but simply because they think these things are wrong. Though we sometimes say that the strong take what they can and the weak grant what they must, this is simply not the case. The strong could probably take much more than they do. The importance of good conscience should not be underestimated, even in the supposedly cutthroat world of international politics.

States also abide by international law because it is in their interests to do so, which we refer to as **utilitarian compliance.** Even when some benefit may be gained by violating a law in specific instances, nations recognize that in the long run they benefit from upholding the law. Take an example that sometimes infuriates people—international laws that prohibit nations from trying and punishing foreign diplomats who commit crimes. This is known as **diplomatic immunity.** Typically, these are relatively harmless but nonetheless annoying violations, such as United Nations diplomats who park their cars wherever they want in New York and rack up tens of thousands of dollars in unpaid parking tickets. But occasionally there are more egregious examples—foreign diplomats have abused children and killed people in drunk driving accidents—but cannot be prosecuted or even arrested in the United States or other countries. In these cases, the host government has two options: first, it can ask

---

identitive compliance The fact that people and nations usually abide with laws not out of fear of punishment but because the laws embody norms that are viewed as right.

utilitarian compliance When people or states abide by laws because they think it is in their interests to do so.

diplomatic immunity The principle that nations cannot try and punish diplomats of other nations who violate their domestic laws. This is an example of an international law that emerged first through custom but was eventually codified in treaties.

the diplomat's government to waive that person's diplomatic immunity and allow him or her to be arrested and tried; or second, the diplomat can be declared a *persona non grata* and expelled from the country. Despite these (admittedly rare) horror stories, it remains in the interest of the United States, and of other countries, to respect the norm of diplomatic immunity. But why? Because U.S. diplomats are stationed all over the world in nations where laws and legal systems might not be to our liking. Without diplomatic immunity, a U.S. diplomat caught with alcohol or a *Playboy* magazine in some countries might be subject to draconian punishments, and might be tried in corrupt legal systems. Thus, the overall benefits of abiding by diplomatic immunity vastly outweigh the occasional costs.

A related motivation for state compliance with international law is a *fear of chaos*. The point here is that nations do not calculate on a law-by-law basis whether their interests are served by compliance or violation. There is a value to international law that transcends such narrow calculations. States also benefit from the preservation of a certain measure of international order and stability. Even when some immediate benefit might be gained by violating a given rule, states recognize that they have a more fundamental, long-term interest in upholding the general system of international law. "The ultimate explanation of the binding force of all law," according to Brierly, "is that man, whether he is a single individual or whether he is associated with other men in a state, is constrained, in so far as he is a reasonable being, to believe that order and not chaos is the governing principle of the world in which he has to live."[28] The preservation of order depends on reciprocity—if you expect others to abide by the rules, you need to abide by them yourself. If states begin violating some laws in order to gain an advantage, doing so encourages other states to do likewise when they might benefit. If the entire system begins to unravel, the costs are almost certain to outweigh the gains from the initial violation.

States also abide by international law because of the fear of punishment. This might seem odd given the absence of a central political authority to enforce laws and carry out the punishment. The mere fact that there is no centrally imposed punishment does not mean there is no punishment; it simply requires that punishment be imposed in a decentralized fashion by other states. International law recognizes a right of **reprisal** or retaliation—that is, the right of states to take actions that would otherwise be impermissible in response to another state's violation of international law. For example, when Iranian radicals took U.S. diplomats hostage in 1979 with the approval and support of the Iranian government, this was universally recognized as a violation of longstanding international law. As a result, the United States had the right to take actions that would normally not be allowed in reprisal, such as seizing Iranian assets in the United States. Furthermore, international law recognizes a right of **collective reprisal.** Even though it was the United States' diplomats who were taken hostage, all nations had a right to take actions to punish Iran. The right to punish is not restricted to the state whose rights were violated because it is the obligation of all states to uphold international law.

The Iranian hostage case provides an example of yet another reason states usually abide by international law: in the event that a state's rights are violated in the future, other nations are less likely to come to its aid if that state has violated international law in the past. States need to care about their reputations, something Iran would soon find out. Several years after the hostage crisis, Iran found itself embroiled in a bitter

reprisal An act that is normally a violation of international law but that is permitted as a response to another nation's violation of international law.

collective reprisal Under international law, the ability or obligation for all states to punish those who violate international law (as opposed to only those states whose rights were violated).

An American diplomat paraded by his captors in Iran after the 1979 takeover of the United States embassy. This was clear violation of international law. When Iran complained a few years later about Iraqi use of chemical weapons (also a violation of law), the international response was not what Iran hoped.
SOURCE: Hulton Archive/Getty Images

war with Iraq. During the course of that war, Iraq used chemical weapons against Iranian targets in clear violation of international law. When Iran protested to the international community that its rights were being violated, there was not much sympathy to be found. Nations cannot violate the rights of others and then expect others to care when their rights are violated. Thus, nations are usually unwilling to be saddled with the reputation of violating international law for fear that their ability to call on the international community for help in the future will be diminished.

Liberalism and the promise of international law Liberals have traditionally seen a greater scope for common interests in international relations than realists. But like realists, liberals recognize that the uncertainties and insecurities of anarchy make it difficult for states to cooperate to achieve their common interests. This is one of the valuable functions of international law. Because nations usually do comply, international law gives states some reasonable assurance, if not a guarantee, about how other states will behave. International law lessens some of the uncertainties of anarchy by promoting predictability, reliability, and regularity. As Hedley Bull explains, "international law provides a means by which states can advertise their intentions with regard to the matter in question [and] provide one another with a reassurance about their future policies in relation to it."[29] Thus, it is not that states only abide by international law when it is in their interests to do so, but rather that a system of law makes it possible for states to achieve common interests that would be unattainable without international law.

Though they agree that self-interest is a powerful motive for state compliance with international law, liberals are more likely to interpret state behavior as resulting from mixed motives, including ethical and moral considerations. When we look at the reasons that people generally abide by law in domestic society, motives other than self-interest are probably even more important. Is it self-interest that stops people from assaulting, killing, and robbing each other? No. People refrain from such activities because they believe they are wrong. Similarly, is it self-interest that stops nations from attacking each other more often? Probably not. For liberals, the emphasis on self-interest and/or fear of punishment is an unduly pessimistic assessment of state motivations. Remember that liberals view people as essentially rational, reasonable, ethical, and moral beings. Because states are collections of people, state behavior reflects many of the same traits. This perspective provides a much more optimistic vision of the potential of international law.

There are limits to liberal optimism, however. Most liberals have long since abandoned the utopian view of international law that informed the Kellogg-Briand Pact and other attempts to transform international politics through legalistic fiats. There is a recognition that international law cannot completely ignore the realities of power politics. Nonetheless, liberals find the realist view of international law too limiting. Utopian idealism does not have to be replaced by a dismissive cynicism. Though international law cannot bring world peace, it can significantly ameliorate the imperatives of power politics. One reason for this more robust view of international law is that liberals have never accepted the realist conception of international politics as a relentlessly competitive arena in which self-interested states are constantly jockeying for advantage. The realist inclination to reduce all aspects of international politics to relations of power provides a caricature of how the world works. There has always been more to international politics than narrow national interests—there is also restraint, common interests, enlightened self-interest, and, yes, even morality and altruism.

Constructivism, law, norms, and the national interest For constructivists, the relationship between international law and national interests is a bit more complicated than realists (or liberals) suggest. To say that states abide by international law primarily (and perhaps only) when it is in their national interest to do so ignores what constructivists consider the most important issue: how and why nations arrive at their definitions of the national interest. The national interest is not something nations discover like scientists do the law of physics. It is not an objective fact; *national interest* is a subjective and variable social construction. Nations think about their national interests today very differently than they did in centuries past. They also reject as unacceptable, even unthinkable, practices that used to be routine for advancing national interests. David Lumsdaine cites a few examples: "Two centuries ago it was acceptable to wage war with hired foreign mercenaries; now it is not. Killing and enslaving the inhabitants of conquered countries, a common if brutal practice in Thucydides' day, would make a state a total outlaw today. Wars to acquire territory, normal enough in the seventeenth century, are increasingly regarded as unacceptable."[30] Most states today would not dream of doing certain things that were once perfectly legitimate. Why not? Because we adhere to very different notions about what states should be allowed to do; state behavior has changed along with our evolving moral standards.

Realists ask whether international law constrains nations in the pursuit of their national interests, and generally they conclude that it does not. For constructivists, this is not only the wrong answer but also a very simple-minded way of thinking about the relationship between international law and national interests. Once we accept the idea that definitions of the national interest change and evolve over time, a whole new set of possibilities opens up. Is it possible, for example, that prevailing conceptions of morality and rules of law help shape the way nations define their interests? Not only is it possible, but it seems self-evidently to be the case. Thus, the relationship among national interests, state behavior, and international law is more complicated than is often believed. "Norms are not simply an ethical alternative to or constraint on self-interest," Audie Klotz tells us, "rather, in the constructivist view . . . norms play an explanatory role. . . . thus international actors—even great powers such as the United States—inherently are socially constructed; that is, prevailing global norms. . . . partially define their interests."[31] We noted earlier that laws, domestic and international, are typically obeyed because people identify with the norms of behavior they embody (the identitive basis of compliance). This is consistent with the constructivist view that states behave on the basis of shared understandings (i.e., norms) of what is appropriate behavior. So merely looking for instances where international legal norms constrained state behavior underestimates their importance; we also need to appreciate how legal norms influence definitions of national interest in the first place.

CONCLUSION

Discussions of international law used to be defined by the extreme positions: at one end of the spectrum, international law was dismissed as a nonexistent or worthless sham; at the other, international law was presented as an alternative to power politics and the use of force. Contemporary thinking about international law generally rejects both positions in favor of a more nuanced view. There is, in fact, a substantial amount of agreement in the debate over the value of international law. At a general level, Peter Malanczuk comes closest to summarizing prevailing opinion: "The role of international law in international relations has always been limited, but it is rarely insignificant."[32] There is also a consensus that the vast majority of states abide by international law the vast majority of the time. But there are still differences, particularly concerning the motives for compliance, that reflect underlying disagreements about the forces that shape state behavior.

Realists argue that states are primarily motivated by concerns about power and national interest. International anarchy requires that states prioritize power and interests because those that do not will suffer at the hands of those who do. The scope for moral behavior is severely limited in the competitive arena of international politics. The fact that states usually comply with international law is seen as perfectly consistent with this view. For realists, this compliance is driven largely by considerations of national interest, and when there is a conflict between international law and national interests, the latter will certainly prevail. States do not obey international law out of moral commitment. Sometimes the moral and legal course of action is also in the national interest, but this is merely a happy coincidence.

Liberals and constructivists are united in rejecting realist attempts to explain everything in terms of power and national interest. Although morality may or may not be the predominant reason for compliance with international law, it is certainly not the insignificant factor that realists would have us believe. The realist argument, however, is very difficult to counter, largely because the concept of national interest is so vague and elastic that it can account for almost anything states do. Those who are convinced that calculations of national interest dictate how states behave will always be able to explain their actions in these terms. The "national interest" is like those ink-blot tests that psychologists show patients and ask them to tell what they see. You can usually see pretty much anything you want—if you want to see a tiger, there it is; if you want to see your mother, there she is. If a state abides by international law, you can show that it was in its national interest to do so; if it violated the same law, you could show how that, too, was in its national interest. The realist position is almost impossible to disprove. But even if we accept the realist position that national interests determine state behavior, this only leads to the more fundamental question of how states arrive at their definitions of national interests. Conceptions of national interest do not exist independent of international laws and norms. Certainly, definitions of national interest are reflected in laws and norms, but these laws and norms also influence how states think about their national interests.

POINTS OF VIEW

Should the United States Accept the International Criminal Court?

Since the end of World War II, a number of treaties and conventions have outlawed particularly egregious violations of human rights—crimes against humanity, genocide, and other war crimes. Until recently, however, there was no international judicial body designed to prosecute *individuals* suspected of engaging in these proscribed behaviors. The International Court of Justice hears cases against *states,* not individuals. Typically, the ICJ has created ad hoc courts to hear cases against individuals, such as the one trying those suspected of mass killings in the former Yugoslavia. During the 1990s, there was a movement to establish a permanent court to deal with such cases. These efforts were successful, and on July 17, 1998, 120 nations voted in favor of the Rome Statute of the International Criminal Court (ICC). Only seven nations voted against the establishment of this court, including China, Israel, Iraq, and the United States. As of September 2002, eighty-one countries had ratified the statute; the United States was not among them. The Clinton administration claimed to support the idea of the ICC but opposed some provisions of the actual treaty. In 2002, the Bush administration announced its opposition and its decision not to seek ratification of the Rome Statute.

The following documents deal with the controversy over the Bush administration's decision. The remarks by John Bolton, Undersecretary of State for Arms Control and International Security, lay out the administration's concerns about the ICC and its reasons for opposing the treaty. Law professor Joanne Mariner finds fault with the administration's analysis of the treaty and its decision on several levels. What are the main points of disagreement in terms of the specifics of the ICC? More important, how does their disagreement on the ICC reflect a more fundamental difference on the role and value of international law versus the importance of national sovereignty?

The United States and the International Criminal Court

John R. Bolton, Under Secretary for Arms Control and International Security
Aspen Institute, Berlin, Germany, September 16, 2002

The topic I have been asked to speak on is the United States' view of the role of treaties. I thought I would use the International Criminal Court (ICC) as a case study.

For a number of reasons, the United States decided that the ICC had unacceptable consequences for our national sovereignty. Specifically, the ICC is an organization whose precepts go against fundamental American notions of sovereignty, checks and balances, and national independence. It is an agreement that is harmful to the national interests of the United States, and harmful to our presence abroad.

U.S. military forces and civilian personnel and private citizens are currently active in peacekeeping and humanitarian missions in almost 100 countries at any given time. It is essential that we remain steadfast in preserving the independence and flexibility that America needs to defend our national interests around the world. As President Bush said,

> The United States cooperates with many other nations to keep the peace, but we will not submit American troops to prosecutors and judges whose jurisdiction we do not

accept.... Every person who serves under the American flag will answer to his or her own superiors and to military law, not to the rulings of an unaccountable International Criminal Court.

In the eyes of its supporters, the ICC is simply an overdue addition to the family of international organizations, an evolutionary step ahead of the Nuremberg tribunal, and the next logical institutional development over the ad hoc war crimes courts for the Former Yugoslavia and Rwanda. The Statute of Rome establishes both substantive principles of international law and creates new institutions and procedures to adjudicate these principles. The Statute confers jurisdiction on the ICC over four crimes; genocide, crimes against humanity, war crimes, and the crime of aggression. The Court's jurisdiction is "automatic," applicable to covered individuals accused of crimes under the Statute regardless of whether their governments have ratified it or consent to such jurisdiction. Particularly important is the independent Prosecutor, who is responsible for conducting investigations and prosecutions before the Court. The Prosecutor may initiate investigations based on referrals by States Parties, or on the basis of information that he or she otherwise obtains.

So described, one might assume that the ICC is simply a further step in the orderly march toward the peaceful settlement of international disputes, sought since time immemorial. But in several respects, the court is poised to assert authority over nation states, and to promote its prosecution over alternative methods for dealing with the worst criminal offenses.

The United States will regard as illegitimate any attempts to bring American citizens under its jurisdiction. The ICC does not fit into a coherent international "constitutional" design that delineates clearly how laws are made, adjudicated or enforced, subject to popular accountability and structured to protect liberty. There is no such design. Instead, the Court and the Prosecutor are simply "out there" in the international system. Requiring the United States to be bound by this treaty, with its unaccountable Prosecutor, is clearly inconsistent with American standards of constitutionalism and the standards for imposing international requirements....

Numerous prospective "crimes" were suggested at Rome and commanded wide support from participating nations. This includes the crime of "aggression," which was included in the Statute, but not defined. Although frequently easy to identify, "aggression" can at times be something in the eye of the beholder. For example, Israel justifiably feared in Rome that certain actions, such as its initial use of force in the Six Day War, would be perceived as illegitimate preemptive strikes that almost certainly would have provoked proceedings against top Israeli officials. Moreover, there seems little doubt that Israel will be the target of a complaint in the ICC concerning conditions and practices by the Israeli military in the West Bank and Gaza. Israel recently decided to declare its intention not to become a party to the ICC or to be bound by the Statute's obligations.

A fair reading of the treaty leaves one unable to answer with confidence whether the United States would now be accused of war crimes for legitimate but controversial uses of force to protect world peace. No U.S. President or his advisers could be assured that he or she would be unequivocally safe from the charges of criminal liability.

... My concern goes beyond the possibility that the Prosecutor will target for indictment the isolated U.S. soldier who violates our own laws and values by allegedly committing a war crime. My concern is for our country's top civilian and military leaders, those responsible for our defense and foreign policy. They are the ones potentially at risk at the hands of the ICC's politically unaccountable Prosecutor....

[An] alternative, of course, is for the parties themselves to try their own alleged war criminals. Indeed, there are substantial arguments that the fullest cathartic impact of the prosecutorial approach to war crimes occurs when the responsible population itself comes to grips with its past and administers appropriate justice. The Rome Statute pays lip service to the doctrine of "complementarity," or deference to national judicial systems, but this is simply an assertion, unproven and untested. It is *within* national judicial systems where the international effort should be to encourage the warring parties to resolve questions of criminality as part of a comprehensive solution to their disagreements. Removing key elements of the dispute to a distant forum, especially the emotional and contentious issues of war crimes and crimes against humanity, undercuts the very progress that these peoples, victims and perpetrators alike, must make if they are ever to live peacefully together.

Take Cambodia. Although the Khmer Rouge genocide is frequently offered as an example of why the ICC is needed, its proponents offer inadequate explanations why the Cambodians themselves should not try and adjudicate alleged war crimes committed by the Khmer Rouge regime. To exempt Cambodia from responsibility for this task implies the incurable immaturity of Cambodians and paternalism by the international community. Repeated interventions, even benign ones, by global powers are no substitute for the Cambodians coming to terms with themselves. That said, we could see a role for the UN to cooperate with Cambodia in a Khmer Rouge tribunal to provide technical assistance and to ensure that credible justice is achieved.

In the absence of the means or political will to address grave violations, the United States has supported the establishment and operation of ad hoc tribunals such as those in Yugoslavia and Rwanda. Unlike the ICC, these are created and overseen by the UN Security Council, under a UN Charter to which virtually all nations have agreed.

As the ICC comes into being, we will address our concerns about the ICC's jurisdictional claims using the remedy laid out for us by the Rome Statute itself and the UN Security Council in the case of the peacekeeping force in the former Yugoslavia. Using Article 98 of the Rome Statute as a basis, we are negotiating agreements with individual States Parties to protect our citizens from being handed over to the Court. Without undermining the Court's basic mission, these agreements will allow us the necessary protections in a manner that is legally permissible and consistent with the letter and spirit of the Rome Statute.

In order to promote justice worldwide, the United States has many foreign policy instruments to utilize that are fully consistent with our values and interests. We will continue to play a worldwide leadership role in strengthening domestic judicial systems and promoting freedom, transparency and the rule of law. As Secretary Powell has said: "We are the leader in the world with respect to bringing people to justice. We have supported a tribunal for Yugoslavia, the tribunal for Rwanda, trying to get the tribunal for Sierra Leone set up. We have the highest standards of accountability of any nation on the face of the earth."

We respect the decision of States Parties to join the ICC, but they in turn must respect our decision not to be bound by jurisdictional claims to which we have not consented. Signatories of the Statute of Rome have created an ICC to their liking, and they should live with it. The United States did not agree to be bound, and must not be held to its terms.

Bureau of Public Affairs, U.S. Department of State. Accessed at: www.state.gov/t/us/rm/13538.htm

The Case for the International Criminal Court

Joanne Mariner
July 08, 2002

In stepping up its campaign against the International Criminal Court, the United States is now threatening an array of drastic measures. Endangering the international presence in Bosnia, warning of a possible boycott of United Nations peacekeeping missions, and pledging a policy of total noncooperation with the court's prosecutions, Washington's stubborn enmity toward the court has led it to take actions that anger even its closest allies.

So what is the nature of this "threat" to American interests, as Secretary of Defense Donald Rumsfeld recently described it? Does the ICC undermine American sovereignty and jeopardize our national security? Is the United States justified in seeking full immunity from the court's activities because of the serious dangers inherent in any assertion of the court's jurisdiction, even over U.N. peacekeepers?

Washington's actions presuppose that the answers to these questions is yes. It would be foolish and ill-advised to alienate so many of our allies, particularly at a time when our national security depends on international cooperation, if the stakes were not extremely high.

But a review of the ICC's history, rules, and structure presents a very different picture than that understood by Washington. Rather than a court that wrongly threatens U.S. interests, the evidence suggests that the United States is wrongly damaging an international tribunal, thoughtlessly undermining international legal standards, and unwisely subverting the development of international justice.

A Court for the World's Worst Criminals

The International Criminal Court, whose underlying treaty came into force this past July 1, has jurisdiction over the world's worst criminals: those who have committed genocide, crimes against humanity and war crimes. It will also have jurisdiction over the crime of aggression, if and when a definition is decided upon in the future.

Most of the definitions of crimes in the court's treaty were already well-established in international law when the treaty was drafted. In addition, there is now a substantial body of case law from existing international war crimes tribunals to flesh out their meanings. Finally, the Elements of Crimes, drafted subsequent to the court's underlying treaty, further specifies the breadth of the ICC's subject matter jurisdiction.

In terms of the temporal limitations, the court will only have jurisdiction over crimes committed after the treaty's entry into force. In other words, there is no possibility that the court will be used to right all the wrongs of the past. It is not a court for Idi Amin, but instead for the Idi Amins of the future.

Developments in the U.S. Position

There is nothing preordained about the current U.S. hostility toward the ICC. Indeed, it was not always so: the U.S. was an early and enthusiastic supporter of the idea of an international criminal court. In the early 1990s, the U.S. Congress passed resolutions in favor of the court's establishment, and high-level Clinton Administration officials were active participants in the process of drafting the court's treaty.

What finally turned the United States against the court was other countries' refusal to allow the U.N. Security Council to be the court's gatekeeper. Under the rules proposed by the United States, the Security Council was to have a veto over the court's docket. Because of the U.S. power on the Security Council, Washington was assured that a Security Council–controlled court could would pose no threat to its interests.

Although such a court would, in principle, target those responsible for human rights crimes the world over, in practice, it could never prosecute an American citizen in the face of U.S. opposition, or, indeed, prosecute the citizen of any member of the Security Council in the face of the member's opposition. In this way, a handful of countries would have been exempted from norms applicable to all the rest.

Although this proposal was rejected at the 1998 Rome Conference where the ICC treaty was negotiated, the treaty did include the "Singapore compromise," by which the Security Council may delay a prosecution for twelve months if it believes the ICC would interfere with the Council's efforts to further international peace and security. Under this compromise provision, the Security Council must pass a resolution requesting the court not to proceed; an individual permanent member cannot block an investigation by exercising its veto.

In refusing to sign the ICC treaty at the Rome Conference, the U.S. found itself quite isolated. Only China, Iraq, Libya, Qatar, Yemen and Israel joined in boycotting the court, while 120 nations voted in its favor. Although the outgoing Clinton Administration did finally sign the ICC treaty in late December 2001, it continued to insist that the court was flawed. By signing the treaty, however, the U.S. would be able to remain engaged in shaping the new institution.

In other countries, ratification efforts have proceeded at a rapid pace, beyond the hopes of the court's most optimistic supporters. To date, seventy-four countries, including every country in the European Union, have ratified the ICC treaty.

U.S. Unilateralism

The U.S. may have failed to undermine the court's universality at the Rome Conference, but it has not given up in its quest to be totally exempt from court's jurisdiction. Moreover, the U.S. position with regard to the court is symptomatic of a broader unwillingness to be subject to the same international legal norms that bind other countries.

Although in the wake of the September 11 atrocities U.S. officials called for global coalition-building and multilateral cooperation, Washington's actions belie this approach. Now, perhaps more than ever in the past, the United States seems to be willing to force its agenda on the rest of the world—to substitute unilateral power for global consensus.

Those who portray the ICC as a rogue court should wonder instead whether, in persisting in its efforts to sabotage the court, the U.S. is acting more and more like a rogue state.

SOURCE: *FindLaw Newsletters,* accessed at: http://jurist.law.pitt.edu/forum/forumnew31.htm

CHAPTER SUMMARY

- Despite the absence of a world government, most agree that there is a body of rules and norms of behavior that comprise international law.

- International law has often been viewed from two different (and extreme) positions. Skeptics see international law either as nonexistent or as a worthless sham that is easily ignored when it clashes with power and interests. Its more enthusiastic supporters have sometimes seen international law as a powerful tool to shape and change the behavior of states for the better.

- There are several major sources of international law, the most important being customs and treaties or conventions. Decisions of international legal bodies and writings of widely recognized legal authorities are secondary sources of international law.

- The major weakness or limitation of international law is the conflicting and often vague provisions in international treaties and conventions as well as a legal system that lacks compulsory jurisdiction and an accepted hierarchy.

- The ability of nations, particularly the most powerful, to ignore and escape the restrictions of international law provides the most vivid illustration of the weakness of international law.

- Supporters point out that in the vast majority of instances nations scrupulously abide by international law for a variety of reasons (e.g., they agree with the laws, it is in their self-interest, and they fear punishment by other states). This fact is often obscured by some of the more dramatic failures of international law, such as the attempt to "outlaw war" in the 1920s.

- Even supporters recognize that international law has its limits, as does domestic law. An effective legal code needs to reconcile itself to actual behavior of individuals and/or states and not to try to radically remake them according to abstract moral principles.

- International law also has profound impact on how states define their national interest and what types of actions they consider acceptable in pursuit of these national interests.

- In general, realists are most skeptical of the value of international law, whereas liberals and constructivists believe it is, and can be, an important force shaping the behavior of states.

CRITICAL QUESTIONS

1. What are the similarities and differences between domestic and international law?

2. How do liberal, constructivist, and realist perspectives on international law differ?

3. How can international law exist in an anarchic environment?

4. Critics are able to point to frequent violations of international law to illustrate its impotence, especially when it comes to limiting the actions of great powers. How might supporters of international law respond to this line of criticism?

5. How is international law "enforced"?

KEY TERMS

collective reprisal 233
compulsory jurisdiction 226
customary law 224
diplomatic immunity 232
Grotius, Hugo (1583–1645) 222
identitive compliance 232
International Court of Justice (ICJ) 227
judicial hierarchy 228
Kellogg-Briand Pact (1928) 229
natural law tradition 230
optional clause 227
positive law tradition 230
reprisal 233
utilitarian compliance 232

FURTHER READINGS

The essential reference work in international law that provides the texts of most important treaties is Burns H. Weston, Richard A. Falk, and Hilary Charlesworth (eds.), *Supplement of Basic Documents to International Law and World Order* (St. Paul, MN: West, 1997). Excellent overviews of the sources, content, strengths, and weaknesses of international law are J. R. Brierly, *The Law of Nations: An Introduction to the International Law of Peace* (Oxford: Oxford University Press, 1963), and Peter Malanczuk, *Akehurst's Modern Introduction to International Law* (New York: Routledge, 1997). For conflicting views of the role of international law, see Lewis Henkin, Stanley Hoffman, and Jeanne Kirkpatrick, *Right vs. Might: International Law and the Use of Force* (New York: Council on Foreign Relations, 1991).

A theoretically challenging discussion of international law from a constructivist perspective is Friedrich V. Kratochwil, *Rules, Norms and Decisions: On the Conditions of Practical and Legal Reasoning in International Relations and Domestic Affairs* (Cambridge: Cambridge University Press, 1989).

INTERNATIONAL LAW ON THE WEB

www.icj-cij.org
Website of the International Court of Justice provides information on current and past cases before the court as well as international law more generally.

www.un.org/law
The United Nation's international law website offers a wealth of information on international legal bodies as well as treaties.

www.asil.org
Website of the American Society of International Law provides information on all aspects of international law, including how it relates to current events.

www.yale.edu/lawweb/avalon/avalon.htm
Maintained by the Yale Law School, this site posts texts of almost every significant treaty and legal document of the last five hundred years.

www.law.nyu.edu/library/foreign_intl/
A site containing links to a wide variety of sources on all aspects of international law.

www.public-international-law.net
deals with international law generally but focuses on international treaty law.

NOTES

[1] Cited in Mark V. Kauppi and Paul R. Viotti, *The Global Philosophers: World Politics in Western Thought* (New York: Lexington Books, 1992), p. 165.

[2] See Kauppi and Viotti, *Global Philosophers,* pp. 172–74.

[3] Catha Nolan, *The Longman Guide to World Affairs* (New York: Longman, 1995), p. 177.

[4] Hedley Bull, *The Anarchical Society: A Study of Order in International Politics* (New York: Columbia University Press, 1977), p. 127.

[5] See J. L. Brierly, *The Law of Nations: An Introduction to the International Law of Peace* (Oxford: Oxford University Press, 1963), p. 56.

[6] E. H. Carr, *The Twenty Years' Crisis, 1919–1939* (New York: Harper & Row, 1964), p. 171.

[7] David J. Bederman, *International Legal Frameworks* (New York: Foundation Press, 2001), p. 23.

[8] Ibid., pp. 23–24.

[9] Hans Morgenthau, *Politics among Nations* (New York: Alfred A. Knopf, 1968), p. 269.

[10] Ibid., p.193.

[11] See Robert Pastor, *Condemned to Repetition: The United States and Nicaragua* (Princeton: Princeton University Press, 1987), p. 257; and David P. Forsythe, *The Politics of International Law: U.S. Foreign Policy Reconsidered* (Boulder: Lynne Rienner Publishers, 1990), pp. 31–63.

[12] Morgenthau, *Politics among Nations,* p. 277.

[13] Bederman, *International Legal Frameworks,* p. 153.

[14] Brierly, *Law of Nations,* p. 48.

[15] Francis Anthony Boyle, *Foundations of World Order* (Durham: Duke University Press, 1999), p. 7.

[16] Peter Malanczuk, *Akehurst's Modern Introduction to International Law* (New York: Routledge, 1997), p. 29.

[17] B. V. A. Roling cited in ibid., p. 33.

[18] Cited in Carr, *Twenty Years' Crisis,* p. 176.

[19] Malcolm N. Shaw, *International Law* (Cambridge: Cambridge University Press, 1997), p. 3.

[20] See Bederman, *International Legal Frameworks,* pp. 4–5.

[21] Lea Brilmayer, *American Hegemony: Political Morality in a One-Superpower World* (New Haven: Yale University Press, 1994), p. 98.

[22] Malanczuk, *Akehurst's Modern Introduction to International Law,* p. 16.

[23] Brierly, *Law of Nations,* p. 54.

[24] In Kauppi and Viotti, *Global Philosophers,* p. 151.

[25] Stanley Michalak, *A Primer in Power Politics* (Wilmington, DE: Scholarly Resources, 2001), p. 3.

[26] Morgenthau, *Politics among Nations,* p. 265.

[27] Carr, *Twenty Years' Crisis,* p. 176.

[28] Brierly, *Law of Nations,* p. 56.

[29] Bull, *The Anarchical Society,* p. 142.

[30] David Lumsdaine, *Moral Vision in International Politics: The Foreign Aid Regime* (Princeton: Princeton University Press, 1993), p. 26.

[31] Audie Klotz, "Norms Reconstituting Interests: Global Racial Equality and U.S. Sanctions Against South Africa," *International Organization* 49, no. 2 (Summer 1995): 460.

[32] Malanczuk, *Akehurst's Modern Introduction to International Law,* p. 6.

THE UNITED NATIONS AND HUMANITARIAN INTERVENTION

This chapter explores the complex moral and political issues raised by the debate over humanitarian intervention. Advocates of humanitarian intervention come mainly from a liberal perspective, arguing that states forfeit their sovereignty rights when they violate or fail to protect the basic rights of their citizens. Though willing to make rare exceptions, they strongly prefer that interventions take place under the auspices of international organizations such as the United Nations because this framework increases legitimacy and reduces opportunities for abuse. Opponents of humanitarian intervention, often reflecting a realist perspective, believe that sovereignty should remain a principle of international order. The primary obligation of states is to the interests and well-being of their own citizens, not that of the citizens of other states. Furthermore, no matter how noble the ideal of humanitarian intervention is in theory, in practice it will become another tool for the powerful to impose their will and values. Because the United Nations is merely another arena, rather than an alternative, for power politics, its participation will not solve the problem of abuse.

How effective can international organizations be in an anarchic world of independent states? When, if at all, is it acceptable for one state or group of states to interfere in the domestic affairs of another state? What role should moral considerations, as opposed to calculations of national interest, play in international affairs? These are some of the most enduring questions in international relations, raising profound empirical and normative issues that divide policymakers and theorists alike. Stated in such general terms, however, these issues often become unwieldy and abstract. It is sometimes more useful to approach these types of questions through the lens of more concrete policy debates. Perhaps no debate is better suited for these issues than the one that has raged since the end of the Cold War over humanitarian intervention. Because most advocates of humanitarian intervention favor a critical role for the United Nations, it addresses the capabilities and limits of international organizations. Intervention of any sort inevitably involves outside interference in the domestic affairs of states. And the suggestion that states should be prepared to intervene in defense of human rights, not their national interest, brings questions of morality and international politics into focus. Thus, the problems of international organizations, sovereignty, and morality are all thrown into sharp relief by the debate over humanitarian intervention.

When the United Nations was founded in the immediate aftermath of World War II, memories of two devastating total wars and the failure of the interwar League of Nations were still fresh. An effective international organization was considered essential to avoiding another global war. Unfortunately, the United Nations fell victim to the superpower Cold War rivalry. Nowhere was the impact of the Cold War more evident than on the UN Security Council, whose five permanent members—the United States, the Soviet Union, China, France, and Britain—each possessed a veto that could be used to block any action or resolution. The ten nonpermanent members of the Council are elected for two-year terms by the UN General Assembly, in which each member state has one vote. Because virtually every issue during the Cold War was seen through the prism of the U.S.-Soviet conflict, each superpower tended to oppose anything supported by the other. The geopolitics of the Cold War combined with the veto power usually produced paralysis. With the end of the Cold War in 1989–1990, many hoped that the United Nations might be freed of the geopolitical shackles that had restrained it for so long, allowing the organization to fulfill its original promise. As Michael Barnett notes, "the atmosphere at the UN during the early 1990s was positively triumphant."[1]

Perhaps no event did more to shatter this optimism than the organization's inaction in face of the Rwandan genocide in 1994. Like many other African states, Rwanda is characterized by a division between ethnic groups, the majority Hutus and minority Tutsis. The animosity and suspicion between them is largely a legacy of colonialism. The Germans and Belgians had imposed this classification while fueling the notion that the Tutsis were somehow superior to the Hutus. Dividing the native population in this way was part of a strategy facilitating external domination: divide and conquer. After independence, the Hutu-controlled government discriminated against the Tutsi minority, treating them as second-class citizens. This simmering conflict eventually erupted into a civil war that lasted from 1990 until the signing of a ceasefire in February 1993. At this point the United Nations became involved in monitoring the ceasefire and negotiating a settlement of the conflict. A small force of 2,500 was sent to help maintain the peace. The precarious peace began to unravel on April 6, 1994, when a plane carrying the Hutu president of Rwanda was shot down as

Decaying corpses of Tutsi victims of ethnic violence provide a grisly reminder that genocide is not just a thing of the past. Despite the scale of the barbarity, the United Nations did nothing to halt it.
SOURCE: © Baci/CORBIS

it approached Kigali airport. Hutu extremists used this as an excuse to incite violence against the minority Tutsis. Within days, it was clear to UN officials in Rwanda that a systematic campaign, not merely spasmodic violence, was under way. The head of UN peacekeeping forces "understood that Hutu extremists were carrying out ethnic cleansing . . . [and] emphasized to headquarters the magnitude and scale of the crimes."[2] Over the course of the next few weeks, between 500,000 and 1,000,000 Tutsis were slaughtered in a horrific orgy of violence.

The tale of how officials in New York, Washington, and elsewhere failed to recognize and/or admit what was going on in Rwanda is both complicated and depressing. Suffice it to say that no significant action was taken to prevent or halt the genocide in Rwanda. The post–Cold War optimism concerning the United Nations and the international community's willingness to defend basic human rights was replaced by doubt and soul searching. If humanitarian action was not forthcoming in one of the most egregious and obvious violations of human rights since the Holocaust, it was hard to hold out much hope for and effective response to the next such catastrophe.

Sovereignty, Human Rights, and the United Nations

The idea of national sovereignty was codified in the Peace of Westphalia (1648). At the time it was seen as the only feasible solution to the religious conflict that gave rise to the bloody Thirty Years War (1618–1648). By making each ruler the sole authority on questions of religion over the territory they controlled, the monarchs of Europe devised a formula they could live with. This provision should not be confused with religious tolerance, however. Monarchs frequently engaged in brutal repression of subjects who did not share their faith, and this was deemed to be nobody else's business. Because rulers did not recognize the rights of their own subjects, they could hardly be expected to care about the rights of another monarch's subjects. Sovereignty was intended to restore international order, not protect individual rights. For the monarchs of Europe, constantly meddling in each other's affairs was a recipe for disorder, and what they craved most of all after three decades of war was order. In practice, of course, nations were not always as respectful of each other's sovereignty as the rhetoric and treaties suggested. This was particularly true outside the confines of Europe, where "lesser" races and non-Christians were deemed undeserving of the benefits of civilization. A large measure of hypocrisy and double standards has always surrounded the practice of sovereignty.

All of this began to change with the Enlightenment and the growth of liberalism, which introduced the notion of individual rights into political discourse. The first task for liberalism was establishing the principle that governments needed to respect the rights of their own subjects in the domestic sphere. In the 1700s and 1800s, liberalism helped erode the foundations of absolutist monarchism, ushering in an era of political democracy, limited government, and individual rights. But even though individuals increasingly gained rights in the domestic realm, they still lacked rights under international law. If a government refused to respect the rights of its people, this still did not provide a justification for violating the norm of sovereignty.

It took the horrors of the Holocaust and World War II to finally shake the bedrock principle of national sovereignty. As advancing allied armies liberated the concentration camps, it became clear that the Nazi atrocities were beyond anyone's wildest imagination. When those responsible were prosecuted at the **Nuremberg war crimes trials,** their defenses were predictable. Some claimed that the charges were all lies. Those a little further down the chain of command said they were just following orders and would have risked their own lives if they had refused participation. Those who issued the orders needed a different defense. Confronted with the evidence of Nazi crimes, one of Hitler's deputies, Hermann Goering, shouted, "But that was our right! We were a sovereign state and that was strictly our business."[3] There were two problems with this defense. First, many of these crimes took place on territory acquired through aggression and could not be considered under the legitimate control of the German state. Second, even claims of sovereignty proved unacceptable in the face of such barbarism. The limits of sovereignty had finally been exceeded. The Nuremberg trials (and similar trials in Tokyo for Japanese leaders) represented the first time in history that "a legal proceeding attempted to make government leaders internationally responsible as individuals for crimes against humanity covering so much

Nuremberg war crimes trials Post–World War II trials in which top officials of Nazi Germany were tried for violations of international law, including massive violations of human rights.

time, so many nations, or so many people, *including their own citizens* [emphasis added]."[4] Goering was convicted of crimes against humanity but cheated the executioner by taking his own life.

After Nuremberg sovereignty could no longer be considered absolute, but it was also not irrelevant. Clearly some actions were now beyond legitimate claims of sovereignty, but it was unclear exactly where the line between would be drawn. Since World War II the tension between individual rights and national sovereignty has remained unresolved. This can be seen in the **United Nations Charter** (1945), which obliges "all members [to] refrain in their international relations from the threat or use of force against the territorial integrity or political independence of any state." The organization as a whole faces the same restriction as member states: "Nothing contained in the present Charter shall authorize the United Nations to intervene in matters which are essentially within the domestic jurisdiction of any state."[5] Prohibitions against intervention are even more explicit in the Charter of the Organization of American States (OAS): "No state or group of states has the right to intervene, directly or indirectly, *for any reason whatever,* in the internal or external affairs of any other state [emphasis added]."[6] You cannot get any clearer than that. The only instance in which the United Nations, acting through the Security Council, could authorize forceful intervention in a state's domestic affairs is when "international peace and security" were threatened. This rather vague and nebulous phrasing has been subject to some fairly expansive interpretations over the years. The real dilemma, however, concerns large-scale human rights abuses that do not pose any wider threat to peace and security.

While seeming to strengthen norms of national sovereignty, the UN Charter also "reaffirm[s] faith in fundamental human rights, in the dignity and worth of the human person, in the equal rights of men and women." In addition to the UN Charter, the "non-binding" **Universal Declaration of Human Rights** (1948) specifies an almost comically long and detailed list of rights, including the right to "rest and leisure." But this recognition of individual rights raises the obvious question: What good are treaties guaranteeing human rights if outside forces are prohibited from intervening to protect those rights? This is tantamount to laws protecting children from abuse that also forbid anyone from entering private houses to stop the abuse.

As a result, many have concluded that lofty treaties protecting human rights are hollow charades without a right of **humanitarian intervention,** which is defined as the uninvited interference by a state, states, or international organization in the domestic affairs of another state in order to prevent and/or end abuses of human rights. The *humanitarian* part of the equation speaks to the primary motivation, and *intervention* means that action was undertaken without the consent of the target state. This is not to be confused with other uses of force that the United Nations has typically undertaken, such as peacekeeping operations, which generally occur with the consent of the relevant parties in order to preserve a peace that has already been achieved. It is also different than interventions that happen to produce collateral humanitarian benefits. U.S. intervention in Afghanistan in the wake of the 2001 terrorist attacks, for example, may have "liberated the Afghan people from the Taliban and impending starvation, but that was just frosting on the cake. They were never what this war was about."[7] The same could be said of the 2003 invasion of Iraq. Though there were obvious humanitarian benefits from the ousting of Saddam Hussein, the

United Nations Charter (1945) The founding document of the United Nations that appears to enshrine the principle of state sovereignty by prohibiting forceful external intervention unless the Security Council finds a threat to international peace sufficient to authorize intervention.

Universal Declaration of Human Rights (1948) A nonbinding United Nations declaration that recognizes a long list of basic human rights. Combined with the United Nations Charter, it revealed an emerging tension between the principles of state sovereignty and human rights.

humanitarian intervention Uninvited intervention by external actors into the domestic affairs of a state with the primary motive of ending or preventing violations of human rights.

invasion was motivated and justified in terms of security and the United States' national interests.

The debate over humanitarian intervention covers a lot of ground, but three questions are paramount. First, should states forfeit their right to sovereignty if they engage in massive human rights violations? Second, if intervention is justified, who has the right to intervene? Can states act on their own (**unilateral intervention**), or must intervention be sanctioned by some international organization, namely the United Nations (**multilateral intervention**)? Finally, if such interventions need to be endorsed by the UN, and the Security Council in particular, is the organization equipped to carry out this mission effectively?

THE UNITED NATIONS SHOULD INTERVENE TO PROTECT HUMAN RIGHTS

To its supporters, the case for recognizing a right of humanitarian intervention is clear when some of the abuses the world has witnessed in recent decades are taken into consideration. When Pol Pot's Khmer Rouge kill 2 million of their fellow Cambodians and 800,000 Rwandans are slaughtered in the span of few weeks, what possible logic can excuse or condone the inaction of those who had the power to prevent and/or end these tragedies yet sat on the sidelines? Is there really anyone who thinks it was a bad thing that Vietnam violated Cambodia's sovereignty in 1979 and finally put Pol Pot and his henchmen out of business? Even those who condemned Vietnam in public were probably applauding in private. By some estimates, as few as 5,000 troops deployed to Rwanda in 1994 could have saved a few hundred thousand lives.[8] In retrospect, what cold calculus could possibly justify nonintervention?

Because state sovereignty is usually cited as the primary obstacle to intervention, supporters of humanitarian intervention begin by challenging this foundational premise of international law. In reality, they argue, the practice of sovereignty has always been at variance with the lofty protections afforded by treaties and conventions. State sovereignty has never been as sacrosanct as some now pretend. Furthermore, the world community has long abandoned even the abstract principle of absolute and unconditional sovereignty.

The limits of sovereignty Like most controversial issues, humanitarian intervention requires that we make a choice between competing values: If there is a conflict between the rights of individuals and the sovereignty of states, which takes precedence? Is sovereignty a license for states to do whatever they want to their citizens, or do states that abuse their citizens surrender their right to sovereignty? Advocates of humanitarian intervention themselves realize the existence of a tradeoff in which the right to intervene necessitates a diminished right to sovereignty. UN Secretary-General Kofi Annan implicitly recognizes as much when he poses the question: "If humanitarian intervention is, indeed, an unacceptable assault on sovereignty . . . how should we respond to a Rwanda . . . to gross and systematic violations of human rights that offend every precept of our common humanity?"[9] Note Annan's formulation: he concedes that humanitarian intervention *is* an "assault on sovereignty"; the only question is whether it is an *acceptable* or *unacceptable* assault on sovereignty.

Advocates of humanitarian intervention see no reason why we should view sovereignty as an inviolable absolute. In the first place, the idea that states have consistently respected each other's sovereignty since the Peace of Westphalia is based on either a willful fabrication or inexcusable ignorance of history. Over the past four hundred years, states have routinely meddled in each other's domestic affairs for a host of reasons. Some of these interventions were even "humanitarian" in nature, such as those undertaken to protect Christian minorities from mistreatment in the Ottoman Empire during the 1800s.[10] Most interventions were motivated by less admirable concerns, such as undermining strategic rivals, exacerbating ethnic conflicts, or crushing revolutionary governments.[11] Given this huge gap between rhetoric and practice, the newfound reverence for the principle of national sovereignty when it comes to saving people from outrageous assaults on their basic human rights seems like little more than a convenient and hypocritical evasion of moral responsibility.

But even if the principle of sovereignty had been scrupulously adhered to, so what? The mere fact that we have done something for four hundred years is a fairly lame reason to continue to do so. Sovereignty is not a law of physics that we have no choice but to abide by; it is a social custom or practice like slavery and dueling that can (and should) be changed if it is inconsistent with contemporary mores and norms. As David Forsythe explains, "State sovereignty is not some immutable principle decreed in fixed form once and for all time . . . it is an idea devised by social beings. It can change along with changing circumstances."[12]

In fact, we long ago discarded the idea, both in principle and practice, that states possessed some automatic right to have their sovereignty respected. Sovereignty is no longer seen as a divine gift as it was in the age of Louis XIV. Monarchical absolutism has been replaced by **popular sovereignty,** or the principle that governments derive their legitimacy from their citizens. Citizens provide the only legitimate basis of authority and hence sovereignty. Because it is the people who grant legitimacy, any state that denies basic rights to its citizens can hardly claim to be legitimate in their eyes. And if a state becomes illegitimate in the eyes of its own citizens, there are no grounds for other states to recognize its legitimacy. In this case, why should other states feel obligated to respect sovereignty of an illegitimate state? Penelope Simons summarizes the essential point: "States receive their legitimacy from the will of the people. Hence, sovereignty is not an inherent right of states but, rather, derives from individual rights. Thus, when sovereignty comes into conflict with human rights, the later must prevail."[13]

popular sovereignty The principle that governments must derive their legitimacy from the people over whom they rule. Embodied in the French and American revolutions, this assertion challenged the principle of the divine right of kings.

The right (obligation?) to intervene It is one thing to argue that states engaged in violations of basic human rights lose their right to sovereignty, but is this sufficient for establishing that others have a right to intervene? That is, does the absence of a right to sovereignty necessarily entail a right of intervention? Not directly. The right of intervention derives not from the target state's loss of sovereignty but from the rights of those who are being abused. Lea Brilmayer is certainly correct when she notes that "the victims themselves have a right of resistance to crimes perpetrated against them . . . [and that] other groups in the same society have a good claim (if not in fact an obligation) to come to the aid of the victims." But if we accept the proposition that "victims within states, and locals who would assist them, have a right of resistance, then it is hard to imagine why they should not able to summon outside help."[14]

Nazi leaders on trial for war crimes at Nuremberg. The precedent of these trials marked a turning point in the evolution of international human rights law.

Because the state's sovereignty has been surrendered once it violated the rights of its citizens, it no longer provides any obstacle to outside intervention. And if the victims of abuse have a right to ask outsiders for help, it would be downright perverse if outsiders lacked the right to come to their assistance. Thus, the right of outsiders to intervene to protect human rights is a natural extension of a principle that virtually no one rejects—that people and groups within nations are entitled to resist when their rights are violated, even when the perpetrator is their own government. If a state's internal sovereignty is not absolute, its external sovereignty cannot be viewed as absolute, either.

The trickier question is whether outsiders have any positive *obligation* (as opposed to a mere right) to come to the aid of citizens of other countries whose rights are being violated. Even among those who support a right of humanitarian intervention, there is disagreement on the issue of obligation. To use Brilmayer's terminology, if intervention is only a right, it becomes tantamount to an act of *charity,* but if intervention is obligatory, it is a *duty.* There are a number of approaches to dealing with this question. One could argue that states only have obligations to their own citizens and that although they are entitled to assist citizens of other states, they are not obliged to do so. The issue is whether moral obligations are limited or conditioned by national boundaries. Are people and states part of a seamless global human community in which duties and obligations transcend national borders, or are nations distinct moral communities? Nicholas Wheeler is among those who sees a moral obligation to intervene: "Once it is accepted that there is nothing natural or given about sovereignty as the outer limits of our moral responsibilities, it becomes possible to argue for a change in moral horizons. . . . [in which case] governments are responsible not only for protecting the human rights at home but also for defending them abroad."[15]

Who should intervene? Once we accept the premise that outsiders have a right and/or obligation to intervene in defense of human rights, some critical issues remain to be resolved. Most important, who has the right to intervene? Does any external actor have the right to intervene whenever it thinks a state is violating its citizens' rights, or does intervention need to be conducted by the international community as a whole (or at least with its sanction)? Although this is also a matter of some debate even among those predisposed to favor humanitarian intervention, the weight of opinion leans toward opposing any right of unilateral intervention. And even those who concede that in some very rare instances (which we will discuss shortly) unilateral intervention may be acceptable, it is always seen as preferable that intervention be multilateral. In the current international system, "multilateral" is a synonym for the United Nations and the "sanction" would be some authorization from the Security Council (though there is also a debate about whether regional organizations such as NATO or the OAS can offer sufficient authorization).

If violations of rights are occurring, why should it matter whether one nation, five nations, one hundred nations, or Microsoft, for that matter, stop them? The moral imperative would seem to dictate that human rights be defended, with the issue of exactly who defends them being of little moral consequence. Why, then, the almost reflexive preference for multilateral action? The commitment to multilateralism is motivated by a desire to minimize a series of interrelated practical and political problems that arise from recognizing a right of humanitarian intervention. Those who agree that human rights are a legitimate international concern but nonetheless worry about recognizing a right of intervention harbor several fears. They worry that nations will only intervene in defense of human rights when abuses occur in areas of strategic interest (e.g., in Yugoslavia but not Rwanda), that humanitarian rationales will be little more than cynical fig leafs offered by great powers for interventions motivated by more narrow and selfish concerns, and that selective and opportunistic intervention will breed skepticism and erode international legitimacy.

If decisions about humanitarian intervention are left in the hands of individual states, there is likely to be tremendous variation (that is to say, inconsistency) in the standards and criteria guiding these interventions. Placing the decisions in the hands of a single, centralized international body increases the likelihood that a consistent standard can be developed and applied. The requirement for some authorization from an international body would also act as a check on those states that might be inclined to abuse a right of intervention by claiming humanitarian justifications for less noble interventions. This requirement is particularly critical in terms of reassuring the weaker, more vulnerable members of the international community that a right of intervention will not become license for meddling by great powers. This is why Bernard Kouchner, a co-founder of the Nobel Peace Prize–winning humanitarian organization Doctors Without Borders, insists that "humanitarian intervention will never be the action of a single country or national army playing policeman to the world. . . . humanitarian intervention will be carried out by an impartial, multinational force acting under the authority of international organizations and controlled by them."[16] Gareth Evans and Mohamed Sahnoun make it clear the requirement for multilateral sanction is based not on any moral requirement but rather the political necessity of building an international consensus on the legitimacy of intervention: "As a matter of *political reality* . . . it would be impossible to build a consensus around any set of proposals for military intervention that acknowledged the validity of any intervention not authorized by the Security Council or General Assembly [emphasis added]."[17]

Essentially what we are talking about here is trying to establish an international equivalent of the domestic **rule of law,** or the principle that rules need to be applied even-handedly to all. Consistency is important because in the realm of moral principles "selectivity is prima facie morally suspect."[18] Principles applied inconsistently are not really principles at all. And laws that are selectively enforced only against certain people are not only morally suspect, but can become politically suspect as well. As George Kennan notes, "a lack of consistency implies a lack of principle in the eyes of much of the world."[19] A unilateral right of intervention is a virtual invitation to inconsistency. Thus, in order to provide consistent implementation, minimize opportunities for abuse, and sustain international legitimacy, humanitarian interventions need to be conducted by, or at least with the sanction of, the world's most inclusive organization, the United Nations.

Even its defenders realize, however, that the United Nations is not a perfect organization. Sometimes the United Nations fails to act, as in the case of the Rwandan genocide. No amount of institutional reform can guarantee consistent UN action in defense of human rights. It would seem odd if the requirement for organizational sanction became so absolute that it trumped the defense of human rights. After all, if it is impermissible to sacrifice people because of a commitment to an abstract principle of sovereignty, it would appear equally impermissible to sacrifice them because of a commitment to multilateralism. Faced with the choice between human rights and a requirement for multilateral action or sanction, which should prevail? Given the moral case for humanitarian intervention, the answer seems clear: human rights win every time. But does this mean that we should explicitly recognize the legitimacy of unilateral intervention? Jim Whitman provides a typical example of hesitancy in taking the argument that far: "It is a reasonable expectation that the international legal system should be sufficiently flexible to accommodate specific instances of law-breaking which clearly serve the interests of justice, particularly those which address serious and large-scale humanitarian emergencies."[20] That is, unilateral interventions should remain against international law, but occasional violations of this law should be tolerated in the interests of justice. This is Nicholas Wheeler's position: "Whether there is a new legal custom supporting unilateral humanitarian intervention is beside the point, since, when acts of brutality offend the conscience of humanity, those with the power to end this have a moral responsibility to act."[21]

Following the same logic, Jules Lobel and Michael Ratner concede that "there may, of course, be certain extreme cases of genocide where one country's veto blocks the Security Council from authorizing the use of force." In such cases, they agree that "a nation or group of nations may need to intervene without U.N. authorization in order to save lives." But in their view, tacitly accepting the occasional unilateral intervention is a "less dangerous alternative than permitting an 'escape clause' on the prohibition of the unilateral use of force, an exception that would likely be widely and dangerously abused."[22] UN Secretary-General Kofi Annan himself confessed that he would have been hard pressed to object to a unilateral intervention that stopped the Rwandan genocide, even without any endorsement from the United Nations. This position appears to concede a right to unilateral humanitarian intervention but also an unwillingness to formally recognize or codify such a right. Unilateral intervention should generally remain prohibited, but in rare cases it should be met with a "wink and a nod."

Liberalism and humanitarian intervention It is probably not surprising that the calls for recognizing a right of humanitarian intervention resonate mostly with a liberal perspective on international politics. As with individual rights and popular sovereignty at the domestic level, "the international law of human rights is based on liberalism."[23] The move for a more humane and moral international politics is in many respects a continuation of the liberal revolutions that have remade domestic political orders over the past few centuries. The primacy of individual rights and the view that governments receive their legitimacy from their citizens both strike deep cords with liberal social and political philosophy. Without the liberal assumptions of individual rights and popular sovereignty, it is difficult to see how a case for humanitarian intervention could be constructed. At an even more fundamental level, arguments for humanitarian intervention rest on a profoundly liberal vision of a common humanity, a world in which the moral obligations and people and states are not limited by artificial and transitory lines on a map. Why should a person in Maine be willing to defend the rights of someone 2,500 miles away in California whom they may never meet, but not someone who may live just 10 miles from them across the border in Canada?

The growing salience of human rights and proposals for humanitarian intervention not only give hope to liberals, but also provide constructivists with some confirmation that international politics is shaped, and can be changed, by prevailing and evolving norms. As long as citizens and leaders believed that sovereignty was an absolute that should not be violated, the possibility of humanitarian intervention was precluded. The acceptance of norms of human rights and popular sovereignty provides a foundation for changing state practices. One sees elements of this conviction in Forsythe's observation that sovereignty is a social construction, an idea that sets limits to the actions states are willing to consider. Social constructions, however, can be replaced with other constructions. We may be in the middle of a process in which some fundamental ideas or norms about international politics are being transformed, and the increasing willingness to consider humanitarian intervention may be part of this evolution. As Daniel Thomas argues, "International human rights norms affect the behavior, the interests, and the identity of states by specifying which practices are (or are not) considered appropriate by international society."[24] Altered norms can change how nations define themselves, their identities, and their interests, from exclusive national communities to a universal human community.

The Case against Humanitarian Intervention

Negatives can usually be rephrased as positives; thus, the case *against* humanitarian intervention is also an argument in *favor* of the principle of sovereignty. In many respects, the case for sovereignty remains much the same as it was in 1648. At that time, the absence of a religious consensus in Europe necessitated acceptance of sovereignty and nonintervention if any sort of international order was to be preserved. Today, with respect to humanitarian intervention versus sovereignty, the problem is the absence of a universally accepted standard of human rights and the inability to specify with any precision what rights are to be considered basic and how great the violation needs to be in order to justify intervention. But even if it were possible to reach nearly universal agreement on some minimal definition of basic rights, there are reasons to doubt whether the United Nations or any other organization can possibly implement a consistent and impartial doctrine of humanitarian intervention. The critique of humanitarian intervention is both moral and political.

The problem of moral diversity Considering the dilemmas of humanitarian intervention, Bhikhu Parekh begins with the uncontroversial observation that "a humanitarian act is intended to address what is regarded as a violation of the minimum that is due human beings." Even though he supports a limited right of intervention, Parekh continues and makes the somewhat more controversial point that "since views about the latter are culturally conditioned, *no definition of humanitarian intervention can be culturally neutral.*"[25] As a result, any doctrine of humanitarian intervention will necessarily be based on a certain vision of human rights and morality that might not be shared by those upon whom it is imposed. This harsh reality is often avoided because it smacks of an extreme moral relativism in which there is no such thing as right and wrong. Actually, it is just a recognition of the fact that people and cultures do not always agree on what is right and wrong. Though there may be a natural tendency to assume that others do (or at least should) adhere to our moral standards, in fact "there is no universal morality . . . rules about morality vary from place to place."[26] As long as this is the case, the norm of sovereignty serves the same purpose today that it did for the authors of the Peace of Westphalia: it provides a basis for order in a diverse world.

One test of the legitimacy and practicality of humanitarian intervention is whether its advocates are willing to accept restrictions on their nation's sovereignty. This is a touchy point because nations have always been more protective of their own sovereignty than that of others. But if a consensus actually exists on the moral principles guiding intervention, there should be little concern about intervention in your own nation's affairs. Frank Ching touches on this issue when he asks, "If the same doctrine [of humanitarian intervention] had been enunciated in an earlier era, would today's proponents have been in favor? Would the U.S. agree that other countries had the right to punish it for practicing slavery? Would Britain, France, Italy, Belgium, and other European countries agree that others had the right to bomb them to protect the human rights of their colonial subjects?"[27]

Ching's rhetorical questions highlight several problems that inevitably arise with the practice of humanitarian intervention. One is the issue of double standards—the strongest advocates of intervention are often unwilling to concede that others have a right to intervene in their affairs. Second, in raising the issue of how moral norms change over time, Ching touches on the problem of cultural relativism. If notions of morality vary from one era to another, they can also be expected to vary from one culture to another. Like the norm of sovereignty, conceptions of human rights are also social creations.

The magnitude of this problem becomes evident once we move beyond the "easy" but relatively rare example of outright genocide. Apart from this exception, it becomes very difficult to delineate a list of basic human rights. Bernard Kouchner adopts an extreme form of moral universalism: "everywhere, human rights are human rights . . . if a Muslim woman in Sudan opposes painful clitoral excision, or if a Chinese woman opposes the binding of her feet, her rights are being violated." In the face of such abuses, he proposes that we "establish a forward-looking right of the world community to actively interfere in the affairs of sovereign states to prevent the explosion of human rights violations."[28] This sort of universalism denies the culturally specific nature of rights and gives critics of humanitarian intervention the chills. The application of a single moral code in which "human rights are human rights everywhere," leading to a norm of "active interference" in the domestic affairs of states could provide a license for endless intervention and meddling.

Frank Ching's questions also reflect a sentiment shared by many non-Western governments that "there is something not quite right when the same countries that perpetrated unspeakable offences against human rights should now set themselves up as the arbiters of human rights, in some cases condemning countries that they had previously oppressed."[29] Many in the Third World especially detect an element of ethnocentrism and fear that humanitarian intervention will be nothing more than imperialism with a happy face. Notice the examples Kouchner cites—clitoral excision in Somalia and foot binding in China. Virtually all the cases where humanitarian intervention has been suggested lie outside the confines of Western Europe and North America (the former Yugoslavia being the only possible exception) and are directed against weaker powers. Are there never any violations of human rights in Paris, Connecticut, Russia, or China that the world needs to worry about? Many nations and societies have long been on the receiving end of outside intervention, which was often accompanied by noble rhetoric of spreading the virtues of civilization and Christianity. These nations had to fight long and hard to achieve their independence. Having finally achieved the sovereignty they were denied for so long, they are now told that the time has come to give it up. It is easy to understand why they are hesitant to surrender their hard-won sovereignty to nations whose motives they have good reason to doubt.

To be fair, supporters of humanitarian intervention have a fairly good response to these concerns about moral diversity and moral imperialism. Lea Brilmayer admits that "the cultural relativity argument is hard to rebut directly. . . . there is no denying that some moral norms vary from one culture to another. Certain societies ban marriage to second cousins, the consumption of alcohol, or the use of mind-altering drugs; others encourage them." Nonetheless, she thinks that "the philosophical power of the argument is vastly overrated." A doctrine of humanitarian intervention does not require that all societies have precisely the same conception of morality on each and every issue. Merely because cultures differ in their evaluations of *some* behaviors does not mean that they differ in their evaluation of *all* behaviors. It is on those points of moral agreement that a doctrine of humanitarian intervention can be erected. The fact that two cultures might disagree about foot binding is irrelevant if they agree that genocide is indeed a crime.

Brilmayer uses the conflict in the former Yugoslavia to illustrate her point: "If the United States [or anyone else] were to intervene, its actions could hardly be criticized on cultural relativism grounds. For it would be hard to argue that the murder of civilians, gang rape, and deliberate starvation are considered innocent activities in the Balkans." There are some abuses of human rights that are universally recognized as such. Those who have been charged with crimes against humanity in the former Yugoslavia have not defended themselves by claiming that their culture accepts the actions they are charged with. Their defense is that they did not commit the acts attributed to them: the disagreement is about the facts, not the morality or immorality of the alleged acts. Under close scrutiny, the cultural relativism objection is revealed to be a disingenuous debating trick in which moral consensus is ignored by references to trivial and meaningless moral differences. Thus Brilmayer is able to dispose of the problem quite easily: "For relativism to be an objection, it is not enough that morality may *in theory* differ from culture to culture; morality must *in fact* differ. . . . Most human rights abuses involve the perpetration of harms that are undeniably wrong in the eyes of all parties to the dispute."[30]

Once this point is appreciated, fears that humanitarian intervention will inevitably be a form of moral imperialism also fall apart. If outside forces intervened to stop mass gang rapes in the former Yugoslavia, the interveners could hardly be charged with imposing their morality on a culture that accepts systematic rape. And if the United Nations had intervened in Rwanda, it would be almost insulting to charge that it was imposing its moral code against genocide on a culture that accepted genocide.

From abstraction to action The dilemmas, however, become somewhat more severe when we move from the agreement on abstract moral principles to implementing a policy of humanitarian intervention. We may agree that it is violation of basic rights for a government to kill its political opponents, but does this mean that ten assassinations should trigger intervention? Exactly how great must the violation of rights be before intervention becomes permissible? Some draw the line at genocide, which is precisely defined in several international treaties and conventions. But few are willing to restrict the right of intervention to cases that meet the strict definition of genocide. Most usually include the more flexible category of "gross," "egregious," and "massive" violations of human rights or, to use Michael Walzer's famous formulation, acts that "shock the conscience of humanity." But what specific actions rise to these levels? The devil, as usual, is in the details. Stephen Solarz and Michael O'Hanlon provide a commendable attempt to confront this thorny issue, arguing that humanitarian intervention should be considered "only to stop extreme violence when the death rate reaches or threatens to reach at least tens of thousands a year." They cite the usual examples of Rwanda in 1994 and Pol Pot's Cambodia in the 1970s but eliminate virtually every other possible case because they "were simply not bloody enough to justify outside military intervention."[31] Critics pounce on such apparently crass head counting because it appears to relinquish the high ground by turning a moral cause into an accounting exercise. What moral calculus requires us to protect someone being killed with 100,000 of his fellow citizens but not someone being killed with only 5,000 others? There are answers to this uncomfortable question, but they are messy ones that dull the moral luster of humanitarian intervention. But there is no avoiding the problems of moving beyond the tidy moral plane in which words such as "gross" and "massive" need not be defined with any precision. Say "massive rights violations" and people nod their heads in agreement. For some, however, 5,000 deaths might be "massive"; for others, it may not be "massive" until the figure reaches 100,000. Thus, even with agreement in principle, there is still a lot of leeway for inconsistency and selectivity in practice.

The problem of power The more fundamental dilemma is a familiar one in the history of international relations, which provides many examples of noble moral projects (such as treaties outlawing war in the 1920s) that proved to be miserable failures. The general problem is "the antagonistic relationship between an ideal system of norms and the reality of power politics."[32] The dilemmas pile up as we move beyond the purely normative analysis and "take into consideration the unequal constellation of power under which humanitarian intervention [will be] practiced."[33] The fact is that nations with the power to conduct and resist interventions will surrender much less of their sovereignty than nations lacking equivalent power. As a result, "any right of state intervention, however clearly delineated, would in fact and perception empower the already powerful."[34] *In theory,* accepting the principle of humanitarian intervention erodes every nation's sovereignty. *In practice,* however, there is no danger that foreign troops will land in the United States to stop the death penalty or in China to save the Tibetans.

On one level, advocates of humanitarian intervention are aware of the difficulties resulting from the "reality of power politics." Taking decisions about intervention away from individual states and placing them under the authority of the United Nations is designed to lessen this precise problem. Recall Bernard Kouchner's assurance that humanitarian intervention would be "impartial." What will ensure this impartiality? The fact that intervention would not be unilateral and that it would only occur under the auspices of the United Nations. The unstated assumption is that individual states are "partial" and the United Nations is "impartial," which means untainted by national interests and differences in power. Skeptics find this an untenable leap of faith. They view the United Nations as merely another arena for, rather than an escape from, power politics. Because it is merely an organization of independent states, it cannot help but be influenced by the relative power of its members. Hans Kochler gets to the heart of the matter: "We have to admit that the step from *idealistic vision* to the *realization* of an international policy of intervention cannot be responsibly made . . . an implementation of the doctrine outside the realm of power politics . . . is impossible. Any act of humanitarian intervention, *whether exercised on a unilateral, regional or multilateral level,* will be determined by the interests of the power(s) initiating it."[35] It is with good reason that the president of Algeria asks, "Is interference valid for only weak states or for all states without distinction?"[36] Can anyone but the hopelessly naïve believe that all states will be equally liable to intervention, regardless of their power?

We need not even look very deeply to see the impact of power politics because it is built into the Security Council's structure. The five permanent members are always represented and can scuttle any intervention with a simple "no" vote. As Stanley Michalak explains, "The United Nations was explicitly designed so that it would be unable to act against any of the permanent members or even against their pleasure."[37]

This is one reason that NATO intervention in the former Yugoslavia was conducted without the authorization of the Security Council. Everyone knew that Russia or China would have vetoed any intervention because "each has ethnic minorities whose treatment might be used by other countries as an excuse for military intervention."[38] Power can be abused for political reasons not only by conducting interventions but also by preventing them. Stanley Hoffman states the problem bluntly: "Too many states among UN members have bloody domestic records, and they can be expected to block any proposal for collective intervention."[39] Many see this as an argument for reforming the United Nations and the Security Council. The obstacle, of course, is that the United States, Russia, and China are not likely to look kindly on reforms that erode their power. The difficulty of altering rules and procedures that give some nations greater influence is itself a reflection of the United Nations' lack of immunity from the very power politics that advocates of humanitarian intervention hope it will transcend.

In the final analysis, the United Nations is an organization of independent states. It is not a world government, it does not have its own armed forces, and it relies on voluntary contributions from members to fund and implement its operations. Nations can refuse to provide troops for humanitarian intervention and they can withhold their financial support. The United Nations can only act consistently and impartially if its members, particularly those with the wealth and resources to conduct interventions, are willing to act consistently and impartially.

The limits of moral action Debates about humanitarian intervention focus on two basic issues. First, do states have the right or obligation to intervene in the affairs of other states in order to defend human rights? Second, can we devise mechanisms for implementing a policy of humanitarian intervention that lives up to its moral impulses? Though realists will disagree on some specific issues, they have generally been skeptical of humanitarian intervention on both these counts.

George Kennan provides a typical realist response to the suggestion that states should risk their citizens' interests and even lives to defend the rights of others. He draws a distinction between how we should think about individual versus state morality. If individuals chose to barge into homes to defend people being attacked, that is their right because the only life they are putting at risk is their own. But if the president of the United States decides to send troops into Rwanda because he wants to protect lives, this is more problematic because he is risking the lives of others, people whose interests he is supposed to protect. As a result, Kennan argues that the "commitments and moral obligations of governments are not the same as those of the individual. Government is an agent, not a principal. Its primary obligation is to the interests of the national society it represents." He draws an analogy between governments and lawyers: "No more than the attorney vis-à-vis the client, nor the doctor vis-à-vis the patient, can government attempt to insert itself into the consciences of those whose interests it represents."[40] Samuel Huntington reflected this view when he argued that "it is morally unjustifiable and politically indefensible that members of the [U.S.] armed forces should be killed to prevent Somalis from killing each other."[41]

Rather than relying on the proposition that states *should not* act for moral reasons, most realists (and many Marxists and feminists interestingly) prefer to emphasize that they *will not*. Though it may be regrettable, states are simply not willing to incur substantial economic and human costs in order to defend the rights of others when their own national interest is not involved. John Mearsheimer notes that "despite claims that American foreign policy is infused with moralism, Somalia (1992–93) is the only instance during the past one hundred years in which U.S. soldiers were killed in action on a humanitarian mission." And in this case the public's reaction to a small number of American casualties was so great "that they immediately pulled all U.S. troops out of Somalia and then refused to intervene in Rwanda in the spring of 1994, when ethnic Hutu went an a genocidal rampage against their Tutsi neighbors."[42] Making a similar point about the former Yugoslavia, Henry Kissinger observes a "vast gap between the rhetoric and the means with which to back it up. Allies' pronouncements have ritually compared Milosevic to Hitler. But the transparent reluctance to accept casualties signaled that the Alliance would not make the commitment necessary to overthrow the accused tyrants."[43] Realists see in calls for humanitarian intervention something we have witnessed before: moral pronouncements that are easily and readily abandoned the moment they clash with perceptions of national interests or threaten to actually cost anything.

Though liberals are generally predisposed to support a right of humanitarian intervention and realists are inclined to be skeptical or opposed, other perspectives display less unity. Feminists certainly welcome an international discourse that elevates human rights to a central place, but they frequently express some dismay with exactly how these rights are conceptualized. In particular, some feminists argue that prevailing notions of rights often ignore the deprivations that women are routinely subjected to around the world. Why, they ask, did the plight of women under Afghanistan's Taliban regime only become a matter of tremendous concern after September 11, 2001? And now that the women in Afghanistan may have been liberated to some degree, what about the women of Saudi Arabia, whose status is only slightly better than under the Taliban? Indeed, feminists were deeply divided on the question of whether the use of force in Afghanistan was justifiable.[44] Many feminists are also uncomfortable with using military intervention or force to protect human rights, since militarism is seen as an integral part of domestic and international systems of oppression. This is not to say that feminists would never see military force as justified (except for those who combine their feminism with pacifism), but there is a strong presumption against it in most feminist analysis.

A definitive Marxist position is also difficult to identify. In general, however, Marxists find it hard to imagine that a doctrine of humanitarian intervention can be applied consistently and impartially in the current international system. Such a policy is almost certainly going to be used by the dominant powers to pursue their interests vis-à-vis the poor, weak, and vulnerable of the world. According to John Pilger, "humanitarian intervention is the latest brand name for imperialism as it begins its return to respectability."[45] Marxists, like realists, have a deep appreciation for the role of power in politics. Instances of intervention motivated by genuine humanitarian motives are likely to remain the extremely rare exception, making Marxists hesitant to embrace or endorse any right of intervention. Most Marxists would also share the view that military force is almost never a tool for advancing or protecting human rights. This reluctance to support humanitarian military intervention in principle does not mean that no intervention can ever be justified. Marxists and others on the left were, for example, divided on the issue of NATO intervention in Yugoslavia.

CONCLUSION

Though we cannot turn back the clock and bring to life the victims of genocide in Rwanda and the Khmer Rouge in Cambodia, we are almost certainly going to be faced with similar human catastrophes in the future. Evans and Shanoun offer a prediction and ask a question: "It is only a matter of time before reports emerge again from somewhere of massacres, mass starvation, rape and ethnic cleansing. And the question will arise again in the Security Council: What do we do? This time the international community must have answers." Reflecting the sober soul-searching that followed the Rwandan genocide, they claim that "few things have done more harm to its shared ideal that people are all equal in worth and dignity than the inability of the community of states to prevent these horrors. In the new century, there must be no more Rwandas."[46]

The next Rwanda will once again test the limits of human compassion. But it is not only in our time that people have wondered whether there are limits. More than two centuries ago, in *The Theory of Moral Sentiments*, Adam Smith pondered the same question that still haunts us today. He wondered how a perfectly decent and moral European would react to two hypothetical events: first, tragedy in China that resulted in the deaths of millions; and second, an accident that cut off his own finger. With regard to the death of millions on the other side of the world, Smith speculated that the average person would feel sorry and utter all the appropriate sympathies about the tragic loss of life. Nonetheless, he would soon go on with his life "as if no such accident happened." Upon losing a finger, however, this same person would obsess endlessly about his comparatively "paltry misfortune." This juxtaposition led Smith to ask a pointed question: "To prevent, therefore, this paltry misfortune to himself, would a man of humanity be willing to sacrifice the lives of millions of his brethren, provided he had never to see them?" Merely to ask the question suggests a harsh judgment. Perhaps it is a sign of how little has changed that this same question comes to mind as we witness contemporary human tragedies that the world does nothing to stop. But maybe the growing acceptance of humanitarian intervention suggests how far we have come. Either way, the fundamental question today remains what it was for Adam Smith: Are there limits to human compassion? The answer is still in doubt.

POINTS OF VIEW

Should the United Nations Prepare for Humanitarian Interventions?

The 1994 genocide in Rwanda was one of the great human tragedies of the post–World War II era. If this was not a case that merited humanitarian intervention, it is difficult to imagine one that would. However, the world for the most part did nothing. These two essays present opposing points of view on the issue of intervention. Charles Krauthammer discusses the world's failure to respond and proposes something that has been suggested on several occasions—the creation of a standing military force under the control of the Security Council to intervene in such cases. David C. Unger, on the other hand, opposes United Nations intervention, even in cases such as Rwanda. What are the main points of disagreement between the writers? To what extent do their positions reflect or move beyond the rationales for and against intervention discussed in this chapter? To what extent would a force of the kind Krauthammer proposes solve some of the intervention-related problems we have discussed? What problems would remain even after the creation of a United Nations force? Are you more inclined to agree with Krauthammer or Unger?

Stop the Genocide in Rwanda

Charles Krauthammer

For all of the hyperbolic use of such terms as genocide and holocaust to describe Bosnia, the worst violence on earth today is occurring in Rwanda. Unlike Bosnia, where the combatants are fighting over four or six or nine percent more territory, in Rwanda the issue is not territory but existence. This is a tribal war of extermination, of mass murder at a Hitlerian rate. Between 200,000 and 400,000 have been massacred in seven weeks—as many as have died in all two years of the Bosnian civil war.

Yet Bosnia has a vocal, articulate constituency. Rwanda has none. Bosnians are white, European, familiar, Rwandans are black, African, foreign. For Western intellectuals, Sarajevo evokes Spanish Civil War romance, Kigali evokes nothing more than Heart of Darkness nihilism.

It is a curious humanitarianism, however, that advocates humanitarian intervention on grounds of familiarity, race and romance. What counts is the scale of the violence and the suffering. Rwanda is the one unequivocal case of genocide occurring in the world today and genocide demands intervention.

But by whom? The best answer, but unfortunately of use only to future Rwandas, would be a small U.N. army, as first proposed by U.N. Secretary-General Trygve Lie in 1948. The current chief advocate for the idea is former U.N. undersecretary Brian Urquhart. Urquhart is a humanitarian realist. He knows that where individual Great Powers have no interests, they will in the end not intervene. It is the godforsaken places that need a U.N. army made up not of units cobbled together from existing national armies but of individuals enlisting under the U.N. flag in a U.N. uniform.

Such an intercession force could be rapidly deployed to danger zones on order of the Security Council. No need with each crisis to canvass for a new set of volunteers. No need to patch together Malaysian and Moroccan, Pakistani and Italian units into some rickety uncoordinated force. A small mobile U.N. legion would be ready to go anywhere, and quickly.

But what to do for Rwanda today? The best answer is a regional force drawn from African countries. Three African states—Ghana, Senegal and Ethiopia—have already volunteered troops for Rwanda peacekeeping. One wishes, however, that one particular African state—the leading African state—were on that list too.

South Africa is sub-Saharan Africa's regional superpower, an advanced industrialized country with a powerful army and the proven ability to fight far from home. It is doubly blessed by having such an army now commanded by the man who carries more moral authority than any national leader on the planet, Nelson Mandela. As the leading black African state, South Africa should be granted the authority—and most urgently encouraged—to lead an African response to an African tragedy.

Only South Africa has the power and prestige to head a regional intervention into Rwanda. It would be objected, of course, that the new South Africa, barely weeks old, has other problems. This would be yet another added to a full plate.

True. But all countries have problems and Rwanda's neighbors all have full plates. Which is why they turn away and Rwandan genocide goes on unchecked without the most minimal outside effort to do anything beyond evacuating whites. (That was done immediately.)

Moreover, intervention need not mean active participation in Rwanda's civil war. Entering Kigali with the intention of stopping the war and separating the combatants is too ambitious and difficult an objective. The most urgent need, as the relief agencies on the scene have insisted, is far less dangerous and costly: the establishment of havens for the feeding and protection of those threatened with massacre.

The outside world could help South Africa by lightening the economic burdens of leadership. South Africa is already reducing military expenditures. Why does not the world community, through, say, a financial pool established by the G-7 countries, create a fund for these units of the South African army dedicated to African peace-keeping?

One could even imagine South Africa being given eventual trusteeship of a place like Rwanda. At the time of Somalia's crackup, trusteeship was raised as a way of establishing effective and internationally recognized authority over failed states like Somalia.

But tinged as it is with the memory of imperialism, trusteeship by the Great Powers would not have a chance of gaining worldwide support. Trusteeship by a country like South Africa would. And there is precedent. After World War I, the white government of South Africa was given trusteeship over the former German colony of Southwest Africa (today Namibia). Why not grant the majority black government of South Africa trusteeship over some of the wreckages of the post-colonial era?

But what if South Africa declines to lead in Rwanda? Then America should step in as the last resort. Somalia again? Yes, but this time we do it right: in and out in 90 days. No nation-building fantasies, just rescue and protection. Create the havens, then turn them over to the multinational African force. Genocide demands no less.

UN Troops Cannot Stop Genocide

David C. Unger

What can the world do when hundreds of thousands of innocent civilians are slaughtered because of their race, religion, class or tribe? It happened this year in Rwanda and is still happening in Bosnia. Recently, it has happened in Cambodia, Indonesia and the Kurdish areas of Iraq.

Typically, the world does very little. This passivity outrages compassionate people everywhere. Increasingly, those demanding armed action against genocide have made the United Nations their chosen instrument. The urge to defend innocent victims reflects humanity at its best. But the task is rarely as simple as it looks. And U.N. military intervention is, in most cases, the wrong tool.

Genocide usually comes as an accompaniment to civil war, invasion or other forms of political and military conflict. And an outside intervention that looks humanitarian to the rest of the world often looks partisan to one or more of the contending armies. In Bosnia, the crimes against Muslim civilians are part of a battle for territory. In Somalia, food supplies were hijacked as part of a struggle to succeed a fallen dictator. In Rwanda, Hutu militias slaughtered Tutsis while a Hutu-led army tried to fend off the Tutsi-led rebels who now run the country.

Even if a U.N. force limits itself to imposing a cease-fire, it becomes the strategic ally of the side currently losing and the enemy of the side that feels victory in its grasp. When one or more contenders resent and resist a U.N. presence, U.N. forces are left with only two bad choices: become directly involved in the conflict or abruptly withdraw. Somalia has illustrated the high costs of both choices. In Rwanda, though the new Government remembers French troops as protectors of a murderous regime, direct conflict has been avoided.

The U.N. was not designed as a world government and should not be mistaken for one. It has no army of its own and relies on voluntary troop contributions from member states. That proved no problem when the big powers wanted to make a stand against aggression in the Persian Gulf war. But who offers troops can be an issue when the U.N. enters internal disputes.

The U.N. was designed to resolve conflicts between nations and needs to proceed cautiously when extending its mandate into any country's internal affairs. Historically, it has done best by intervening only after contending parties reach a mutually acknowledged stalemate. It can then play the role of neutral peacekeeper, monitoring agreements the parties have already reached. Cambodia, the most successful recent mission, followed this pattern, as did those that won U.N. peacekeepers the 1988 Nobel Peace Prize.

But the results have been mixed at best in recent missions driven by televised images of suffering and well-meaning demands to do something about it. When intervention preceded effective diplomacy in Bosnia, peacekeepers felt obliged to exercise a blind neutrality that equated those who torched villages and raped women with those who defended the victims. In Somalia, the U.N. added to the violence by wrongly waging war against Gen. Mohammed Farah Aidid, only to see its mission then gutted by unilateral withdrawals. The truth is that the outside world often cannot do much militarily about genocide until the local combatants are ready for peace.

The global community is not totally helpless. Sanctions, diplomacy and denunciations put useful pressure on the bloodthirsty. In extreme cases, nearby nations and other interested parties may usefully mount a military rescue, understanding in advance the risk of becoming combatants. In those instances, if diplomacy has failed and the motives of those involved seem strictly humanitarian, the U.N. should bless the intervention. But it should also build safeguards into its mandate to assure that would-be peacemakers do not worsen the existing violence.

That cautious prescription will not, and should not, satisfy the compassionate, or still their demands for action. Nearly 50 years after the defeat of Nazi genocide, the world, to all our shame, has not yet found a morally and militarily adequate response to this recurring crime against humanity.

CHAPTER SUMMARY

- The current debate over the wisdom of humanitarian intervention touches three of the most enduring issues in international politics: (1) the importance of state sovereignty, (2) the utility of international organizations, and (3) the relative importance of morality versus power and national interest in foreign policy.

- Though state sovereignty has been a central element of international order since the Peace of Westphalia (1648), the horrors of World War II led many to argue that massive human rights violations could not be ignored or excused by assertions of sovereignty.

- Since the end of World War II, a series of international agreements has established the principle that there are limits to sovereignty, though the line between acceptable and unacceptable violations of sovereignty have remained unclear.

- Building on liberal principles of popular sovereignty and human rights, supporters of humanitarian intervention argue that states that violate or fail to protect their citizens' basic rights forfeit their right to sovereignty. In these cases, outside actors have a legitimate right to intervene in defense of basic human rights. The right of outsiders to intervene is a logical extension of the right of domestic actors to defend their own rights.

- Those who favor humanitarian interventions generally prefer that they be undertaken within the framework of the United Nations. This is preferable for two reasons. First, it reduces the chances that individual nations will use or abuse a right humanitarian intervention as a cover for more selfish objectives. Second, it will assure the weak nations of the world that the strong will not be allowed to intervene at will.

- Drawing on realist assumptions about the inevitability of power politics, critics argue that any doctrine of humanitarian intervention will necessarily reflect the power and values of the strong. Implementing a policy of humanitarian intervention untainted by power and national interest is impossible.

- The requirement for United Nations action is often based on the naïve assumption that the organization is an alternative to power politics when it is actually just another venue for power politics.

- Opponents of humanitarian intervention reject the idea that the governments of some states are required to intervene to protect the rights of citizens of other states. The primary obligation of a government is to protect the interests of its citizens, not the citizens of other states. States are not justified in risking the lives of their citizens to defend the rights of citizens of other states.

- The legal, political, and moral issues raised by the debate over humanitarian intervention have been with us for centuries. The end of the Cold War and recent tragedies such as the ethnic genocide in Rwanda have merely increased their salience.

CRITICAL QUESTIONS

1. Should U.S. soldiers be placed in danger to prevent massive abuses of human rights, even when there is no clear "national interest" at stake?

2. Is a consistent policy of nonintervention preferable to one of selective intervention?

3. Is humanitarian intervention inevitably a form of cultural and moral imperialism?

4. Would other nations ever be justified intervening in U.S. domestic affairs to prevent what they perceive as violations of human rights?

5. Should nations be allowed to decide on their own whether to conduct a humanitarian intervention, or must there be some international sanction?

KEY TERMS

humanitarian intervention 249
multilateral intervention 250
Nuremburg war crimes trials 248
popular sovereignty 251
rule of law 254
unilateral intervention 250
United Nations Charter (1945) 249
Universal Declaration of Human Rights (1948) 249

FURTHER READING

A good place to begin considering the role of morality in international politics is Stanley Hoffman's *Duties beyond Borders: On the Limits and Possibilities of Ethical International Politics* (Syracuse, NY: Syracuse University Press, 1981), and Lea Brilmayer's *Justifying International Acts* (Ithaca, NY: Cornell University Press, 1989). Brilmayer's *American Hegemony: Political Morality in a One-Superpower World* (New Haven, CT: Yale University Press, 1994) is particularly useful for thinking about humanitarian intervention in the post–Cold War World. An excellent introduction to the topic of human rights in international politics is David P. Forsythe's *Human Rights in International Relations* (Cambridge: Cambridge University Press, 2000). A more detailed historical treatment is Paul Lauren Gordon, *The Evolution of International Human Rights* (Philadelphia: University or Pennsylvania Press, 1998). On the more specific question of humanitarian intervention, Nicholas Wheeler provides the best discussion in *Saving Strangers: Humanitarian Intervention in International Society* (Oxford: Oxford University Press, 2001). Finally, an excellent, if somewhat depressing, account of the failure to intervene is Michael Barnett's *Eyewitness to a Genocide: The United Nations and Rwanda* (Ithaca, NY: Cornell University Press, 2002).

HUMANITARIAN INTERVENTION ON THE WEB

www.hrw.org
   Website of Human Rights Watch, which monitors and publicizes human rights abuses worldwide.

www.amnesty.org
   Website of Amnesty International, perhaps the most famous and influential international human rights organization.

www.dfait-maeci.gc.ca/iciss-ciise/menu-en.asp
   Website of the International Commission on Intervention and State Sovereignty, maintained by the Canadian Department of Foreign Affairs.

www.policylibrary.com/humanitarianintervention
   Resources site for literature and information in humanitarian intervention.

www.pbs.org/wgbh/pages/frontline/shows/evil
   Based on *Frontline*'s documentary about the Rwandan genocide, this site discusses its historical background as well as the international response.

www.ictr.org
   Details the proceedings of the International Criminal Tribunal for Rwanda, which is trying to bring those responsible for the genocide to justice.

NOTES

[1] Michael Barnett, *Eyewitness to a Genocide: The United Nations and Rwanda* (Ithaca, NY: Cornell University Press, 2002), pp. 22–23.

[2] Ibid., p. 109.

[3] Paul Lauren Gordon, *The Evolution of International Human Rights* (Philadelphia: University of Pennsylvania Press, 1998), p. 210.

[4] Ibid., p. 209.

[5] A text of the United Nations Charter can be found at www.un.org

[6] Cited in Lea Brilmayer, *Justifying International Acts* (Ithaca, NY: Cornell University Press, 1989), p. 105.

[7] Clifford Owen, "Humanitarian Wars Are a Past Luxury," *National Post*, February 15, 2002, p. A22.

[8] Scott R. Feil, *Preventing Genocide: How the Early Use of Force Might Have Succeeded in Rwanda* (Washington, DC: Carnegie Commission on Preventing Deadly Conflict, 1998).

[9] Cited in Olivia Ward, "In Defense of Human Rights— Debate Rages over When, If Ever, International Intervention in a Sovereign Nation Is Justified," *Toronto Star*, February 18, 2001, p. 1.

[10] See Martha Finnemore, "Constructing Norms of Humanitarian Intervention," in *The Culture of National Security: Norms and Identity in World Politics*, ed. Peter Katzenstein (New York: Columbia University Press, 1996), pp. 161–165. Also see Steven Krasner, *Sovereignty: Organized Hypocrisy* (Princeton: Princeton University Press, 1999), pp. 73–126.

[11] See Cynthia Weber, *Simulating Sovereignty* (Cambridge: Cambridge University Press, 1995), pp. 61–91.

[12] David P. Forsythe, *Human Rights in International Relations* (Cambridge: Cambridge University Press, 2000), p. 20.

[13] Penelope Simons, *Humanitarian Intervention: A Review of the Literature*, Ploughshares Working Paper 0-12, p. 6.

[14] Lea Brilmayer, *American Hegemony: Political Morality in a One-Superpower World* (New Haven: Yale University Press, 1994), p. 152.

[15] Nicholas Wheeler, *Saving Strangers: Humanitarian Intervention in International Society* (Oxford: Oxford University Press, 2000), p. 294.

[16] Bernard Kouchner, "Humanitarian Intervention—A New Global Moral Code Must Emerge," *Toronto Star*, October 20, 1999, p. 1.

[17] Gareth Evans and Mohamed Sahnoun, "The Responsibility to Protect," *Foreign Affairs* 81 (November/December 2002): 107.

[18] Brilmayer, *American Hegemony*, pp. 161–62.

[19] George Kennan, "Morality and Foreign Policy," *Foreign Affairs* 64 (Winter 1985/86): 45.

[20] Jim Whitman, "A Cautionary on Humanitarian Intervention," *GeoJournal* 34 (October 1994): 170.

[21] Nicholas Wheeler, *Saving Strangers: Humanitarian Intervention in International Society* (Oxford: Oxford University Press, 2001), p. 294.

[22] Jules Lobel and Michael Ratner, "Humanitarian Military Intervention."

[23] Forsythe, *Human Rights in International Relations,* p. 217.

[24] Daniel C. Thomas, *The Helsinki Effect: International Norms, Human Rights and the Demise of Communism* (Princeton: Princeton University Press, 2001), p. 281.

[25] Bhikhu Parekhh, "Rethinking Humanitarian Intervention," *International Political Science Review* 18 (1997): 54–55.

[26] R. J. Vincent, *Human Rights and International Relations* (Cambridge: Cambridge University Press, 1986), p. 37.

[27] Frank Ching, "UN: Sovereignty or Rights?" *Far Eastern Economic Review* (October 21, 1999): 40.

[28] Kouchner, "Humanitarian Intervention," p. 1.

[29] Ching, "UN: Sovereignty or Rights?", p. 40.

[30] All quotes in these two paragraphs are from Brilmayer, *American Hegemony,* pp. 148–49.

[31] Stephen Solarz and Michael E. O'Hanlon, "Humanitarian Intervention: When is Force Justified?" *The Washington Quarterly* 20 (Fall 1997): 8.

[32] Hans Kochler, *Humanitarian Intervention in the Context of Modern Power Politics* (Vienna: International Progress Organization, 2001), p. 17.

[33] Ibid., p. 7.

[34] Whitman, "Cautionary on Humanitarian Intervention," p. 171.

[35] Kochler, *Humanitarian Intervention,* p. 17.

[36] In Ching, "UN: Sovereignty or Rights?" p. 40.

[37] Stanley Michalak, *A Primer in Power Politics* (Wilmington, DE: Scholarly Resources, 2001), p. 29.

[38] Ching, "UN: Sovereignty or Rights?" p. 40.

[39] Stanley Hoffman, "America Goes Backward," *New York Review of Books* 50 (June 12, 2003). Accessed at: http://www.nybooks.com/articles/16350

[40] Ibid.

[41] Michael J. Smith, "Humanitarian Intervention: An Overview of Ethical Issues," *Ethics and International Affairs* 12 (1998): 63.

[42] John Mearsheimer, *The Tragedy of Great Power Politics* (New York: W. W. Norton, 2001), p. 47.

[43] Henry Kissinger, "A New World Disorder," *Newsweek* (May 31, 1999), p. 41.

[44] See Sharon Lerner, "Feminists Agonize over War in Afghanistan," *The Village Voice,* October 31–November 6, 2001) Accessed at: www.villagevoice.com/issues/1044/lerner.php

[45] John Pilger, "Humanitarian Intervention," *The New Statesman* (June 28, 1999), p. 8.

[46] Evans and Sahnoun, "The Responsibility to Protect," p. 99.

NUCLEAR PROLIFERATION

This chapter focuses on the debate over the consequences and desirability of nuclear proliferation. In its simplest form, the essential issue is whether nuclear weapons have been, and will be, a force for peace and stability. Those who favor (or at least do not fear) nuclear proliferation claim that because nuclear weapons substantially increase the potential costs of war, they also reduce the likelihood of war. Realists in particular are attracted to this logic of peace through nuclear deterrence. But there is disagreement on how much proliferation is desirable. Advocates of limited proliferation argue that nuclear deterrence contributes to stability only under certain conditions. More extreme proliferation proponents predict that nuclear weapons are stabilizing in almost any setting. These two versions of the pro-proliferation position remain minority stances. More common is opposition to any further spread of nuclear weapons. Nuclear weapons cannot eliminate the chances for war (purposeful or accidental) even if they do reduce them. Because the consequences of nuclear war would be so devastating, it is not a gamble worth taking. But even in the face of these disagreements, there is one point of consensus: the spread of nuclear weapons to nonstate actors would be a disaster because deterrence ceases to be an option in facing an enemy lacking any identifiable territory or assets that can be targeted or destroyed.

The Cold War was marked by continual fear of nuclear catastrophe. From silly grade school drills in which children were taught to hide under their desks (as if that would provide any protection from a nuclear blast) to popular movies, such as *The Day After,* that portrayed the consequences of a nuclear war in graphic terms, the Cold War was almost synonymous with the nuclear arms race. Given the near equation of the Cold War with the threat of nuclear war, it is easy to understand why concern about nuclear weapons waned when the Cold War came to an end. The reprieve would prove short lived. Eventually people began to realize that the passing of the Cold War did not eliminate the nuclear danger. More than a decade after the collapse of the Soviet Union, there are still thousands of nuclear weapons in the world—more than enough to end life as we know it—and headlines reflect new fears, including possible nuclear war between Pakistan and India as well as Iranian and North Korean efforts to acquire nuclear weapons. Popular entertainment provides images of terrorist organizations destroying U.S. cities, a scenario that took on added credibility after the attacks of September 11, 2001. Even though the likelihood of a nuclear exchange between the major powers has undeniably diminished, this scenario has been replaced by new, and perhaps more real, dangers.

The current fear of nuclear proliferation has become great enough to produce a fundamental shift in U.S. strategic doctrine. In the months leading up to the 2003 invasion of Iraq, the Bush administration claimed that the consequences of nuclear and other weapons of mass destruction falling into the hands of rogue nations were so dire that the United States reserved the right to use military force to prevent this from happening. Needless to say, the idea of preemptive military action to prevent nations from acquiring nuclear weapons has been controversial. And the legitimacy of preemptive war under international law is, to put it mildly, questionable. When Israel destroyed an Iraqi nuclear reactor in 1981 on the grounds that Iraqi nuclear weapons would pose an immediate threat to its security, the United States and most other nations condemned the attack as a violation of international law. Though there were several rationales for the 2003 invasion of Iraq, the possibility that the Hussein regime might acquire nuclear weapons was high on the list. The new U.S. doctrine represents one of the more stunning strategic turnarounds in recent memory. If anything, it appears more expansive than the one used to justify the Israeli attack. Israel, after all, only destroyed the reactor in a surgical strike (killing one person); it did not attempt to alter the Iraqi regime.[1]

THE REALITY OF PROLIFERATION
AND NONPROLIFERATION

Though we worry a lot about nuclear proliferation these days, it is important to remind ourselves that there is some good news: the problem could be much worse than it is. As of 2003, only eight countries possessed nuclear weapons: the United States, Russia, Britain, France, China, Israel, Pakistan, and India (see map 11.1). South Africa, which had a small nuclear arsenal in the 1980s, remains the only nation to develop nuclear weapons only to abandon them (though a few former Soviet republics inherited nuclear weapons upon the Soviet Union's breakup and returned them to

The nuclear age began in August of 1945 with the dropping of a nuclear bomb on Hiroshima, Japan, followed by a second bomb dropped days later on Nagasaki (pictured). It was now possible to destroy an entire city and its people in a matter of seconds.
SOURCE: © Bettmann/CORBIS

Russia). In many respects, it is remarkable that only nine nations have demonstrated the ability and desire to build nuclear weapons. As James Carroll notes, "We could just as easily be living in a world with nuclear weapons as common, say, as high-tech fighter aircraft—with countries like Egypt, Indonesia, Australia and numerous others armed with nukes."[2] Thus, it is worthwhile to begin looking at the debate over nuclear proliferation by asking why more nations have not been interested in joining the nuclear club.

"Nuclear proliferation," explains Mitchell Riess, "is a function of two variables: technological capability *and* political motivation . . . capability without motivation is innocuous . . . [and] motivation without capability is futile [emphasis added]."[3] Early predictions that perhaps two dozen nations would acquire nuclear weapons were based on a form of technological and political determinism. The assumption was that any nation with the scientific and economic wherewithal to build nuclear weapons would not long refrain from doing so. Politically, it was difficult to imagine that a nation would have the ability to build nuclear weapons but exercise voluntary restraint. As one observer asks, "When in history . . . [have] so many nations had the capability to produce a powerful weapon, and chosen not to exercise it?"[4] Aside from the interesting example of chemical and biological weapons (which many nations could build), the extent of nuclear nonproliferation has few historical parallels.

MAP 11.1

Nuclear Status

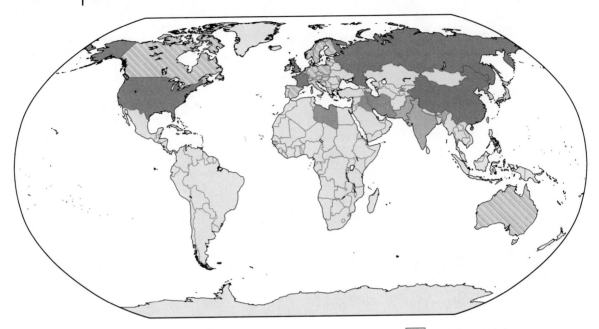

Nuclear Weapon States

Abstaining Countries

These industrialized countries have the technological base, but thus far not the desire, to develop nuclear weapons. A number have installations under international inspection that can produce weapons-grade nuclear material.

High-Risk States

North Korea, Iran, Iraq, and Libya have taken steps in the past several years to acquire nuclear weapons capabilities.[1]

Iraq and Libya are no longer considered high risk states as a result of developments in 2003 and 2004.

Non-NPT Nuclear Weapon States

These nations (India, Israel, and Pakistan) are believed to be able to deploy one or more nuclear weapons rapidly or to have deployed them already.

Recent Renunciations

Several nations in this category had, or were believed to have had, active nuclear-weapon programs during the 1980s, but recently renounced such activities by opening all of their nuclear facilities to international inspection and by joining the non-proliferation regime. Following the Soviet breakup, Belarus, Kazakhstan, and Ukraine acceded to the NPT as non–nuclear weapon states, and cooperated in the removal of all remaining nuclear weapons to Russia.

[1] Given the events of 2003, Iraq and Libya would no longer be classified as high-risk states.
SOURCE: The Carnegie Endowment for International Peace, accessed at www.ceip.org/files/nonprolif/map/default.asp

nuclear abstainers Nations with the economic and technological ability to build and maintain nuclear weapons who have chosen not to acquire them.

nuclear umbrella When one nation promises to employ its nuclear arsenal in order to defend another nation from attack.

Fortunately, predictions of twenty or more nuclear powers by 2000 proved wrong. The list of **nuclear abstainers**—that is, nations that have the ability to build nuclear weapons but have chosen not to—is a long one. A 2002 Carnegie Foundation report pointed to forty nations that can develop nuclear weapons but have not.[5] For many abstainers, such as Germany and Japan, the American **nuclear umbrella** might provide the explanation. Because they are allies of the United States, it is understood that any attack on them would be treated as an attack on the United States, requiring the appropriate response. Thanks to the United States, most Western European nations and some Asian nations, particularly Japan and South Korea, have had no reason to build their own weapons. But this cannot account for all the abstainers, since others (e.g., Sweden and Switzerland) do not enjoy the benefits of U.S. protection.

Perhaps part of the explanation can be found in the international legal obstacles to proliferation, namely, the **Nuclear Non-Proliferation Treaty** (**NPT**).[6] Signed in 1968 by forty-eight nations, including the United States and the Soviet Union, the agreement was designed to prevent what many feared most—a world with dozens of nuclear powers (technically the treaty did not come into effect until 1970). Since 1968, the list of signatories has grown to 187 nations. Parties to the treaty agree not to provide technological or material assistance that would allow other nations to build nuclear weapons. Those nations not already possessing nuclear weapons agreed to forego them in the future. Nations possessing nuclear weapons made vague promises to work toward reducing their levels, but there was no requirement that existing nuclear powers eliminate their weapons. The NPT is an *arms control treaty,* not a *disarmament treaty,* and essentially tried to preserve the nuclear status quo as it existed in 1968.

How successful has the NPT been in preventing proliferation? The answer depends on how we measure "success." On one level, it can be seen as a great success: only three (four, if we include South Africa) nations have joined the nuclear club since 1968. And if we judged international treaties by the number of nations that sign on, the NPT would have to be considered a smashing success. Only three nations have refused to sign—Israel, India, and Pakistan. Very few treaties have gained such wide ascent. But it is unclear whether the treaty prevented any nation from getting nuclear weapons. Though "Egypt, Sweden, Italy and Switzerland gave up serious nuclear weapons program upon signing,"[7] the most comprehensive study of nuclear non-proliferation concludes that all potential nuclear powers "had chosen to give up their nuclear options prior to joining the Nuclear Non-Proliferation Treaty."[8] It is possible that the treaty merely formalized decisions that had already been made.

Evaluating the success of the NPT also raises the question of enforcement—what happens if a nation violates the agreement? The **International Atomic Energy Agency** (**IAEA**) is charged with monitoring compliance with the NPT. It was the IAEA that conducted inspections for evidence of a nuclear weapons program in Iraq during the winter of 2002–2003 (the inspections for chemical and biological weapons were carried out by a separate team assembled by the United Nations). The IAEA, however, has no powers to enforce the treaty and must approach the U.N. Security Council to impose sanctions if violations are uncovered. This difficulty of enforcement is compounded by a provision allowing any signatory to withdraw from the treaty with only three months notice "if it decides that extraordinary events . . . have jeopardized the supreme interests of its country." And who decides what constitutes an extraordinary event or supreme interest? Each state decides for itself. In January 2003 North Korea announced its decision to exercise its right to withdraw from the NPT, citing this provision of the treaty.

In the final analysis, the problem of nuclear proliferation is not really *how many* nations possess nuclear weapons, but *which* nations. Headlines announcing that Norway had exploded its own nuclear bomb would not exactly leave the world in fear at the prospect of the Norwegian prime minister with his or her finger on the nuclear trigger. Clearly, the spread of nuclear weapons into the hands of certain nations would provoke more anxiety than others. But before we get to details about why some nations might provide cause for greater concern, it might come as something of a

Nuclear Non-Proliferation Treaty (1968) Agreement designed to prevent the spread of nuclear weapons. Existing nuclear powers promised not to aid others in acquiring nuclear weapons, and those without nuclear weapons agreed not to build them. Only three nations have not signed the NPT—Israel, India, and Pakistan.

International Atomic Energy Agency (IAEA) Organization charged with monitoring compliance with the Nuclear Non-Proliferation Treaty.

surprise to learn that there is even a debate about nuclear proliferation. Are there actually people who view nuclear proliferation as desirable? In a word, yes, some serious analysts consider nuclear weapons a powerful force for peace and stability. For **proliferation optimists,** more nuclear powers may be a desirable goal, though there is disagreement about how much proliferation is desirable. This perspective contrasts with the more common argument of **proliferation pessimists** that the consequences of using nuclear weapons are potentially so disastrous that their proliferation should be prevented if at all possible. The basic debate addressed in this chapter is whether, and under what circumstances, nuclear weapons might be a force for peace and stability. Three basic positions are presented: the case for nearly limited proliferation, the argument for nearly unlimited proliferation, and the case against any further proliferation.

proliferation optimists
Those who believe that the spread of nuclear weapons can contribute to international peace and stability.

proliferation pessimists
Those who believe that any spread of nuclear weapons is undesirable and should be prevented.

THE CASE FOR LIMITED PROLIFERATION

Debates about the consequences of nuclear proliferation derive in part from disagreements about the impact of nuclear weapons during the Cold War. John Mearsheimer has been particularly influential in setting the terms of the debate. In 1990, just as the Cold War was coming to an end, he claimed that the United States would soon miss the good old days of Cold War stability and predictability.[9] As the United States basked in the glory of victory, it seemed ridiculous to claim that this country would grow nostalgic for the Cold War. But Mearsheimer's position was quite simple. In retrospect, he argued, the Cold War was a period of almost unprecedented great power peace, particularly in Europe, where two total wars had been waged in the three decades preceding 1945. Tens of millions of battlefield and civilian deaths were a testament to the instability of the pre–Cold War world. Despite the intensity of the Cold War superpower rivalry, there was never any direct military engagement between the United States and the Soviet Union. What accounted for this enduring peace in the face of intense rivalry? Mearsheimer identified three critical factors: bipolarity (i.e., only two major powers with which lesser powers were aligned); a rough balance of power between the two superpower alliances; and the presence of nuclear weapons. This last feature is most relevant to the debate over nuclear proliferation.

How did nuclear weapons help keep the peace? Mearsheimer bases his analysis on the plausible assumption that nations start wars because they expect to win them. Only in rare instances do nations start wars they anticipate losing (e.g., if they know they are about to be attacked anyway and think they might get some advantage by going first). Winning means that the expected benefits of war exceed the costs. Historically, however, nations have frequently miscalculated, often losing wars they initiated and expected to win. Before the nuclear era, decision makers confronted two major problems that contributed to the "fog" of war calculations. First, it was easy to misjudge the likely effects of using conventional weapons. Second, it was also easy to imagine that conventional weapons might be used in ways that would allow a nation to "win." This is where the benefits of nuclear weapons come into play. With weapons of such incredibly destructive potential, there is no doubt that their use would result in such tremendous destruction that it would be impossible to reach the conclusion that war would bring more benefits than costs. Nuclear weapons impose a clarity on strategic calculations that conventional weapons do not. By so obviously raising the potential costs of war relative to any conceivable benefits, nuclear weapons dramatically reduced the chances that either the United States or the Soviet Union would risk their use. As Charles Krauthammer concludes, "Deterrence has a track record. For the entire postwar period it has maintained the peace between the two superpowers, preventing not only nuclear but conventional war as well."[10]

Mearsheimer worried that the post–Cold War world would resemble Europe on the eve of World War I, hence the clever title of his article, "Back to the Future." No longer would there be only two major powers—a new, multipolar order would emerge. There was no assurance that a balance of power would be achieved among the major powers. And, perhaps worst of all, many of these powers would not have nuclear weapons. That is, the post–Cold War world was reverting back to a world like the one that produced World War I and World War II. Though he did not predict a repetition of the world wars, Mearsheimer saw trouble coming.

In order to deal with this situation, Mearsheimer advocated a "managed proliferation" of nuclear weapons, especially to Germany. When he was writing in 1990, the Soviet Union still existed as a unified nation. It seemed clear to Mearsheimer that Germany and the Soviet Union would emerge as the dominant powers in Europe. Like all great powers, Germany and the Soviet Union would eventually find themselves in conflict. Because Germany could not rely forever on the United States to provide a nuclear deterrent, stability in Europe required that Germany possess its own nuclear deterrent. Mearsheimer believed this was not only desirable, but also inevitable. And if it was going to happen, it should preferably occur in a "managed" and orderly fashion during a period of relative international calm.

The Soviet Union's demise in 1991 did not alter Mearsheimer's opinion about the wisdom of a German nuclear arsenal, but it did create a new dilemma. The Soviet Union's collapse left a sizable number of nuclear weapons on the territory of some newly independent states, most notably Ukraine. What should be done with weapons Ukraine inherited from the Soviet Union? Consistently applying his logic, Mearsheimer advised Ukraine to keep its nuclear weapons. Russia, after all, would continue to maintain a nuclear arsenal well into the future. Ukraine and Russia were bound to come into conflict at some point. If both had nuclear weapons, the chances they would go to war would be greatly diminished. Mearsheimer was nothing if not consistent.[11]

Mearsheimer's immediate focus was on the future of Europe, and he did not address fully the question of nuclear proliferation elsewhere. His logic could certainly be applied to Asia in terms of a Japanese nuclear deterrent. Like Germany, Japan could not count on the American deterrent forever, and it had to deal not only with Russia's nuclear arsenal but also China's. But how far can this logic extend? As Jonathan Schell (an opponent of proliferation) asks, "If, as many analysts say, [nuclear] deterrence was a successful solution to the dangers of the Cold War, then why should it not be accepted by all nations prone to conflict?"[12] Mearsheimer was not willing to carry his argument to this logical extreme. His concern that German nuclear weapons be acquired in a managed fashion in tranquil times hinted that other times and settings may be too volatile, or at least less opportune, for proliferation. Though providing the justification for a Ukrainian nuclear deterrent, he argued that "nuclear proliferation does not axiomatically promote peace and can in some cases even cause war." He noted that "smaller European powers might lack the resources to make their nuclear force survivable, and vulnerable nuclear forces would invite a first strike in the event of a crisis."[13] If there are reasons to believe that even some smaller European powers may be ill prepared to build and maintain the necessary nuclear forces, one might conclude that very few countries outside Europe possess the requisite resources. And certainly, North Korea and Iran would not be among them.

THE CASE FOR WIDESPREAD PROLIFERATION

Mearsheimer was not the first to see virtues in nuclear proliferation. More than a decade earlier, and long before the end of the Cold War, Kenneth Waltz laid out the basic thesis that Mearsheimer would later apply to post–Cold War Europe. Waltz, however, did not see the benefits of nuclear proliferation as limited to the small handful of states with the resources of Europe's major powers. In arguing that more nuclear weapons may be better even in the most dangerous of places, Waltz provides an extreme case in favor of nuclear proliferation.[14]

For Waltz, like Mearsheimer, nuclear weapons are good because they increase the potential costs of war, thereby decreasing the chances for war. Waltz is as succinct as possible: "War becomes less likely as the costs of war rise in relation to the possible gains."[15] As long as each side knows that any use of nuclear weapons would result in its own destruction, they will not be used, and situations that might entail their use will be avoided. This is the situation that existed between the United States and the Soviet Union and became known as **mutual assured destruction (MAD).** In order for MAD to exist, both powers need have the ability to absorb an attack by the other side and have enough nuclear weapons left over to inflict unacceptable destruction in retaliation. This entails having an **invulnerable second-strike** capability—that is, nuclear weapons which the other side cannot knock out in a first strike. The United States and the Soviet Union accomplished this by putting a lot of nuclear weapons in places where the other side could not effectively attack them (e.g., underground in missile silos and underwater in submarines). Mearsheimer's concern that lesser powers may not be able to build and maintain invulnerable forces focuses on this issue.

Waltz agrees that invulnerable nuclear forces are the key to stable nuclear deterrence. But in his view it is relatively easy to build and maintain an invulnerable second-strike capability. Take an example from recent headlines, Pakistan and India. Waltz claims that they do not need hundreds or thousands of very expensive nuclear weapons in submarines and fortified silos in order to maintain deterrence. A small handful of weapons could do the job because "once a country has a small number of deliverable warheads of uncertain location, it has a second strike force."[16] Pakistan would need only ten or twenty nuclear weapons to inflict incredible damage and casualties on India. Nuclear weapons landing in Bombay and Calcutta alone could kill millions of people. Add three or four more large cities and this would certainly raise the potential costs of war to an unacceptable level. So in order for stable nuclear deterrence (MAD) to exist between Pakistan and India, all each country needs is a few nuclear weapons that the other side cannot locate and target. A few well-concealed or mobile missiles would do the trick. This is where Mearsheimer and Waltz part company: Mearsheimer views nuclear deterrence as a good thing, but he thinks it is expensive and difficult. Waltz agrees that nuclear deterrence is a good thing, but unlike Mearsheimer he thinks it is relatively cheap and easy. For Waltz, any nation with the

mutual assured destruction (MAD) A strategic reality and doctrine in which any use of nuclear weapons would inevitably entail one's own destruction. Achieved when each party possess an invulnerable second-strike (retaliatory) capability.

invulnerable second strike Nuclear weapons that cannot be destroyed in a preemptive attack, providing the ability to respond to any attack with a second (retaliatory) strike.

resources to get nuclear weapons in the first place is almost certainly capable of acquiring enough invulnerable weapons to create stable deterrence.

Fears that Iraq or North Korea might get nuclear weapons, however, are not always based solely on assessments of their ability to build stable deterrents. Even with the necessary weapons, some measure of rationality is essential for deterrence to hold. Decision makers must understand the futility of using nuclear weapons. The description of these countries as rogue states implies doubts about the rationality of the leaders of potential nuclear powers. It is not unusual to hear students or politicians state bluntly that these people or leaders are "crazy." In academic debates these concerns lurk beneath the surface, though even Mearsheimer cites the dangers of "irrational decision-making" as one of the reasons he is only willing to go only so far in supporting proliferation (apparently he loses little sleep worrying about irrationality in Berlin or Kiev).

Waltz sees no reason to assume that so-called leaders will prove less rational or prudent than Joseph Stalin or Mao Tse Tung. In fact, one of the best things about nuclear deterrence is that it does not require an incredible level of rationality to understand the harsh realities. Certainly Saddam Hussein misjudged or miscalculated the consequences of his invasion of Kuwait in 1990. He assumed that other nations would complain but would do little to reverse his conquest. This was a reasonable and rational calculation—wrong, but reasonable. Even rational people miscalculate on occasion. Though the rulers of some potential nuclear nations might be dictatorial, brutal, and evil, there is no reason to assume they are also irrational. Comparing these supposedly "crazy" leaders to some recent U.S. presidents, Waltz wondered why "we continually worry about the leaders of 'rogue' states—the likes of Qaddafi, Saddam and Kim Il Sung." Though supposedly irrational, "they have survived for many years, despite great internal and external dangers." Somewhat tongue in cheek, Waltz goes on to suggest that "their cognitive skills. . . . are more impressive than those of, say, Jimmy Carter or George Bush [the first one]. Given all the advantages of presidential incumbency, Carter and Bush managed to stay in office for only four years." As a result, he doubts that "hardy political survivors in the Third World [are] likely to run the greatest of all risks by drawing the wrath of the world down on them by accidentally or in anger exploding nuclear weapons they may have."[17]

Exactly what are we worried about? Those concerned about nuclear proliferation do not always specify clearly what they are worried about. Are they worried that new nuclear powers will use these weapons against the United States or that they will use them against each other? These two problems need to be dissected separately. Waltz is worried least about the prospect that new nuclear nations will attack the United States. The reason is simple: the overwhelming power of its nuclear deterrent. Any nation that used nuclear weapons against the United States or its armed forces could rest assured of being on the receiving end of a devastating response. Nuclear missiles come with a "return address"; the question of nuclear weapons in the hands of nonstate actors is much trickier and will be explored shortly. Whatever one thinks about some of the world's more unsavory dictators, it is probably safe to assume they have no desire to rule over a parking lot.

Even in the case of Saddam Hussein, there is evidence that he could have been deterred. In the final round of diplomacy before the first Gulf War, U.S. Secretary of

State James Baker met with Iraqi Foreign Minister Tariq Aziz in Geneva, Switzerland. The prospect of Iraqi use of chemical and/or biological weapons in the coming war was a matter of great concern (nuclear weapons were not really in the cards yet). Saddam Hussein had already demonstrated his willingness to use chemical weapons, both against his own people and in the Iran-Iraq war in the early 1980s. Baker felt compelled to warn Iraq that any use of chemical or biological weapons would "demand the strongest possible response" from the United States. Just in case there was any mistaking what this meant, Baker reminded Aziz that the United States had nuclear weapons (as if there was any chance he had forgotten).[18] Lo and behold, Saddam Hussein refrained from using chemical and biological weapons, even when faced with a humiliating defeat. Though Saddam Hussein is no longer in power, the lesson that deterrence worked in the first Iraq war remains valid.

But even if nuclear weapons are not used against the United States, might new nuclear powers use their weapons against each other? Again, Waltz thinks it will generally be easy for stable deterrence to emerge as nuclear weapons proliferate. There is some evidence that appears to support the position that nuclear weapons will play the same role for smaller nuclear powers that they did for the United States and Soviet Union. After examining the Indian-Pakistani crisis of 1990, Devin Haggerty concludes that "New Delhi and Islamabad were deterred from war by their recognition of each other's nuclear capabilities . . . [which] lends further support to the already impressive evidence that the chief impact of nuclear weapons is to deter war between their possessors."[19] Nonetheless, even Waltz concedes that in the final analysis "no one can say that nuclear weapons will never be used." Though he is confident that new powers are extremely unlikely to use their weapons against the major nuclear powers, Waltz seems to grant a somewhat greater possibility that they might use them against each other. What then? In what some might consider a callous and/or cavalier response, Waltz answers that "if such states use nuclear weapons, the world will not end. The use of nuclear weapons by lesser powers would hardly trigger them elsewhere."[20] So even though the detonation of a few nuclear devices in New Delhi or Karachi would be a tragedy for the inhabitants of these cities, this would pose no risk to the world's major nuclear powers. The world would not end. Opponents of nuclear proliferation do not take great comfort in the mere fact that the world would survive.

THE CASE AGAINST NUCLEAR PROLIFERATION

Much of the case in favor of nuclear proliferation relies on the argument that nuclear weapons served to stabilize U.S.-Soviet relations during the Cold War. The fifty years of major power peace is contrasted with two world wars that killed millions in the decades before the nuclear era. Those who have a less benign view of nuclear proliferation usually reject this analysis of the Cold War peace. The problem is a familiar one by now: we cannot assume that because we had nuclear weapons and peace that we had peace *because* of nuclear weapons. To use the familiar cliché, correlation does not prove causation.

Alternative interpretations of the Cold War peace relegate nuclear weapons to a much less important, and perhaps completely irrelevant, role. Historian John Lewis Gaddis, who coined the description of the Cold War as the "long peace," lists nuclear weapons as only one of many factors that helped the superpowers avoid war. He accords much greater weight to the simplicity of bipolarity, the essentially conservative nature of political leadership in both societies, the emergence of norms of peaceful competition between the two countries, and their geographical distance from each other.[21] Others go one step further, arguing that nuclear weapons were completely irrelevant. For John Mueller, the two world wars were enough to convince U.S. and Soviet leaders that even a conventional war would have imposed costs that exceeded any potential gains. Using a colorful metaphor to illustrate the comparative destructiveness of conventional and nuclear war, Mueller observes that "a jump from the fiftieth floor is probably quite a bit more horrible to think about than a jump from the fifth floor, but anyone who finds life even minimally satisfying is extremely unlikely to do either."[22]

Of course, as Robert Malcolmson explains, it is impossible to offer any final, definitive answer to the question of whether nuclear weapons kept the Cold War peace: "perhaps the nuclear threat played a major role in deterring war, perhaps it did not: the fact is, we do not know and never will." Though Malcolmson believes it likely that "the fear of nuclear catastrophe probably did impose some restraint on the actions of the superpowers," he wonders whether "it is possible to establish the relative importance of this restraining fear." Because we cannot provide firm answers to these questions, relying on the supposedly pacifying impact of nuclear weapons is a rather shaky basis for increasing the number of nations with their fingers on the nuclear trigger. No matter how compelling the argument might seem, "the proposition that nuclear deterrence kept the peace is not a matter of knowledge, it is a matter of belief and often rather dogmatic belief."[23]

The gamble of proliferation One of the most effective strategies in any debate is to take your opponent's best argument and turn it against them. Proliferation optimists rest much of their case on the seemingly commonsensical notion that because nuclear weapons increase the potential costs of war, their possession reduces the chances for war. Even if this fundamental point is granted, opponents of proliferation see a weakness. Mearsheimer and Waltz do not, and really cannot, argue that nuclear weapons *eliminate* the chances for war. As Waltz is honest enough to admit, "No one can say that nuclear weapons will never be used." At best, nuclear weapons only reduce the chances for war. But by how much? Do nuclear weapons lower the odds of another Indian-Pakistani war by 10 percent, 50 percent, or 90 percent? No one can claim to know. This uncertainty is important because it highlights that advocates of proliferation are willing to make a tradeoff. They admit that an Indian-Pakistani war with nuclear weapons would be much more destructive than one without them—indeed, this is the very crux of their argument—but in their view the reduced chances of war are worth taking the risk of a much more destructive war. Proliferation proponents, to put it crudely, are willing to "play the odds," though without knowing exactly what these odds are. But, critics wonder, do nuclear weapons reduce the chances for war enough, given the potentially horrific consequences of their use? As Steven Miller concludes, "Even a small risk war despite nuclear weapons makes nuclear proliferation too dangerous to contemplate . . . when one considers the stakes and risks involved, the gamble is too great."[24]

Why worry about Iraq and Pakistan but not Germany? Why would proliferation of nuclear weapons to some states elicit greater anxiety than proliferation to others? Many within the Third World see a mildly racist double standard: as long as nuclear weapons remain in the hands of Northern (i.e., white) nations, there is no problem; it is only when all those different-looking people in Asia and the Middle East get them that Westerners need to worry. Ahmed Hashim suggests that such fears are based on "hoary clichés about the irrationality and callousness of leaders and peoples in the Middle East."[25] From this perspective, the insistence of preventing any further proliferation reinforces a **nuclear apartheid** that gives current nuclear powers an enduring strategic advantage. Most opponents of proliferation, of course, would reject such charges, insisting that there are good reasons to be concerned.

nuclear apartheid A term used by critics of attempts to create two classes of nations—those allowed to possess nuclear weapons and those who cannot be trusted with them.

From the perspective of the United States at least, Germany or Israel with nuclear weapons is less troubling than Iran or Iraq because they are allies. It only stands to reason that nuclear weapons in the hands of friends are less worrisome than in the hands of hostile nations. But concerns about proliferation to developing countries go beyond considerations of their political allegiances. The fact that all nations currently pursuing nuclear weapons are relatively poor causes the most concern. This is because their relative poverty will influence how many nuclear weapons they are likely to build as well as what kind. The fear is that poor nations will be able to afford only a small number of the most basic and worst types of nuclear weapons. This will bring all the drawbacks and risks of nuclear weapons but none of the benefits, introducing weapons of mass destruction into volatile situations where nations lack the technological and financial resources to maintain adequate deterrents.

Mutual assured destruction in the U.S.-Soviet context came about because each nation had thousands of nuclear weapons based in places that the other could not get to, such as underground silos and submarines. This meant that any attack would be met with a devastating counterattack. Consequently, there was never any incentive to use nuclear weapons first. The two powers spent billions and billions of dollars and rubles building these arsenals. Proliferation pessimists worry that new nuclear powers will never be able to do likewise. Iran, North Korea, Pakistan, and India are likely to have arsenals measured in the dozens or hundreds, not thousands. These weapons will be stationed above ground rather than in invulnerable silos or submarines because this placement is easier and cheaper. This being the case, we cannot assume the pacifying effects of nuclear weapons during the Cold War will be replicated in new contexts.

So what if two opponents have only a few nuclear weapons? Wouldn't just five or six nuclear explosions create enough damage to increase costs of war beyond any possible gains? On an objective level, the answer is probably yes. But this does not matter. What matters is whether those making decisions about war and peace believe it to be true. In the final analysis, deterrence is largely psychological in that it relies on decision makers' beliefs and expectations about the likely consequences of certain actions. One nation's fifty or a hundred nuclear weapons will only deter if potential aggressors are convinced those weapons will be used and the damage inflicted will be unacceptable. When a nation has 25,000 nuclear weapons, it is almost impossible to reach any other conclusion. Things may be very different with only a few dozen weapons. Proliferation opponents worry that with only a handful of weapons nuclear powers might come to believe, however incorrectly, that a limited nuclear war might be winnable.

Kim Jong Il, the reclusive dictator of communist North Korea. His pursuit of nuclear weapons became a symbol of the dangers of nuclear proliferation.
SOURCE: © AFP/CORBIS

History is replete with examples of leaders who were unable to recognize what in hindsight appears obvious. The leaders of Europe on the eve of World War I failed to grasp the potential horrors of the war that awaited them, even though they were aware of each other's huge armies with massive quantities of weapons. In 1914, deterrence failed miserably. During the crisis between India and Pakistan in the spring and summer of 2002, some observers were disturbed by what they saw as widespread "nuclear denial." Among the general population there was little awareness of what nuclear weapons could actually do. Even among some in the military there was a disturbingly cavalier attitude toward the possible consequences of nuclear war. One Pakistani general, asked about fears of nuclear war, responded, "I don't know what you're worried about. You can die crossing the street, hit by a car, or you could die in a nuclear war. You've got to die someday anyway."[26] Though we should not draw too large an inference from the off-the-cuff remarks of a single general, such comments certainly do not reveal an appreciation of the devastation nuclear weapons could bring. Kenneth Waltz may be correct about the futility of using even a few weapons, but unfortunately he will not be making the decisions. We need not assume rampant irrationality in order to worry that miscalculations, misperceptions, and wishful thinking might lead to the failure of deterrence in a crisis or war between bitter rivals.

A very delicate balance of terror[27] Even for basically rational decision makers, nuclear arsenals consisting of a few weapons in vulnerable positions create several basic problems. In addition to the possibility that a nuclear war with only a few weapons might be viewed as "winnable," there are serious dilemmas relating to what strategists call **crisis stability,** or the likelihood that a crisis will escalate to (nuclear) war. One fear is that in a crisis between nations with relatively small nuclear arsenals there will

crisis stability The presence or absence of incentives to initiate military action in the event of crisis.

be a strong temptation for both sides to launch a **preemptive strike**—that is, an initial attack intended to eliminate the nuclear forces of the other side before it has a chance to use them. If two enemies have thousands of weapons in many different places, as was the case with the United States and the Soviet Union, a preemptive attack would be futile. There would be no possibility of actually eliminating all the other side's weapons, and whatever weapons remained would surely be launched in retaliation. With only a small number of weapons in vulnerable places, a preemptive attack becomes a feasible, even attractive, option.

To make matters even worse, there will also be strong pressures to adopt a policy of **launch on warning**—that is, to fire one's weapons the moment one suspects an attack is underway. The reasoning here is that if one side waits for an attack to be completed before they respond, they may find themselves with few or no weapons left to retaliate. They could be placed in a "use them or lose them" situation. And since there may be only 4 or 5 minutes warning of an attack from Pakistan on India or vice versa, the time pressures on decision makers will be intense. And when the warning time is so short that decisions need to be almost instantaneous, the danger of inadvertent nuclear war increases dramatically. Again, the situation is different from that of the superpowers in the Cold War, when it would have taken about 30 minutes for missiles from the United States to reach the Soviet Union or vice versa. Even though 30 minutes might not be a lot of time to make a decision on which the future of humanity rests, it was sufficient to allow mistaken indications that an attack was underway (and there were several such incidents during the Cold War) to be detected before any rash decisions were made regarding retaliation.[28]

As a result of these crucial differences, critics of nuclear proliferation believe that we cannot extrapolate the U.S.-Soviet experience into the most likely scenarios for future nuclear proliferation. Even if nuclear weapons did produce, or at least contribute to, the superpower peace, it was only because the United States and the Soviet Union had the money and technology to build a lot of the right kinds of weapons. They also had the technology and time that allowed them to avoid rash, impulsive decisions that might have led to war by mistake. It was a balance of terror, to be sure, but it was a stable balance of terror. Nuclear proliferation will produce more balances of terror in the world, but these are likely to be delicate, fragile, and unstable.

Terrorists, black markets, and nuclear handoffs There is one aspect of nuclear proliferation that everyone agrees on: the acquisition of nuclear weapons by nonstate actors, particularly terrorist groups, would be an unmitigated disaster. Even those who do not worry much about so-called rogue states armed with nuclear weapons concede that this would be a problem of a different order. It is not hard to figure out why there is such a consensus on this point. When we are dealing with states, there is always at least the possibility of deterrence. Even leaders we despise and whose rationality might be doubted have assets that can be targeted and whose destruction can be threatened in order to prevent them from using their weapons. The threat of utter annihilation is plausible and easily understood. With nonstate actors the problem, as Carl Builder explains, is that "an opponent cannot be deterred by the threat of nuclear weapons if that opponent has no definable society to threaten."[29] Presumably, these groups would not go to the trouble of getting nuclear weapons unless they were willing to use them, and since the option of deterrence would not exist, nothing would prevent them from doing so.

Opponents of proliferation argue that we cannot treat proliferation to states and nonstate actors as if they were separate, unrelated problems. The proliferation of nuclear weapons to other states increases the likelihood of proliferation to nonstate actors. How so? We need to remember that building nuclear weapons is no easy feat. States with a lot of resources at their disposal often require decades before they are finally successful. The problem is not the difficulty of knowing how to build a bomb—a few hours on the Internet will yield the necessary plans. The big obstacle is getting one's hands on the *fissile material*—that is, the fuel that feeds the explosion, plutonium or highly enriched uranium (HEU). These are not naturally occurring substances and are very difficult and expensive to produce. It is very unlikely that a nonstate actor could manufacture either plutonium or HEU on its own. If a terrorist group does get nuclear weapons, there are two likely routes—acquiring either the fissile material or a completed weapon from state actors. This could occur either voluntarily, as a so-called handoff from a sympathetic regime or some faction within it, or through a black market in stolen fuel or weapons. Thus, there is a potential connection between nuclear proliferation to states and the likelihood that terrorist organizations might also get them. It only stands to reason that more nuclear powers, more nuclear weapons, and more nuclear fuel in the world will only increase the chances that weapons will wind up in the wrong hands. And since the dangers of these weapons in the hands of nondeterrable actors are so immense, we need to prevent anything that increases this risk, including proliferation to other states.

The other weapons of mass destruction Concern about nuclear weapons proliferation is often expressed in the context of **weapons of mass destruction (WMD)** more generally, a category that includes chemical and biological weapons as well as radiological weapons or "dirty bombs." Chemical weapons include such things as nerve gas or other substances that disable or kill people who are exposed. Biological weapons involve the release of bacteria or viruses that cause disease. Radiological weapons are conventional bombs that would spread radioactive material. In the leadup to the 2003 Iraq war, for example, the Bush administration emphasized possible Iraqi chemical and biological weapons, not nuclear weapons. Though Iraq was suspected of having a nuclear weapons program, most thought it would be some time before that country could have any nuclear weapons.

weapons of mass destruction (WMD) A general category of unconventional weapons including nuclear, chemical, biological, and radiological weapons.

On one level there are good reasons to be more worried about these other WMDs. One good thing about nuclear weapons is that they are both difficult and expensive to build. But because chemical and biological weapons are easier and cheaper to build, other states and organizations are more likely to acquire them than nuclear weapons. This is why biological weapons are often referred to as the "poor man's nuke." This is not to say that it is easy to make usable biological weapons—there are still many obstacles to growing biological agents and converting them into a weaponized form. Chemical weapons, the easiest to manufacture, were used almost a century ago when soldiers in World War I confronted mustard gas on the battlefield. Though they are certainly frightening, it would be difficult for chemical weapons to achieve nuclearlike destructiveness. For this reason, it might be a mistake to classify them as genuine weapons of mass destruction. A successful biological attack with a highly infectious agent, on the other hand, could produce casualties of nuclear proportions.

Unlike nuclear weapons, however, there is no real debate about the merits of chemical and biological weapons proliferation. No one seriously argues that the world would be a better and more stable place with more biological weapons. One reason is that although a nuclear bomb would produce great damage, its effects can be contained and calculated. But once an infectious biological agent is released into the human population, there is no controlling its eventual course. It is almost impossible to know where the agent will travel, which people it will kill, or how many. Because these weapons are so inherently unpredictable, it is difficult to imagine how they would fit into any rational policy of deterrence.

CONCLUSION

The debate over whether the spread of nuclear weapons contributes to peace and stability is largely an in-house discussion among realists. Kenneth Waltz, who advocates widespread proliferation, and John Mearsheimer, who favors more limited proliferation, are both self-described realists. Other realists oppose any further proliferation. This divergence among realists illustrates something we have seen already: debates exist not only between and among different perspectives, but also within them. Despite shared assumptions, people can arrive at different conclusions.

Both Mearsheimer and Waltz agree that nuclear deterrence can be a powerful force for peace. They also agree that nuclear deterrence works because it increases the costs of war, making it less likely that war will be initiated. The connections between this argument for nuclear deterrence and the realist worldview are easy to discern. Realists have always emphasized the inevitability of conflict among nations. International conflict, like social conflict in general, can never be entirely eliminated. Politics is about the management of conflict, not its elimination. In the absence of a central government to deal with disputes among nations, the distribution of power becomes a critical factor influencing whether conflicts lead to war. Realists have generally seen a balance of power between antagonists as the most stable situation. When a balance of power exists, neither side can be confident of prevailing in a war, which decreases the likelihood that war would be initiated. States are deterred from going to war because of the fear that they might lose. The argument that nuclear weapons are a stabilizing force is an understandable extension of this basic logic. Conflicts are prevented from escalating to war not by eliminating the underlying cause of the dispute but by convincing both sides they have much more to lose than gain. Thus, nuclear weapons deter war in much the same way as the balance of power. The logic is quintessentially realist.

Acceptance of the general argument, however, does not always lead to agreement on specific issues. This is because additional questions need to be answered before general principles can be translated into policy: What constitutes an adequate deterrent? Which nations have the capacity to build a sufficient deterrent? The basic assumptions of realism do not provide answers to these questions. Because realists make different judgments on these issues, they do not agree on whether nuclear weapons decrease or increase the danger of war between Ukraine and Russia or India and Pakistan. An essentially realist argument can be made either way. The basic principles of realism (or any other perspective) provide a general framework, not a detailed road map, for thinking about international problems.

Even though realists have dominated discussions about the consequences of nuclear proliferation, they have not monopolized it. Liberals have also weighed in on the question, generally opposing proliferation in favor of strengthening the NPT and other international efforts to control the spread of nuclear weapons. But liberal opposition to proliferation usually does not focus on the ability or inability of nations to build an adequate deterrent. Liberal opposition to proliferation derives from a deeper unease with nuclear deterrence itself. Stripped to its barest essentials, the case for nuclear deterrence is an argument for peace based on fear. Peace is not brought about by accommodation, reconciliation, or resolving the issues that produced conflict in the first place. Peace prevails because nuclear weapons make war too horrible to contemplate. For realists, who view some measure of international conflict as inevitable, the logic of peace through deterrence or fear makes sense. But liberals have always been uncomfortable with the notion that that peace is preserved by making the costs of war ever more horrific. Liberals would rather bring about peace by finding a way to resolve the issue(s) that create hostility. A peace based on the mutual threat of total destruction is not a long-term solution to anything and merely perpetuates and exacerbates conflict. For liberals, the debate over proliferation raises issues that go well beyond worries about crisis stability. As Jonathan Schell explains, "The principle strategic question is whether the doctrine of deterrence, having been framed during the cold war, will now be discredited as logically absurd and morally bankrupt or, on the contrary, recommended to nations all over the world."[30] For Schell, the narrow focus on the consequences of proliferation obscures the more important question. The most pressing issue is not whether *any more* nations should get nuclear weapons, but whether *any* nation should have them in the first place.

POINTS OF VIEW

Do Indian and Pakistani Nuclear Weapons Help Prevent War?

In the summer of 2002, tensions between India and Pakistan were on the rise. This was part of their ongoing conflict over the province of Kashmir, which India currently controls. Because both India and Pakistan have nuclear weapons, this crisis was particularly worrisome. Many feared the world was on the brink of its first war between nuclear powers. The following editorials present very different views of the crisis. Ernest Lefever argues that these fears were overblown. Indeed, he claims that the crisis can be seen as a positive development. Why? How does his argument in favor of "sabre rattling" echo the arguments for nuclear proliferation and even move beyond them? Does his logic suggest support for limited or unlimited nuclear proliferation? Salil Tripathi, however, was much more worried about the prospects for nuclear war. Why is Tripathi not as confident as Lefever about avoiding nuclear war? Why does he think the U.S.-Soviet experience is not a good model for the Pakistani-Indian conflict? Whose arguments do you find more persuasive?

Nuclear Saber-Rattling Helps Blow Off Steam

Ernest W. Lefever
June 4, 2002

Strange as it may seem, a little nuclear saber-rattling over the Kashmir conflict may be a good thing. During the last two weeks, the leaders of India and Pakistan have brandished their nuclear-tipped missiles and made veiled threats to use them. Pakistan President Pervez Musharraf and Indian Prime Minister Atal Behari Vajpayee have felt compelled to look and act fearsome.

Like animals that show their fangs or inflate themselves with air to appear more menacing to adversaries, both men have resorted to this hallowed ritual of political rivals, which more often than not has prevented a deadly showdown. Leaders of the U.S., Britain, Russia and China have warned of a possible 12 million immediate deaths in a nuclear exchange. India's nuclear force is substantially larger than Pakistan's though each has the capacity to destroy one another's capital. To underscore their concern, Washington and other governments have ordered or strongly recommended the evacuation of their nationals from India and Pakistan.

With all this noise, sometimes bordering on hysteria, one might conclude that we are on the verge of a catastrophic nuclear war. But we are not. The well-documented history of the nuclear era—and virtually all other evidence—suggests that such a war will not erupt. The provocative words on both sides are part of an elaborate ritual.

Now, as always, leaders confronting a crisis communicate with one another not only through quiet diplomatic channels but also by a public ritualized code. This coded confrontation is often a substitute for lethal conflict, a kind of foreplay that can end in a fragile peace if not in a mutual embrace.

Such brinkmanship has had an honored place in the nuclear era. Over the weekend, brinkmanship began to bear fruit in the softened rhetoric on both sides.

Musharraf said that nuclear war was unthinkable. Neither "side is that irresponsible," and no "sane individual" should even think of initiating such a war, "whatever the pressures."

He called for a no-war pact with India and the elimination of nukes from South Asia.

The Indian prime minister said India will not use nuclear weapons first, but he saw no immediate need for a face-to-face meeting with Pakistan's president.

For its part, Washington is dispatching Defense Secretary Donald Rumsfeld and other officials to the region to caution restraint. Though not publicly announced, they will also recommend ways for each side to tighten its control and safeguard systems to minimize an accidental launch.

More important than the immediate posturing by India and Pakistan is the fact that both sides are increasingly aware of the lessons learned by Washington and Moscow since the dawn of the nuclear era. Many of those who studied in the U.S. have adopted the esoteric vocabulary of the nuclear balance. Among the understandings they learned are these:

- The atom-bombing of Japan in 1945 was a one-time measure, tragic but justified because it ended a brutal war and saved up to a million lives, mostly Japanese.

- Shortly after the Soviet Union acquired the atom bomb, both Washington and Moscow realized that the basic purpose of their respective stockpiles was to prevent their use. As it turned out, the delicate nuclear balance of terror also prevented a conventional war.

- The 1962 Cuban missile crisis demonstrated the stabilizing impact of nuclear deterrence and reinforced the tendency of the superpowers to rely on less-lethal means for managing conflict. Further, President Kennedy and Soviet Premier Nikita Khrushchev negotiated by deeds without the necessity for face-to-face talks.

- After the Soviet Union fell, the threat of nuclear war receded even further. Both sides increasingly recognized the merit of minimum deterrence, the view that each side needed only enough nuclear weapons to make a first strike against it too costly to the other. What rational Kremlin leader would initiate a nuclear attack if the assumed millions of his people would perish in retaliation?

To what extent have the leaders of India and Pakistan internalized these vital lessons? And do they have the requisite attributes—common sense, prudence and courage—to resist the passions of the moment? I believe they do.

Say No to Armageddon: Time for Statesmanship

Salil Tripathi
May 31, 2002

There is an alarming and dangerous complacency in South Asia about the possibility of a nuclear war. Indian and Pakistani leaders resent any implication that their nuclear weapons could lie in immature, untrained or irresponsible hands. They believe such implications are racist, and that the world should trust the Cold War-like deterrent effect of nuclear weapons and the wisdom of the two governments. Sadly, neither assumption can be made in the current context in the subcontinent. World leaders anxiously lining up to visit Islamabad and New Delhi clearly think otherwise. The world is nervous about an India-Pakistan conventional war turning nuclear, either by accident or design.

India joined the nuclear club in 1974. It reaffirmed its nuclear status in 1998, at least partly because it wanted to be taken seriously as a regional, if not global power. India's move that year also forced Pakistan to make its clandestine nuclear program public. Indian leaders felt their country deserved a place at the head table of International affairs, given India's size, strategic significance and democratic society. They resented the importance given to post-Mao China and felt their regional and global ambitions were being scuttled because Pakistan demanded parity with India, though it is only a 10th its size.

In the nuclear context, Indian leaders argued that the non-proliferation treaty was fundamentally flawed and discriminatory, for it contained no time-table or incentive for the five declared nuclear powers to reduce or eliminate their arsenal while restricting the rights of other nations to develop nuclear weapons. Trust us, Indian and Pakistani leaders argued after their 1998 tests; we can be as responsible with weapons of mass destruction as the United States and the Soviet Union were during the Cold War.

One should not be so sanguine. It is true that the U.S. and the U.S.S.R. did not use nuclear weapons. But that sense of security is false, for it lulls us into believing that the next Cold War also will remain on drawing boards and in simulations. True, South Asian leaders have been using the jargon of cold warriors effectively—nuclear deterrence, command-and-control systems, no-first-use, early-warning capability and so on. But as an Indian official says: "The leaders in both countries have singularly failed to prepare and educate their people about what this game is all about. I am extremely uncomfortable about the fact that neither India nor Pakistan has even begun a process of public debate and transparency about the command-and-control system, and about nuclear doctrine. It is essential to think these things through and come to a public consensus on such matters, in order to contain the danger."

Indeed, the parallel with the Cold War is flawed on several counts. Take geography. The distance between the U.S. and the Soviet Union was vast (except in the Pacific Ocean). This meant that there was adequate time to verify rumors and check intentions. Lines of communication existed between heads of state and generals in forward positions to prevent a misunderstanding from turning into a catastrophe. However, a nuclear missile fired by either India or Pakistan will cross the border within minutes, making such checks almost impossible.

Another reason is ideology. The Cold War was an ideological battle; the more visceral tendencies that can be unleashed by religious passions were largely absent. But India and Pakistan's shared history is not only troubled and tragic, the leaders of each country have justified their nuclear-weapon program in religious terms. Pakistan's Gen. Pervez Musharraf has routinely clothed his belligerent arguments in religious garb. India, currently ruled by a Hindu nationalist-led coalition, ends an official paper on its nuclear policy with a quotation from the Gita, the ancient Hindu religious text. It says, "Action is a process to reach a goal; action may reflect tumult but when measured and focused, will yield its objective of stability and peace."

Then there is preparedness. During the Cold War, the U.S. and the U.S.S.R. played out elaborate game-theory scenarios to anticipate each other's moves. However artificial such simulations might seem, both countries made preparations to handle the logistical nightmare that would follow a nuclear attack. The game theorists played out their scenarios with a lucid awareness of what they were dealing with.

Now it may very well be that India and Pakistan have mapped out defense-related game-theory scenarios. But their logistic preparedness can never be adequate. After all, the two countries are among the poorest in the world, with inadequate infrastructure even at the best of times. To be sure, India appears to be making adequate defense preparations: According to *Jane's Defence Weekly,* its strategic nuclear command will be placed in the southern city of Thiruvananthapuram in June. And the army is inducting an integrated field shelter that can withstand any nuclear, biological or chemical attack according to reports in the Indian press.

But still, a U.S. Defense Department study speculates that a nuclear war in South Asia will mean nine to 12 million deaths, with two to seven million injured. Not only would that mean the two nations will need every hospital bed in their own countries, but even the additional medical infrastructure of the Middle East and Southeast Asia may not be enough to cope.

But it just doesn't have to be that way. Nor can it be allowed to turn out that way. Reducing the current tension along the border will require pragmatism. Gen. Musharraf has shown he possesses this—notice the speed with which he dumped the Taliban. It will also need wily statecraft. Indian Prime Minister Atal Bihari Vajpayee once was famous for this. Even if the two leaders may not want to, they will have to rise to the occasion and not allow their baser instincts to prevail. The nuclear doctrine of South Asia is too important to be held hostage to the wishes of fundamentalists who want to live out their misanthropic fantasies. There are times when statesmanship is thrust upon leaders. This is such a time.

The Asian Wall Street Journal, May 31, 2002.

CHAPTER SUMMARY

- Despite current fears about nuclear proliferation, the past few decades are remarkable for the number of nations that have refrained from developing nuclear weapons, even when they have the financial and technological ability to do so. The reasons for this restraint are many—the U.S. "nuclear umbrella," the Nuclear Non-Proliferation Treaty, and the absence of any compelling strategic rationale being important factors.

- The fact that relatively few nations have pursued nuclear weapons is of little comfort if these are the ones we need to worry most about. The debate over the consequences of nuclear proliferation raises the question of whether we really need to be that fearful. Some even argue that a world with more nuclear weapons might be more peaceful and stable.

- There are essentially three major positions in the debate over nuclear proliferation: the case for limited spread of nuclear weapons, a more extreme argument for virtually unlimited proliferation, and the more common opposition to any further proliferation.

- Those who favor proliferation claim that nuclear weapons were a force for stability during the Cold War and can be in other settings. By increasing the potential costs of war, nuclear weapons have the effect of reducing the chances for war. In this sense, nuclear deterrence "works."

- Those who favor only limited proliferation argue that although nuclear deterrence works, it is difficult and expensive. Very few nations have the ability to build and maintain an adequate nuclear deterrent. The case for more widespread proliferation rests on the assumption that only a few nuclear weapons would be sufficient, making nuclear deterrence relatively easy and cheap.

- The debate about how much proliferation is desirable usually pits realists against other realists. Though attracted to the logic of deterrence, realists disagree among themselves about exactly what is needed for deterrence to work.

- Opponents of proliferation point out that even if nuclear weapons reduce the chances for war, they do not eliminate them. And because war with nuclear weapons would be so horrible, this is not a risk worth taking. Proliferation pessimists also worry more about the "rationality" of the leaders of rogue states and the danger of accidental launches from countries with primitive command and control systems.

- Whatever the disagreements concerning the spread of nuclear weapons to other states, there is consensus that it would be a disaster if nonstate actors acquired nuclear weapons. When an actor lacks any territory or assets that be easily targeted and destroyed, deterrence is not an option.

CRITICAL QUESTIONS

1. Would the world be a better and safer place without nuclear weapons?

2. Are there legitimate reasons to worry about a handful of Indian and Pakistani nuclear weapons but not thousands of American nuclear weapons?

3. Why do states and nonstate actors pose fundamentally different problems in terms of nuclear proliferation?

4. Is the United States (or any nation) justified in using force to prevent other nations from acquiring nuclear weapons?

5. Can the arguments in favor of nuclear proliferation be applied to other weapons of mass destruction?

KEY TERMS

crisis stability 281
International Atomic Energy Agency (IAEA) 273
invulnerable second strike 276
launch on warning 282
mutual assured destruction (MAD) 276
nuclear abstainers 272
nuclear apartheid 280
Nuclear Non-Proliferation Treaty (1968) 273
nuclear umbrella 272
preemptive strike 281
proliferation optimists 274
proliferation pessimists 274
weapons of mass destruction (WMD) 283

FURTHER READINGS

Since much of the debate about nuclear proliferation relies on assessments about the impact of nuclear weapons during the Cold War, it is useful to begin by looking at the U.S.-Soviet experience. Two excellent surveys are Richard Smoke, *National Security and the Nuclear Dilemma, 1945–1991*

(New York: McGraw-Hill, 1992), and Ronald Powaski, *Return to Armageddon: The United States and the Nuclear Arms Race, 1981–99* (Oxford: Oxford University Press, 2000). In terms of the debate over proliferation, Kenneth Waltz's essay, "The Spread of Nuclear Weapons: More May Be Better," *Adelphi Papers,* vol. 17 (Oxford: Oxford University Press, 1981), is the best place to begin because this seminal article set the terms for the entire debate. Differing views of the impact of nuclear weapons on the "peace" of the Cold War are presented by John Mearsheimer, "Back to the Future: Political Instability in Europe after the Cold War, *International Security* 15 (Summer 1990): 5–56, and John Mueller, "The Essential Irrelevance of Nuclear Weapons," *International Security* 13 (Fall 1988): 55–79. The best overall presentation of the debate is Scott D. Sagan and Kenneth N. Waltz, *The Spread of Nuclear Weapons: A Debate Renewed* (New York: W. W. Norton, 2003). An excellent collection of essays dealing with individual countries is Peter R. Lavoy, Scott D. Sagan, and James Wirtz, eds., *Planning the Unthinkable: How New Powers will Use Nuclear, Chemical and Biological Weapons* (Ithaca, NY: Cornell University Press, 2001).

NUCLEAR PROLIFERATION ON THE WEB

www.armscontrol.org
Website of the Arms Control Association provides information and news on all aspects of nuclear weapons, including nuclear proliferation.

www.nuclearfiles.org/hinonproliferationtreaty
Provides the test of the Nuclear Non-Proliferation Treaty as well as other information about nuclear weapons, including the history of the nuclear arms race.

www.ceip.org/files/nonprolif
Website maintained by the Carnegie Endowment for International Peace provides the latest news on nuclear, chemical, and biological weapons proliferation.

www.lib.berkeley.edu/SSEAL/SouthAsia/nuclear.html
Provides information and news focusing on the nuclear situation between India and Pakistan.

www.nci.org
Perhaps the best source for up-to-date information on nuclear proliferation, this is the website of the Nuclear Control Institute.

NOTES

[1] See Louis Rene Beres and Yoash Tsiddon-Chatto, "Reconsidering Israel's Destruction of Iraq's Osiraq Nuclear Reactor," *Temple International and Comparative Law Journal* 9, no. 2 (1995): 437–440; and by the same authors, "Sorry Seems to Be the Hardest Word," *Jerusalem Post,* June 5, 2003, p. 37A.

[2] James Carroll, "The President's Nuclear Threat," *Boston Globe,* October 1, 2002, p. A15.

[3] Mitchell Reiss, *Without the Bomb: The Politics of Nuclear Nonproliferation* (New York: Columbia University Press, 1988), p. 247.

[4] Quoted in Jim Walsh, "Understanding the Nuclear Puzzle," *International Studies Review* 13, no. 1 (Fall 2001): 177.

[5] Drake Bennett, "Critical Mess: How the Neocons Are Promoting Nuclear Proliferation," *The American Prospect* (July/August 2003): 50.

[6] The full text of the treaty can be found at www.state.gov/www/global/arms/treaties/npt1.html. A list of signatories is available at the same site.

[7] Bennett, "Critical Mess," p. 50.

[8] T. V. Paul, *Power versus Prudence: Why Nations Forgo Nuclear Weapons* (Montreal: McGill-Queens University Press, 2000), p. 151.

[9] John Mearsheimer, "Why We Will Soon Miss the Cold War," *The Atlantic* (August 1990): 35–50. A more detailed and scholarly version of the argument is presented in John Mearsheimer, "Back to the Future: Political Instability in Europe after the Cold War," *International Security* 15, no. 1 (Summer 1990): 5–56.

[10] Charles Krauthammer, "On Nuclear Morality," in *Nuclear Arms: Ethics, Strategy, Politics,* ed. R. James Woolsey (San Francisco: Institute for Contemporary Studies, 1984), p. 15.

[11] Mearsheimer's advice was not followed and Ukraine did return its inherited weapons to Russia.

[12] Jonathan Schell, "The Gift of Time: The Case for Abolishing Nuclear Weapons," *The Nation* (February 9, 1998): 21.

[13] John Mearsheimer, "The Case for a Ukrainian Nuclear Deterrent," *Foreign Affairs* 72, no. 3 (Summer 1993): 51.

[14] Kenneth Waltz, "The Spread of Nuclear Weapons: More May Be Better," Adelphi Papers, vol. 17 (Oxford: Oxford University Press, 1981). The argument contained here was later refined and incorporated into Scott Sagan and Kenneth Waltz, *The Spread of Nuclear Weapons: A Debate* (New York: W. W. Norton, 1995).

[15] Sagan and Waltz, *Spread of Nuclear Weapons,* p. 3.

[16] Ibid., p. 109.

[17] Ibid., p. 97.

[18] Lawrence Freedman and Efraim Karsh, *The Gulf Conflict, 1990–1991: Diplomacy and War in the New World Order* (Princeton: Princeton University Press, 1993), p. 255. The "reminder" about nuclear weapons was revealed in the PBS *Frontline* documentary, "The Gulf War" (January, 1996).

[19] Devin T. Haggerty, "Nuclear Deterrence in South Asia: The 1990 Indo-Pakistani Crisis," *International Security* 20, no. 3 (Winter 1995/96): 82, 114.

[20] Sagan and Waltz, *Spread of Nuclear Weapons,* pp. 16–17.

[21] John Lewis Gaddis, *The Long Peace: Inquiries into the History of the Cold War* (New York: Oxford University Press, 1987), pp. 215–45.

[22] John Mueller, *Retreat from Doomsday: The Obsolescence of Major Power War* (New York: Basic Books, 1988), p. 116.

[23] Robert W. Malcolmson, *Beyond Nuclear Thinking* (Montreal: McGill-Queens University Press, 1990), p. 89.

[24] Steven Miller, "The Case against a Ukranian Nuclear Deterrent," *Foreign Affairs* 72, no. 3, (Summer 1993): 80.

[25] Ahmed Hashim, "The State, Society and the Evolution of Warfare in the Middle East: The Rise of Strategic Deterrence?" *Washington Quarterly* 18, no. 4 (Autumn 1995): 69.

[26] Cecilia Dugger, "Eyeball to Eyeball, and Blinking in Denial," *New York Times,* June 2, 2002, Section 4, p. 1.

[27] This section subtitle is, of course, taken from Albert Wohlstetter's seminal article, "The Delicate Balance of Terror," *Foreign Affairs* 37 (1959): 211–34.

[28] Scott Sagan discusses some of the scarier near-misses in *The Limits of Safety: Organizations, Accidents and Nuclear Weapons* (Princeton: Princeton University Press, 1993).

[29] Quoted in Alvin and Heidi Toffler, *War and Anti-War* (New York: Warner Books, 1995), p. 198.

[30] Schell, "Gift of Time," p. 22.

CHAPTER TWELVE

INTERNATIONAL TERRORISM

Given the events of September 11, 2001, it is understandable that terrorism would become one of the critical problems of international relations in the eyes of most Americans. Even though the magnitude of these attacks was unprecedented, terrorism has been around for a long time. So, too, have debates about almost every aspect of terrorism—the meaning and definition of terrorism, its causes, consequences, and morality. This chapter focuses primarily on policy responses to terrorism. It identifies two different strategies of response that emerged in the post–September 11 debate. A *cosmopolitan* approach treats terrorist attacks as criminal acts against humanity as a whole, requiring a legal and international response. This needs to be accompanied by a long-term strategy addressing the root causes of terrorism, such as global poverty and discontent. The cosmopolitan strategy resonates with important strands of liberal, Marxist/radical, and feminist thought. A *statist* approach treats terrorist attacks as acts of war that might require a forceful response not only against terrorist organizations but also against states that actively support or passively tolerate them. Advocates of a statist response are more inclined to see terrorism as rooted in a fundamental conflict of values, not social and economic conditions that can be eliminated by reform. This approach obviously has much in common with a realist worldview.

What is terrorism and who are the terrorists? What motivates individuals and groups to engage in terrorism? Can terrorism ever be morally justified? Does terrorism work? What policies and strategies should nations pursue to deal with the problem of terrorism? These are some of the enduring conceptual, empirical, theoretical, moral, and political issues that come to mind as we try to understand and respond to terrorism. And, as is usually the case, the problems become more complex as we realize that these questions are interrelated—for example, assumptions about terrorist motivations are tied to policy recommendations; and definitions of terrorism influence moral evaluations. Though many societies have wrestled with these matters for decades, they have taken on added significance, especially for the United States, as a result of the events of September 11, 2001.

Though the term *terrorism* is of relatively recent origin (it was used for the first time during the French Revolution), the phenomenon is probably as old as political violence itself. It is possible to find acts in the ancient world that would meet contemporary definitions of terrorism. In this sense the attacks of September 11, 2001 are merely the latest chapter in the very long history of terrorism. Though it is important to place contemporary events in their larger historical context, it would be a mistake to view the September 11 attacks as "only" the most recent manifestation of an age-old phenomenon. For the United States, of course, September 11 had a special significance because this country was the target. The larger significance of the attacks on the World Trade Center and the Pentagon derives from their magnitude. As Martha Crenshaw notes, "the September 11 assaults . . . [were] unprecedented in the history of terrorism."[1] The attacks represented much more than a minor escalation in the scale of violence; this was violence of a whole other order. Though the difference between these attacks and previous terrorist acts might be just a matter of degree, there comes a point where differences of degree become great enough to become differences in kind.

TERRORISM: THE DEFINITIONAL ANGST

terrorism The indiscriminate use or threat of violence to advance social, political, economic, or religious objectives by creating a climate of fear.

What exactly is **terrorism?** This seems like a simple enough question for which there should be some straightforward answer, but things are rarely as easy as they first appear. Like so many of the critical concepts in international relations, terrorism has no universally accepted definition. Paul Pillar sees a "collective definitional angst" among policymakers and scholars who deal with terrorism.[2] Given the highly charged connotations of the labels *terrorism* and *terrorist*, it should come as no surprise that definitional issues would prove contentious. It is hard to think of a more emotionally laden term in the current political environment. Nations and groups are understandably anxious to define terrorism so as to exclude their own actions but include those of their opponents. There is a strong political incentive to adopt a definition that can be employed cynically and selectively. If you can make the terrorist label stick to your enemies, you have already won a political victory. Thus, one harsh critic charges that in the case of U.S. anti-terrorist policy, "the condemnatory label [is] being deployed to the enemies of U.S. interests while being withheld from U.S. friends and clients, no matter how opprobrious their conduct might otherwise be."[3] The battle over how to define terrorism is almost as intense as the struggle against terrorism itself.[4]

Even those more detached from contemporary political conflicts have difficulty settling on a definition. One of the most exhaustive and authoritative studies of modern terrorism required more than a hundred pages to survey and compare the various definitions.[5] Walter Laqueur, exasperated by the proliferation of definitions, concludes that "any definition of political terrorism venturing beyond noting the systematic use of murder, injury and destruction or threats of such acts toward achieving political ends is bound to lead to endless controversy." As a result, "it can be predicted with confidence that the disputes about a comprehensive, detailed definition of terrorism will continue for a long time, that they will not result in a consensus and that they will make no notable contribution toward the understanding of terrorism."[6]

In some respects, this debate exaggerates the difficulty of providing a definition. Certainly there are differences at the margins, such as whether a single act (e.g., an assassination) can count as terrorism or whether it needs to be part of a pattern of violence. Such differences, however, should not be allowed to obscure the widespread agreement, perhaps even consensus, on the basic components of terrorism. Although some acts may fall within certain definitions of terrorism but not others, many acts also fall unambiguously into virtually all definitions. It is impossible, for example, to find a definition of terrorism that would not include the attacks of September 11, 2001. Certainly gray areas exist, but there are also black and white areas that few, if any, question.

What elements of terrorism are common to most definitions? First, terrorism involves the threat or use of violence. Though people sometimes worry about *cyberterrorism,* in which a society is targeted by having its communications and information systems disrupted, most still see violence or force as a defining feature of terrorism. Second, this violence must be carried out in the furtherance of some broader political or social objective. A mugger might use deadly force, but this is usually done for personal gain, not to advance a political or social agenda. Third, it usually does not matter *who* is harmed by terrorist violence because "terrorism is specifically designed to have far-reaching psychological effects beyond the immediate victims or objects of the terrorist attack."[7] When a suicide bomber blows up a bus and kills a dozen people, precisely which dozen people are killed is of little consequence. The terrorist is not trying to kill those people specifically. In this sense the targets are random, and the randomness is what creates fear: it leads everyone to worry about whether they might be the next target. If a terrorist group were only trying to knock off a specific group of people (e.g., U.S. senators), those of us who were not part of that group would have little to fear (though some terrorist groups have targeted specific individuals). Cindy Combs reflects the consensus on these points, defining terrorism as "involv[ing] an act of violence, an audience, the creation of a mood of fear, innocent victims, and political goals or motives."[8] Even Conor Gearty, who expresses doubts that a meaningful definition of terrorism can be agreed on, presents a very similar definition: "By terror, we mean the launching of reckless or consciously indiscriminate attacks on civilians in order to communicate a message to a third party, who will invariably be the real enemy."[9]

Once we move beyond these essential elements, the controversy heats up. Bruce Hoffman, for example, includes all of these aspects in his definition but goes on to add that terrorism is something conducted by "a subnational group or non-state entity."[10] This addition raises the whole issue of whether terrorism should be defined simply by the nature of the act or also by the nature of the group. If Hoffman's definitional amendment is accepted, it basically inoculates states from any charges of terrorism. Given that the term *terrorism* first appeared in the aftermath of the French Revolution to describe the policies of the revolutionary government during the so-called "reign of terror," it would seem odd to argue that states, by definition, could not commit acts of terrorism. But Louis Rene Beres agrees with Hoffman: "Definitions that do not refer specifically and exclusively to insurgent organizations [non-state actors] broaden the meaning of terrorism to unmanageable and useless levels."[11] This is the definitional issue on which there is the greatest divergence of opinion.

Terrorism or terrorisms? Once we have reached some measure of agreement, if not total consensus, on what constitutes terrorism, we need to consider whether it is useful to view terrorism as an undifferentiated phenomenon or whether it is better to recognize that not all terrorist groups are the same. There is no easy answer to this question, but the problem is familiar. Sometimes it makes sense to group together similar things, whereas other times it is better to draw some distinctions. For some purposes we might want to lump all felons together, and for other purposes grouping robbers with mass murderers might obscure more than it illuminates. These sorts of distinctions and classifications are neither right nor wrong; they are simply more or less useful. Similarly, sometimes it might be helpful to speak in general about terrorist groups, whereas at other times it is important to recognize significant differences because they can be critical for shaping policy responses.

In the sense that they have all engaged in acts that meet most definitions of terrorism, the Irish Republican Army (IRA), Al-Qaeda, and Aum Shinrikyo can all be considered terrorist organizations. But does it really make sense to analyze these groups as if they represent the same phenomenon? Probably not. They are very different in terms of their motives, goals, and objectives as well as the type of terrorist attacks committed. The IRA can be viewed as a very traditional terrorist group, a movement with relatively modest political objectives fighting against what its members see as outside domination. Its tactics are also very traditional, involving small-scale bombings that cause at most several dozen casualties. Nationalist or separatist groups like the IRA "have tended to calibrate their use of violence, using enough to rivet world attention but not so much as to alienate supporters abroad or members of their base community."[12]

Al-Qaeda ("the base"), on the other hand, has much more expansive political and social goals that are deeply infused with, and motivated by, a particular form of religious (Islamic) fundamentalism. Not only are its objectives broader and more ambitious than those of the IRA, but its tactics and the scale of its attacks are on a very different level. The IRA had no desire to destroy Great Britain, but merely to get the British out of Northern Ireland. There is no reason to believe that the IRA would ever contemplate crashing airliners into buildings or using chemical, biological, or nuclear weapons, even if it had the capability to do so. This is what made the attacks of September 11, 2001 so significant. They were certainly not the first terrorist attacks directed against the United States, even on its own territory. What was new was the scale of the attack. Thus, even though the phenomenon of terrorism may be as old as human history, September 11 suggests that we may be dealing with something very different than what we are used to. This is particularly significant because religiously motivated terrorist organizations have been increasing in number since the 1980s.

The Aum Shinrikyo's 1995 sarin gas attack on the Tokyo subway demonstrated the dangers of chemical attacks by terrorist groups.
Source: © Tokyo Shimbun /CORBIS SYGMA

According to Hoffman, "only two of the sixty-four [terrorist] groups active in 1980 could be classified as predominantly religious in character." The majority were ethnic or nationalist in nature, such as the IRA or Basque separatists (ETA) in Spain. By 1995, however, religious groups "account[ed] for nearly half (twenty-six, or 46 percent) of the fifty-six known, active international terrorist groups."[13] Thus, the mix of international terrorist groups may be changing in favor of those inclined to use greater levels of violence and more unconventional modes of attack. The majority of this chapter focuses on debates over appropriate responses to this form of terrorism.

In addition to organizations that fuse fundamentalist religious doctrine with political objectives, there are also groups such as Aum Shinrikyo (the "Supreme Truth"), the bizarre Japanese doomsday cult that conducted a Sarin nerve gas attack on the Tokyo subway in March 1995, killing twelve and sending almost 5,000 people to the hospital. Before this attack, Aum Shinrikyo had also released botulinum toxin and anthrax from building tops and trucks in Japanese cities. Fortunately, however, these biological attacks failed (and since many of the cult's members were well-trained scientists, this says something about the difficulty of carrying out biological attacks). These attacks were intended to spark what the cult's leader predicted would be an apocalypse and nuclear war that would usher in heaven on earth. The cult's members believed they would somehow escape destruction.[14]

CHAPTER 12 *International Terrorism* 297

These organizations may prove particularly dangerous because they possess few, if any, internal constraints on their use of violence. Most terrorist organizations use violence in pursuit of an identifiable end or objective, and as a result there usually comes a point where the level of violence would simply be too much, where it works against the organization's objectives. For doomsday cults, violence may effectively become an end in itself and there might never be such a thing as too much. Luckily, there are not many cults with Aum Shinrikyo's financial resources and technological capabilities.

The recognition of the diversity of terrorist groups simultaneously complicates and simplifies the problem. It complicates things because it means that generalizations about terrorism or terrorist groups are difficult to come by. As Walter Laqueur tells us, "The problem of terrorism is complicated. What can be said without fear of contradiction about a terrorist group in one country is by no means true for other groups at other times in other countries."[15] There is unlikely to be a single explanation that accounts for the IRA, Al-Qaeda, and Aum Shinrikyo. Although this fact makes any grandiose theories about terrorism problematic, the diversity of terrorism might be good news in terms of policy responses because it allows us to cut the problem up into more manageable pieces. The so-called "war on terrorism" can then be transformed into a war on *terrorisms,* particularly those that pose the greatest threat. The goal of eliminating all terrorism might be morally laudable, but it also is so expansive as to be practically daunting, if not impossible; dealing with just a part of the problem is likely to be difficult enough.

Frameworks for understanding How does terrorism fit into the study of international relations? What do different perspectives on international politics have to offer us for understanding and dealing with the problem of terrorism? The prevailing wisdom is that international relations theories do not really tell us very much. John Mearsheimer, when asked what realism contributes to our understanding of terrorism, answers, "Not a whole heck of a lot. Realism, as I said before, is really about relations among states, especially among the great powers . . . al-Qaeda is not a state, it's a non-state actor, which is sometimes called a transnational actor . . . [as a result] realism does not have much to say about the *causes* of terrorism." But merely because terrorist organizations are nonstate actors, it does not follow that theories of international relations offer nothing in terms of thinking about the problem of international terrorism. Terrorist organizations must still operate within states, their targets are often states, their objectives usually involve changing state policies, and their activities take place within the same international system in which states operate. Though international relations focuses on the behavior of states, everyone has always been aware that nonstate actors can affect international politics. It was, for example, the assassination of the Austro-Hungarian archduke in July 1914 by a member of a radical Serbian nationalist (terrorist) group that set in motion the chain of events leading to the outbreak of World War I. Thus, while he concedes the limited relevance of realism for explaining the causes of terrorism, Mearsheimer points out that "terrorism is a phenomenon that will play itself out in the context of the international system. So it will be played out in the state arena, and, therefore, all of the realist logic about state behavior will have a significant effect on how the war on terrorism is fought."[16]

We also need to remember that most theories of international relations have their intellectual roots in more foundational social and political theories or philosophies.

Even though realism focuses on conflicts among states, it is informed by a deeper vision of the nature and causes of social conflict. International conflict is simply a specific manifestation or form of social conflict. Because terrorism is a form of social conflict, the beliefs that shape their basic worldview will also influence how realists approach the problem of terrorism. The same can be said of liberals, feminists, and Marxists. Like realism, none of these perspectives offers a well-developed theory of the causes of terrorism: there is no distinctive feminist or liberal explanation for terrorism. Nonetheless, when people from these different perspectives think about the problem of terrorism, their underlying beliefs and assumptions provide the intellectual foundation for their analysis. Mearsheimer expected "realist logic [to] have a significant effect on how the war on terrorism is fought." This statement suggests that those who adhere to alternative (e.g., liberal, feminist, and Marxist) logics will have very different ideas about how to fight the "war on terrorism."

Though it might be a slight simplification to reduce the debate over responses to contemporary terrorism to just two alternatives, Daniele Archibugi and Iris Young certainly capture two of the dominant orientations, drawing a distinction between what they label the **statist** versus the **cosmopolitan interpretation** or **response:** "The attacks on the World Trade Center and the Pentagon in September 2001 can appear within two different frames of interpretation. The first [the statist perspective] sees them as attacks on the United States as a state and its people. The second [the cosmopolitan perspective] views them as crimes against humanity. The difference in interpretation is not merely technical, but political, and each implies different strategies of reaction."[17]

In highlighting the relationship between "frames of interpretation" and "strategies of reaction," Archibugi and Young stress a point that has been made throughout this book: underlying beliefs, assumptions, and worldviews shape people's analyses of particular issues in ways that predispose them to favor certain policy responses and oppose others. This is consistent with Mearsheimer's observation that realist "logics" will influence how the war on terrorism is fought. But in dealing with the problem of international terrorism, what exactly are the different strategies of reaction, and how do they reflect alternative logics or frames of interpretation? Archibugi and Young's distinction between statist and cosmopolitan responses is as good a place to start as any.

statist interpretation or response Views terrorist attacks as acts of war and assumes that the most effective strategy for combating terrorism requires putting pressure on those states that actively support or passively tolerate terrorist organizations.

cosmopolitan interpretation or response Conceptualizes terrorist attacks as criminal acts requiring an international, multilateral response within the context of international law and organizations. As a long-term strategy, it involves addressing the root causes of terrorism, which are usually identified as poverty, inequality, and discontent.

THE COSMOPOLITAN RESPONSE

One of the first questions to emerge in the wake of September 11 was how the attacks should be viewed. The initial response, quickly embraced by the Bush administration, was to characterize them as acts of war. Even those willing to accept the terminology of war, however, concede that it is somewhat problematic. As Nicholas Lehman explains, "Traditional wars are fought by military means and have definite endings. . . . [but] terror . . . will never sit at a desk and sign an unconditional surrender."[18] If this was a war, it was not a war like World War II because "war" in this sense usually describes armed conflict between/among states. Whatever Al-Qaeda is, it is not a state. Though clearly not a traditional war, this is also not a purely metaphorical war such as the "war" on poverty or cancer. Al-Qaeda and other groups are organizations capable of and willing to use deadly force against the United States and others.

Terrorist groups may not be states, but they are capable of inflicting damage like states at war.

Regardless of the merits, the rhetoric of war has stuck, and there are those who remain critical and prefer to approach the problem of terrorism from a different perspective. The criticism does not arise from the failure of this war to meet the definition found in dictionaries but rather from a concern that the language and terminology of war brings with it policies that might not be appropriate, particularly the reliance on military force. But if it is not useful to view the attacks of September 11 as acts of war, how should they be seen? What is the alternative? Archibugi and Young propose that "the events [of September 11] be conceptualized as crimes, not as acts of war." In the words of someone who shares this sentiment, "we need to hold those behind the terrible atrocities in New York and Washington. But we need a law enforcement model, not a military model." A parallel is drawn to the 1990 bombing of the Murrah Federal Building in Oklahoma City. The U.S. government did not declare itself at war with Timothy McVeigh or the domestic organizations he associated with. Though widely described as an act of terrorism, it was viewed as a criminal act, not an act of war. Conceptualizing the September 11 attacks as crimes against humanity (and not merely against the United States) is the starting point for a cosmopolitan response, which has two essential elements.

The first task relates to the culprits and organizations responsible for the September 11 attacks. Consistent with criminal or law enforcement models, the United States and the international community as a whole should have sought "the establishment of an international tribunal with the authority to seek out, extradite, or arrest and try those responsible for the September 11 attack and those who commit or are conspiring to commit future attacks."[19] In the same vein, Samina Ahmed urged the United States to "refrain from any unilateral and precipitous military action. It must create a unified international coalition, with strong Islamic representation, to bring Bin Laden and other terrorists within the Taliban-controlled territory of Afghanistan to justice."[20] The proposed tribunal would be similar to the one dealing with those accused of human rights violation during the war in the former Yugoslavia. From this perspective, Al-Qaeda and similar groups would be classified as international criminal organizations, and the full range of international law enforcement bodies (e.g., Interpol) would be mobilized to put it out of business. Though most who favor this strategy would admit that international legal and law enforcement institutions are not as strong and well developed as domestic ones, they are seen as strong enough, and the threat of international terrorism also provides an opportunity to strengthen these institutions. Perhaps, as the old cliché goes, necessity is the mother of invention. Furthermore, on a purely practical level there is no alternative to increased international cooperation to combat transnational terrorism.

International legal responses directed at people and organizations involved in specific terrorist acts, however, is something of a band-aid approach because it deals with the problem of terrorism only after harm has already been done (or is imminent). As a result, there is a second, and in the long run more important, element of a cosmopolitan strategy directed at the deeper causes of terrorism, the so-called *root causes*. According to Andrew Johnston, "You can write off the terrorist attacks of Sept[ember] 11 as the crazed act of a fanatical gang hell-bent on causing mayhem at any cost. Or you can try to understand the attack's root causes by taking a closer look at the world whose fragile ecology of power they upset."[21] The implication, of course, is that the root causes need to be identified in the hope that they can be eliminated or, at the very least, ameliorated.

The general proposition that we should eliminate the root causes of terrorism appears so commonsensical that it is hard to imagine any disagreement. The problem is that doing so requires that we identify what the root causes are. Given the diverse nature of contemporary terrorism, it is not surprising that the list of potential root causes is quite long, some applying to terrorism in general and others specifically to terrorism motivated by Islamic fundamentalism. With regard to the latter, many cite a long history of Western, especially U.S., support for repressive and authoritarian regimes in the Arab world, often placing this pattern in the context of a long history of Western and Christian hostility to Islam reaching all the way back to the Crusades. Israeli treatment of the Palestinians, U.S. support for Israel, and the stationing of U.S. troops in Saudi Arabia are presented as the most recent manifestations of this broader historical pattern. This combination of historical and contemporary events helps explain a widespread sense of frustration throughout much of the Islamic world as well as the focusing of these sentiments on the United States.

At a more general level, terrorism is commonly portrayed as a response to poverty and global economic inequality. This is why Jared Diamond urges that "we must feed the hands that could bite us" in the wake of September 11. "When people cannot solve their own problems," Diamond argues, "they strike out irrationally, seeking foreign scapegoats, or collapsing into civil war over limited resources. By bettering conditions overseas, we can reduce chronic future threats to ourselves." To cope with these underlying causes, he proposes that the United States "single out three strategies—providing basic health care, supporting family planning and addressing such widespread environmental problems as deforestation."[22] Similarly, Robert Hinde is convinced that "overpopulation, poverty and political dislocation are no doubt important background factors in the genesis of terrorism." Reiterating Thomas Homer-Dixon's prediction, he warns that "as disparities of wealth and opportunity on our planet widen, the problem is certain to get worse."[23] No less a figure than James Wolfenson, president of the World Bank, essentially equates the war on terrorism with a war on poverty, arguing that "the war [on terrorism] will not be won until we have come to grips with the problem of poverty and sources of discontent." Even though "this war is viewed in terms of the face of Bin Laden . . . [and] the terrorism of Al Qaeda . . . these are just symptoms." The underlying cause "is the discontent seething in Islam and, more generally, in the world of the poor. Winning the war means tackling the roots of protest."[24]

Archibugi and Young also focus on poverty. After outlining the steps necessary to strengthen international legal institutions, they settle on just one recommendation as the core of their cosmopolitan strategy: "narrow global inequalities." Despite noting that "there are many poor places that appear not to nurture people who join international terrorist organizations," they believe "there is no doubt that such indifference amid affluence fosters resentment in many corners of the world and endangers peace and prosperity for many outside the shanty towns."[25] In this view, the moral imperative for improving the lot of the world's poor (which presumably would exist regardless of any connection between poverty and terrorism) proves consistent with the interests of the United States as a form of "enlightened self-interest." In the final analysis, the failure to address the problem of global poverty will come back to haunt the wealthy and powerful: "No justice, no peace."[26]

There is, however, more to justice than the alleviation of poverty. In a world where political and economic forces are inevitably intertwined, the economic causes of terrorism are not easily divorced from political institutions and dynamics. "Ultimately," we are told, "the creation of a more peaceful and just world order implies changes in *political, economic and social* institutions [emphasis added]."[27] It is not merely poverty that fuels terrorism, but a more profound sense of exclusion and domination at the domestic and international levels. Domestically, the absence of democracy and lack of respect for human rights contribute to a sense of resentment while foreclosing nonviolent means of dissent. Though he concedes there may be some need to work with nondemocractic regimes to combat the most immediate terrorist threats (a concession many from the cosmopolitan perspective are unwilling to make), Tony Karon argues that "in the long term, eliminating the root cause of terror will involve, if not complete democracy, at least allowing the citizens of Middle Eastern countries some voice [in] their governance."[28] Internationally, the dominance of a small handful of nations (primarily the United States) possessing tremendous economic, political, and military power only exacerbates the problem because "the willingness of the United States to wield [its power] asymmetrically and with only the thinnest veneer of multilateralism elicits hostile reactions from all over the world."[29] Again, the only long-term strategy to deal with the root causes of terrorism is a wholesale reform of those international and domestic institutions that perpetuate the inequities and injustices that sustain terrorist organizations by providing fertile breeding grounds of anger and discontent. Attempts to combat terrorism with the sort of forceful response entailed by the statist model will only make the problem worse. As Betty Williams, a Nobel Peace Prize winner who founded the World Centers of Compassion for Children, maintains, "From my long experience with terror and violence in Northern Ireland, I know that a war on terrorism and violence cannot bring anything, but breed and increase terror and violence."[30]

The intellectual roots of a cosmopolitan strategy What are the underlying assumptions of a cosmopolitan strategy? To what extent is it shaped by different theoretical perspectives on international politics? What logic does it embody? Recall that the cosmopolitan and statist strategies were presented as competing approaches to terrorism. The statist strategy, about which we will have more to say shortly, obviously refers to an approach informed by realism. Consequently, the cosmopolitan strategy finds its intellectual roots among the alternatives to realism. The suggestion that a law enforcement model, relying on international law and organizations, forms the basis of a response to the attacks of September 11 provides an obvious indication of strategy's underlying assumptions. Those who are skeptical of the effectiveness of the international legal system, after all, are unlikely to place it at the center of the solution to the problem of international terrorism. Liberals (and constructivists) have historically been more inclined to see international law and organizations as effective embodiments of shared values and interests (see chapter 7). Thus, it makes sense to view this component of a cosmopolitan strategy as being derived from an essentially liberal logic of international politics.

The proposal that we deal with terrorism by addressing its root causes is a little ambiguous in terms of its intellectual foundations, reflecting elements of liberalism, Marxism, and feminism. In particular, the belief that we can eliminate terrorism by tackling the problem of poverty and inequality appeals to all three of these perspectives. On a general level, this is consistent with the liberal view of social conflict as arising from faulty but reformable social, political, and economic conditions and institutions. There is also a (usually unarticulated) assumption that the root causes of terrorism can be eliminated once they have been identified. The possibility that we might identify the root causes only to conclude that there is little we can do about them is rarely seriously entertained. The guiding vision is that greater material prosperity, respect for human rights, and democratic government (all liberal values) will provide the antidote to terrorism. If the denial of justice leads to violence, then the provision of justice will lead to its elimination. The corollary of Archibugi and Young's "No justice, no peace" must be "If justice, then peace."

The cosmopolitan approach resonates with other perspectives as well. Finding the roots of terrorism in poverty and economic inequality is consistent with the Marxist view that social conflict is almost always rooted in economic conflict. This is particularly the case if the international inequalities are placed within a broader analysis or critique of capitalism and globalization. Even when conflicts do not appear to be economic on their face, Marxists assume that there is usually a critical economic foundation. Focusing on the Marxist analysis of civil violence more generally, James Rule explains that we should "expect, for every mobilization on behalf of religious or other nonmaterial ends, to find some antecedent frustration to the material interests of groups among whom the mobilization occurs."[31]

Feminists have also expressed sympathy for a cosmopolitan approach and deep reservations about a statist response stressing military force. Not surprisingly, however, feminists are anxious to expand the "poverty as the root cause of terrorism" thesis to include all institutions and patterns of domination, including the oppression of woman. It is, they point out, no coincidence that regimes with some of the worst records when it comes to the rights of women (e.g., the Taliban in Afghanistan) are associated with support for terrorist violence. Amy Caiazza draws the connection: "Even if we dismiss the claim that women's rights are central to human rights, there are centuries of evidence that physical, political and economic violence against women is a harbinger of other forms of violence." Thus, "we should pay particularly close attention to those who are effective opponents of violence against women. By doing so, we would be more likely to address the root causes of terrorism and violence at home and around the world."[32] J. Ann Tickner (taking the connection between poverty and terrorism for granted) draws our attention to "the poor treatment of women as one of the major reasons for the region's [the Middle East] lack of development."[33] And since poverty and the lack of development are a root cause of terrorism, it follows that the poor treatment of women is one of the major reasons for terrorism. Though feminists disagreed about the use of military force against the Taliban regime in Afghanistan, it is fair to say that feminists generally favor a cosmopolitan strategy over the statist approach.[34]

THE STATIST RESPONSE

The cosmopolitan approach frames terrorist attacks such as those of September 11 as criminal acts, fearing that portraying them as acts of war will lead to unilateral and counterproductive military responses that leave the "root" causes of terrorism undisturbed. There is no question that terrorist acts usually violate domestic and international law, making them criminal acts by definition. "The fundamental problem," according to Steven Pomerantz, "is that international terrorism is not *only* a crime. It is also, for all intents and purposes, an act of war, and the United States needs to treat it as such."[35] Although admitting that "my view may [be] in the minority" among his fellow law professors, Anthony D'Amato's assessment is similar to Pomerantz's: "Sept[ember] 11th occasioned an attack on the United States itself by people who seem to be engaged in an outright war against us. . . . It may be a new concept of 'war,' but it is one that builds upon, and extends, the classic concept."[36] There is agreement that terrorist attacks are not acts of war in the sense that we normally think of war, but they are also not "crimes" in the way we normally think of crime, either. Neither label is without its problems. Those who prefer to view terrorist attacks as acts of war do not shy away from the implications of doing so. Pomerantz recognizes that this "means, for starters, a significantly more aggressive diplomatic posture."[37] In words that are sure to make Archibugi and Young cringe, Charles Krauthammer argues that "half-measures are for wars of choice, wars like Vietnam. In wars of choice, losing is an option. You lose and you still survive as a nation." The war on terrorism, however, is different: "Losing is not an option. Losing is fatal. This is no time for restraint and other niceties. This is a time for righteous might."[38]

Though it is important to note the critical differences between cosmopolitan and statist strategies, they should not be presented as caricatured alternatives that share no common ground. Advocates of a statist approach would certainly not object to seeing Osama Bin Laden in the docket before a tribunal, and those favoring a cosmopolitan strategy might admit that in certain instances, however rare, a state may have to use military force to deal with specific terrorist threats. The debate revolves around points of emphasis and general predispositions: Should attacks such as those of September 11 be viewed *primarily* as crimes against humanity or as acts of war? Should international legal and organizational avenues be pursued as *primary* or merely *supplementary* components of an antiterrorism strategy?

A statist strategy would deemphasize the legal and international organizational elements of an antiterrorism policy. Though international organizations and law may occasionally be useful (e.g., in tracking and reducing the flow of financial resources to terrorist organizations), it would be a mistake to view them as substitutes for state action. It is on this point that the realist basis of a statist strategy starts to reveal itself: statist criticisms of a law enforcement model echo all the familiar realist arguments about the limits of international law and organizations. Archibugi and Young correctly note that states often treat terrorist acts as criminal acts, but all of their examples (e.g., the attack in Oklahoma City) are domestic in nature. Pomerantz is in full agreement that "when it comes to terrorism at home, law enforcement and the criminal justice system—our only available options—have been effective." But the suggestion that a similar approach be applied at the international level ignores the fundamental differences between international and domestic society. At the national level, law enforcement agencies and legal institutions are sufficiently developed and powerful to deal with such problems. At the international level, the parallel agencies and institutions have not advanced beyond the most rudimentary stage. As we discussed in the chapter on international law, the basic elements of an effective international legal system are simply not present.

There are good reasons to doubt the effectiveness of international organizations, where debate often takes precedence over action. In the wake of the 1972 Palestine Liberation Organization (PLO) massacre of Israeli athletes at the summer Olympic Games in Munich, Germany, the United Nations attempted to fashion a coordinated set of policies dealing with terrorism at an international level. The resulting debate and failure to craft and implement effective international measures demonstrated why the international community accomplished so little before September 11. If there is to be an international effort to combat terrorism, there needs to be some agreement on what it is and that it is bad. After protracted discussion, the United Nations could not even get past the point of defining terrorism. Particularly problematic were the actions of national liberation movements. Activities that the United States considered terrorism were often viewed by many in the developing world as legitimate responses to oppression and domination, the only tool available to the weak in the face of power. Condemnations of terrorism were commonplace, but the apparent consensus disappeared when the United Nations tried to move beyond vague generalities. "The resultant definitional paralysis," Hoffman explains, "throttled UN efforts to make substantive progress on international cooperation against terrorism."[39]

Despite these problems, there was some modest progress on a few fronts. During the 1960s and early 1970s, several treaties tried to deal with hijacking and the safety of commercial aviation. The PLO's taking of Israeli hostages at the 1972 Olympics eventually led to adoption of the International Convention Against the Taking of Hostages (1979), though even this small achievement was marred by the fact that only ninety-seven nations have ratified the agreement. And, as with most international agreements, states are free to withdraw (with one year's notice in this case).[40] International police agencies such as Interpol try to keep track of known terrorists, but much intelligence remains in the hands of national law enforcement bodies that may or may not share it with others. The general problem here should be familiar by now: it is difficult to craft an effective international response in a world of sovereign states. These efforts obviously did nothing to prevent the September 11 attacks, and those who prefer a statist strategy see little reason to think things have changed.

"It's the Clash, Not the Cash"[41] For statists, the desire to combat terrorism by eliminating its "root causes" is a deceptively attractive solution. The first problem is that we really have no idea what the root causes are. The common hypothesis that poverty and inequality lead to terrorism is usually asserted as matter of faith without any careful or compelling evidence. Even Archibugi and Young, who advocate narrowing of global economic inequalities, concede that the link between poverty and terrorism is not straightforward. Most poor societies are not sources of terrorism, and affluent societies are not immune. If we look at the terrorists themselves, we find little support for the poverty-causes-terrorism thesis. Economists Alan Krueger and Jitka Maleckova, in one of the few systematic studies of this issue, examined the backgrounds of 126 members of the militant wing of Hezbollah, a terrorist organization headquartered in Lebanon. They found that "compared to the general population from the same age group and region, the Hezbollah militants were actually slightly less likely to come from impoverished households, and were more likely to have attended secondary school."[42] The lack of connection between poverty and terrorism is striking with regard to the attacks of September 11. "Poverty did not breed the terrorists of September 11," Helle Dale tells us, "the politics of radical Islam did." This is evidenced by the fact that "the 19 hijackers were not poor or uneducated, they were motivated by religious fanaticism and apparently some bizarre expectations of their rewards in heaven." And the people who planned the attack did not lack for privilege: "Is Osama Bin Laden a poor man? Certainly not. He's the son of a Saudi family wealthier than most Americans will ever dream of becoming.[43] If those who hijacked the planes and crashed them into their targets are at all representative, Sean Wilentz notes wryly, we would be more justified concluding that "money, education and privilege" are the root causes of terrorism.[44] There may, of course, still be lots of good reasons to work for the reduction of poverty in the world, but its causal role in creating and sustaining terrorism is, at best, much more complicated than often suggested.

But even if poverty and inequality were the root causes of terrorism, we would face a further problem. Like virtually every other potential root cause, global poverty is not something that is likely to disappear in the near future; regardless of what we do, global poverty will not be eradicated in the next ten or twenty years. The threat of terrorism is in the present, whereas the elimination of global poverty is, being optimistic, sometime in the distant future. This fact raises the difficult question of what we do about terrorism between now and the day when justice and equality are finally realized. Too often, statists fear, the demand that we attack the root causes of terrorism is a self-righteous excuse or cover designed to allow people to avoid meaningful actions and hard choices.

This is not to imply that statists refrain from thinking about the causes of terrorism. Any attempt to respond to terrorism rests on some notion of what drives it, even if those forces are not readily amenable to alteration. Rather than seeing international terrorism as a response to poverty and economic deprivation, proponents of a statist response are more likely to see terrorism as a manifestation of fundamental conflicts of interests and values. Some even make explicit reference to Samuel Huntington's controversial prediction that the post–Cold War world would be marked by a **clash of civilizations** as opposed to nations. Though the world remains divided into distinct states, the fault lines of conflict will be between civilizations that embrace "different views on the relations between God and man . . . as well as different views of the relative importance of rights and responsibilities, liberty and authority, equality and hierarchy."[45] Huntington identified seven major civilizations—"Western, Confucian, Japanese, Islamic, Hindu, Slavic-Orthodox, Latin American and possible African." From this perspective, the attacks of September 11 can be seen as an extreme manifestation of this emerging civilizational conflict. "Read in the wake of September 11," Stanley Kurtz muses, "it is more clear than ever that Huntington's book is filled with . . . useful generalizations. . . . in large measure the world is already living out the truth of Huntington's thesis."[46] In a similar vein, Michael Howard takes direct issue with the poverty thesis: "This is not a problem of poverty as against wealth, and I am afraid that it is symptomatic of our Western materialism to suppose that it is. It is a far more profound and intractable confrontation between a theistic, land-based and tradition culture, in places little different from the Europe of the Middle Ages, and the secular values of the Enlightenment."[47] If a terrorist organization is engaged in an effort to undermine and perhaps destroy secular, liberal civilization, then no concession or change of policy will reduce the threat.

Description of the threat as "intractable" in this context is revealing. Statists are not only skeptical that we can put our finger on what the root causes of terrorism are,

clash of civilizations
The thesis, popularized by Samuel Huntington, that civilizational conflicts based on competing social and political values are replacing traditional national conflicts as the defining feature of contemporary international politics.

Representatives of Afghanistan's Taliban regime reject United States demands to hand over Osama Bin Laden and others connected to the September 11th attacks. The Taliban would become the first victim of the statist strategy of "regime change" in the war on terrorism.
SOURCE: © AFP/CORBIS

they are also less sanguine about our ability to eliminate those root causes once we find them. There tends to be a lot more talk of intractable conflict in a statist perspective, and given its realist foundations, this should come as no surprise. When someone describes conflicts as "intractable," there is a good chance we are dealing with a realist. This perspective contrasts with the liberal inclination to view social conflict as an outgrowth of social, economic, and political conditions that can be altered in a manner that will eliminate the conflict. The notion that we should (or even can) eradicate inequality and injustice in order to end the threat of terrorism strikes statists and realists as a utopian evasion. Thus, on one level this debate is simply a contemporary manifestation of the enduring clash between liberal optimism and realist (conservative) pessimism on questions of social conflict.

Even though the Bush administration's policies after the September 11 attacks followed the logic of a statist response, it quickly tried to discourage attempts to frame events in terms of a clash of civilizations. Even though Secretary of State Colin Powell portrayed the attacks as an assault on "civilization" (that is, civilization in general, not any particular civilization), he insisted there was "no connection or relationship to any faith."[48] Speaking to the UN Security Council two months after the attacks, Powell was even more explicit: "This was not about a clash of civilizations or religions; it was an attack on civilization and religion themselves."[49] Publicly at least the administration interpreted the attacks as the work of an evil person and organization perverting the values and ideas of Islam. Skeptics were quick to wonder whether these denials were politically motivated with an eye to not alienating moderate Arab governments whose cooperation might be needed in the short run.[50]

States still matter One may lament the lack of viable alternatives to states' acting to defend themselves against threats to their security and citizens, but for statists this is the unavoidable reality we need to come to terms with. The need or hope for alternatives does not automatically bring them into being. As a result, responses to terrorism need to be crafted within the limitations of the existing state system. Fortunately, there is much that states can do. Certainly nonstate adversaries pose challenges that more traditional state-to-state conflicts do not, but we should not leap to the conclusion that states are powerless to act against terrorist organizations merely because they are not states. Jack Spencer reminds us that terrorist "groups could never pull off these sophisticated operations if there were no place where they could support their networks." Terrorist groups may not be states, but terrorists, terrorist training facilities, and terrorist financial resources are all located within the borders of states. Consequently, the war on terrorism is "essentially . . . [a] war with states that support terrorism."[51] Several years before the September 11 attacks, Steve Pomerantz suggested the same course of action: "If a state is the victim of private actors such as terrorists, it [can] try to eliminate these groups by depriving them of sanctuaries and punishing states that harbor them. The national interest of the attacked state will therefore require either armed interventions against governments supporting terrorism or a course of prudence and discreet pressure on other governments."[52]

As the Bush administration tried to give meaning to the "war on terrorism," Vice President Dick Cheney provided the rationale for a statist response: "To the extent that we define our task broadly . . . including those who support terrorism, then we get at states. And it's easier to find them than it is to find bin Laden."[53] This same sentiment informed President Bush's warning that the United States would "make no distinction between the terrorists who committed these acts and those who harbor them." From the statist perspective, the war on terrorism is, even if indirectly, still a conflict among states. And one deals with this threat according to the same logic that guides responses to traditional threats—by "exacting a price for terrorism so as to make it less likely that terrorist will want to strike again." These costs need to be imposed not only on the terrorists themselves but also on states that provide active support or passively permit them to operate. In President Bush's words, "we have to force countries to choose."[54] The option of last resort would be "regime change": "If you replace the states that do support terrorism with those that don't, you deny terrorists the kind of support that allows them to mount big operations against us."[55]

This is the crux of the statist response: getting at terrorist organizations by using the traditional tools of statecraft against those states within whose borders they operate. Will this allow us to eliminate terrorism? Certainly not. It is unrealistic to assume that we can ever totally eradicate terrorism. The focus needs to be on those organizations that pose the most immediate threat. Although "we can never be immune from terrorist violence," Pomerantz concedes, "we can . . . raise the price for those who attack us and the nations that sponsor and support them. In doing so, we can expect to make the cost high enough to significantly reduce the number of international terrorist incidents directed against the United States." This statement summarizes the statist strategy nicely, and it is easy to see how its underlying logic is quintessentially realist. First, there is the admission that we will never eliminate all terrorism and to hope otherwise is a fantasy, which reflects a realist impatience with sweeping declarations of ridding the world of terrorism. Second, we need to deal with terrorist organizations as threats to the national interest that must be either defeated or deterred. Third, states continue to be the critical players on the global level, even when it comes to controlling the actions of nonstate actors such as terrorist organizations.

CONCLUSION

Neither terrorism nor the debate over appropriate responses is going away anytime soon. In fact, there are important elements of the debate that this chapter has not even touched on, such as whether the war on terrorism requires restrictions on domestic civil liberties. If anything, we can probably expect terrorism to worsen before it gets better because "the number of intensely aggrieved groups will almost certainly grow in the coming decades of rapid technological, and hence social, change."[56] And it is this very technological change and the easy dissemination of knowledge that gives individuals and groups the ability to cause harm and destruction on a scale previously unimaginable. Technological and social change provides both motives and means.

Policy debates will remain intense for at least two important reasons. First, they reflect competing visions of international society and, at an even more fundamental level, differences about the nature and dynamics of social conflict. Second, and this point cannot be stressed too heavily, "the menu for policy options in the war on terrorism is loaded with short-term/long-term tradeoffs."[57] Examples of these tradeoffs abound. Democracy in the Middle East may be an essential part of long-term strategy to reduce terrorism, but in the short run we might have to deal with some nondemocratic regimes to diffuse the most immediate threats. But if the United States is seen as supporting nondemocratic regimes, this could increase hostility and the risk of future terrorist attacks in the long run. Similarly, the use of military force may be needed to destroy or diminish the capabilities of a terrorist group or its state sponsor, but if this reinforces certain negative images of the United States, long-term threats may increase. Most people are probably attracted to elements of both the cosmopolitan and statist strategies because they each embody desirable short- and long-term objectives that may run counter to each other. Policy debates are always the hardest to resolve when they require tradeoffs among equally valued and beneficial objectives. But no useful purpose is served by failing to recognize the need to make tradeoffs. All good things do not always come together.

POINTS OF VIEW
How Should the War on Terrorism Be Fought?

Sometimes it is people's immediate reactions to events, expressed before they have time to think too much, that provide the best insight into their thinking. In these situations, comments are likely to be almost reflexive manifestations of underlying beliefs and predispositions. The following essays by Robert Kagan and Sienho Yee provide this sort of immediate response in the wake of September 11, 2001. Written within days (and just hours, in Kagan's case) of those dramatic attacks, these were early examples of the competing orientations that would define debates over the appropriate response to the attacks. And although Archibugi and Young did not make direct references to either Kagan or Lee, it is easy to see how their positions fit nicely into the statist versus cosmopolitan frameworks they identified. How and to what extent do these essays reflect the themes and assumptions of the statist and cosmopolitan strategies? Whose position do you find most persuasive and why? How would Kagan and Lee respond to each other's arguments? Do we need to view these positions as alternatives, or is it possible to create a single coherent strategy that incorporates the strong points of each position?

We Must Fight This War

Robert Kagan
September 12, 2001

Sept. 11, 2001—the date that will live in infamy, the day the post–Cold War era ended, the day the world for Americans changed utterly. In the coming days, as rescuers pick through the rubble in New York, in Washington, in Pittsburgh and who knows where else across the besieged United States, as the bodies of thousands of dead Americans are uncovered and as the rest of us weep over the destruction of innocent human life, our friends and loved ones, we may begin to hear analyses as to why this "tragedy" has befallen us. There will no doubt be questions raised, sins of omission and commission in the Middle East alluded to. Even yesterday, as the flames still burned, the BBC opined that the attacks came because the United States had failed to get a "grip" on the Middle East. Nothing in that is strange or odd. After Pearl Harbor, almost exactly 60 years ago, there were those who argued, with perhaps even more persuasiveness, that then, too, the United States had somehow invited the Japanese attack. After all, had we not embargoed Japan's vital oil supply?

One can only hope that America can respond to yesterday's monstrous attack on American soil—an attack far more awful than Pearl Harbor—with the same moral clarity and courage as our predecessors did. Not by asking what we have done to bring on the wrath of inhuman murderers. Not by figuring out ways to reason with, or try to appease those who have spilled our blood. Not by engaging in an extended legal effort to arraign, try and convict killers, as if they were criminals and not warriors. But by doing the only thing we now can do: Go to war with those who have launched this awful war against us. Over the past few years there has been a nostalgic celebration of "The Greatest Generation"—the generation that fought for America and for humanity in the Second World War. There's no need for nostalgia now. That challenge is before us again. The question today is whether this generation of Americans is made of the same stuff.

Please let us make no mistake this time: We are at war now. We have suffered the first, devastating strike. Certainly, it is not the last. The only question is whether we will now take this war seriously, as seriously as any war we have ever fought, whether we will conduct it with the intensity and perseverance it requires. Let's not be daunted by the mysterious and partially hidden identity of our attackers. It will soon become obvious that only a few terrorist organizations are capable of carrying out such a massive and coordinated strike. We should pour the resources necessary into a global effort to hunt them down and capture or kill them. It will become apparent that those organizations could not have operated without the assistance of some governments, governments with a long record of hostility to the United States and an equally long record of support for terrorism. We should now immediately begin building up our conventional military forces to prepare for what will inevitably and rapidly escalate into confrontation and quite possibly war with one or more of those powers. Congress, in fact, should immediately declare war. It does not have to name a country. It can declare war against those who have carried out yesterday's attack and against any nations that may have lent their support. A declaration of war would not be pure symbolism. It would be a sign of will and determination to see this conflict through to a satisfactory conclusion no matter how long it takes or how difficult the challenge.

Fortunately, with the Cold War over, there are no immediate threats around the world to prevent us from concentrating our energies and resources on fighting this war on international terrorism as we have never fought it before.

Pay Tribute to Reason and Think Long-term: Reflections on the 9-11 Tragedy

Sienho Yee

As the entire nation is preparing for some immediate, perhaps military, responses to the 9-11 Tragedy, some reflections on the long-term results of any possible responses may be sobering and beneficial.

As we know well, conflicts are inevitably manifestations of disharmony in society, and so it behooves us to consider what sorts of disharmony may have led to this tragedy and what antidotes would be most effective.

It is no secret that there exist in the world certain resentments and hostility against the United States. Whether such sentiments are justifiable or whether they are right or wrong is unimportant; what matters is whether such sentiments did in fact cause or contribute to the 9-11 Tragedy. It is obviously beyond anyone's capability to answer this question; some of the suicide notes left behind by the attackers, when made public, may give us a hint. Here I shall assume that such sentiments had something to do with the 9-11 Tragedy and speculate as to what we can do about this.

Such resentments and hostility may have also built up because of the perceived injustice that the United States has allegedly inflicted upon the world, the perceived unfairness that the United States has allegedly perpetrated, the perceived disregard that the United States has allegedly paid to the rule of law in the world, and the perceived go-it-alone and high-handed attitude that the United States government and citizens have allegedly exhibited towards the world at large and towards some segment of the world in particular.

Without necessarily personally endorsing such perceptions, one might give as examples the following acts and conduct of the United States: refusing to pay its United Nations dues; pulling out of various international negotiations; walking out of the Racism Conference; its attitude toward the expansion of Israeli settlements in traditionally Palestinian territories; its role in the continuing sanctions on Iraq and the resulting misery of the Iraqi children and women; and its bombing of the Sudanese pharmaceutical plant without giving sufficient evidence for its alleged connection with bin Laden.

If such resentments and hostility toward the United States are the ultimate if not proximate cause for terrorism against the United States, immediate bombing retaliation may only satisfy the yearning for justice; it will not solve any problem. In fact, it will leave behind a long-term spiral of hatred and violence, against which anticipatory or preventive self-defense, whether lawful or not, will not be effective in modern life: the source of perpetrators can be unlimited and their ingenuity knows few bounds.

Under such circumstances, any effective response to the 9-11 Tragedy has to have three components: first, improve security measures to prevent future attacks; second, hunt down and punish the perpetrators; and three, project the image of a fair and rule of law friendly United States. Being an ivory-tower academic, I shall not speculate on how to improve security measures or hunt down the perpetrators. I shall here offer some thoughts on how the government can project the image of a fair and rule of law friendly United States in the immediate term as well as in the long term.

First of all, in attempting to punish the perpetrators, we must always give judicial process a chance. The magic power that an impartial judicial process has on building a rule of law society needs no emphasizing. . . . Such a course of action would show the world the United States is a fair and just nation and with tremendous strength. . . .

Secondly, the United States must lead the world to find a fair solution to the conflict between "Palestine" and Israel. The spiral of violence and hatred has been going on there for too long and the world seems to be inflicted with a sense of resignation. We must recognize that it is no longer a problem confined to the Israelis and the Palestinians. And I have a hunch, though I cannot prove it, that as long as this conflict lasts, there will be no end to terrorism in the world, despite the conspiracy of the world to keep silent on this score. The United States must act even-handedly in solving this conflict. . . .

The United States government may have to reconsider its perception of national interest, the content of its foreign policy, and the ways and means of conducting its foreign policy. Every measure should be taken to ensure the United States act fairly and humbly in the world and shake off its image of "speak loudly and carry a big stick." Without attempting to provide a full recipe for how to act fairly and humbly, one can think of the following: building coalition and rallying support from around the world (which the United States has done from time to time) for its policy and plans for action; participating in international efforts rather than walking out; applying the same standard to the world without asking for exceptions for itself or its own citizens; and generally paying respect to the rule of law in the world.

More specifically, one may say that it would help if the United States ratifies the Rome Statute of the International Criminal Court and reaccept the jurisdiction of the International Court of Justice under the optional clause. Submitting oneself to the judgment of judicial tribunals has enormous positive effect on the perception of fairness. Sending the dispute on bin Laden to the International Court of Justice for a decision on the Taliban's duty to surrender him would be a big step in convincing the world of the fairness of the wounded giant—the United States. Finally, increasing assistance to the poor countries to reduce poverty and to improve education can be a most effective weapon against terrorism.

Fourthly, every nation in the world has to learn a lesson from the Tragedy and might need to reconsider its recent re-moralization in international relations and international law. The shrill voices of moral superiority, pitting "us" against "them," the "liberal" against the "non-liberal," normally contribute to the general atmosphere of hatred and hostility. On the other hand, as Montesquieu long ago taught us, soft manners and morals help to elevate humanity. Faced with a grim reality, we should not sacrifice our lives on the altar of some abstract sense of righteousness. To me, life is supreme.

One cannot be sure whether we could ever stamp out terrorism. One can only hope that the measures proposed above will go some way in the right direction to preventing terrorism, in the long term.

SOURCE: *The Jurist,* accessed at: http://jurist.law.pitt.edu/forum/forumnew31.htm

CHAPTER SUMMARY

- Though definitions of terrorism are often controversial and politically charged, there is a consensus that terrorism has several essential components: (1) the use or threat of violence to create a climate of fear, (2) indiscriminate targeting of civilians (because the audience is the real "target"), and (3) a larger social or political objective. There is less agreement about whether terrorism should be defined to exclude states and include only nonstate actors as possible perpetrators.

- Even though terrorist acts and groups share some things in common, it is probably more useful to classify terrorist groups according to their motivations, goals, and objectives rather than to treat terrorism as a single, undifferentiated phenomenon. Strategies that might be effective in dealing with some organizations may prove useless for others with different objectives and *modi operandi*.

- In the aftermath of the September 11 attacks, debate naturally focused on possible responses to terrorism. Archibugi and Young argue that two basic alternatives shaped the public debate.

- The cosmopolitan response encompasses both short- and long-term elements. In the short term, the specific attacks need to treated as criminal acts necessitating an international legal response to capture and prosecute those responsible while using the full range of tools available to the international community to destroy the organization's ability to operate.

- The longer-term goal of a cosmopolitan strategy lies in addressing the underlying root causes of terrorism, which are normally identified as the poverty, inequality, and discontent that breed resentment and drive people to desperate acts.

- The suggestion that terrorism be approached from an international legal perspective and the desire to deal with the root causes of terrorism makes a cosmopolitan approach attractive to liberals as well as many feminists and Marxists.

- The statist response views terrorist attacks as acts of war and threats to national security. Although there may be useful legal and multilateral elements of an effective response, the emphasis must be on destroying the terrorist organization's ability to act by any means available. The focus of these efforts should be not only the terrorist organizations themselves but also the states that support or permit them to operate.

- Although the logic of tackling the root causes of terrorism is attractive, statists are skeptical of the commonly accepted idea that poverty leads to terrorism. At a minimum, the connection between poverty and terrorism is very complicated. Statists are more inclined to see terrorism, especially of the type perpetrated by Al-Qaeda, as motivated by a fundamental conflict of values and visions.

- This view of the underlying conflict and the inclination to view terrorism as a national security issue to be addressed within the framework of state relations resonates more with the realist perspective.

- Despite the fact that they are portrayed as alternative approaches, it might be useful to think about whether and how elements of these apparently opposing strategies might be melded into a single coherent strategy. The critical obstacle that must be overcome to achieve this fusion is that many of the short-term responses called for by a statist approach appear to work against many of the long-term goals of the cosmopolitan approach.

CRITICAL QUESTIONS

1. How would you define terrorism? According to your definition, could the United States' use of atomic bombs against Japan to end World War II be considered terrorism? Why or why not?

2. Do you think terrorism can ever be justified? Could terrorist acts by opposition groups in Germany designed to undermine the Nazi regime between 1933 and 1945 be justified? Why or why not?

3. Would you agree or disagree with the often-heard cliché, "One man's terrorist is another man's freedom fighter"?

4. Why might a terrorist group's goals and objectives matter in thinking about how it should be dealt with?

5. Though a crude "poverty leads to terrorism" hypothesis seems not to fit the evidence, many continue to feel that some connection must exist. How can we think about the relationship between poverty and terrorism in a more complicated and sophisticated fashion?

KEY TERMS

clash of civilizations 306
cosmopolitan interpretation or response 299
statist interpretation or response 299
terrorism 294

FURTHER READINGS

The literature on terrorism has grown considerably since the events of September 11, 2001, but it is still useful to consult some of the major works that appeared before these events. Alex Schmid's *Political Terrorism: A Reference Guide* (New Brunswick, NJ: Transaction Books, 1984) is still a standard reference. Walter Laqueur's *Terrorism* (Boston: Little, Brown, 1977) remains insightful. Bruce Hoffman's *Inside Terrorism* (New York: Columbia University Press, 1998) is particularly good on the history and evolution of terrorism. For exhaustive coverage of terrorism in the Middle East, see Richard Chasdi's twin volumes, *Serenade of Suffering: A Portrait of Middle East Terrorism, 1968–1993* (New York: Lexington Books, 1999) and *Tapestry of Terror: A Portrait of Middle East Terrorism, 1994–1999* (New York: Lexington Books, 2002). The classic exploration of the dilemmas terrorism poses for democratic states is Paul Wilkinson, *Terrorism and the Liberal State* (New York: Macmillan, 1977). It will come as no surprise that many works on terrorism have appeared since September 11, 2001. Bob Woodward's *Bush at War* (New York: Simon & Schuster, 2002) provides a good first look at the United States' response. A controversial reaction from the political left (which has been criticized by many normally considered on the left) is Noam Chomsky, *9/11* (Boston: Seven Stories Press, 2001). Other interesting attempts to come to terms with the broader dilemmas in responding to terrorism include Jean Bethke Elshtain, *Just War against Terror: The Burden of American Power in a Violent World* (New York: Basic Books, 2003), Paul Berman, *Terrorism and Liberalism* (New York: W. W. Norton, 2003), and Thomas Friedman, *Longitudes and Attitudes: Exploring the World after September 11* (New York: Farrar Straus Giroux, 2002). And a recent collection of essays dealing with a range of largely moral and ethical issues is James P. Sterba, ed., *Terrorism and International Justice* (Oxford: Oxford University Press, 2003). A collection of feminist perspectives is Susan Hawthorne and Bronwyn Winter, eds., *September 11, 2001: Feminist Perspectives* (Melbourne, Australia: Spinfex, 2002).

TERRORISM ON THE WEB

www.terrorismanswers.com/home
Website maintained by the Council on Foreign Relations. Deals with many aspects of 9/11 and terrorism more generally in a question-and-answer format.

www.terrorism.com
Website of the Terrorism Research Center, Inc. includes a wealth of information on terrorism and terrorist groups worldwide.

www.terrorismfiles.org
Contains recent news as well as information on the history of terrorism and most terrorist organizations.

www.fas.org/irp/threat/terror.htm
Website maintained by the Federation of American Scientists. Contains many useful links to news and documents.

www.state.gov/s/ct/rls/pgtrpt/2001/html
The State Department's most recent annual report on terrorist activity around the world.

www.jurist.law.pitt.edu/terrorism.htm
Updates and essays on legal aspects of responses to terrorism after September 11, 2001.

www.ssrc.org/sept11/essays
The Social Science Research Council's website containing essays and research analyzing the events of September 11, 2001 and terrorism more broadly.

NOTES

[1] Martha Crenshaw, "Why America? The Globalization of Civil War," *Current History* (December 2001): 425.

[2] Paul Pillar, *Terrorism and U.S. Foreign Policy* (Washington, DC: Brookings Institution Press, 2001), p. 5.

[3] Conor Gearty, *The Future of Terrorism* (London: Phoenix Books, 1997), p. 34.

[4] For a more protracted discussion of the problems of definition, see Thomas J. Brady, "Defining International Terrorism: A Pragmatic Approach," *Terrorism and Political Violence* (Spring 1998): 90–107.

[5] Alex Schmid, *Terrorism: A Research Guide* (New Brunswick, NJ: Transaction Books, 1984).

[6] Walter Laqueur, *Terrorism* (Boston: Little, Brown, 1977), p. 79.

[7] Bruce Hoffman, *Inside Terrorism* (New York: Columbia University Press, 1998), pp. 42–43.

[8] Cindy Combs, *Terrorism in the Twenty-First Century* (Upper Saddle River, NJ: Prentice Hall, 2003), p. 10.

[9] Gearty, *Future of Terrorism*, p. 53.

[10] Hoffman, *Inside Terrorism*, p. 43.

[11] Louis Rene Beres, "The Meaning of Terrorism—Jurisprudential and Definitional Clarifications," *Vanderbilt Journal of Transnational Law* 28 (March 1995): 243.

[12] Council on Foreign Relations, "Terrorism: Q & A," at www.terrorismanswers.com.

[13] Hoffman, *Inside Terrorism*, pp. 90–91.

[14] On Aum Shinrikyo, see Jessica Stern, "Terrorist Motivations and Unconventional Weapons," *Planning the Unthinkable: How New Powers Will Use Nuclear, Chemical and Bio-*

logical Weapons, ed. Peter Lavoy, Scott Sagan, and John Wirtz (Ithaca, NY: Cornell University Press, 2000), pp. 205–209.

[15] Laqueur, *Terrorism,* p. 134.

[16] "A Conversation with John Mearsheimer," University of California at Berkeley, April 8, 2002. Transcript at: http://globetrotter.berkeley.edu/people2/Mearsheimer/mearsheimer-con5.html

[17] Daniele Archibugi and Iris Young, "Toward a Global Rule of Law," *Dissent* (Spring 2002): 27.

[18] Nicholas Lehman, "The War on What?" *The New Yorker* (September 9, 2002): 14.

[19] Michael Ratner and Jules Lobel, "An Alternative to the Use of U.S. Military Force," *Jurist: The Legal Resources Network.* Online forum accessed at: http://jurist.law.pitt.edu/forum/forumnew32.htm

[20] Quoted in Foreign Policy in Focus press release, "World Trade Center/Pentagon Attack: Expert Statements," (September 18, 2001). Accessed at: http://www.fpif.org/media/releases/2001

[21] Andrew Johnston, "Disparities of Wealth Are Seen as Fuel for Terrorism," *International Herald Tribune,* December 20, 2001, p. 8.

[22] Jared Diamond, "Why We Must Feed the Hands That Could Bite Us," *Washington Post,* January 13, 2002, p. B01.

[23] Robert A. Hinde, "Root Causes of Terrorism," *Pugwash Online.* Accessed at: www.pugwash.org/september11/hinde.htm

[24] "The War against Terrorism Will Be Won by Eliminating Poverty," interview with James Wolfenson, December 7, 2001. Accessed at: www.worldback.org/html/extdr/extrme/jdwint120701b.htm

[25] Archibugi and Young, "Toward a Global Rule of Law," p. 31.

[26] Ibid., p. 32.

[27] Ibid., p. 28.

[28] Tony Karon, "Can Democracy Be a Weapon against Terrorism?" *Time* (September 28, 2001): 18.

[29] Archibugi and Young, "Toward a Global Rule of Law," p. 27.

[30] "Bush and Sharon 'Creating Terrorism,'" *Gulf News,* November 2, 2003. Accessed at: www.gulf-news.com/Articles/news.asp?ArticleID=77025

[31] James B. Rule, *Theories of Civil Violence* (Berkeley: University of California Press, 1988), p. 71.

[32] Amy Caiazza, "Why Gender Matters in Understanding September 11: Women, Militarism and Violence," IWPR (Institute for Women's Policy Research) publication no. 1908 (November 2001), p. 1.

[33] J. Ann Tickner, "Feminist Perspectives on 9/11," *International Studies Perspective,* 3 (2002): 346.

[34] Another example is Mary Riddell, "Feminised Face of War," *The Guardian,* September 23, 2001, p. 24.

[35] Steven L. Pomerantz, "The Best Defense," *The New Republic* (July 31, 1998): 14.

[36] Anthony D'Amato, comment attached to Ratner and Lobel, "Alternative to the Use of U.S. Military Force," p. 2.

[37] Pomerantz, "Best Defense," p. 15.

[38] Charles Krauthammer, "Not Enough Might," *Washington Post,* October 30, 2001, p. A21.

[39] Hoffman, *Inside Terrorism,* p. 32.

[40] Accessed at: www.nti.org/e_research/official_docs/inventory/pdfs/hostage.pdf

[41] This phrase is found in Daniel Pipes, "God and Mammon: Does Poverty Cause Militant Islam?" *The National Interest* (Winter 2001/02): 21.

[42] Alan B. Krueger and Jitka Maleckova, "The Economics and the Education of Suicide Bombers: Does Poverty Cause Terrorism?" *The New Republic* (June 24, 2002): 21.

[43] Helle Dale, "Poverty and Terrorism," *Washington Times,* March 20, 2002, p. 24.

[44] Cited in Pipes, "God and Mammon," p. 17.

[45] Samuel Huntington, "The Clash of Civilizations?" *Foreign Affairs* 72, no. 3 (Summer 1993): 32.

[46] Stanley Kurtz, "The Future of 'History,'" *Policy Review* 113 (June 2002). Accessed at: www.policyreview.org/JUN02/kurtz.html

[47] Cited in Pipes, "God and Mammon," p. 21.

[48] Colin Powell, statement before the Senate Foreign Relations Committee, October 25, 2001. Accessed at: http://www.state.gov/secretary/rm/2001/5751.htm

[49] Colin Powell, statement before the United Nations Security Council, November 12, 2001. Accessed at: http://www.state.gov/secretary/rm/2001/6049pf.htm

[50] See Marc Erikson, "It IS a Clash of Civilizations," *Asia Times,* November 28, 2001. Accessed at: http://www.atimes.com/c-asia/CK28Ag01.html

[51] Cited in David Masci and Kenneth Jost, "War on Terrorism," *Global Issues* (Washington, DC: CQ Press, 2003), p. 80.

[52] Pomerantz, "Best Defense," p. 14.

[53] Bob Woodward, *Bush at War* (New York: Simon & Schuster, 2002), p. 43.

[54] Ibid., p. 33.

[55] The quote is from Dan Goure and is cited in Masci and Jost, "War on Terrorism," pp. 80–81.

[56] Robert Wright, "A Real War on Terrorism," part of nine-part series on www.slate.com (September 6, 2002), p. 2.

[57] Ibid., p. 3.

THE GLOBAL COMMONS

Not all issues and debates fall neatly into existing frameworks and perspectives. The complex bundle of issues surrounding global population growth, resource depletion, and environmental degradation is a case in point. Although it might be useful to think about a realist perspective on nuclear proliferation, for example, it is nonsensical to speak of a realist position on global warming. But the issues are no less important merely because they cannot be analyzed within familiar categories. The debate over the future of the global commons emerged from fears that a world of limited resources could not sustain an unlimited population. On one side of the debate are those who believe there is a limit to the level of population our world can support and that we are at or close to that limit. As we approach or exceed this limit, the strains in terms of resources scarcity (e.g., fossil fuels such as oil) and damage to the environment (e.g., global warming) will be increasingly evident. Others reject this pessimistic assessment. Even if there is some theoretical limit to growth, the world is not near, and is unlikely to come close to, that limit. These analysts tend to argue that dire warnings of resource depletion and environmental crises are, at a minimum, wildly exaggerated. Furthermore, human ingenuity and scientific progress will almost certainly allow us to overcome the obstacles usually cited as creating limits to growth.

At some point on October 12, 1999, the United Nations estimated that the world passed a new milestone: the birth of its 6 billionth person.[1] It had taken almost 10,000 years of recorded human history (from 8,000 B.C.E. until sometime shortly after 1800) for the world to reach a population of 1 billion (see table 13.1). It took until roughly 1950 for global population to reach 2.5 billion. A mere fifty years later, it stood at 6 billion people. At the same time as they were recording the arrival of the world's 6 billionth citizen, newspapers were also filled with news of rising oil prices, holes in the ozone layer, the destruction of rainforests, endangered species, increasing global temperatures, and famine and disease in sub-Saharan Africa. Taken together, these stories seemed to point in the direction of one unavoidable conclusion: the world is rapidly approaching the point (if it has not already passed it) where there would be more people than our resources and environment can support. If we can barely support 6 billion people, what will we do with 8, 10, 15, or 20 billion?

Periodically throughout human history, people have worried about the availability of sufficient resources to sustain given levels of population, but it was not until the early years of the industrial revolution that some began to worry about the problem on a global scale. One of the earliest and influential examinations of the problems posed by increasing population can be found in the writings of **Thomas Malthus** (1766–1834). In his *An Essay on the Principle of Population* (1789), Malthus predicted a dire future for humankind. The basic problem was that population was growing geometrically (1,2,4,8,16) while food production grew arithmetically (1,2,3,4,5). If these trends were extrapolated into the future, the point would eventually be reached where there would be too many people and too little food. As a result, famine would become commonplace, and this in turn would lead to all sorts of social and political unrest. Famine and disease would eventually reduce population to sustainable levels, but the process would not be pretty. It was a gloomy vision.

Many of his contemporaries worried about the implications of Malthus's ideas. They feared his analysis would be used to deny aid and assistance to the poor on the grounds that it would merely contribute to further overpopulation (Malthus did tend to worry about the breeding habits of the lower classes). It is a fine line to cross from the notion that we have too many people to the belief that some people are expendable. Anyone who has ever seen or read Charles Dickens's *A Christmas Carol* remembers the scene where two men solicit Scrooge on Christmas Eve, seeking aid for the poor. Scrooge inquires whether the workhouses and orphanages he supports with his taxes are still in operation. When told that many poor would rather die than go to these places, Scrooge responds that if they would rather die, they best do so and decrease the "surplus population." This is the sort of thinking that led Malthus's critics, which included Karl Marx, to conclude that he was a tool of the ruling class and an enemy of the poor.

History has not been kind to Malthus and his predictions. The key flaw was his assumption that existing trends in population growth and food production would extend unaltered into the future. Although population growth continued at an even faster rate than Malthus anticipated, revolutions in farming techniques and technology led to an even more dramatic increase in the food supply. Rather than having population growth outstrip the food supply, the reality was exactly the opposite. For more than a century after Malthus, the productivity of the industrial revolution eased

Malthus, Thomas (1766–1834) Predicted (in 1789) that population growth would soon outstrip increases in the food supply, leading to a host of social, economic, and political crises. Though he proved to be wrong, his arguments foreshadowed many of those made almost two hundred years later by the Club of Rome.

Six billion people and counting. How many people will the world have by 2100? How many more people can it support?

SOURCE: © Carl and Ann Purcell/CORBIS

concerns about the availability of food and other resources. Economic growth and greater productivity provided the answer to the problem of population growth.

Beginning in the 1950s and 1960s, there was a revival of the sorts of concerns raised by Malthus a century and a half earlier, though the exact focus was somewhat different. Why did people start to worry about these issues again? The most important reason was the dramatic increase in global population during the 1950s and 1960s.[2] During these two decades, global population grew at almost 2 percent a year (see table 13.2). This seems like a small figure, but it is more than twice the historical average. The problem seemed even worse when this growth rate was "disaggregated." Although 2 percent was the global growth rate, some areas of the world were approaching 5 percent, and this was largely in poor Third World nations seen as least able to sustain a rapidly growing population.

In addition to the global population explosion, resource shortages began to raise concerns about the long-term sustainability of existing levels of consumption. The most dramatic of these were the oil and gas shortages in the 1970s that created long lines at gas stations. Though the cause of gas lines had more to do with politics than actual resource limits, the problem of resource availability entered the public consciousness. The final element for the resurgence of concerns about population growth and resources was the emergence of the modern environmental movement in the 1960s and 1970s. As J. R. McNeill explains, "Between 1960 and 1990 a remarkable and potentially earth-shattering (earth-healing?) shift took place. For millions of people

TABLE 13.1 How many people have ever lived on Earth?

Year	Population
8000 B.C.E.	5,000,000
1 C.E.	300,000,000
1200	450,000,000
1650	500,000,000
1750	795,000,000
1850	1,265,000,000
1900	1,656,000,000
1950	2,516,000,000
1995	5,760,000,000

SOURCE: Population Reference Bureau estimates.

TABLE 13.2 Historical world population growth rates

Period	Annual Percentage Growth
1750–1800	0.4
1800–1850	0.5
1850–1900	0.5
1900–1920	0.6
1920–1930	1.0
1930–1940	1.1
1940–1950	1.0
1950–1960	1.9
1960–1970	2.0
1970–1980	1.8
1980–1981	1.7

SOURCE: Barry Hughes, *World Futures: A Critical Analysis of Alternatives* (Baltimore: Johns Hopkins University Press, 1985).

swamps long suited for draining became wetlands worth conserving. Nuclear energy, once expected to fuel a cornucopian future, became politically unacceptable. Pollution no longer signified industrial wealth but became a crime against nature and society. . . . Environmentalism had arrived."[3] This conjunction of population growth, perceptions of resource depletion, and the growth of a vocal and powerful environmental movement set in motion a new debate about the future of the world.

TOO MANY PEOPLE, TOO FEW RESOURCES

In 1968, a group of concerned scientists, both natural and social, came together in Rome and began a project that would shape future debate about the problems of population growth and resources. Known as the **Club of Rome,** they wanted to bring together existing knowledge about population growth, technology development, food production, energy supplies and consumption, and the environment in order to examine "the present and future predicament of man."[4] The result was a study entitled *Limits to Growth.* On one level, their argument resembled that of Thomas Malthus. The most important similarity was the focus on population growth. Their basic conclusion can be stated simply: a world of limited resources cannot sustain an unlimited number of people. Whereas Malthus emphasized the problem of food, the Club of Rome focused on other concerns as well. The good thing about food is that it is a **renewable resource**—that is, we grow new food all the time and we can figure out ways to increase food production. Much more problematic for the Club of Rome was the consumption of **nonrenewable resources.** Oil provides an obvious example—there is only a certain amount of oil in the world and when it is gone there will be no more, at least not for millions of years until the earth produces more. Many elements of the environment are also in a sense nonrenewable resources: people need clean air, water, and a hospitable environment in order to live. If the environment is destroyed, a necessary "resource" for life will be gone.

As the title of its study suggests, the Club of Rome believed that there was a limit to the number of people the world's resources and environment could sustain. In the abstract, this is a point with which few could disagree. It would be hard to imagine how the earth could support a few trillion people. The real question is: How many people can the world sustain, and how close are we to that limit? Was this merely a theoretical problem to be faced far down the road, or was it nearly upon us? The Club of Rome's answer was unequivocal: "If present growth trends in world population, industrialization, pollution, food production, and resource depletion continue unchanged, the limits to growth on this planet will be reached sometime in the next one hundred years."[5] Once these limits to growth were surpassed, "the most probable result will be a rather sudden and uncontrollable decline in both population and industrial capacity" and a declining standard of living for everyone in the world.[6] Though coming 170 years later, with some alterations in focus and emphasis, the underlying logic of the argument was the same as Malthus's reasoning.

Population growth Simply stated, population grows because more people are born every year than die. If 1,000 people are born in a year and 1,000 people die, the population growth rate is zero. In somewhat more complicated terms, population growth is the difference between what demographers refer to as the *crude birth rate* (the number born per 1,000 in population) and the *crude death rate* (the number who die per 1,000 in population). If 40 children are born in one year for every 1,000 people and 22 die, the net gain in population is 18 per 1000, or 1.8 percent.

A figure like 1.8 percent does not sound like a very high rate of growth: a 1.8 percent interest on your savings account, 1.8 percent inflation, or 1.8 percent unemployment would be considered quite low. When it comes to population growth, however, 1.8 percent is in fact very large. We can see how large by comparing it to historical

Club of Rome A group of social and natural scientists created in 1968 to examine the future "predicament" of humankind. Their 1972 study, *Limits of Growth,* helped shape the debate over the interrelated issues of global population growth, resources depletion, and environmental degradation.

renewable resources Resources whose supply can be increased within a meaningful time frame.

nonrenewable resources Limited or finite resources that cannot be replaced once used.

TABLE 13.3	Doubling time	
Growth rate (% per year)	**Doubling time (years)**	
0.1	700	
0.5	140	
1.0	70	
2.0	35	
4.0	18	
5.0	14	
7.0	10	
10.0	7	

SOURCE: Donella Meadows, Dennis Meadows, Jorgen Randers, and William W. Behrens, *Limits to Growth* (New York: Universe Books, 1972), p. 22.

rates of growth (see table 13.1). Over the past two and half centuries, global population has rarely grown by much more than 1 percent. It is only in the second half of the twentieth century that population growth rates have approached 2 percent. So 1.8 percent is large compared to the historical norm. But one gets a better appreciation for the significance of 2 percent growth if we look at population **doubling time,** which is the number of years it would take population to double at given rates of growth. If population grows at a rate of .5 percent a year, which was typical prior to the twentieth century, it would take 140 years for the population to double. When population grows at 2 percent a year, however, its takes only 35 years for population to double (see table 13.3). Thus, if global population continues to grow at 2 percent, the world will go from 6 to 12 billion people well within the lifetime of today's average college student (indeed, well before they even retire). These are rates of growth well beyond those that caused Malthus to worry.

The limited nature of many resources and the limited ability of our environment to withstand the consequences of economic growth and production means that there is a limit to the number of people the world can sustain at a reasonable standard of living. The Club of Rome referred to this limit as the world's **carrying capacity.** The only long-term solution is to reach a level of population at or below this carrying capacity and then keep it there. Eventually the world must reach a state of **zero population growth** (ZPG). In the simplest terms, this means that we need to have the same number of people dying each year as are being born. There is no escaping the need for an eventual end to population growth. Because population results from more people being born than dying, there are only two logical ways to achieve ZPG: reduce the number of people being born or increase the number of people dying. Stated in such stark terms, we begin to see the difficulty of the problem.

Resources and the environment   Although the Club of Rome was also worried about the availability of food and arable land (i.e., land suitable for agricultural production), the problem was much broader. The general problem is that people not only consume resources but also produce waste and pollution. Some of the resources people con-

doubling time The number of years it takes population to double at a given rate of growth.

carrying capacity Term employed by the Club of Rome to indicate the maximum level of population that the world's resources and environment could sustain.

zero population growth A situation in which a population's crude birth rates (number of births per 1,000 people) equals crude death rates (number of deaths per 1,000 people).

sume are renewable in the sense that we can make more, such as food. But even with renewable resources there is a problem if these resources are being used more rapidly than they can be renewed. We grow more food each season, farm animals are bred to increase their numbers, and fish spawn in the oceans and rivers, but there are still limits in terms of how much the supply of food can reasonably be expanded. Renewable does not mean infinite. Other resources are finite in that the available quantity is set and we cannot make any more. We may be able to find more of these resources, but we cannot create more. The Club of Rome was concerned with the whole spectrum of resources.

Availability of resources, however, is only half of the problem, and maybe not the most troublesome half. Even if there were enough land, food, oil, coal, and so on for 15 or 20 billion people, we need to take account of the consequences of this level of consumption. Farming land, burning oil, chopping down forests, operating factories, and the other elements of human consumption and production create byproducts, some of which have an environmental impact. And our environment is also a "resource" in a broader sense. Clean air, clean water, and a hospitable climate are things people need to survive as much, if not more so, than a supply of oil. In this sense, we also "consume" our environment.

The list of environmental concerns is long. **Global warming** is the one that has received the most coverage in recent years. According to the theory of global warming, burning of fossil fuels (e.g., coal, oil, and gas) releases carbon dioxide (CO_2) and other **greenhouse gases,** such as methane, into Earth's atmosphere, some of which is absorbed by the world's oceans and forests. This is one of the reasons that widespread deforestation is a problem: the destruction of forests diminishes Earth's ability to absorb these harmful gases. This accumulation of greenhouse gases has led to an increase in average global temperature over the last 100 years, a period coinciding with the industrial revolution, of about 1 degree Fahrenheit. Some of the consequences of this warming are clearly discernible, including a lengthening of growing seasons, earlier flowering of trees, and shifts in plant and animal habitats. Although the implications of warming for human beings has been quite limited thus far, J. R. McNeill explains that if predictions of global warming "prove correct, this warming implies vast changes in evaporation and precipitation, a more vigorous hydrological cycle making for both more droughts and more floods. The consequences for agriculture, while difficult to predict, would be sharp. Human health would suffer from the expanded range of tropical diseases. Species extinction would accelerate . . . [and] for some low-lying countries, such as the Maldives, it could also be the last chapter."[7]

The theory of global warming, however, is not just about the empirical fact of warming, but also its causes. The consensus of scientific opinion is that recent warming exceeds normal temperature fluctuations and must be traced, at least in part, to human activity. The most comprehensive study of this issue is provided by the Intergovernmental Panel on Climate Change (IPCC), an organization established in 1988 involving more than 2,500 leading climatologists from around the world. The IPCC's 1995 study concluded that "the balance of evidence suggests that there is a discernable human influence on the global climate." And in 2001 the IPCC's judgment was even less equivocal: "There is new and stronger evidence that most of the warming observed over the past 50 years is attributable of human activities."[8]

One of the more alarming aspects of global warming is that most of the world's greenhouse gases are produced by a small percentage of its population—those

global warming The problem of rising global temperatures brought on by the emission of greenhouse gases (especially carbon dioxide).

greenhouse gases Gases resulting from the burning of fossil fuels, especially carbon dioxide (CO_2), that build up in the upper atmosphere. It is the accumulation of these gases that lead to global warming.

The destruction of the Brazilian rainforest has become the most potent symbol of the environmental problems confronting our world.
SOURCE: © Stephanie Maze/CORBIS

wealthy and technologically advanced enough to support a lifestyle that requires the consumption of large quantities of fossil fuels. An average family of four in Seattle contributes much more to global warming than a family of ten in Bangladesh. As the majority of the world's population pursues economic development and replicates the consumption patterns of the industrialized North, the problem is likely to get much worse before it gets better. A world of 10 or 12 billion people living the lifestyle to which we have become accustomed in the United States would dramatically worsen the problem of global warming. This is one reason that likely scenarios for the next century are direr than the 1 degree warming of the last century. In 1995, the IPCC predicted that global temperature would increase between 1.8 and 6.3 degrees Fahrenheit, though by 2001 it raised this estimate to an increase of 2.5 to 10.4 degrees.[9]

Global warming may be the most overriding and widely publicized environmental problem, but it is by no means the only one. There is also the reduction of Earth's ozone layer and the appearance of an ozone hole over Antarctica. Though ozone is considered a pollutant at ground levels (major cities issue "ozone alerts" on bad pollution days), a thin layer of ozone in the stratosphere screens out the sun's harmful ultraviolet rays, which contribute to a variety of medical conditions from skin cancer to cataracts. The depletion of ozone is the result of emissions of chlorofluorocarbons (CFCs). Even though the ozone holes are currently located over unpopulated or sparsely populated areas, this is another potentially dangerous consequence of human industrial activity (though successful attempts have been made in the last two decades to reduce the use and production of CFCs).

We can add to this list concerns about *biodiversity* with the extinction of animal, insect, and plant species; the shrinking of the world's major rainforests; acid rain; the erosion of farmland; the availability of fresh drinking water; and the use of toxic chemicals that are finding their way into the human food chain. Some of these problems are truly of global nature (such as global warming, obviously), whereas others are more localized (access to fresh drinking water). The technical details and scientific debates involved in many of these issues quickly become a mind-numbing array of data, statistics, charts, and tables that are almost impossible for a nonspecialist to sort out. But the overall picture is that of a fragile ecosystem suffering a series of substantial shocks in a relatively short period as a result of human economic and industrial activity. The combined affect is that we have reached a point where, to paraphrase the title of former Vice President Al Gore's environmental manifesto, the "earth is in the balance."[10]

Population growth and the tragedy of the commons To some extent, the problem can be dealt with on the resource and environment side of the equation through greater efficiency and cleaner production processes. But the problem cannot be finally solved on this side of the equation. Resource and environmental problems are merely a manifestation of the underlying pressures of global population growth. No lasting solution can be found to these problems if global population continues to spiral out of control. Although many try to avoid tackling this issue head on, there are others for whom this is the central issue.

In order to begin considering solutions to a problem, we need to appreciate its underlying dynamics. In considering the dilemmas raised by population growth, resource usage, and environmental degradation, many have found it useful to think of them as *commons* problems, invoking the metaphor of the **tragedy of the commons** to illustrate these complicated issues in simple terms.

The metaphor of the tragedy of the commons attempts to explain why people overuse common resources to the point of destruction or depletion, referring back to a time when many towns had areas known as commons (if you have been to Boston, you may have visited its central park, still known as the Boston Common). Commons were tracks of land that were open to all who wanted to graze their animals. It was "common" property, as opposed to private property, from which nonowners could be excluded. In the case of the commons, each person had to make decisions about the size of the herd they would graze on the land. The difficulty arose from the fact that the individual herders enjoyed the full benefit of each additional animal they grazed (the animals belonged to them) even though they only bore a portion of the costs of raising each animal. When the animal was fed on the commons, the costs were shared by all. The benefits of each additional animal were privatized, but the costs were socialized. This being the case, there was always a rational incentive for each herder to increase the size of his herd. But as herds got larger and larger, eventually too many animals would be grazing and the commons would be destroyed. In a sense, the carrying capacity of the commons was exceeded, with a predictable result.[11]

Many argue that the problems laid out by the Club of Rome are similar in nature. The commons in this case is not grazing land per se but all the resources we need to sustain the human "herd"—energy supplies, food, clean air, clean water, and so on. These are our global commons. If we run out of oil because of excessive consumption, it is gone for everyone, whether you used it or not. If the environment is destroyed, it

tragedy of the commons
A metaphor in which actors fail to restrain their use of common resources, eventually depleting those resources for all. Often used to conceptualize the issues of global population growth, resources depletion, and environmental degradation.

is destroyed for everyone, regardless of whether you polluted it or not. Though the basic structure of the problem may be the same, real-world solutions are a little harder to come by.

Garrett Hardin on restricting the commons Confronted with the dilemma of slowing the growth in global population, most are inclined to favor voluntary programs that encourage smaller families, such as greater access to birth control. Others argue that there is a need to deal with the root causes of population growth, such as poverty and the second-class status of women. Some, however, have advanced more radical proposals designed to directly control or regulate population growth. Perhaps the most controversial figure on this front is Garrett Hardin.

Garrett Hardin has been influential in framing the issues raised by the Club of Rome as analogous to the tragedy of the commons. He is not as shy in proposing solutions. Hardin begins by pointing out the obvious: if the world has too many people, it is because people are having too many children. The only solution is to get people to have fewer children. The decision to have children is a private one that has social consequences. In Hardin's view, behaviors that have social consequences should be open to social regulation. Most people continue to believe, however, that procreation is not something that should be subject to government regulation. This is a luxury that we can no longer enjoy, according to Hardin. Arguing that we need to relinquish the "freedom to breed," he makes his case in the starkest terms: "The most important aspect of necessity that we must now recognize is the necessity of abandoning the commons in breeding. No technical solution can rescue us from the misery of overpopulation. Freedom to breed will bring ruin to all . . . the only way we can preserve and nurture other and more precious freedoms is by relinquishing the freedom to breed, and that very soon . . . only so can we put an end to this aspect of the tragedy of the commons."[12]

What would restrictions on procreation entail in practice? Visions of infanticide and coerced abortions immediately come to mind, but very few (and certainly not Hardin) suggest such draconian measures. Once there is agreement that procreation is a legitimate target of social or government regulation, a number of devices to reduce population growth are possible. Interestingly, few people have problems with government policies intended to encourage people to have more children. Many countries have tax policies that provide incentives for bigger families, especially in parts of Europe and Asian that have low birth rates. People seem more reluctant, however, to use the same type of policies to discourage large families. But, Hardin would ask, why is it acceptable to offer tax benefits for second and third children but not to impose tax penalties for additional children? The discussion of policy details, however, comes after the acceptance of the legitimacy and necessity of social and political regulation of population growth.

Even more controversial has been Hardin's opposition to proposals for the establishment of an **international food bank** to offer rapid assistance to countries in the event of famine. Famine, in Hardin's view, is a sign of overpopulation. Nations and regions that experience repeated and severe famines have failed to come to grips with the problem of controlling their population growth. If the international community rushes in with food aid, this merely allows people to survive and the population to grow even further, resulting in what Hardin refers to as a **population escalator.** This aid only rescues societies from their inability or unwillingness to control their popu-

international food bank
Proposed as means of responding to famines around the world. The idea was to create a ready stock of food that could be shipped rapidly to areas in need, thus saving thousands of lives. Opposed by Garrett Hardin because he thought such aid would increase the population of areas that were already overpopulated.

population escalator
Garrett Hardin's term to describe the effect of an international food bank. Refers to the steady increases in population that would result every time external assistance was offered to deal with recurring famines.

lation. Although feeding starving people might seem the moral thing to do, the inevitable result is continued overpopulation and an endless cycle of famines. In typically provocative terms, he advises that "it is essential that those in power resist the temptation to convert extra food into extra babies."[13] Given the limited supply of food and other resources, Hardin urges that we need to view the world as akin to a lifeboat that has enough food and water to support ten people but aboard which fourteen people have climbed. In this case there are two options: share the food and water among all fourteen, which means no one will survive, or recognize the need to reduce the population to ten so that some can make it. If we see the world's resources as a commons to be shared by all, the inescapable and logical result, in Hardin's view, is ruin for all.

Needless to say, Hardin's approach to dealing with the problems of the global commons is not universally accepted. Even among those who agree with the basic logic and details laid out by the Club of Rome, Hardin's solutions are considered extreme. Most would rather tackle the problem through the less coercive means that Hardin views as inadequate. These are largely in-house criticisms—that is, debates about appropriate solutions among those who see the fundamental problem in similar ways. Others reject Hardinesque solutions because they disagree with the underlying assumptions of a looming crisis brought on by global population growth. As a result, they also reject Hardin's metaphor of the earth as a lifeboat without sufficient resources to sustain those onboard. If they wanted to be as provocative as Hardin, the critics might suggest that a better metaphor would be that some of the people on the lifeboat want to eat like gluttonous fat pigs on their way to shore and are prepared to deny others food in the process. These critics of the Club of Rome see a world of plenty, not a world of limits.

A WORLD OF PLENTY

Examining competing visions of the future, Barry Hughes distinguishes **neotraditionalists** from **modernists.** The neotraditionalist approach is embodied in the analysis and predictions of the Club of Rome and Garrett Hardin. The label *neotraditionalism* stems from a distinction often drawn between so-called traditional and modern societies. Traditional societies tend to accept a fatalistic view that people are constrained by natural forces and limits, whereas modern societies are characterized by a faith in people's ability to overcome and master the limits imposed by nature. The notion that people need to adjust to inherent limits to growth is, according to Hughes, a traditionalist perspective. This view of the future is rejected by what he calls *modernists,* analysts who believe people have the intellectual and technological capacity to overcome the limits and problems that supposedly restrict human and economic growth. Modernists believe that the Club of Rome, like Malthus before them, is wrong, and largely for the same reasons.[14]

Malthus was clearly wrong in his time. The three decades since the initial report of the Club of Rome have not borne out some if its direr predictions for the twentieth century. Were Malthus and the Club of Rome merely a little (or, in the Malthus's case, a lot) ahead of their time, or were their analyses and predictions fundamentally flawed? Do their analyses need to be slightly updated and revised, or fundamentally altered? Modernists think the latter, arguing that visions of scarcity and ecological

neotraditionalists Those, like the Club of Rome and Garrett Hardin, who believe that the world is rapidly approaching (or is already at) its limits to growth.

modernists Those who reject the analysis presented by the Club of Rome. Argue that even if there is a limit to the population the world can support, it is not even close to that limit. Generally have a great faith in science's ability to solve problems and overcome what are often portrayed as limits to growth.

disaster accompanying exponential population growth have been wrong historically and are likely to continue to be wrong. Recall the abstract principle underlying the Club of Rome: there is a limit to the number of people that the world's resources and environment can support. Specifically, they argued that the world was at or very close to that limit. There are several possible reactions to the Club of Rome. First, one can reject even the abstract principle and believe there is no theoretical limit to the number of people the world can sustain. Second, one can accept the conclusion that there is a limit and we are close to it. Finally, one can agree that there is a theoretical limit but simply argue that we are not yet near that limit and are unlikely to reach it. Modernists tend to adopt this last position (though some might prefer the first).

The modernist vision of the future rests on a few critical assumptions. First, global population is likely to level off at about 8 to 9 billion people by the end of the century. Second, many of the supposed limitations to population and economic growth are likely to be overcome by human ingenuity and technological advances. Third, many of the problems cited by the Club of Rome are the result of bad policies, not any inherent limits to growth. In sum, the predictions of the Club of Rome are likely to be seen a hundred years from now in much the same manner people now see Malthus's predictions: fundamentally flawed because they take existing trends and extrapolate them into the future without accounting for human adaptability, intelligence, and technology.

How many people will we have? Graphs that show global population growing at rapid rates well into the future are indeed scary. The doubling of population every thirty-five or forty years as far as the eye can see would pose major problems. Fortunately, modernists argue, this is not likely to happen. Adhering to what is known as the **theory of demographic transition,** they see population growing in spurts that eventually level off, not in a consistently exponential fashion. The dramatic increase in global population in the middle and later half of the twentieth century was an unusual occurrence that will not be sustained.

According to the theory of demographic transition, high rates of population are usually the result of social, medical, economic, and scientific advances that increase life expectancy and reduce infant mortality. As people start to live longer and more children survive infancy, population grows rapidly. This is what Europe experienced in the first half of the twentieth century, thanks to the improvements that came from the industrial revolution (increased food supply, better sanitation, improved medical knowledge). The problem is that increasing life expectancy and decreasing infant mortality are not initially matched by declining birth rates. If the crude death rate declines but the crude birth rate remains the same, you get population growth. Eventually, however, birth rates also begin to come down. This brings birth rates in line with death rates, causing population to level off (see table 13.4 and figure 13.1). Unfortunately, this may take a generation or two.

But why do birth rates eventually decline in response to changes in life expectancy and infant morality? First, the same advances that altered life expectancy and infant mortality are part of a larger pattern of economic growth that leads to greater wealth and affluence. And if there is an iron law of demography, it is that wealth and fertility (childbearing) are *inversely* related. That is, across societies and within them, wealthy people have fewer children. This seems odd to many because wealthy people and so-

theory of demographic transition Claims that periods of great population growth tend to be followed a leveling off of population. The same technological, economic, and social changes that cause population to grow in the first place by reducing death rates usually have long-term effects that result in declining birth rates.

TABLE 13.4

A hypothetical demographic transition (1)

	Crude birth rate	Crude death rate	Growth rate (%)
Stage I	40/1,000	38/1,000	.2
Stage II	40/1,000	22/1,000	1.8
Stage III	24/1,000	22/1,000	.2

SOURCE: Author.

FIGURE 13.1

A hypothetical demographic transition (2)

SOURCE: *Demographic Transition—Geography,* September 9, 1998, http://geography.about.com/library/weekly/aa090798.htm

cieties would be able to afford more children. The critical part of the explanation is the changing economic motivation for having children. In poor societies, children are economic assets. In many Third World societies, children work and contribute economically to the family by their early teens. Because poor societies also tend to lack welfare benefits to support people in old age, parents anticipate the need to have their children support them. As societies and people become more affluent, they have children largely for the emotional and psychological benefits of procreation. And for many parents, two children provide all the emotional benefits they can tolerate. Thus, affluence eventually reduces birth rates.

A second reason for declining birth rates is more straightforward. When many children die in infancy or at very young ages, people need to have more children to assure that some make it to adulthood. As infant mortality declines and life expectancy rises, there is less need to have a lot of children to assure the survival of a few. In countries like the United States, parents expect every child they have to make it to adulthood: it is an unusual tragedy when a parent buries a child. Throughout most of human history and in many parts of the contemporary world, the death of a child is not so unusual. Finally, economic growth and industrialization also tend to alter the role of women in society. As women become more educated, as they work outside the home and have an independent source of income, and as they have access to birth control, they tend to have fewer children. This is a point stressed by feminists and nonfeminists alike: improving the status of women is one of the keys to reducing population growth.[15]

On a global level, different regions progress through this demographic transition at different times and rates. The advanced industrialized world has already gone through the cycle. Population grew at a rapid rate during the first half and middle of the twentieth century and then leveled off in North America, Europe, and Japan. In Western Europe many nations are faced with birth rates so low they worry about their ability to afford the generous welfare benefits that elderly citizens enjoy.[16] Much of the population growth we see today is occurring in the Third World, which is experiencing now what Europe experienced a generation or two ago.

Though Europe has completed the demographic transition, large parts of the world are in the middle of it. The expectation is that the same pattern will manifest itself and birth rates will decline, bringing population growth under control. Indeed, in many parts of the Third World this appears to be happening. And given the availability of artificial birth control, the demographic transition can occur quite rapidly. In Taiwan and South Korea, for example, crude birth rates in 1960 were about 40 per 1,000. A mere fifteen years later, in 1975, the birth rate was 25 per 1,000, and by 2001 it was down to 14 per 1,000.[17] Taking into account these trends, more recent estimates are that global population will continue to increase until about 2075, when it reaches approximately 9 billion and will stabilize around that number (see table 13.5).[18] Thus, though a doubling of population every thirty-five years would be a nightmare, this is almost certainly not going to happen.

But even if one accepts the prediction that world population is likely to level off at around 9 billion people by the end of the century, this is still a lot of people. The question still remains: can the world's resources and environment sustain indefinitely a population of 9 or 10 billion people? Modernists think so. An exhaustive survey of modernist responses to the resource and environmental concerns of the neotraditionalists is more than we can accomplish here. But let us look at a few issues to get a feel for the modernist perspective: food, energy resources, and global warming.[19]

A world awash in food Certainly there are starving people in the world. Though we might assume this is because there is not enough food to go around, we would be wrong. More than enough food is being produced in the world to feed all of its people. If there is a problem, it is one of distribution, not supply. We need to be careful to differentiate problems that stem from bad policies and social, political, and economic conditions from those that derive from inherent resource limits.

If we look at some crude figures for global food production, we can see that the supply of food has actually been increasing faster than population. Table 13.6 shows trends in global production of fish, meat, soybean, and grain from 1950 to the mid-1990s in aggregate and per capita (per person). The aggregate figures are pretty amazing: an almost 300 percent increase in grain production, 800 percent increase in soybeans, 400 percent in meat, and 500 percent in fish over the course of forty-five years. Perhaps even more important are the per capita (per person) figures. Since the period

TABLE 13.5

Forecasted population sizes

Year	Median world and regional population sizes (millions)				
	2000	**2025**	**2050**	**2075**	**2100**
World total	6,055	7,827	8,797	8,951	8,414
North Africa	173	257	311	336	333
Sub-Saharan Africa	611	976	1,319	1,522	1,500
North America	314	379	422	441	454
Latin America	515	709	840	904	934
Central Asia	56	81	100	107	106
Middle East	172	285	368	413	413
South Asia	1,367	1,940	2,249	2,242	1,958
China region	1,408	1,608	1,580	1,422	1,250
Pacific Asia	476	625	702	702	654
Pacific OECD	150	155	148	135	123
Western Europe	456	478	470	433	392
Eastern Europe	121	117	104	87	74
European part of the former USSR	236	218	187	159	141

SOURCE: From Wolfgang Lutz, Warren Sanderson, and Sergei Scherbov, "The End of World Population Growth," *Nature,* 412, August 2, 2001, p. 544. Used by permission of *Nature,* and the author.

between 1950 and 1995 was one of unprecedented population growth that is unlikely to be repeated, it would be even more amazing if food production kept pace. The data reveal that increases in food production were *greater* than increases in population. The world produces twice as much grain, three times more soybeans, twice as much meat, and more than twice the amount of fish per person in 1995 than in 1950. The population explosion, dramatic as it was, has been dwarfed by the food explosion. For modernists, this is a tremendous accomplishment that most people are completely unaware of. Consistent and repeated predictions that increases in the food supply would soon be reversed and prices would begin to climb have proven wrong time and time again. On this issue at least, Malthus is still wrong.

Modernists remain optimistic about the future. Increases in the food supply are likely to continue, thanks to improvements in agricultural technology that will continue to increase yields. We also have no idea what the genetic revolution will bring. Perhaps we will see a greater reliance on disease-resistant crops or grains engineered to have higher concentrations of essential nutrients (e.g., strains of rice much higher in vitamin A). When these improvements in food production are coupled with declining rates of population growth, the problem of feeding the world's people is the least of our worries. But even some who recognize this achievement and concede that previous predictions were wrong warn that this increase in food production has come at a cost—in terms of soil erosion and possible overuse of fresh water through irrigation—and may not be sustainable.

TABLE 13.6

Vital signs

World fish harvest, 1950–94			World meat production, 1950–95		
Year	Total (mill. tons)	Per capita (kilograms)	Year	Total (mill. tons)	Per capita (kilograms)
1950	21	8.6	1950	44	17.2
1955	29	10.4	1955	58	20.7
1960	40	12.5	1960	64	21.0
1965	54	16.1	1965	81	24.2
1966	57	16.7	1966	84	24.5
1967	61	17.2	1967	86	24.5
1968	64	18.0	1968	88	24.8
1969	63	17.4	1969	92	25.5
1970	66	17.8	1970	97	26.2
1971	66	17.5	1971	101	26.7
1972	62	16.1	1972	106	27.4
1973	63	16.0	1973	105	26.8
1974	67	16.7	1974	107	26.6
1975	66	16.2	1975	109	26.7
1976	69	16.6	1976	112	26.9
1977	68	16.1	1977	117	27.6
1978	70	16.3	1978	121	28.2
1979	71	16.2	1979	126	28.8
1980	72	16.2	1980	130	29.1
1981	75	16.6	1981	132	29.2
1982	77	16.7	1982	134	29.0
1983	78	16.4	1983	138	29.4
1984	84	17.6	1984	142	29.7
1985	86	17.7	1985	146	30.1
1986	93	18.8	1986	152	30.8
1987	95	18.9	1987	157	31.2
1988	99	19.4	1988	164	32.1
1989	100	19.2	1989	166	31.9
1990	98	18.5	1990	171	32.4
1991	98	18.2	1991	173	32.1
1992	99	18.1	1992	175	31.9
1993	102	18.4	1993	177	31.9
1994	109	19.3	1994	184	32.7
			1995 (prel)	192	33.4

SOURCES: FAO, *Yearbook of Fishery Statistics: Catches and Landings* (various years); 1994 data, FAO, Rome, private communication, January 25, 1996.

SOURCES: FAO, *1948–1985 World Crop and Livestock Statistics* (1987); FAO, *FAO Production Yearbooks 1988–1991;* USDA, *Livestock and Poultry: World Markets and Trade,* October 1995.

SOURCE: Lester Brown, Christopher Flavin, and Hal Kane, *Vital Signs,* 1996 (New York: W. W. Norton, 1996), pp. 25, 27, 29, 31.

World soybean production, 1950–95				World grain production, 1950–95		
Year	Total (mill. tons)	Per capita (kilograms)		Year	Total (mill. tons)	Per capita (kilograms)
1950	17	6		1950	631	247
1955	19	7		1955	759	273
1960	25	8		1960	847	279
1965	32	9		1965	917	274
1966	36	11		1966	1,005	294
1967	38	11		1967	1,029	295
1968	42	12		1968	1,069	301
1969	42	12		1969	1,078	297
1970	44	12		1970	1,096	296
1971	47	12		1971	1,194	316
1972	49	13		1972	1,156	299
1973	62	16		1973	1,272	323
1974	55	14		1974	1,220	304
1975	66	16		1975	1,250	306
1976	59	14		1976	1,363	328
1977	72	17		1977	1,337	316
1978	78	18		1978	1,467	341
1979	94	21		1979	1,428	326
1980	81	18		1980	1,447	325
1981	86	19		1981	1,499	331
1982	94	20		1982	1,550	336
1983	83	18		1983	1,486	317
1984	93	20		1984	1,649	346
1985	97	20		1985	1,664	343
1986	98	20		1986	1,683	341
1987	103	21		1987	1,612	321
1988	95	19		1988	1,564	306
1989	106	21		1989	1,685	324
1990	103	20		1990	1,780	336
1991	106	20		1991	1,696	315
1992	116	21		1992	1,776	316
1993	117	21		1993	1,703	307
1994	136	24		1994	1,745	309
1995 (prel)	125	22		1995 (prel)	1,680	293

SOURCES: USDA, "Production, Supply, and Demand View" (electronic database), January 1996; USDA, "Oilseeds: World Markets and Trade," October 1995.

SOURCES: USDA, World Grain Database (unpublished printouts), 1991; USDA, "Production, Supply, and Demand View" (electronic database), January 1996; USDA, "World Agricultural Supply and Demand Estimates," January 1996; USDA, Grain: World Markets and Trade, January 1996.

Energy resources: The myth of scarcity The good thing about food is that we can always grow more. Other things people consume are, however, finite: once we have used it all, we will have to wait millions of years for the earth to replenish our supply. The finite resource that immediately springs to mind is energy or, to be more precise, fossil fuels such as oil, natural gas, and coal. We are undoubtedly using these resources more rapidly than the Earth is making more, so there is no escaping the logical conclusion that we will run out of them someday. Even if world population stabilizes at 9, 10, or 11 billion people, this does nothing to prevent the depletion of oil, gas, and coal, though it will take a little longer than if we had 15 or 10 billion people. Fewer people simply gives us more time, not more resources.

How do modernists respond to this seemingly cruel and inevitable logic of resource depletion? There are essentially two major arguments. First, the supply of these fossil fuels is greater than most believe and we are likely to have more than sufficient supplies well into the future. Second, modernists make the distinction between the supply of energy and the supply of fossil fuels. The latter may indeed be finite, but the former is infinite. Fossil fuels have provided us with most of our energy in the industrial age (and this is likely to remain the case for some time to come), but there are many other potential sources of energy, many of which are unlimited, and technological advances are likely to allow us to exploit these sources before we need them.

The bad thing about making predictions is that they may not come true. Make too many bad predictions and people start to question them all. Few predictions have fared as poorly as those concerning the depletion of fossil fuels. In 1891, the U.S. Geological Survey indicated that we were unlikely to find much oil in Kansas and Texas. As recently as 1981, the U.S. Department of Energy predicted that by the end of the century the price of oil would double or triple.[20] In 1972, the authors of *Limits to Growth* estimated that we would exhaust all known existing reserves of petroleum by 1992.[21] Not only were these predictions wrong, they were shockingly so. Needless to say, we did not run out of oil in 1992. Nor do trends in the price of oil indicate any increasing scarcity. In constant 2000 dollars (that is, adjusted for inflation), the price of oil *declined* by more than 50 percent from the early 1980s to 2000.[22] Looking at the price of gasoline in the United States, we again fail to see evidence of scarcity and rising prices. As the *Chicago Tribune* reported in April 2000, "While retail gas averaged $1.57 a gallon last month . . . that still compares favorably with inflation-adjusted prices from 1920 ($2.53), 1930 ($2.03), 1940 ($2.23), 1950 ($1.88), 1970 ($1.56), 1980 ($2.51) and 1990 ($1.58)." Slightly tongue in cheek, the *Tribune* went on to compare the price of gas to a gallon of Coca-Cola ($1.87) and Ben and Jerry's Chunky Monkey Ice Cream ($26.32), hardly essential or finite resources.[23] The constantly predicted depletion of oil and the soaring prices that would accompany its increasing scarcity have failed to materialize time and time again. Every new prediction is held up by modernists as the latest example of the proverbial boy who cried wolf. Modernists contend that the fossil fuels on which we now depend remain plentiful and are likely to remain so. We are constantly finding new reserves as well as developing new technologies that allow us to extract more oil more efficiently.

But there remains the unavoidable conclusion that one day these fossil fuels will be exhausted. We can quibble about how long that will take, but there is no escaping the reality of eventual depletion. What then? Modernists stress that fossil fuels and energy are not one and the same. Running out of fossil fuels does not mean the end our energy supply. A host of theoretical alternatives to fossil fuels—hydroelectric, nuclear, solar, wind, and so on—are available. There are two problems at present. The technology in these areas is not advanced enough and the energy produced through alternative means is generally more expensive than fossil fuels. The coming decades are likely to produce improvements in the technologies of alternative energy sources, most of which are potentially infinite. Furthermore, when fossil fuels do become genuinely scarce, their price will begin to rise. As the cost of fossil fuel derived energy increases, alternative sources will become more attractive and profitable. We may run out of fossil fuels, but we will never run out of "energy." This optimism and belief in technology is expressed by Lomborg: "The important point . . . on energy is to stress not only that there are ample reserves of fossil fuels but also that the potentially unlimited renewable energy resources definitely are within our economic reach."[24]

Global warming—But so what? There is no single modernist response to theories of global warming, though the responses do share varying degrees of skepticism about what they see as exaggerated predictions of imminent environmental catastrophe. To understand the range of responses, we need to break down the issue into several distinct questions. First, is global warming occurring at all? Second, if so, what is causing it? And third, how much warming are we likely to see and with what effects?

A small number of skeptics go so far as to question whether global warming is occurring at all. Debates on this issue can get very technical because they involve the reliability of different methods of measuring temperature. When most people think of temperature, they think of what the weather reporter says. This is ground temperature that can be read from a thermometer in the backyard. These measures do tend to show an increase in global temperature. But temperature is also measured in the upper atmosphere by weather balloons and satellites. Some climatologists consider these more accurate and reliable because ground temperatures are skewed by the **heat island effect,** in which buildings, concrete, and roads in urban areas "trap" heat, making the problem of warming seem worse than it really is. According to the theory of global warming, temperatures at higher elevations should also be on the rise. In reality, these measures appear to show a much more modest increase or no clear trend at all.[25] These issues aside, most scientists agree that surface temperatures have risen over the last hundred years.

The major bones of contention are the cause, extent, and likely consequences of this warming. The theory of global warming asserts not merely that temperatures are rising but that this increase is a result of human activity. Critics are quick to point out, however, that global temperature has fluctuated throughout history. No one denies this fact. Increases and decreases in global temperature are nothing new. The issue is whether current warming is occurring on a scale or with a rapidity different from previous warmings. Unfortunately, no one was recording temperature 18,000 years ago, so we need to look at indirect indicators of temperature, such as the accumulation of ice in Greenland, to get some sense of global climate thousands of years ago. But these indicators are open to different interpretations. A 2003 survey conducted by Harvard scientists concluded that global temperatures appear to have been significantly higher during the Middle Ages than they are today.[26] The problem here is that systematic records of temperature begin in the second half of the 1800s, and there is not much doubt about the temperature increases since then. But if the period between 1300 and 1850 was unusually cool, using temperature records beginning in the late 1800s as a baseline for measuring warming of the last century might be misleading.[27] There is,

heat island effect The tendency for buildings, concrete, and asphalt to "trap" heat in highly populated areas. Some argue that the resulting temperatures create a misleadingly exaggerated impression of global warming.

however, consensus on at least one major point: the concentration of CO_2 in the atmosphere has been increasing. Even the Bush administration's Environmental Protection Agency, which has been criticized for its equivocal position on global warming, concludes that "there is *no doubt* this atmospheric buildup of carbon dioxide and other greenhouse gases is largely the result of human activities."[28]

Even if one grants that warming is occurring and that human activity is causing it, the next questions become: How much is temperature likely to rise, and with what consequences? These questions are hard to answer because predictions about global temperature are derived from complex models of how the world's climate works. These models need to incorporate many elements of a very complicated system, including not only greenhouse gases and temperature but also oceans, forests, cloud cover, evaporation rates, precipitation, and so on. Changes in one element of the climate affect others, and we are not quite sure about how all these elements interact. Remember the IPCC's prediction that by 2100 global temperature will increase between 2.5 and 10.4 degrees Fahrenheit. This is a substantial range. For some, even the smallest increase is cause for concern. According to Al Gore, "even *small* changes in global average temperatures can have *enormous* effects on climate patterns. And *any* disruption in climate patterns can dramatically affect the distribution of rainfall, the intensity of storms and droughts, the directions of prevailing winds and ocean currents, and the appearance of erratic weather patterns [emphasis added]."[29] In Gore's view, the world's environment is a finely balanced, fragile, and interrelated system in which adverse changes in one area, even small, can have "enormous" repercussions for the larger environment.

Others present a more benign vision of a *slightly* warmer world. In a somewhat provocative passage entitled "The Case for Global Warming" (see box 13.1), Greg Easterbrook sees no reason to assume that today's average global temperature is necessarily the ideal, though he admits an increase of 4 or 5 degrees, not to mention 10, could have disastrous consequences. The response to this optimism is that since we cannot know for certain which predictions will prove correct, it is prudent to do what we can now because the consequences are potentially so dire. Because it may take decades for policies to curb greenhouse gases to have an effect, we cannot wait until every last global warming skeptic is convinced. Operating on the assumption (or hope) that warming will remain mild with mostly positive consequences would represent a tremendous gamble with the future of the planet.

The good news In general, modernists reject the chorus of what they consider to be doomsday predictions of population growth, resource depletion, famines, and environmental degradation. Such predictions have been notoriously wrong in the past and need to be viewed with deep skepticism today. The problems are either nonexistent (food availability), greatly exaggerated (global warming), capable of "solving themselves" (population growth), or amenable to technological solutions (energy). Furthermore, the endless recitation of problems only serves to obscure the evidence of a better life for virtually everyone on the planet. On whatever measure one chooses to focus on, human life is better today than it was a hundred years ago, and is likely to be better a hundred years from now. As a result, Bjorn Lomborg anticipates that "children born today—in both the industrialized world and developing countries—will live longer and be healthier, they will get more food, a better education, a higher

The Case for Warming

Gregg Easterbrook

Here's an aspect of the greenhouse controversy that drives environmentalists to distraction: Is global warming bad? The high range of doomsday predictions for a warmer Earth would be fearsome. But mild warming is probably in society's interest, particularly if present trends hold and the warming comes in wintertime or on summer nights.

No one contends that the warming of the past century has done the slightest harm. The prime results of that mild warming, higher crop yields and lower energy consumption, are powerful pluses. What was the economic bottom line on the 1980s, the "hottest years on record"? Agriculture was strong throughout the world. Most developing nations produced sufficient food for domestic consumption. In 1986 India—India!—briefly entered the food export market. Energy consumption was soft, winter peak demand being a key variable in power needs. In turn, energy prices declined. By 1994, in real-dollar terms gasoline cost less in the United States than during the 1950s, a period enshrined in collective memory as Energy Heaven. High agricultural yield and soft energy demand are especially important to the Third World. Farm yields stave off malnutrition, while most developing nations are fuel importers whose populations suffer when oil prices rise.

"I have a hard time following why longer growing seasons, lower energy use and fewer subzero days in North Dakota are the new apocalypse," says Michaels, of the University of Virginia. He argues that up to a global increase of around three degrees Fahrenheit, an artificial greenhouse effect will be benign. Pessimists try to wave away such arguments. Paul Allen of the Natural Resources Defense Council has said that mere discussion of benefits from global warming is "preposterous." Yet the notion of gains from warming is not without respectable backing. The Intergovernmental Panel on Climate Change has estimated that a 3.5-degree Fahrenheit warming would increase agricultural yields in the former Soviet Union by 40 percent, in China by 20 percent, in the United States by 15 percent. Even at this point, global temperatures would remain below their level for most of Earth's history.

Gregg Easterbrook, *A Moment in the Earth* (New York: Penguin, 1996) pp. 301–302.

standard of living, more leisure time and far more possibilities—without the global environment being destroyed. And that is a beautiful world."[30] The difference in vision between this view and that of the Club of Rome could not be starker.

Conclusion

Many of the critical debates about the future of the global commons are scientific and empirical in nature. It is not always useful to think about these questions using the same categories we used to look at other issues. There is no realist or liberal position on whether the accumulation of greenhouse gases is likely to raise global temperatures to dangerous levels. There is no feminist or Marxist position on whether technological advances will reduce our reliance on fossil fuels. Realists, liberals, Marxists, and feminists can be found among the ranks of both modernists and neotraditionalists. But even when the basic debate is scientific, there are likely to be political and social dimensions as well, if only because solutions will have to be formulated and implemented in the political realm. When we look at the political and social aspects of global commons problems, these perspectives do have insights to offer.

Realists have usually focused on what we sometimes refer to as "high politics"—namely, issues of war, peace, and national security, not problems of resource depletion and the environment. But we should not assume that the logic of realism must be limited to questions of war and peace. The realist emphasis on the fundamental distinction between domestic and international politics is critical for thinking about solutions to global commons problems. There are, of course, many domestic issues similar to global commons problems. Concerns about water quality and air pollution have been around for over a century. But until recently environmental issues were conceptualized in local, not global, terms. At the domestic level, there are governments that can impose solutions by regulating emissions and punishing those who violate environmental laws. At the international level, however, there is no central authority to do likewise. Even though the issues might be different, realists see another manifestation of a familiar dilemma: how do we achieve socially desirable outcomes that require cooperation in a world of sovereign states? Furthermore, for realists the problem is not simply obstacles to cooperation; there is also the likelihood that resource scarcities will be a new source of conflict among nations. In parts of the world where fresh water is in short supply, it is not too far fetched to envision conflicts, even wars, over this vital resource. It is one of the cruel ironies of international relations (and social relations generally) that conditions requiring greater cooperation simultaneously provide new opportunities for conflict.

Though aware of the difficulties, liberals are more optimistic than realists about the prospects for international cooperation. If there is any silver lining to emerging resource and environmental crises, it is the recognition that every nation ultimately has an interest in preserving those common resources that are essential for sustaining life as we know it. Global warming, after all, knows no national, ethnic, class, or religious boundaries. If the world's environment is destroyed, everyone suffers. And there are signs that this common threat can spur nations into action, a prime example being the Montreal Protocol of 1987. As a response to mounting evidence of a thinning ozone layer, twenty-two nations agreed to cut their use of CFCs (which were largely responsible for ozone depletion) in half by 1998. When new data indicated that the problem was worse than anticipated, the timetable for phasing out CFCs altogether was accelerated. The most developed nations agreed to end all use of CFCs by 2000 and developing nations promised to do the same by 2010 (169 nations had signed on by 2000). And in an unprecedented move, wealthy nations promised to help developing nations pay the costs associated with phasing out CFCs. Although the jury is still out on whether these agreements have halted ozone depletion (CFC use has declined dramatically), liberals look to this experience as a model for international collaboration addressing other global environmental problems, though everyone recognizes that greenhouse gases and global warming will be much more difficult to tackle, largely because there were relatively inexpensive alternatives for CFCs (used mainly for cooling and refrigeration).

Marxists have also explored the problems of the global commons, and it should come as no surprise by now that they see them as intimately related to the operation of capitalism. To the extent that global capitalism produces and perpetuates a system of global economic inequality, the environmental and population problems that derive from global poverty are seen, in a deeper sense, as the consequence of global capitalism. But it is also the fundamental logic of capitalism that is at fault. Capitalism's emphasis on the pursuit of profit drives patterns of production and consumption that inevitably sacrifice everything else, including the environment. John Foster Bellamy argues that because capitalism is "caught up in this unrelenting process of accumulation and creative destruction, the system runs roughshod over each and every thing that stands in its path." As a result, "the exponential growth of capitalism and the increasing consumption of raw materials and energy that goes with it have resulted in a rapidly compounding environmental problem."[31] In this analysis the environmental tragedy of the commons is yet another manifestation of the tragedy of global capitalism. The only long-term solution is to be found not in technological fixes but rather "far-reaching socioeconomic transformations" that alter the underlying economic and social dynamics that have brought us to this point.[32]

Feminists accept the proposition that far-reaching social and economic changes are essential if global disaster is to be avoided. As one might expect, an essential (perhaps the essential) change required is improvement in the status of women, particularly in the developing world, where population growth rates remain high. The most recent United Nations report, *The State of World Population 2001*, released in November 2001, places special emphasis on improving women's access to education, economic opportunity, and reproductive health services, including birth control, as a means of reducing population growth. Many of these proposals are in line with the dynamics suggested by demographic transition theory.

Even people who offer very different explanations of how we got to this point can agree on one thing: the problems of the global commons are perhaps the most difficult we will face in the decades ahead. The scientific debates continue to rage and may not be finally resolved until it is too late to do much about the problems. And even if there was universal agreement on the empirical facts, the anarchic nature of international politics presents challenges to crafting an effective international response. But if the threats to the global commons are as great as some fear, they cannot be dealt with by nations acting on their own.

POINTS OF VIEW
Should the Kyoto Treaty Be Ratified?

One of the most controversial policy issues in recent years has been the Kyoto Treaty on global warming. Signed in 1997 by the Clinton administration, the treaty was designed to reduce the emission of the greenhouse gases that cause global warming. In 2001, however, President George W. Bush announced that he would not submit the treaty for Senate ratification. This policy reversal by the United States unleashed a chorus of criticism abroad, especially in Europe. The Kyoto process and treaty highlight many of the general issues raised in this chapter: the uncertainties of scientific models and predictions, ideological disagreements about solutions (to the extent problems are recognized at all), the global nature of the problems and necessary solutions, and the obstacles to dealing with these problems in a world of sovereign states.

Here you will find two statements. The first is by then Vice President Albert Gore expressing support for the Kyoto process shortly before the agreement was signed. The second is the text of President George W. Bush's statement announcing his decision not to seek Senate ratification of the agreement. How would you place these two statements into the larger debate about the future of the global commons? To what extent do Bush and Gore reflect the differing views presented in this chapter? What are the main points of disagreement between them? What lessons can we learn from the Bush administration's decision in terms of the obstacles to solving commons problems on a global scale?

Remarks as Prepared for Delivery for Vice President Al Gore

Kyoto Climate Change Conference, December 8, 1997

We have reached a fundamentally new stage in the development of human civilization, in which it is necessary to take responsibility for a recent but profound alteration in the relationship between our species and our planet. Because of our new technological power and our growing numbers, we now must pay careful attention to the consequences of what we are doing to the Earth—especially to the atmosphere.

There are other parts of the Earth's ecological system that are also threatened by the increasingly harsh impact of thoughtless behavior:

The poisoning of too many places where people—especially poor people—live, and the deaths of too many children—especially poor children—from polluted water and dirty air; the dangerous and unsustainable depletion of ocean fisheries; and the rapid destruction of critical habitats—rain forests, temperate forests, borial forests, wetlands, coral reefs, and other precious wellsprings of genetic variety upon which the future of humankind depends.

But the most vulnerable part of the Earth's environment is the very thin layer of air clinging near to the surface of the planet, that we are now so carelessly filling with gaseous wastes that we are actually altering the relationship between the Earth and the Sun—by trapping more solar radiation under this growing blanket of pollution that envelops the entire world.

The extra heat which cannot escape is beginning to change the global patterns of climate to which we are accustomed, and to which we have adapted over the last 10,000 years.

Last week we learned from scientists that this year, 1997, with only three weeks remaining, will be the hottest year since records have been kept. Indeed, nine of the 10 hottest years since the measurements began have come in the last 10 years. The trend is clear. The human consequences—and the economic costs—of failing to act are unthinkable. More record floods and droughts. Diseases and pests spreading to new areas. Crop failures and famines. Melting glaciers, stronger storms, and rising seas.

Our fundamental challenge now is to find out whether and how we can change the behaviors that are causing the problem.

To do so requires humility, because the spiritual roots of our crisis are pridefulness and a failure to understand and respect our connections to God's Earth and to each other.

Each of the 160 nations here has brought unique perspectives to the table, but we all understand that our work in Kyoto is only a beginning. None of the proposals being debated here will solve the problem completely by itself. But if we get off to the right start here, we can quickly build momentum as we learn together how to meet this challenge. Our first step should be to set realistic and achievable, binding emissions limits, which will create new markets for new technologies and new ideas that will, in turn, expand the boundaries of the possible and create new hope. Other steps will then follow. And then, ultimately, we will achieve a safe overall concentration level for greenhouse gases in the Earth's atmosphere.

This is the step-by-step approach we took in Montreal 10 years ago to address the problem of ozone depletion. And it is working.

This time, success will require first and foremost that we heal the divisions among us.

The first and most important task for developed countries is to hear the immediate needs of the developing world. And let me say, the United States has listened and we have learned.

We understand that your first priority is to lift your citizens from the poverty so many endure and build strong economies that will assure a better future. This is your right: it will not be denied.

And let me be clear in our answer to you: we do not want to founder on a false divide. Reducing poverty and protecting the Earth's environment are both critical components of truly sustainable development. We want to forge a lasting partnership to achieve a better future. One key is mobilizing new investment in your countries to ensure that you have higher standards of living, with modern, clean and efficient technologies.

That is what our proposals for emissions trading and joint implementation strive to do.

To our partners in the developed world, let me say we have listened and learned from you as well. We understand that while we share a common goal, each of us faces unique challenges.

You have shown leadership here, and for that we are grateful. We came to Kyoto to find new ways to bridge our differences. In doing so, however, we must not waiver in our resolve. For our part, the United States remains firmly committed to a strong, binding target that will reduce our own emissions by nearly 30 percent from what they would otherwise be—a commitment as strong, or stronger, than any we have heard here from any country. The imperative here is to do what we promise, rather than to promise what we cannot do.

All of us, of course, must reject the advice of those who ask us to believe there really is no problem at all. We know their arguments; we have heard others like them throughout history. For example, in my country, we remember the tobacco company spokesmen who insisted for so long that smoking did no harm. To those who seek to obfuscate and obstruct, we say: we will not allow you to put narrow special interests above the interests of all humankind.

So what does the United States propose that we do?

The first measure of any proposal must be its environmental merit, and ours is environmentally solid and sound.

It is strong and comprehensive, covering all six significant greenhouse gases. It recognizes the link between the air and the land, including both sources and sinks. It provides the tools to ensure that targets can be met—offering emissions trading, joint implementation and research as powerful engines of technology development and transfer. It further reduces emissions—below 1990 levels—in the years 2012 and beyond. It provides the means to ensure that all nations can join us on their own terms in meeting this common challenge.

It is also economically sound. And, with strict monitoring and accountability, it ensures that we will keep our bond with one another.

Whether or not agreement is reached here, we will take concrete steps to help meet this challenge. President Clinton and I understand that our first obligation is to address this issue at home. I commit to you today that the United States is prepared to act—and will act....

So let us press forward. Let us resolve to conduct ourselves in such a way that our children's children will read about the "Spirit of Kyoto," and remember well the place and the time where humankind first chose to embark together on a long-term sustainable relationship between our civilization and the Earth's environment.

In that spirit, let us transcend our differences and commit to secure our common destiny: a planet whole and healthy, whose nations are at peace, prosperous and free; and whose people everywhere are able to reach for their God-given potential.

Global Climate Change

George W. Bush

Good morning.

I've just met with senior members of my administration who are working to develop an effective and science-based approach to addressing the important issue of global climate change. This is an issue that I know is very important to the nations of Europe, which I will be visiting for the first time as president. The Earth's well-being is also an issue important to America. And it's an issue that should be important to every nation and every part of our world.

The issue of climate change respects no border. Its effects cannot be reined in by an army nor advanced by any ideology. Climate change with its potential to impact every corner of the world is an issue that must be addressed by the world.

The Kyoto Protocol was fatally flawed in fundamental ways. But the process used to bring nations together to discuss our joint response to climate change is an important one....

My Cabinet-level working group has met regularly for the last 10 weeks to review the most recent, most accurate and most comprehensive science. They have heard from scientists offering a wide spectrum of views. They have reviewed the facts, and they have listened to many theories and suppositions.

The working group asked the highly respected National Academy of Sciences to provide us the most up-to-date information about what is known and about what is not known on the science of climate change.

First, we know the surface temperature of the Earth is warming. It has risen by 0.6 degrees Celsius over the past 100 years. There was a warming trend from the 1890s to the 1940s; cooling from the 1940s to the 1970s; and then sharply rising temperatures from the 1970s to today.

There is a natural greenhouse effect that contributes to warming. Greenhouse gases trap heat and thus warm the earth because they prevent a significant portion of infrared radiation from escaping into space.

Concentration of greenhouse gases, especially CO_2, have increased substantially since the beginning of the industrial revolution. And the National Academy of Sciences indicates that the increase is due, in large part, to human activity. Yet, the academy's report tells us that we do not know how much effect natural fluctuations in climate may have had on warming.

We do not know how much our climate could or will change in the future. We do not know how fast change will occur or even how some of our actions could impact it....

And finally, no one can say with any certainty what constitutes a dangerous level of warming and therefore what level must be avoided. The policy challenge is to act in a serious and sensible way, given the limits of our knowledge. While scientific uncertainties remain, we can begin now to address the factors that contribute to climate change....

A growing population requires more energy to heat and cool our homes, more gas to drive our cars, even though we're making progress on conservation and energy efficiency and have significantly reduced the amount of carbon emissions per unit of GDP. Our country, the United States, is the world's largest emitter of manmade greenhouse gases. We account for almost 20 percent of the world's manmade greenhouse gas emissions.

We also account for about one-quarter of the world's economic output. We recognize a responsibility to reduce our emissions. We also recognize the other part of the story, that the rest of the world emits 80 percent of all greenhouse gases, and many of those emissions come from developing countries.

This is a challenge that requires a 100 percent effort, ours and the rest of the world's.

The world's second largest emitter of greenhouse gases is China, yet China was entirely exempted from the requirements of the Kyoto Protocol. India and Germany are among the top 10 emitters, yet, India was also exempt from Kyoto....

Kyoto is, in many ways, unrealistic. Many countries cannot meet their Kyoto targets. The targets themselves are arbitrary and not based upon science. For America, complying with those mandates would have a negative economic impact with layoffs of workers and price increases for consumers. And when you evaluate all these flaws, most reasonable people will understand that it's not sound public policy. That's why 95 members of the United States Senate expressed a reluctance to endorse such an approach.

Yet, America's unwillingness to embrace a flawed treaty should not be read by our friends and allies as any abdication of responsibility.

To the contrary, my administration is committed to a leadership role on the issue of climate change. We recognize our responsibility and will meet it at home, in our hemisphere and in the world. . . .

I also call on Congress to work with my administration to achieve the significant emission reductions made possible by implementing the clean energy technologies proposed in our energy plan. Our working group study has made it clear that we need to know a lot more.

The U.N. Framework Convention on Climate Change commits us to stabilizing concentrations at a level that will prevent dangerous human interference with the climate, but no one knows what the level is. The United States has spent $18 billion on climate research since 1990, three times as much as any other country and more than Japan and all 15 nations of the EU combined. . . .

America is a leader in technology and innovation. We all believe technology offers great promise to significantly reduce emissions, especially carbon capture, storage and sequestration technologies. So we're creating the National Climate Change Technology Initiative to strengthen research at universities and national labs, to enhance partnerships in applied research, to develop improved technology for measuring and monitoring gross and net greenhouse gas emissions and to fund demonstration projects for cutting-edge technologies such as bio-reactors and fuel cells.

Even with the best science, even with the best technology, we all know the United States cannot solve this global problem alone. We're building partnerships within the Western Hemisphere and with other like-minded countries. . . .

As we analyze the possibilities, we will be guided by several basic principles. Our approach must be consistent with the long-term goal of stabilizing greenhouse gas concentrations in the atmosphere. Our actions should be measured as we learn more from science and build on it. Our approach must be flexible to adjust to new information and take advantage of new technology. We must always act to ensure continued economic growth in prosperity for our citizens and for citizens throughout the world.

We should pursue market-based incbetween 1950 and 1995 was one of unprecedented population growth that is unlikely entives and spur technological innovation.

And finally, our approach must be based on global participation, including that of developing countries whose net greenhouse gas emission now exceed those in the developed countries.

CHAPTER SUMMARY

- In recent decades, people have increasingly begun to worry about the interrelated issues of global population growth, resources depletion, and environmental degradation.

- Though Thomas Malthus feared the consequences of population growth more than two centuries ago, these same concerns emerged in somewhat different form in the 1960s and 1970s.

- The terms of the debate were set in 1972, when the Club of Rome released its study *Limits to Growth,* predicting that in the following century the world would reach the maximum level of population its resources and environment could support. If population did not level off before that point, the result would be a declining standard of living for all in the world.

- The issues raised by the Club of Rome are conceptualized using the metaphor of the tragedy of commons, which attempts to illustrate why people often overuse common resources. On a global scale, the "commons" in question are limited natural and environmental resources.

- If this vision of the future is correct, the only long-term solution lies in restraining population growth. Exactly how this is to be accomplished is often a matter of some controversy. Garrett Hardin has argued that the first critical step is recognizing the need for government policies that restrict population and encourage people to have fewer children.

- Not everyone accepts the Club of Rome's analysis of the "predicament" facing humankind. In opposition to this *neotraditionalist* vision is a *modernist* view.

- Modernists present a more optimistic assessment, claiming the problems highlighted by the Club of Rome are mostly nonexistent, exaggerated, or solvable.

- Drawing on the theory of demographic transition, modernists predict that global population will level off at about 8–9 billion by the end of the century.

- On the question of natural resource depletion, modernists are skeptical of predictions of imminent exhaustion. These sorts of predictions have a very poor track record. Most resources (e.g., fossil fuels) remain sufficiently plentiful to sustain our population until scientific progress leads us to feasible and unlimited substitutes.

- On environmental issues, modernists also fear that many problems, such as fears of global warming, are being exaggerated. Those environmental problems that do exist have technological solutions. We have the ability to sustain the world's probable population with a minimal effect on the global environment.

- Though it may not seem very useful to view debates over the future of the global commons in terms of the perspectives we have focused on for other issues (e.g., realism, liberalism), we should not assume they have nothing to offer. Some perspectives do speak to some of the fundamental problems, such as feminism's emphasis on the status of women as a major determinant of population growth rates. Other perspectives have more to offer in terms of understanding the possibilities for finding solutions for global problems.

CRITICAL QUESTIONS

1. In what sense are global environmental problems "commons" issues?

2. Why are commons problems so much more difficult to solve at the global level than the domestic level?

3. Modernists often assume that global population will level off as developing nations replicate the demographic trends of the developed world. Are there reasons to think this might not be the case?

4. Why is the underlying problem of global population growth so difficult to solve?

5. What are the similarities and differences between the Club of Rome and Thomas Malthus?

KEY TERMS

carrying capacity 322
Club of Rome 321
doubling time 322
global warming 323
greenhouse gases 323
heat island effect 335
international food bank 326
Malthus, Thomas (1766–1834) 318
modernists 327
neotraditionalists 327
nonrenewable resources 321
population escalator 326
renewable resources 321
theory of demographic transition 328
tragedy of the commons 325
zero population growth 322

FURTHER READINGS

A good place to begin is with the landmark study that shaped much of the debate for the past few decades: Donella Meadows, Dennis Meadows, Jorgen Randers, and William W. Behrens, *Limits to Growth* (New York: Universe Books, 1972). The Worldwatch Institute publishes a popular collection of essays every year entitled *State of the World* (New York: W. W. Norton, annual) dealing with the issues raised in the larger debate about population growth, environmental problems, and resources depletion. Another fairly comprehensive overview is John Dryzek and David Schlosberg, eds., *Debating the Earth: An Environmental Politics Reader* (Oxford: Oxford University Press, 1998). A popular statement of concern echoing the views of the Club of Rome is Albert Gore's *Earth in the Balance: Ecology and the Human Spirit* (New York: Houghton Mifflin, 1992). Garrett Hardin's *Living within Limits: Ecology, Economics and Population Taboos* (Oxford: Oxford University Press, 2000) is a thought-provoking, if controversial, exploration of many of these issues. The classic response to arguments about growing resource scarcity was presented in Julian Simon and Herman Kahn, *The Resourceful Earth* (Oxford: Basil Blackwell, 1984). Bjorn Lomborg's *The Skeptical Environmentalist: Measuring the Real State of the World* (Cambridge: Cambridge University Press, 2001) is an extremely controversial attempt to counter what he sees as exaggerated concerns about population growth, resources, and environmental degradation.

THE GLOBAL COMMONS ON THE WEB

www.ipcc.ch
> Official website of the Intergovernmental Panel on Climate Change, the leading organization examining the problems of global warming.

www.law.pace.edu/env/energy/globalwarming.html
> An excellent site covering all aspects and sides of the debate over global warming.

www.bbc.co.uk/science/hottopics/climatechange/kyototreaty.shtml
> The British Broadcasting Company's informative site on global warming, particularly good on the controversy over the Kyoto Treaty.

www.popnet.org
> Resources with considerable information and links to other sources on global population trends and dynamics.

NOTES

[1] "And Baby Makes 6 Billion," *San Francisco Examiner*, October 11, 1999.

[2] See Paul R. Ehrlich, *The Population Bomb* (New York: Ballantine, 1968), is a classic early statement of concern about population growth.

[3] J. R. McNeill, *Something New under the Sun: An Environmental History of the Twentieth-Century World* (New York: W. W. Norton, 2000), p. 340.

[4] Donella H. Meadows, Dennis Meadows, Jorgen Randers, and William W. Behrens, *Limits to Growth* (New York: Universe Books, 1972), p. 9.

[5] Ibid., p. 23

[6] Ibid., p. 23.

[7] McNeill, *Something New under the Sun*, pp. 110–111.

[8] Citations from the Union of Concerned Scientists website on global warming: http://www.ucsusa.org/global_environmental/globalwarming/page.cfm?pageID=497

[9] Ibid.

[10] Albert Gore, *Earth in the Balance* (New York: Houghton Mifflin, 1992).

[11] There are numerous statements of the tragedy of the commons. See, for example, Elinor Ostrom, *Governing the Commons: The Evolution of Institutions for Collective Action* (Cambridge: Cambridge University Press, 1990), and Garrett Hardin, "The Tragedy of the Commons," *Science* (1968), pp. 243–48.

[12] Hardin, "Tragedy of the Commons," p. 248.

[13] Garrett Hardin, *Managing the Global Commons* (San Francisco: Freeman, 1977), p. 269.

[14] Barry Hughes, *World Futures: A Critical Analysis of Alternatives* (Baltimore: Johns Hopkins University Press, 1985). For more on the distinction between traditional and modern societies, see Daniel Lerner, *The Passing of Traditional Society: Modernizing the Middle East* (New York: The Free Press, 1958). Different labels have also been used to describe these competing perspectives, such as eco-optimists and eco-pessimists, neomalthusians and cornucopians, and so on.

[15] On the theory of demographic transition, see: John I. Clarke, *The Future of Population* (London: Phoenix, 1997) and Hughes, *World Futures*, pp. 73–76.

[16] See Nicholas Eberstadt, "The Population Implosion," *Foreign Policy* (March-April 2001), pp. 42–53, and Carolyn Lynch, "Population Loss Trends Cited," *Washington Post* (March 22, 2000), p. A28.

[17] Hughes, *World Futures*, p. 75. Year 2001 figures from the Population Reference Bureau (www.prb.org).

[18] Wolfgang Lutz, Warren Sanderson, and Sergei Scherbov, "The End of World Population Growth," *Nature* 412

(August 2, 2001): 543–45. The authors concede a high-end prediction population of about 12 billion. The figures in table 13.5 represent the most likely population figures.

[19] The classic statement of modernism is Julian Simon and Herman Kahn, *The Resourceful Earth* (Oxford: Blackwell, 1984). See also Gregg Easterbrook's *A Moment on the Earth: The Coming Age of Environmental Optimism* (New York: Viking, 1995), and Ronald Bailey, ed,. *The True State of the Planet* (New York: The Free Press, 1995). A more recent study is sure to become the new classic statement of modernism: Bjorn Lomborg, *The Skeptical Environmentalist: Measuring the Real State of the World* (Cambridge: Cambridge University Press, 2001).

[20] Hughes, *World Futures,* pp. 104–105.

[21] Meadows et. al., *Limits to Growth,* p. 58. There are also predictions concerning the depletion of other natural resources as well, not a single one of which has proven correct.

[22] Lomborg, *Skeptical Environmentalist,* p. 123 (figure 65).

[23] Nick Pachetti, "Crude Economics," *Chicago Tribune Magazine* (April 23, 2000), p. 36.

[24] Lomborg, *Skeptical Environmentalist,* p. 132.

[25] See Kim McDonald, "Debate over How to Gauge Global Warming Heats Up Meeting of Climatologists," *Chronicle of Higher Education* (February 5, 1999), A17–18.

[26] Brian Matthews, "Middle Ages Were Warmer than Today, Say Scientists," *Daily Telegraph* (April 6, 2003). Accessed at: www.dailytelegraph.co.uk

[27] See Brian M Fagan, *The Little Ice Age: How Climate Made History, 1300–1850* (New York: Basic Books, 2001).

[28] Accessed at: http://yosemite.epa.gov/oar/globalwarming.nsf/content/climateuncertanties.html

[29] Gore, *Earth in the Balance,* p. 91.

[30] Lomborg, *Skeptical Environmentalist,* p. 352.

[31] John Foster Bellamy, "Capitalism's Environmental Crisis—Is Technology the Answer?" *Monthly Review* (December 2000).

[32] Ibid. See also James O'Connor, "Capitalism, Nature, Socialism: A Theoretical Introduction," *Debating the Earth: The Environmental Politics Reader,* ed. John Dryzek and David Schlosberg (Oxford: Oxford University Press, 1998), pp. 438–57.

CREDITS

14 [map] Copyright 2001, Christos Nussli, www.euratlas
.com. Reprinted by permission. 89 From UNESCO and human rights: standards-setting instruments, major meetings,
publications, © UNESCO 1999. Reproduced by permission
of UNESCO. 92 "Hard-Wired for War? Violence Part of
Being Human" from ABCNEWS.com. Reprinted courtesy
of ABCNEWS.com. 98 [fig.] http://users.erols.com /
mwhite28/govt 99 [fig.] http://users.erols.com/mwhite28/
govt 100 [fig.] http://users.erols.com/mwhite28/govt
116 James P. Pinkerton, "Bush Mixes Democracy and Hypocrisy," Newsday, June 5, 2003, p. A37. Reprinted by permission of the author. 128 [fig.] Reprinted from Stephen
Walt, The Origins of Alliances. Copyright © 1987 by Cornell
University. Used by permission of the publisher, Cornell
University Press. 129 [fig.] From World Politics by
A.F.K. Organski, 1968, p. 369. Reprinted by permission
of the Estate of Abramo F.K. Organski. 163 Patrick Buchanan and Ralph Nader, "The Battle in Seattle," transcript
from November 28, 1999, Time and Yahoo!Chat. © 1999
Time Inc. reprinted by permission. Reproduced with permission of Yahoo! Inc. © 2004 by Yahoo! Inc. Yahoo! and
the Yahoo! logo are trademarks of Yahoo! Inc. 165 Originally published in The New York Times, December 1, 1999.
Copyright © 1999 The New York Times Co. Reprinted by
permission. 179 [fig.] © 2001 The Economist Newspaper
Ltd. All rights reserved. Reprinted with permission. Further
reproduction prohibited. www.economist.com 187 "How
agriculture subsidies in rich countries hurt poor nations,"
by Wole Akande, YellowTimes.org, October 19, 2002. Reprinted by permission of YellowTimes.org and the author.
189 "The Poor's Best Hope—Trading for Development,"
Economist, June 22, 2002. © 2002 The Economist Newspaper Ltd. All rights reserved. Reprinted with permission.
Further reproduction prohibited. www.economist.com
207 [fig.] This Way Up, from "Bottom Feeders," by Daniel
Drezner, Foreign Policy, Nov./Dec. 2000, p. 67. 217 "Globalization—Coming to Your Town?" by Sherry Peters, Toronto Star, March 3, 2002 Sunday Ontario Edition. Reprinted by permission of the author. 241 "The Case for the
International Criminal Court," by Joanne Mariner, Find
Law's, July 8, 2002. This column originally appeared on
FindLaw.com. http://findlaw.com. Reprinted by permission. 263 "Stop the Genocide in Rwanda" by Charles
Krauthammer, The Washington Post, May 27, 1994. Copyright 1994 The Washington Post. Reprinted by permission.
265 Originally published in The New York Times, July 31,
1994. Copyright © 1994 The New York Times Co. Reprinted
by permission. 272 [map] Reprinted by permission of the
publisher from Deadly Arsenals: Tracking Weapons of Mass
Destruction, Joseph Cirincione, Miriam Rajkumar, and Jon
Wolfsthal (Washington, DC: Carnegie Endowment for International Peace, 2002) www.ceip.org 286 "Nuclear Saber-
Rattling Helps Blow Off Steam," by Ernest W. Lefever, Los
Angeles Times, June 4, 2002, p. 13. Reprinted by permission
of the author. Ernest W. Lefever, a senior fellow at the Ethics
and Public Policy Center in Washington, D.C., is the author
of Nuclear Arms in the Third World and other books on
U.S. foreign policy. 287 Asian Wall Street Journal [staff pro-
duced copy only] by Salil Tripathi. Copyright 2002 by Dow
Jones & Co Inc. Reproduced with permission of Dow Jones
& Co Inc via Copyright Clearance Center. 310 Robert
Kagan, "We Must Fight This War," Washington Post, September 12, 2001, p. A31. Reprinted by permission of the author. 311 "Pay Tribute to Reason and Think Long-Term:
Reflections on the 9-11 Tragedy," by Professor Sienho Yee,
University of Colorado School of Law. Reprinted by permission of Jurist, University of Pittsburgh School of Law.
322 [table] From Donella H. Meadows, Jorgen Randers,
and Dennis Meadows, Limits to Growth—The 30-Year Up-
date, p. 23. Copyright © 2004. Reprinted by permission of
the authors. 329 [fig.] From Demographic Transition—Geography, September 7, 1998. Reprinted by permission of
Matt Rosenberg. 332–333 [tables] "World Fish Harvest,
1950–94", "World Meat Production, 1950–95", "World
Soybean Production, 1950–95", "World Grain Production,
1950–95", from Vital Signs 1996: The Trends That Are
Shaping Our Future by Lester R. Brown, Christopher Flavin
and Hal Kane. Copyright © 1996 by the Worldwatch Institute. Used by permission of W. W. Norton & Company,
Inc. 337b "The Case for Warming," from A Moment On
The Earth by Gregg Easterbrook, copyright © 1995 by
Gregg Easterbrook. Used by permission of Viking Penguin,
a division of Penguin Group (USA) Inc.

INDEX

GLOBAL POLITICS
IN A CHANGING WORLD

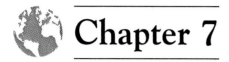

Chapter 7

TIES THAT BIND: THE RISE OF TRANSNATIONAL INSTITUTIONS

The widening violence of postmodern war, the growing problem of terrorism, the dark shadow of weapons of mass destruction, the expanding danger of state failure, the spread of democratic values and institutions, and the increasing power of intergovernmental organizations all testify to the turbulent transformation under way in global politics today, and to the simultaneous fragmentation and integration of politics that is taking place. Perhaps the most striking evidence of this transformation, though, is the growing importance of *transnational institutions*. Reflecting the heightened importance of issues that transcend national frontiers and the growing political activity of ordinary citizens, especially in the advanced economic areas of the world like North America and Europe, transnational institutions are changing how the global political agenda is set and empowering individuals and groups to solve a wide range of problems.

Transnational institutions link together people in different societies, enhancing cooperation and encouraging global and regional responses to the challenges posed by transnational issues. In this way, they act to integrate global politics. Transnational organizations are as varied as the Catholic Church, General Motors, the Boy Scouts, the Irish Republican Army, Greenpeace, the Cali drug cartel, the International Political Science Association, Shell Oil, Doctors Without Borders, and Amnesty International. What these organizations have in common is that their membership consists of ordinary individuals in more than one country. Transnational organizations are thus different from more traditional *intergovernmental organizations (IGOs)* like those discussed in the preceding chapter, whose members are sovereign states.

The proliferation of transnational organizations is even more explosive than that of intergovernmental organizations. This growth is creating a rapidly thickening web of institutions that bind peoples across state frontiers, fundamentally alter the nature of global politics, and reflect both the desire and ability of individuals to take their fate in their own hands. Classically, states and their governments served to mediate the wishes of citizens whose knowledge of and interest in foreign affairs was at most episodic. The growing interdependence of peoples, the erosion of state capacity, the availability of new electronic technologies that provide access to information and allow citizens to communicate easily across vast distances, growing literacy, and the seeming impotence of governments to solve problems have all

accelerated transnational activity and the tendency and ability of ordinary people to take responsibility for their own future.

The variety of transnational groups is astounding. Among the most powerful are transnational corporations (TNCs), like Chevron or Microsoft, whose business activities span national boundaries, involving people from different societies in networks of economic activities. Other transnational organizations are motivated by goals other than economic profit. They work for environmental ends or human rights, serve educational or humanitarian purposes, and bring together people with similar professions. Together, such groups are bringing about what has been described as an "associational revolution." The spreading network of nonprofit groups is encouraged by the grassroots activities of citizens, the actions of public and private institutions, and sometimes even by official government policies. This revolution, which is taking place in the developing world and the former Soviet bloc as well as in the West, reflects growing citizen activism and participation at a time of declining state efficacy. Dramatic improvements in communication technology and the globalization of economic growth also facilitate and stimulate this associational revolution.

The expansion of transnational institutions and groups represents an exciting, if sometimes troubling, aspect of today's turbulent political transformation. Involving ordinary people, solving ordinary people's problems, and interacting with intergovernmental organizations and states, NGOs and TNCs represent powerful forces on the global political scene and promise to play an important role in addressing the new issues emerging on the world stage.

7.1 Power Shift

Jessica T. Mathews

In the first selection, Jessica T. Mathews, formerly of the prestigious New York–based Council on Foreign Relations and now head of the Carnegie Endowment for International Peace, argues that states are increasingly "sharing powers" with nongovernmental organizations as state sovereignty weakens. In her view, technological innovation, especially in computers and telecommunications, is the most important factor in the decline of states and the rise of nonstate actors because governments no longer enjoy a monopoly on information. Moreover, the new technology has made it easy for people who are physically remote to communicate and make common cause for political ends, thereby reducing government control.

Not only is the number of NGOs growing geometrically, but governments are relying upon them more and more for human and financial resources and for expertise. "Increasingly," Mathews argues, "NGOs are able to push around even the largest governments." The weakening of states has costs and dangers, Mathews observes, but she concludes that "nation-states may no longer be the natural problem-solving unit."

The Rise of Global Civil Society

The end of the Cold War has brought no mere adjustment among states but a novel redistribution of power among states, markets, and civil society. National governments are not simply losing autonomy in a globalizing economy. They are sharing powers—including political, social, and security roles at the core of sovereignty—with businesses, with international organizations, and with a multitude of citizens groups, known as nongovernmental organizations (NGOs). The steady concentration of power in the hands of states that began in 1648 with the Peace of Westphalia is over, at least for a while.

The absolutes of the Westphalian system—territorially fixed states where everything of value lies within some state's borders; a single, secular authority governing each territory and representing it outside its borders; and no authority above states—are all dissolving. Increasingly, resources and threats that matter, including money, information, pollution, and popular culture, circulate and shape lives and economies with little regard for political boundaries. International standards of conduct are gradually beginning to override claims of national or regional singularity. Even the most powerful states find the marketplace and international public opinion compelling them more often to follow a particular course.

The state's central task of assuring security is the least affected, but still not exempt. War will not disappear, but with the shrinkage of U.S. and Russian nuclear arsenals, the transformation of the Nuclear Nonproliferation Treaty into a permanent covenant in 1995, agreement on the long-sought Comprehensive Test Ban treaty in 1996, and the . . . entry into force of the Chemical Weapons Convention in 1997, the security threat to states from other states is on a downward course. Nontraditional threats, however, are rising—terrorism, organized crime, drug trafficking, ethnic conflict, and the combination of rapid population growth, environmental decline, and poverty that breeds economic stagnation, political instability, and, sometimes, state collapse. The nearly 100 armed conflicts since the end of the Cold War have virtually all been intrastate affairs. Many began with governments acting against their own citizens, through extreme corruption, violence, incompetence, or complete breakdown, as in Somalia.

These trends have fed a growing sense that individuals' security may not in fact reliably derive from their nation's security. A competing notion of "human security" is creeping around the edges of official thinking, suggesting that security be viewed as emerging from the conditions of daily life—food, shelter, employment, health, public safety—rather than flowing downward from a country's foreign relations and military strength.

.The most powerful engine of change in the relative decline of states and the rise of nonstate actors is the computer and telecommunications revolution, whose deep political and social consequences have been almost completely ignored. Widely accessible and affordable technology has broken governments' monopoly on the collection and management of large amounts of information and deprived governments of the deference they enjoyed because of it. In every sphere of activity, instantaneous access to information and the ability to put it to use multiplies the number of players who matter and reduces the number who command great authority. The effect on the loudest voice—which has been government's—has been the greatest.

By drastically reducing the importance of proximity, the new technologies change people's perceptions of community. Fax machines, satellite hookups, and the Internet connect people across borders with exponentially growing ease while separating them from natural and historical associations within nations. In this sense a powerful globalizing force, they can also have the opposite effect, amplifying political and social fragmentation by enabling more and more identities and interests scattered around the globe to coalesce and thrive.

These technologies have the potential to divide society along new lines, separating ordinary people from elites with the wealth and education to command technology's power. Those elites are not only the rich but also citizens groups with transnational interests and identities that frequently have more in common with counterparts in other countries, whether industrialized or developing, than with countrymen.

Above all, the information technologies disrupt hierarchies, spreading power among more people and groups. In drastically lowering the costs of communication, consultation, and coordination, they favor decentralized networks over other modes of organization. In a network, individuals or groups link for joint action without building a physical or formal institutional presence. Networks have no person at the top and no center. Instead, they have multiple nodes where collections of individuals or groups interact for different purposes. Businesses, citizens' organizations, ethnic groups, and crime cartels have all readily adopted the network model. Governments, on the other hand, are quintessential hierarchies, wedded to an organizational form incompatible with all that the new technologies make possible. . . .

. . . Both in numbers and in impact, nonstate actors have never before approached their current strength. And a still larger role likely lies ahead.

Dial Locally, Act Globally

No one knows how many NGOs there are or how fast the tally is growing. Published figures are badly misleading. . . . In fact, it is impossible to measure a swiftly growing universe that includes neighborhood, professional, service, and advocacy groups, both secular and church-based, promoting every conceivable cause and funded by donations, fees, foundations, governments, international organizations, or the sale of products and services. The true number is certainly in the millions, from the tiniest village association to influential but modestly funded international groups like Amnesty International to larger global activist organizations like Greenpeace and giant service providers like CARE, which has an annual budget of nearly $400 million.

Except in China, Japan, the Middle East, and a few other places where culture or authoritarian governments severely limit civil society, NGOs' role and influence have exploded in the last half-decade. Their financial resources and—often more important—their expertise, approximate and sometimes exceed those of smaller governments and of international organizations. "We have less money and fewer resources than Amnesty International, and we are the arm of the UN for human rights," noted Ibrahima Fall, head of the UN Centre for Human Rights, in 1993. "This is clearly ridiculous." Today NGOs deliver more official development assistance than the entire UN system (excluding the World Bank and the International Monetary Fund). In many countries they are delivering the services—in urban and rural community development, education, and health care—that faltering governments can no longer manage.

The range of these groups' work is almost as broad as their interests. They breed new ideas; advocate, protest, and mobilize public support; do legal, scientific, technical, and policy analysis; provide services; shape, implement, monitor, and enforce national and international commitments; and change institutions and norms.

Increasingly, NGOs are able to push around even the largest governments. When the United States and Mexico set out to reach a trade agreement, the two governments planned on the usual narrowly defined negotiations behind closed doors. But NGOs had a very different vision. Groups from Canada, the United States, and Mexico wanted to see provisions in the North American Free Trade Agreement on health and safety, transboundary pollution, consumer protection, immigration, labor mobility, child labor, sustainable agriculture, social charters, and debt relief. Coalitions of NGOs formed in each country and across both borders. . . .

Technology is fundamental to NGOs' new clout. The nonprofit Association for Progressive Communications provides 50,000 NGOs in 133 countries access to the tens of millions of Internet users for the price of a local call. The dramatically lower costs of international communication have altered NGOs' goals and changed international outcomes. Within hours of the first gunshots of the Chiapas rebellion in southern Mexico in January 1994, for example, the Internet swarmed with messages from human rights activists. The worldwide media attention they and their groups focused on Chiapas, along with the influx of rights activists to the area, sharply limited the Mexican government's response. What in other times would have been a bloody insurgency turned out to be a largely nonviolent conflict. "The shots lasted ten days," José Angel Gurría, Mexico's foreign minister, later remarked, "and ever since, the war has been . . . a war on the Internet."

NGOs' easy reach behind other states' borders forces governments to consider domestic public opinion in countries with which they are dealing, even on matters that governments have traditionally handled strictly between themselves. At the same time, cross-border NGO networks offer citizens groups unprecedented channels of influence. Women's and human rights groups in many developing countries have linked up with more experienced, better funded, and more powerful groups in

Europe and the United States. The latter work the global media and lobby their own governments to pressure leaders in developing countries, creating a circle. of influence that is accelerating change in many parts of the world.

Out of the Hallway, Around the Table

In international organizations, as with governments at home, NGOs were once largely relegated to the hallways. Even when they were able to shape governments' agendas . . . their influence was largely determined by how receptive their own government's delegation happened to be. Their only option was to work through governments.

All that changed with the negotiation of the global climate treaty, culminating at the Earth Summit in Rio de Janeiro in 1992. With the broader independent base of public support that environmental groups command, NGOs set the original goal of negotiating an agreement to control greenhouse gases long before governments were ready to do so, proposed most of its structure and content, and lobbied and mobilized public pressure to force through a pact that virtually no one else thought possible when the talks began.

More members of NGOs served on government delegations than ever before, and they penetrated deeply into official decision-making. They were allowed to attend the small working group meetings where the real decisions in international negotiations are made. The tiny nation of Vanuatu turned its delegation over to an NGO with expertise in international law (a group based in London and funded by an American foundation), thereby making itself and the other sea-level island states major players in the fight to control global warming. ECO, an NGO-published daily newspaper, was negotiators' best source of information on the progress of the official talks and became the forum where governments tested ideas for breaking deadlocks.

Whether from developing or developed countries, NGOs were tightly organized in a global and half a dozen regional Climate Action Networks, which were able to bridge North-South differences among governments that many had expected would prevent an agreement. United in their passionate pursuit of a treaty, NGOs would fight out contentious issues among themselves, then take an agreed position to their respective delegations. When they could not agree, NGOs served as invaluable back channels, letting both sides know where the other's problems lay or where a compromise might be found.

As a result, delegates completed the framework of a global climate accord in the blink of a diplomat's eye—16 months—over the opposition of the three energy superpowers, the United States, Russia, and Saudi Arabia. The treaty entered into force in record time just two years later. . . .

The influence of NGOs at the climate talks has not yet been matched in any other arena, and indeed has provoked a backlash among some governments. A handful of authoritarian regimes, most notably China, led the charge, but many others share their unease about the role NGOs are assuming. Nevertheless, NGOs have worked their way into the heart of international negotiations and into the day-to-day operations of international organizations, bringing new priorities, demands for procedures that give a voice to groups outside government, and new standards of accountability.

One World Business

The multinational corporations of the 1960s were virtually all American, and prided themselves on their insularity. Foreigners might run subsidiaries, but they were never partners. A foreign posting was a setback for a rising executive.

Today, a global marketplace is developing for retail sales as well as manufacturing. Law, advertising, business consulting, and financial and other services are also marketed internationally. Firms of all nationalities attempt to look and act like locals wherever they operate. Foreign language skills and lengthy experience abroad are an asset, and increasingly a requirement, for top management. Sometimes corporate headquarters are not even in a company's home country.

Amid shifting alliances and joint ventures, made possible by computers and advanced communications, nationalities blur. Offshore banking encourages widespread evasion of national taxes. Whereas the fear in the 1970s was that multinationals would become an arm of government, the concern now is that they are disconnecting from their home countries' national interests, moving jobs, evading taxes, and eroding economic sovereignty in the process.

The even more rapid globalization of financial markets has left governments far behind. Where governments once set foreign exchange rates, private currency traders, accountable only to their bottom line, now trade $1.3 trillion a day, 100 times the volume of world trade. The amount exceeds the total foreign exchange reserves of all governments, and is more than even an alliance of strong states can buck.

Despite the enormous attention given to governments' conflicts over trade rules, private capital flows have been growing twice as fast as trade for years. International portfolio transactions by U.S. investors, 9 percent of U.S. GDP in 1980, had grown to 135 percent of GDP by 1993. Growth in Germany, Britain, and elsewhere has been even more rapid. Direct investment has surged as well. All in all, the global financial market will grow to a staggering $83 trillion by 2000, a 1994 McKinsey & Co. study estimated, triple the aggregate GDP of the affluent nations of the Organization for Economic Cooperation and Development.

Again, technology has been a driving force, shifting financial clout from states to the market with its offer of unprecedented speed in transactions—states cannot match market reaction times measured in seconds—and its dissemination of financial information to a broad range of players. . . .

More and more frequently today, governments have only the appearance of free choice when they set economic rules. Markets are setting de facto rules enforced by their own power. States can flout them, but the penalties are severe—loss of vital foreign capital, foreign technology, and domestic jobs. Even the most powerful economy must pay heed. . . .

The forces shaping the legitimate global economy are also nourishing globally integrated crime—which UN officials peg at a staggering $750 billion a year,

$400 billion to $500 billion of that in narcotics, according to U.S. Drug Enforcement Agency estimates. Huge increases in the volume of goods and people crossing borders and competitive pressures to speed the flow of trade by easing inspections and reducing paperwork make it easier to hide contraband. Deregulation and privatization of government-owned businesses, modern communications, rapidly shifting commercial alliances, and the emergence of global financial systems have all helped transform local drug operations into global enterprises. The largely unregulated multi-trillion-dollar pool of money in supranational cyberspace, accessible by computer 24 hours a day, eases the drug trade's toughest problem: transforming huge sums of hot cash into investments in legitimate business.

Globalized crime is a security threat that neither police nor the military—the state's traditional responses—can meet. Controlling it will require states to pool their efforts and to establish unprecedented cooperation with the private sector, thereby compromising two cherished sovereign roles. If states fail, if criminal groups can continue to take advantage of porous borders and transnational financial spaces while governments are limited to acting within their own territory, crime will have the winning edge. . . .

Leaps of Imagination

After three and a half centuries, it requires a mental leap to think of world politics in any terms other than occasionally cooperating but generally competing states, each defined by its territory and representing all the people therein. Nor is it easy to imagine political entities that could compete with the emotional attachment of a shared landscape, national history, language, flag, and currency.

Yet history proves that there are alternatives other than tribal anarchy. Empires, both tightly and loosely ruled, achieved success and won allegiance. In the Middle Ages, emperors, kings, dukes, knights, popes, archbishops, guilds, and cities exercised overlapping secular power over the same territory in a system that looks much more like a modern, three-dimensional network than the clean-lined, hierarchical state order that replaced it. The question now is whether there are new geographic or functional entities that might grow up alongside the state, taking over some of its powers and emotional resonance. . . .

For Better or Worse?

A world that is more adaptable and in which power is more diffused could mean more peace, justice, and capacity to manage the burgeoning list of humankind's interconnected problems. At a time of accelerating change, NGOs are quicker than governments to respond to new demands and opportunities. Internationally, in both the poorest and richest countries, NGOs, when adequately funded, can outperform government in the delivery of many public services. Their growth, along with that of the other elements of civil society, can strengthen the fabric of the many still-fragile democracies. And they are better than governments at dealing with problems that grow slowly and affect society through their cumulative effect on individuals—the "soft" threats of environmental degradation, denial of human rights, population growth, poverty, and lack of development that may already be causing more deaths in conflict than are traditional acts of aggression.

As the computer and telecommunications revolution continues, NGOs will become more capable of large-scale activity across national borders. Their loyalties and orientation, like those of international civil servants and citizens of non-national entities like the EU, are better matched than those of governments to problems that demand transnational solutions. International NGOs and cross-border networks of local groups have bridged North-South differences that in earlier years paralyzed cooperation among countries.

On the economic front, expanding private markets can avoid economically destructive but politically seductive policies, such as excessive borrowing or overly burdensome taxation, to which governments succumb. Unhindered by ideology, private capital flows to where it is best treated and thus can do the most good. . . .

There are . . . many reasons, however, to believe that the continuing diffusion of power away from nation-states will mean more conflict and less problem-solving both within states and among them.

For all their strengths, NGOs are special interests, albeit not motivated by personal profit. The best of them, the ablest and most passionate, often suffer most from tunnel vision, judging every public act by how it affects their particular interest. Generally, they have limited capacity for large-scale endeavors, and as they grow, the need to sustain growing budgets can compromise the independence of mind and approach that is their greatest asset.

A society in which the piling up of special interests replaces a single strong voice for the common good is unlikely to fare well. Single-issue voters, as Americans know all too well, polarize and freeze public debate. In the longer run, a stronger civil society could also be more fragmented, producing a weakened sense of common identity and purpose and less willingness to invest in public goods, whether health and education or roads and ports. More and more groups promoting worthy but narrow causes could ultimately threaten democratic government.

Internationally, excessive pluralism could have similar consequences. Two hundred nation-states is a barely manageable number. Add hundreds of influential nonstate forces—businesses, NGOs, international organizations, ethnic and religious groups—and the international system may represent more voices but be unable to advance any of them.

Moreover, there are roles that only the state—at least among today's polities—can perform. States are the only nonvoluntary political unit, the one that can impose order and is invested with the power to tax. Severely weakened states will encourage conflict, as they have in Africa, Central America, and elsewhere. Moreover, it may be that only the nation-state can meet crucial social needs that markets do not value. Providing a modicum of job security, avoiding higher unemployment, preserving a livable environment and a stable climate, and protecting consumer health and safety are but a few of the tasks that could be left dangling in a world of expanding markets and retreating states. . . .

Finally, fearsome dislocations are bound to accompany the weakening of the central institution of modern society. The prophets of an internetted world in which national identities gradually fade, proclaim its revolutionary nature and yet believe the changes will be wholly benign. They won't be. The shift from national to some other political allegiance, if it comes, will be an emotional, cultural, and political earthquake.

Dissolving and Evolving

Might the decline in state power prove transitory? Present disenchantment with national governments could dissipate as quickly as it arose. Continuing globalization may well spark a vigorous reassertion of economic or cultural nationalism. By helping solve problems governments cannot handle, business, NGOs and international organizations may actually be strengthening the nation-state system.

These are all possibilities, but the clash between the fixed geography of states and the nonterritorial nature of today's problems and solutions, which is only likely to escalate, strongly suggests that the relative power of states will continue to decline. Nation-states may simply no longer be the natural problem-solving unit. Local government addresses citizens' growing desire for a role in decision-making, while transnational, regional, and even global entities better fit the dimensions of trends in economics, resources, and security.

The evolution of information and communications technology, which has only just begun, will probably heavily favor nonstate entities, including those not yet envisaged, over states. The new technologies encourage noninstitutional, shifting networks over the fixed bureaucratic hierarchies that are the hallmark of the single-voiced sovereign state. They dissolve issues' and institutions' ties to a fixed place. And by greatly empowering individuals, they weaken the relative attachment to community, of which the preeminent one in modern society is the nation-state.

If current trends continue, the international system 50 years hence will be profoundly different. During the transition, the Westphalian system and an evolving one will exist side by side. States will set the rules by which all other actors operate, but outside forces will increasingly make decisions for them. In using business, NGOs, and international organizations to address problems they cannot or do not want to take on, states will, more often than not, inadvertently weaken themselves further. Thus governments' unwillingness to adequately fund international organizations helped NGOs move from a peripheral to a central role in shaping multi-lateral agreements, since the NGOs provided expertise the international organizations lacked. At least for a time, the transition is likely to weaken rather than bolster the world's capacity to solve its problems. If states, with the overwhelming share of power, wealth, and capacity, can do less, less will get done.

Whether the rise of nonstate actors ultimately turns out to be good news or bad will depend on whether humanity can launch itself on a course of rapid social innovation, as it did after World War II. Needed adaptations include a business sector that can shoulder a broader policy role, NGOs that are less parochial and better able to operate on a large scale, international institutions that can efficiently serve the dual masters of states and citizenry, and, above all, new institutions and political entities that match the transnational scope of today's challenges while meeting citizens' demands for accountable democratic governance.

7.2 Learning to Live with NGOs

P. J. Simmons

The increasing power and influence of NGOs raises critical questions about their nature and whether they will be a force for good or evil. In the next selection, P. J. Simmons of the Carnegie Endowment for International Peace builds on Mathews's analysis, looks at the roles NGOs play, warns about the dangers as well as benefits inherent in increasing NGO strength, and explores how to incorporate NGOs into the international system in ways that take advantage of the integration they provide without creating unnecessary dangers.

In the summer of 1994, U.S. environmental advocacy groups were getting ready to celebrate. The United States was about to join almost 90 other nations in ratifying the Convention on Biodiversity, which enjoyed broad support from U.S. environmentalists, agro-business groups, and the biotechnology sector. After hearings characterized in the press as a "love fest," members of the Senate Foreign Relations Committee were almost unanimously prepared to back the treaty. Then a group of agricultural and trade nongovernmental organizations (NGOs) previously uninvolved in the debate weighed in, warning that ratification could, in effect, destroy U.S. agriculture. As the *Chicago Tribune* reported in September 1994, evidence later surfaced that some of this opposition was based on a virulent misinformation campaign claiming, among other things, that treaty advocates were all foes of farming, logging, and fishing. But by then, the biodiversity treaty had been relegated to the back of a long line of treaties competing for congressional attention.

At a time when NGOs are celebrating their remarkable success in achieving a ban on landmines and creating an International Criminal Court (ICC), it may seem churlish to recall a four-year-old episode that many would likely regard as a defeat. But amid the breathless accounts about the growing power of NGOs, the failure of the biodiversity treaty is a useful reminder of the complexity of the role that these groups now play in international affairs. Embracing a bewildering array of beliefs, interests, and agendas, they have the potential to do as much harm as good. Hailed as the exemplars of grassroots democracy in action, many NGOs are, in fact, decidedly undemocratic and unaccountable to the people they claim to represent. Dedicated to promoting more openness and participation in decision making, they can instead lapse into old-fashioned interest group politics that produces gridlock on a global scale.

The question facing national governments, multilateral institutions, and national and multinational corporations is not whether to include NGOs in their deliberations and activities. Although many traditional centers of power are fighting a rear-guard action against these new players, there is no real way to keep them out. Instead, the real challenge is figuring out how to incorporate NGOs into the international system in a way that takes account of their diversity and scope, their various strengths and weaknesses, and their capacity to disrupt as well as to create.

Why NGOs Matter

. . . In 1948, for example, the UN listed 41 consultative groups that were formally accredited to cooperate and consult with the UN Economic and Social Council (ECOSOC); in 1998, there were more than 1,500 with varying degrees of participation and access. Until recently, NGOs clustered in developed and democratic nations; now groups sprout up from Lima to Beijing. They are changing societal norms, challenging national governments, and linking up with counterparts in powerful transnational alliances. And they are muscling their way into areas of high politics, such as arms control, banking, and trade, that were previously dominated by the state.

In general terms, NGOs affect national governments, multilateral institutions, and national and multinational corporations in four ways: setting agendas, negotiating outcomes, conferring legitimacy, and implementing solutions.

Setting Agendas   NGOs have long played a key role in forcing leaders and policymakers to pay attention. In the early 1800s, U.S. and European bodies such as the British and Foreign Anti-Slavery Society were driving forces behind government action on the slave trade; by the turn of the century, groups such as the Anglo-Oriental Society for the Suppression of the Opium Trade were leading an influential antidrug movement that culminated in the 1912 Hague Opium Convention. In 1945, NGOs were largely responsible for inserting human-rights language in the UN Charter and have since put almost every major human-rights issue on the international agenda. Likewise, NGO activism since the 1960s and 1970s successfully raised the profile of global environmental and population issues.

Instead of holding marches or hanging banners off buildings, NGO members now use computers and cell phones to launch global public-relations blitzes that can force issues to the top of policymakers' "to do" lists. Consider the 1997 Nobel Prize–winning campaign by NGOs to conclude a treaty banning landmines over the objections of the United States. The self-described "full working partnership" between the Canadian government and a loose coalition of more than 350 humanitarian and arms-control NGOs from 23 countries was key to the negotiations' success. But what seized the attention of the public and policymakers was the coalition's innovative media campaign using the World Wide Web, faxes, e-mail, newsletters, and even *Superman* and *Batman* comic books. Treaty supporters won the signatures of 122 nations in 14 months. When several coalition members announced plans for a follow-on campaign against small arms, the U.S. government sprang into action, meeting with 20 other countries in July 1998 to launch official talks on a possible treaty.

Negotiating Outcomes   NGOs can be essential in designing multilateral treaties that work. Chemical manufacturing associations from around the world helped set up an effective verification regime for the 1997 Chemical Weapons Convention that could be supported by industries and militaries. Throughout the various sessions of negotiations on climate change, groups such as the Environmental Defense Fund and the World Business Council for Sustainable Development have helped craft compromise proposals that attempt to reconcile environmental and commercial interests; meanwhile, NGOs have been instrumental in helping government negotiators understand the science behind the issues that they seek to address.

NGOs can also build trust and break deadlocks when negotiations have reached an impasse. In 1990, a sole Italian NGO, the Comunità di Sant'Egidio, started the informal meetings between the warring parties in Mozambique that eventually led to a peace settlement. During talks in 1995 to extend the Treaty on the Non-Proliferation of Nuclear Weapons, NGOs from several countries working with the South African government delegation helped forge a compromise that led to the treaty's permanent extension.

Conferring Legitimacy   NGO judgments can be decisive in promoting or withholding public and political support. The World Bank learned this lesson in the early 1990s, albeit the hard way. After decades of watching the bank do business with only a handful of NGOs and brush off demands for change, more than 150 public-interest NGOs took part in a sustained campaign to spur greater openness and accountability and to encourage debt reduction and development strategies that were more equitable and less destructive to the environment. Today, partly as a result of this high-profile pressure, about half of the bank's lending projects have provisions for NGO involvement—up from an average of only 6 percent between 1973 and 1988. The bank has even included NGOs such as Oxfam International in once sacrosanct multilateral debt relief discussions—against the wishes of many World Bank and International Monetary Fund (IMF) officials. Even the IMF is beginning to change its tune. In June 1998, the IMF Board of Directors met with several NGO leaders to discuss their proposals to increase the fund's transparency.

Making Solutions Work   NGOs on the ground often make the impossible possible by doing what governments cannot or will not. Some humanitarian and development NGOs have a natural advantage because of their perceived neutrality and experience. The International Committee of the Red Cross, for example, is able to deliver health care to political prisoners in exchange for silence about any human-rights violations that its members witness. Other groups such as Oxfam International provide rapid relief during and after complex humanitarian disasters—with and without UN partners. Moreover, as governments downsize and new challenges crowd the international agenda, NGOs increasingly fill the breach. Willy-nilly, the UN and nation-states are depending more on NGOs to get things done. Total assistance by and through international NGOs to the developing world amounted to about $8 billion in 1992—accounting for 13 percent of all development assistance and more than the entire amount transferred by the UN system.

International NGOs also play critical roles in translating international agreements and norms into domestic realities. Where governments have turned a blind eye, groups such as Amnesty International and the Committee to Protect Journalists call attention to violations of the UN Declaration on Human Rights. Environmental NGOs police agreements such as the Convention on International Trade in Endangered Species, uncovering more accurate data on compliance than that provided by member nations. Perhaps one of the most vital but overlooked NGO roles is to promote the societal changes needed to make international agreements work. Signatories of the Organization for Economic Cooperation and Development's 1997 Bribery Convention, for example, are counting on the more than 80 chapters of Transparency International to help change the way their societies view bribery and corruption.

Increasingly, however, NGOs operate outside existing formal frameworks, moving independently to meet their goals and establishing new standards that governments, institutions, and corporations are themselves compelled to follow through force of public opinion. The UN moratorium on driftnet fishing in 1992 and the U.S. International Dolphin Conservation Act of 1994, for example, largely codified changes in fishing practices that NGOs had already succeeded in promoting and then winning from commercial fisheries. More recently, even as governments and multilateral institutions slowly begin to consider measures to promote the sustainable use of forests, the environmental NGO Greenpeace led a European consumer boycott that persuaded a leading Canadian logging company to announce that it would change the way that it harvests trees.

The Rise of the "Global Idiots"?

Despite the demonstrated capacity of NGOs to do good, their growing power on the ground has exposed them to heightened criticism, some of it justified. . . . In the Sudan and Somalia, NGOs have subsidized warring factions by making direct and indirect payments to gain access to areas needing assistance. In other conflict settings such as Ethiopia and Rwanda, NGO-constructed roads and camps for civilian assistance have instead been used by combatants.

Other longer-term concerns loom for these service-delivery NGOs. The UN High Commissioner for Refugees warned in 1996 that if national governments continue to favor NGOs over multilateral agencies in donor assistance, they may undermine important systems of coordination and cooperation in large-scale emergencies. Intense competition among NGOs in the relief sector has also pushed the sector toward a form of oligopoly that threatens to crowd out smaller players, especially local NGOs in developing countries. Eight major groups now control about 50 percent of the relief market. . . .

But on balance, the record for such NGOs is surely no worse than that of governments. NGOs are increasingly aware of these weaknesses and are moving to address them by adopting codes of conduct and pledging to "do no harm." Moreover, given their origins as grassroots groups, NGOs tend to be wary of organizations that become too big; this innate suspicion can serve as a mechanism for self-regulation.

Yet, the greatest challenges created by the growing influence of NGOs are not in the field but in the arena of public opinion and the corridors of power. Today, in a phenomenon that one environmental activist bemoaned as the "rise of the global idiots," any group with a fax machine and a modem has the potential to distort public debate—witness the demise of not just the biodiversity treaty but the Multilateral Agreement on Investment (MAI), which for all its apparent shortcomings still deserved more reasoned consideration than it received. . . . Even legitimate, well-established groups sometimes seize on issues that seem designed more to promote their own image and fundraising efforts than to advance the public interest: In 1995, for example, Greenpeace continued to attack the Royal Dutch/Shell Group for its plans to sink an oil rig (the Brent Spar) in the North Sea, even after independent scientific analyses showed that the environmental effects of doing so would be inconsequential. Steeped in a culture that encourages adversarial attitudes to the powers that be, many NGOs seem best suited to confrontation, a characteristic that some U.S. policymakers seized on in noting that the NGO coalition against landmines might have won U.S. support (and hence a stronger treaty) if it had been more patient and willing to compromise.

The Limits of Democracy

Governments, multilateral institutions, and corporations face inherent dilemmas in trying to work with NGOs. At their most fundamental level, these dilemmas hinge on two key questions: Who should participate, and how? On the one hand, opening up the floodgates to allow equal access to every group would frustrate decision making. More than 1,500 NGOs were accredited at the 1992 United Nations Conference on the Environment and Development in Rio de Janeiro, for example. Trying to include them all was impossible, so in the final days of the conference, government delegates increasingly retreated behind closed doors. On the other hand, narrowing the field fairly is extraordinarily difficult because no one algorithm or set of criteria can objectively rank the worth of an NGO to a participatory process. . . .

Some traditional centers for power have done a better job than others at tackling these kinds of questions about participation. Among nation-states, Canada stands out for its role in forging an alliance with NGOs on the landmine ban. As Foreign Minister Lloyd Axworthy has said, "Clearly, one can no longer relegate NGOs to simple advisory or advocacy roles. . . . They are now part of the way decisions have to be made." . . . The U.S. record in working with NGOs is mixed: generally good in areas such as the environment and relatively poor in areas such as arms control and regional issues. China represents another extreme, having chosen to banish NGO delegates at the Fourth International Women's Conference in Beijing in 1995 to a site one hour's drive away from the main negotiations.

Most multinational corporations are still struggling to figure out how to handle NGO participation. . . . Still, there are grounds for optimism: A 1998 survey of 133 NGOs found that while many rated their current relationships with corporations as "antagonistic" or "nonexistent," most predicted the development of cooperative relationships in the future. The changing attitude toward NGOs of the Royal Dutch/Shell Group may be a case in point. Stung by fierce NGO campaigns on the Brent Spar episode and its operations in Nigeria, where its ties to the dictatorship of General Sani Abacha made it a target for human-rights groups, Shell has adopted a new Statement of General Business Principles that includes commitments on human rights and the environment; in regions such as Latin America, it now consults with NGOs to ensure that its oil operations take environmental and social factors into account. . . .

Perhaps most important in the long run are systems to formalize existing means of two-way communication between decision-making institutions and "stakeholders." Although NGOs still see much room for improvement at the World Bank, it has produced better decisions and is rated accountable by more NGOs because it no longer simply provides a sounding board mechanism for selected groups to air their views. The bank now disseminates more detailed information about its decisions and activities so outside groups can weigh in. And it uses a variety of techniques to elicit feedback and track NGO expertise—including surveys, advisory groups, public meetings, and private meetings with staff. Consequently, the bank is more apt to consult and partner with the right groups when designing and implementing specific projects. Because the system is more open, groups that cannot participate directly are more likely to judge the decision-making process as accountable—even if they disagree with the results.

Letting NGOs Be NGOs

Many governments and institutions—including the WTO, IMF, and several UN bodies—will continue to resist more public participation, arguing that their issues require great secrecy. . . .

The challenge facing NGOs is more subtle but no less important. As these groups acquire the access and influence that they have long sought, they must not lose the qualities that have made them a source of innovation and progress. Some analysts already fear that formerly independent NGOs may become more beholden to national governments as they come to rely more on public-sector funding— which now accounts for around 40 percent of NGO budgets versus only 1.5 percent in 1970. And many of the schema for increasing NGO involvement may simply foster predictable and bureaucratic behavior among civil society representatives, potentially dulling the passion and richness of views that can emanate from narrowly focused groups. They may also cut off NGOs from the informal channels through which they have traditionally been most influential.

Instead, NGOs, governments, and multilateral institutions need to devise systems of public participation that draw on the expertise and resources of NGOs, their grassroots connections, sense of purpose and commitment, and freedom from bureaucratic constraints. Those NGOs that have seen the most rapid growth in their power will have to contend with inevitable limits on their influence and access. Those governments and institutions that have resisted the advance of these new players will have to permit an unprecedented level of public scrutiny and participation. Over time, this messy process of give-and-take promises to transform the way that international affairs are conducted. Yet as it plays out, both sides may realize that the new system that they have sought to create or resist is in many respects no different from the clash of competing interests that has characterized democracies since their inception.

 NGOs and States

7.3 NGOs: Sins of the Secular Missionaries

The Economist

The combination of weakening or failing states and the growing capacity of NGOs has meant that in some cases NGOs have stepped in to provide basic services, such as education and health care, that states are failing to provide. Where states are failing, NGOs seem to be the big growth industry, as the following article from *The Economist* suggests. In some cases, these NGOs are closely linked to other states, and are carrying out assistance operations that these states could not conduct without clearly violating sovereignty. Thus while NGOs may find themselves at loggerheads with IGOs, and while NGOs may be infringing on the sovereign responsibilities of failing states, NGOs and nonfailing states—and NGOs and businesses—are developing complex, symbiotic relationships. Indeed, the boundaries between states, NGOs, and businesses are becoming increasingly unclear.

A young man thrusts his crudely printed calling card at the visitor. After his name are printed three letters: NGO.

"What do you do?" the visitor asks.

"I have formed an NGO."

"Yes, but what does it do?"

"Whatever they want. I am waiting for some funds and then I will make a project."

Once little more than ragged charities, non-governmental organisations (NGOs) are now big business. Somalia, where that exchange took place, is heaven for them. In large parts of the country, western governments, the United Nations and foreign aid agencies cannot work directly; it is too dangerous. So outsiders must work through local groups, which become a powerful source of patronage. "Anybody who's anybody is an NGO these days," sighs one UN official.

And not just in Somalia. NGOs now head for crisis zones as fast as journalists do: a war, a flood, refugees, a dodgy election, even a world trade conference, will draw them like a honey pot. Last spring, Tirana, the capital of Albania, was swamped by some 200 groups intending to help the refugees from Kosovo. In Kosovo itself, the ground is now thick with foreign groups competing to foster democracy, build homes and proffer goods and services. Environmental activists in Norway board whaling ships; do-gooders gather for the Chiapas rebels in Mexico.

In recent years, such groups have mushroomed. A 1995 UN report on global governance suggested that nearly 29,000 international NGOs existed. Domestic ones have grown even faster. By one estimate, there are now 2 million in America alone, most formed in the past 30 years. In Russia, where almost none existed before the fall of communism, there are at least 65,000. Dozens are created daily; in Kenya alone, some 240 NGOs are now created every year.

Most of these are minnows; some are whales, with annual incomes of millions of dollars and a worldwide operation. Some are primarily helpers, distributing relief where it is needed; some are mainly campaigners, existing to promote issues deemed important by their members. The general public tends to see them as uniformly altruistic, idealistic and independent. But the term "NGO," like the activities of the NGOs themselves, deserves much sharper scrutiny.

Governments' Puppets?

The tag "Non-Governmental Organisation" was used first at the founding of the UN. It implies that NGOs keep their distance from officialdom; they do things that governments will not, or cannot, do. In fact, NGOs have a great deal to do with governments. Not all of it is healthy.

Take the aid NGOs. A growing share of development spending, emergency relief and aid transfers passes through them. According to Carol Lancaster, a former deputy director of USAID, America's development body, NGOs have become "the most important constituency for the activities of development aid agencies." Much of the food delivered by the World Food Programme, a UN body, in Albania last year was actually handed out by NGOs working in the refugee camps. Between 1990 and 1994, the proportion of the EU's relief aid channeled through NGOs rose from 47 percent to 67 percent. The Red Cross reckons that NGOs now disburse more money than the World Bank.

And governments are happy to provide that money. Of Oxfam's £98 million ($162 million) income in 1998, a quarter, £24.1 million, was given by the British government and the EU. World Vision U.S., which boasts of being the world's "largest privately funded Christian relief and development organisation," collected $55 million-worth of goods that year from the American government. Médecins Sans Frontières (MSF), the winner of last year's [1999's] Nobel peace prize, gets 46 percent of its income from government sources. Of 120 NGOs which sprang up in Kenya between 1993 and the end of 1996, all but nine received all their income from foreign governments and international bodies. Such official contributions will go on, especially if the public gets more stingy. Today's young, educated and rich give a smaller share of their incomes away than did—and do—their parents.

In Africa, where international help has the greatest influence, western governments have long been shifting their aid towards NGOs. America's help, some $711 million last year, increasingly goes to approved· organisations, often via USAID. Europe's donors also say that bilateral aid should go to NGOs, which are generally more open and efficient than governments. For the UN, too, they are now seen as indispensable. The new head of the UN's Development Programme says the body "will put a lot more emphasis on relations with NGOs." Most such agencies now have hundreds of NGO partners.

So the principal reason for the recent boom in NGOs is that western governments finance them. This is not a matter of charity, but of privatisation: many "non-governmental" groups are becoming contractors for governments. Governments prefer to pass aid through NGOs because it is cheaper, more efficient—and more at arm's length—than direct official aid.

Governments also find NGOs useful in ways that go beyond the distribution of food and blankets. Some bring back useful information, and make it part of their brief to do so. Outfits such as the International Crisis Group and Global Witness publish detailed and opinionated reports from places beset by war or other disasters. The work of Global Witness in Angola is actually paid for by the British Foreign Office.

Diplomats and governments, as well as other NGOs, journalists and the public, can make good use of these reports. As the staff of foreign embassies shrink, and the need to keep abreast of events abroad increases, governments inevitably turn to private sources of information. In some benighted parts of the world, sometimes only NGOs can nowadays reveal what is going on.

Take, for example, human rights, the business of one of the biggest of the campaigning NGOs, Amnesty International. Amnesty has around 1 million members in over 162 countries, and its campaigns against political repression, in particular against unfair imprisonment, are known around the world. The information it gathers is often unavailable from other sources.

Where western governments' interests match those of campaigning NGOs, they can form effective alliances. In 1997, a coalition of over 350 NGOs pushed for, and obtained, a treaty against the use of landmines. The campaign was backed by the usual array of concerned governments (Canada, the Scandinavians) and won the Nobel peace prize.

NGOs are also interesting and useful to governments because they work in the midst of conflict. Many were created by wars: the Red Cross after the Battle of Solferino in 1859, the Save the Children Fund after the First World War, MSF after the Biafran war. By being "close to the action" some NGOs, perhaps unwittingly, provide good cover for spies—a more traditional means by which governments gather information.

In some cases, NGOs are taking over directly from diplomats: not attempting to help the victims of war, but to end the wars themselves. Some try to restrict arms flows, such as Saferworld, which is against small arms. Others attempt to negotiate ceasefires. The Italian Catholic lay community of Sant' Egidio helped to end 13 years of civil war in Mozambique in 1992. International Alert, a London-based peace research group, tried the same for Sierra Leone in the mid-1990s. Last year, Unicef (a part of the UN) and the Carter Centre, founded by ex-President Jimmy

Carter, brought about a peace deal of sorts between Uganda and Sudan. There are now roughly 500 groups registered by the European Platform for Conflict Prevention and Transformation. "Civil war demands civil action," say the organisers.

Larger NGOs have pledged not to act as "instruments of government foreign policy." But at times they are seen as just that. Governments are more willing to pay groups to deliver humanitarian aid to a war zone than to deliver it themselves. Last autumn, America's Congress passed a resolution to deliver food aid to rebels in southern Sudan via USAID and sympathetic Christian groups (religious NGOs earn the label RINGOs, and are found everywhere).

Perhaps the most potent sign of the closeness between NGOs and governments, aside from their financial links, is the exchange of personnel. In developing countries where the civil service is poor, some governments ask NGOs to help with the paperwork requested by the World Bank and other international institutions. Politicians, or their wives, often have their own local NGOs. In the developed world, meanwhile, increasing numbers of civil servants take time off to work for NGOs, and vice versa: Oxfam has former staff members not only in the British government, but also in the Finance Ministry of Uganda.

This symbiotic relationship with government (earning some groups the tag GRINGO) may make the governments of developing countries work better. It may also help aid groups to do their job effectively. But it hardly reflects their independence.

NGOs can also stray too close to the corporate world. Some, known to critics as "business NGOs," deliberately model themselves on, or depend greatly on, particular corporations. Bigger ones have commercial arms, media departments, aggressive head-hunting methods and a wide array of private fund-raising and investment strategies. Smaller ones can be overwhelmed by philanthropic businesses or their owners: Bill Gates, the head of Microsoft, gave $25 million last year to an NGO that is looking for a vaccine for AIDS, transforming it overnight from a small group with a good idea to a powerful one with a lot of money to spend.

The Business of Helping

In 1997, according to the OECD, NGOs raised $5.5 billion from private donors. The real figure may well be higher: as leisure, travel and other industries have grown, so too have charities. In 1995 non-profit groups (including, but not only, NGOs) provided over 12 percent of all jobs in the Netherlands, 8 percent in America and 6 percent in Britain.

Many groups have come to depend on their media presence to help with fund-raising. This is bringing NGOs their greatest problems. They are adapting from shoebox outfits, stuffing envelopes and sending off perhaps one container of medicines, to sophisticated multi-million-dollar operations. In the now-crowded relief market, campaigning groups must jostle for attention: increasingly, NGOs compete and spend a lot of time and money marketing themselves. Bigger ones typically spend 10 percent of their funds on marketing and fund-raising.

The focus of such NGOs can easily shift from finding solutions and helping needy recipients to pleasing their donors and winning television coverage. Events at Goma, in Congo, in 1994 brought this problem home. Tens of thousands of refugees from Rwanda, who had flooded into Goma, depended on food and shelter from the UN High Commissioner for Refugees and from NGOs. Their dramatic plight drew the television cameras and, with them, the chance for publicity and huge donations. A frantic scramble for funds led groups to lie about their projects. Fearful that the media and then the public might lose confidence in NGOs, the Red Cross drew up an approved list of NGOs and got them to put their names to a ten-point code of conduct.

Since then, NGOs have been working hard to improve. More than 70 groups and 142 governments backed the 1995 code of conduct, agreeing that aid should be delivered "only on a basis of need." "We hold ourselves accountable to both those we seek to assist and those from whom we accept resources," they pledged. Yet in Kosovo last year there was a similar scramble, with groups pushing to be seen by camera crews as they worked. Personnel and resources were even shifted there from worse wars and refugee crises in Africa.

As they get larger, NGOs are also looking more and more like businesses themselves. In the past, such groups sought no profits, paid low wages—or none at all— and employed idealists. Now a whole class of them, even if not directly backed by businesses, have taken on corporate trappings. Known collectively as BINGOs, these groups manage funds and employ staff which a medium-sized company would envy. Like corporations, they attend conferences endlessly. Fund-raisers and senior staff at such NGOs earn wages comparable to the private sector. Some bodies, once registered as charities, now choose to become non-profit companies or charitable trusts for tax reasons and so that they can control their spending and programmes more easily. Many big charities have trading arms, registered as companies. One manufacturing company, Tetra Pak, has even considered sponsoring emergency food delivery as a way to advertise itself.

Any neat division between the corporate and the NGO worlds is long gone. Many NGOs operate as competitors seeking contracts in the aid market, raising funds with polished media campaigns and lobbying governments as hard as any other business. Governments and UN bodies could now, in theory, ask for tenders from businesses and NGOs to carry out their programmes. It seems only a matter of time before this happens. If NGOs are cheap and good at delivering food or health care in tough areas, they should win the contracts easily.

Good Intentions Not Enough

It could be argued that it does not matter even if NGOs are losing their independence, becoming just another arm of government or another business. GRINGOs and BINGOs, after all, may be more efficient than the old sort of charity.

Many do achieve great things: they may represent the last hope for civilians caught in civil wars, for those imprisoned unfairly and for millions of desperate refugees. There are many examples of small, efficient and inspirational groups with great achievements: the best will employ local people, keep foreign expertise to a minimum, attempt precise goals (such as providing clean water) and think deeply about the long-term impact of their work. Some of these grow into large, well-run groups.

But there are also problems. NGOs may be assumed to be less bureaucratic, wasteful or corrupt than governments, but under-scrutinised groups can suffer from the same chief failing: they can get into bad ways because they are not accountable to anyone.

Critics also suspect that some aid groups are used to propagate western values, as Christian missionaries did in the 19th century. Many NGOs, lacking any base in the local population and with their money coming from outside, simply try to impose their ideas without debate. For example, they often work to promote women's or children's interests as defined by western societies, winning funds easily but causing social disruption on the ground.

Groups that carry out population or birth-control projects are particularly controversial; some are paid to carry out sterilisation programmes in the poor parts of the world, because donors in the rich world consider there are too many people there. Anti-"slavery" campaigns in Africa, in which western NGOs buy children's freedom for a few hundreds dollars each, are notorious. Unicef has condemned such groups, but American NGOs continue to buy slaves—or people they consider slaves—in southern Sudan. Clearly, buying slaves, if that is what they are, will do little to discourage the practice of trading them.

NGOs also get involved in situations where their presence may prolong or complicate wars, where they end up feeding armies, sheltering hostages or serving as cover for warring parties. These may be the unintended consequences of aid delivery, but they also complicate foreign policy.

Even under calmer conditions, in non-emergency development work, not all single-interest groups may be the best guarantors of long-term success. They are rarely obliged to think about trade-offs in policy or to consider broad, cross-sector approaches to development. NGOs are "often organised to promote particular goals . . . rather than the broader goal of development," argues Ms. Lancaster. In Kosovo last spring [1999], "many governments made bilateral funding agreements with NGOs, greatly undermining UNHCR's [United Nations High Commissioner for Refugees] ability to prioritise programmes or monitor efficiency," says Peter Morris of MSF. This spring in Kosovo, "there were instances of several NGOs competing to work in the same camps, duplication of essential services," complains an Oxfam worker.

And whatever big international NGOs do in the developing world, they bring in western living standards, personnel and purchasing power which can transform local markets and generate great local resentment. In troubled zones where foreign NGOs flourish, weekends bring a line of smart four-by-fours parked at the best beaches, restaurants or nightclubs. The local beggars do well, but discrepancies between expatriate staff and, say, impoverished local officials trying to do the same work can cause deep antipathy. Not only have NGOs diverted funds away from local governments, but they are often seen as directly challenging their sovereignty.

NGOs can also become self-perpetuating. When the problem for which they were founded is solved, they seek new campaigns and new funds. The old anti-apartheid movement, its job completed, did not disband, but instead became another lobby group for southern Africa. As NGOs become steadily more powerful on the world scene, the best antidote to hubris, and to institutionalisation, would be this: disband when the job is done. The chief aim of NGOs should be their own abolition.

Pathogens

9.5 Together, in Sickness and in Health

Natalie Angier

Disease is increasingly a transnational security problem. To be sure, transnational epidemics are hardly new. Many more people died during the influenza epidemic of 1919 than had been killed in World War I, and diseases like bubonic plague, cholera, malaria, smallpox, and typhoid decimated populations with little regard for national identity or borders. However as AIDS (acquired immune deficiency syndrome) demonstrates, plagues now can cross borders and spread rapidly via modern transportation systems. Other transnational problems, like drug abuse, changing sexual mores, and economic underdevelopment, exacerbate the difficulties of controlling the epidemic. In turn, AIDS exacerbates other transnational problems, like poverty. Thus, "solving" the AIDS problem, or the problem of other infectious diseases like malaria and drug-resistant tuberculosis, is likely to require both a global approach and serious progress in resolving a complicated nexus of global economic, environmental, and social problems.

According to United Nations experts, one in every one hundred sexually active adults in the world is infected with HIV, the virus that causes AIDS, and nine of every ten of them are unaware that they have contracted the virus. More than five million people are infected each year. The virus has swept across Africa, following trade routes and ignoring borders. Although Africa has been the worst afflicted continent to date, the AIDS epidemic is truly global in scope, and Asia threatens to inherit this unhappy distinction in the near future.

In the following selection, Natalie Angier describes the accelerated spread of pathogens that comes with globalization. She focuses in particular on three killer diseases—malaria, AIDS, and tuberculosis—and their rapid transnational spread. These diseases show no respect for borders and, where they are endemic, have caused serious economic and social disruption, which in turn create more ripple effects that cross borders, undercutting prospects for happy, healthy lives around the globe. Thus both directly and indirectly these diseases weaken the global fabric of human security. In today's increasingly tightly linked and interdependent world, nations will have to cooperate to solve these problems. As Angier notes, however, globalization, as well as speeding the spread of diseases and complicating national efforts, may help in the search for cures.

Not long ago, my older brother, Joe, flew in from Los Angeles for a family gathering at my home outside Washington, looking paler than a dieting vampire and muttering that he might be "coming down with something." The rest of us eyed him warily, washed our hands compulsively and broke out the echinacea and vitamin C.

By the time my brother-in-law, Dave, had flown back to Oregon, he was too sick to return to work. My daughter and I also took to bed for a day or two, but then gamely pulled ourselves together to attend a big party at my mother's apartment in Manhattan—after which we collapsed once more in fevered, achy near-delirium. Later my mother told me that party guests from two different states had called to complain that I had given them some sort of "bug."

And so from one humble plucking of the kinship bond came an Attila-scale distribution of the season's flu virus, itself a strain that most likely had its genesis in Asia. My story is hardly unusual, and that is exactly my point. Today, diseases as common as the cold and as rare as Ebola are circling the globe with near telephonic speed, making long-distance connections and intercontinental infections almost as if by satellite. You needn't even bother to reach out and touch someone. If you live, if you're homeothermic biomass, you will be reached and touched. Microbes are, after all, members of the most ancient, zealous and Darwinically gilded 24–7 delivery consortium. They travel by land, sea, air, nose, blows, glove, love, sewage, steerage, rat backs, hat racks, uncooked burritos, overlooked mosquitoes.

And, oh, how they love the global village. How readily, for microbes, that village feels like home. Whether it's the recent outbreak of cholera in Buenos Aires, after years during which Latin America was free of the disease, or the debut in the emergency rooms of Manhattan of an African-born illness like West Nile fever, the globalization of disease is an unavoidable byproduct of the high holy multicultural hustle. And though microbes have always had the traveling bug, in centuries past, it at least took a few weeks or months for sailors to deliver a ship of rats bearing fleas with bubonic-plague bacteria from the Orient to Europe. Nowadays, a mosquito infested with the malaria parasite can be buzzing in Ghana at dawn and dining on an airport employee in Boston by cocktail hour.

Every day brings fresh evidence of how intimate are the links that lash together nations, peoples, bodies, species. One land's meat, for example, seems every land's poison, as hapless Britain has struggled with a double whammy on its livestock. Since 1988, nearly 180,000 cases of bovine spongiform encephalopathy—a.k.a. mad cow disease—have been reported in British cattle, along with several thousand cases elsewhere in Europe, raising fears that we're eating tainted hamburgers capable of delivering into our brains the deadly agent of Creutzfeldt-Jakob disease, and prompting the Department of Agriculture to ban animal protein products from Europe. Vegetarianism has beckoned even more brightly in the last few weeks with the televised images of macabre mass barbecues, as Britain, the Netherlands and a number of other countries have struggled to combat the recent outbreak of foot-and-mouth disease among their livestock. Nearly five million animals in Britain and hundreds of thousands elsewhere in Europe have been killed or await execution, resulting in meat, dairy and leather shortages worldwide, not to mention the tanning of the political hide of the British prime minister, Tony Blair.

"The globalization of health and disease is an incontrovertible fact," said Christopher J. Murray, a policy director with the World Health Organization in Geneva and an author of an influential report, "The Global Burden of Disease." "The travel and interaction between continents, and the exchange of people, animals, animal products, food products, disease vectors, are all vastly greater than in the past, and so is the potential for pathogens to move quickly from one place to another."

"Today I can be in a place like Mecca, where there's an outbreak of meningitis, and I would not know I was sick with it until I got home," said David L. Heymann, executive director in charge of communicable diseases at the World Health Organization in Geneva. "And think of all the people I'll expose on my trip back." Especially given the robustly recycled vaporous substances that passes for air in a modern jetliner.

The United States can give as well as it gets. In 1998, nearly 1,500 athletes from around the world competed in a triathalon in Springfield, Ill., where they were exposed during the swim portion of the event to leptospirosis bacteria, which can cause fever, chills, jaundice, meningitis and kidney failure. Of these, 72 sought medical attention, and the Centers for Disease Control and Prevention spent many weeks tracking down all the participants to warn them of possible symptoms and to seek immediate treatment should they arise, before permanent organ damage set in. Moreover, there was some risk of infected people releasing leptospirosis microbes into local water supplies through urination, further dispensing America's inadvertent gift to the spirit of international competition. "There's no epidemic in even the smallest corner of the globe that the world can afford to ignore," said Jacquelyn C. Campbell, a professor at Johns Hopkins School of Medicine's Board on Global Heath. "We're so interconnected that an isolationist's perspective is no longer an option."

A true understanding of that growing interconnectedness has to include the developing world, where most of the people on the planet live and where infectious diseases account for almost half the deaths each year. Half of those deaths can be attributed to three "pedestrian" yet persistently devastating diseases: malaria, HIV/AIDS and tuberculosis. Malaria kills more than one million people annually, the overwhelming majority of them children in sub-Saharan Africa. Many millions of other people living in more than 90 countries suffer from malaria, sometimes contracting it repeatedly year after year. Though they don't die of the disease, the debility and cost are enormous. By one estimate, Africa's gross domestic product would be $100 billion greater today than it is if malaria had been eliminated. And the warming global climate is carrying those malaria-bearing mosquitoes north. So is the 2:43 out of Kinshasa: planes landing in Charles de Gaulle Airport have recently been found to be carrying more than a few non-paying passengers, leading European airlines to step up their preflight extermination efforts.

Sub-Saharan Africa also has taken the most brutal jackhammering from the AIDS epidemic. Of the 35 million people living with HIV or AIDS in the world, 25 million are in sub-Saharan Africa. Of the 5.4 million people who are newly infected with the virus each year, 4 million live in sub-Saharan Africa. Helen Epstein, a former instructor at Makere University School of Medicine in Uganda, wrote recently in *The New York Review of Books* that "the AIDS epidemic in Africa may turn out to be the worst health crisis in the history of the human race." Thanks to the effectiveness of new drug regimens, Westerners have developed the false sense that AIDS is no longer a lethal disease. But apart from the fact that nobody knows how long patients on the new drug regimens will survive before the virus finally outmutates the current armamentarium, these drugs are expensive and difficult to take.

Moreover, the AIDS epidemic in Africa is unlikely to remain confined to Africa: the strains of HIV running rampant there, if left unchecked, are sure to gain novel malevolence that would allow them to spread elsewhere and overwhelm whatever resources we have devoted to defeating our Western-bred strains. And keep in mind that other highly populous countries like China and India are just beginning to feel the brunt of the disease. There's a perversely poetic loopiness at work: a disease that presumably had its origins in Africa made its first angry mark in America, then exploded in Africa, and is now moving onward, outward and back again, cat's-cradle style. It's not "Africa's" health crisis alone.

The only sane response to the world's AIDS crisis remains prevention—a response that hardly attracts an ounce of attention, let alone pounds, dollars or rubles. Last year, a total of $165 million from all sources was devoted to AIDS prevention in sub-Saharan Africa, compared with the $2.5 billion estimated as necessary to do even a perfunctory job. "When you see $9 billion going into the response to Creutzfeldt-Jakob disease, where you would expect a few hundred or maybe a few thousand cases at the most, while other, far greater public health problems are seriously neglected, we have to ask if we're getting the bang for our health bucks that we ought to get," said Joshua Lederberg, a Nobel-laureate infectious-disease expert at Rockefeller University. Don't look to the United States to swoop in and fix it: of the top 20 industrialized nations, the United States devotes the smallest percentage of its gross domestic product to battling these international epidemics.

But disease isn't the only thing moving around the globe with increasing speed, binding far-flung countries together in a mutual medical destiny. Medicines and methods of treatment are also part of the worldwide exchange. Pharmaceutical companies in the United States and Europe export a vast array of medications—from penicillin to protease inhibitors—to the developing world. And by seeking out alternative, local solutions from around the world, those companies, along with the best-endowed Western hospitals and research facilities, are beginning to level the balance of trade.

Where their citizens' health is concerned, some developing nations clearly have the edge over us on doing much more at fire-sale prices. In Chile, for example, the per-capita income today is about $5,000, the same as it was in the United States in the year 1900. But while the average life expectancy in our country a century ago was 47, in Chile today it is 76—pretty much the same as ours is now. And while Cuba remains an economic backwater, Castro's commitment to universal health care has paid off: the infant mortality rate there is the lowest by far in Latin America. (Meanwhile, the United States, which has the finest available health care, was ranked 54th by the

World Health Organization in terms of equality of access.) Whatever our squeamishness over methodology, we have a lot to learn from these countries and from others that have demonstrated successes in treating disease with a fraction of our resources.

We also have a lot to learn about the potential medical applications of herbs and extracts native to obscure corners of the continents. Seeking them out and bringing them back to the lab for study—bioprospecting, as these hunting expeditions have come to be known—has become a big business unto itself, incorporating the quest not only for flora, fauna and fungi, but even for exotic human genes to which biotech companies now routinely purchase the rights in hopes they will yield some insight, and some profit.

Globalization has also underscored a potentially universal source of human strength: in the tribe. We are clansfolk at heart, hardly past the mutual flea-plucking stage, and evolved to traffic comfortably with a few scores of people at best. As a result, global health care workers have found that the most effective health programs are local and inclusive. For example, says Patricia L. Rosenfield of the Carnegie Corporation in New York and a former member of the Board on Global Health, "Thailand has one of the most effective AIDS programs in the world because they take the power of the community seriously." Their education efforts are concentrated locally on individual villages, schools, groups of prostitutes. The lesson of "think global, nag local" can work here too: when doctors in Minnesota took the time to contact families whose children need follow-up booster shots, the overall effectiveness of the local vaccination program rose markedly. And tuberculosis outbreaks in both Africa and New York have been tamed by keeping an eye on infected people and ensuring that they take their medications every day.

As a number of articles in this issue make clear, the world is moving beyond the old polarities of ancient and modern, global and vernacular, high-tech and no-tech. We're not just mixing our microbes; we're hybridizing our medical traditions. Elisabeth Rosenthal describes a promising treatment being used at Memorial Sloan-Kettering Cancer Center that was developed by a folk healer in rural China. Matthew Steinglass visits a tribal doctor in South Africa who dispenses Western analgesics along with his herbal potions. In an article about a family of noble Italian lineage whose members suffer from an exceedingly rare genetic disease called fatal familial insomnia, D. T. Max describes the insights that the affliction has yielded into the general nature of prions, rogue proteins believed to be responsible for a number of brain disorders, mad cow disease among them.

It's not always easy to admit that other tribes are more enlightened than we are. America refuses to adopt the metric system, by gum, and we're way behind most countries of the world when it comes to the promotion and acceptance of the finest form of disease prevention known to medicine—breast-feeding. Sara Corbett describes the outrage and disgust that a Delaware woman elicits because she nurses her 4-year-old twins, though in many traditional societies breast-feeding children of 4, 5, 6 years of age is considered a sign of superlative mothering. And despite the sustained scoffery of American doctors, a number of "folk" remedies may be every bit as worthy as their mainstream pharmaco-counterparts, as Sheryl Gay Stolberg makes clear in her discussion of herbs like black cohosh, widely used in Europe but not here, to treat the symptoms of menopause.

In the end, then, the great global agora of medicine is all about barter: buying, selling, swapping, titting, tatting, seducing and swindling. We import a malign parasite here, we export a rotten fast-food franchise there. Merck donates medicines for river blindness to Africa. Americans fly to Thailand for discount plastic surgery. Through the Internet, too, we've become an obligate if virtual superorganism, busy bees without borders, compulsively foraging through a billion sites for sensation, guidance, palliatives or cures for lupus, chronic fatigue syndrome, nailbiting, insomnia, narcissism.

There is something unnerving about the distending column of health information ricocheting through our cyberhive, much of it unexpurgated, unedited and unconfirmed. At the same time, there is something glorious—OK, I'll call it miraculous—about anybody anywhere having free, instant computer access to Medline and all the papers published in thousands of medical journals around the world. Our modems have become medical devices, and as fast as microbes can move nowadays, ideas, Google willing, will always outrun them.

9.6 New Strain of Sovereignty

Christopher Caldwell

In the final selection of this chapter, Christopher Caldwell describes some of the problems in trying to limit the spread of disease in a globalizing world. He discusses the SARS epidemic that started in China and spread through much of Asia and into Canada and applies insights from this experience to other diseases. While sovereign states may still claim the right to decide the policies by which epidemics are treated within their own borders, increasingly the international community feels a stake in intervening, and a variety of international institutions may become involved.

These problems are widespread. Recently, for instance, objections to polio vaccination by Muslim leaders in northern Nigeria resulted not only in an outbreak there but to the spread of this disease to other countries where it had been eliminated. As a consequence, this disease that had been on the verge of global eradication is again on the rise.

This week, a second patient was hospitalised in China's Guangdong province with severe acute respiratory syndrome. Three Hong Kong journalists who returned home after visiting Guangdong to report on SARS are now in hospital, too, after showing symptoms. The disease that infected more than 8,000 people last winter and killed 774 of them is back. The Chinese patient is a waitress in a restaurant that serves civet cat, which is both a regional delicacy and, accord-

"New Strain of Sovereignty," by Christopher Caldwell, *Financial Times*, January 9, 2004. Reprinted by permission of the author.

ing to studies done last spring, a likely incubator for SARS. So the Chinese government has undertaken a search for the offending animals and claims to be drowning them by the thousand in disinfectant.

In addition to rousing the fury of Brigitte Bardot and other animal-rights activists, China's measures are worrying the Geneva-based World Health Organisation, which played a leading role in combating last year's outbreak. For one thing, it is not certain that civet cats are the main vector of disease to humans—or how exactly the disease spreads at all. The authorities could be squandering a chance to learn about SARS. Or worse: Agence France Presse has reported a rumour that some of the cats are being bludgeoned to death. If so, the authorities risk spreading SARS through the very measures meant to contain it. At a time when so much of the world is mobile, such reports raise troubling questions: if China—or any other afflicted country—were doing a bad job of tackling a fast-moving epidemic, what would we do about it?

China's record on SARS is mixed. Last winter it treated the outbreak with an efficiency made possible by its Communist party chain of command, setting up roadblocks across the country and rigorously enforcing quarantine and isolation. Last summer that efficiency was enhanced, with the creation of an internet-based SARS-reporting programme linking the country's 60,000 hospitals. China's record of sharing information about the virus, however, is poor. It stonewalled the WHO when researchers first inquired about the disease in November 2002 and it ordered reporters and editors to content themselves with reproducing the health ministry's official SARS updates. Last week the authorities arrested seven employees of the Southern Metropolis Daily newspaper, which has done investigative reporting on the latest SARS outbreak.

The fact that SARS broke out in China may have led us to underestimate the threat that similar diseases can pose to world order. China is a "strong state" in two senses: it can control its populace and enforce quarantines; and it is, by virtue of its size and military strength, invulnerable to foreign invasion and occupation. A SARS outbreak in a weak state might look very different. An epidemic leading to hundreds of deaths, as SARS did last spring, in a state that was highly populated, open to the world via air travel and relatively unsophisticated in its epidemiology could prompt the United Nations Security Council to take up the matter. After all, western leaders are constantly apologising for not having "done more" in big political crises, from Rwanda to Bosnia. Medical crises and political crises differ but the cases for intervening might not, if a given epidemic were sufficiently deadly and fast-moving.

In a medical intervention, the military principle that Robert Kagan, the American foreign policy expert, laid out in his book *Power and Weakness* might prove generally applicable: countries would split along the lines of their competences, not their ideologies. The U.S., with its centres for disease control and its unrivalled research hospitals, would claim leadership. But, in contrast to recent disputes, Europe would be united in sympathy to American arguments. In field medical capabilities, there is no "gap" between the two continents, of the sort that exists in military technology. Europe would thus claim a role more befitting its self-image.

But other countries would protest. For now, international law seems to grant a right to medical incompetence within one's own borders. Despite the highest AIDS case load on the planet, for instance, South Africa's President Thabo Mbeki turned his country into the public health equivalent of a rogue state, refusing for years to acknowledge a link between the disease and HIV and spurning advanced anti-retroviral drugs in his official pronouncements. The outrage was confined to AIDS activists and a few pressure groups. One wonders how long this right to incompetence will be granted by an ever more ambitious UN.

In a sense, then, it is lucky that a regime for influencing the conduct of afflicted states arose almost spontaneously out of last winter's crisis: the WHO's travel warnings. These have the effect of shutting down much international commerce and trade. The warnings from last winter's SARS outbreak are estimated to have cost the economies of Hong Kong and other hard-hit states $18 billion. While these warnings are applied according to strictly medical criteria, any opacity in public health reporting or stubborn obscurantism in treatment would make their imposition more likely.

Like a bond-rating agency, the WHO holds the economic fate of institutions and people in its hands and has shown itself willing to use that power ruthlessly. Last winter, its SARS experts discussed their hopes of limiting economic damage in the affected countries but did not consult those countries' sovereign governments in order to do so. The result was a series of turf battles, such as the one between the WHO and Jean Chretien, the former Canadian prime minister, over whether Canada's quarantines were sufficient to spare it a travel warning.

These are not just medical questions. The WHO now has a great deal of de facto authority—but it has not yet acquired a firm and permanent accountability to go with it. As elsewhere in the global economy, sovereignty is shifting in strange ways that nobody expected—in this case, out of the parliamentary chamber and into the laboratory. As the WHO changes from a kind of medical advisory board to a kind of regulator, it will gain the potential to do a great deal of good while sparing the world the frictions of international power politics. But it will also face temptations of high-handedness, which it will be up to the world's democracies to check.

Chapter 11

POVERTY AND DEVELOPMENT

As interdependence transforms the global security agenda, poverty emerges as one of the most pressing issues in world politics. Approximately 3.2 billion people live in low-income economies (economies with per capita gross national product [GNP] of $725 or less), in many cases at the edge of survival. Although every society has its rich and poor, the gap between the world's industrialized North (the rich First World nations of North America, Western Europe, Australia, and Japan and the ex-communist Second World nations of Eastern Europe and the former Soviet Union) and the economically less-developed nations of the world's South (Latin America, Asia, and Africa) is enormous. The developing countries, home to four-fifths of the world's population, earn only about one-fifth of the world's GNP. Although India and China account for large numbers of the world's poor, twenty-nine of the fifty poorest countries in the world are located in sub-Saharan Africa, including the ten poorest. These regions are burdened by high population growth, widespread disease, poor education systems, and subsistence agricultural economies. In many of the poorest societies, wealth and land are concentrated in the hands of a small elite, creating huge disparities within these societies. Rural poverty and underemployment encourage immense migrations to urban centers, where people live in wretched conditions in "shanty towns" and "favelas" without sanitation or pure water.

These problems are worsening rather than disappearing. Since 1980, the gap between rich and poor has widened rather than narrowed. During this period the income of roughly a quarter of the world's population has declined, and in forty-three countries average incomes are actually lower than they were in 1970. During the 1980s (sometimes called the "lost decade"), per capita income in Latin America fell by 7 percent. In sub-Saharan Africa, per capita GNP dropped by 10 percent, and real prices for major export commodities, notably tea, coffee, cocoa, and cotton, fell by more than 50 percent in real terms. Many African countries confronted a mountain of debt and were forced to use up all or most of their earnings from exports merely to pay interest on that debt. Overall, during the last three decades, the share of global income enjoyed by the richest 20 percent of the world's population rose from 70 to 85 percent, while the share of the poorest 20 percent declined from 2.3 to 1.4 percent.

Poverty is associated with a variety of serious problems. Approximately 17 million people die each year in the developing world from curable diseases like malaria, and 90 percent of all those infected with HIV, the virus that causes AIDS, live in these countries. Approximately 500 million people in the developing world are chronically malnourished, including more than a third of the children.

The world's poor are, in large measure, either left out of the economic globalization discussed in the previous chapter or are its victims. Globalized markets and transnational corporations may provide opportunities, stimulating economic development and creating new or higher-paying jobs. In some parts of the world, however, this economic development has proceeded only slowly, if at all, and gaps between the world's rich and the world's poor continue to widen. And where economic development has proceeded, it has come at a price, threatening social stability and traditional values and straining the environment. Integrating the world's poor into the global economy, and doing so in a way that does not perpetuate poverty, thus represents a major challenge in today's world. The new integrative institutions and actors discussed in preceding chapters—intergovernmental organizations, nongovernmental organizations, transnational corporations, international law, and the web of complex interdependence that is resulting in increased interstate cooperation—all play an important role in this development process.

The way in which the world deals with poverty is likely to determine whether the coming decades are peaceful and stable or violent and dangerous. Poverty produces frustration and anger, directed both at the governments of developing countries and at citizens of wealthy countries. It is from the densely packed slums of the developing world's "megacities" (urban centers with a population of more than ten million) that angry young terrorists emerge determined to take revenge on their own rulers or on wealthy foreigners and to make the world take notice of their plight. Civil war, lawlessness, and refugees are some of the consequences of urban overcrowding, unemployment, and poverty.

The problems of global poverty and underdevelopment thus draw together a number of the strands we have been exploring: how the disintegration of some political institutions and the rise of others, like a global economy, are transforming life, and how a whole new set of issues is making its way onto the global security agenda.

11.1 Human Development—Past, Present and Future

United Nations Development Program

The first selection in this chapter, excerpted from a United Nations study of global poverty and underdevelopment, describes the effort to create "an environment in which people can develop their full potential and lead productive, creative lives." As this study documents, economic growth has varied dramatically around the globe.

Human development is about much more than the rise or fall of national incomes. It is about creating an environment in which people can develop their full potential and lead productive, creative lives in accord with their needs and interests. People are the real wealth of nations. Development is thus about expanding the choices people have to lead lives that they value. And it is thus about much more than economic growth, which is only a means—if a very important one—of enlarging people's choices.

Fundamental to enlarging these choices is building human capabilities—the range of things that people can do or be in life. The most basic capabilities for human development are to lead long and healthy lives, to be knowledgeable, to have access to the resources needed for a decent standard of living and to be able to participate in the life of the community. Without these, many choices are simply not available, and many opportunities in life remain inaccessible.

This way of looking at development, often forgotten in the immediate concern with accumulating commodities and financial wealth, is not new. Philosophers, economists and political leaders have long emphasized human well-being as the purpose, the end, of development. As Aristotle said in ancient Greece, "Wealth is evidently not the good we are seeking, for it is merely useful for the sake of something else."

In seeking that something else, human development shares a common vision with human rights. The goal is human freedom. And in pursuing capabilities and realizing rights, this freedom is vital. People must be free to exercise their choices and to participate in decision-making that affects their lives. Human development and human rights are mutually reinforcing, helping to secure the well-being and dignity of all people, building self-respect and the respect of others. . . .

Human development challenges remain large in the new millennium. Across the world we see unacceptable levels of deprivation in people's lives. Of the 4.6 billion people in developing countries, more than 850 million are illiterate, nearly a billion lack access to improved water sources, and 2.4 billion lack access to basic sanitation. Nearly 325 million boys and girls are out of school. And 11 million children under age five die each year from preventable causes—equivalent to more than 30,000 a day. Around 1.2 billion people live on less than $1 a day (1993 PPP [Purchasing Power Parity] US$), and 2.8 billion on less than $2 a day. Such deprivations are not limited to developing countries. In OECD [Organization for Economic Cooperation and Development] countries more than 130 million people are income poor, 34 million are unemployed, and adult functional illiteracy rates average 15 percent.

The magnitude of these challenges appears daunting. Yet too few people recognize that the impressive gains in the developing world in the past 30 years demonstrate the possibility of eradicating poverty. A child born today can expect to live eight years longer than one born 30 years ago. Many more people can read and write, with the adult literacy rate having increased from an estimated 47 percent in 1970 to 73 percent in 1999. The share of rural families with access to safe water has grown more than fivefold. Many more people can enjoy a decent standard of living, with average incomes in developing countries having almost doubled in real terms between 1975 and 1998, from $1,300 to $2,500 (1985 PPP US$). . . .

Behind this record of overall progress lies a more complex picture of diverse experiences across countries, regions, groups of people and dimensions of human development. . . .

Regional Contrasts in the Pace of Progress   All regions have made progress in human development in the past 30 years, but advancing at very different paces and achieving very different levels. East Asia and the Pacific has made rapid, sustained progress in most areas, from expanding knowledge to improving survival to raising standards of living. South Asia and Sub-Saharan Africa lag far behind other regions, with human and income poverty still high. The adult literacy rate in South Asia is still 55 percent and in Sub-Saharan Africa 60 percent, well below the developing country average of 73 percent. Life expectancy at birth in Sub-Saharan Africa is still only 48.8 years, compared with more than 60 in all other regions. And the share of people living on less than $1 a day is as high as 46 percent in Sub-Saharan Africa and 40 percent in South Asia, compared with 15 percent in East Asia and the Pacific and in Latin America.

The Arab States also lag behind in many indicators, but have been making the most rapid progress. Since the early 1970s life expectancy at birth has improved by 14 years and the infant mortality rate by 85 per 1,000 live births, and since 1985 the adult literacy rate has risen by 15 percentage points—faster progress than in any other region.

Differences among regions and countries are particularly marked in economic growth, which generates public resources to invest in education and health services and increases the resources people have to enjoy a decent standard of living and improve many other aspects of their lives. In 1975–99 per capita income quadrupled in East Asia and the Pacific, growing 6 percent a year. The growth rate in South Asia exceeded 2 percent. Two countries that together account for a third of the world population did well: per capita income in China grew at an impressive 8 percent a year, and in India at an average rate of 3.2 percent. OECD countries had average growth of 2 percent a year, raising already high incomes to an average of more than $22,000 (PPP US$).

But in the Arab States and Latin America and the Caribbean growth has been slower, averaging less than 1 percent. Most devastating has been the performance of Sub-Saharan Africa, where already low incomes have fallen; in 1975–99 GDP per capita growth in the region averaged −1 percent. Madagascar and Mali now have per capita incomes of $799 and $753 (1999 PPP US$)—down from $1,258 and $898 (1999 PPP US$) 25 years ago. In 16 other Sub-Saharan countries per capita incomes were also lower in 1999 than in 1975. In Eastern Europe and the Commonwealth of Independent States (CIS) too, incomes have dropped sharply. Since 1990 per capita incomes have declined in 16 countries—in 4 by more than half. . . .

Unequal Incomes

Income is a very important means of enlarging people's choices and is used in the HDI [Human Development Index] as a proxy for a decent standard of living. Income growth has varied considerably among countries in recent decades, more so than trends in many human development indicators. The distribution of the world's income, and the way this is changing, are thus a vital issue deserving special consideration.

Income levels across countries have been both diverging and converging—with some regions closing the income gap and others drifting away. In 1960 there was a bunching of regions, with East Asia and the Pacific, South Asia, Sub-Saharan Africa and the least developed countries having an average per capita income around ⅑ to ⅒ of that in high-income OECD countries. Latin America and the Caribbean fared better, but still had just ⅓ to ½ of the per capita income of these OECD countries.

The impressive growth in East Asia and the Pacific is reflected in the improvement in the ratio of its income to that of high-income OECD countries, from around ⅒ to nearly ⅕ over 1960–98. The relative income in Latin America and the Caribbean stayed about the same. Income in South Asia—after worsening in the 1960s and 1970s, then improving significantly in the 1980s and 1990s—remains about ⅒ of that in OECD countries. In Sub-Saharan Africa the situation has worsened dramatically: per capita income, around ⅑ of that in high-income OECD countries in 1960, deteriorated to around 1/18 by 1998.

Despite a reduction in the relative differences between many countries, absolute gaps in per capita income have increased. Even for East Asia and the Pacific, the fastest growing region, the absolute difference in income with high-income OECD countries widened from about $6,000 in 1960 to more than $13,000 in 1998 (1985 PPP US$).

Within-Country Inequality—What's Hiding Behind Average Incomes?   Also important is income inequality within countries, which may affect long-term prosperity. Although there are reasonable data on within-country inequality for points in time, the data are not based on uniform surveys across countries and so comparisons must be treated with care. But even very rough comparisons reveal a lot about within-country inequality. . . .

Latin American and Caribbean countries have among the world's highest income inequality. In 13 of the 20 countries with data for the 1990s, the poorest 10 percent had less than 1/20 of the income of the richest 10 percent. This high income inequality places millions in extreme poverty and severely limits the effect of equally shared growth on poverty. So Latin America and the Caribbean can reach the Millennium Declaration's development target of halving poverty by 2015 only if the region generates more growth and that growth disproportionately benefits poor people. . . .

China and India—two countries with low but rapidly growing per capita incomes and large populations—deserve special consideration. In China inequality has followed a U-shaped pattern, with inequality falling until the mid-1980s and rising since. The story is better in India, with inequality falling until recently, and then coming to a halt.

Many countries in Sub-Saharan Africa have high levels of income inequality. In 16 of the 22 Sub-Saharan countries with data for the 1990s, the poorest 10 percent of the population had less than ⅒ of the income of the richest 10 percent and in 9 less than 1/20. Despite the pressing need to understand what is happening to income inequality over time in this poor region, trend data on income distribution remain too limited to draw conclusions.

Most countries in Eastern Europe and the CIS have relatively low inequality—though there are notable exceptions, such as Armenia and the Russian Federation. . . .

Among OECD countries there is also diversity in income inequality, from the low levels in Austria and Denmark to the relatively high levels in the United Kingdom and the United States. Still, in global terms income inequality among these countries is relatively low. What about trends over time? Results from a variety of country and cross-country studies suggest that income inequality increased in many OECD countries between the mid- to late 1980s and mid- to late 1990s. While data for earlier periods are more limited, these countries seem to have experienced a U-shaped change in inequality, with declines in the 1970s changing to increases in the 1980s and 1990s. The constant level in Canada and slight improvement in Denmark are exceptions to the apparent trend.

World Inequality Another measure of inequality looks both between and within countries—lining up all the world's people from richest to poorest (in real purchasing power) regardless of national boundaries. A recent study. . . compares the poorest and richest people across the globe, giving a much more complete picture of world inequality than a simple comparison of country averages would. Based on household surveys for 1988–93, the study covers 91 countries (with about 84 percent of the world's population) and adjusts income levels using purchasing power parity conversions. The disadvantage is that the study relies entirely on household budget survey data that are not necessarily comparable and are limited in their scope. Nevertheless, the study produced some powerful results.

♦ World inequality is very high. In 1993 the poorest 10 percent of the world's people had only 1.6 percent of the income of the richest 10 percent.

♦ The richest 1 percent of the world's people received as much income as the poorest 57 percent.

♦ The richest 10 percent of the U.S. population (around 25 million people) had a combined income greater than that of the poorest 43 percent of the world's people (around 2 billion people).

♦ Around 25 percent of the world's people received 75 percent of the world's income (in PPP US$).

Inequality and Mobility Two societies with the same income inequality could differ greatly in the mobility and opportunity facing individual members—and in the mobility and opportunity that children have relative to their parents. A focus on mobility helps to identify the factors that block the opportunities of poor people and contribute to the intergenerational transmission of poverty. . . .

In every country family background significantly influences the length of children's schooling. Children with wealthier, better-educated parents are always likely to do better. But there is substantial variation across countries and periods, depending on macroeconomic conditions and public education policies.

An emphasis on basic schooling in public spending enhances intergenerational mobility in Latin America. There, a person needs at least 10 years of schooling to have a 90 percent or higher probability of not falling into poverty or of moving out of poverty. And having just 2 years less schooling means 20 percent less income for the rest of a person's active life. . . .

The Millennium Declaration's Goals for Development and Poverty Eradication

As the world entered the new millennium, heads of state and government gathered at the United Nations General Assembly to lay out their vision for the world. The leaders of the summit adopted the United Nations Millennium Declaration, recognizing their "collective responsibility to uphold the principles of human dignity, equality and equity at the global level." Among the many objectives set out by the declaration are specific, quantified and monitorable goals for development and poverty eradication by 2015:

◆ To halve the proportion of the world's people living on less than $1 a day.

◆ To halve the proportion of the world's people suffering from hunger.

◆ To halve the proportion of the world's people without access to safe drinking water.

◆ To achieve universal completion of primary schooling.

◆ To achieve gender equality in access to education.

◆ To reduce maternal mortality ratios by three-quarters.

◆ To reduce under-five mortality rates by two-thirds.

◆ To halt and begin to reverse the spread of HIV/AIDS, malaria and other major diseases.

These goals build on the international development goals, which include three more targets—namely, to reduce infant mortality rates by two-thirds, to provide access for all who want reproductive health services and to implement national strategies for sustainable development by 2005 to reverse the loss of environmental resources by 2015.

What are the prospects for achieving these goals? The good news is that for universal primary education and gender equity in education, many developing countries have already achieved the goals or are on track to do so. Because of the importance of education to so many areas of development, these bright prospects strengthen the possibilities for accelerating progress towards the other goals. . . . Furthermore, over 60 percent of the world's people live in 43 countries that have met or are on track to meet the goal of halving the number of people who are hungry.

The bad news is that in other areas more than half the countries for which data are available will not achieve the goals without a significant acceleration in progress. Many of these are least developed countries in Sub-Saharan Africa. While 50 countries have achieved or are on track to achieve the safe water goal, 83 countries with 70 percent of the world's people are lagging or far behind. And while 62 countries are on track to reduce maternal mortality by three-quarters, 83 are lagging or far behind. In income poverty, more than 40 percent of the world's people live in countries that are on track to meet the goal. But they are concentrated in 11 countries, including India and China, while 70 countries are far behind or slipping. Though these countries contain only a third of the world's people, they constitute more than half of all developing countries. Without China and India,

9 countries, with 5 percent of the world's people, would be on track to halve the proportion of people living in extreme income poverty. The situation is perhaps most serious for under-five mortality. While 66 countries are on track to meet the goal, 83 countries with around 60 percent of the world's people are lagging or far behind—and in 10 under-five mortality rates are increasing. While there is not comparable trend data on the prevalence of HIV/AIDS to do a full analysis, the global prevalence of HIV/AIDS among adults is still on the rise, with only a handful of countries, such as Uganda and possibly Zambia, showing signs of decline.

 # Who Are the Poor?

11.2 Killing for Scratch on BMW Reveals China's Wealth Gap

Jonathan Watts

One of the consequences of economic globalization has been the widening of gaps in wealth *within,* as well as between, countries. Nowhere is this growing gap more evident than in China where a few individuals have become extremely rich through global trade and business, leaving farther and farther behind hundreds of millions of mainly rural Chinese peasants. In the following selection, Jonathan Watts of the British *Guardian* tells the extraordinary story of how a newly wealthy wife of a businessman in the city of Harbin became infuriated by a peasant woman who had accidentally scratched the wing-mirror of her BMW and then intentionally ran over the peasant woman. As this story indicates, in many cases globalization and economic development bring with them growing inequities in societies, inequities that raise not only troubling moral questions but worries about long-term political stability.

I t was the smallest of prangs, but the minor traffic accident between a top-of-the-range BMW and a rickety farmer's tractor has prompted the Chinese authorities into drastic action to prevent a head-on collision between the top and bottom classes of its increasingly divided society.

"The BMW incident," as it is now widely known, forced the authorities to hold a retrial and made the propaganda ministry slam the brakes on Internet chatrooms filled with public resentment.

This thoroughly modern Chinese tale of social inequality, dubious justice and appalling driving began innocuously one day last October when Liu Zhongxia, a peasant woman, and her husband Dai Yiquan were rattling through Harbin, in Heliongjiang province, in a tractor piled high with onions.

A few years ago they would have enjoyed the freedom of almost empty roads, but China's booming economy is increasing the traffic at the rate of more than 20 percent a year. In one of the many changes of direction prompted by oncoming cars, Mr. Liu scratched the wing-mirror of a new BMW X5, prompting an altercation which has still to die down six months later.

The details of the road rage incident have become the stuff of myth, but according to the local media, the driver of the BMW, Su Xiuwen, hit Mrs. Liu with her purse and screamed: "How can you afford to scratch my car?"

The furious woman—the wife of a business tycoon—then got back in her car, slammed her foot on the accelerator and ran over Mrs. Liu, killing her and injuring a dozen other bystanders.

Public anger at this display of petulance was only increased by the trial on December 20 [2003], when Mrs. Su was cleared of manslaughter and given a suspended sentence. In a hearing that lasted only two hours, the court accepted her claim that she had accidentally put her car into the wrong gear.

But with little faith in the judicial system, many people are convinced that the case was decided by bribes.

Not one witness turned up to testify, not even Mr. Dai, who accepted an out-of-court settlement of 80,000 RMB (£6,000)—equivalent of eight years wages—for the death of his wife.

He told reporters he had had little choice. "I told police that she drove into the crowd on purpose," he said. "But no one dared stand up as a witness. I had to give up because I was helpless. I have no money, no power."

The same could not be said of Mrs. Su, whose husband, Guan Ming Bo, has earned a fortune as a property developer. As well as buying a car worth £60,000, the couple splashed out on a personalised license plate bearing the number 6666, which is considered auspicious in China. They also admitted buying Mrs. Su's licence by paying an experienced driver to take the driving test on her behalf.

Millions were willing to believe the rumours circulating on the Internet that Mrs. Su has threatened to run people down before the accident, and that she had been able to escape punishment because her husband was related to a senior official in the local authority.

While such accusations lack evidence and have been denied by the parties involved, they fit a growing public belief that wealth equals corruption in a country that once prided itself on communist equality but is now racked by suspicions that officials are exploiting their control of land, the courts and the media to grow rich and escape justice.

The feeling is particularly strong in Harbin, the heart of the rust-belt in northeastern China, where millions of workers have been laid off from state-owned enterprises since the switch to a market economy.

But it is spreading everywhere with the growing unease about the disparity between the urban rich and the rural poor, which rose last year to a record 4:1.

"If it were a rich family who lost a member like that, they would pursue justice in the courts," a woman who gave her name as Mrs. Yang said in Beijing yesterday.

"But the poor don't have the power to fight back."

Public anger was apparent on the Internet, which is now accessible by 78 million people and has become the main outlet for dissent. At the peak of interest after the trial, more than 200,000 comments were posted on chatroom sites.

Fearful that the BMW affair might become a cause célèbre, the authorities ordered newspapers to play down or stop their coverage. The national propaganda department also instructed major chatrooms to tone down the contributions they were receiving.

To placate opinion, Heilongjiang province ordered a retrial. But it was reported this week that the outcome was the same. With newspaper and website editors now under orders to dampen the emotions aroused by the affair, the verdict has been given scant coverage. But experts said it was unlikely to be the last China heard of such disturbances.

"This case highlights the growing social concern about the gap in economic status," said Qu Wen Yong, a Heilongjiang University sociologist. "People believe the rich can influence the law behind the scenes with money. More cases like the BMW furore are likely to happen in the future."

 # Aid and Good Governance

11.3 Who Helps the World?

Karen DeYoung

Although private capital is an important source of development, foreign aid is critically important in relieving poverty, building basic infrastructure, and providing for education in many parts of the developing world. But since the end of the Cold War, the United States, never generous by international standards, has given less and less foreign development aid. As Karen DeYoung of the *Washington Post* points out in the next article, the United States now gives less than one-tenth of 1 percent of its gross national product. (This is about as much as it spends to buy one aircraft carrier and its associated airplanes.) How and where this money, and money given by private donors, is spent is controversial. Aid supporters point out that it is cheaper to help with development than to respond to the crises that occur when development fails. Critics point to waste.

From *The Washington Post National Weekly Edition,* December 13, 1999. © 1999, The Washington Post, reprinted with permission.

While America has enjoyed one of its most prosperous decades ever in the 1990s, it also has set a record for stinginess. For as long as people have kept track, never has the United States given a smaller share of its money to the world's poorest.

Although the size of its economy makes America a major foreign aid donor— and Americans as individuals are generous givers to domestic and foreign emergencies—the country is the most parsimonious in the world when its charity is measured as a fraction of available riches. In 1997, the U.S. government spent about $7 billion on traditional, nonmilitary foreign aid, or less than one-tenth of 1 percent of the $8.1 trillion gross national product. That was the lowest percentage of any donor country and less than half the proportion that America spent just 10 years earlier.

But the United States is far from the only country giving less; declining generosity has become a worldwide trend. Overall international foreign assistance has fallen sharply since the end of the Cold War, dropping 21 percent in inflation-adjusted terms between 1992 and 1997.

The reasons for the decline are not hard to find. Critics have long said that foreign assistance was wasted by bloated aid agencies pouring money into the pockets of corrupt Third World governments.

When the Soviet Union collapsed, Western powers no longer felt the need to purchase the Cold War loyalty of such governments. With a less threatening world beyond their borders, donor nations came under pressure to attend to problems at home.

"All they want is to give the taxpayers' money away to foreign countries and be damned what happens at home," Republican Rep. Harold Rogers of Kentucky said in a floor speech last month [November 1999] as Congress slashed President Clinton's foreign aid budget request.

The shrinking amount of aid has imposed a rigid new calculus on where the assistance goes. Major natural disasters and strategically important trouble spots—Turkish earthquakes, Balkan wars and Middle East peace agreements—have continued to attract international largess, particularly when television cameras are on hand to broadcast the need and document the good deeds.

The principal loser in this equation has been Africa, where the impact of declining funds and shifting priorities is felt in increasingly scarce resources to combat hunger, homelessness and disease.

The United Nations aid agencies, which depend on voluntary contributions from member nations, are the primary dispensers of assistance to Africa. This year, donors have provided less than three-fifths of the $800 million UN request for emergencies in sub-Saharan Africa. The UN target had already been reduced by nearly a third from last year after donors complained it was too high.

In September, the UN's World Food Program announced it would curtail its feeding program for nearly 2 million refugees in Sierra Leone, Liberia and Guinea after receiving less than 20 percent of requested funding.

An emergency appeal during the summer to feed and shelter at least 600,000 Angolans who had been displaced in that country's long-standing civil war—a number nearly equal to Kosovo's refugees of last spring—brought minimal initial response and predictions of mass starvation.

In Africa's Great Lakes region of Congo, Burundi and Rwanda, where overlapping wars have been raging for years, nearly 4 million people are crowded into refugee camps or hiding in the hills far from roads and towns. Nearly all farmers or herders, they are without land and livestock, and in many cases without access to health services or other humanitarian assistance. This year, the United Nations estimated it would need $278 million to take care of them. By late October, only 45 percent of that amount had been donated.

Africa also has been largely bypassed by the mushrooming flows of private investment funds that have offset the decline in foreign aid in other regions, such as East Asia and Latin America, where investors have seen better potential returns. Africa's problems seem an old story, with disasters declared with dulling regularity, victims located far from anyone's strategic ken or camera range, savage wars and governments that rob their own people. Because things seem to have gotten worse, rather than better, critics of foreign aid tend to view money sent to Africa as wasted on a lost cause.

But to the proponents and practitioners of foreign aid, this depressing logic condemns the world's most needy to falling ever further behind precisely because they have been unable to get ahead.

It is, says Mark Malloch Brown, director of the United Nations Development Program (UNDP), "a very Darwinian situation."

The 1990s have been a demoralizing decade for the professional aid community—those in government, multinational and private agencies who determine where funds are needed and how they should be spent, lobby donors to come up with the money and deliver the aid to the field.

Not only was overall funding down, but the largest aid undertakings were notorious failures.

In Somalia, a combined military-humanitarian intervention collapsed in lethal firefights and recrimination.

In Bosnia, programs to feed the victims of atrocities became a grotesque smoke screen to conceal the lack of political will to stop the killings.

In the case of Rwanda, the international community ended up feeding and supplying the very perpetrators of genocide.

The aid agencies got much of the blame. If they couldn't succeed in places like Somalia and Rwanda, where the money was flowing freely, why give them more? After Rwanda, says Francisco Hochschild, special assistant to UN Humanitarian Coordinator Sergio Vieria de Mello, "budgets started shrinking."

But then, Hochschild says, "Kosovo turned up to save everybody."

If the selection of those deserving of foreign assistance is Darwinian, then the people of Kosovo are among the world's fittest. The survival and safe return of 730,000 Kosovo Albanians was "one of the most spectacular reverse population movements in contemporary history," UN High Commissioner for Refugees Sadako Ogata said last summer.

But in fundamental ways, Kosovo confirmed the worst fears of aid officials, that they have become active participants in a process that concentrates assistance on the most strategically located and widely televised crises, often at the expense of the most needy.

The hundreds of millions of dollars spent on Kosovo refugees and the crush of aid agencies eager to spend it "was almost an obscenity," says Randolph Kent, who worked with the United Nations in the Balkans until last summer, when he became the coordinator of UN aid programs for Somalia. Some aid workers called the Kosovo Albanians "the Pampers refugees" in an exaggerated reference to material comforts unavailable to Africans.

The need in Kosovo was undeniably large and urgent. But many aid officials acknowledge that a large part of their eagerness came from "the CNN effect"—the symbiotic relationship among donor governments, foreign aid agencies and television. The aid agencies know they are in a business that must justify its existence in ways that those supplying the money can see and approve. Television coverage both reflects and promotes high-level donor interest, so aid agencies' activities tend to follow the cameras. . . .

"What Kosovo highlighted" for both government and private donors, says the UN's Hochschild, "was that some . . . were happy to [pay to] set up camps at huge expense, with soldiers, in front of the TV cameras. That's what they're not willing to do in Angola and in Central Africa," where the media rarely ventures.

But donors who contributed heavily for Kosovo now have less left for other regions. "Kosovo doesn't mean we're going to get less for Africa" this year, says Thomas H. Fox, AID's assistant administrator for policy. "But it might prevent our being able to make a successful case for more" in the future.

"What you're looking at is not a bottomless pot of gold, but a very limited amount of money available throughout the world for crisis. If it happens to be somewhere in Europe, everybody else is out of luck," says Neville Pradham, a Geneva-based appeals coordinator for ACT, the private emergency aid agency supported by Protestant churches worldwide. The response of churches and their parishioners to ACT appeals for Africa, he says, has been disappointing.

Many Africans believe the disparity in aid has deeper roots than the strategic imperatives of donor nations and the news judgment of the media.

During a UN Security Council meeting with more than a dozen representatives of African countries in September, speaker after African speaker implied or charged outright that racism played a major role in the level of aid to the continent and the decreased willingness of the West to become involved in helping Africa settle its conflicts.

A citizen of Congo was no less deserving than someone from Kosovo or East Timor, says Andre Mwamba Kapanga, the representative of the Democratic Republic of the Congo. "The color of his skin," he says, "does not make him a substandard being."

Nigerian representative Ibrahim Gambari called on the Security Council to compare the world's response to the Kosovo crisis—where he said the international community spent $1.50 per day per refugee—to the response to conflicts in Sierra Leone and Rwanda, where he said the daily expenditure per refugee was 11 cents.

In a speech in August to the Veterans of Foreign Wars, President Clinton included a brief plug for increased U.S. foreign aid to Africa.

"These efforts don't make a lot of headlines. I'll bet most of you don't know much about them," Clinton told the veterans. "That's good, because the point is to avoid headlines . . . about famine and refugee crisis and genocide, and to replace them, instead, with stories of partnership and shared prosperity. These are the stories we can write now . . . if Congress will invest only a tiny portion of what we spend on defense on avoiding war in the first place."

Clinton's point was one that aid scholars and practitioners make repeatedly—that giving foreign aid now is cheaper, both in moral and monetary terms, than what might be necessary if Africa's "basket cases" are allowed to fester. But it is an argument that makes little headway in Congress, where there is widespread doubt about whether foreign aid really works.

"The United Nations has declared that 70 countries—aid recipients all—are now poorer than they were in 1980," responds aid critic Doug Bandow of the libertarian Cato Institute. "An incredible 43 were worse off than in 1970. Chaos, slaughter, poverty and ruin stalked Third World states, irrespective of how much foreign assistance they received." Except for Haiti, all of the 13 foreign aid failures he cites—Somalia, Sierra Leone, Liberia, Angola, Chad, Burundi, Rwanda, Uganda, Zaire, Mozambique, Ethiopia and Sudan—were in sub-Saharan Africa.

AID and UN officials reply that, with the exception of Haiti and Somalia, both scenes of expensive military interventions as well as aid, the amount of assistance received by these countries pales beside that bestowed elsewhere—to Egypt, Israel, India, Pakistan, Indonesia and the Philippines, among others now considered aid success stories. And according to AID statistics, it is thanks in large part to foreign aid that world literacy rose by nearly 50 percent in the last third of this century, infant mortality was halved, life expectancy tripled and 71 more nations have become "free or partly free."

But the skepticism of Bandow and others is strengthened by severely troubled situations like the one in Central Africa. At least two, and sometimes three, wars are simultaneously being fought in the region, ethnic strife has led to the slaughter of thousands of people including numerous aid workers, and the parties seem impervious to pleas to stop.

Even where there is peace in Africa, corruption often siphons off both domestic and foreign resources at staggering levels. According to the World Bank, nearly 40 percent of Africa's aggregate wealth has fled to foreign bank accounts. Of the 20 countries most highly indebted to the U.S. government, 15 are in sub-Saharan Africa.

In an appeal for funds this fall, UN Secretary General Kofi Annan acknowledged that there sometimes seems little promise that aid to Africa will accomplish much. "There are, in short, places where the widely held view of Africa as a region in perpetual crisis is not just an image, but an all-too-grim and painful reality," he said.

"But there are also places, more than is commonly recognized, where we are witnessing dramatic changes for the better," he added. While problems persist in Sierra Leone, Sudan, Somalia and elsewhere, he says, the international community must "seize this moment" to engage with those parts of a society prepared to turn a corner. . . .

As funding continues to fall, alarmed aid organizations have slimmed down their staffs and their ambitions. They have also begun to rethink the foreign aid business in search of innovative ways to solicit money and more intelligent ways to spend it. . . .

Others have advocated small steps in the field, away from the massive development projects of the past and direct support for inept governments and toward microloans, health projects administered by local villagers and education programs for small business entrepreneurs.

AID, the U.S. government development agency, is looking for ways to take advantage of new data indicating that Americans are far more supportive of foreign aid than the aid-averse Congress thinks they are, but are wildly misinformed about how much the government spends. Although the figure is currently less than 1 percent of GNP, most respondents in opinion polls guess it is about 15 percent, and suggest 5 percent would be about right.

Aid leaders such as Brown, World Bank President James D. Wolfensohn and James H. Michel, the outgoing chair of the development committee of the Organization for Economic Cooperation and Development, have all called on donor nations to help look for new strategies to reverse the trends and reject what Wolfensohn, too, has called the "Darwinian theory of development whereby we discard the unfit by the wayside."

The donor governments have said they share the concern, and have pledged to do something about it. Pressure has mounted within the G-7 group of the world's leading industrialized nations for Third World debt forgiveness. Britain, Canada and Germany have made substantive moves in that direction, although Clinton's proposal to do the same in next year's budget was rejected by Congress.

Several years ago, the OECD, which groups 21 of the world's richest countries, set a goal of cutting in half the world's poverty by 2015. To back up the pledge, members agreed in 1996 to raise their individual annual aid expenditures to at least seven-tenths of 1 percent of GNP—a commitment later made by the G-7 as well.

By last year, however, the same four countries that consistently score at the top of the proportional generosity scale—Denmark, Norway, the Netherlands and Sweden—remain the only ones to meet the OECD individual funding target. Fifteen of the 21 OECD donors, including all G-7 members but France, weren't even halfway there. Five gave less than the year before.

11.4 How to Make Aid Work

The Economist

As development dollars get scarcer, the question of how to make aid work becomes more pressing. In the next selection, *The Economist* examines the question of why aid sometimes fails to have much effect and why sometimes it works well.

"The poor always ye have with you," said Jesus, and 2,000 years of history have not proven him wrong. People who live permanently hungry, racked by parasites and forced to walk miles each day to fetch water, are more numerous now than ever before. Roughly 1.2 billion people—a fifth of the world's population—subsist on less than $1 a day. On June 18th, [1999] at a summit in Cologne, the rich world's leaders came up with a plan to ease their plight.

Under the "Cologne Initiative" the G8 group of industrialised countries agreed to provide more debt relief, more quickly, to more poor countries. This, it is hoped, will release resources for health and education and generally make life in the Third World less miserable. Tony Blair, Britain's prime minister, spoke of "the biggest step forward in debt relief and help to the poorest countries that we have seen for many years." Perhaps. But that depends on how it is put into practice.

The initiative is directed at the clumsily-named Heavily Indebted Poor Countries (HIPCs). The first comprehensive HIPC debt-relief plan dates from 1996. It aimed to reduce the debts of countries that maintained good economic policies to a "sustainable" level. This is calculated for most countries as a stock of debt (discounted to reflect its present value) equal to no more than 200–250% of annual exports. Alternatively, for extremely open economies, sustainability could be defined as a ratio of debt to government revenue of 280%.

Unfortunately, the original HIPC plan proved slow (only Uganda, Bolivia and Guyana have benefited so far) and stingy (in many cases the amount of debt service actually paid was likely barely to budge). Led by bishops, rock stars and charities, a loud campaign emerged to push for more and faster debt relief. The Scriptures call for forgiveness of debts every 50 years, some noted, reckoning that the next mass write-off was due in the year 2000.

The Cologne Initiative may fall short of millennial salvation but it is an improvement on its predecessor. The criteria for defining HIPCs have been broadened: a sustainable debt burden now implies a debt/export ratio of 150% or a debt/revenue ratio of 250%, and it will be easier to qualify for the second.

Under the new plan 33 countries (with a total of 430 million inhabitants) are likely to be eligible for debt relief, compared with 26 under the original plan. And relief should arrive more quickly: the G8 have agreed to shorten the time a country must follow good policies before its debts are cut and to offer "cash-flow" relief in the meantime. Creditors also promised to include for the first time some $20 billion worth of concessional loans in the debt calculation. When added to earlier pledges, the G8 claim, their efforts could reduce the stock of nominal HIPC debt by up to $70 billion: from some $130 billion today to as little as $60 billion. Viewed in present-value terms, the initiative itself offers debt reduction of $27.5 billion, which is more than double the $12.5 billion available before.

That is a big change—if it attracts genuinely new aid money. The G8 say that the IMF's share of financing debt relief should come from selling up to 10 million ounces of gold and reinvesting the proceeds. But America's Congress must approve that arrangement, and a number of lawmakers have said that they want no part of a gold sale. There is also talk of using World Bank profits, though these are unlikely to cover the Bank's proposed whack of $5 billion. Conspicuously absent are financial commitments from the rich countries: the G8 merely promised to consider new contributions "in good faith." The debt-relief plan will be put to the annual IMF–World Bank meetings in September for agreement on its structure and financing.

The danger is that the promised relief for HIPC debtors will either prove elusive or come at the expense of other aid and other recipients. Official aid flows have been broadly stagnant anyway throughout the 1990s—in part because aid has produced so few successes and so many mistakes. But there is hope in the fact that this initiative comes at a time when many donors—not least the World Bank—are rethinking their whole approach to aid. History offers one outstanding clue: if relief is not carefully aimed at countries with a genuine commitment to sound economic management, it will be wasted.

Unhelpful Help

Over the past 50 years rich nations have given $1 trillion in aid to poor ones. This stupendous sum has failed spectacularly to improve the lot of its intended beneficiaries. Aid should have boosted recipient countries' growth rates and thereby helped millions to escape from poverty. Yet countless studies have failed to find a link between aid and faster economic growth. Poor countries that receive lots of aid do no better, on average, than those that receive very little.

Why should this be? In part, because economic growth has not always been donors' first priority. A sizeable chunk of Saudi Arabian aid, for example, aims to tackle spiritual rather than material needs by sending free Korans to infidels. During the Cold War, the Soviet Union propped up odious communist despots while America bankrolled an equally unsavoury bunch of anti-communists. Keeping thugs like North Korea's Kim Il Sung and Liberia's Samuel Doe in power hardly improved the lives of their hapless subjects. Even today, strategic considerations often outweigh charitable or developmental ones. Israel gets the lion's share of American aid largely for historical reasons, and millions of American voters support it. Egypt gets the next biggest slice for recognising Israel. Russia and Ukraine receive billions to ensure that they do not sell their surplus nuclear warheads.

Even where development has been the goal of aid, foul-ups have been frequent. Big donors like to finance big, conspicuous projects such as dams, and sometimes fail to notice the multitudes whose homes are flooded. Gifts from small donors are often strangely inappropriate: starving Somalis have received heartburn pills; Mozambican peasants have been sent high-heeled shoes. Poor research can render aid worthless: a fish farm was built for Mali in canals that were dry for half the year. The Turkana nomads of north-western Kenya, long pestered with ill-planned charitable projects, refer to foreign aid workers and their own government alike as *ngimoi:* "the enemy."

Aid faces further hurdles in recipient countries. War scuppers the best-laid plans. A shipment of vaccines was destroyed in Congo when rebels cut the power supply to the capital, shutting down the refrigerators where the medicines were stored. In Afghanistan, Taliban zealots have closed aid-financed hospitals for employing female doctors. Less spectacularly but more pervasively, corruption, incompetence and foolish economic policies can often be relied on to squander any amount of donor cash. One example, Zambia, speaks for many.

At independence in 1964, Zambia seemed poised for success. The second-richest country in Africa, it had a popularly elected government committed to helping the poor, big copper mines and a generous stream of aid. Most donors believed that the main obstacle to Third World development was lack of capital, and that giving poor governments cash to invest would spur rapid growth. It was not so simple.

Zambia's first president, Kenneth Kaunda, set up a one-party socialist state and nationalised everything from dry-cleaners to car-part retailers. His officials told farmers what to grow, bought their crops and sold them at heavily subsidised prices. Mr. Kaunda assumed that the copper mines would provide an inexhaustible source of revenue, however badly managed. Zambians came to see government loans as a perk of freedom from colonial rule.

In the mid-1970s, the price of copper tumbled, and it became harder to pay for all this. Foreign donors picked up the slack. As Mr. Kaunda's economic policies grew worse, aid climbed steadily, reaching 11 percent of real GDP by the early 1990s. IMF loans were tied to free-market reforms, but these were enacted reluctantly and frequently reversed.

Donors agitated for free elections and in 1991 Frederick Chiluba, a former union leader and avowed economic reformer, became president. Aid began to flow again, but Mr. Chiluba's zeal to privatise was soon dampened by the discovery that state-owned firms provided ministers with lucrative opportunities for patronage. Corruption is becoming as great a brake on growth as socialism was under Mr. Kaunda. William Easterly of the World Bank says that, if aid had had the predicted accelerating effect on growth between 1961 and 1994, Zambia's income per head would now be more than $20,000. In fact, it has dawdled at around $400.

Growth and Poverty

GDP is not a foolproof measure of well-being. Wealth may be unevenly spread, so that a high average disguises widespread wretchedness. Nor does GDP take account of the hidden costs of pollution, for example. But when GDP grows, social indicators tend to improve with it.

In Thailand, where income per capita tripled between 1966 and 1990, the proportion of the population living in poverty fell from more than half to just 2 percent. Infant mortality fell by two-thirds. Slower-growing countries did less well: in India, income per head doubled, infant mortality fell by half and half the population stayed stuck in poverty. In no-growth countries such as Ethiopia, all the advances in modern medicine and the efforts of foreign donors could not effect more than a 27 percent drop in infant mortality over the same period.

Until recently, the fastest-growing emerging economies were clustered in East Asia whereas the disaster zones were disproportionately African. This led many to conclude that culture was the best predictor of economic success. Actually, sound policies and institutions, backed by liberal helpings of aid, are usually a better guide.

Take Botswana. Zambia's neighbour was, at independence in 1966, one of the world's poorest countries. One British official called it "a useless piece of territory." To begin with, aid financed virtually all government investment and much of its recurrent expenditure too. Then prospectors found diamonds under the Botswanan desert. Unlike many African governments, Botswana's did not squander the windfall. Diamond dollars were ploughed into infrastructure, education and health. Private business was allowed to grow; foreign investment was welcomed. Aid projects were approved only if they were sustainable and did not duplicate the work of others.

From 1966 to 1991, Botswana's economy grew faster than almost any other in the world. It helped that its government was unusually honest and competent. Cabinet ministers did not award themselves huge pensions, mansions and public contracts. In Zambia, government bigwigs drive Mercedes limousines. Those in Botswana choose locally-assembled Hyundai sedans. Even the president, Festus Mogae, has been seen doing his own shopping.

Botswana abolished exchange controls this year. Its budget is usually in surplus and GDP per head tops $3,000. The country remains vulnerable to swings in the price of diamonds, but it has made a better job of diversifying than most third-world mineral producers. Their task completed, donors are packing their bags.

Cash Advances or Advice?

The reason that aid has worked in Botswana but not in Zambia is simple. Botswana had good economic policies, soundly administered. Zambia did not. A recent study by the World Bank sorted 56 aid-receiving countries by the quality of their economic management. Those with good policies (low inflation, a budget surplus and openness to trade) and good institutions (little corruption, strong rule of law, effective bureaucracy) benefited from the aid they got. Those with poor policies and institutions did not. Badly run countries showed negligible or negative growth, and no amount of aid altered this. Well run countries that received little aid grew steadily, with GDP per head increasing by 2.2 percent a year. Well run countries with a lot of aid grew faster, at 3.7 percent per head a year.

Several things explain these differences. In countries with poor management, aid is sometimes stolen. Its effectiveness is often limited anyway by the fact that it tends to displace, rather than complement, private investment. In countries with good management, aid "crowds in" private investment: if an economy is growing fast, the returns on road-building or setting up a new airline are likely to be high. A poorly managed, stagnant economy offers private investors fewer opportunities.

It seems clear that aid should be directed towards countries with good management and lots of poor citizens. Yet many donors continue to behave as if it were not. Bilateral aid has tended to favour allies and ex-colonies. A 1998 study by Alberto Alesina and David Dollar found that a former colony with a closed economy received about twice as much assistance as a non-colony with an open one. Undemocratic ex-colonies also received twice as much as democratic non-colonies. On some figures, countries with poor management got just as much bilateral aid as those with good management. (Nordic aid was an exception to this dismal trend.)

Can aid persuade countries with bad policies and institutions to adopt good ones? It is not easy. For years the IMF and World Bank have made their loans conditional on policy reform, but the record is mixed, to put it kindly. Governments often agree to cut subsidies or tackle corruption, but later backtrack. Zimbabwe's president, Robert Mugabe, frequently promises one thing to donors and the opposite to domestic interest-groups. Kenya's Daniel arap Moi is skilled at selling the same reforms several times. Even when recipients blatantly flout aid conditions, donors often hand over the money anyway, for fear of sparking an economic collapse or even bloodshed.

Good policies cannot be imposed on unwilling pupils. Attaching conditions to aid can strengthen the arm of governments that are trying to push through wise but unpopular measures. Broadly, however, reforms rarely succeed unless a government considers the reform programme essential, and its own. A recent study by David Dollar and Jakob Swensson found that elected governments were much more likely to implement reforms than unelected ones, and new regimes more likely than old ones.

For countries with foolish leaders, a better approach than offering money is offering ideas. The architects of successful reforms in Indonesia in the 1970s, and in several Latin American countries in the 1980s and 1990s, were largely educated abroad, often at aid-givers' expense. The crash course in market economics given to top African National Congress members before they won South Africa's first all-race elections in 1994 helped turn them from Marxists into fiscal conservatives. Ethiopia's new leaders took degrees in business administration in the mid-1990s.

Rethinking Aid

A condition of the G8's new debt-relief plan is that the cash it frees be spent on worthy things like education and health. The World Bank is well aware of the difficulties in ensuring that this actually happens but many donors are not. Aid-givers often finance specific projects, such as irrigation and the building of schools. Since the schools are usually built and the ditches dug, donors are satisfied that their money has served its intended purpose. But has it? Probably not.

Most evidence suggests that aid money is fungible—that is, that it goes into the pot of public funds and is spent on whatever the recipient wants to spend it on. If donors earmark money for education, it may cause the recipient government to spend more on education, or it may make available for something else the money that it would otherwise have spent on education.

If the government is benign, the alternative may be agriculture or tax cuts. If the government is crooked, donors' funds may be spent on shopping trips to London for the president's wife or fighter planes to strafe unpopular minorities. The important factor is not the donor's instructions but the recipient's priorities. A 14-country study published by the World Bank in 1998 showed that each extra aid dollar aimed at agriculture, for example, actually decreased total agricultural spending by five cents.

This does not mean that donors should never support specific projects. Sometimes the real value of a donor-financed dam or telephone network lies in the technology that is transferred, and the advice given on how to operate and maintain the infrastructure. But the fact of fungibility suggests that aid-giving could be greatly simplified if most took the form of unconditional "balance-of-payments support." That is, cash.

Rich countries should be much more ruthless about how they allocate their largesse, whether earmarked or not. Emergency relief is one thing. But mainstream aid should be directed only to countries with sound economic management. The HIPC debt-relief plans, to their credit, do this. More donors should follow suit. Aid should also favour countries with large numbers of very poor citizens. India, Vietnam, Mozambique and Uganda, among others, meet both conditions. Many countries that receive substantial aid, such as Zimbabwe, Kenya and Russia, do not.

According to the World Bank, an extra $10 billion in aid could lift 25 million people a year out of poverty—so long as it went to poor countries that manage their economies well. The same sum spread across the current cast of aid recipients would lift only 7 million out of destitution. In other words, aid could work if it were properly directed. And if taxpayers in rich countries saw their money actually doing some good, they might be happy to give more of it.

 Microlending

11.5 Africa's Women Go to Work

The Economist

Many cures for global poverty have been proposed, but none has been more than partially successful. In recent years, however, a new strategy has been widely praised: providing small loans to poor individuals and families to allow them to set up small businesses, often at home. Such microlending was pioneered by Mohammad Yunus through his Grameen Bank in Bangladesh. Involving a profound shift away from the policy of most banks to make loans only to those with collateral, the new strategy has been particularly helpful to poor women. Not only have many people started small businesses but, contrary to conventional wisdom, they have faithfully repaid their loans. The following selection from *The Economist* discusses the concept.

On a steamy morning in a Kampala slum, the men are getting drunk. They sit in circles around pots of brown, sludgy millet beer, sucking it through long wooden straws to heighten the buzz and, through a filter, to strain out the lumps. Seven local women support their families by running the Otim bar. They brew the booze, too, in a large oil drum with the Shell logo still visible on the side. The business has grown rapidly, mainly because the owners, despite being poor, have access to credit.

Microcredit—lending small sums to poor people to set up or expand small businesses—is an effective way to alleviate poverty. The poor cannot usually borrow from commercial banks, because they lack collateral. Loan sharks lend without security, but often at interest rates of 10–20 percent a day. Hawkers who borrow from sharks to buy a day's stock often have to hand over most of their profits. Failure to repay can result in broken legs.

Microlenders try to satisfy poor people's hunger for credit less brutally. Since the 1970s, organisations, such as the Grameen Bank in Bangladesh and Accion International in Latin America, have encouraged poor borrowers to form groups to cross-guarantee each other's loans. In the Grameen model, one of a group of rural women takes out a microscopic loan, often as little as $25, to start a business. Only when she repays it can the next woman in the group borrow. Peer pressure makes sure that default rates are minimal.

The idea has spread. All told, about 14 million poor people now borrow from microlenders, a number that has increased by over 80 percent in the past two years, according to the Microcredit Summit Campaign (MSC), a lobbying group. Each borrower is thought to support about five family members. Most borrowers are women. Microlenders prefer to lend to women because they are likely to use additional income to feed and clothe their children. Men, as the proprietors of the Otim bar can testify, may blow the spare cash on booze.

Microcredit works better than handouts for two reasons. First, it fosters enterprise rather than dependency. Second, a well-run microcredit scheme can be self-sustaining. Repayment rates of over 98 percent are common.

The business plans backed by microfinanciers tend to be breathtakingly simple. Take Pakmogda Zarata, a successful microentrepreneur from Burkina Faso, one of Africa's poorest countries. Ms. Zarata runs a restaurant in a marketplace near Ouagadougou, the capital. The place cost almost nothing to build: roughly-hewn logs prop up a ceiling of thatch and old dustbin liners; there are no walls to speak of.

The menu is unpretentious. "We only serve rice," she says, "but we do cook it." By taking out a series of small loans from the local branch of the Fédération des Caisses Populaires du Burkina Faso, the country's main microlender, Ms. Zarata was able to buy rice wholesale rather than retail. Her profits rose. She now employs seven people, can pay her children's school fees, and swaggers around town on a second-hand motorcycle.

As microfinance has globalised, it has run into local problems. Not all poor communities are as tight-knit as those in rural Bangladesh. The urban poor, being more mobile, do not always know their neighbours well enough to act as guarantors for them. In the shanty towns of Africa and Latin America, something called "stepped lending" often works better. A would-be borrower puts up a little money of her own. The microfinancier lends her roughly the same amount again. If she repays promptly, she can raise a larger loan. The better her credit record becomes, the more she can borrow. The carrot of more credit discourages defaults as effectively as peer pressure does in villages.

The MSC hopes to see 100 million poor borrowers receiving microloans by 2005. To reach such an ambitious target, microlenders will need much more capital. Support from donors is buoyant, but not enough. To expand faster, microlenders need to tap capital markets. This is not easy. Many microlenders break even, but few produce the kind of returns that might entice hard-nosed capitalists to give them their backing.

Some, however, are credit-worthy enough to borrow at commercial rates. In Bolivia, BancoSol, a microlender with over 70,000 clients, has issued $5 million in bonds backed by its lending portfolio, $2 million of which were bought by foreigners. Commercial banks can sometimes be persuaded to take equity stakes in microlenders, partly to make contact with up-and-coming small businessmen with a sound credit history. For example, two Peruvian banks own shares in Mibanco, Peru's first for-profit microlender. According to Accion International, perhaps 50 of the world's 7,000–10,000 microlenders can cover their own operating and financial costs unaided.

In many poor countries, however, disease makes this difficult. In Africa, AIDS often causes borrowers to default, either because they are too ill to work, or because their family's medical bills have soared. A survey of microborrowers in 14 African countries found that 95 percent had trouble paying medical bills, 77 percent had trouble paying for funerals, and half had difficulties finding money to look after orphans, usually the children of relations who had died of AIDS.

Microlenders often try to tackle this through education. In Burkina Faso, where diarrhoea is a killer, those who want to get their hands on a loan must first learn about washing them. In eastern and southern Africa, many microlenders promote condoms.

A more challenging idea is to combine microcredit with micro–health insurance. FINCA, a microlender in Uganda, runs a pilot scheme allowing members free treatment for a range of problems at a mission hospital in Kampala, in return for a small quarterly fee. The scheme is popular, but racks up big losses. Before it can be duplicated, FINCA needs to find ways to encourage healthy people to join the scheme, and discourage frivolous visits to the doctor. If micro-insurance can be made to work, the Internet will ensure that the idea is swiftly copied. Globalisation is not just for the rich.

Suggested Discussion Topics

1. Why should citizens in wealthy countries be concerned about the fate of the poor living elsewhere? In what ways do poverty and underdevelopment pose problems for the global community? Do you think we should regard poverty and underdevelopment as security issues? Why or why not?
2. One way to reduce global poverty would be to allow poor people to move to wherever the jobs are, regardless of national borders. How do you feel about this idea? Why? Be prepared to argue either side of this question: that the United States, for example, should allow open immigration, or that countries should strictly limit immigration.
3. If people cannot move freely to jobs, then employers are likely to move jobs to wherever labor is most readily and most cheaply available, if they are able to do so. Is this a good thing? Again, be prepared to argue either side in a debate.
4. In recent decades, economic development has rocketed ahead in East Asia and, at best, inched forward in sub-Saharan Africa. Why has development proceeded unevenly around the globe? What are the dangers of continued uneven development? Do you think economic development will become more or less uneven during your lifetime? Explain your reasoning.
5. Explain why microlending works. What do you see as the limits to microlending?
6. Who should play the lead role in promoting economic development: states, nongovernmental organizations, or private corporations? What does your answer imply about the strategies for development that will be pursued? What does it imply about which institutions will be powerful in everyday life?
7. What, in your view, are the most important reasons that aid has not ended global poverty or narrowed the gap between rich and poor nations? Drawing on all of the readings in this chapter, outline your own plan for making development aid more effective.

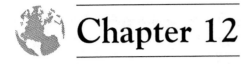

Chapter 12

ENVIRONMENTAL ISSUES AND THE GLOBAL COMMONS

Perhaps no contemporary issues more clearly reflect the new security agenda, present a greater challenge to the global system, and demand greater cooperation among societies and political actors around the world than do environmental issues. Among the most perilous of environmental trends are depletion of the ozone layer, deforestation and desertification, loss of biodiversity, and global warming. Collectively, they are as much a threat to human security and survival as are weapons of mass destruction. They represent challenges that have no respect for national sovereignty or national frontiers and that are beyond the ability of any single state, however powerful, to overcome. Thus, when it comes to the global environment, human beings, regardless of nationality, have linked fates, and our continued existence as a species rests upon our ability to cooperate in confronting and overcoming environmental degradation.

To the extent that people compete for scarce resources, environmental issues promote political fragmentation and conflict. The solution to environmental problems, however, demands greater global collaboration and the creation of integrative political institutions that facilitate this collaboration.

Although humankind has faced environmental challenges before, population growth and rapid modernization have placed unprecedented stress on the world in which we live. Two problems are clear. First, more people—all of whom are demanding a higher standard of living—means greater competition for increasingly scarce natural resources such as water, land, and food. Human efforts to provide sustenance, clothing, shelter, and all the comforts and luxuries that make life pleasant have had a dramatic impact on the world's ecosystems. In an attempt to turn the environment to productive use, humans have cleared land of native plant and animal species, dammed rivers for energy or water supplies, pumped water from underground aquifers, and hunted and fished certain species to the brink of extinction or beyond.

Two centuries ago, Thomas Malthus (1766–1834) predicted that population growth would outstrip food supply, causing massive famine. That the catastrophe he predicted did not occur owes much to the ability of science to increase food production. But even with improved technology, the population explosion of the last two centuries has taxed the capacity of the environment, as humans in some places have exploited renewable resources (such as fresh water, fish, and forests) past their "carrying capacity," have used other natural resources in ways that have led to their degradation (for example, farming processes that have led to soil erosion and loss of fertile topsoil), and have begun to damage highly fragile ecosystems (such as rain forests or arctic regions). In the absence of more suitable land, for example, large tracts of the Amazon jungle have been cleared for cattle ranching. This exploitation of the rain forest, however, has yielded little by way of long-term food production—the land quickly becomes compacted and nutrients leach away, leaving it unsuitable for agriculture—but has resulted in the extinction of innumerable species and created local environmental wounds that will take centuries or longer to heal. Although rates of population growth have begun to ease in recent decades, the world's population continues to explode, and many observers doubt that the world and its delicate ecology can sustain human population growth indefinitely.

Second, population growth and demands for higher standards of living are also straining the environment's capacity to cope with the waste products human societies generate. More people, all making and using more things, translates into more air, water, and soil pollution. On the local level, this has meant cities in which the air is dangerous to breathe and land and groundwater that are contaminated with toxic chemicals. Regionally, it has meant phenomena such as the acid rain (caused by sulfur emissions from the burning of carbon fuels) that has devastated flora and fauna across much of central Europe and parts of northeastern North America. And globally, the byproducts of human agriculture and industry threaten to result in massive climate change, as depletion of the ozone layer allows more of the sun's ultraviolet radiation to reach the Earth and as greenhouse gases such as carbon dioxide build up and produce a global warming that could melt polar icecaps, raise ocean levels, swamp island countries, and inundate coastal areas around the world.

This double-barreled environmental problem—increasing pollution and shortages of resources—is clearly growing and is inextricably tied to the development problems discussed in the previous chapter. The United Nations projects that world population will increase from 5.7 billion in 1992 to 12.5 billion in the middle of the next century. In the last half century, the world's population has doubled and its economy has increased fivefold. In a world of global markets, shortages of food and water cease to be a matter of purely local or national concern, and the destruction of environmental capital, through overuse or by contamination with waste products, reduces the world's long-term carrying capacity for everyone.

The need for international action is obvious. Concerns about the consequences of unfettered growth provided the impetus for the 1992 UN–sponsored Conference on Environment and Development (Earth Summit) in Rio de Janeiro and the 1994 UN–sponsored Conference on Population and Development in Cairo. Many of the most difficult environmental problems facing the world today transcend national borders, and solving them requires international cooperation or transnational action. Two examples illustrate this. Sulfur dioxide released by power plants in the United States precipitates out of the air as sulfuric acid, or acid rain, killing trees and increasing the acidity of lakes and streams hundreds of miles downwind: across the border in Canada. Determining whether American consumers should pay more for their electricity, or how much more they should pay, in order to save Canadian forests and fisheries is a matter for international, rather than national, negotiation. Global warming caused by the increased release of greenhouse gases from the burning of carbon fuels and the clearing of forests offers a second example. Although environments all around the world are likely to be affected, the most dramatic human suffering may well be caused by increased drought in sub-Saharan Africa, the disappearance of low-lying Pacific islands, and the inundation of highly populated coastal regions in East Asia. The principal contributors to global warming, however, have not been the nations of these areas, but the industrialized nations of Europe and North America and the nations presently clearing tropical rain forests. In general, reaching agreement on who should pay the costs, or who should forego the benefits, of exploiting natural resources will be highly contentious.

12.1 The Tragedy of the Commons

Garrett Hardin

Over thirty years ago, biologist Garrett Hardin outlined what he described as "the tragedy of the commons." Hardin noted that resources that are owned "in common," like the world's atmosphere and its oceans, tend to be overused, even to the point of environmental collapse. Although no one wants this outcome, in the absence of "ownership" that would make it rational for individuals to take responsible care of common resources, it is rational for each user to exploit them. Understanding this tragedy of the commons, and the need for some sort of international agreement or regulation—mutual coercion, Hardin would say—to prevent it, is the starting place for any discussion of today's environmental dangers.

The tragedy of the commons develops in this way. Picture a pasture open to all. It is to be expected that each herdsman will try to keep as many cattle as possible on the commons. Such an arrangement may work reasonably satisfactorily for centuries because tribal wars, poaching, and disease keep the numbers of both man and beast well below the carrying capacity of the land. Finally, however, comes the day of reckoning, that is, the day when the long-desired goal of social stability becomes a reality. At this point, the inherent logic of the commons remorselessly generates tragedy.

As a rational being, each herdsman seeks to maximize his gain. Explicitly or implicitly, more or less consciously, he asks, "What is the utility *to me* of adding one more animal to my herd?" This utility has one negative and one positive component.

1) The positive component is a function of the increment of one animal. Since the herdsman receives all the proceeds from the sale of the additional animal, the positive utility is nearly +1.

2) The negative component is a function of the additional overgrazing created by one more animal. Since, however, the effects of overgrazing are shared by all the

herdsmen, the negative utility for any particular decision-making herdsman is only a fraction of −1.

Adding together the component partial utilities, the rational herdsman concludes that the only sensible course for him to pursue is to add another animal to his herd. And another; and another. . . . But this is the conclusion reached by each and every rational herdsman sharing a commons. Therein is the tragedy. Each man is locked into a system that compels him to increase his herd without limit—in a world that is limited. Ruin is the destination toward which all men rush, each pursing his own best interest in a society that believes in the freedom of the commons. Freedom in a commons brings ruin to all. . . .

Pollution

In a reverse way, the tragedy of the commons reappears in problems of pollution. Here it is not a question of taking something out of the commons, but of putting something in—sewage, or chemical, radioactive, and heat wastes into water; noxious and dangerous fumes into the air; and distracting and unpleasant advertising signs into the line of sight. The calculations of utility are much the same as before. The rational man finds that his share of the cost of the wastes he discharges into the commons is less than the cost of purifying his wastes before releasing them. Since this is true for everyone, we are locked into a system of "fouling our own nest," so long as we behave only as independent, rational, free-enterprisers.

The tragedy of the commons as a food basket is averted by private property, or something formally like it. But the air and waters surrounding us cannot readily be fenced, and so the tragedy of the commons as a cesspool must be prevented by different means, by coercive laws or taxing devices that make it cheaper for the polluter to treat his pollutants than to discharge them untreated. We have not progressed as far with the solution of this problem as we have with the first. Indeed, our particular concept of private property, which deters us from exhausting the positive resources of the earth, favors pollution. The owner of a factory on the bank of a stream—whose property extends to the middle of the stream—often has difficulty seeing why it is not his natural right to muddy the waters flowing past his door. The law, always behind the times, requires elaborate stitching and fitting to adapt it to this newly perceived aspect of the commons.

The pollution problem is a consequence of population. It did not much matter how a lonely American frontiersman disposed of his waste. "Flowing water purifies itself every 10 miles," my grandfather used to say, and the myth was near enough to the truth when he was a boy, for there were not too many people. But as population became denser, the natural chemical and biological recycling processes became overloaded, calling for a redefinition of property rights. . . .

Mutual Coercion Mutually Agreed Upon

The social arrangements that produce responsibility are arrangements that create coercion, of some sort. . . .

. . . Taxing is a good coercive device. To keep downtown shoppers temperate in their use of parking space we introduce parking meters for short periods, and traffic fines for longer ones. We need not actually forbid a citizen to park as long as he wants to; we need merely make it increasingly expensive for him to do so. Not prohibition, but carefully biased options are what we offer him. . . .

Coercion is a dirty word to liberals now, but it need not forever be so. As with the four-letter words, its dirtiness can be cleansed away by exposure to the light, by saying it over and over without apology or embarrassment. To many, the word *coercion* implies arbitrary decisions of distant and irresponsible bureaucrats; but this is not a necessary part of its meaning. The only kind of coercion I recommend is mutual coercion, mutually agreed upon by the majority of the people affected.

To say that we mutually agree to coercion is not to say that we are required to enjoy it, or even to pretend we enjoy it. Who enjoys taxes? We all grumble about them. But we accept compulsory taxes because we recognize that voluntary taxes would favor the conscienceless. We institute and (grumblingly) support taxes and other coercive devices to escape the horror of the commons. . . .

Recognition of Necessity

Perhaps the simplest summary of this analysis of man's population problems is this: the commons, if justifiable at all, is justifiable only under conditions of low-population density. As the human population has increased, the commons has had to be abandoned in one aspect after another.

First we abandoned the commons in food gathering, enclosing farm land and restricting pastures and hunting and fishing areas. These restrictions are still not complete throughout the world.

Somewhat later we saw that the commons as a place for waste disposal would also have to be abandoned. Restrictions on the disposal of domestic sewage are widely accepted in the Western world; we are still struggling to close the commons to pollution by automobiles, factories, insecticide sprayers, fertilizing operations, and atomic energy installations. . . .

Every new enclosure of the commons involves the infringement of somebody's personal liberty. Infringements made in the distant past are accepted because no contemporary complains of a loss. It is the newly proposed infringements that we vigorously oppose: cries of "rights" and "freedom" fill the air. But what does "freedom" mean? When men mutually agreed to pass laws against robbing, mankind became more free, not less so. Individuals locked into the logic of the commons are free only to bring on universal ruin: once they see the necessity of mutual coercion, they become free to pursue other goals. I believe it was Hegel who said, "Freedom is the recognition of necessity."

The Problem of Collective Action

12.2 Global Problems and Local Concerns

The World Bank

Our first selection uses the critical issues of the diminishing ozone layer and global warming to illustrate the problem of achieving collective action in a world divided among sovereign nation-states. The first of these provides something of a model of adaptive change and cooperation through a process of learning, building a capacity for action, and compromising between domestic and international interests. As this analysis by the World Bank observes, however, the problem of warming has been less amenable to collective action than the ozone issue. Despite some progress, the institutions needed to coerce individual states into modifying their behavior for the benefit of humanity as a whole are still being developed.

Social and environmental problems often spill over national boundaries. . . . However, there is one big difference: at the global level, there is no central authority to enforce agreements. Nations have to devise ways to keep themselves on agreed paths. . . .

Designing Institutions to Solve Global Problems

Who would have thought that leaky refrigerators, fire extinguishers, and aerosol spray cans could seriously damage the entire biosphere? The story of how stratospheric ozone depletion was diagnosed as a problem, and how the global community organized to address it, illustrates how *adaptive, learning institutions* can successfully address global issues.

Refrigerators began using chlorofluorocarbons (CFCs) around 1930. By 1970 the world used about 1 million tons of these substances each year as coolants, as propellants in aerosol cans, and for manufacturing. In that year, James Lovelock used recently invented techniques to detect trace amounts of CFC in the atmosphere over London. His request for a grant to measure CFC concentrations over the Atlantic was denied: "One reviewer commented that even if the measurement succeeded, he could not imagine a more useless bit of knowledge."

Lovelock persisted, though, and showed that CFCs were detectable far from land. Four years later, chemists F. Sherwood Rowland and Mario Molina realized that even tiny concentrations of CFCs could, theoretically, erode the stratospheric ozone layer that shields life from ultraviolet radiation, an insight that won them the 1995 Nobel Prize in chemistry. It was known, too, that CFCs had a long lifetime in the atmosphere and that increased exposure to ultraviolet radiation would increase the risk of skin cancer. Although a definitive cause-and-effect relationship had not yet been demonstrated, circumstantial evidence was strong enough in the early 1980s to support a precautionary approach to the threat of ozone depletion. The Vienna Convention (1985) committed the nations of the world to addressing the problem, but imposed no obligations.

Meanwhile, scientists had been monitoring stratospheric ozone since the 1920s in a widening global network that extended to Antarctica in 1957. A scientist at the British Antarctic Station, noticing declining ozone readings in the late 1970s, published definitive data by 1984. Shortly thereafter, dramatic satellite images of the Antarctic ozone "hole" captured public attention. This deepening evidence prompted the Montreal Protocol of 1987, an out-growth of the Vienna Convention, to impose obligations on developed countries to reduce the use of ozone-depleting substances. The Montreal Protocol also set up panels to assess the impacts of ozone depletion and the technology and economics of mitigating ozone-depleting substances.

By 1990 there was firmer evidence of a causal impact of chlorine and bromine compounds on ozone. In that year the London Protocol to the Vienna Convention took effect. Under this protocol, developing countries agreed to take on obligations, with a grace period, and developed countries underwrote a trust fund to assist them.

The process remains dynamic. Two more amendments to the Vienna Convention have been adopted. Technical panels, involving multistakeholder cooperation, have helped identify technological approaches to phasing out ozone-depleting substances. More than $1.3 billion have been committed to help developing countries. The result: a foreseeable reduction in atmospheric concentrations of ozone-depleting substances and an eventual recovery of the ozone layer.

The problem of protecting the global ozone layer was, for a variety of reasons, easier to tackle than other global problems. The production and use of ozone-depleting substances is not central to any economy—unlike greenhouse gases, whose production is deeply embedded in the energy and transport sectors. It has been easy to find less harmful substitutes for most substances, at modest cost. The political economy of reaching agreement has also been favorable. At the national level, the wealthy industrial nations responsible for most production were also those at the greatest risk from skin cancer, in part because ozone depletion is far more severe at temperate than tropical latitudes. And the corporations that produced most ozone-depleting substances also produced most substitutes.

The record of success in tackling this problem provides both hope and inspiration for other global initiatives. It also shows the key components in global problem-solving:

♦ Pick up signals of the problem and agree on its nature.
♦ Build local capacity and international networks to support adaptive learning.
♦ Reconcile domestic and international interests.

These components are explored in detail below, together with an emerging fourth:

♦ Harness decentralized mechanisms to establish incentives for socially responsible actions.

Pick up Signals of the Problem and Agree on Its Nature   Solving problems requires some consensus on the facts and on the costs and impacts of action (or inaction). The first step is to detect the problem and put it on the public agenda. . . . But detection is not enough. Especially where dispersed interests need to be mobilized, activists (sometimes including scientists) can put a problem on the public agenda. . . .

The next step is achieving some consensus on the problem's gravity, threats, and potential solutions. At the outset, activists use data to demand action, and defenders of the status quo attack the data and interpretation as inaccurate, incomplete, and biased. Progress in resolving the issue requires better information and some consensus on the diagnosis. This is not always easy. To understand such problems as acid rain and global warming, we need to understand how thousands of factories and millions of households behave—and how chemicals mix and react across the entire atmosphere. These processes can be understood only through sophisticated simulation models, and the models can be validated only against rich and accurate observations of physical, biological, and social systems. There is scope for honest disagreement on interpreting data and models. And naturally, each stakeholder group will promote interpretations favorable to its own interests. What is needed is a credible, legitimate forum for fostering consensus on diagnosis and action.

Combining credibility and legitimacy in a policy institution is a fine balancing act, especially for global issues. . . . How can this be done?

The IPCC [Intergovermental Panel on Climate Change] is one example. The IPCC was chartered by the World Meteorological Organization and the United Nations Environment Programme (UNEP) to assess the risk of human-induced climate change. It has produced three large assessments, carried out by an international team of volunteer experts, who evaluate and synthesize the vast and sometimes contradictory scientific literature through an elaborate set of working groups, subgroups, and reviews. Because the reports are thick, densely technical documents, attention focuses on distilling summaries for policymakers. Each summary is approved, line by line, by representatives of all IPCC member governments in a forum where scientists can defend their conclusions. The process results in political buy-in to scientific findings. Over the past 10 years, the IPCC's work has contributed greatly to promoting consensus on the nature and causes of climate change. . . .

Learning and Adapting   The diagnostic process is most effective when it feeds into an adaptive process of balancing interests, setting goals, taking actions, and learning from results. The Convention on Long-Range Transboundary Air Pollution (CLRTAP) illustrates adaptive learning. This Convention has forged increasingly ambitious agreements among European nations (including economies in transition) on reducing emissions that cause acid rain, eutrophication, ground-level ozone, and other environmental problems. It has done so in part by encouraging the collection, harmonization, and analysis of data on emissions and environmental conditions. This process has fostered communication among policymakers and scientists, facilitated agreement on an operational definition of goals, and promoted a rational, cost-effective approach to achieving those goals.

The CLRTAP and the Montreal Protocol illustrate the appeal of adaptive learning in forging international agreements. Countries are averse to taking on binding commitments when there is great uncertainty about the costs or impacts, about their ability to induce citizens to comply, and about the compliance of other parties. Adaptive learning allows countries—and groups whose behavior is targeted for change—to understand the problem and to acquire confidence in their own ability and others' to deal with it.

Two routes are available:

♦ One route is through "soft law": nonbinding statements of principles and sometimes targets. By gradually establishing norms, soft law lays the foundation for negotiation on binding arrangements. Nonbinding but ambitious targets can also encourage experimentation that would be too risky under a binding regime.

♦ The other route is to start with a binding agreement that is easy to achieve, but that sets up a process that allows parties to learn more about costs and benefits and to build confidence in their partners' behavior and in newly created institutions.

For both routes, the seemingly mundane requirement of reporting can be key. Reporting—for greenhouse gas emissions under the Kyoto Protocol, for consumption of ozone-depleting substances under the Montreal Protocol, or for compliance with labor standards under the International Labour Organisation—deepens domestic understanding of the problem and strengthens external confidence in the country's commitment to compliance.

Build Local Capacity for Assessment, Negotiation, and Action   How can a hundred or more governments, representing billions of people, forge sustainable agreements that touch those people's lives? These agreements need to balance the diverse interests of groups that cut across national boundaries. International labor standards affect the workers, owners, and customers of low-wage assembly plants. The Montreal Protocol touches multinational and local chemical companies, people who risk developing skin cancer, and poor families that dream of affording a small used refrigerator. Negotiations on climate change affect coal miners, oil companies, Sahelian herders, atoll dwellers, car owners, and wind turbine entrepreneurs.

To work, these agreements must reconcile interests within and between countries. This requires mobilizing concern, and demands for action, among the many who would gain some benefit from the agreement, but who are less vocal than the few who perceive their main interests to be at risk. It thus requires creative ways of framing problems and solutions to increase the perceived congruence of interests, within and across countries. And it often depends on strengthening the capabilities of people and organizations in the developing world to assess options, to negotiate provisions, and to finance and undertake actions. . . .

Reconcile Domestic and International Interests—with Commitments and Cash
International agreements are possible because of the overlap between domestic and global interests—and because participating nations agree that the benefits they gain outweigh the costs that they accept. But environmental and social agreements usually involve balancing opposing domestic interests, often supporting a broad constituency of dispersed interests against one that is more narrowly focused but influential. And national compliance is not usually achieved with the simple stroke of an executive pen, requiring instead the cooperation of a multitude of citizens, government officials, corporate leaders, and others. Think, for instance, of the issues surrounding worker rights, pollution, and protection of privately owned wetlands or forests. A nation that agrees to international commitments on these issues has to deploy domestic carrots and sticks to coax its citizens into compliance. However, international agreements themselves can help provide some of those carrots and sticks. . . .

Financial transfers are often designed to align local actions with global interests. Many international agreements recognize that developing countries may be unable to finance their commitments to improve the global environment, even when those commitments provide some domestic benefits. The GEF [Global Environment Fund] has approved about $2.7 billion in grants to reduce ozone-depleting substances, mitigate climate change, protect biodiversity, and protect international waters. Depending on how the Kyoto Protocol is implemented, developing countries and economies in transition could get billions of dollars annually in market payments that would promote clean energy technologies.

Standards, Certification, and Performance Reporting—Inducing Socially Responsible Behavior   How can society reward people, firms, organizations, and governments that behave well? Locally, a community might patronize merchants who are friendly, civic-minded, and environmentally responsible—and do so happily even if their prices are a bit higher than those of less respectable competitors. Outside the community, the scope for doing this diminishes, as information about reputation thins. . . . An emerging set of institutions and networks tries to fill this gap by generating information about performance, using that information to set up incentives for socially responsible behavior. . . .

Various initiatives are beginning to publicize information about environmental and social performance—and there is some evidence of firms responding. Indonesia's government-led PROPER program, which instituted audited self-reporting of firms' pollution levels, has now been emulated in China, India, the Philippines, and Vietnam. . . . Nongovernmental evaluation and certification systems are developing quickly. . . .

There has been rapid growth in mutual funds and other investment vehicles that screen investments on social and environmental performance. In 1984, $40 billion in professionally managed assets were socially screened; in 2001, $2 trillion, of

$19 trillion in professionally managed assets. The growing demand for socially responsible investment and the growing supply of environmental and social performance indicators can interact in a virtuous circle. Better information enables more discerning investment; greater interest in ethical investment elicits better information. Similarly, as certification starts to become the norm in an industry, non-certified products find it harder to compete.

Who sets the standards and defines the indicators—and how? This is crucial to the future of such "bottom-up" approaches to regulation. Already there are disputes about how strictly to set standards for certification. Overly lax standards could defeat the purpose of certification. But so too could overly strict standards, if they are too expensive for firms to adopt and for outsiders to monitor. . . . This tradeoff is of crucial interest in trade negotiations, especially where developing countries fear that onerous standards would freeze them out of export markets. . . .

Mitigating and Adapting to Risks of Climate Change

People are changing the planet's climate. Burning fossil fuels—and to a lesser but important extent, deforestation and other land use practices—releases CO_2 and other greenhouse gases (GHGs). Accumulating more rapidly in the atmosphere than can be removed by natural sinks, these gases trap heat, changing climate in complex ways, with widespread impacts. This is quintessentially a global problem because GHGs mix rapidly in the atmosphere and have the same impact on climate change regardless of where they are emitted. And it is a long-term problem because the great inertia in social, economic, and physical systems means that it would take decades to moderate the rate of change substantially.

Because of its characteristics, climate change has been a particularly difficult problem to solve. It has been difficult for society to pick up signals—to understand the causes, magnitude, and consequences of climate change. . . .

Dispersion of interests in mitigating climate change has been a barrier to achieving agreement on actions. Many of the people most vulnerable to climate change are poor, live in remote regions—or have not even been born. Even the vulnerable wealthy—owners of oceanfront property, for instance—may not yet rank climate change among their greatest current concerns. The voice of these numerous but diffuse interests is weaker than that of industries and consumers, especially wealthy ones, that are heavily reliant on fossil fuels and would bear the burden of control costs. Finally, climate change is an extreme example of the commitment problem. . . . Mitigation of climate change will require a concerted, decades-long effort.

With these barriers in mind this section starts by reviewing the consequences and sources of climate change. Using this information, it assesses institutional aspects of undertaking the long-run mitigation of climate change. Then, it examines issues related to adapting to the climate change that past actions have already made inevitable—and that lack of progress in mitigation will exacerbate.

Consequences and Causes of Climate Change   Climate change is already here. Over the past century, mean global surface temperature has increased by 0.4° to

0.8° Celsius (C). According to the IPCC, GHGs released by human action are likely to have been responsible for most of the warming of the past 50 years. Other observed changes are consistent with this warming. Sea levels rose 10 to 20 centimeters over the past century. Over the past 50 years, the summer extent of arctic sea-ice has shrunk by 10 percent or more, and its thickness by 40 percent. Outside the polar regions, glaciers are retreating, affecting mountain ecosystems and water flows. Droughts have become more frequent and intense in Asia and Africa. Many of the world's coral reefs have been damaged by bleaching, associated with higher sea temperatures. Animals and plants have shifted their geographic ranges and behavior. Extreme weather events may have increased.

Unchecked, these impacts are predicted to intensify, posing risks of varying kinds for different countries. Impacts will fall heavily on many developing countries, including those that have not contributed to climate change. They are physically vulnerable. Climate-sensitive agriculture bulks large in their economies. And they have less institutional capacity to adapt to change.

Low-lying islands and coastal areas everywhere will be exposed to flooding and storm damage. Bangladesh, for instance, may be severely hit. A recent study predicts that by 2030 an additional 14 percent of the country would become extremely vulnerable to floods caused by increased rainfall. A 10-centimeter increase in sea level would permanently inundate 2 percent of the country, with the additional effect of making floods more severe and longer lasting. Saltwater intrusions, and more severe dry seasons, will reduce fresh water availability in coastal areas. As coastal populations swell worldwide, a 40-centimeter rise in the sea level would increase the number of coastal dwellers at risk of annual flooding by 75 to 206 million—90 percent of them in Africa and Asia. The starkest local impacts are faced by the low islands of the Pacific, some of which could lose their freshwater and be largely inundated during storm surges if sea levels rise.

Climate change could damage developing-country agriculture. Even taking into account crop substitution possibilities, one study finds that a 2°C temperature increase decreases the value of Indian agricultural land by 36 percent. Arid and semi-arid areas in Africa and Asia will probably face higher temperatures. Feedback between vegetation loss and reduced rainfall could result in faster desertification.

Impacts on industrial countries are thought to be mixed, but may be generally negative. Agricultural productivity will likely improve, in the medium term, in some northern areas. But southern Europe will likely suffer drier summers; much of Europe could experience river flooding. The Atlantic coast of the United States will be vulnerable to rising sea levels, and Australia will likely be more subject to drought.

Current understanding also depicts the global climate as a finely balanced mechanism that goes awry when stressed, with prehistoric instances of 10°C global temperature changes occurring within the span of a decade. There is a risk of catastrophic consequences of climate change that could be irreversibly set in motion during this century. There could, for instance, be an abrupt failure of the great ocean "conveyor belt" currents that warm the North Atlantic and mix deep with surface waters. Biodiversity losses could be massive as habitat fragmentation makes it impossible for plants and animals to migrate in response to rapidly changing temperatures.

The risks are difficult to evaluate, but they affect industrial as well as developing countries and are credible enough to demand attention. At the very least they put a premium, or option value, on maintaining lower levels of atmospheric GHGs while the world more carefully examines the consequences and develops options for mitigation.

What drives climate change? GHGs have built up in the atmosphere as a consequence of 250 years of emissions from burning fossil fuel, deforestation, and other sources. Currently, about 40 percent of the human-induced heating effect is from increased atmospheric concentrations of methane (from landfills, rice paddies, and cows), nitrous oxide (from industry and agriculture), and halocarbons such as CFCs. The remaining 60 percent is CO_2. Of the approximately 28.2 billion tons of annual CO_2 emissions, 23.1 billion are from energy and other industrial sources. This component is closely linked to income, across countries, though there is considerable variation in emissions per dollar of GDP and emissions per capita among the wealthier countries. The remaining 5.1 billion tons come from tropical deforestation. . . .

Mitigating Climate Change   Concerned about climatic risks, most of the world's nations agreed in 1992 to the UNFCCC [UN Framework Commission on Climate Change]. The convention's objective is defined as the "stabilization of greenhouse gas concentrations in the atmosphere at a level that would prevent dangerous anthropogenic interference with the climate system." But the Convention itself did not quantify this level or specify how to achieve it.

As a first step the Kyoto Protocol to the UNFCCC was negotiated in 1997. This agreement would require industrial nations and economies in transition—the Annex B countries—to accept specified limits on emissions of GHGs for 2008–2012. The Protocol would decrease compliance costs by allowing Annex B countries to trade their emissions allowances. It would also allow these countries to purchase emissions reductions from developing countries, the reductions being reckoned against assumed "business as usual" levels, since the developing countries' emissions were not capped. The subsequent Marrakech Accords of 2001 allowed for developing countries to generate emissions reductions from forestry projects in only a limited way. . . .

It is important to recognize that the Protocol's commitments for 2008–2012, even if observed by all major emitters, would be only a first step toward the UNFCCC goal. . . .

If the world is to stabilize atmospheric concentrations and provide good living standards to all its citizens, it must switch in the long run to energy technologies (such as wind, solar power, and hydrogen, among others) that emit near-zero net amounts of CO_2. Simple arithmetic shows why. The world's population is now expected to stabilize at about 9 billion around mid-century. Suppose that people then aspire to the current lifestyle of a prosperous country. Among the prosperous countries, Norway has one of the lowest ratios of CO_2 emissions per capita from energy, owing in part to ample use of hydropower. Yet if the global population of 2050 emitted CO_2 on average at this rate, the total would be about 2.5 times current global emissions, which would greatly exceed the planetary absorptive capacity.

Between now and the time the world switches entirely to near-zero-emissions technologies, GHGs will accumulate in the atmosphere. The amount of damage, and the risk of catastrophic changes, will be related to the cumulative amount. To reduce the damage, the world needs to accelerate the shift to lower-emissions energy technologies, increase the efficiency of energy use, and reduce the emissions of GHGs.

Although these actions provide some immediate side benefits in addition to their cumulative effect on reducing climate damages, they involve costs. Because emissions reductions represent a global public good, burden sharing is inevitably contentious. To facilitate global coordination in this effort, a strategy has to reduce the overall cost of mitigating emissions and seek to align local and global interests as far as possible. It also has to avoid free-rider problems. This requires further institutional innovation at both national and global levels. . . .

Conclusion

The distinctive feature of global problems is the lack of a central authority for coordination and enforcement. Despite this obstacle, there are encouraging examples of successful transnational institution building to tackle transborder environmental problems. Success has been greatest in cases such as stratospheric ozone and acid rain, where the problem can be made operational in precise technical terms; where international action can therefore focus on tightly defined interventions; and where the perceived benefits of collective action have been high, for key actors, relative to the cost. It will be more difficult for other environmental and social problems—where the relationship between action and impact is less well understood, and where the costs and benefits of action do not coincide.

12.3 North Sea Cod Crisis Brings Call for Nations to Act

Craig Smith

The dumping of chlorofluorocarbons and carbon dioxide into the world's atmosphere—and the consequent depletion of the ozone layer and global warming—represent one type of challenge posed by a "global commons" outside the jurisdiction of any single sovereign state: pollution. A second type of challenge posed by the "global commons," and a second example of the need for global institutions to deal with a global environment is overconsumption. Like the overuse of a common pasture by livestock owners, the overuse of the world's ocean by fishermen threatens to destroy a common resource on which they all rely. While everyone would benefit from more careful stewardship of the oceans, individual fishermen, communities, and nations are loathe to cut back on their own exploitation of it. Studies show that populations of key species of fish around the globe have been reduced to such levels that it is unclear whether they can rebound—and yet fishing continues. For the following article, Craig Smith of the *New York Times* traveled to a fishing village in Denmark to document the tension between the common good and the incentives of individual communities and the gradual evolution of international regulation.

Gilleleje, Denmark—The cod are disappearing from the deep gray waters that stretch to the horizon from this gull-festooned town, a stark reminder that there is a finite number of fish in the sea and that man's growing appetite for seafood, if left unchecked, could eventually drive many species to extinction.

Scientists warned last month [October 2002] that unless almost all commercial fishing in the North Sea was banned, the cod stock might soon collapse, meaning that the number of cod necessary to repopulate the overfished region could fall so low that the popular food fish might never recover.

"The cod are now so depleted we're not really sure of their population dynamics," said Henrik Sparholt, a fisheries assessment scientist at the International Council for the Exploration of the Sea, which has advised closing the North Sea to most fishing indefinitely.

Mr. Sparholt said the number of North Sea cod was at its lowest level ever and was half of what was considered the minimum for assured propagation.

The cod crisis is one of many facing the international community as countries compete for thinning stocks in the world's once fish-thick seas. Fish are the last food source hunted on a large scale in the wild, and the United Nations warns that the world's 17 main fisheries are fished at or above sustainable levels.

None of the endangered species of fish affects so many countries and so many people or has such historic significance as cod. Once known as "beef of the sea," it is the world's most popular food fish and was a driving force in the development of the global economy.

Thanks to their lethargic swimming style, cod are easy to catch and have the whitest flesh of all white-fleshed fish. The meat is low in fat, high in protein and easily filleted.

The low fat content makes it easy to cure and made it the perfect fish for marine provisions and international trade before the invention of refrigeration. The Massachusetts Bay Colony was established, in part, to make money by selling cod to England.

Cod stocks have collapsed before. The fish was once so abundant off the northeastern coast of North America that the Italian explorer John Cabot reported catching them with a bucket in 1497.

But after 500 years of increasingly intensive fishing and repeated warnings that the cod were endangered, they suddenly all but disappeared more than a decade ago. Despite a fishing ban, they have yet to come back in significant numbers.

Thinning cod stocks in the North Sea have worried scientists for years now, and though the European Union had fiddled with quotas and the sizes of net holes—larger holes let younger fish survive until they can spawn—it has been slow to offer the fish adequate protection.

Part of the problem is that harsher measures would devastate the economies of towns like Gilleleje, where cod fishing is the biggest industry.

"I'm 57, and I have to work another 10 years because I have no pension," said Peter Andersen, winding a heavy green net onto the winch of his 56-foot blue and white trawler docked at the town's nearly empty harbor. "I wouldn't earn a living if I couldn't fish cod."

Hunching against a bitter wind, Mr. Andersen says increasingly restrictive quotas on cod catches have already shortened his annual fishing season from 10 months to 5. He supplements his income by catching lobster but says too many fishing boats are doing the same for the lobster to last if the cod industry is shut down.

Demand for cod rose sharply in the early 1900's after Clarence Birdseye developed his method for freezing food and the fish industry began filleting fish by machine. Then, in 1962, the owner of a McDonald's franchise in Cincinnati invented the Filet-O-Fish sandwich for Catholics who did not eat meat on Friday. Demand for cod surged again.

Today it is eaten in almost every country in the world. To meet demand, competing Danish and Scottish fishing fleets use nets that drag across the seabed and can sweep a mile or more of water free of fish in a matter of hours.

There are some areas where cod remain plentiful—around Iceland and in the Barents Sea—but the rest of the world's major stocks, relatively distinct populations of the fish that live in a particular region, are thinning rapidly or are already depleted. In the early 20th century it was not unheard of for fishermen to catch man-sized, 200-pound cod, but such old fish are rare these days.

Last year the European Commission put forward a plan devised to help North Sea cod stocks recover, but the fishery ministers of European Union members countries have bickered over the plan because it uses limits on the length of time that fishermen can spend fishing cod instead of quotas on the quantity they can catch.

The switch, intended to combat the chronic underreporting of catches, is unpopular because it could leave some countries with less fish than others if their fishermen were unlucky.

While the ministers argue, the International Council for the Exploration of the Sea says the situation has grown increasingly dire. The council, which makes policy recommendations to its 19 member countries, advised last month that until the cod recover, fishing should be banned altogether for most fish in the North Sea, the Irish Sea and the waters west of Scotland.

Because many cod are caught as a "bycatch" by crews fishing for other species in the region, the council's scientists want the ban extended beyond cod.

Franz Fischler, the European commissioner responsible for agriculture, rural development, and fisheries, has blasted the European Union's fishery ministers for letting the situation go so far.

"It is galling after repeatedly warning of the dire consequences of inaction," he said in a speech delivered after the council made its advice public, "to see our worst fears realized."

Mr. Fischler said that if the European Commission's own scientific committee backs the council's advice when it delivers its report on cod stocks next Monday, he will propose a ban on cod, haddock and whiting fishing in the area, and substantial reductions in the quotas for other fish, until the ministers can agree on a longer-term solution.

But many marine biologists worry that politicians lack the will to sacrifice jobs for cod. With stocks so low, Mr. Sparholt says, anything less than a total, indefinite ban may leave the cod population vulnerable to nature's periodic environmental shocks, like changes in water temperature or a sudden drop in the food supply. . . .

But even if the North Sea cod are saved, the pressure will likely move to other fisheries to meet the voracious appetite for fish sticks, fish and chips and fried fish sandwiches—or it will go to other species. The more plentiful pollock, for example, is increasingly being used as a substitute for cod.

12.4 Once Targeted by Protesters, Home Depot Plays Green Role

Jim Carlton

As a rule environmental issues have pitted conservationists against corporations that seek inexpensive natural resources to make their products. The following selection describes how one major transnational corporation, Home Depot, the world's largest single retailer of lumber, has made a virtue of necessity by coming to the defense of Chile's old growth forests and in doing so has become a valuable and valued ally of local conservationists.

Concepción, Chile—High on a ridge above this coastal city stands a forest of ancient araucaria trees, bending in the wind. Native forests like this one, once in constant danger of being razed, now are more likely to remain undisturbed.

Their unlikely protector: Home Depot Inc.

The world's largest retailer of lumber, Home Depot buys almost 10 percent of Chile's annual wood exports. Most of the lumber comes from tree farms of non-

Wall Street Journal. Eastern Edition by Jim Carlton. August 6, 2004. Copyright 2004 by *Dow Jones & Co Inc* in the format Textbook via Copyright Clearance Center.

native pine and eucalyptus that the Chilean timber industry planted on denuded land—including places where large swaths of ecologically diverse native forest had been clear-cut or burned down.

In the past few years, Home Depot has begun lobbying governments and loggers to stop overcutting forests from Asia and Africa to the Americas. In Chile, Home Depot recently brokered a pact to deter landowners from converting native forests into the very kind of tree farms the retailer depends on.

Home Depot is part of a growing rapprochement between American corporations and the global activists who traditionally clashed with them. From 1997 to 1999, environmental groups organized protests against the company, charging it was failing to ensure that its wood didn't come from endangered forests. Activists picketed hundreds of Home Depot stores, hung banners at its corporate headquarters in Atlanta and demonstrated at shareholder meetings.

Home Depot was afraid the protests might lead to a consumer backlash and sliding sales. It had already started an internal push to follow better environmental practices. So the company agreed to stop using products from endangered forests. It created a new executive position—environmental global project manager. The man appointed to the post, Roland "Ron" Jarvis, has the authority to sever logging contracts with any supplier whose practices harm endangered forests or otherwise hurt the environment.

Citing the destruction of tropical forests in Indonesia, Mr. Jarvis slashed Home Depot's purchases of wood there. He also played mediator between Chilean environmentalists and Chile's two largest timber producers, Empresas CMPC SA and Celulosa Arauco y Constitución SA, persuading them to overcome years of acrimony and negotiate face-to-face for the first time.

For retailers, working with green groups can be a fairly inexpensive way to ingratiate themselves with customers and rid themselves of negative publicity. Home Depot says the cost of its initiatives is small relative to the $64.8 billion in sales the company had last year. Mr. Jarvis says 95 percent of its wood comes from North America, so the impact on the bottom line from switching overseas suppliers is minor.

Still, many environmentalists applaud this newfound activism, saying it represents the fruit of "markets campaigns" that some activists have carried out over the past decade. Instead of seeking environmental change through government legislation or the courts, these activists target specific corporations through boycotts and protests. They then persuade those companies to pressure their suppliers and business partners to change their practices, creating a "green" domino effect through an industry.

Office-supply giant Office Depot Inc., after an activists' campaign against it, canceled purchases from an Indonesian paper supplier that activists say was using trees from the country's endangered forests. Office Depot officials said the campaign didn't motivate their decision. Home-improvement retailer Lowe's Cos. joined Home Depot and several other U.S. companies in pressuring Canada to declare logging off-limits in great swaths of the Great Bear Rainforest in British Columbia.

"If you've got Home Depot carrying your water, you're going to get a lot farther than as just an environmental group," says Randy Hayes, president of the Rainforest Action Network, an environmental group in San Francisco.

The retailers that have made reforms say it is too early to see any impact on the environment, but Home Depot says it has seen a modest impact in sales from customers who are aware of its environmental stands. It says it sold $30,000 of green-certified wood to build ramps at this year's X Games, an extreme-sports event that started yesterday in Los Angeles. The protests directed against the companies have ceased.

The markets campaigns don't always work. Even proponents of the campaigns admit that the agreements generally aren't legally binding. Sometimes pressure from giant U.S. corporations isn't enough to make countries change environmentally harmful logging practices.

In bowing to the environmentalists' demands, Home Depot agreed to give preference to wood that had been logged in an environmentally friendly way. It first used guidelines from the Forest Stewardship Council, a body now based in Bonn, Germany, that certifies trees as properly harvested. But Home Depot realized it couldn't meet demand with council-certified wood alone. It needed to identify forests around the world that were endangered and persuade suppliers not to log there.

That proved to be a challenge. "If you asked us when we started this program how much of our wood came from the Brazilian rain forest, we didn't know," recalls Mr. Jarvis, an athletic 44-year-old who was recruited by Home Depot cofounder Pat Farrah to become environmental manager in June 2000.

Formerly the head of Home Depot's merchandising business in the Southeast U.S. and Puerto Rico, Mr. Jarvis spent the first few months getting educated. He met officials from the State Department and Department of Agriculture and sat through a global forestry summit in Rome, where he huddled with timber executives from 30 countries.

Six months later, he had learned enough to begin enforcing Home Depot's new green policy. In Indonesia, Home Depot's main supplier was cutting trees in a slash-and-burn fashion, razing entire swaths of the country's rain forest to get the lumber it wanted. "We asked them to stop, but they said they would continue," he recalls. In response, Mr. Jarvis cut 90 percent of Home Depot's purchases of Indonesian lumber. The remaining purchases came from suppliers who didn't slash and burn. Mr. Jarvis hoped rewarding those suppliers would pressure others to change their methods but that hasn't happened yet, he says.

In the African nation of Gabon, a Home Depot supplier also used slash-and-burn methods in a jungle that is home to the endangered lowland gorilla. Mr. Jarvis pulled all of Home Depot's contracts there when the company's suppliers declined to change their practices. He shifted the buying to tree plantations in Brazil and Central America.

In late 2002, an environmentalist named Aaron Sanger phoned Mr. Jarvis. Coordinator of the Chilean wood campaign for San Francisco–based Forest Ethics, Mr. Sanger warned that the expansion of Chilean tree farms was wiping out the country's natural forests.

Chilean activists had started complaining about the decline of native forests soon after the dictatorship of Gen. Augusto Pinochet ended in 1989. In 1974, Mr.

•

Pinochet instituted subsidies for tree farms, aiming to build a large wood-products industry. While the plantations grew to generate more than $2 billion a year in Chilean exports, environmental activists and native Mapuche Indians living near the tree farms fought to rein in their growth. They said the farms sucked up water and caused erosion.

"We can't even graze our animals there," because the tightly-packed plantation groves provide too much shade for grass to grow, said Julio Alarcon, a 62-year-old herdsman, as he warmed his hands over a campfire in a native forest surrounded by tree farms in the central Chilean highlands.

The tree plantations were an example of the conundrum Home Depot faced. It wanted the lumber, but it couldn't say it was observing its environmental policy's promise of "efficient and responsible use of wood and wood products" if native Chilean forests continued to be cleared.

Mr. Sanger asked Home Depot to work with Chile's biggest timber companies, CMPC and Arauco, on solutions. By late 2002, Mr. Sanger was organizing a campaign encouraging North American buyers to boycott Chilean wood. More than a dozen companies eventually joined the boycott.

Mr. Jarvis agreed to look into the situation. He called two Chilean executives— Hernan Fournies of CMPC and Charles Kimber of Arauco—and asked for their side of the story. The Chileans accused the environmentalists of exaggerating claims. Environmentalists said some three million acres of native forests had been removed by fire and logging to make way for plantations of mostly radiata pine. The executives asserted that the real figure was less than a million acres. They also said they were no longer doing the conversions, but were planting tree farms mainly on former ranch and farm land.

Mr. Jarvis then asked if the companies had ever sat down with their critics in Chile to discuss the problem. He was surprised to find they had not.

"So I threw out the idea of bringing both sides to the table to talk these issues out," says Mr. Jarvis. The Chilean logging companies reluctantly agreed. "Of course, we have to listen to what our customers want," Mr. Fournies says.

Mr. Jarvis suggested a meeting outside Chile, where the two sides had clashed repeatedly. The previous year, Chilean police had shot and killed a 17-year-old Mapuche boy as he and several of his tribesmen tried to take over a CMPC tree farm.

Both sides agreed to meet May 1, 2003, at Home Depot's Atlanta headquarters. "I thought to myself, 'Maybe we will have a blood bath,'" Mr. Fournies recalls. Mr. Jarvis posted an armed guard outside the fourth-floor meeting room.

The timber executives wore casual attire to try to fit in with the activists. The executives remember being pleasantly surprised at seeing all of the environmentalists dressed in business suits. One woman from the Rainforest Action Network showed colleagues where she had scaled a building to hang a banner attacking Home Depot four years earlier.

Twenty-three people, including Mr. Jarvis, sat around folding tables, the environmentalists on one side and the timber executives on the other. The CMPC executives bristled when Malu Sierra, a fiery activist from Santiago, began lecturing them on the need to do more to protect the forests because the companies were "so rich" and, in her view, had a history of hurting the environment. An equally outspoken executive named Daniel Contesse, vice president of CMPC's forestry operations, recalls that he started to jump to his feet to rebut Ms. Sierra.

From his corner, Mr. Sanger says, he quietly interjected: "We can't agree on the past, but we can agree on the future—to protect the native forests of Chile."

That helped set an amicable mood for the rest of the four-hour meeting, the Chilean timber officials say. The two sides came away from Atlanta with plans to work on a forestry accord. In the meantime, the logging companies agreed to enact stronger conservation measures and the environmentalists agreed to stop targeting Arauco and CMPC in their boycott campaign.

The next big meeting was in Chile in July, where CMPC and Arauco executives had invited the environmentalists to inspect the companies' forests, sawmills and nature preserves. The environmentalists were impressed, in part, by the companies' expressed desire to preserve the country's remaining natural forest. At the tour's end, Mr. Sanger told the lumber executives, "We have learned you are as passionate about the native forests as we are."

A hurdle arose when the two sides sat down to hammer out the details of their agreement. The companies wanted to emphasize in the statement that they had been following conservation practices for a while. The environmentalists bristled at that language, Mr. Jarvis says. "I basically told both sides, 'If you want to win on this, you have to give,'" Mr. Jarvis recalls. So the environmentalists agreed to give the companies some praise in the statement.

After one more meeting at Home Depot's headquarters in Atlanta and further telephone consultations, the two sides were ready to announce their agreement on Nov. 12. Although the companies insisted they weren't doing forest conversions themselves, they agreed not to keep buying land that landowners had deforested recently. CMPC said it wouldn't buy properties razed after 1993, while Arauco said it wouldn't purchase land cleared after 2002.

So far, everyone has adhered to the agreement. Mr. Jarvis says he's now preparing to spread Home Depot's activism. "I think that maybe this is a template we can use in other countries," he says, naming Indonesia as a possible next target.

Environmental Degradation
and International Conflict

12.5 On the Threshold: Environmental Changes as Causes of Acute Conflict

Thomas F. Homer-Dixon

Shortages and environmental degradation may actually bring nations and peoples into conflict with each other. Virtually all of the projected growth in world population will take place in the developing world, and this is where Thomas Homer-Dixon, a Canadian political scientist and the author of the next selection, believes that environmental degradation is most likely to overwhelm political institutions and produce violence. Homer-Dixon reviews the arguments of environmental optimists and pessimists, revealing himself to be something of a pessimist in the process. Third World countries are, he argues, more vulnerable to environmental pressures than wealthy countries. He identifies seven interrelated environmental problems that afflict developing countries: greenhouse warming, ozone depletion, soil acidification, deforestation, soil erosion, water pollution, and fish depletion. These problems, in his view, have a series of social consequences—reduced agricultural production, economic decline, population displacement, and disrupted institutions—that in turn foster conflict and violence. Homer-Dixon links environmental degradation to three types of conflict: simple scarcity conflicts that arise over the distribution of diminishing resources like fresh water, group-identity conflicts involving the collision of different ethnic and cultural groups, and relative-deprivation conflicts associated with inequalities within societies. He concludes by drawing out the implications of these conflicts for international security, arguing that the developed countries cannot isolate themselves from the effects of conflicts in the developing world.

How might environmental change lead to acute conflict? Some experts propose that environmental change may shift the balance of power between states either regionally or globally, producing instabilities that could lead to war. Or, as global environmental damage increases the disparity between the North and the South, poor nations may militarily confront the rich for a greater share of the world's wealth. Warmer temperatures could lead to

Thomas F. Homer-Dixon, "On the Threshold: Environmental Changes as Causes of Acute Conflict," *International Security*, 16:2 (Fall 1991), pp. 76–116. © 1991 by the President and Fellows of Harvard College and the Massachusetts Institute of Technology.

contention over new ice-free sea-lanes in the Arctic or more accessible resources in the Antarctic. Bulging populations and land stress may produce waves of environmental refugees that spill across borders with destabilizing effects on the recipient's domestic order and on international stability. Countries may fight over dwindling supplies of water and the effects of upstream pollution. In developing countries, a sharp drop in food crop production could lead to internal strife across urban-rural and nomadic-sedentary cleavages. If environmental degradation makes food supplies increasingly tight, exporters may be tempted to use food as a weapon. Environmental change could ultimately cause the gradual impoverishment of societies in both the North and South, which could aggravate class and ethnic cleavages, undermine liberal regimes, and spawn insurgencies. Finally, many scholars indicate that environmental degradation will "ratchet up" the level of stress within national and international society, thus increasing the likelihood of many different kinds of conflict and impeding the development of cooperative solutions.

Which of these scenarios are most plausible and why? . . .

. . . [P]oor countries will in general be more vulnerable to environmental change than rich ones; therefore, environmentally induced conflicts are likely to arise first in the developing world. In these countries, a range of atmospheric, terrestrial, and aquatic environmental pressures will in time probably produce, either singly or in combination, four main, causally interrelated social effects: reduced agricultural production, economic decline, population displacement, and disruption of regular and legitimized social relations. These social effects, in turn, may cause . . . scarcity disputes between countries, clashes between ethnic groups, and civil strife and insurgency, each with potentially serious repercussions for the security interests of the developed world.

I do not hypothesize that the causal links between these variables will be tight or deterministic. As anti-Malthusians have argued for nearly two centuries, numerous intervening factors—physical, technological, economic, and social—often permit great resilience, variability, and adaptability in human environmental systems. . . . [I]n particular . . . free-market mechanisms may permit developing countries to minimize the negative impacts of environmental degradation. But I suggest that, as the human population grows and environmental damage progresses, policymakers will have less and less capacity to intervene to keep this damage from producing serious social disruption, including conflict. . . .

The Range of Environmental Problems   Developing countries are likely to be affected sooner and more severely by environmental change than rich countries. By definition, they do not have the financial, material, or intellectual resources of the developed world; furthermore, their social and political institutions tend to be fragile and riven with discord. It is probable, therefore, that developing societies will be less able to apprehend or respond to environmental disruption.

Seven major environmental problems . . . might plausibly contribute to conflict within and among developing countries: greenhouse warming, stratospheric ozone depletion, acid deposition, deforestation, degradation of agricultural land, overuse and pollution of water supplies, and depletion of fish stocks. These problems can all be crudely characterized as large-scale human-induced problems, with long-term and often irreversible consequences, which is why they are often grouped together under the rubric "global change." However, they vary greatly in spatial scale: the first two involve genuinely global physical processes, while the last five involve regional physical processes, although they may appear in locales all over the planet. These seven problems also vary in time scale: for example, while a region can be deforested in only a few years, and severe ecological and social effects may be noticeable almost immediately, human-induced greenhouse warming will probably develop over many decades and may not have truly serious implications for humankind for half a century or more after the signal is first detected. In addition, some of these problems (for instance, deforestation and degradation of water supplies) are much more advanced than others (such as greenhouse warming and ozone depletion) and are already producing serious social disruption. . . .

Many of these problems are causally interrelated. For instance, acid deposition damages agricultural land, fisheries, and forests. Greenhouse warming may contribute to deforestation by moving northward the optimal temperature and precipitation zones for many tree species, by increasing the severity of windstorms and wildfires, and by expanding the range of pests and diseases. The release of carbon from these dying forests would reinforce the greenhouse effect. The increased incidence of ultra-violet radiation due to the depletion of the ozone layer will probably damage trees and crops, and it may also damage the phytoplankton at the bottom of the ocean food chain. . . .

Four Principal Social Effects   Environmental degradation may cause countless often subtle changes in developing societies. These range from increased communal cooking as fuelwood becomes scarce around African villages, to worsened poverty of Filipino coastal fishermen whose once-abundant grounds have been destroyed by trawlers and industrial pollution. Which of the many types of social effect might be crucial links between environmental change and acute conflict? . . .

. . . I hypothesize that four principal social effects may, either singly or in combination, substantially increase the probability of acute conflict in developing countries: decreased agricultural production, economic decline, population displacement, and disruption of legitimized and authoritative institutions and social relations. These effects will often be causally interlinked, sometimes with reinforcing relationships. For example, the population displacement resulting from a decrease in agricultural production may further disrupt agricultural production. Or economic decline may lead to the flight of people with wealth and education, which in turn could eviscerate universities, courts, and institutions of economic management, all of which are crucial to a healthy economy.

Agricultural Production   Decreased agricultural production is often mentioned as potentially the most worrisome consequence of environmental change. . . .

The Philippines provides a good illustration of deforestation's impact. . . . Since the Second World War, logging and the encroachment of farms have reduced the virgin and second-growth forest from about sixteen million hectares to 6.8–7.6 million hectares. Across the archipelago, logging and land-clearing have accelerated erosion, changed regional hydrological cycles and precipitation patterns, and decreased the land's ability to retain water during rainy periods. The resulting flash floods have damaged irrigation works while plugging reservoirs and irrigation channels with silt. These factors may seriously affect crop production. For example, when the government of the Philippines and the European Economic Community commissioned an Integrated Environmental Plan for the still relatively unspoiled island of Palawan, the authors of the study found that only about half of the 36,000 hectares of irrigated farmland projected within the Plan for 2007 will actually be irrigable because of the hydrological effects of decreases in forest cover.

. . . [T]he degradation and decreasing availability of good agricultural land . . . deserve much closer attention than they usually receive. Currently, total global cropland amounts to about 1.5 billion hectares. Optimistic estimates of total arable land on the planet, which includes both current and potential cropland, range from 3.2 to 3.4 billion hectares, but nearly all the best land has already been exploited. What is left is either less fertile, not sufficiently rainfed or easily irrigable, infested with pests, or harder to clear and work.

For developing countries during the 1980s, cropland grew at just 0.26 percent a year, less than half the rate of the 1970s. More importantly, in these countries arable land per capita dropped by 1.9 percent a year. In the absence of a major increase in arable land in developing countries, experts expect that the world average of 0.28 hectares of cropland per capita will decline to 0.17 hectares by the year 2025, given the current rate of world population growth. Large tracts are being lost each year to urban encroachment, erosion, nutrient depletion, salinization, waterlogging, acidification, and compacting. The geographer Vaclav Smil, who is generally very conservative in his assessments of environmental damage, estimates that two to three million hectares of cropland are lost annually to erosion; perhaps twice as much land goes to urbanization, and at least one million hectares are abandoned because of excessive salinity. In addition, about one-fifth of the world's cropland is suffering from some degree of desertification. Taken together, he concludes, the planet will lose about 100 million hectares of arable land between 1985 and 2000.

. . . Coastal cropland in countries such as Bangladesh and Egypt is extremely vulnerable to storm surges. Such events could become more common and devastating, because global warming will cause sea levels to rise and might intensify storms. . . .

Economic Decline   If we are interested in environment-conflict linkages, perhaps the most important potential social effect of environmental degradation is the further impoverishment it may produce in developing societies. . . .

Agriculture is the source of much of the wealth generated in developing societies. Food production soared in many regions over the last decades because the green revolution more than compensated for inadequate or declining soil productivity; but some experts believe this economic relief will be short-lived. . . . Damage to the soil is already producing a harsh economic impact in some areas. . . .

Population Displacement   Some commentators have suggested that environmental degradation may produce vast numbers of "environmental refugees." Sea-level rise may drive people back from coastal and delta areas in Egypt; spreading desert may empty Sahelian countries as their populations move south; Filipino fishermen may leave their depleted fishing grounds for the cities. The term "environmental refugee" is somewhat misleading, however, because it implies that environmental disruption could be a clear, proximate cause of refugee flows. Usually, though, environmental disruption will be only one of many interacting physical and social variables, including agricultural and economic decline, that ultimately force people from their homelands. For example, over the last three decades, millions of people have migrated from Bangladesh to neighboring West Bengal and Assam in India. While detailed data are scarce (in part because the Bangladeshi government is reluctant to admit there is significant out-migration), many specialists believe this movement is a result, at least in part, of shortages of adequately fertile land due to a rapidly growing population. Flooding, caused by deforestation in watersheds upstream on the Ganges and Brahmaputra rivers, might also be driving people from the area. In the future, this migration could be aggravated by rising sea-levels coupled with extreme weather events (both perhaps resulting from climate change).

Disrupted Institutions and Social Relations　　The fourth social effect especially relevant to the connection between environment change and acute conflict is the disruption of institutions and of legitimized, accepted, and authoritative social relations. In many developing societies, the three social effects described above are likely to tear this fabric of custom and habitual behavior. A drop in agricultural output may weaken rural communities by causing malnutrition and disease, and by encouraging people to leave; economic decline may corrode confidence in the national purpose, weaken the tax base, and undermine financial, legal, and political institutions; and mass migrations of people into a region may disrupt labor markets, shift class relations, and upset the traditional balance of economic and political authority between ethnic groups.

The Capacity of Developing Countries to Respond . . .

Can developing countries respond to environmental problems effectively enough to avert these negative social effects? . . .

Over the long term, the capacity of developing countries to respond effectively to the consequences of environmental change on agriculture will depend on complex interactions within each society. . . . Of particular importance are the society's prevailing land-use practices, land distribution, and market mechanisms within the agricultural sector. Market factors are especially relevant today as numerous developing countries are relinquishing state control over the marketplace, reducing government spending, and removing impediments to foreign investment. Economists often contend that—in a market economy with an efficient price mechanism— environmentally induced scarcity will encourage conservation, technological innovation, and resource substitution. . . . Many economists point to the success of the green revolution, which was often driven by market forces; it involved both new technologies and the substitution of petroleum resources (in the form of fertilizer) for inadequate or degraded nutrients in the soil. This argument supports the policies for market liberalization and "structural adjustment" currently promoted by international financial and lending institutions, such as the International Monetary Fund and World Bank. Below, however, I suggest why these policies will not be an effective response to environmental scarcity in the future.

Cornucopians and Neo-Malthusians   Experts in environmental studies now commonly use the labels "cornucopian" for optimists . . . and "neo-Malthusian" for pessimists. . . . Cornucopians do not worry much about protecting the stock of any single resource, because of their faith that market-driven human ingenuity can always be tapped to allow the substitution of more abundant resources to produce the same end-use service. . . . Neo-Malthusians are much more cautious. For renewable resources, they often distinguish between resource "capital" and its "income": the capital is the resource stock that generates a flow (the income) that can be tapped for human consumption and well-being. A "sustainable" economy, using this terminology, is one that leaves the capital intact and undamaged so that future generations can enjoy an undiminished income stream.

Historically, cornucopians have been right to criticize the idea that resource scarcity places fixed limits on human activity. Time and time again, human beings have circumvented scarcities, and neo-Malthusians have often been justly accused of "crying wolf." But in assuming that this experience pertains to the future, cornucopians overlook seven factors.

First, whereas serious scarcities of critical resources in the past usually appeared singly, now we face multiple scarcities that exhibit powerful interactive, feedback, and threshold effects. An agricultural region may, for example, be simultaneously affected by degraded water and soil, greenhouse-induced precipitation changes, and increased ultraviolet radiation. . . . Second, in the past the scarcity of a given resource usually increased slowly, allowing time for social, economic, and technological adjustment. But human populations are much larger and activities of individuals are, on a global average, much more resource-intensive than before. This means that debilitating scarcities often develop much more quickly: whole countries may be deforested in a few decades; most of a region's topsoil can disappear in a generation; and critical ozone depletion may occur in as little as twenty years. Third, today's consumption has far greater momentum than in the past, because of the size of the consuming population, the sheer quantity of material consumed by this population, and the density of its interwoven fabric of consumption activities. The countless individual and corporate economic actors making up human society are heavily committed to certain patterns of resource use; and the ability of our markets to adapt may be sharply constrained by these entrenched interests. . . .

The fourth reason that cornucopian arguments may not apply in the future is that the free-market price mechanism is a bad gauge of scarcity, especially for resources held in common, such as a benign climate and productive seas. . . .

The fifth reason is an extension of a point made earlier: market-driven adaptation to resource scarcity is most likely to succeed in wealthy societies, where abundant reserves of capital, knowledge, and talent help economic actors invent new technologies, identify conservation possibilities, and make the transition to new production and consumption patterns. Yet many of the societies facing the most serious environmental problems in the coming decades will be poor; even if they have efficient markets, lack of capital and know-how will hinder their response to these problems.

Sixth, cornucopians have an anachronistic faith in humankind's ability to unravel and manage the myriad processes of nature. There is no *a priori* reason to expect that human scientific and technical ingenuity can always surmount all types of scarcity. . . . Perhaps most important, scientific and technical knowledge must be built incrementally—layer upon layer—and its diffusion to the broader society often takes decades. Any technical solutions to environmental scarcity may arrive too late to prevent catastrophe.

Seventh and finally, future environmental problems, rather than inspiring the wave of ingenuity predicted by cornucopians, may instead reduce the supply of ingenuity available in a society. The success of market mechanisms depends on an intricate and stable system of institutions, social relations, and shared understandings. . . . Cornucopians often overlook the role of *social* ingenuity in producing the complex legal and economic climate in which *technical* ingenuity can flourish. Policymakers must be clever "social engineers" to design and implement effective market mechanisms. Unfortunately, however, the syndrome of multiple, interacting, unpredictable, and rapidly changing environmental problems will increase the complexity and pressure of the policymaking setting. It will also generate increased "social friction" as elites and interest groups struggle to protect their prerogatives. The ability of policymakers to be good social engineers is likely to go *down*, not up, as these stresses increase. . . .

Although we must be careful not to slip into environmental determinism, when it comes to the poorest countries on this planet we should not invest too much faith in the potential of human ingenuity to respond to multiple, interacting, and rapidly changing environmental problems once they have become severe. The most important of the seven factors above is the last: growing population, consumption, and environmental stresses will increase social friction. This will reduce the capacity of policymakers in developing countries to intervene as good social engineers in order to chart a sustainable development path and prevent further social disruption. Neo-Malthusians may underestimate human adaptability in *today's* environmental-social system, but as time passes their analysis may become ever more compelling.

Types of Conflict

. . . [S]evere environmental degradation will produce three principal types of conflict. . . .

Simple Scarcity Conflicts   Simple scarcity conflicts . . . may arise over three types of resource in particular: river water, fish, and agriculturally productive land. These renewable resources seem particularly likely to spark conflict because their scarcity is increasing rapidly in some regions, they are often essential for human survival, and they can be physically seized or controlled. . . .

The current controversy over the Great Anatolia Project on the Euphrates River illustrates how simple scarcity conflicts can arise. By early in the next century, Turkey plans to build a huge complex of twenty dams and irrigation systems along the upper reaches of the Euphrates. This $21 billion project, if fully funded and built, would reduce the average annual flow of the Euphrates within Syria from 32 billion cubic meters to 20 billion. The water that passes through Turkey's irrigation systems and on to Syria will be laden with fertilizers, pesticides, and salts. Syria is already desperately short of water. . . . Much of the water for its towns, industries, and farms comes from the Euphrates, and the country has been chronically vulnerable to drought. Furthermore, Syria's population growth rate, at 3.7 percent per year, is one of the highest in the world, and this adds further to the country's demand for water. . . .

Group-Identity Conflicts   Group-identity conflicts . . . are likely to arise from the large-scale movements of populations brought about by environmental change. As different ethnic and cultural groups are propelled together under circumstances of deprivation and stress, we should expect intergroup hostility, in which a group would emphasize its own identity while denigrating, discriminating against, and attacking outsiders. The situation in the Bangladesh-Assam region may be a good example of this process; Assam's ethnic strife over the last decade has apparently been provoked by migration from Bangladesh.

As population and environmental stresses grow in developing countries, migration to the developed world is likely to surge. . . . People will seek to move from Latin America to the United States and Canada, from North Africa and the Middle East to Europe, and from South and Southeast Asia to Australia. This migration has already shifted the ethnic balance in many cities and regions of developed countries, and governments are struggling to contain a xenophobic backlash. Such racial strife will undoubtedly become much worse.

Relative-Deprivation Conflicts   . . . [A]s developing societies produce less wealth because of environmental problems, their citizens will probably become increasingly discontented by the widening gap between their actual level of economic achievement and the level they feel they deserve. . . . Lower-status groups will be more frustrated than others because elites will use their power to maintain, as best they can, access to a constant standard of living despite a shrinking economic pie. At some point, the discontent and frustration of some groups may cross a critical threshold, and they will act violently against other groups perceived to be the agents of their economic misery or thought to be benefiting from a grossly unfair distribution of economic goods in the society. . . .

. . . Although relative-deprivation conflicts will tend to be domestic, we should not underestimate their potentially severe international repercussions. . . . For example, highly centralized dictatorships threatened by revolutionary actions, purges, and strikes are especially prone to engage in external war and belligerence. . . . External aggression may also result after a new regime comes to power through civil strife: regimes born of revolution, for example, are particularly good at mobilizing their citizens and resources for military preparation and war.

While environmental stresses and the conflicts they induce may encourage the rise of revolutionary regimes, other results are also plausible: these pressures might overwhelm the management capacity of institutions in developing countries, inducing . . . widespread social disintegration. They may also weaken the control of governments over their territories, especially over the hinterland. . . . The regimes that do gain power in the face of such disruption are likely to be extremist, authoritarian, and abusive of human rights. Moreover, the already short time horizons of policymakers in developing countries will be further shortened. These political factors could seriously undermine efforts to mitigate and adapt to environmental change. Soon to be the biggest contributors to global environmental problems, developing countries could become more belligerent, less willing to compromise with other states, and less capable of controlling their territories in order to implement measures to reduce environmental damage.

If many developing countries evolve in the direction of extremism, the interests of the North may be directly threatened. Of special concern here is the growing disparity between rich and poor nations that may be induced by environmental change. Robert Heilbroner notes that revolutionary regimes "are not likely to view the vast difference between first class and cattle class with the forgiving eyes of their predecessors." Furthermore, these nations may be heavily armed, as the proliferation of nuclear and chemical weapons and ballistic missiles continues. Such regimes, he asserts, could be tempted to use nuclear blackmail as a "means of inducing the developed world to transfer its wealth on an unprecedented scale to the underdeveloped world."[1] Richard Ullman, however, argues that this concern is overstated. Third World nations are unlikely to confront the North violently in the face of the "superior destructive capabilities of the rich."[2] In light of the discussion in this article, we might conclude that environmental stress and its attendant social disruption will so debilitate the economies of developing countries that they will be unable to amass sizeable armed forces, conventional or otherwise. But the North would surely be unwise to rely on impoverishment and disorder in the South for its security.

12.6 Receding Aral Sea Offers Fertile Ground for Conflict

David Stern

In the following selection, British journalist David Stern describes one of the world's great man-made environmental tragedies, the virtual disappearance of the Aral Sea owing to the abuse of its water for agriculture by the former Soviet Union. The article suggests that the disappearance of the Aral Sea is already having detrimental

---

[1] Robert Heilbroner, *An Inquiry into the Human Prospect* (New York: Norton, 1980), pp. 39 and 95. These North-South disputes would be the international analogues of domestic relative-deprivation conflicts.
[2] Richard Ullman, "Redefining Security," *International Security*, Vol. 8, No. 1 (Summer 1983), p. 143.

consequences for the economies and societies of the region. The problem is likely to increase as states selfishly compete for the water that used to flow to the sea, and the potential for conflict over this water continues to increase.

T he countryside in the western Uzbek region of Karakalpakstan is as white as the snow in a Christmas scene, but the reality is not so picturesque. The soil is laden with salt—a result of the steady drying-up of the nearby Aral Sea and a catastrophic loss of water in its main source the Amu Darya river.

This is ground zero of one of the world's most extreme examples of regional water abuse, an issue which will be one of the main points on the agenda at the Group of Eight summit in the French spa town of Evian next week [June 2003]. The Aral Sea has been inexorably disappearing since the 1960s, when Soviet planners tapped the waters of the Amu Darya and Syr Darya rivers to help fulfil grandiose plans for cotton production.

Today what was once the fourth largest inland body of water is now less than one-fifth of its original size. The sea's shores have retreated more than 150km.

The plight of the Aral is nothing new. Untold numbers of international conferences and possibly hundreds of millions of dollars—as well as thousands of lines of newsprint—have been devoted to the subject. Each year environmentalists and government officials meet and agree that more must be done and the countries of the region must co-operate. Still the sea continues to recede.

The disaster is almost entirely man-made. "The fact is that the region's basin has enough water. We have over 2,500 cubic meters per capita per year which even for irrigated agriculture should be sufficient," says Juerg Kraehenbuehl of the Swiss Agency for Development and Co-operation.

The problem, says Mr Kraehenbuehl, is an antiquated, decaying infrastructure, with masses of unlined irrigation canals, and gross mismanagement of water resources. "It's a catch-as-catch can system with each upstream country and region taking as much as it is able," he says.

The sea's disappearance is just one more result of the fractious former Soviet states' inability to agree among themselves. Kyrgyzstan needs the water to power its hydroelectric stations, since it lacks the energy resources of its neighbours. Uzbekistan, Tajikistan and Kyrgyzstan fight over limited resources in the Ferghana Valley, the region's breadbasket. Kazakhstan is also a big agricultural producer and shares the Aral Sea with Uzbekistan.

Jacques Chirac, the French president, in a message to the World Water Forum in March, voiced concern that the 21st century could be a period of "tension and water wars." Nowhere is this threat greater than in central Asia.

For environmentalists the greatest areas of worry lie to the west and south. Turkmenistan, which already uses four to five times the amount of water that it should, plans to dig a 3,460 sq km, $6 billion . . . artificial lake in the heart of the desert.

"Receding Aral Sea Offers Fertile Ground for Conflict," by David Stern, *Financial Times,* May 28, 2003. Reprinted with permission of *Financial Times.*

This could prove a catastrophic drain on resources and increase the chance of conflict with neighbouring Uzbekistan, experts say. Likewise Afghanistan, which so far has not realised its agricultural potential because of its recent political turmoil, is expected to increase consumption.

And as the sea dies, economic and social tensions rise. In a bazaar in the Uzbek village of Takhtakupir a handful of tradesmen offer cheap household goods and car parts. There are few buyers though. Those that do venture a purchase can do so only on credit and the traders themselves say that they can support their families only by borrowing.

At a nearby, collective farm, most of the fields are unusable. Marat, a farm worker, says that today he works on only 40 hectares, compared with 400–500 in the past. Drinking water is heavily salinated and full of heavy metals and pesticides.

In the town hospital the number of cases of respiratory illness and anaemia have soared, doctors say. Especially acute is the level of tuberculosis, a "poor person's disease," in the words of one, which affects those who suffer from lowered immunity brought on by poor diet. According to Médecins sans Frontières, the disease sees Karakalpakstan ranked 11th in the world.

"All of the region's economy is based on the idea that people live in a river delta. And people here still live as if they were in a river delta—but the river doesn't exist anymore," says Jean Takken of MSF's Karakalpakstan office.

 # The Transnational Web of Development and Environmental Protection

12.7 Energy Project vs. Environmentalists in Peru

Juan Forero

The final selection in this chapter provides a complex and fascinating case study of the various interests that clash in environmental issues. It describes the efforts of environmentalists to prevent an international organization, the Inter-American Development Bank, from providing loans to the government of Peru for developing natural gas resources in an environmentally sensitive area along its coast. For its part, the government, claiming that the project is vital to the region's economic development, is allied with several large private energy firms that seek to exploit the gas deposits.

Paracas, Peru—In the barren moonlike landscape outside this coastal hamlet, workers in hard hats are busily laying cables and constructing giant holding tanks for natural gas liquids. An alliance that includes well-known names in energy like Hunt Oil of Texas and Pluspetrol of Argentina then plans to lay two miles of pipe along the ocean floor to a loading platform for tankers.

The development in Paracas, about three hours' drive south from Lima, is part of an ambitious project, which could cost up to $3.6 billion, to export butane, propane and, eventually, natural gas to California. Peruvian officials say the development, 20 years in the making, would be a crucial engine for growth as the country, which is resource rich but cash poor, tries to transform itself into an energy exporter.

But a surging environmental movement—led by activists from the United States—is pushing hard to halt construction at this plant, which is still in its early stages, and force it to move elsewhere.

Asserting that the plant is a danger to the country's only marine reserve, a sanctuary for sea turtles, rare penguins and sea lions only 4.3 miles to the south, environmental groups won a big victory on Aug. 28 [2003]. That was when the Export-Import Bank, a credit agency of the United States government, rejected a $214 million loan, citing concerns about the environment.

Now, the Inter-American Development Bank is set to vote on Sept. 10 on $75 million in additional financing that, if rejected, could place at least another $60 million in syndicated loans in jeopardy.

Peruvian government officials and operators of the Camisea project—named for the region where the wells are—said they had lined up $225 million in optional financing from a Peruvian bank and promised to finish the project. . . .

But an adverse decision could be a serious blow to the project's image and set a precedent sought by environmentalists—that multinational lending agencies, particularly those dependent on American money, ensure rigorous environmental standards before providing big loans.

"Camisea is a key test for the international financial institutions and the United States government," said Senator Patrick Leahy of Vermont, the ranking Democrat in the foreign operations subcommittee of the Appropriations Committee and a leading critic of the project. "The issue is whether the Inter-American Development Bank, financed with U.S. taxpayer dollars, will protect a pristine area."

Alliance engineers and officials in President Alejandro Toledo's government, which says the project would increase gross domestic product 0.8 percent a year, assert that the highest environmental standards have been exceeded. They accuse environmental groups of exaggerating deficiencies in a quest to terminate the project.

"We had 18 public meetings," said Jaime Quijandría, the economy minister. "Problems came up, but not the kinds of problems that are being raised now."

Mr. Quijandría added: "We are certain there is not going to be any environmental damage."

Project officials and government officials admit errors in the development, but say that standards were improved as environmentalists and consulting firms hired by the multi-national lenders raised concerns.

Alejandro Segret, general manager of TGP in Peru, noted that the pipeline construction, which his company is leading, will be underground, to be covered by jungle.

"Our focus was always to minimize the environmental and social damage," he said. "This is one of the most transparent projects there has been in this country."

But environmental groups like Amazon Watch, Conservation International and the World Wildlife Fund and a collection of grass-roots groups have warned of environmental devastation. And some of their concerns have been echoed by some officials at the Export-Import Bank, the Inter-American Development Bank and by some members of Congress.

The Camisea fields, discovered a generation ago by Shell, were envisioned as one of the largest energy developments in Latin America.

Shell eventually dropped out, and the project has been developed by companies like Hunt Oil of Texas; Pluspetrol of Argentina; Techint, which owns TGP; the SK Corporation of South Korea; Sonatrach, an Algerian state-owned company, and Tractebel, the Belgian energy giant. The companies are developing gas fields thought to hold 13 trillion cubic feet of natural gas and condensate, including butane and propane, an enormous amount. Wells are being developed in the lower Urubamba region of the Peruvian Amazon, along with a gas-and-liquids separation plant and two pipelines stretching across the Andes.

One pipeline, 445 miles long, is projected to transport gas to Lima by August, lowering electricity rates and improving air quality. The other, 335 miles long, leads to this 600-acre site. All this will cost $1.6 billion.

Another $2 billion will be spent to build a plant to liquefy the natural gas and, by 2007, become a major supplier to the United States. A leading candidate for the job would be Halliburton, another Texas company, a Hunt Oil official said.

Both companies have close ties to the Bush administration (Vice President Dick Cheney was chief executive of Halliburton). The administration's energy policy calls for diversifying the sources of America's energy imports and reducing dependence on the Middle East.

But the project cuts through some of the world's most pristine jungles, home not only to rare species of birds and animals but also to indigenous tribes. Wells are being developed in the Nahua Kugapakori Indigenous Reserve, a region established to protect three tribes living in virtual isolation from modern Peru.

"These populations depend exclusively on the territory where they live, the river, the woods," said Beatriz Huertas, adviser to a tropical forest Indian organization. "But the new contacts cause sickness, transmission of disease and death."

Environmentalists also say that the project has led to serious soil erosion, the contamination of rivers and the killing of fish and that developers have cut through communities without providing adequate reimbursement.

Reports from the United States Agency for International Development and an environmental assessment memo from the Export-Import Bank show that the United States has had deep concerns about a lack of transparency, about environmental studies that are called shoddy or insufficient and a lack of knowledge of native groups in the region.

An environmental assessment by the Export-Import Bank says access roads and other paths cut into the jungle "have produced significant direct negative impacts."

The report also says "deforestation, human population growth and consequent losses of biodiversity" are "by far the most significant potential negative effects."

Regarding the Paracas site, the Export-Import Bank report says that while oceanographic conditions were taken into account in choosing the site, no adequate assessments of the social or environmental impacts were conducted on five other alternative sites, contradicting government officials and project officials.

A July memo from the United States Agency for International Development recommended that the Treasury Department, which determines the vote at the Inter-American Development Bank, withhold support for the loan.

Environmentalists concede that much of the work on the Camisea project is complete. Indeed, Norberto Benito, general manager of Plus-petrol in Peru, said the well sites, the pipeline and the gas-and-liquids separation plant are largely done, with about $1.2 billion already spent. . . .

Government officials and the project's sponsors say halting construction is unthinkable. Closing down here and moving to another site would cost an estimated $100 million.

"No way," said Roberto Dañino, the Peruvian ambassador in Washington, who has lobbied hard for the project.

Mr. Dañino says the plant is exactly where it needs to be, in a region with a natural harbor and slight embankment that makes the plant safe from tidal waves.

On first glance, the site does not look like much. The coastline around here is already polluted, thanks to a string of fish meal plants that spew waste into the ocean. And the bone-dry, dusty land around the plant is covered with mounds of empty shells of marine life discarded by the plants.

But just to the south is the hamlet of Paracas, with its hotels, seafood restaurants and a fishing fleet that is dependent on fishing grounds loaded with mackerel, anchovies and other fish. And nearby is the Paracas reserve, a 135,000-acre land-and-sea sanctuary popular with Peruvians and foreigners.

"Paracas is a big tourist destination and visitors could stop coming," said Adalberto Campos, owner of a small hotel. "We wonder what dangers it could bring. We knew nothing about the level of pollution we could have."

Suggested Discussion Topics

1. In what ways does the environment represent a security problem? What conflicts over resources, or over the impact of pollution, do you expect to see during your lifetime? Will these be more likely to affect economically developing nations or nations in the developed world? Why?
2. Despite repeated predictions over the years that environmental catastrophe or mass starvation is just around the corner, the world has so far avoided disaster. Why do environmental pessimists think that this time we really have reason to worry? Do you think these environmental pessimists are right? Why or why not?

3. If everyone wants a clean, healthy environment, why is it so difficult to achieve this goal? What kinds of agreements, institutions, and organizations might be useful in helping to prevent the overuse of natural resources or pollution?

4. Is the environment a global problem, or is it a local or national one? Explain your reasoning. Who should have responsibility for protecting the environment and for determining and enforcing environmental standards?

5. What connection do you see between economic development and the environment? Does economic development result in increasing scarcity of resources, such as food and clean water? Will it lead to additional pollution as members of developing nations gradually attain the lifestyle, and levels of consumption, of the world's richer citizens? Why or why not?

6. What role should transnational corporations—for example, Home Depot—play in dealing with environmental problems? If a host state—for example, Indonesia or Gabon—says that slash-and-burn forest management is acceptable, and that such agricultural techniques are appropriate given the resources of the nation and the needs of its people, should transnational corporations insist on higher standards? If the future development of the timber industry in Chile is decided at a meeting in Atlanta, Georgia, in which the participants are representatives of U.S.-based transnational corporation Home Depot, two private Chilean logging companies, and various transnational environmental NGOs, then what is the role of the "sovereign" state of Chile? To whom is Home Depot answerable? To whom are the Chilean logging companies answerable? To whom are the NGOs answerable? In a classroom discussion, be prepared to play the role of a Home Depot representative, a logging company official, an environmentalist, a Chilean logger, and the Chilean minister of agriculture.

7. If Peru is a sovereign state, why doesn't it simply go ahead with its joint venture with Hunt Oil and Pluspetrol? What kind of power or leverage does each of the actors in this story possess? Be prepared to play the role of each of these actors in a classroom simulation. If you were Peruvian, how would you feel about the influence and power of the U.S. government? Why?

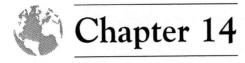

Chapter 14

GENDER AND GLOBAL POLITICS

Historically, the study of global politics has focused on the activities of states: that is, on the interaction among groups of individuals who are divided and organized according to their citizenship. Individuals define their own identity and the identity of "others" in a number of ways, however. "Us" and "them" distinctions are constructed on a variety of different superficial but observable markers, for example, language, religion, clothing, and skin color or other physical features. As we saw in the previous chapter, these other socially constructed identities can be important in global politics, dividing or uniting people in ways that can make it easy or difficult to solve shared problems and develop institutions that create security for oneself and one's own group without threatening the security of others.

In recent years, gender has become an increasingly important identity and source of division in global politics. Dividing the world along gender lines—dividing people into male or female categories and allotting different roles and opportunities to them simply because of the category they fall into—has a number of consequences for global politics.

First, because nearly all societies are dominated by men, women as a group find themselves discriminated against. Most states are ruled by men, and many states do not offer women equal legal or economic status. Even in countries in which the state attempts to treat men and women equally, social institutions, typically dominated by men, discriminate against women and limit their choices, denying them career and lifestyle options available to men.

Historically, gender-based discrimination has had an impact not only on women's quality of life but also on their chances of survival. In traditional agricultural societies, parents preferred male children who would carry on the family name and support their parents in old age. By contrast, female children were regarded as economic burdens. In such societies, it was not uncommon for female babies to be "exposed," that is, left outside the home to die. Their only crime was that they would grow up to be women rather than men. And even today, in some countries, including India and China, modern medical techniques such as ultrasound and amniocentesis are used to identify female fetuses, which are then aborted. More widely around the world, families discriminate against their daughters in providing education, health care, and even nourishment, saving family resources for the males in the household. Estimates of the number of "missing" women in today's world—individuals who were killed or allowed to die simply because they were female—fall in the range of 60 to 100 million. As a result populations in some parts of the world are increasingly skewed. The overabundance of young men and scarcity of women promises to cause social and political problems.

Gender-based discrimination extends into the most personal aspects of life, with consequences that affect not only individual happiness but the well-being of society as a whole. In many societies, women are forced to bear children, regardless of their preferences, and are denied access to birth control. In such societies, maternal mortality rates remain relatively high. Perhaps even more shocking, some African societies still encourage (and others tolerate) the genital mutilation of young women to prevent them from ever enjoying sex.

Discrimination also extends into the economic realm. Around the world, societies undervalue "women's work," jobs that are assigned to women. In most countries women are paid less than men for the same work. Even today, in some Islamic countries women cannot leave home without an escort, cannot hold jobs outside the home, and cannot drive a car. Not surprisingly, women and children make up the bulk of the poorest of the world's poor.

To focus solely on the victimization of women, however, would be to miss much of why gender is so important in global politics. A second consequence of dividing the world along gender lines and of men's control over political and social power is that women's insights are ignored, and problems are defined and addressed exclusively in ways that men see them. Feminist scholars argue that the tendency of men to see relationships as competitive and to define situations in zero-sum terms—that is, to assume that one side can gain only at the expense of the other—has resulted in a global political system that is unnecessarily conflictual. Alternative views of politics—views that are more natural for women, that give less emphasis to boundaries, separateness, and autonomy in relationships—are ignored or ridiculed. If only men could be more like women; that is, if only males were trained to value the things that women value, instead of being taught to despise them, politics would be transformed. Men, like women, are trapped in the gender roles and identities that society has constructed for them, and this limits their ability to solve the problems they face. Equally important, some feminists argue, men's efforts to retain dominance over women traps them in certain mindsets and behavior patterns that prevent the discovery of creative, cooperative solutions to shared problems. Because men are taught that being a man means dominating (dominating women, dominating weaker men, dominating nature), they ignore or reject options that would undercut rigid power hierarchies, even in their own minds.

A third consequence of gender-based divisions is that women have often been excluded from the political process of developing and implementing solutions to the world's problems. Women have been seen as the target or object of (man-made) state policies rather than as equal and active participants in problem solving. Addressing today's global security problems, such as economic underdevelopment, overpopulation, pollution, and resource depletion, requires the full involvement of both women and men. Indeed, an abundance of research has shown that the surest way to accelerate economic development is to provide women with education, contraceptive information, and access to credit, and to allow them the same freedom to make choices that men have.

To whatever degree the new issues on today's security agenda are global issues—problems that threaten us collectively and require a transnational or global effort to solve—the way individual societies around the world define women's roles becomes a matter of global concern. If women are denied capital (the tools needed to be productive), the education needed to make more productive use of their labor, and the freedom to make decisions for themselves simply because they are women, then many of today's security problems are likely to be insoluble, with tragic consequences for all. And if successful resolution of many of today's problems requires women's thinking—that is, finding the kinds of solutions that women are taught to look for—then exclusion of women from power, and the socialization of men to think as men, may prove disastrous. Many feminists therefore reason that the inclusion of women in positions of power and authority, where they can join fully in solving today's problems, is a critical step.

As we noted in earlier chapters, one of the important developments in today's global transformation has been the rise of a global network of problem-solving nongovernmental organizations, working side by side with the existing structure of sovereign states. These NGOs tend to be relatively nonhierarchic and to focus on finding cooperative solutions. Perhaps not surprisingly, these NGOs have in many cases been relatively open to women's participation and women's solutions: Even while states have generally remained dominated by men, some NGOs have offered a parallel avenue for women's inclusion in problem solving and for women's insights to be heard.

At the heart of most feminist analyses of global politics is a critique of patriarchy. Patriarchy—a construction of gender roles that concentrates social and political power in the hands of men—perpetuates gender-based stereotypes and increasingly is a source of conflict in global politics. Patriarchy is not simply an infringement on human rights, victimizing individuals because they are women, but has also resulted in a distorted, conflictual view of politics and, by disempowering women, has served as an obstacle to solving some of the world's most pressing problems.

Gender-based identities are hardly new; what is new, and what may be contributing to today's turbulent global transformation, is an increased awareness of the problems posed by patriarchy, its human costs, and the barriers it creates to human fulfillment and security. Growing recognition of gender inequality was apparent at the UN-sponsored Fourth World Conference on Women that convened in Beijing in September 1995. At the conference, Hillary Clinton voiced the view of most of the 50,000 people who had gathered from over 180 countries when she declared that women's rights were also human rights. The preamble of the final conference declaration denied claims that national or religious customs could justify unequal treatment of women: "It is the duty of states, regardless of their political, economic and cultural systems, to promote and protect all human rights and fundamental freedoms." The final declaration of the conference declared the "full realization of all human rights and fundamental freedoms of all women" to be "essential for the empowerment of women." The declaration included demands that women be permitted to control their own sexuality; that violence against women, including rape in wartime, domestic abuse, genital mutilation, and sexual harassment in the workplace, be ended; that an end be brought to discrimination against female infants and girls; and that women be provided access to credit.

Gender identities thus promise to play an important role in global politics. Our ability to build integrative political institutions will depend in large measure on our ability to overcome "we/they" distinctions based on gender and to recognize how gender-based identities have shaped (and limited) how we approach collective dilemmas.

14.1 Women, the State, and War: Feminist Incursions into World Politics

Franke Wilmer

Increasingly, feminist scholars are offering students of world politics insights into the importance of gender identity and gender construction in understanding conflict and violence around the globe and an alternative framework for conceptualizing world affairs. In the first selection in this chapter, Professor Franke Wilmer of Montana State University provides an overview of feminist perspectives on global politics. She points out that gender is an important factor in many cultures and helps determine what individuals can or cannot do. In most societies, men are dominant, and they view the world in terms of stereotypic opposites. As a result, positive qualities are associated with masculinity and negative ones with femininity. When thinking about global politics, men tend to focus on abstractions like states and classes. Women, she says, unlike men, view people as individuals and focus on real people and what happens to them when thinking about global politics.

Wilmer observes that women rarely appear in accounts of global politics. "Where are they?" she asks, and answers that although their activities are frequently ignored in men's accounts, women are everywhere: providing men for wars, caring for children, working without pay, fostering peace movements, fighting as soldiers, and being coerced to provide sexual services. She then asks how women's perspectives differ from men's and argues that one important difference is that, whereas men see interstate war to be the greatest threat in global politics, women see violence in general—whether interstate, within families, or in other settings—to be the key problem. Much of the violence in the world, including organized warfare, feminists argue, grows out of men's dominance of women; that is, violence is "part of a more pervasive social process in which male dominance is reproduced in social organizations ranging from the family to the state." Males, feminists argue, find it necessary to assert their masculinity and their independence from women over and over again. Their assertion of independence is complicated by the fact that most male children are cared for by women. In adulthood the assertion of

independence may take the form of preoccupation with sovereignty and boundaries, including those of the nation-state. It reflects, Wilmer argues, men's fear of
being "reengulfed" by women.

More than any other issue, the reconceptualization of war as a "problem"
during the twentieth century, rather than an acceptable option for implementing the foreign policy goals of states, provided the impetus for international relations to develop as a distinct field of academic inquiry. For the most
part, until the first half of the twentieth century international relations as such was
subsumed by the discourse of diplomatic history. Until women as feminists recently
entered the academy, however, we all seemed oblivious to the fact that all of these
discourses, as well as the institutions they produced and legitimated, were conducted from a *masculine* perspective.

Those engaged in academic projects which speak to the masculinization of "public" life[1] are now commonly referred to as "feminists." One aspect of feminism is
that it signals an analysis undertaken from the cognitive perspective of women. But
more importantly, the presentation of a distinctly feminist perspective as a special
case or approach to international relations or world politics implicitly reveals that
both the discourses about and the conduct of politics in the West (and by its hegemony, much of "the" world today) have proceeded from a masculine perspective.
The study of international relations has been conducted largely by and from (until
very recently) the cognitive perspective of men. Therefore, a course on international relations that does not take into account feminist research, theory, and perspectives is really a course on "masculinist international relations."

We Are All Gendered

While I do not want to perpetuate a masculinist perspective that the world and our
knowledge about it can be conveniently divided into a dichotomous representation
of masculine and feminine, one of the most important insights of feminist scholars
has been to reveal the process of *gendering*. To the extent that individuals have
been socialized as male and female and identify themselves as male and female,
their behavior and the ways they think about the world will reflect those differences. Men have built states distinguished from other kinds of polities by their
"monopoly of force," and men have defined politics as a struggle over and management of coercive power. Men, in other words, have created both states and war,
without which there would be no "international relations," as we know it, to study.

Revealing the gendered nature of how we think and act is but one of the many
contributions of feminist scholarship. The issue of *gendering* is a good place to begin
because it helps us think about how and why patterns of gendered social relations

---

[1] I use quotes because the distinction between public and private is one of the dichotomies called into question by feminist theorizing.

This article is an original contribution prepared for this text.

have marginalized (or rendered invisible in some cases) women. What are the consequences of marginalization; how and why do women's perspectives differ from men's; and why are women's perspectives significant? These issues will be taken up as a way of organizing the rest of this essay. But first, there are at least four consequences that thinking about the process of gendering reveals that are particularly important for framing a discussion of feminism and world politics.

The first is the notion that identity categories such as "masculine" and "feminine" are *socially constructed*. Of course, there are biological differences, but what is important is the *meaning* associated with difference, indeed, the way difference itself is constructed, not the "differences" themselves. Women have the potential to bear children; men do not. Women have the potential to lactate; men do not. Men and women are biologically characterized in general by different hormone mixes. This much is cross-cultural. But cross-cultural analysis also reveals that the significance assigned to biological difference varies. Furthermore, how these categories are constructed through social processes and interactions becomes the basis for legitimating and even institutionalizing certain configurations of gender relations. Patriarchy (a community in which the father is the supreme authority in the family, clan, or tribe), for example, posits the dominance of women by men and the privileging of masculine over feminine as the basis for social order. A social order constructed in terms of the complementarity of gender roles and relationships, on the other hand, sees the interdependence of women and men and feminine/masculine as the bases for social order.

A second contribution of feminist scholarship is to highlight differences commonly ascribed to masculine and feminine. Typically, masculine and feminine are spoken of in terms of positive and negative attributes. What masculine "is," feminine "is not," and vice versa. Men are aggressive, women are submissive. A submissive man is less manly, more feminine. An aggressive women is unfeminine. Masculine is: rational, resolute, competitive, assertive, calculating, disciplined, restrained, physical, detached. Feminine is: emotional, flexible, cooperative, compliant, intuitive, undisciplined, expressive, verbal, passive, caring. And so on. To be "masculine" is to be "not feminine."

Thus a third contribution is to eliminate dichotomous thinking about gender (as well as other identity issues). Such thinking, called "essentialism," ascribes to individuals immutable qualities owing to their membership in mutually exclusive categories: male/female, nature/culture, rational/irrational. The problem with such thinking is that it stereotypes people and so hides their individuality. What is worse is that usually that which is male/masculine is viewed as superior to female/feminine.

Feminist thinking demands that we attend to the particular, and formulate alternatives to dichotomous thinking. I have recently begun to incorporate feminist research and perspectives into my courses wherever it seems relevant. After a recent lecture on international relations theory when I concluded with a feminist critique of militarization, a student approached me at the end of class. "One thing I do not understand," she said, "is what the feminist position on the military is. Some feminists critique the military, while others want to gain admission to it on the same basis and in the same capacities as men." I explained that one of the most important revelations of feminist thinking is to reject homogenized categories and male-female stereotypes altogether and to focus instead on the diversity of stand-points taken by *real people*. For feminists the actors in international relations are not states, regimes, classes, or movements. Instead, the real actors are people. Feminists resist categories wherever possible because categories deny the subject-status of people, relegating them instead as a category of objects. How does this produce a different reading of world politics and a different methodology for making sense of world politics?

Cynthia Enloe begins her book *The Morning After: Sexual Politics at the End of the Cold War* with the sentence: "Now that the war is over, Esmerelda has had her IUD removed." "Esmerelda," she goes on,

> is a Salvadoran woman who spent many of her young adult years as a guerrilla in the Farbundo Marti National Liberation Front, the FMLN. She pounded out tortillas and washed her boyfriend's clothes as well as wielding a gun. Now it was the "morning after." . . . Her country's strife had been brought to an end by a peace accord signed by government men and opposition men up in New York, under the watchful eye of the men from Washington. So Esmerelda was going to hand her gun over to the United Nations peacekeepers and try to remake her life. One of her first postwar acts was to have her IUD taken out. During the war her guerrilla tasks had made it seem politically irresponsible to get pregnant. But now she was being urged by men in the political leadership to imagine her postwar life as one devoted to being a good mother.
>
> Some Salvadoran women, however, had quite a different vision of postwar relationships between their country's women and men. They were imagining an end to police rape and domestic violence. Men's violence against women had escalated under the pressures of a civil war fueled by Cold War anxieties.[2]

From her analysis of the significance of both Esmerelda's "personal" choice to use an IUD during the war and to remove it afterward, and of women's political activism both during the war and following the peace accords, Enloe concludes that "the civil wars in Central America and the global Cold War, which intensified so many local conflicts during the last forty years, have not come to a neat end. They must have ending processes, ones not as elegant or as conclusive as, say, an operatic grand finale. These messier processes may go on for years, even generations."[3]

Enloe's point is that when we only look at men's experiences and the institutions and events designated as significant by men, we will miss something critical about international relations in general, and in this case, war and violence in particular. We will not see the continuing processes of postwar conflict as they affect the lives of *people*, and we will therefore not perceive, for instance, the necessity of postconflict reconciliation among *people*, in *communities*, and in *relationships*. We will not see how the "event" of signing a peace accord or treaty among categories of people (mostly men) called "governments" and "rebels" takes place within a historical and social context of continuous relationships, man to woman, family to community, one generation to the next. It is not simply a matter of "seeing" women's perspec-

---

[2] Cynthia Enloe, *The Morning After: Sexual Politics at the End of the Cold War* (Berkeley: University of California Press, 1993), p. 1. Copyright © 1993 The Regents of the University of California. Reprinted by permission.
[3] Ibid., p. 2.

tives. Missing the "personal" is missing the human, historical, and social context in which the conflict emerged, became violent, and became part of the interpretive framework in which configurations of power and human relationships continued after "the war." When we ignore the personal we fail to understand the social, psychological, and historical processes in which conflict, civil strife, social injustice, dominance, and power relations repeatedly erupt. It is not enough, Enloe argues, to demilitarize our institutions. We must demilitarize ourselves, our self-consciousness, ·the ways in which masculinity and femininity are constructed in relation to the maintenance of the garrison state if we are to find a stable world order the morning after the Cold War.

Finally, feminist explorations into the construction of feminine and masculine identity have done the most interesting and important work on the question of how identity is politicized and the consequences of politicization. Ultimately, global politics features groups whose adherents distinguish between "themselves" and "others." Ending conflict necessarily entails overcoming the opposition between people posed by "self/other" distinctions.

To summarize thus far, then, feminist scholarship has made at least five important contributions to the study of world politics. First, it reveals the gendered nature of how we think and act. Second, it focuses on the socially constructed aspect of gendered identity. Third, it highlights the mutually constitutive nature of feminine/masculine constructions. Fourth, it shows how dichotomous categorization generates stereotypes. And finally, feminist scholarship has opened new avenues for interdisciplinary work on the problem of identity.

The remainder of the essay will provide an overview of the questions that have guided feminist scholarship in recent decades. In the mid-1980s feminist perspectives were just beginning to find their way into political science, and somewhat later entered into examinations of international relations. Since then there has been a literal explosion of research.

The "Invisibility" Questions: Where Are the Women?

Women have never been *absent* in world politics. They have, however, for the most part, been *invisible* within the discourse conducted by men from a masculine perspective about politics and the world. Women, along with slaves and children, were the noncitizens who "achieved the production and reproduction that was a precondition of the public"[4]—in other words, generated the resources required for the development of ancient Greek city-states, modern European states, and the settler states in North America, Australia, and New Zealand. Women's unpaid labor within the family, like the unpaid labor of slaves, contributed to the accumulation of wealth in industrial societies (concentrated in the hands of men). Without

---

[4] V. Spike Peterson, "Security and Sovereign States: What's at Stake in Taking Feminism Seriously?" in Peterson, ed., *Gendered States: Feminist (Re)Visions of International Relations Theory* (Boulder: Lynne Reinner, 1992), p. 36.

mothers socialized as "good citizens" to value the sacrifice of their sons in war, there could be no reliable military defense of the state. Enloe draws attention to the Russian women who undertook hunger strikes and formed civic organizations to resist the conscription of young Russian men as a critical factor in undermining the military support on which the Soviet regime relied for legitimacy and essential support.

Another way of rendering women visible historically is to study the contributions of specific women. Joan D'Arc, Catherine de Medici, Catherine the Great, Queens Victoria and Elizabeth I, Indira Gandhi, Clara Barton, and Golda Meir are not "invisible," although they have been scarcely considered in their roles as political actors and as women, as particular women.

In the twentieth century women have played an enormous role in fostering and sustaining peace movements, disarmament initiatives, and the processes that led to the creation of the League of Nations and the United Nations. Elise Boulding reports that the first "women's peace groups with international contacts date back to 1852 (Anglo-American Olive Leaf Circles)," that between 1880 and 1900 five international women's organizations were founded, and that the "first great congress of women" occurred at the Chicago Exposition in 1893.[5] The Women's International League for Peace and Freedom was founded in 1915 "to seek disarmament, social and economic justice, and an end to all war."[6] Women organized successful petition drives leading to the 1930 European Conference on Disarmament and the Limited Test Ban Treaty of 1963.

In 1981 "thirty-six women and a 'few' men and 'children'" initiated a protest against basing American nuclear weapons in England by camping out at Greenham Common in England. The camp lasted more than two years—through two winters. It generated a series of court cases in which women protesters were charged with "behavior likely to cause a breach of the peace" under an obscure 1361 act as well as a court case in the United States (rejected by a U.S. appeals court) against then President Ronald Reagan, undermined public support for the basing program, and opened the "mainstream" disarmament movement to "feminist argument and practice."[7] An International Women's Peace Camp in 1985 in Geneva highlighted the continued deep commitment of women to and their exclusion from international disarmament processes, and in 1986 the U.S. National Women's Conference to Prevent Nuclear War convened in Washington, D.C.

Women are economically and physically coerced into sexual tourism and slavery, and the provision of sexual services to men stationed at foreign military bases. They are rape victims in men's wars of emasculation, diplomatic wives, maids, nannies, and campesinas. Women are soldiers, revolutionaries, and the nucleus around which the social structure of the family revolves. Women's invisibility, like the invisibility of other marginalized "groups" (with women as a "class" cutting across

---

[5] Elise Boulding, *Women in the Twentieth Century World* (New York: John Wiley and Sons, 1977), p. 188.
[6] Catherine Foster, *Women for All Seasons: The Story of the Women's International League for Peace and Freedom* (Athens: University of Georgia Press, 1989), p. 7.
[7] Christine Sylvester, *Feminist Theory and International Relations in a Postmodern Era* (Cambridge: Cambridge University Press, 1994), p. 193.

all groups), renders our efforts to understand the causes, consequences, and possible futures of international relations incomplete and in all likelihood, inaccurate.

The "Voice" Question:
What Are Women's Perspectives on Global Politics?

There is no monolithic "women's perspective," but rather a variety of shared and particular perspectives about women and world politics. Women are directly concerned with the rights of children, and many of the issues highlighted by women's activism fall into the realm conventional international relations calls "low politics" (and which is marginalized in relation to men's concern with the "high" politics of militarization). Women, of course, have many of the same concerns men have. Women wish to live in secure and peaceful social environments, with equal opportunities to participate in and benefit from an economic life that provides basic needs, and where one's contribution to social processes is limited only by one's choices and aptitude. Women's conception of security, however, may be different than men's. Women, as men, do not wish for war. But they also wish to be physically secure within spheres (men have) designated as "private," like the home.

National security, for example, includes not only freedom from attack by other states but freedom from attack within the domestic sphere of marriage, family, and intimate relationships. During the height of the Vietnam War, an average of 5,750 Americans were killed annually. Around 1,500 women are murdered every year by husbands or boyfriends in a "war against women" that has been going on much longer and continues with no end in sight. If 1,500 Americans were killed each year in an "international" war, the public would be outraged.

National security means living in a social world in which one feels secure against the threat of rape. In the United States, 1.3 women are raped every minute—78 per hour, 1,872 per day, 56,160 per month, and 683,280 per year.[8]

According to the FBI, attacks on women by intimates result in more injuries requiring hospital treatment than robbery, mugging, rape, and automobile accidents combined.[9] The U.S. Department of Justice reports that on yearly average, women are victims of 572,032 violent acts committed by intimates, compared to 48,983 attacks against men in intimate relationships.

Children's security is inseparable from women's security. Where violence is directed toward women, children are observers, or victims themselves. When women lack basic resources, children are malnourished or hungry, homeless, and lacking in basic health care. Fifty percent of all homeless women and children in the United States have taken to the streets because of domestic violence; women who leave violent partners are at a 75 percent higher risk of being murdered by them than those who remain in the relationship.

---

[8] Chris Bartley, *Sexual Assault Information Page* (1997), www.cs.utk.edu.
[9] *Myths and Facts About Domestic Violence* (1997), www.iquest.net/~gtemp/dv_facts.htm.

Feminist scholarship argues that these data suggest the central problem of international relations is not "war," but *violence*. Defining the problem as "war" focuses our attention on certain institutions—the state and military—and how these institutions "behave." Thus research programs like The Correlates of War project at the University of Michigan ask question such as: Are states more likely to go to war when they are in alliances? Are states less likely to go to war when power is "balanced" among them? Are democratic states more war-prone than nondemocratic states? And so on. Other studies focus on human behavior as a cause of war, but the fact that the "humans" studied and theorized about are (socially gendered) masculine and that they act as they do within socially constructed and *gendered* institutions is not regarded as significant in these accounts, if it is considered at all. War—groups of men (or states built and governed by men) carrying out institutionalized violence against other groups of men—is made to seem normal by this historical account (written largely by men) of interstate relations.

From a feminist perspective, the problem is *gendered* human violence, and the state and war are consequences of the way in which men are gendered, the way in which men are masculinized in relation to violence. Feminist perspectives problematize the distinction between "good" and "bad" violence implicit in concepts of the state and war. "Good" violence—the use of force in defense of family and community—supports order and social stability, whereas "bad" violence—that is, antisocial uses of force, violence that is disruptive of existing relationships—threatens national and international social order.

But what if the social order itself is violent, or is constructed in such a way as to legitimate and even require violence (or "coercion")? In its relations with indigenous peoples, British imperial authorities evaluated how "developed" an indigenous people's political system was by whether or not the social order relied on coercion: that is, by the extent to which it was organized to carry out violence.[10] Such a construction of violence and the identification of "good violence" as a political "necessity" carried on by "good men" not only obscures questions of interpersonal violence and structural violence, but sanctions violence itself as a necessary social behavior. Order in social groups, from the family to the state, is perceived as depending on a willingness to use violence to exert control. The "problem" then becomes regulating it (the good violence/bad violence problem). Violence is viewed as a normal component of maintaining social order. The question is not asked whether the basis of the social order itself—patriarchy—is constructed to require violence. Yet as some feminists point out, patriarchy can be interpreted as institutionalized violence: By its nature patriarchy is "a means to maintain privilege and hierarchy, so physical violence is used to demonstrate power or superiority."[11]

---

[10] It was on this basis that Australian Aboriginal peoples, for example, were determined not to have constituted political entities capable of occupying the land, leaving the land, conveniently, as "unoccupied." The High Court of Australia in 1993 overturned this doctrine and has begun a process of reconciling Aboriginal land claims.

[11] Betty Reardon, ed., *Women and Peace* (Albany: State University of New York Press, 1993), p. 41.

The roots of violence, institutional, structural and direct, private and public, from the perspective of some feminist scholars lie in the construction of social dominance in the form of patriarchy, which is then reproduced in gendered states, gendered state violence, and gendered international relations. Patriarchy is the institutionalization of unequal gender relations where *men* and *masculine* dominate *women* and *feminine*.

War—which, viewed as a problem, has provided the main impetus for the development of international relations as a distinct field of study—is, from a feminist perspective, part of a more pervasive social process in which male dominance is reproduced in social organizations ranging from the family to the state to interstate relations and regimes. More importantly, male dominance both constructs and limits the way we think about the actors and problems within the sphere called "international relations" or "world politics." At least until very recently. Instead of viewing war as either an enduring feature or a bounded problem in world politics, feminists tend to view war as one of many forms of violence. From the perspective of some feminists (particularly peace researchers and advocates of nonviolence), violence represents a failure of humanity. "Solving the problem of war" may be less a matter of "scientifically" studying war than changing the way we, living in gendered states, think about ourselves in relation to violence. By constructing nonviolent mechanisms for dispute resolution, by adopting nonviolent strategies to maintain social order, and by restructuring our thinking so that privilege, hierarchy, and violence are unacceptable in interpersonal, familial, communal, and social relations, we can collapse many points along the continuum of violence.

The "Significance" Question: What Is Signified by Man/Woman?

After acknowledging gender inequality and demanding equality in public spheres, feminists began to wrestle with the question: What difference does difference make? Are "men" and "women" merely receptacles for sets of ascribed characteristics, the former privileged and the latter the residue of "qualities society does not wish to promote as public virtues"?[12] Does acknowledging difference lend legitimacy to the continued domination of men/masculine over women/feminine?

The building and legitimating of the nation-state itself was a masculine project. The state is constructed as *boundaried* and (militarily) *defended* territory. Or, as Enloe says, "States had militaries; that's how you could tell they *were* states."[13] Feminists have explored the psychoanalytic implications of masculine identity's reliance on, even obsession with, boundaries and autonomy as a consequence of the need for the masculine self to emerge in opposition to the feminine caretaker

---

[12] Sylvester, *Feminist Theory and International Relations in a Postmodern Era*, p. 23.
[13] Enloe, *The Morning After*, p. 246.

as the original "other" against which infantile autonomy must struggle. Sovereignty, the bounded state, and autonomous political actors as the basic components of the state system are directly linked to the way in which masculine identity is formulated. Masculine identity, formulated under conditions of female-monopolized early childhood, is chronically at risk of feminization. The identification of the infant as a bounded self, according to this view, is always initially formulated in relation to the mother or "woman" as long as women are primary caretakers of infants. By some accounts, for girls this produces less anxiety, because for them the development of identity as "self" and "feminine" occurs in the same turn. The self is "mirrored" in a feminine other. For boys, however, gendered identity requires a further differentiation from the "other." Self is mirrored first in a feminine other, and subsequently a distinctly masculine identity must also be constructed. Behind the construction of a man as masculine lies his original identification with the female (m)other, so that sustaining masculine identity relies on his reminding himself and others that he is "not-feminine." This explains the prevalence of patriarchy as well as misogyny, and by some accounts, is reproduced in virtually all of men's activities, including the construction of the state as a *militarized* and thus *masculinized* institution. Thus to demilitarize the state necessitates no less than a reconstruction of masculine identity.

In this vein, Christine Di Stefano argues that, owing to the male's childhood struggle for autonomy against primarily feminine caretakers, adult masculinity, at least in the Western tradition, has been concerned with the maintenance and defense of boundaries as a mechanism for securing autonomy. The notion of sovereignty, as well as the state it sustains, reflects this preoccupation with securing autonomy. "Within this symbolic frame of meaning," Di Stefano writes, "maternal and natural reengulfment become the constitutive threats to autonomy, masculinity, and 'civilization' itself."[14] Is this fear of "reengulfment" at work in the idea of the state as a bounded territory (never quite) secured by a ready military? Is fear of "reengulfment" at work in the perception of international relations as anarchic, as an environment in which one must always imagine and expect attacks by powerful adversaries who wish to violate the boundaries of one's state, where one must be prepared to fight and win imagined potential wars? Is this fear at work in domestic politics, revealed as resistance to regional and international organization? Does the idea of a fear of "reengulfment" help explain the growing support, in the aftermath of the Cold War, for fringe groups in the United States which believe that the United Nations is really an instrument for the development of a world government that will invade and conquer the country?

Male efforts to protect masculinity appear in support for the military. "Man" or "masculine" and "warrior" are inseparable. That is, the qualities that make a "good" warrior are indistinguishable from those that "make a man masculine." Male mili-

---

[14] Christine Di Stefano, *Configurations of Masculinity: A Feminist Perspective on Modern Political Theory* (Ithaca: Cornell University Press, 1991), p. 51.

tary recruits must be bound to male state officials and military officers. "The glue," Enloe says, "is camaraderie; the base of the glue is masculinity."[15] And nothing reflects this masculinization gone amok in the U.S. military better than Marine "pin-hazing."[16]

Taking a step further, some feminist theorists argue that "woman" and "feminine" have been used to signify chaos, and "man" and "masculine" to signify order in Western political philosophy. In this reading, state building aims to bring order out of chaos, indeed, to control chaos; it represents the triumph of (masculine) rational culture over (feminine) irrational anarchy. Women/feminine as anarchy/chaos/unpredictable/irrational is the problem for *masculinist* constructions of world politics. And man as statesman and soldier fights his foe with order, predictability, and rationality. Attempts to solve the problems of world politics which are emotional, flexible, cooperative, relationship-oriented, intuitive, verbal, and caring (as feminized qualities) are dismissed as "unrealistic" in favor of those which are rational, resolute, competitive, dominance-oriented, calculating, physical, and tough. The portrayal of world politics as hostile legitimates a male "protection racket." Men in control of states portray—even create—an international environment that is hostile in order to legitimize the state and the state's (and therefore predominantly men's) monopoly of force as a defense against anarchy.

Conclusion

The necessity of rethinking sovereignty, the state, and war is apparent. A growing number of global problems—the stalling out of "development" in the less-developed countries, terrorism, environmental degradation, nuclear proliferation—have less to do with preserving "territorial integrity" (the objective of a militarized state) than with deeply embedded and complex relationships and perceptions of dominance, struggles for dominance, perpetual fear of domination, and struggles against domination. Territorially organized states that, by the doctrine of sovereignty, may use any means necessary in "defense" of their interests/autonomy may not be suited to our contemporary needs for problem solving. Feminists are providing important critiques of the state and state system that call into question the cognitive and philosophic underpinnings of international relations. Is war the problem and the state the solution? Or is the way the state is currently constructed—reproducing a certain conception of masculinity—the problem, and violence and domination consequences of that construction of the state?

---

[15] Enloe, *The Morning After*, p. 52.

[16] Reuters reported February 1, 1997, on a broadcast newsfilm which showed Marine paratroopers at Camp Lejeune, North Carolina, "writhing and crying out in pain as others pounded the spiked medals into their chests through tee-shirts."

The Real Gender Gap

14.2 No Daughters Need Apply

Rick Weiss

The devaluation of women is nowhere more clearly revealed than in the age-old practice in some Asian countries of killing daughters or letting them die, supplemented by the newer practice of selectively aborting female fetuses. The following selection describes this process and some of its effects.

The long-standing custom in some Asian countries of allowing girls to die soon after birth, either by neglect or by outright infanticide, appears to have become increasingly common in recent years as women opt for smaller families, according to new studies.

The new research on demographic data from India, China and Taiwan suggests that biases against girls are not disappearing even as those countries' birth rates approach those of Western nations. The work also indicates that women are increasingly using prenatal sex-determination tests and selective abortions to ensure that they give birth to boys.

"As fertility has declined, sex preferences have stayed constant," says Nancy Williamson, director of the women's studies project at Family Health International, a Durham, N.C.–based nonprofit organization specializing in reproductive health in developing countries. As a result, the latest figures show that boy-to-girl ratios are continuing to increase in several Asian countries, Williamson and others said May 9 [1996] in New Orleans at the annual meeting of the Population Association of America.

Sex selection is an old practice in many Asian countries, reflecting the significantly higher value those societies place on boys and men. While male-to-female ratios among children in Western countries are roughly 1 to 1, those in several Asian countries range from 106 to 114 boys for every 100 girls. Because countries such as China and India are so populous, such differences can add up to millions of "missing" girls.

The details of what happens to these girls are often vague. In some cases the girls are killed soon after birth, but in many cases their demise is more subtle—the result of deeply ingrained cultural practices that increase female death rates during the first few years of life. In India, for example, women and girls traditionally do not eat until the men and boys have had their fill. When food supplies are short, that can lead to reduced survival of girls compared with boys.

Harvard University researcher Monica Das Gupta and colleague Mari Bhat used census data and hospital records to calculate the rate of sex discrepancy in India, and to determine how much of it is likely to be due to prenatal testing and abortion. Such testing allows a woman to learn the sex of her fetus during the second trimester by ultrasound, and then to have a late-stage abortion if the sex is not to her liking.

Das Gupta's analysis indicates that more than 1 million girls were lost due to selective abortions between 1981 and 1991, chiefly during the second half of that decade because the technology was not widely available before then. In addition, however, about 4 million girls "disappeared" during their first four to six years of life, or about 36 girls for every 1,000 born. That's about the same rate documented during the previous decade, suggesting that selective abortion is not substituting for female infanticide, but supplementing it. "It has been an additive effect," Das Gupta says. "And in 1991 to the year 2000 we should expect to see more of it."

Judith Banister of the U.S. Census Bureau describes a new analysis of data from China, a country with a long history of skewed sex ratios. Using Chinese census figures from the past decade, she has calculated that about 1.5 million female fetuses had been selectively aborted between the mid-1980s and 1990. By the beginning of this decade, she says, such abortions were responsible for about 50 percent of that country's annual shortfall of girls, which has been estimated by others at half a million.

"We see a rising number of girls missing for this reason, but it doesn't stop the other categories," including infanticide, abandonment and selective neglect, Banister says.

Shelley Clark of Princeton University presented evidence that sex selection is also widespread in Taiwan. Along with that country's steady economic development, she says, the average number of children per family has dropped from 5.75 in 1960 to 1.7, mostly as a result of contraceptive use. The ratio of boys to girls is 107 to 100.

Clark's analysis of data on birth order and family size indicates that contraceptives are being used to shape the sex ratios in families. Women who already have a couple of sons are likely to start using contraceptives, she and her colleagues found, while those who keep having daughters do not.

Sex discrimination takes a toll on mothers as well as children, says Leila E. Caleb, a research fellow at the Population Council in New York. Caleb interviewed 312 women living in a slum outside Delhi, India, during the weeks after they gave birth. She found that women who gave birth to girls had significantly fewer visits and less assistance from friends and extended family members—an indication of the lower import given to such births.

The researchers say more highly educated Asian women are less likely to express strong preferences for boys, suggesting there is hope that the trend may eventually decline. But the cultural and economic roots of male preference run deep. Meanwhile, they say, the growing availability of prenatal testing and abortion—long a rallying cry for feminists concerned about reproductive rights in the Third World— may be working against the interests of female children.

14.3 A Surplus of Men, A Deficit of Peace

Valerie M. Hudson and Andrea Den Boer

This selection by two insightful political scientists picks up on the previous essay, exploring the consequences of the gender inequality that occurs when "one child is allowed to live while another is actively or passively killed." The authors of this selection make a persuasive connection between the resulting surplus of males in a population and the problems of domestic and international peace and security. Looking particularly at emerging conditions in Asia, the authors argue that "young surplus males" are a source of belligerence and strife both at home and abroad and that action should be taken immediately to bring an end to preferential sex selection of fetuses and newborn babies.

International security and stability rest in large measure on the internal security of nations. Analysts have long examined factors such as arms transfers and ethnic violence in this regard, but the list now includes variables that were not traditionally viewed as related to national security. Unemployment rates, water tables and river flows, infant mortality, migration patterns, infectious disease epidemiology, and a whole host of other variables that tap into the general stability of a society are now understood to affect security. . . .

. . . One overlooked wellspring of insecurity, we argue, is exaggerated gender inequality. Security scholarship is theoretically and empirically impoverished to the extent that it fails to inquire into the relationship between violence against women and violence within and between societies. . . .

Admittedly, there is probably no society in which women do not experience some gender inequality, meaning subordinate status or inferior treatment in political, legal, social, or economic matters. Indeed, what would constitute a perfect society between men and women is a controversial topic with which we are not concerned here. However, *exaggerated* gender inequality is hard to miss: We define it to be present when, because of gender, one child is allowed to live while another is actively or passively killed.[1] Offspring sex selection, almost universally used to favor male offspring, indicates that the life of a female in the society is not only not valued but actually despised. There can be no greater evidence of the extremely unequal and subordinate status of women in a society than the presence of prevalent offspring sex selection therein.

---

[1] "Passive killing" refers to such phenomena as withholding food from a newborn or abandoning a newborn in the wild. Though not an active killing, such as smothering a child, the intent to kill is clear, and so is termed passive killing.

Valerie M. Hudson and Andrea Den Boer, "A Surplus of Men, A Deficit of Peace: Security and Sex Ratios in Asia's Largest States," *International Security*, 26:4 (Spring 2002), pp. 5–38. © 2002 by the President and Fellows of Harvard College and the Massachusetts Institute of Technology.

If violence against women within a society bears any relationship to violence within and between societies, then it should be possible to see that relationship at work in societies where violence against women is exaggerated—that is, where offspring sex selection is prevalent. Specifically, internal instability is heightened in nations displaying exaggerated gender inequality, leading to an altered security calculus for the state. Possibilities of meaningful democracy and peaceful foreign policy are diminished as a result. . . .

Selection against female offspring produces an excess proportion of males in society: surplus males. Given the long history of son preference in China, it is not surprising that the Chinese have a special term for such surplus males: *guang gun-er* (also transliterated as *guanggun, guangguer,* or *guanguen*), alternatively translated as "bare sticks" or "bare branches," indicating those male branches of a family tree that would never bear fruit because no marriage partner might be found for them. . . .

Who are these young surplus males? First, they are not equivalent to the bachelors of the West. Single men in the West are not surplus males: Indeed they can and often do form semipermanent attachments to women and produce children in that context. Surplus males, on the other hand, do not have such possibilities. In a marriage market where women are scarce and thus able to "marry up," certain characteristics of young surplus males are easily and accurately predicted. They are liable to come from the lowest socioeconomic class, be un- or underemployed, live a fairly nomadic or transient lifestyle with few ties to the communities in which they are working, and generally live and socialize with other bachelors. In sum, these young surplus males may be considered, relatively speaking, losers in societal competition.

The behavior of young surplus males also follows a broadly predictable pattern. Theory suggests that compared with other males in society, bare branches will be prone to seek satisfaction through vice and violence, and will seek to capture resources that will allow them to compete on a more equal footing with others. These theoretical predictions are substantiated by empirical evidence so vast and so compelling as to approach the status of social science verity. Cross-culturally, an overwhelming percentage of violent crime is perpetrated by young, unmarried, low-status males. . . .

Some may question whether marital status plays an important role in such behavioral dispositions, but this is another widely confirmed research finding. David Courtwright notes, "It is when young men cannot or do not marry that socially disruptive behavior is intensified."[2] . . .

In conclusion, there is both strong theory and persuasive historical evidence that the bare branches of high sex-ratio societies can contribute significantly to intrasocietal violence. In some cases, this domestic threat has led governments to create foreign policy initiatives designed to disperse bare branches. The strategies that bare branches choose to better their position in society erode the stability of the societies in which they live. . . .

---

[2] David T. Courtwright, *Violent Land* (Cambridge, MA: Harvard University Press, 1996), p. 202.

The Security Logic of High Sex-Ratio Societies

The repercussions of artificially high sex ratios pose grave problems of insecurity for a society which, in turn, create vexing policy dilemmas for governments. . . .

High sex-ratio societies will tend to develop authoritarian political systems over time, for these are better equipped to deal with possible large-scale intrasocietal violence created by society's selection for bare branches. As Christian Mesquida and Neil Weiner note, "Choice of political system made by the members of a population is somewhat restricted by the age composition of its male population."[3] Robert Wright is even more blunt: "Few things are more anxiety-producing for an elite governing class than gobs of [unmarried] and childless men with at least a modicum of political power. . . . Leaving lots of men without wives is not just inegalitarian: it's dangerous. . . . A nation, in which large numbers of low-income men remain mateless, is not the kind of country many of us would want to live in."[4] . . .

. . . Speaking more generally about Asia, however, we are on the cusp of the time period wherein these larger proportions of bare branches will become socially active. As they do, we believe that governments in such societies will begin their predicted shift toward greater authoritarianism. In countries with high sex-ratio societies that are not ethnically homogeneous, such as India, this shift may start as rule by the majority ethnic group which group will, in turn, actually promote interethnic violence.

Indeed, governments of high sex-ratio societies must often cultivate a political style crafted to retain the allegiance and respect of its bare branches. This tends to be a swaggering, belligerent, provocative, martial style—to match that of the bare branches themselves. In the rhetoric accompanying such a posture, there is inevitably an "other," who is weak and contemptible and whose attempt to find a place in society or in the international order must be opposed. The society is then enjoined to muster its strength so that these "insults" can be answered with appropriate action. Though all governments at one time or another may engage in these types of tactics, they take on a particular urgency for governments of high sex-ratio societies. These governments understand that its bare branches are a formidable club—if it is in your hand it can be very useful, but if it is poised over your head, it may constitute a greater threat than external enemies. . . .

There is only one short-term strategy for dealing with a serious bare-branch problem: Reduce their numbers. There are several traditional ways to do so: Fight them, encourage their self-destruction, or export them. Longer-range strategies to address the problem, such as decreasing offspring sex selection, are also viable (and laudable), but are not likely to improve the government's situation for a generation or more. Furthermore, though economic prosperity is useful in placating disgruntled members of society, including bare branches, no amount of wealth will turn

---

[3] Christian G. Mesquida and Neil I. Weiner, "Human Collective Aggression," *Ethology and Sociobiology,* Vol. 17, No. 4 (1996), p. 257.

[4] Robert Wright, *The Moral Animal* (New York: Pantheon, 1994), pp. 98–101.

surplus males into nonsurplus males. . . . Prosperity is thus no panacea in this situation, though economic downturns are likely to trigger violent resource capture by bare branches.

Governments will always seek to suppress societal violence that threatens their authority. Indeed the government may actually recruit bare branches into military or police units that are used to fight bare-branch criminals. . . .

Another approach is to simply let bare branches destroy each other, either turning a blind eye when rivals dispatch one another or encouraging ethnic divisions that will lead to intergroup violence. Once again, however, the level of societal dislocation may in the end threaten the government, as it will appear that the government has lost control over the level of violence in society. A second variant of this strategy is to provide large, dangerous public works that pay well. Building intercontinental railways or huge new dams, reclaiming vast tracts of swampland or desert—if done the old-fashioned way using primarily manual labor—can both occupy and sustain bare branches, while also ensuring significantly increased mortality among that population subgroup. Nevertheless, there may be a limit to how many such works can be undertaken by a given society.

Finally, governments seek to send bare branches elsewhere. "Elsewhere," in the government's perspective, may include distant frontier regions of the country or may in fact be other countries. This may be a peaceful export of colonists to a frontier or an exodus of migrant workers to other nations. There is, however, a martial variant of this strategy as well: a strategy that has been consciously used in history to reduce bare-branch numbers. If the bare branches threaten national security if they live at home, the government may prefer to let them die in some glorious national cause far from home instead. . . .

Conclusions

. . . In a way, the very type of government to which a nation can aspire may be tied to the status of women in society. When that status is very low, the possibilities for a full and meaningful democracy and for a peaceful foreign policy are distinctly less. High sex-ratio societies, denoting a very low status for women, cannot be expected to emulate normal sex-ratio societies either in terms of their form of government or in terms of their tendency toward peacefulness. Any attempts at that emulation may prove, historically speaking, to be short-lived. And any attempts by scholars from normal sex-ratio societies to project their own security logic onto a high sex-ratio society will lead to miscalculation. High sex-ratio societies simply have a different security calculus. . . .

. . . The relationship we see is not straightforward cause and effect: Strife and war obviously take place within and between normal sex-ratio cultures as well. Nevertheless, exaggerated gender inequality, as we have seen, may provide an aggravating catalyst to the mix of insecurity factors leading to conflict. All we have found suggests that high sex-ratio societies in contexts of unequal resource distribution and generalized resource scarcity breed chronic violence and persistent social disorder and corruption. . . .

... The scale on which sex ratios are being artificially altered in Asia today is, generally speaking, unprecedented in human history. What are the consequences of this vast demographic shift? What happens to societies that explicitly *select* for increasing and disproportionate numbers of bare branches? We suggest that societies with young adult sex ratios of approximately 120 and above are inherently unstable, and both China and India are, at this writing, nearing that level and will probably surpass that level in the next two decades.[5] We stand at the threshold of a time in which these young surplus males will increasingly figure into the deliberations of Asian governments. Not only the nations of Asia, but the nations of the world will want to pay close attention to the ramifications of Asia's spiraling sex ratios and the policy choices they force upon Asian governments. How ironic it would be if women's issues, so long ignored in security studies as simply irrelevant, became a central focus of security scholars in the twenty-first century.

 Women and NGOs

14.4 Ladies, You Have No Choice

Don Hinrichsen

While the development of a global network of NGOs has been critical in addressing issues such as violence against women and in empowering women, not all NGOs advocate greater gender equality. As the following selection documents, some NGOs have pressured the American state and attacked international organizations, arguing against the women's rights agenda, particularly with regard to family planning. This selection describes how the administration of George W. Bush, at the urging of these conservative NGOs, has attacked international agencies that assist women, accusing these agencies, often wrongly, of fostering policies that favor abortion. Although the right to abortion is constitutionally guaranteed to

---

[5] In the historical time periods we examined, sex ratios of greater than 120 have been noted. With regard to China and India, such very high sex ratios were usually regionally or temporally bounded (a particular region would embrace female infanticide for a time). Never before in history, however, have entire nations engaged in such high rates of offspring sex selection. It is the new, cheap technology that allows for this heightened and nationwide prevalence. Thus the scale (in terms of what percentage of the country's population is practicing offspring sex selection) is unprecedented in human history. Also, never before have China and India had such huge populations. For example, China's population at the turn of the twentieth century was about 460 million persons. Today it is more than 1.2 billion persons. The combination of these two factors means that the sheer number of bare branches being created in Asia is also unprecedented in human history. Yet, given the pockets of high sex ratios in history, we can also say with some confidence that societies that reach and exceed 120 males per 100 females in the young-adult age group are inherently unstable.

American women, no such guarantee exists for women globally, and the administration's assault on a variety of humanitarian and aid agencies—public and private—has set back efforts to help women out of poverty, reduce violence in their lives, and provide them with greater autonomy and better health care.

Every Friday morning, Stirling Scruggs receives a fax that the sender, an organization called C-FAM, may or may not have intended for him to receive. C-FAM is the Catholic Family and Human Rights Institute, based in New York near the United Nations, a behind-the-scenes anti-abortion group that has established itself as one of the most vociferous factions in the U.S. culture wars. . . . It's [Scruggs's] job, as director of the Information and External Relations Division of the United Nations Population Fund (UNFPA), to watch out for disinformation being disseminated through the United States and abroad by a network of shadowy anti-choice organizations of which C-FAM is one. . . .

The newly arrived fax alleges that the UN Population Fund was complicit in the forced sterilizations of poor, indigenous women in Peru during the presidency of Alberto Fujimori. The allegation comes from another group in the network, called the Population Research Institute (PRI), which is based in the horse-country town of Front Royal, Virginia. This assertion, says Scruggs, is "total fiction." C-FAM, he says, is passing along PRI's charges as part of an orchestrated campaign to discredit the UN in general and UNFPA in particular. . . .

C-FAM's use of fax rather than e-mail may seem quaint, but the group's influence is both calculated and potent. The "Friday Fax of Misinformation," as Scruggs ruefully calls it, is circulated to a network of other, like-minded, groups that will in turn do their best to provoke the rage of fellow anti-abortionists all over the world. It also goes to certain members of the U.S. Congress and selected members of the media who can be counted on to promote the group's anti-choice agenda.

That agenda, says the UN's Scruggs, is not simply to oppose abortion. Rather, the anti-abortion rhetoric is a kind of code for something more pervasive. "These groups are not just anti-abortion, they are anti-women, and oppose population policies and programs in general," says Scruggs. "They hate us because we have been very effective in promoting women's rights and providing poor communities with the information and means to voluntarily plan their families. The pity is that refuting these lies takes up valuable staff time—time we could be using to carry out our primary mandate, saving the lives of poor women, men, and adolescents."

Behind their innocuous-sounding names and claims to represent "pro-life" interests, C-FAM and its network of like-minded groups—others include the Pro-Life Action League, American Life League, Campaign Life Coalition, Concerned Women for America, and National Right to Life Committee—have lobbied heavily against women's rights to make their own decisions about having or not having children. . . .

C-FAM's president, Austin Ruse, is one of a growing number of figures who are apparently bent on undermining all aid to developing countries by organizations that even mention the words "family planning," "reproductive health," "women's rights," or "free, informed choice." He has reportedly told supporters that reproductive health is just a "cover-up for abortionists" and that efforts to achieve reproductive health and establish rights for poor women is a "feminist conspiracy" to "destroy the family."

A particular target, for Ruse, is the Beijing Platform of Action, a product of the Fourth World Conference on Women, held in Beijing, China, in 1995. In the typically bland but well-meaning language of UN delegates everywhere, the Platform calls for actions "to eradicate persistent and increasing burden of poverty on women; to remove the obstacles to women's full participation in public life and decision-making; to eliminate all forms of violence against women; to ensure equal access for girl children and women to education and health services; to promote economic autonomy for women; and to encourage an equitable sharing of family responsibilities." To Ruse, this is "*one of the most radical and dangerous documents you can imagine*" (italics added). . . .

The pit-bull of this labyrinthine assemblage is the Population Research Institute, which was set up in 1989 by Benedictine priest Father Paul Marx. . . . Sometime in the mid-1990s, Marx recruited a man named Steven Mosher to run PRI. Marx is perhaps best known for his assertion that the success of the abortion rights movement in the United States and elsewhere is the work of Jews. In a 1993 newsletter to supporters, Marx wrote: "Today, certain members of this people whose ancient religion and culture managed to survive Auschwitz and Buchenwald are presiding over the greatest Holocaust in the history of the world. American Jews have been leaders in establishing and defending the efficient destruction of more than 30 million preborn [sic] children in this country." . . .

During the 1990s, the views of Mosher, Ruse, and their network made steady but quiet inroads into the thinking of the increasingly conservative U.S. Congress. . . . "These groups have been around for the past decade," points out Richard Snyder, chief of UNFPA's External Relations Branch. "The difference is that now they have an ear in the White House." . . . And on his first day in office, Bush gave them their first reward—reactivating a discredited Reagan-era policy called the "global gag rule," according to which no organization can receive U.S. family planning assistance if it performs abortions, provides counseling and referral for abortions, or lobbies to make abortion legal or more available in its own country.

The next target to be put in the White House crosshairs was UNFPA. The Congress allocated $34 million to the Population Fund in 2002. But then Mosher's PRI issued a report alleging that UNFPA aid funds were being used for coercive abortions and sterilizations in China. Congressman Chris Smith, a Republican from New Jersey . . . became very excited about the report—even though it actually contained no hard evidence. . . . Smith dispatched a letter to Bush urging that the funding be withheld. Bush . . . decided to withhold the funds. His reason, he said, was the Kemp-Kasten Amendment to the 1985 foreign aid bill [officially the Foreign Operations, Export Financing, and Related Programs Appropriations Act], which stipulates that no funds can be allocated to any organization or program "which supports or participates in the management of a program of coercive abortion or sterilization." . . .

. . . In April 2002, a three-member group of British parliamentarians—one of them a conservative Catholic—visited China and found no evidence of misconduct by UNFPA. The next month, a three-person team was sent by the U.S. State Department. Embarrassingly for Bush, the U.S. team found "no evidence that UNFPA has knowingly supported or participated in the management of a program of coercive abortion or involuntary sterilization in the PRC. Indeed, UNFPA has registered its strong opposition to such practices." All told, in the past decade there have been more than 160 UN monitoring missions to China. None of them confirmed the PRI report that had so excited Congressman Smith and so galvanized George Bush. . . .

The Death Toll Your News Channel Doesn't Discuss

Despite the fact that every scientific study ever to address the issue has rated condoms as one of the most effective means of halting the spread of HIV/AIDS and other sexually transmitted infections (STIs), the Bush regime has entered into an implicit alliance with the Vatican to preach abstinence-only programs. One immediate consequence has been a significant drop in the number of condoms shipped to poor developing countries by USAID, which, under Clinton, was one of the two largest donors of condoms in the world (the other was UNFPA). According to Population Action International, an NGO based in Washington, D.C., Bush's partisan policies have ended life-saving shipments of condoms and other contraceptive supplies to 16 of the poorest developing countries in Africa, Asia, and the Pacific. Family planning agencies in another 13 countries, nearly all in sub-Saharan Africa, no longer get condoms and contraceptives from USAID because they will not agree to the conditions set forth in the global gag rule. With funds in short supply, donor governments now provide only one-eighth of the number of condoms needed to effectively combat the spread of HIV/AIDS. . . .

IPPF [International Planned Parenthood Federation] predicts that the number of women who die from unsafe abortions every year—estimated minimally at 70,000 by the World Health Organization—will soar due to Bush's policies. Making abortion illegal, or difficult to obtain, does not stop abortion from happening. In the Philippines, an overwhelmingly Catholic nation where abortions are completely illegal, IPPF estimates there are half a million a year. Many of them take place in unsafe, unsanitary conditions. At just one hospital in Addis Ababa, capital of Ethiopia—another country where abortion is illegal—a study found that half of all female deaths were from botched back-street abortions.

Perhaps the ultimate tragedy in this saga is the loss in reproductive health and family planning services to poor women—ironically, the very services that can prevent abortions from taking place. IPPF points to just a few of the programs it had to cut: In Bangladesh 14 clinics in poor neighborhoods had to be closed; in Nepal, over $700,000 has been lost for family planning, safe motherhood, and contraceptive services; in Cambodia over $3 million has been lost for HIV/AIDS prevention and counseling; in Kenya three clinics servicing 56,000 clients, mostly poor women of reproductive age, had to close; and in eastern Nepal, the local branch of IPPF had to close clinics and cut back services for over 300,000 people, endangering their health and welfare. . . .

On a much larger scale, UNFPA calculates that the loss of $34 million, about 13 percent of its total budget, is having a devastating effect on programs in some of the poorest countries in which the Fund works. In Bangladesh, where close to 70 percent of pregnant women receive no medical care before, during, or after childbirth, programs to train doctors to deal with obstetric emergencies had to be cancelled. In Kenya, where the Fund was working with the Catholic Church to prevent teenagers from contracting the HIV virus, the project had to be shelved when funds dried up. Overall, UNFPA estimates that the loss of U.S. funding will result in 2 million unwanted pregnancies, 800,000 abortions, and more than 81,000 deaths.

 ## Female Genital Mutilation

14.5 Is It Crime or Culture?

The Economist

As the preceding article makes clear, patriarchy is deeply rooted in many cultures, including America's. On a number of specific issues, however, there is a growing divide between world opinion and the cultural practices of particular societies. Behavior that the modern world regards as human rights abuses against women is still widespread in traditional societies, and these societies consider international pressure to end such practices as a form of cultural imperialism.

Genital mutilation is perhaps the clearest example. In much of Africa, women who come of age are forced to go through a painful procedure misnamed "genital circumcision." The purpose is to reduce a woman's capacity for sexual pleasure and, it is believed, the possibility that she will have sexual relations with anyone other than her husband. The practice is most widespread in parts of East Africa— the Sudan, Ethiopia, Eritrea, and Somalia—where over 80 percent of women are subjected to it, and across a broad swath of the Sahelian region to West Africa. The following selection from *The Economist* describes the practice of genital mutilation and the extent to which it continues to exist in Africa.

If Article 299A of Senegal's penal code were fully applied, some 1–2 million Senegalese would now go to jail. The amendment, which parliament passed last month, makes it a crime to carry out female genital mutilation (circumcision) or to encourage anybody else to do so. The practice is defined by the World Health Organisation as "the partial or total removal of the external female genitalia or other injury to the female genital organs whether for cultural or other non-therapeutic reasons." Excision of the clitoris and labia minora are the commonest forms; infibulation—the stitching of the vaginal opening except for a small hole for menstrual blood—is the most extreme version. A staggering 137 million in at least 28 African countries have been mutilated in this way. Could Senegal help bring an end to this horrifying practice?

First signs are not encouraging. For a start, say critics, the government changed the law only to please American sensitivities. It carefully sent drafts to local offices of western aid organizations, particularly to the United States Agency for International Development. It pushed the law through just one month before the American State Department's annual report on human rights was due to be released. This report lists those African governments that have banned female circumcision, and is used as a guide to allocating American aid.

It is already clear that the ban will not be enforced. "I would rather die than be forced to stop what I believe in," declares Mountaga Tall, the supreme spiritual leader of northern Senegal's Toucouleur people. Other traditional leaders say they too will ignore the ban. In defiance of the law just before it was passed, one southern village reportedly circumcised 120 girls *en masse*.

No other African country that has recently banned female circumcision, including Egypt, Ghana and Burkina Faso, dares enforce the law. In Guinea, female genital mutilation carries the death penalty, but it has never been applied. Governments fear a repetition of the bloody rebellions of colonial days. Groups in favour of female circumcision helped build support for the Mau Mau uprising in Kenya in the 1950s. When colonial law banned cutters from performing the procedure, girls would defiantly conduct what was called *Ngaitana,* or "I cut myself."

In any event, argue some Senegalese opponents of female genital mutilation, by criminalising the practice the government will undermine delicate local efforts to discourage it. Last year one organisation, called Tostan, had some success informing hundreds of villages of the health risks and encouraging open discussion of the matter. No fewer than 31 villages then publicly declared that they would stop the tradition, and more were planning to follow. But now Tostan has had to suspend its work. Villagers say the ban has turned friends and relations into criminals, and fiercely resist the idea that they are being forced into giving up the practice. The issue has also exposed a split among aid workers on the ground, who tend to oppose criminalisation, and those in distant western capitals that make policy, who back it.

"Criminal law works only when the criminals are the minority," says Gerry Mackie, a political scientist from Oxford University. "It is not possible to criminalise the entire population without the methods of mass terror." To apply this sort of law in Senegal, goes this argument, would be quite different to doing so in France, where on February 2nd [1999] a trial began against Hawa Gréou, a Malian, for mutilating girls of Malian origin there.

The debate about female genital mutilation, like polygamy and witchcraft, is highly charged. Some Africans, indignant at the way western critics denounce the tradition as barbaric and primitive, defend it in the name of cultural tradition. After all, they say, it is mostly women—not men—who carry out and defend the practice.

The best way to bring about change, argue many campaigners, is to avoid cultural judgment and concentrate on health. The cultural meaning of the practice anyway varies across the belt of Africa from Senegal to Somalia, among Muslims and Christians, where it is widely practised. It is considered, variously, a cleansing ritual, a female rite of passage, a guarantor of chastity, a boost to fertility or to male sexual pleasure, and a cure for "sexual deviance." Its health risks, however, are plain. According to the WHO, these range from urine retention and haemorrhage to the formation of abscesses and dermoid cysts the size of a football, not to mention painful sex and even more painful childbirth.

In some places, Africans seem to have been quietly putting an end to the tradition. In Guinea, for instance, Aja Tounkara Diallo Fatimata, the chief "cutter" in the capital Conakry, used to be reviled by western human-rights groups. Then, a few years ago, she confessed that she had never actually cut anybody. "I'd just pinch their clitorises to make them scream," she said, "and tightly bandage them up so that they walked as though they were in pain."

Female opponents in Sudan and Egypt say they favour education over criminalisation. Rather than ban the practice altogether, both countries decided to restrict it to qualified doctors. But in Egypt, American pressure proved too great for an aid-hungry government, and the law now makes genital mutilation a crime. The trouble, as officials admit, is that the ban has driven the practice, unsafely and unhygienically, into illegal shadows.

Suggested Discussion Topics

1. Are gender identities important? If you believe they are, give examples from your life. If you believe they are not, explain your view. Feminist scholars have pointed out that the importance and meaning of being a man or a woman are constructed by societies. Explain what this means. Are the categories male and female constructed by societies? Explain why or why not.

2. How does a feminist account of global politics differ from a masculinist one? Make the strongest argument you can that our political institutions, such as war, and our understanding of global politics are influenced by gender. Now make the strongest argument you can that they are not influenced by gender.

3. What is patriarchy and how does it affect relationships such as those between individuals and states or between states themselves? Does patriarchy legitimate oppression and violence? Why or why not?

4. Are underdevelopment and poverty gender issues? Why or why not? Do you think giving women more control over their lives and equal access to social and political power would help resolve problems such as economic development, the environment, and overpopulation? If you think so, explain how and why. If not, explain why not.

5. Is violence against women a global problem? Why have women organized transnational networks to put violence against women on the global political agenda? What difference do NGOs and transnational networks make?

6. Is female genital mutilation a cultural practice that countries should be able to allow their citizens to practice, or is it a violation of basic human rights? Should the United States grant political asylum to women fleeing from societies that engage in this practice? The United States sometimes imposes economic sanctions or breaks diplomatic ties with states that violate the human rights of their people. Should the United States do so in the case of states that allow or encourage female genital mutilation?

7. Why do some families, particularly in the developing world, prefer sons to daughters? What measures, if any, should they be allowed to take to act on this preference? Should they be allowed to abort a fetus just because it is female? Should they be allowed to feed sons more than daughters? Should they be allowed to favor sons over daughters in schooling? Should states or international groups have the right to intervene in family life to prevent these practices?

8. Are gender rights and gender discrimination global issues? Or should they be dealt with by each society as it sees fit? Are transnational women's groups a healthy development or a sign of Western cultural imperialism and an infringement of sovereignty and a threat to cultural integrity? Should intergovernmental organizations become involved in legislating gender rights? What if a majority of states in the UN concluded that the United States discriminated against women by failing to provide adequate public funding for abortion? Should the United States have to change its laws?

9. Should the United States support international agencies and NGOs that provide medical assistance to women around the world, even if these agencies and NGOs provide information on abortion? U.S. courts have determined that American women have a right to abortion. In other countries where abortion is legal, should the United States support organizations that provide this medical service? Or should the United States seek to deny to non-American women a right that is guaranteed to American women?

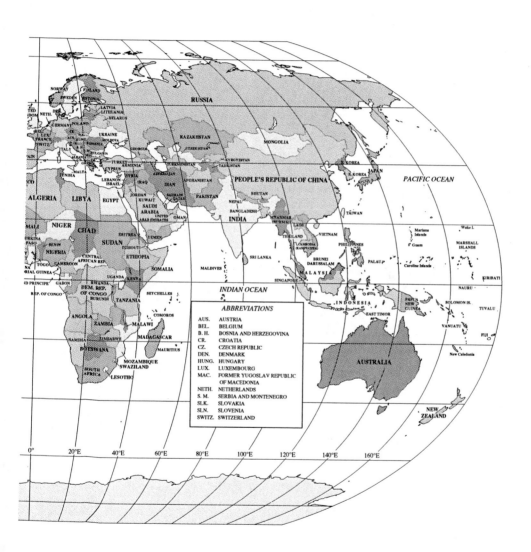

NORWAY FINLAND
SWEDEN ESTONIA
LATVIA
LITHUANIA
BELARUS
GERMANY POLAND
UKRAINE
RUSSIA

NETH.
DEN.
BEL.
LUX.
FRANCE
SWITZ.
ITALY

KAZAKHSTAN
UZBEKISTAN
MONGOLIA

GEORGIA
ARMENIA
AZERBAIJAN
TURKMENISTAN
KYRGYZSTAN
TAJIKISTAN

N. KOREA
S. KOREA
JAPAN

PACIFIC OCEAN

ALGERIA   LIBYA   EGYPT

TURKEY
CYPRUS
SYRIA
LEBANON
ISRAEL
IRAQ
IRAN
JORDAN
KUWAIT
SAUDI
ARABIA
BAHRAIN
QATAR
UNITED
ARAB EMIRATES
OMAN

AFGHANISTAN
PAKISTAN

PEOPLE'S REPUBLIC OF CHINA

NEPAL
BHUTAN
BANGLADESH
INDIA
MYANMAR
(BURMA)

TAIWAN

MALTA
TUNISIA

MALI   NIGER   CHAD
BURKINA
FASO
NIGERIA
BENIN
TOGO
CAMEROON
CENTRAL
AFRICAN REP.
SUDAN

ERITREA
DJIBOUTI
YEMEN

ETHIOPIA
SOMALIA

LAOS
THAILAND
VIETNAM
CAMBODIA
(KAMPUCHEA)

PHILIPPINES

Mariana
Islands

Guam

Wake I.

MARSHALL
ISLANDS

SRI LANKA
MALDIVES

BRUNEI
DARUSSALAM

PALAU

Caroline Islands

KIRIBATI

RIAL GUINEA
D PRINCIPE   GABON
REP. OF CONGO

UGANDA
RWANDA
DEM. REP.
OF CONGO
BURUNDI
KENYA
TANZANIA

SEYCHELLES

INDIAN OCEAN

MALAYSIA

SINGAPORE

INDONESIA

EAST TIMOR

PAPUA
NEW
GUINEA

NAURU

SOLOMON IS.

TUVALU

VANUATU

FIJI

ANGOLA
ZAMBIA
NAMIBIA
ZIMBABWE
BOTSWANA

MALAWI
COMOROS

MOZAMBIQUE
SWAZILAND
SOUTH
AFRICA
LESOTHO

MADAGASCAR
MAURITIUS

AUSTRALIA

NEW
ZEALAND

New Caledonia

ABBREVIATIONS

AUS.	AUSTRIA
BEL.	BELGIUM
B. H.	BOSNIA AND HERZEGOVINA
CR.	CROATIA
CZ.	CZECH REPUBLIC
DEN.	DENMARK
HUNG.	HUNGARY
LUX.	LUXEMBOURG
MAC.	FORMER YUGOSLAV REPUBLIC
	OF MACEDONIA
NETH.	NETHERLANDS
S. M.	SERBIA AND MONTENEGRO
SLK.	SLOVAKIA
SLN.	SLOVENIA
SWITZ.	SWITZERLAND

0°   20°E   40°E   60°E   80°E   100°E   120°E   140°E   160°E